Social Science Research

A Cross Section of Journal Articles for Discussion and Evaluation

Sixth Edition

Turner C. Lomand

Editor

Pyrczak Publishing

P.O. Box 250430 • Glendale, CA 91225

"Pyrczak Publishing" is an imprint of Fred Pyrczak, Publisher, A California Corporation.

This edition was prepared in collaboration with Randall R. Bruce.

Project Director: Monica Lopez.

Editorial assistance provided by Cheryl Alcorn, Jenifer Dill, Brenda Koplin, Erica Simmons, and Sharon Young.

Cover design by Robert Kibler and Larry Nichols.

Printed in the United States of America by Malloy, Inc.

ISBN 1-884585-87-6

Contents

Continued →

Combined Qualitative/Quantitative Research

Meta-Analysis

Notes

Introduction to the Sixth Edition

The research articles in this book will help students learn how to read and evaluate published research. The articles were selected because they are clearly written, employ straightforward research designs, deal with interesting topics, and, as a group, illustrate a variety of methodological techniques.

The articles represent a cross section of social science research. Although sociology, social work, social psychology, and criminal justice are most heavily represented, some works from other related disciplines are also included.

Learning How to Read Research

Social science students, instructors, researchers, and practitioners all read far more research than they conduct. The ability to comprehend research reports is clearly a useful skill, but it is not a skill most individuals acquire naturally. It needs to be learned. Like most learned skills, an individual gets better through instruction and practice. A classroom teacher can provide instruction, but learning to fully comprehend research reports also requires practice. Structured practice is exactly what this collection of articles and the associated questions provide.

Evaluating Research

All the research articles in this collection make a contribution to the advancement of knowledge in their fields. However, none of them are examples of perfect research. Perfect research eludes researchers for three primary reasons.

First, there is no perfect way to sample. Some groups, such as successful criminals, are difficult to locate. Even if they can be located, some of the people a researcher wants to include in a sample are unwilling or unable to participate. In addition, due to time and budgetary limitations, many researchers make do with samples of convenience such as the students in the classes they teach.

Second, there is no perfect way to measure the key variables of interest to social scientists. For example, if a researcher conducts interviews using a tape recorder, he or she can review the material as often as needed to obtain accurate

transcripts and reliable interpretations. However, the presence of an audiotape recorder may influence what the respondents are willing to tell the researcher. Using alternatives such as taking notes or relying on the interviewer's memory are likely to lead to an incomplete record. In short, researchers often have to select among imperfect ways to measure the variables of interest.

Finally, interpreting and drawing implications from data involve subjectivity. Trained researchers may have honest differences of opinion on how to do this for a given set of data.

For the reasons stated above, important decisions in the social sciences should be based on the *body of relevant research*. Thus, before generalizing from the results of any given article in this book, students should examine the results of other published research on the same topic.

Reading Statistics

Most of the articles in this book employ relatively simple statistical procedures. There are exceptions, however. It is almost certain that every reader will encounter some statistical techniques with which he or she is not familiar. This happens not just to students but to professionals as well. Unless directed differently by an instructor, in these situations students should focus on the author's *interpretation* of the statistics in the narrative of the report.

The Appendix

For most students, primary instruction in reading research articles comes from a classroom instructor. Appendix A may help in that instruction. It contains an excellent article that explains the purpose of each part of a standard research article: heading, abstract, introduction, method, results, and discussion.

Factual and Discussion Questions

The *Factual Questions* at the end of each article address major points of the article, particularly methodological issues. These questions can be answered directly from the article itself. The lines in each article are numbered, which should help in documenting answers. These questions should help students recognize the types of information in research articles that are substantively important and should be noticed.

The *Questions for Discussion* draw attention to methodological issues on which there may be honest differences of opinion. There are no right or wrong answers to these questions. However, students should be prepared to provide reasons for their answers if they are discussed in class.

Evaluation Criteria

At the end of each article are 13 basic evaluation criteria that require quality ratings. These may also be used as the basis for classroom discussions. Depending upon the objectives for a research methods class, some instructors may require students to apply a more detailed set of criteria when evaluating the articles.

New to the Sixth Edition

Many of the articles from the Fifth Edition have been retained. The new articles that have been added to the Sixth Edition are Articles 1, 12, 21, 26, 28, 29, 35, and 36.

Acknowledgment

Robert F. Szafran pioneered this reader in the social sciences. In his capacity as editor of the First Edition, he established many structural elements that guided the development of this edition. His contribution is greatly appreciated.

Feedback

I welcome your feedback on this collection and am especially interested in receiving suggestions for improving the next edition of this book. You can write to me care of the publisher using the address on the title page of this book or by e-mailing messages to me via Info@Pyrczak.com.

Turner C. Lomand
Editor

Article 1

Adolescent Internet Usage in Taiwan: Exploring Gender Differences

CHIEN-HUANG LIN
National Central University, Taiwan

SHU-FEN YU
National Central University, Taiwan

ABSTRACT. The purpose of this study was to explore gender differences in adolescent Internet accessibility, motives for use, and online activities in Taiwan; 629 5th- and 6th-graders were surveyed. Findings revealed that the gap in gender differences with regard to Internet use has decreased in this generation. Even though the Internet is the most recent form of major media in the world, it has become the second most important medium as perceived by boys and girls. No gender difference was found in adolescents' motives for using the Internet. The ranking of relative importance of motives for adolescents going online was searching for information, followed by socializing, and boredom avoidance for both boys and girls. However, a gender difference in online activities seems to persist. Searching for homework information and playing games were the most popular online activities for all adolescents. However, while girls tended to view the Internet more as a means of searching for information and e-mailing friends, boys tended to use it more for playing games and downloading software.

From *Adolescence*, *43*, 317–331. Copyright © 2008 by Libra Publishers, Inc. Reprinted with permission.

Introduction

The preteens and teens of today are the first widely "wired" generation. According to a report released by eMarketer (2004), the number of preteens and teens online in the United States grew steadily from 26.6 million in 2000 to 34.3 million in 2003, when nearly one-half of all youngsters were online. The report further points out that preteens and teens comprise over 20% of the American online population. A recent survey (Forrester Research, 2005) revealed that consumers between the ages of 12 and 17 in North America were often online daily and averaged almost 11 hours per week. The trend is similar in Taiwan. According to a survey by Taiwan Network Information Center (2008), the Internet population in Taiwan has reached 15 million. Among them, Internet users under the age of 20 accounted for about 2.86 million. Moreover, the two groups with the highest rates of Internet usage were 12- to 15-year-olds (98%) and 16- to 20-year-olds (95.6%). It appears that the Internet has become not only part of adolescents' daily life but one of the most important media.

The popularity of the Internet among adolescents raises many challenges to the academic community as well as to market researchers. Due to their greater buying power, most research has focused on the Internet behavior of adults while research on adolescents has been relatively neglected. Monitoring adolescent Internet behavior is important, in part, because they may encounter undesirable content, such as pornography or online harassment. Additionally, many online games contain a large amount of violence. Though the advantages provided by the Internet are indispensable for modern life, its possible negative influences cannot be dismissed. More knowledge about adolescents' behaviors may provide parents and teachers with the information necessary to guide them in their Internet use and help them avoid the dangers.

The purpose of this study was to explore gender differences in adolescent Internet accessibility, motives for use, and online activities in Taiwan.

Theoretical Background and Hypotheses
Accessibility to the Internet

Some studies have indicated that while males tend to highlight the value of using the Internet as well as their proficiency, females tend to express more negative attitudes toward computers and the Internet (e.g., Durndell & Haag, 2002; Kadijevich, 2000; Whitley, 1997). In part because of such findings, computers and the Internet may be considered a masculine domain. Two factors may help explain this phenomenon. One is the ability to master computers and the Internet; it is undeniable that males had more opportunities to use technology products such as the Internet. The result was that males have used the Internet more often and for a longer time than have females (Clemente, 1998; Kraut et al., 1998; Bruce, 1988). The other factor could be embedded in the contents of the Internet, much of which was not targeted at females when the Internet first gained prominence. Clemente (1998) pointed out that, at least in the mid-1990s, the Internet simply did not have what most females wanted or needed. Giacquinta, Bauer, and Levin (1993) concluded much the same about the limited participation of women in early home computing: "Clearly, for the majority of these women, the design, marketing, and interpretation of

1

home computer hardware and software did not address their needs or the reality of their lives. Mothers view time in the home very differently; time required to master computer activities is a burden rather than an escape or pastime" (p. 90). Since its content did not satisfy the needs of women, they tended to view the Internet as less important and used it less often than did males.

Recently, some researchers (e.g., Schumacher & Morahan-Martin, 2001) have argued that the gap has narrowed now that females have acquired more experience with the Internet and more content related to women's interests has become available. Empirical studies support this view. Hunley et al. (2005) reported that the amount of time spent on the computer was similar across genders. Tsai and Lin (2004) found no significant gender differences in adolescents' Internet self-efficacy, suggesting that both genders were competently mastering it. Nevertheless, education policies might play an important role in bridging the remaining gap. For example, in order to equip youngsters with the skills necessary to master technology and information resources in 2001, the Ministry of Education in Taiwan required computer and Internet classes starting in the 5th grade in every public elementary school. Since then, both boys and girls at school have had equal opportunity to access the Internet. For this new generation, the gender gap should have narrowed.

H1: There is no gender difference in accessibility to the Internet and its importance.

Motives for Using the Internet

Most studies investigating the motives for using media have focused on television (e.g., Rubin, 1977; Condry, 1989) and computers (e.g., Livingstone & Bovill, 1999). Rubin (1977) found that while "Viewing for arousal" was the most important reason to watch television for 9-year-olds, "Viewing to pass time" was the major motive among 13- to 17-year-olds. Investigating children's motives for using computers, Livingstone and Bovill (1999) reported that computers were most often used for playing games, word processing, drawing, and doing math or number work. Research specifically examining the motives for using the Internet, however, has only examined adults (e.g., Ferguson & Perse, 2000; Papacharissi & Rubin, 2000; Perse & Dunn, 1998). Ferguson and Perse (2000) found that entertainment was the most salient motive for visiting the Web, followed by passing time, acquiring social information, and relaxation. Similarly, Papacharissi and Rubin (2000) reported that information seeking and entertainment were equally important motives for using the Internet. As far as we know, only one study has investigated adolescent motives. Surveying 8- to 13-year-old children in the Netherlands, Valkenburg and Soeters (2001) found that boys and girls did not differ significantly in their motives for going online. They further pointed out that affinity to computers,

seeking information, and entertainment were the three most important motives for children to use the Internet. Their study showed that while older children more often reported going online for information, younger children mentioned using the Internet to avoid boredom more often than did older children. However, since motives can vary by age and conditions in a country, such as culture and economic development, these findings may not be applicable to Taiwan. This study uses the following research questions:

1. What are adolescents' motives for using the Internet?
2. Is there a gender difference in their motives for using the Internet?

Online Activities Among Adolescents

Although the literature suggests that the gender difference in computer use is closing, there continues to be a gender gap in online activities and in the content that is accessed (Clemente, 1998). Due to the importance of school and recreation in adolescent life, it seems reasonable that searching for homework information and online entertainment would be their most popular Internet activities. The Internet provides users with information about almost anything in mere moments. Moreover, in order to train teens how to master the Internet, certain school homework assignments in Taiwan require them to look for information online. These factors make the Internet an excellent tool in the eyes of teens. In addition to providing information, entertainment also attracts adolescents. A wide variety of games on the Internet appeals to adolescents' desires (e.g., for social contact, viewing violence, role-playing, and exploration).

Some findings from marketing reports and academic research support the idea that searching for information and playing games are the most common online activities for adolescents. For example, Hunley et al. (2005) pointed out that girls most often used the computer for homework. Surveying 6- to 11-year-old children, eMarketer (2005) found that game playing (42.6%) and searching for homework information (23.1%) were the most popular online activities for adolescents. Similarly, a study conducted by Mediamark Research (2005) reported game playing (42.6%) and "Did stuff for school/homework (23.1%)" as the top online activities for children ages 6 to 11. However, the report also indicated that boys (28.9%) were more likely to play games than were girls (11.1%). A Griffiths, Davies, and Chappell study (2004) also supported that boys tended to play games more often than did girls. Similarly, investigating adolescent perception and attitudes toward the Internet, Tsai and Lin (2004) found that while males tended to consider the Internet more as a "toy," females tended to view it as a tool or as technology with which to accomplish a task. Hunley et al. (2005) found that 46% of 10th-grade adolescents reported that searching for information on the Internet for school purposes was their main reason for going online. These findings may indicate that females tend to hold a more pragmatic view of the Internet, while males tend to focus more on enjoyment.

180   A greater focus on socializing may be another cause for gender differences. Literature suggests that girls view close relationships as more important (Gilligan, 1982; Buhrmester, 1996). Tsai and Lin's study (2004) indicated that female adolescents expressed
185 greater confidence in using the Internet for general or communication purposes. Conducting a survey of Internet users over 15 years of age in the United States, Hoffman, Kalsbeek, and Novak (1996) found that females were more likely to use the Internet for e-
190 mailing, while males were more likely to download software. It is possible that female adolescents tend to use e-mail to fulfill their need for social contact with friends. As to why males more often download software, online games may be behind this behavior. Some
195 games, especially those on children's Web sites, require the player to download software. Since male adolescents tend to spend more time playing online games, it may lead to their spending more time downloading materials. In one final point of difference, girls more
200 frequently surf for information about idols (Valkenburg & Soeters, 2001).

Based on the above findings, the following hypotheses about adolescent Internet behavior are proposed.

205   H2: Searching for information and playing games are the two most popular Internet activities among adolescents.

H3: Girls search for information on the Internet more often than do boys.

210   H4: Boys play games more often.

H5: Girls use e-mail more often.

H6: Boys download software more often.

H7: Girls use the Internet to surf for information about idols more often.

Method

Sample

215   The experience with the Internet of 634 5th- and 6th-grade Taiwanese school children in this study ranged from six months to two years. The sampling process was as follows: First, 10 municipal elementary schools were drawn randomly from Taipei City, Tai-
220 wan. Then, one class of each 5th and 6th grade was drawn randomly from the chosen schools. All students in the chosen classes were then asked to fill out a questionnaire. Finally, 629 effective questionnaires were obtained. Our sample consisted of 337 5th-graders and
225 290 6th-graders; 347 were boys and 282 girls.

Questionnaire and Measurements

Before the survey, a focus group of 5 5th- and 5 6th-graders with an even number of each gender was conducted in order to develop the questions about online activities and motives that were to be used in the
230 questionnaire of this study, which consisted of four parts. In the first part, subjects were asked to report on the accessibility of computers and the Internet at home, their experience with the Internet (i.e., how long they had been using it), the amount of time spent on the
235 Internet weekly, and the location of the Internet. The second part asked subjects to indicate their three most frequent online activities from nine items: searching for homework information, playing games, e-mailing, downloading software, visiting children's Web sites,
240 chatting with friends, reading news, visiting idols' Web sites, and others. The third part aimed at detecting subjects' motives for using the Internet. Subjects were requested to rate how much each of the following statements was similar to their own reasons for using
245 the Internet on a 1–5 Likert scale, where 1 represents "Strongly disagree," and 5 stands for "Strongly agree." These statements were developed from the focus group:

1. I use the Internet because the content is interesting.
250   2. I use the Internet because it has become a habit for me.
3. I use the Internet because my parents or teachers ask me to search for information.
4. I use the Internet for killing time.
255   5. I use the Internet for learning new things.
6. I use the Internet because it enables me to escape loneliness and have the company of others.
7. I use the Internet because my parents use it.
8. I use the Internet for finding subjects to talk about
260   with friends.
9. I use the Internet for approaching my idols (to chat with and e-mailing them, or searching for news about idols).
10. I use the Internet because I have nothing else to do.

265   These statements were entered into a principal components analysis with varimax rotation. The analysis yielded three factors with eigenvalues higher than 1.0, which explained 53.27% of the variance. The three factors were labeled socializing (items 6, 8, and 9; ei-
270 genvalues = 1.96), boredom-avoidance (items 4 and 10; eigenvalues = 1.79), and information acquisition (items 1, 2, 3, 5, 7; eigenvalues = 1.58).

The last part of the questionnaire asked the subjects about their grade, sex, and views on the importance of
275 media today. Five types of media (i.e., television, newspapers, radio, magazines, and the Internet) were included. Subjects were asked to rate each on a 1–5 Likert scale, where 1 stands for "Very unimportant," and 5 stands for "Very important."

Results

Gender Differences in Internet Accessibility

280   To investigate gender differences in Internet accessibility in Taiwan, we conducted a series of cross-tabulations on each of the categories. The frequencies and percentages are shown in Table 1. Over 94% reported having computers, and around 90% had Internet
285 access at home. Regarding their experience with the Internet, subjects were classified into two major groups. Around 35% of the boys and girls had less than one year of experience with the Internet, while 42% had at least 2 years of experience. This phenomenon
290 probably resulted from the fact that computer and Internet courses had been taught in Taiwanese schools starting in the 5th grade.

Table 1
Gender Difference in the Internet Accessibility

	Boys		Girls		
	Frequency	%	Frequency	%	χ^2
Home with computer					.01
Yes	329	94.8	267	94.7	
No	18	5.2	15	5.3	
Home with Internet					.11
Yes	314	90.5	253	89.7	
No	33	9.5	29	10.3	
Internet access location					23.88**
Home	255	73.5	221	78.4	
School	38	11.0	40	14.2	
Public library	10	2.9	9	3.2	
Internet coffee shop	31	8.9	2	0.7	
Friend's house	4	1.2	6	2.1	
Other	9	2.6	4	1.4	
Experience with Internet					.27
Less than one year	120	34.7	97	34.8	
1 to 2 years	74	21.4	64	22.9	
Over 2 years	152	43.9	118	42.3	
Weekly online time					8.83*
Less than an hour	137	39.5	134	47.5	
1 to 5 hours	143	41.2	109	38.7	
5 to 10 hours	30	8.6	25	8.9	
Over 10 hours	37	10.7	14	5.0	

Note. $N = 625$ to 629; *$p < .05$, **$p < .001$.

It is interesting to note that gender differences appeared in the categories of weekly online time and the
295 Internet access locations. Most subjects' weekly online time fell either into the category of "Less than an hour (boys: 39.5%; girls: 47.5%)" or "1 to 5 hours (boys: 41.2%; girls: 38.7%)." Ten percent of the boys reported spending over 10 hours surfing on the Internet weekly:
300 This percentage indicates that boys tend to spend more time than girls on the Internet (χ^2 (3, $N = 629$) = 8.83, $p < .05$). Furthermore, Table 1 indicates that while girls tend to go online mostly at home and school, boys visit Internet coffee shops with greater frequency than do
305 girls (χ^2 (5, $N = 629$) = 23.88, $p < .001$).
    Table 2 shows the mean scores of the importance of media as perceived by the subjects. A series of *t*-tests on the mean scores of media with gender as the between-subjects factor was conducted. Results revealed
310 no gender difference in subjects' view of the impor-

tance of television and the Internet. In contrast, for media such as newspapers ($t(626) = 2.67$, $p < .01$), ra-dio ($t(626) = 2.52$, $p < .05$), and magazines ($t(627) = 2.57$, $p < .05$) there was a significant difference, with
315 boys tending to view these media as more important than do girls. Furthermore, both genders held the same hierarchy of importance of media types. To examine the difference in their views of media types, a one-way analysis of variation (ANOVA) on the mean scores of
320 media as the between-subjects factor was conducted for each gender. The results of pairwise comparisons showed that the differences among ratings for television, Internet, and newspapers reached a significant level for both genders. Thus, for both boys and girls,
325 television was ranked as the most important media, followed by the Internet, radio, and newspapers and magazines.

Table 2
Gender Difference in the Perceived Importance of Media

	Boys		Girls		
Media	M	SD	M	SD	t
Television	4.14	2.24	3.98	1.91	.99
Internet	3.94	2.25	3.65	1.78	1.79
Newspapers	3.58	2.19	3.16	1.72	2.67**
Radio	3.37	2.40	2.93	2.01	2.52*
Magazines	3.31	2.38	2.87	1.95	2.57*

Note. $N = 629$; *$p < .05$, **$p < .01$.

In sum, the results show that girls as well as boys had equivalent access to the Internet at home. There
330 was no discernable difference in their experience in and opportunities for using the Internet. Only the amount of time spent on the Internet and Internet access locations showed gender differences. This implies that the gap between genders in Internet use has de-
335 creased in this generation. Both boys and girls not only had the same opportunity to access the Internet, but also viewed it as the second most important media. Thus, hypothesis 1 is supported.

Motives for Using the Internet

Table 3 shows mean scores of motives for using the
340 Internet. To examine the differences between the three categories of motives (i.e., information acquisition, socializing, and boredom avoidance), a one-way ANOVA on the mean scores of motives as the between-subjects factor was conducted for boys and girls
345 separately. The results of the pairwise comparisons showed that while the differences among the three categories reached a significant level for girls, only the differences between the ratings of information and so-cializing as well as the differences between the ratings
350 of information and boredom avoidance reached significant levels for boys. This implies that the major motive for girls was to go online for information acquisition, followed by socializing and boredom avoidance. Though boys also reported that searching for informa-
355 tion was their main motivation for going online, social-

4

izing and boredom avoidance tied as their second ranked motive.

Table 3
Gender Difference in Motives for Using the Internet

Motive	Boys		Girls		
	M	SD	M	SD	t
Information acquisition	3.63	.71	3.66	.63	−.49
Sociability	2.73	.96	2.69	.83	.47
Boredom avoidance	2.61	1.24	2.44	1.07	1.83

Note. N = 629

To investigate the gender differences in the motives for Internet usage, a series of t-tests on the mean scores of children's motives for using the Internet with gender as the between-subjects factor was conducted. The t scores ranged from −.49 for information acquisition to 1.83 for boredom avoidance, and none of them reached a significant level. This implies that there were no gender differences in motives for using the Internet.

On a less general level aside from the data presented in Table 3, gender differences appeared in specific motives that fall under the three broad categories of motives. In the information acquisition category, girls more frequently than boys mentioned the motive of going online as a way to approach their idols, t (627) = −2.14, $p < .05$. Furthermore, under the category of socializing, a greater number of boys reported that the Internet allows them to have the company of others, t (627) = 2.71, $p < .001$. The last specific motive with a gender difference barely reached the significant level. In the boredom avoidance category, more boys than girls reported that they used the Internet because they had nothing else to do, t (626) = 1.94, $p = .053$.

Gender Differences in Online Activities

To investigate gender differences in online activities, we conducted a series of cross-tabulations on each of the surveyed activities. Table 4 shows the frequencies and percentages. As expected, searching for information for homework and playing games were among the top three online activities for both boys and girls. While the percentage of time girls spent searching for homework information was higher than that of boys (χ^2(1, N = 629) = 11.49, $p < .01$), boys reported playing more games than did girls (χ^2(1, N = 629) = 24.27, $p < .001$). Furthermore, survey results showed that girls spent a higher percentage of their time using e-mail than did boys (χ^2(1, N = 629) = 30.47, $p < .001$). The percentage of downloading software among boys was almost double that of girls (χ^2(1, N = 629) = 50, $p < .001$). It is also interesting to note that girls tend to visit their idols' Web sites more often than do boys (χ^2(1, N = 634) = 17.79, $p < .001$). Thus, hypotheses 2 to 7 are supported.

Table 4
Gender Difference in Online Activities

	Boys		Girls		
	Frequency	%	Frequency	%	χ^2
Searching for information	185	53.3	188	66.7	11.49*
Playing games	210	60.5	115	40.8	24.27**
E-mailing	109	31.4	150	53.2	30.47**
Downloading software	177	51.0	66	23.4	50.00**
Visiting children's Web sites	65	18.7	66	23.4	2.06
Chatting	56	16.1	47	16.7	.03
Reading news	48	13.8	36	12.8	.15
Visiting idols' Web sites	1	0.3	10	3.5	9.61*

Note. N = 629; *$p < .01$ **$p < .001$.

Discussion

The purpose of this study was to explore gender difference in adolescent Internet usage in Taiwan, with a focus on Internet accessibility, motives, and online activities. The results supported the view that the gap in gender differences in Internet use has decreased in this generation. Both genders appear now to have equivalent resources and experience in accessing the Internet. Even though the Internet is the most recent form of major media, it has become the second most important medium in the opinion of adolescents. Furthermore, no gender differences were found in adolescents' motives for using the Internet. The ranking of the relative importance of motives for adolescents going online was searching for information, followed by socializing, and boredom avoidance for both boys and girls.

However, some gender differences in online activities among adolescents seem to have persisted. Searching for homework information and playing games were the two most popular online activities for all adolescents. While girls viewed the Internet more as a tool for searching for information and e-mailing friends, boys tended to use it for entertainment purposes (i.e., playing games and downloading software). These findings are consistent with those of Hunley et al. (2005).

However, the findings here seem to raise more issues than they resolve. Since this study should be considered exploratory, it may serve as a reference for future research. The results of this study reveal that adolescents today use the Internet almost daily. Unfortunately, the high frequency of Internet usage may increase the number of adolescents exposed to harassment (British Broadcasting Corporation, 2002) and pornography (Cameron et al., 2005; Valkenburg & Soeters, 2001). Finkelhor, Mitchell, and Wolak (2000) found that youths were exposed to unwanted sexual material (25%), sexual solicitation (19%), and harassment (6%). Future research could explore the relationship between the amount of time spent on the Internet and the experiences of encountering harassment or pornographic contents. Studies could also focus on adolescents' responses to these experiences and the effect they have on them.

The responses from adolescents in this study established that playing games is one of the most popular online activities. A study by Griffiths et al. (2004)

445 pointed out that adolescent online game players tended to sacrifice time that could be spent on their education. This study also found that compared to adults, adolescent gamers were more interested in violent games. This raises the possibility that this exposure might have

450 a deleterious effect on their problem resolution methods. Future studies might examine the relationship between playing violent games and the use of violence in real life. Results of this study also show that socializing and boredom avoidance are two major motives for ado-

455 lescents' online activities. Future research might examine the relationship between their motives and the kinds of online games adolescents play.

Parents, educators, policy makers, and scholars have long been concerned with the possible negative

460 influence of media messages on children. Finkelhor et al. (2000) found that some youth are taking risks on the Internet, such as engaging in sexual conversations, seeking out X-rated sites, posting their own pictures, or harassing other Internet users. This study further

465 pointed out that the rates are not high compared to other more risky behaviors, such as using drugs, drinking alcohol, or stealing, but they do reflect a new dimension of deviance that needs to be understood and addressed. As the number of adolescents online and the

470 importance of the Internet continue to increase, so does the need for appropriate guidance (Dorman, 1997). However, until now research regarding parental mediation has focused only on television (e.g., Atkin, Greenberg, & Baldwin, 1991; Krcmar, 1996; Nathanson,

475 1999), and parental mediation patterns concerning adolescent Internet usage still remain unknown. There is a need to provide guidance for parents in teaching their children how to take advantage of the Internet without becoming a victim of it.

References

Atkin, D., Greenberg, B. S., & Baldwin, T. F. (1991). The home ecology of children's television viewing: Parental mediation and the new video environment. *Journal of Communication, 41*, 40–52.

British Broadcasting Corporation. (2002). Youngsters targeted by digital bullies. Retrieved May 5, 2003, from: http://news.bbc.co.uk/hi/english/uk/newsid_1929000/1929944.stm

Bruce, M. (1988). Home interactive telematics: New technology with a history. In F. Van Rijn & R. Williams (Eds.), *Concerning home telematics: Proceedings of the IFIP TC 9 Conference on Social Implications of Home Interactive Telematics* (pp. 83–93).

Buhrmester, D. (1996). Need fulfillment, interpersonal competence, and the developmental contexts of early adolescent friendship. In W. M. Bukowski, A. F. Newcomb, & W. W. Hartup (Eds.), *The company they keep: Friendship in childhood and adolescence* (pp. 158–185), Cambridge: Cambridge University Press.

Cameron, K. A., Salazar, L. F., Bernhardt, J. M., Burgess-Whitman, N., Wingood, G. M., & DiClemente, R. J. (2005). Adolescents' experience with sex on the Web: Results from online focus groups. *Journal of Adolescence, 28*, 535–540.

Clemente, P. C. (1998). *State of the Net: The new frontier.* New York: McGraw-Hill.

Condry, J. C. (1989). *The psychology of television.* Hillsdale, NJ: Erlbaum.

Dorman, S. M. (1997). Internet safety for schools, teachers, and parents. *Journal of School Health, 67*, 355.

Durndell, A., & Haag, Z. (2002). Computer self-efficacy, computer anxiety, attitudes towards the Internet and reported experience with the Internet, by

gender, in an East European sample. *Computers in Human Behavior, 18*, 521–535.

eMarketer. (2004). The online population among American adolescents and children increases dramatically. Retrieved January 9, 2006, from: http://www.emarketer.com/Report.aspx?kids_may04

eMarketer. (2005). What do kids love to do? Retrieved December 10, 2005, from: http://www.emarketer.com/Article.aspx?1003699

Ferguson, D. A., & Perse, E. M. (2000). The World Wide Web as a functional alternative to television. *Journal of Broadcasting & Electronic Media, 44*, 155–174.

Finkelhor, D., Mitchell, K., & Wolak, J. (2000). Online victimization: A report on the nation's youth. National Center for Missing & Exploited Children. Retrieved November 28, 2005, http://www.unh.edu/ccrc/youth_Internet-infopage.html

Forrester Research. (2005). Entertainment grabs youth's online time: Gaming sites get the greatest play with consumers. Retrieved December 8, 2005, http://www.forrester.com/Research/Document/Excerpt/0,7211,373352,00.html

Giacquinta, J. B., Bauer, J., & Levin, J. E. (1993). *Beyond technology's promise: An examination of children's educational computing at home.* Cambridge, UK: Cambridge University Press.

Gilligan, C. (1982). *In a different voice: Psychological theory and women's development.* Cambridge, MA: Harvard University Press.

Griffiths, M. D., Davies, M. N. O., & Chappell, D. (2004). Online computer gaming: A comparison of adolescent and adult gamers. *Journal of Adolescence, 27*, 87–96.

Hoffman, D. L., Kalsbeek, W. D., & Novak, T. P. (1996). Association for Computing Machinery. *Communications of the ACM, 39*(12), 36–46.

Hunley, S. A., Evans, J. H., Delgado-Hachey, M., Krise, J., Rich, T., & Schell, C. (2005). Adolescent computer use and academic achievement. *Adolescence, 40*(158), 307–318.

Kadijevich, D. (2000). Gender differences in computer attitude among ninth-grade students. *Journal of Educational Computing Research, 22*, 145–154.

Kraut, R., Lundmark, V., Patterson, M., Kiesler, S., Mukopadhyay, T., & Scherlis, W. (1998). Internet paradox: A social technology that reduces social involvement and psychological well-being? *American Psychologist, 53*(9), 1017–1031.

Krcmar, M. (1996) Family communication patterns, discourse behavior, and child television viewing. *Human Communication Research, 23*, 251–277.

Livingstone, S., & Bovill, M. (1999). *Young people, new media. Report of the research project children, young people, and the changing media environment.* London: London School of Economics and Political Science.

Mediamark Research. (2005). Mediamark Research Inc. releases its first-ever survey of children ages 6–11. Retrieved January 9, 2006, from: http://www.mediamark.com/mri/docs/press/pr_11-21-05_KidsStudy.htm

Nathanson, A. I. (1999). Identifying and explaining the relationship between parental mediation and children's aggression. *Communication Research, 26*, 124–143.

Papacharissi, Z., & Rubin, A. M. (2000). Predictors of Internet use. *Journal of Broadcasting & Electronic Media, 44*, 175–196.

Perse, E. M., & Dunn, D. G. (1998). The utility of home computers and media use: Implications of multimedia and connectivity. *Journal of Broadcasting & Electronic Media, 42*, 435–456.

Rubin, A. M. (1977). Television usage, attitudes and viewing behaviors of children and adolescents. *Journal of Broadcasting, 21*, 355–369.

Schumacher, J., & Morahan-Martin, J. (2001). Gender, Internet and computer attitudes and experiences. *Computers in Human Behavior, 17*, 95–110.

Taiwan Network Information Center. (2008). 2008 Internet Broadband Usage in Taiwan. Retrieved March 7, 2008, from: http://www.twnic.net.tw/download/200307/0801.pdf

Tsai, C., & Lin, C. (2004). Taiwanese adolescents' perceptions and attitudes regarding the Internet: Exploring gender differences. *Adolescence, 39*(156), 725–734.

Valkenburg, P. M., & Soeters, K. E. (2001). Children's positive and negative experiences with the Internet: An exploratory survey. *Communication Research, 28*(5), 652–675.

Whitley, B. E. (1997). Gender differences in computer-related attitudes and behavior: Meta-analysis. *Computers in Human Behavior, 13*, 1–22.

About the authors: *Chien-Huang Lin*, Department of Business Administration, National Central University, Taiwan. *Shu-Fen Yu*, Department of Information and Communication, Ming Chuan University, Department of Business Administration, National Central University, Taiwan.

Address correspondence to: Shu-Fen Yu, Department of Information and Communication, Ming Chuan University, 250 Sec. 5, Chung Shan N. Rd., Taipei 111, Taiwan, R.O.C. E-mail: sfyu@mcu.edu.tw

Exercise for Article 1

Factual Questions

1. What is the third hypothesis?

2. How many of the participants were 6th-graders?

3. What did the researchers conduct in order to develop the questions for their survey?

4. What percentage of the girls spent over 10 hours online?

5. Was there a significant difference between boys and girls in the perceived importance of the Internet? If yes, at what probability level?

6. Was there a significant difference between boys and girls in the frequency of playing games on the Internet? If yes, at what probability level?

Questions for Discussion

7. Is it important to know that the selection of school and classes was done at random? Explain. (See lines 218–221.)

8. Table 2 presents the results of *t* tests. What is your understanding of the general purpose of such tests?

9. The researchers summarize the results in four tables. How helpful are the tables in helping you comprehend the results?

10. Do you agree with the researchers that the findings raise more issues than they resolve? (See lines 424–425.)

11. In your opinion, is this survey sufficiently important that it should be replicated with a sample from the United States? Explain.

Quality Ratings

Directions: Indicate your level of agreement with each of the following statements by circling a number from 5 for strongly agree (SA) to 1 for strongly disagree (SD). If you believe an item is not applicable to this research article, leave it blank. Be prepared to explain your ratings. When responding to criteria A and B below, keep in mind that brief titles and abstracts are conventional in published research.

A. The title of the article is appropriate.
SA   5   4   3   2   1   SD

B. The abstract provides an effective overview of the research article.
SA   5   4   3   2   1   SD

C. The introduction establishes the importance of the study.
SA   5   4   3   2   1   SD

D. The literature review establishes the context for the study.
SA   5   4   3   2   1   SD

E. The research purpose, question, or hypothesis is clearly stated.
SA   5   4   3   2   1   SD

F. The method of sampling is sound.
SA   5   4   3   2   1   SD

G. Relevant demographics (for example, age, gender, and ethnicity) are described.
SA   5   4   3   2   1   SD

H. Measurement procedures are adequate.
SA   5   4   3   2   1   SD

I. All procedures have been described in sufficient detail to permit a replication of the study.
SA   5   4   3   2   1   SD

J. The participants have been adequately protected from potential harm.
SA   5   4   3   2   1   SD

K. The results are clearly described.
SA   5   4   3   2   1   SD

L. The discussion/conclusion is appropriate.
SA   5   4   3   2   1   SD

M. Despite any flaws, the report is worthy of publication.
SA   5   4   3   2   1   SD

Article 2

A Survey of the Health, Sleep, and Development of Children Adopted from China

MICHAEL A. RETTIG
Washburn University

KELLY McCARTHY-RETTIG
Desoto School District

ABSTRACT. The health, development, and sleeping patterns of 240 children adopted from China were examined using a survey research approach. Eighty percent of the children were 18 months of age or younger when adopted, and 98% of the children were girls. Sixty-two percent of the children were reported to have been developmentally delayed at the time of adoption; of this number, 91% were reported to have had delays in motor development. Of the families, 52% reported that children experienced sleep problems, but only 9% of the total sample experienced significant sleep difficulties. Implications for social workers are also discussed.

From *Health & Social Work, 31*, 201–207. Copyright © 2006 by the National Association of Social Workers. Reprinted with permission.

International adoption is an increasingly popular method for parents seeking to increase the size of their families. For example, Arsonson (2003) reported that there were more than 15,000 international adoptions in
5 the United States in 1998. This was an increase of more than 2,000 from 1997. One of the main sources of international adoption is China. According to the National Adoption Information Clearinghouse (2003), there have been more than 32,000 visas issued for chil-
10 dren being adopted from China since 1995. Given the large number of children coming to this country from China and the general concerns about the psychological and behavioral impact of adoption, it is reasonable to investigate health and developmental outcomes after
15 the adoption.

Information on the postadoptive outcomes of children adopted from China is relevant to social workers, adoption agencies, and other professionals assisting families with international adoption. It is important that
20 these professionals be aware of any potential problems so that families can be prepared for possible child care issues. For example, Shapiro and colleagues (2001) indicated that studies of children of international adoption have shown potential problems with psychological
25 adjustment. These problems may be due to medical or nutritional deprivation, lack of a primary caregiver, or inconsistencies in caregivers. Howe (1997) noted that nearly 25% of adopted children will display some type

30 of behavioral or mental health concern later in life, so it is important to be aware of postadoptive outcomes.

Related Literature

We conducted a search for relevant literature using ERIC and Internet search engines. This search focused on studies relevant to children adopted from China and on reports investigating health, sleep, or developmental
35 problems. Several reports relevant to this investigation were identified.

One potential area of concern regarding international adoptions involves medical concerns. Arsonson (2003), for example, identified and discussed 17 poten-
40 tial medical problems, including malnutrition, rickets, eczema, scabies, lead poisoning, bacterial intestinal infections, tuberculosis, hepatitis B and C, asthma, anemia, and visual or hearing problems. Despite the relatively large number of potential medical problems,
45 Arsonson noted that the children typically have limited long-term medical issues and that these are fairly easily addressed with diagnosis and proper treatment.

Another potential area of concern involves the fact that earlier research has indicated that it is typical for
50 children to present with developmental delays at the time of their adoption (Johnson & Traister, 1999; Miller & Hendrie, 2000; Miller, Kiernan, Mathers, & Klein-Gitelman, 1995). In the Miller and associates study, the mean age of children at arrival was 14
55 months, and they were seen within three months of arrival. These researchers found that approximately 74% of children showed delays in one or more areas of development at the time of their arrival in the United States. Miller and Hendrie assessed the health and de-
60 velopmental status of 452 children in two different groups. Of the 452 children, 98% were girls. They found that 75% of the children had significant developmental delays in at least one area and that the delays were related to length of time children spent in orphan-
65 ages. The longer the time spent in an orphanage, the greater the developmental delays. Delays in gross motor skills were most common (55%), followed by delays in language (43%), socioemotional (28%), and cognitive skills (32%). Miller and Hendrie also found
70 that a number of children had medical problems, including anemia (35%), elevated lead levels (14%), tu-

berculosis (3.5%), and hepatitis B surface antibody (22%). Each of these studies pointed to the need for continued long-term follow-up of the children.

75   A study conducted by Tessler and colleagues (1999) looked at intercountry adoption from a sociological perspective and examined the nature of families adopting children as well as some health and developmental outcomes. Children in this study were adopted
80   from China, Korea, Thailand, Peru, and the United States. Of the 361 families, 332 had adopted children from China. Similar to methods used in this study, the Tessler team set up a Web site and e-mail address through which families could complete questionnaires.
85   They received responses from 526 parents in 361 households in 38 states. Tessler and colleagues found that 97% of the children adopted were girls, and the mean age at adoption was two years. The children came from 15 different provinces across China. Sixty-
90   four percent of the adopted Chinese children were the only child in the family. A number of parents reported that the children lagged in development, especially in gross motor skills. However, they also reported that the children caught up quickly, learned English quickly,
95   adapted easily to new foods, and accepted their new families.

Shapiro and colleagues (2001) indicated that adoptive parents might be unprepared for a child's developmental problems or for possible problems with at-
100 tachment. Haugaard and colleagues (1999) pointed out that professionals and parents involved in the adoption process would benefit from knowing about specific child characteristics that can indicate which transracial children are at the greatest or least risk of short- or
105 long-term problems. Vonk and Angaran (2003) indicated that parents who adopt across race need training in cultural competence to be prepared for the demands of raising the child. They indicated in their survey of adoption agencies that only about half the agencies
110 provided training to facilitate transracial adoption.

Sleep Problems

A review of literature regarding the sleeping patterns of internationally adopted children revealed limited information. However, this also seems to be a potential area of concern given that approximately 25%
115 of children can experience sleep problems (Zuckerman, Stevenson, & Bailey, 1987) and that subpopulations of children, such as those with diagnosed disabilities or other developmental delays, may display greater difficulty with sleeping (Mindell, 1993). Zuckerman and
120 associates indicated that as many as 30% of children can have sleep problems during the first four years of life, with the highest incidence occurring from one to two years of age. They also found that many of these sleep problems do not disappear with age. In their
125 study, children who experienced sleeping problems at eight months of age also experienced sleep difficulties at three years of age.

According to the American Academy of Child and Adolescent Psychiatry (2000), children can experience
130 a variety of different sleep disorders. These can include nightmares, bedwetting, teeth grinding, or difficulty falling asleep. A subgroup of sleep disorders are referred to as parasomnias. These sleep disorders include sleep terrors, sleep talking, and sleepwalking. Para-
135 somnias usually occur during the first third of the night, and individuals have little memory of them.

Hopkins-Best (1998) indicated that sleep issues are among the most commonly reported problems of families of internationally adopted children. She noted that
140 sleeping alone, as is common in the United States, is different from many cultures that focus on a family bed. Although family beds may be more common in China than in the United States, it is uncertain what the sleeping conditions are for children in orphanages.
145 One study that addressed the sleep problems of internationally adopted children directly was conducted by Bishop (2001). This study examined the sleeping patterns of 17 internationally adopted girls (from China and Cambodia) compared with 15 children in nonadop-
150 tive families (seven boys and eight girls). The mean age of the adopted children was nine months; the mean age for the nonadopted children was 14 months. Bishop used a questionnaire to measure the children's sleeping patterns. The results indicated that there was only one
155 significant difference found in the sleep patterns of the two groups of children. The internationally adopted children had longer-duration night wakings than the nonadopted children. Overall, the hypothesis that the adopted children would display more sleep problems
160 than the nonadopted children was not supported.

Method

Participants

Participants in this survey were 240 families who had adopted children from China. Families responded from 35 states. All of the children were adopted between 1992 and 2001. Families responded by e-mail or
165 regular mail.

Procedures

A snowball sampling method was used. The national Families with Children from China (FCC) Web site (www.fwcc.org) was accessed to obtain member contact information. Families receiving the survey
170 were asked to forward it to other families with children adopted from China.

The survey questions were based in part on the interest regarding the health, development, and sleeping habits of children adopted from China and on the re-
175 search questions and format used by Tessler and colleagues (1999). A short introductory letter explaining the survey's purpose and providing contact information was included, as well as information on how to respond. The letter indicated that the results would be
180 made available through publication and that we would ask the FCC site to include this summary as a link.

A pilot test of the survey was sent electronically to 10 FCC families in the immediate geographic area. E-mail addresses for these families were obtained from the local FCC group. Feedback on the questions and methods being used was requested from these 10 families. Families who did not respond within three weeks were sent a follow-up survey. On the basis of this pilot test of the survey, three questions were revised and two additional questions were added to the survey, for a total of 23 questions.

Although not all families who have adopted children from China are members of FCC, it is the largest such organization, and we felt that a large number of families could be reached through it. A list of FCC contacts in several states was compiled, and e-mails were sent asking for permission to contact members. We asked, and hoped, that the contacts would forward the survey to local FCC members. Some of these contacts indicated either that they were not comfortable forwarding the survey or that some local FCC groups had policies about not forwarding e-mails. E-mails were sent to families across the country from April to July 2001.

An electronic database was set up to collect and summarize the information obtained from the surveys. E-mail addresses were used as a primary key to be sure that there were no duplicate survey returns. The surveys were examined using the database's sort capabilities, and reports were generated for each research question.

Results

Responses were obtained from 240 families by e-mail or regular mail, and all responses were obtained between April and August 2001. Responses came from 35 states, including 17 states east of the Mississippi River and 18 states west of the Mississippi River. Mothers responded to the survey in 89% of the returns; fathers, 11%. Children came from 22 different provinces: 19% were adopted from Guangdong, 17% from Hunan, and 14% from Jiangxi; fewer than 10% were adopted from each of the other provinces.

As indicated in Table 1, most of the children in this sample (68%) were adopted in their first year of life, and 80% were 18 months of age or younger when adopted. The vast majority of children adopted were girls (98%) (Table 1). Of the 240 responses, only two indicated that the adopted child was a boy.

The years in which these children were adopted ranged from 1992 to 2001; 38 children were adopted between 1992 and 1995, 90 between 1996 and 1998, and 112 between 1999 and 2001. Almost half the families in this survey reported having other children. Of these, 44% were biological children, 38% were adopted children, 15% were both biological and adopted children, and 3% were stepchildren (Table 2).

Table 1
Characteristics of Children Adopted from China

Survey questions	% Responses
Age of child when adopted	
0–1 year	68
1–2 years	20
2–3 years	5
3–4 years	3
4–5 years	1
> 5 years	1
Gender	
Male	2
Female	98
Length of stay in orphanage	
1–4 months	11
5–9 months	43
10–15 months	29
16–24 months	10
Developmental delays in children	
No	38
Yes	62
Domains of developmental delay	
Motor	91
Language	35
Social	35
2 of 3 areas	35
All 3 areas	18

Note. Rounding error accounts for totals less than 100%.

Table 2
Characteristics of Participants in Survey about Children Adopted from China

Survey questions	% Responses
Survey Respondents	
Mothers	89
Fathers	11
Time period of adoption	
1992–1995	16
1996–1998	38
1999–2001	46
Other children in the family	
No	52
Yes	48
If other children in family	
Biological children	44
Adopted children	38
Both biological and adopted	15
Stepchildren	3

As there have been reports raising concerns about the length of stay in orphanages, we included a question asking how long children had been in an orphanage before adoption. Most of the children in this study (43%) had been in an orphanage for five to nine months (Table 1). One child was reported to have been in an orphanage for 12 years.

Families were also asked whether they had visited the orphanage in China. Only 45% of families reported visiting the child's orphanage. Of these 109 families, 81 were families who adopted children in the age range of birth to one year. Only 24% of families reported that their children spent time living with a foster family before adoption.

Table 3
Problems with Sleep, Eating, Social Interactions, Bonding, or Acceptance Among Children Adopted from China

Area	% of families reporting problems	Extent of problems reported (%)		
		Minor	Some	Many
Sleep	52	68	14	17
Eating	19	60	28	11
Interacting with others	16	11	4	1
Bonding	13	10	2	1
Acceptance	9	7	2	—[a]

[a]Only two families (less than 1%) reported having many problems in this area.

250 Families were asked how much they had been told or knew about their children before adoption and whether this information was correct. Forty-five percent of families reported knowing something about their child, and 17% reported knowing nothing about 255 their child. Of the families who did get some prior information, 33% reported that this information was accurate, and 15% reported that the information was partly correct.

Families were asked whether the children were de-260 velopmentally delayed when adopted and if so, in what areas (language, social, motor, or any combination). Sixty-two percent of families reported that children were developmentally delayed at their arrival in the United States (Table 1). The families reporting devel-265 opmental delays indicated that motor delays were the most common.

Families were asked whether children had any serious medical conditions at the time of adoption. Thirty-two families, or 13% of the total sample, reported that 270 children had medical problems. Of these 32 children, 84% were 0 to two years old when adopted. Three children had positive tuberculosis tests, five tested positive for hepatitis B or C, three had hearing or ear problems, two had visual problems, two had seizures, 275 and two had asthma. Other problems mentioned included high lead levels, rickets, dental decay, dyspraxia, and scabies.

The survey asked whether there had been any problems with the children's sleeping or eating behaviors as 280 well as whether there had been any problems with social interactions, bonding, or acceptance. For each of these items, a scale including the following responses was used: "no problems (less than 25% of the time)," "minor problems (25% of the time)," "some problems 285 (50% of the time)," and "many problems (75% or more of the time)."

Nearly 52% of families reported that children had some degree of sleep problems and that most of these were minor (Table 3). Only 9% of the total sample 290 reported many sleep problems (75% of the time or more). A number of families included comments about their children's sleep patterns, stating that children did not want to sleep alone, that children had night terrors, or that the sleeping problems faded as the children got 295 older.

A relatively small number of families reported problems with diet or eating. The responses indicated that only 19% experienced problems in this area. The majority of children were eating dairy products, al-300 though a few families reported that children were lactose intolerant.

Families were asked whether there had been any problems with children interacting with others, bonding with family members, or being accepted by friends or 305 family. Survey responses indicated that 16% of the families reported problems with social interactions. Only 13% of the sample reported problems with bonding, and again most of these were minor. Very few problems were reported with acceptance of the child 310 (9%). Only two of the 240 families reported having many problems with the acceptance of their child by friends or family members.

Parents were also asked whether their children had been identified as gifted or in need of special education 315 services because of a disability. Seven percent of families reported that children had been identified as gifted; only 4% had been referred for special education services owing to disabilities. These figures need to be viewed with caution given that many of the children in 320 this survey were not yet of school age.

Discussion

What are the postadoptive outcomes of internationally adopted children and, specifically, of children adopted from China? This central question and related questions in this investigation were what we hoped to 325 address with this research. The answers to these questions are important to social workers helping children and families through the adoption process. They are also important for our society as a whole, given the thousands of children being adopted from all over the 330 world.

The focus of this investigation was to obtain information to help children, families, schools, and society to be prepared for possible postadoptive outcomes. These outcomes may often be very positive. Anecdotal 335 comments included in the completed surveys indicated that many of the children are healthy, happy, smart, and social. Given that the children are often adopted into good home environments with loving, well-educated, professional parents, one could easily assume

340 that the long-term outlook for these children is very good.

The results of this study are consistent with those obtained in other studies. First, the majority of children adopted from China are young girls 18 months of age 345 or younger, from a variety of provinces. Consistent with other studies, many of the children displayed developmental delays at the time of adoption. An important point of distinction in future studies is whether the determination of developmental delay was made 350 through an agency or clinic or based on the parents' opinion. In this survey, parents made this determination. None of the families reported a formal determination of developmental delay. However, it is possible that children will display some delays in development, 355 especially in motor skills, at the time of adoption. These delays will very likely be temporary and fade as children get older.

Only 13% of children in this survey were reported as having serious medical problems. As Arsonson 360 (2003) has noted, these medical conditions are usually easily diagnosed, and treatment can begin immediately with very few long-term effects.

Several children were reported to have problems with sleeping. Slightly more than half of the surveys 365 (125 families) reported children having some degree of sleeping problems. Most of these problems were minor, with only 9% of the total sample reporting serious sleep problems. The extent and nature of the sleeping problems was not examined as closely as in research 370 studies focusing specifically on this topic. However, a number of families reported children having a difficult time falling asleep, experiencing night terrors, or not wanting to sleep alone. A more detailed examination of children's sleep problems is warranted and must take 375 into consideration cultural differences between the United States and China. The length of stay in an orphanage or whether children lived in a foster family (and, if so, how long) may be variables to be examined in other studies investigating sleep disorders.

Limitations

380 The sampling technique and procedures used in this study were not effective. This contributed to the study's small sample size and makes generalization of the findings difficult. Given that thousands of children have been adopted from China in the past 10 years, the 385 total number of returns was far short of what we had hoped and represents approximately 1% of all children adopted from China. However, the research questions addressed in this survey are important, and an effective way to reach these families must be found. It is impor- 390 tant to the children, their families, and society that we know as much as possible about any potential problems both before and after the adoption.

Implications for Social Workers and Other Professionals

International adoption presents challenges to the adoptive child, the adoptive parents, and the adoptive 395 extended family. One of the most important things needed to assist in successful postadoptive outcome is information.

Issues that need to be addressed by social workers and families involve information on the child. Children 400 adopted from China may experience abandonment issues that may lead to sleep, bonding, or attachment problems. The children may feel a sense of loss that their native family and country could not take care of them. There may be attachment issues inasmuch as 405 children may have been cared for by several different caregivers in orphanages or foster families before coming to their homes in the United States. There may also be identity problems as children work to discover why they are in their new world. Some problems children 410 experience may be transitional ones that will fade over time, but others may not. Such problems may include sleep, eating, or behavioral problems. Social workers can help families understand that such problems may occur and that these problems may be expected in chil- 415 dren coming from institutional settings (Johnson & Dole, 1999).

The overall lack of information on children and their history is an issue for families. Adoptive families are unlikely to know anything about a child's medical 420 history or prior family background. Even a child's exact birth date may be in question. Parents may also be concerned about the child's developmental delays and what can be done about them as well as about problems that children may experience with diet or sleeping. 425 Social workers can help provide needed information.

A number of suggestions can be made to social workers and educational professionals who work with adoptive children and their families. These suggestions are consistent with those of Judge (1999). First, adop- 430 tive children should receive complete medical and developmental examinations soon after their arrival in the United States. For many children, this may simply be precautionary, but it is important that information be obtained so that when intervention is warranted, it can 435 begin as soon as possible. This examination should also include a follow-up on any information provided on immunizations. Such examinations would appear to be needed for all children adopted internationally.

Second, the children's emotional health should be 440 addressed. Children may experience a sense of loss or attachment issues, and they should be provided with considerable emotional support. It is important that parents provide a consistent, predictable, and well-structured environment (Judge, 1999). Although this is 445 a good suggestion for any family, it is very important for adopted children adapting to their new world. Parents should be encouraged to spend as much time as possible with the child, attend promptly to the child's needs, and provide a supportive, empathic home envi- 450 ronment. Social workers should be prepared to provide families with resource information on sleep disorders or, even thumb sucking, as needed.

It is important to help families identify and locate local, state, and national resources and support groups
455 (Judge, 1999). This could include the FCC, which has many local chapters. It may also involve the use of more experienced parents who can discuss their adoption experiences and help new adoptive families learn what they can expect (Judge, 1999). For example, one
460 local community has an informal mothers' group that meets once a month. This group is made up only of mothers with internationally adopted children who can share their knowledge and experiences. The mothers and families have formed an important bond that also
465 allows the children an opportunity to get together on a regular basis.

In addition, families need to be encouraged to make an effort to learn about the child's native culture and to be prepared for the child's questions about Chinese
470 culture, language, and the adoption. Families should be encouraged to speak in an honest and matter-of-fact manner about the adoption, read books about adoption and China, and be prepared for the child's questions. Social workers could provide families with a list of
475 children's books that address adoption or Chinese culture. Parents should make an effort to learn about and celebrate Chinese holidays such as the Moon Festival or Chinese New Year, as this can be an important way for children to learn about their native country.

References

American Academy of Child and Adolescent Psychiatry. (2000). *Children's sleep problems*. Retrieved July 2004 from www.aacap.org/publications/factsfam/sleep.html

Arsonson, J. E. (2003). *An update on health issues in children adopted from China*. Retrieved May 1999 from www.orphandoctor.com/medical/regional/China/healthissues.html

Bishop, C. T. (2001). *Sleep habits of internationally adopted children*. Unpublished master's thesis, St. Joseph's University, Philadelphia.

Haugaard, J. J., Palmer, M., & Wojslawowicz, J. (1999). International adoption: Children primarily from Asia and South America. *Adoption Quarterly*, *3*, 83–93.

Hopkins-Best, M. (1998). *Toddler adoption: The weaver's craft*. Indianapolis: Perspectives Press.

Howe, D. (1997). Parent-reported problems in 211 adopted children: Some risk and protective factors. *Journal of Child Psychology and Psychiatry and Allied Disciplines*, *38*, 401–411.

Johnson, D. E., & Dole, K. (1999). International adoptions: Implications for early intervention. *Infants & Young Children*, *11*, 34–45.

Johnson, D. E., & Traister, M. (1999). Micronutrient deficiencies, growth failure and developmental delays are more prevalent than infectious diseases in US adopted Chinese orphans. *Pediatric Research*, *45*, 126A.

Judge, S. L. (1999). Eastern European adoptions: Current status and implications for intervention. *Topics in Early Childhood Special Education*, *19*, 244–252.

Miller, L. C, & Hendrie, N. W. (2000). Health of children adopted from China. *Pediatrics*, *105*, E76.

Miller, L. C., Kiernan, M. T., Mathers, M. I., & Klein-Gitelman, M. (1995). Developmental and nutritional status of internationally adopted children. *Archives of Pediatrics & Adolescent Medicine*, *149*, 40–44.

Mindell, J. (1993). Sleep disorders in children. *Health Psychology*, *12*, 151–162.

National Adoption Information Clearinghouse. (2003). *HealthFinder*. Retrieved April 2003 from http://www.calib.com/naic

Shapiro, V., Shapiro, J., & Paret, I. (2001). International adoption and the formation of new family attachment. *Smith College Studies in Social Work*, *71*, 389–418.

Tessler, R., Gamache, G., & Liu, L. (1999). *West meets East: Americans adopt Chinese children*. Westport, CT: Bergin & Garvey.

Vonk, M. E., & Angaran, R. (2003). Training for transracial adoptive parents by public and private adoption agencies. *Adoption Quarterly*, *6*, 53–62.

Zuckerman, B., Stevenson, J., & Bailey, V. (1987). Sleep problems in early childhood: Continuities, predictive factors, and behavioral correlates. *Pediatrics*, *80*, 664–671.

Acknowledgments: Special thanks to Megan, Ryan, and Kate Li Rettig.

About the authors: *Michael A. Rettig*, Ph.D., is professor, Department of Education, Washburn University, 1700 SW College Avenue, Topeka, KS 66621 (E-mail: Michael.rettig@washburn.edu). *Kelly McCarthy-Rettig*, MS, is a teacher in the Desoto School District, Desoto, KS.

Exercise for Article 2

Factual Questions

1. Did the review of literature regarding the sleeping patterns of internationally adopted children reveal much information?

2. From how many states did families respond?

3. For what words does FCC stand?

4. Of the 240 responses, how many indicated that the adopted child was a boy?

5. According to the researchers, why should the findings regarding identification of children as gifted or in need of special education services be viewed with caution?

6. According to the researchers, were the findings of this study consistent with those obtained in other studies?

Questions for Discussion

7. The researchers state that they used "snowball sampling." What do you think this term means? (See lines 166–171.)

8. What is your opinion on defining "no problems" as being "less than 25% of the time"? (See lines 278–286.)

9. In your opinion, how important are the limitations discussed by the researchers? (See lines 380–392.)

10. In your opinion, to what extent are the implications directly based on the data generated by this survey? (See lines 393–479.)

11. In a future study, do you think it would be useful to include a comparison group such as children adopted from within the United States? Why? Why not?

12. If you were to conduct a survey on the same topic, what changes, if any, would you make in the research methodology?

Quality Ratings

Directions: Indicate your level of agreement with each of the following statements by circling a number from 5 for strongly agree (SA) to 1 for strongly disagree (SD). If you believe an item is not applicable to this research article, leave it blank. Be prepared to explain your ratings. When responding to criteria A and B below, keep in mind that brief titles and abstracts are conventional in published research.

A. The title of the article is appropriate.

SA   5   4   3   2   1   SD

B. The abstract provides an effective overview of the research article.

SA   5   4   3   2   1   SD

C. The introduction establishes the importance of the study.

SA   5   4   3   2   1   SD

D. The literature review establishes the context for the study.

SA   5   4   3   2   1   SD

E. The research purpose, question, or hypothesis is clearly stated.

SA   5   4   3   2   1   SD

F. The method of sampling is sound.

SA   5   4   3   2   1   SD

G. Relevant demographics (for example, age, gender, and ethnicity) are described.

SA   5   4   3   2   1   SD

H. Measurement procedures are adequate.

SA   5   4   3   2   1   SD

I. All procedures have been described in sufficient detail to permit a replication of the study.

SA   5   4   3   2   1   SD

J. The participants have been adequately protected from potential harm.

SA   5   4   3   2   1   SD

K. The results are clearly described.

SA   5   4   3   2   1   SD

L. The discussion/conclusion is appropriate.

SA   5   4   3   2   1   SD

M. Despite any flaws, the report is worthy of publication.

SA   5   4   3   2   1   SD

Article 3

Bullies Move Beyond the Schoolyard:
A Preliminary Look at Cyberbullying

JUSTIN W. PATCHIN
University of Wisconsin, Eau Claire

SAMEER HINDUJA
Florida Atlantic University

ABSTRACT. Bullying in a school setting is an important social concern that has received increased scholarly attention in recent years. Specifically, its causes and effects have been under investigation by a number of researchers in the social and behavioral sciences. A new permutation of bullying, however, has recently arisen and become more common: Tech-savvy students are turning to cyberspace to harass their peers. This exploratory article discusses the nature of bullying and its transmutation to the electronic world and the negative repercussions that can befall both its victims and instigators. In addition, findings are reported from a pilot study designed to empirically assess the nature and extent of online bullying. The overall goal of the current work is to illuminate this novel form of deviance stemming from the intersection of communications and computers and to provide a foundational backdrop on which future empirical research can be conducted.

From *Youth Violence and Juvenile Justice*, 4, 148–169. Copyright © 2006 by Sage Publications, Inc. Reprinted with permission.

The home, neighborhood, and school are all recognized as important social and physical contexts within which adolescents develop. Bullying—an all too common form of youthful violence—has historically af-
5 fected only children and teenagers while at school, while traveling to or from school, or in public places such as playgrounds and bus stops. Modern technology, however, has enabled would-be bullies to extend the reach of their aggression and threats beyond this
10 physical setting through what can be termed *cyberbullying*, where tech-savvy students are able to harass others day and night using technological devices such as computer systems and cellular phones. Computers occupy a significant proportion of the homes in which
15 children reside and are frequently used for social, entertainment, academic, and productivity needs (National Telecommunications and Information Administration [NTIA], 2002). Moreover, cellular phones are gaining widespread popularity and use among the
20 younger age groups because they are perceived as a status symbol, allow for conversations with friends in different physical spaces, and provide a virtual tether of sorts for parents, allowing for supervision from afar.

Though they are intended to positively contribute to
25 society, negative aspects invariably surface as byproducts of the development of new technologies such as these. The negative effects inherent in cyberbullying, though, are not slight or trivial and have the potential to inflict serious psychological, emotional, or social harm.
30 When experienced among members of this highly impressionable and often volatile adolescent population, this harm can result in violence, injury, and even death (e.g., Meadows et al., 2005; Vossekuil, Fein, Reddy, Borum, & Modzeleski, 2002) and later criminality for
35 both the initiator and recipient of bullying (e.g., Olweus, Limber, & Mihalic, 1999; Patchin, 2002). One particularly horrendous anecdotal account deserves mention. In May of 2001, viciously offensive messages denigrating and humiliating a high school sophomore
40 girl who suffered from obesity and multiple sclerosis were posted anonymously to an online message board associated with a local high school in Dallas, Texas (Benfer, 2001). In time, the bullying crossed over to the physical world as the victim's car was vandalized,
45 profanities were written on the sidewalk in front of her home, and a bottle filled with acid was thrown at her front door, which incidentally burned her mother. This example vividly depicts how bullying online can lead to physical harm offline.[1]
50 Little research to date has been conducted on cyberbullying. However, research on the correlates of traditional bullying can assist in comprehending the reality and growth of this new phenomenon. To begin, the desire to be and remain popular takes on almost
55 lifelike proportions among kids and teenagers during certain stages of their life, and their self-esteem is largely defined by the way that others view them. Although it is unclear exactly when self-esteem increases or decreases during a child's life (Twenge & Campbell,
60 2001), it unquestionably shapes a child's development in profound ways. According to the social acceptance model, self-esteem stems from the perceptions that others have of the individual (Cooley, 1902). When individuals perceive themselves to be rejected or oth-
65 erwise socially excluded, a number of ill effects can result (Leary, Schreindorfer, & Haupt, 1995). Much research has validated this theory (Leary & Downs,

1995; Leary, Haupt, Strausser, & Chokel, 1998; Leary, Tambor, Terdal, & Downs, 1995) and has pointed to the following potentially negative outcomes: depression (Quellet & Joshi, 1986; Smart & Walsh, 1993), substance abuse (Hull, 1981), and aggression (Coie & Dodge, 1988; French & Waas, 1987; Hymel, Rubin, Rowden, & LeMare, 1990; Paulson, Coombs, & Landsverk, 1990; Stewart, 1985). In addition, low self-esteem tends to be found among chronic victims of traditional bullying (Hoover & Hazler, 1991; Neary & Joseph, 1994; Rigby & Slee, 1993).[2] It is expected that cyberbullying can similarly cripple the self-esteem of a child or adolescent, and without a support system or prosocial outlets through which to resolve and mitigate the strain, the same dysphoric and maladaptive outcomes may result. Despite these solemn possibilities, there has been very little empirical attention to date devoted toward better understanding the electronic variant of this deviance (exceptions include Berson, Berson, & Ferron, 2002; Finn, 2004; Ybarra & Mitchell, 2004).

This research seeks to fill this gap by exploring cyberbullying and examining its potential to become as problematic as traditional bullying—particularly with society's increasing reliance on technology. Its goal is to illuminate this novel form of deviance stemming from the intersection of communications and computers and to provide a foundational backdrop on which future empirical research can be conducted. First, what is known about traditional bullying will be summarized to provide a comparative point of reference. Second, data collected from various media sources will be presented to describe the technology that facilitates electronic bullying and to portray its prevalence. Third, preliminary findings from a pilot study of adolescent Internet users will be presented, highlighting the characteristics of this group and their involvement (both as victims and offenders) in the activity. Finally, suggestions for future empirical research will be offered as guidance for additional exploration of this subject matter.

Traditional Bullying

Bullying Defined

A variety of scholars in the disciplines of child psychology, family and child ecology, sociology, and criminology have articulated definitions of bullying that generally cohere with each other. To begin, the first stages of bullying can be likened to the concept of harassment, which is a form of unprovoked aggression often directed repeatedly toward another individual or group of individuals (Manning, Heron, & Marshal, 1978). Bullying tends to become more insidious as it continues over time and is arguably better equated to violence rather than harassment. Accordingly, Roland (1989) states that bullying is "long-standing violence, physical or psychological, conducted by an individual or a group directed against an individual who is not

able to defend himself in the actual situation" (p. 21).[3] Stephenson and Smith (1989) contend that bullying is

a form of social interaction in which a more dominant individual [the bully] exhibits aggressive behavior, which is intended to and does, in fact, cause distress to a less dominant individual [the victim]. The aggressive behavior may take the form of a direct physical and/or verbal attack or may be indirect as when the bully hides a possession that belongs to the victim or spreads false information about the victim. (p. 45)

Providing perhaps the most panoptic definition, Nansel et al. (2001) asserted that bullying is aggressive behavior or intentional "harm doing" by one person or a group, generally carried out repeatedly and over time and that involves a power differential. Many characteristics can imbue an offender with perceived or actual power over a victim and often provide a sophistic license to dominate and overbear. These include, but are not limited to, popularity, physical strength or stature, social competence, quick wit, extroversion, confidence, intelligence, age, sex, race, ethnicity, and socioeconomic status (Olweus, 1978, 1993, 1999; Rigby & Slee, 1993; Roland, 1980; Slee & Rigby, 1993). Nonetheless, research on the relevance of these differences between bullies and their victims has been inconclusive. For example, differences in physical appearance was not predictive of one's likelihood of being a bully or a victim (Olweus, 1978), but physical shortness (Voss & Mulligan, 2000) and weakness (Leff, 1999) were found to be relevant in other research.

Although the harassment associated with bullying can occur anywhere, the term *bullying* often denotes the behavior as it occurs among youth in school hallways and bathrooms, on the playground, or otherwise proximal or internal to the school setting. Bullies can also follow their prey to other venues such as malls, restaurants, or neighborhood hangouts to continue the harassment. In the past, interaction in a physical context was required for victimization to occur. This is no longer the case thanks to the increased prevalence of the Internet, personal computers, and cellular phones. Now, would-be bullies are afforded technology that provides additional media over which they can manifest their malice. The following sections outline the scope, breadth, and consequences of traditional bullying as a reference point from which cyberbullying can subsequently be viewed and understood.

Extent and Effects of Traditional Bullying

It is unclear exactly how many youth are bullied or bully others on any given day. In 1982, 49 fifth-grade teachers from Cleveland, Ohio, reported that almost one-fourth (23%) of their 1,078 students were either victims or bullies (Stephenson & Smith, 1989). More recently, a nationally representative study of 15,686 students in grades 6 through 10 identified that approximately 11% of respondents were victims of bullying, 13% were bullies, and 6% were both victims and bullies during a year (Nansel et al., 2001). Additional research conducted by the Family Work Institute substantiated these findings through interviews with 1,000 youth in grades 5 through 12. Their study found that 12% of youth were bullied five or more times during the previous month (Galinsky & Salmond, 2002). Finally, the Bureau of Justice Statistics reports that 8% of youth between the ages of 12 and 18 had been victims of bullying in the previous 6 months (Devoe et al., 2002). That said, conservative estimates maintain that at least 5% of those in primary and secondary schools (ages 7–16) are victimized by bullies each day (Björkqvist, Ekman, & Lagerspetz, 1982; Lagerspetz, Björkqvist, Berts, & King, 1982; Olweus, 1978; Roland, 1980).

Many young people are able to shrug off instances of being bullied, perhaps because of peer or familial support or higher self-efficacy. Nonetheless, others are not able to cope in a prosocial or normative manner or reconcile the pain experienced through more serious episodes or actions. Suicidal ideation, eating disorders, and chronic illness have beset many of those who have been tormented by bullies, whereas other victims run away from home (Borg, 1998; Kaltiala-Heino, Rimpelä, Marttunen, Rimpelä, & Rantanen, 1999; Striegel-Moore, Dohm, Pike, Wilfley, & Fairburn, 2002). In addition, depression has been a frequently cited consequence of bullying (e.g., Hawker & Boulton, 2000) and seems to perpetuate into adulthood, evidencing the potentially long-term implications of mistreatment during adolescence (Olweus, 1994). Finally, in extreme cases, victims have responded with extreme violence, such as physical assault, homicide, and suicide (Patchin, 2002; Vossekuil et al., 2002).

Following the fatal shootings at Columbine High School in Littleton, Colorado, in 1999, the educational system was challenged to address bullying because the two teenagers involved in the massacre were reported to have been ostracized by their classmates. Additional school violence research of 37 incidents involving 41 attackers from 1974 to 2000 found that 71% (29) of the attackers "felt bullied, persecuted, or injured by others prior to the attack" (Vossekuil et al., 2002, p. 21). It was also determined that the victimization played at least some role in their subsequent violent outburst. Other less serious but equally as negative outcomes can result from repeated bullying. For example, students who are constantly harassed may attempt to avoid the problems at school as much as possible, leading to tardiness or truancy (BBC News, 2001; Richardson, 2003; Rigby & Slee, 1999). Truancy has been identified as a significant antecedent to delinquency, dropout, and other undesirable outcomes in the juvenile justice literature (Farrington, 1980; Garry, 1996; Gavin, 1997; Nansel et al., 2001). Based on these findings, it is clear that victims of bullies are at risk to have a discontinuous developmental trajectory for many years.

The aggressors in the bullying dyad also appear to be more likely to engage in antisocial activities later in life (Tattum, 1989). For example, approximately 60% of those characterized as bullies in grades six through nine were convicted of at least one crime by the age of 24, compared to 23% who were not characterized as either bullies or victims (Olweus et al., 1999). Further underscoring the relationship between bullying and future criminality, Olweus and colleagues (1999) found that 40% of bullies had three or more convictions by the age of 24, compared to 10% of those who were neither instigators nor victims of bullying.

Based on this brief review, it is clear that both bully victims and offenders are at an increased risk for developmental problems that can continue into adulthood. As such, it is imperative that researchers seek to better understand the antecedents and consequences of bullying behavior, for practitioners to develop and implement antibullying programs in schools, and for societal institutions to better understand the ways in which bullying behaviors are carried out, both in traditional and nontraditional settings.

Cyberbullying

Because of the advent and continued growth of technological advances, the transmutation of bullying has occurred—from the physical to the virtual. Physical separation of the bully and the victim is no longer a limitation in the frequency, scope, and depth of harm experienced and doled out. As instances of bullying are no longer restricted to real-world settings, the problem has matured. Although a migration to the electronic realm is a seemingly logical extension for bullies, little is currently known regarding the nature and extent of the phenomenon. In short, we define *cyberbullying* as willful and repeated harm inflicted through the medium of electronic text. Based on the literature reviewed above, the constructs of malicious intent, violence, repetition, and power differential appear most salient when constructing a comprehensive definition of traditional bullying and are similarly appropriate when attempting to define this new permutation. To be sure, cyberbullies are malicious aggressors who seek implicit or explicit pleasure or profit through the mistreatment of other individuals. Violence is often associated with aggression and corresponds to actions intended to inflict injury (of any type). One instance of mistreatment, although potentially destructive, cannot accurately be equated to bullying, and so cyberbullying must also involve harmful behavior of a repetitive nature. Finally, because of the very nature of the behavior, cyberbullies have some perceived or actual power over their victims. Although power in traditional bullying might be physical (stature) or social (competency or popularity), online power may simply stem from proficiency. That is, youth who are able to navigate the electronic world and utilize technology in a way that allows them to harass others are in a position of power relative to a victim.

A brief editorial published in 2003 in *Journal of the American Academy of Child and Adolescent Psychiatry*
295 pointed to the lack of academic references to this topic despite its anticipated proliferation (Jerome & Segal, 2003). Despite this call for research, very little scholarly attention has been devoted to the topic. In a notable exception, Ybarra and Mitchell (2004) conducted
300 telephone surveys of 1,498 regular Internet users between the ages of 10 and 17, along with their parents, and found that 19% of youth respondents were either on the giving or receiving end of online aggression in the previous year. The vast majority of offenders (84%)
305 knew their victim in person, whereas only 31% of victims knew their harasser in person. This fact is noteworthy; it appears that power and dominance are exerted online through the ability to keep the offender's identity unknown (Ybarra & Mitchell, 2004). When
310 comparing those who were only aggressors to those who had no involvement in online harassment, the former were significantly more likely to be the target of offline bullying, to display problematic behavior, to have low school commitment, and to engage in alcohol
315 and cigarette use. When comparing those who had experience being both an offender and a victim with those who had no involvement in online harassment, the significant differences were the same as above—with the exception of low school involvement. It is interesting
320 to note that real-world variables that play a contributive role in traditional forms of delinquency and crime—such as general deviance, low commitment to prosocial institutions such as school, and substance abuse—are also significantly related to bullying on the Internet.
325 There are two major electronic devices that young bullies can employ to harass their victims from afar. First, using a personal computer, a bully can send harassing e-mails or instant messages, post obscene, insulting, and slanderous messages to online bulletin
330 boards, or develop Web sites to promote and disseminate defamatory content. Second, harassing text messages can be sent to the victim via cellular phones.

Personal Computers

Research by the U.S. Department of Commerce noted that almost 90% of youth between the ages of 12
335 and 17 use computers, and by age 10, youth are more likely than are adults to use the Internet (NTIA, 2002). Demonstrating the broad reach of instant messaging and chat programs, 20 million kids between the ages of 2 and 17 logged onto the Internet in July 2002, and
340 11.5 million used instant messaging programs (NetRatings, 2002). Similarly, according to a study of 1,081 Canadian parents conducted in March 2000, 86% stated that their kids used the Internet, 38% had their own e-mail address, 28% used ICQ (an instant messaging program short for "I seek you"), and 28% regularly
345 spent time in chat rooms (Network, 2001). Indeed,

America Online (AOL, 2002, 2003)—the most popular Internet service provider, with more than 35 million users—states that members join in on more than 16,000
350 chat sessions and send more than 2.1 billion instant messages per day across their network. As a point of reference, 1.9 billion phone calls are made each day in the United States. Finally, the Internet relay channels provide a venue for many other users on a daily basis.
355 For example, on the morning of an average Saturday in May 2005, there were more than 1 million users online in more than 800 chat rooms (Gelhausen, 2005).

Pew Internet and American Life Project (2001) conducted an extensive research endeavor in 2001 to
360 ascertain demographic and behavioral characteristics of teenagers who use the Internet. A telephone survey was administered to 754 children between the ages of 12 and 17 in November and December of 2000. Though not generalizable to the population of online teenagers
365 across the United States because of many methodological limitations, the study paints an interesting picture of the user population and their activities while connected to the Internet. About 17 million youth aged 12 to 17 regularly use the Internet. This figure represents ap-
370 proximately three-fourths (73%) of those in this age bracket.

According to the Pew Internet and American Life Project (2001), approximately 29% of youth younger than 12 regularly go online. Among teenagers, ap-
375 proximately 95% of girls and 89% of boys have sent or received e-mail, and 56% of girls and 55% of boys have visited a chat room. Almost three-fourths of teenagers (74%; 78% of girls and 71% of boys) in the study use instant messaging to communicate with their
380 friends, with 69% using the technology several times a week. Almost half (46%) of respondents who report using instant messaging programs spend between 30 and 60 minutes per session doing so, whereas 21% state that they spend more than 1 hour in the activity in
385 an average online session. Testifying to the benefits of textual communication over verbal communication, 37% used it to say something they would not have said in person. Underscoring the potential for harassment and negative treatment online, 57% have blocked mes-
390 sages from someone with whom they did not wish to communicate, and 64% had refused to answer messages from someone with whom they were angry.

Cellular Phones

In the United States, more than 150 million individuals, including half of the youth between 12 and 17
395 years of age, own cellular phones (Fattah, 2003). It is estimated that 74% of Americans between the ages of 13 and 24 will have a wireless device by 2006 (O'Leary, 2003). Cell phone usage is much higher among teenagers and young adults in Europe compared
400 to the United States, 60% to 85% compared to 25% (O'Leary, 2003). Research estimates that by 2007 nearly 100 million individuals will use the text messag-

ing service on their wireless device (Fattah, 2003). Statistics compiled in November 2001 by UPOC (2001)— a wireless communications firm in the United States— found that 43% of those who currently use text messaging are between the ages of 12 and 17. To note, the text messaging capabilities of cellular phones are being exploited to a greater degree in European and Asian countries. In 2002, approximately 90 billion text messages were sent through the two major telecommunication service providers in China, which equals approximately 246 million per day (CD, 2003). In Europe and Asia, more than 30 billion text messages are sent between individuals each month (Katz, 2002). It is predicted that 365 billion text messages will be sent across western Europe in 2006, up from 186 billion in 2002 (GSMBox, 2002).

Issues Specific to Cyberbullying

Gabriel Tarde's (1903) laws of imitation suggests that new technologies will be applied to augment traditional activities and behaviors. Certain characteristics inherent in these technologies increase the likelihood that they will be exploited for deviant purposes. Cellular phones and personal computers offer several advantages to individuals inclined to harass others. First, electronic bullies can remain virtually anonymous. Temporary e-mail accounts and pseudonyms in chat rooms, instant messaging programs, and other Internet venues can make it very difficult for adolescents to determine the identity of aggressors. Individuals can hide behind some measure of anonymity when using their personal computer or cellular phone to bully another individual, which perhaps frees them from normative and social constraints on their behavior. Further, it seems that bullies might be emboldened when using electronic means to effectuate their antagonistic agenda because it takes less energy and fortitude to express hurtful comments using a keyboard or keypad than using one's voice.

Second, supervision is lacking in cyberspace. Although chat hosts regularly observe the dialog in some chat rooms in an effort to police conversations and evict offensive individuals, personal messages sent between users are viewable only by the sender and the recipient and are therefore outside regulatory reach. Furthermore, there are no individuals to monitor or censor offensive content in e-mail or text messages sent via computer or cellular phone. Another contributive element is the increasingly common presence of computers in the private environments of adolescent bedrooms. Indeed, teenagers often know more about computers and cellular phones than do their parents and are therefore able to operate the technologies without worry or concern that a probing parent will discover their participation in bullying (or even their victimization; NTIA, 2002).

In a similar vein, the inseparability of a cellular phone from its owner makes that person a perpetual target for victimization. Users often need to keep it turned on for legitimate uses, which provides the opportunity for those with malicious intentions to send threatening and insulting statements via the cellular phone's text messaging capabilities. There may truly be no rest for the weary as cyberbullying penetrates the walls of a home, traditionally a place where victims could seek refuge.

Finally, electronic devices allow individuals to contact others (both for prosocial and antisocial purposes) at all times and in almost all places. The fact that most adolescents (83%) connect to the Internet from home (Pew Internet and American Life Project, 2001) indicates that online bullying can be an invasive phenomenon that can hound a person even when not at or around school. Relatedly, the coordination of a bullying attack can occur with more ease because it is not constrained by the physical location of the bullies or victims. A veritable onslaught of mistreatment can quickly and effectively torment a victim through the use of these communications and connectivity tools.

Does Harm Occur?

Of course, cyberbullying is a problem only to the extent that it produces harm toward the victim. In the traditional sense, a victim is often under the immediate threat of violence and physical harm and also subject to humiliation and embarrassment in a public setting. These elements compound the already serious psychological, emotional, and social wounds inflicted through such mistreatment. One might argue that a victim of bullying in cyberspace—whether via e-mail, instant messaging, or cellular phone text messaging—can quickly escape from the harassment by deleting the e-mail, closing the instant message, and shutting off the cellular phone and is largely protected from overt acts of violence by the offender through geographic and spatial distance. Such an argument holds much truth; however, the fact remains that if social acceptance is crucially important to a youth's identity and self-esteem, cyberbullying can capably and perhaps more permanently wreak psychological, emotional, and social havoc.[4] It is not a stretch to say that physical harm, such as being beaten up, might even be preferred by some victims to the excruciating pain they experience from nonphysical harm because the former can heal quicker. Furthermore, it is yet to be determined if there is a causal pathway between cyberbullying and traditional bullying, and so physical harm might very well follow as a logical outcome of a continually increasing desire on the part of the offender to most severely hurt the victim. To be sure, this must be explored in future studies.

With regard to public embarrassment, life in cyberspace is often intertwined with life in the real world. For example, many kids and teenagers spend days with their friends in school and nights with those same friends online through instant message programs and

515 chat channels. That which occurs during the day at school is often discussed online at night, and that which occurs online at night is often discussed during the day at school. There is no clean separation between the two realms, and so specific instances of cyberbully-
520 ing—disrespect, name calling, threats, rumors, gossip—against a person make their way around the interested social circles like wildfire.

Does the mistreatment experienced through online bullying lead to the same feelings that result from tradi-
525 tional bullying, such as self-denigration, loss of confidence and self-esteem, depression, anger, frustration, public humiliation, and even physical harm? This remains to be clearly depicted through empirical research but seems plausible based on the linchpin role of self-
530 esteem among children and teenagers previously described and on anecdotal evidence specifically related to online aggression (BBC News, 2001; Benfer, 2001; Blair, 2003; Meadows et al., 2005; ÓhAnluain, 2002; Richardson, 2003).
535 Because of the widespread availability of electronic devices, there is no lack of participants using the technologies. Their ubiquity provides a seemingly endless pool of candidates who are susceptible to being bullied or to becoming a bully. Unfortunately, however, little
540 is known in terms of how often these technologies are mobilized for deviant purposes. One empirical study has been conducted to date: In 2002, the National Children's Home (NCH, 2002)—a charitable organization in London—surveyed 856 youth between the ages of
545 11 and 19 and found that 16% received threatening text messages via their cellular phone, 7% had been bullied in online chat rooms, and 4% had been harassed via e-mail. Following the victimization, 42% told a friend, 32% told a parent or guardian, and 29% did not reveal
550 the experience to anyone. Because more information is clearly warranted, a study was designed to explore the nature and extent of cyberbullying.

Current Study

Method

The current study involved an analysis of youthful Internet users in an effort to assess their perceptions of
555 and experiences with electronic bullying. It is difficult to individually observe the nature and extent of electronic bullying among adolescent Internet users because of the "private" nature of e-mails, cellular phone text messages, and instant messages and one-on-one
560 chat messages within online chat channels. To be sure, if the instances of cyberbullying occur in a public forum such as a popular chat channel and in the view of all chat room members, then direct observation and consequent analyses may be possible. Most of the time,
565 however, they occur through private (nonpublic), person-to-person communications. A survey methodology was therefore designed to collect data by requiring participants to recall and relate their cyberbullying practices and experiences via a questionnaire that was

570 linked from the official Web site of a popular music artist revered by the target age group. An electronic format was selected as it allows for efficiency in collecting data from a large number of participants (Couper, 2000; McCoy & Marks, 2001; Smith, 1997). The
575 survey was active between May 1, 2004, and May 31, 2004.

The context of the Internet must be considered when dealing with consent issues because forcing all online researchers to comply with traditional proce-
580 dures in this area is unduly onerous, particularly when possible harm is little to none. Because it is impossible to personally obtain informed consent from participants in much online survey research that solicits participants from postings on Web sites, implied consent has gener-
585 ally been accepted (Walther, 2002). This involves the presentation of informed consent information in electronic text (e.g., on a Web page), along with specific actions that must be performed prior to initiation of the survey. These actions often include the checking of a
590 check box (agreeing to participate) and clicking on a *submit* button to send the information to the server. From this, consent can be reasonably inferred (King, 1996). For the current study, researchers instructed participants who were younger than 18 to obtain per-
595 mission from their parent or guardian. Permission was demonstrated by the parent entering his or her initials in a specified box. Again, because of matters of anonymity associated with Internet research, it was impossible to actually verify that adolescents obtained proper
600 permission prior to completing the survey.

With survey research conducted over the Internet, questions also arise as to the reliability of the data (Cho & LaRose, 1999). Participants are self-selected, which introduces some bias as individuals are not randomly
605 chosen for inclusion in the study. Often, a convenience sample, where individuals are chosen because they are available (e.g., because they visit a particular Web site and see a solicitation for research participation), is employed. As a result, the sample obtained may not nec-
610 essarily be representative of all Internet users. Moreover, online demographic groups may not mirror those found in the real world (Witte, Amoroso, & Howard, 2000). Generalization to a larger population then becomes impossible with convenience sampling (Couper,
615 2000), but the technique has demonstrated utility for exploratory studies intended to probe a novel phenomenon. Researchers who seek to tap the resources of the World Wide Web will continue to face these challenging issues. Although these limitations are an unfor-
620 tunate cost of conducting Internet-based research, results from this preliminary study will help to inform a more methodologically rigorous investigation in the future.

The survey went through numerous iterations to op-
625 timize its design and presentation of questions. Prior research has determined that poor design can render dubious the quality of responses and may even affect

completion rate (Crawford, Couper, & Lamias, 2001; Krosnick, 1999; Preece, Rogers, & Sharp, 2002; Schwarz, 1999). Specifics to the survey design bear mentioning. Demographic data were solicited at the beginning of the survey, which has been shown to decrease rates of attrition because individuals are not surprised by more personal questions at the resolution of their participation (Frick, Bachtiger, & Reips, 2001). The survey in its entirety was presented to the respondent on one screen, which has also been shown to increase response rates (Crawford et al., 2001). Although our survey did consist of a vast number of questions, findings related to the relationship between survey length and response rate have been mixed and inconclusive (Brown, 1965; Bruvold & Comer, 1988; Eicherner & Habermehl, 1981; Jobber & Saunders, 1993; Mason, Dressel, & Bain, 1961; Sheehan, 2001; Witmer, Colman, & Katzman, 1999; Yammarino, Skinner, & Childers, 1991).

Incentives to participate in the form of cash or other prizes via a lottery have also been shown to increase response rate; human beings are motivated by the possibility of receiving something in return for their efforts, and this trait is manifested in survey participation as well (Cho & LaRose, 1999; Frick et al., 2001). As such, participants in the current study were entered into a random drawing to win one of three autographed photographs of the musical artist from whose fan Web site they reached the survey. We also specified that the institutional review board at the researchers' university had approved the project to verify its legitimacy and strengthen the trust relationship between the researchers and the potential participants (Cho & LaRose, 1999).

A final point bears mentioning. As the Internet protocol (IP) address and timestamp were recorded with each participant's responses, we were able to eliminate entries where all of the responses were completely the same. This might happen when a respondent fills out the questionnaire, clicks *submit*, goes back to the previous page where all of his or her responses are stored within the survey form, and then clicks *submit* again (and continues in this pattern). To note, there were survey entries from the same IP address but with completely different responses to the questions posed. This was because some Internet service providers route multiple users through one IP address when connecting from their internal network to the external Internet. To summarize, we browsed through all of the data and attempted to determine which entries were fraudulent and which were valid.

Findings

Because this was an Internet-based survey, anyone could participate. Even though the survey was associated with a teen-oriented Web site, individuals from all ages also frequent the site and therefore completed the survey. As noted in Table 1, out of the 571 total respondents, 384 were younger than 18 (67.3%; henceforth referred to as the youth sample). In both groups, the vast majority of respondents were female. This finding is likely attributable to the nature of the Web site on which the survey was linked (a female pop music star). Similarly, the vast majority of respondents were Caucasian. There are several potential interpretations of this finding. First, individuals from different racial and ethnic backgrounds may be less interested in this particular entertainer than are others and may therefore be unlikely to visit the Web site to see the survey solicitation. Alternatively, the overrepresentation of Caucasian respondents could be evidence of the oft-mentioned digital divide, where some populations are not privy to the access and use of technology such as computers and the Internet. As expected, most respondents were between the ages of 12 and 20, and the average age of the youth sample was 14.1. Moreover, more than 70% of respondents from the complete sample were in grades 2 through 12. High school respondents (9th through 12th grade) represented the modal category of respondents for both groups. As might be expected, the vast majority of all respondents came from English-speaking countries (the Web site and survey were written in English), and about 60% of respondents in both groups reported living in the United States. It must be mentioned that because online identity is completely malleable (Hafner, 2001; Turkle, 1995), the demographic data obtained may not be completely accurate because of a lack of trust in our research project, mischief, or purposeful obfuscation. Research performed over the Internet cannot entirely preempt this problem—at least in its current stage of technological development—and so a caveat is justified.

The remainder of the findings discussed relate only to those respondents who were younger than 18 when they completed the survey ($n = 384$). Online bullying was specifically defined on the questionnaire for respondents as behavior that can include bothering someone online, teasing in a mean way, calling someone hurtful names, intentionally leaving persons out of things, threatening someone, and saying unwanted, sexually related things to someone. Table 2 presents the percentage of respondents who have been bullied ("Have you ever been bullied online?"), have bullied others ("Have you ever bullied others while online?"), or have witnessed bullying online ("Have you ever seen other kids bullied online?"). Almost 11% of youth reported bullying others while online, more than 29% reported being the victim of online bullying, and more than 47% have witnessed online bullying. Cyberbullying was most prevalent in chat rooms, followed by computer text messages and e-mail. Bullying using news groups or cellular phones was not as prominent for members of this sample. Indeed, although it is clear that all who responded to the survey have access to a

Table 1
Descriptive Statistics of Survey Respondents

	Complete sample[a]		Youth sample[b]	
	n	%	n	%
Sex				
Female	452	78.3	325	84.6
Male	115	19.9	55	14.3
Missing	10	1.7	4	1.0
Race				
Caucasian	429	74.4	289	75.3
Hispanic	43	7.5	32	8.3
Asian or Pacific Islander	43	7.5	28	7.3
African American	4	0.7	3	0.8
Indigenous or aboriginal	4	0.7	3	0.8
Multiracial	16	2.8	10	2.6
Other race	32	5.5	19	4.9
Missing	6	1.0	0	0.0
Age				
9–11	37	6.4	37	9.6
12–13	110	19.1	110	28.6
14–15	135	23.4	135	35.2
16–17	102	17.7	102	26.6
18–20	128	22.2	—	—
21–25	41	7.1	—	—
26 and older	18	3.1	—	—
Missing	6	1.0	—	—
Grade				
Grades 2–5	25	4.3	24	6.3
Grades 6–8	149	25.8	149	38.8
Grades 9–12	231	40.0	196	51.0
Community college	37	6.4	7	1.8
University	72	12.5	1	0.3
Do not attend school	52	9.0	4	1.0
Missing	11	1.9	3	0.8
Country				
United States	349	60.5	227	59.1
Canada	62	10.7	46	12.0
United Kingdom	53	9.2	35	9.1
Australia	29	5.0	23	6.0
Other or unknown	84	14.6	53	13.8

a. $N = 577$; b. $N = 384$.

computer, it is unknown what proportion of respondents have access to a cellular phone.

Table 2
Percentage of Youth Respondents Who Report Being a Bully, a Victim, or a Witness to Bullying

	Bully	Victim	Witness
Online	10.7	29.4	47.1
In a chat room	7.6	21.9	42.4
Via computer text message	5.2	13.5	15.1
Via e-mail	1.8	12.8	13.8
On a bulletin board	1.0	2.9	13.8
Via cell phone text message	0.8	2.1	6.3
In a newsgroup	0.5	1.6	3.6

Note. N = 384.

As previously described, youth were asked a general question regarding their involvement in online bullying. In addition, youth were asked to relate whether they experienced a number of behaviors that may be associated with bullying. Table 3 presents in-

formation collected from these questions. Notably, 60.4% of respondents have been ignored by others while online, 50.0% reported being disrespected by others, almost 30.0% have been called names, and 21.4% have been threatened by others. In addition, a significant proportion of youth were picked on by others (19.8%) or made fun of by others (19.3%) or had rumors spread about them by others (18.8%).

Table 3
Types of Online Bullying

	Percentage victimized
Ignored by others	60.4
Disrespected by others	50.0
Called names by others	29.9
Been threatened by others	21.4
Picked on by others	19.8
Made fun of by others	19.3
Rumors spread by others	18.8

Note. N = 384.

Table 4
Average Number of Bullying Experiences During Previous 30 Days for Youth Who Reported Being a Victim or a Bully

	Bully			Victim		
	n	*M*	*Max*	*n*	*M*	*Max*
In a chat room	39	1.23	10	83	3.36	50
Via computer text message	30	1.20	6	68	4.65	76
Via e-mail	18	0.39	2	61	4.07	107
On a bulletin board	16	1.50	9	31	2.42	10
Via cell phone text message	9	3.22	23	19	3.37	23
In a newsgroup	2	0.00	0	6	1.67	6

Note. n reflects the number of youth who reported experience in that behavior; *M* is the average number of times the experience occurred in the previous 30 days, and *Max* is the highest number of times the experience was reported during the previous 30 days.

In addition to asking respondents whether they have experienced bullying online, researchers also asked youth how frequently the bullying occurred during the previous 30 days. Table 4 presents summary statistics reflecting the number of youth who reported involvement in the bullying experience, the average number of times the bullying occurred, and the maximum number of times the bullying occurred. For example, 83 youth reported being victimized in a chat room an average of 3.36 times during the previous 30 days. One youth reported being bullied in a chat room 50 times during the previous 30 days. Bullying via computer text messaging and e-mail also occurred frequently during the previous 30 days.

Table 5 demonstrates the negative effects associated with online bullying on victims. For example, 42.5% of victims were frustrated, almost 40.0% felt angry, and more than 27.0% felt sad. Almost one-third (31.9%) reported that it affected them at school, whereas 26.5% reported that it affected them at home. Only 22.1% were not bothered by the bullying they experienced, and less than 44.0% stated that the bullying did not affect them.

Table 5
Effects of Online Bullying

	Percentage yes
I felt frustrated	42.5
I felt angry	39.8
I felt sad	27.4
I was not bothered	22.1
It affected me at school	31.9
It affected me at home	26.5
It affected me with my friends	20.4
It did not affect me	43.4

Note. Responses for youth who reported being bullied online (*N* = 113).

Table 6 describes the response taken by victims of online bullying. Notably, almost 20% of victims were forced to stay offline, whereas almost 32% had to remove themselves from the environment in some capacity or way. Victims also revealed a hesitation to tell authority figures about their experiences. Even though most confided in an online friend (56.6%), fewer than 9.0% of victims informed an adult.

Additional analyses were conducted to attempt to uncover correlates of online bullying. There were no statistically significant associations among age, race, or gender and who is likely to be a victim of online bullying. The lack of relationship among race or gender and victimization may be more a function of the homogeneous nature of the data than any substantive finding and must be further tested. In accordance with intuition, youth who participate in more activities online (represented by a variety score of 13 different activities) were more likely to experience online bullying. Also not surprising, youth who bully others were more likely to be victims of online bullying. In all, 75% of youth who have bullied others online have been victims of bullying, whereas fewer than 25% of youth bullies have never been on the other end of such malicious actions (χ^2 = 42.866; *p* < .001). Future research should seek to better understand what additional factors are associated with online bullying.

Table 6
Response to Online Bullying

	Percentage yes
I tell the bully to stop	36.3
I get away	31.9
I do nothing	24.8
I stay offline	19.5
I bully others	2.7
I tell an online friend	56.6
I tell a friend	25.7
I tell nobody	23.0
I tell my mom and dad	19.5
I tell my brother or sister	16.8
I tell an adult	8.8

Note. Responses for youth who reported being bullied online (*N* = 113).

Discussion

The results of this study point to a number of key issues. First, bullying is occurring online and is impacting youth in many negative ways. Almost 30% of the adolescent respondents reported that they had been victims of online bullying—operationalized as having been ignored, disrespected, called names, threatened, picked on or made fun of, or having had rumors spread by others. Admittedly, being ignored by another person may simply reflect obnoxious behavior that warranted the outcome rather than actual and willful aggression. We were not able to parcel out the stimuli of instances when people were ignored but chose to include a

23

820 measure of it in the current analyses. This is because universal social acceptance is still largely desired by children and adolescents, even if as adults we understand that it is impossible to please everyone at all times. Being ignored would introduce dissonance and instability to the already tenuous relational and social equilibria sought by youths and may accordingly be
825 considered a passive–aggressive form of bullying. Along similar lines, although some of this harassment may be characterized as trivial (e.g., being ignored by others or being disrespected), more than 20% reported being threatened by others. Anger and frustration was a
830 commonly reported emotional response to the harassment. Finally, almost 60% of victims were affected by the online behaviors at school, at home, or with friends.

Several policy implications stem from the aforementioned findings. It is hoped that this harmful phe-
835 nomena can be curtailed by proactively addressing the potentially negative uses of technology. Parents must regularly monitor the activities in which their children are engaged while online. Teachers, too, must take care to supervise students as they use computers in the
840 classrooms. Police officers must investigate those instances of cyberbullying that are potentially injurious and hold responsible parties accountable. Unfortunately, there are no methods to discern which harassment involves simple jest and which has the potential
845 to escalate into serious violence. Future research must analyze case studies and anecdotal stories of cyberbullying experiences to help determine when intervention by authority figures is most appropriate. Overall, parents, teachers, police officers, and other community
850 leaders must keep up with technological advances so that they are equipped with the tools and knowledge to identify and address any problems when they arise.

Limitations of the Current Study

The most notable limitations of this study relate to its administration because data were collected exclu-
855 sively online. With regard to sampling, it is unquestionable that Internet users are dissimilar from those who do not go online. However, Walther (2002, p. 209) argues that concerns related to the generalizability of data collected from the Internet to a target population
860 assume that random samples of Internet users are sought in any study and that a sample obtained from the Internet is able to be generalized to other populations. We would have liked to obtain a random sample of all Internet users younger than 18 to ascertain the
865 extent and prevalence of online bullying, but such a task is impossible as no reliable sampling frame of individuals in cyberspace exists. Thus, we carefully targeted certain Web sites presumably visited by at least some adolescents who have personal experience
870 in the phenomenon. As it turned out, the sample was disproportionately Caucasian and female, and results therefore may be skewed toward these subgroups. As a result, any findings from the research should be very

875 cautiously applied to the larger group of Internet-using youth.

Another issue related to online data collection concerns misrepresentation of age by participants in this research. Undoubtedly, we cannot guarantee that re-
880 spondents honestly indicated their age during participation. Any qualms, though, can be overcome by considering the fallibility of traditional research methods, such as phone surveys or surveys distributed in highly populated settings (e.g., large college classes) or
885 through the mail and even individual, face-to-face administration of questionnaires. A person can lie about his or her age in any of these contexts, and it is unreasonable to assume that a person would be more likely to do so in an online research setting (Walther, 2002).

Directions for Future Research

890 The current study provides the framework for future empirical inquiry on electronic bullying. Indeed, the authors are currently involved in a more comprehensive study that involves both Internet-based research and traditional paper-and-pencil surveys. As
895 with any social scientific endeavor, replication is necessary to more fully understand the phenomena under consideration. There are several questions future research in this area must address. First, data must be collected to more accurately ascertain the scope, preva-
900 lence, and nuances of cyberbullying. For example, it is important to discover whether cyberbullies are simply traditional bullies who have embraced new technologies to accomplish their intentions or if they are youth who have never participated in traditional, school-
905 based bullying. Moreover, do personal computers enable the stereotypical victims of bullies (i.e., those who are smart, physically small, and/or socially challenged) to retaliate using means that ensure their anonymity? It would also be important to determine whether com-
910 monly accepted stimuli for traditional bullying—the need to (a) exert power and dominate, (b) compensate for victimization in another area of one's life, (c) cope with one's insecurities, and (d) attract attention and popularity—are similarly predictive in cyberspace-based instances of the deviance.

915 Also of interest is the extent to which electronic bullying results in harm to adolescents in their physical environments (e.g., at school or in their neighborhoods). Are threats made in cyberspace followed through on the playground? Are victims of cyberbully-
920 ing the same individuals who are also victims of traditional bullying, or are they distinct groups? What about offenders? One could hypothesize that the victims of traditional bullying may turn to the Internet to exact revenge on their schoolyard aggressors. That is, the
925 victim becomes the offender by using his or her technological knowledge to inflict harm on the original bully.

In addition, it is useful to identify whether adults also participate in electronic harassment. Although they

930 may frequent chat rooms to a lesser degree than do children and adolescents, cellular phone use and even instant messaging programs are commonly utilized for both professional and personal purposes. Does electronic harassment occur to the same extent among
935 adults as compared to a population of adolescents? Does it occur in a more controlled and subtle manner or with the same degree of perceivably overt cruelty? Does it occur for fundamentally similar reasons across both groups, or are there factors endemic to youth or
940 adult life that condition and dictate bullying in an online context? These are just some of the important questions that need further examination.

Finally, future research efforts ought to more thoroughly examine the results of this preliminary investi-
945 gation using more rigorous methodology that ensures a more representative sample of responses. As indicated, the intent of this research is to generate scholarly interest in this unique form of adolescent harassment and therefore should be viewed simply as a small, but we
950 think significant, platform on which further research efforts should be built.

Conclusion

The preceding review provides a description of bullying in cyberspace for the purposes of introducing it as a topic meriting academic inquiry and underscoring its
955 often inescapable pernicious nature. Indeed, 74% of the youth in this study reported that bullying occurs online, and almost 30% of the youth reported being victimized by others while online. Some may dismiss electronic bullying as normative behavior that does not physically
960 harm anyone. To be sure, some have this perception regarding traditional bullying, dismissing it as a rite of passage or an inevitable and even instructive element of growing up. Because of the familiarity and memorability of bullying as almost unavoidable in both the
965 schoolyard and neighborhood milieu during one's formative years, perhaps the reader may share those sentiments.

Because no consensus exists when considering whether cyberbullying merits increased attention be-
970 cause of society's continued progression into a wired world, perhaps it should just be considered another contemporary cultural challenge that kids often face when transitioning into adulthood. Conceivably, there is no need to panic when introduced to the concept that
975 online bullying does and will continue to take place as children seek to carve out an identity for themselves and cope with various pressures associated with their development. Alternatively, perhaps there is a need for alarm as both those who bully and those who are bul-
980 lied might yield readily to other criminogenic influences and proceed down a path of deviance online, offline, or both. Regardless, cyberbullying is very real, and it is hoped that this work has highlighted its relevance for the purposes of inspiring additional interest
985 in its etiology and consequences.

End Notes

[1] The interested reader is encouraged to see Blair (2003) or ÓhAnluain (2002) for more examples.

[2] It should be mentioned that research has not identified a link between low self-esteem and the offenders of traditional bullying (Hoover & Hazler, 1991; Rigby & Slee, 1993).

[3] To be sure, females are also bullied to a substantive degree and must not be excluded from any analyses of the phenomenon.

[4] Cyberbullying repercussions have permanence because e-mails can be saved, instant messages and chat conversations can be logged, and Web pages can be archived for an offender, victim, or third party to read over in the future and thereby relive the experience.

References

America Online. (2002). *AOL facts—2002*. Retrieved September 2, 2003, from http://www.corp.aol.com/whoweare/Factbook_F.pdf

America Online. (2003). *Who we are: Fast facts*. Retrieved September 2, 2003, from http://www.corp.aol.com/whoweare/fastfacts.html

BBC News. (2001). *Girl tormented by phone bullies*. Retrieved January 16, 2001, from http://news.bbc.co.uk/1/hi/education/1120597.stm

Benfer, A. (2001). *Cyber slammed*. Retrieved July 7, 2001, from http://www.dir.salon.com/mwt/feature/2001/07/03/cyber_bullies/index.html

Berson, I. R., Berson, M. J., & Ferron, J. M. (2002). Emerging risks of violence in the digital age: Lessons for educators from an online study of adolescent girls in the United States. *Journal of School Violence, 1,* 51–71.

Björkqvist, K., Ekman, K., & Lagerspetz, K. (1982). Bullies and victims: Their ego picture, ideal ego picture, and normative ego picture. *Scandinavian Journal of Psychology, 23,* 307–313.

Blair, J. (2003). New breed of bullies torment their peers on the Internet. *Education Week*. Retrieved February 5, 2003, from http://www.edweek.org/ew/ewstory.cfm?slug=21cyberbully.h22

Borg, M. G. (1998). The emotional reaction of school bullies and their victims. *Educational Psychology, 18,* 433–444.

Brown, M. (1965). Use of a postcard query in mail surveys. *Public Opinion Quarterly, 29,* 635–637.

Bruvold, N. T., & Comer, J. M. (1988). A model for estimating the response rate to a mailed survey. *Journal of Business Research, 16,* 101–116.

CD. (2003). *Thumbs down on mobile messaging*. Retrieved July 22, 2003, from http://www.chinadaily.com.cn/en/doc/2003-07/22/content_247257.htm

Cho, H., & LaRose, R. (1999). Privacy issues in Internet surveys. *Social Science Computer Review, 14 ,* 421–434.

Coie, J. D., & Dodge, K. A. (1988). Multiple sources of data on social behavior and social status in the school: A cross-age comparison. *Child Development, 59,* 815–829.

Cooley, C. H. (1902). *Human nature and the social order*. New York: Scribner.

Couper, M. P. (2000). Web-based surveys: A review of issues and approaches. *Public Opinion Quarterly, 64,* 464–494.

Crawford, S., Couper, M. P., & Lamias, M. (2001). Web surveys: Perceptions of burden. *Social Science Computer Review, 19,* 146–162.

Devoe, J. F., Ruddy, S. A., Miller, A. K., Planty, M., Peter, K., Kaufman, P. et al. (2002). *Indicators of school crime and safety*. Washington, DC: U.S. Department of Education, National Center for Education Statistics, U.S. Department of Justice, Bureau of Justice Statistics.

Eicherner, K., & Habermehl, W. (1981). Predicting the response rates to mailed questionnaires (comment on Herberlien & Baumgartner). *American Sociological Review, 46,* 1–3.

Farrington, D. (1980). Truancy, delinquency, the home, and the school. In L. Hersov & I. Berg (Eds.), *Out of school: Modern perspectives in truancy and school refusal* (pp. 49–63). New York: John Wiley.

Fattah, H. (2003). *America untethered*. Retrieved September 1, 2003, from http://www.upoc.com/corp/news/UpocAmDem.pdf

Finn, J. (2004). A survey of online harassment at a university campus. *Journal of Interpersonal Violence, 19,* 468–483.

French, D. C., & Waas, G. A. (1987). Social–cognitive and behavioral characteristics of peer-rejected boys. *Professional School Psychology, 2,* 103–112.

Frick, A., Bachtiger, M. T., & Reips, U.-D. (2001). Financial incentives, personal information, and dropout in online studies. In U.-D. Reips & M. Bosnjak (Eds.), *Dimensions of Internet science* (pp. 209–219). Lengerich, Germany: Pabst Science.

Galinsky, E., & Salmond, K. (2002). *Youth and violence: Students speak out for a more civil society*. New York: Families and Work Institute.

Garry, E. M. (1996). *Truancy: First step to a lifetime of problems*. Washington, DC: U.S. Department of Justice, Office of Juvenile Justice and Delinquency Prevention.

Gavin, T. (1997). *Truancy: Not just kids' stuff anymore*. Washington, DC: Federal Bureau of Investigation.

Gelhausen, A. (2005). *Summary of IRC networks*. Retrieved May 7, 2005, from http://irc.netsplit.de/networks/

GSMBox. (2002). *Ten years of SMS messages*. Retrieved August 10, 2003, from http://uk.gsmbox.com/news/mobile_news/all/94480.gsmbox

Hafner, K. (2001). *The well: A story of love, death & real life in the seminal online community*. New York: Carrol and Graf.

Hawker, D. S. J., & Boulton, M. J. (2000). Twenty years' research on peer victimization and psychological maladjustment: A meta-analysis review of cross-sectional studies. *Journal of Child Psychology and Psychiatry, 41*, 441–445.

Hoover, J., & Hazler, R. (1991). Bullies and victims. *Elementary School Guidance and Counseling, 25*, 212–219.

Hull, J. G. (1981). A self-awareness model of the causes and effects of alcohol consumption. *Journal of Abnormal Psychology, 90*, 586–600.

Hymel, S., Rubin, K. H., Rowden, L., & LeMare, L. (1990). Children's peer relationships longitudinal prediction of internalizing and externalizing problems from middle to late childhood. *Child Development, 61*, 2004–2021.

Jerome, L., & Segal, A. (2003). Bullying by Internet—Editorial. *Journal of the American Academy of Child and Adolescent Psychiatry, 42*, 751.

Jobber, D., & Saunders, J. (1993). A note on the applicability of the Brurold-Comer model of mail survey response rates to commercial populations. *Journal of Business Research, 26*, 223–236.

Kaltiala-Heino, R., Rimpelä, M., Marttunen, M., Rimpelä, A., & Rantanen, P. (1999). Bullying, depression, and suicidal ideation in Finnish adolescents: School survey. *British Medical Journal, 319*, 348–351.

Katz, A. R. (2002). *Text messaging moves from cell to home*. Retrieved August 15, 2003, from http://www.iht.com/articles/51152.html

King, S. (1996). Researching Internet communities: Proposed ethical guidelines for the reporting of results. *The Information Society, 12*, 119–128.

Krosnick, J. A. (1999). Survey research. *Annual Review of Psychology, 50*, 537–567.

Lagerspetz, K. M. J., Björkqvist, K., Berts, M., & King, E. (1982). Group aggression among schoolchildren in three schools. *Scandinavian Journal of Psychology, 23*, 45–52.

Leary, M. R., & Downs, D. L. (1995). Interpersonal functions of the self-esteem motive: The self-esteem system as a sociometer. In M. H. Kernis (Ed.), *Efficacy, agency, and self-esteem* (pp. 123–144). New York: Plenum.

Leary, M. R., Haupt, A. L., Strausser, K. S., & Chokel, J. T. (1998). Calibrating the sociometer: The relationship between interpersonal appraisals and state self-esteem. *Journal of Personality and Social Psychology, 74*, 1290–1299.

Leary, M. R., Schreindorfer, L. S., & Haupt, A. L. (1995). The role of self-esteem in emotional and behavioral problems: Why is low self-esteem dysfunctional? *Journal of Social and Clinical Psychology, 14*, 297–314.

Leary, M. R., Tambor, E. S., Terdal, S. J., & Downs, D. L. (1995). Self-esteem as an interpersonal monitor: The sociometer hypothesis. *Journal of Personality and Social Psychology, 68*, 518–530.

Leff, S. (1999). Bullied children are picked on for their vulnerability. *British Medical Journal, 318*, 1076.

Manning, M., Heron, J., & Marshal, T. (1978). Style of hostility and social interactions at nursery school and at home: An extended study of children. In A. Lionel, M. B. Hersov, & D. Shaffer (Eds.), *Aggression and antisocial behavior in childhood and adolescence* (pp. 29–58). Oxford, UK: Pergamon.

Mason, W., Dressel, R., & Bain, R. (1961). An experimental study of factors affecting response to a mail survey of beginning teachers. *Public Opinion Quarterly, 25*, 296–299.

McCoy, S., & Marks, P. V., Jr. (2001, August). *Using electronic surveys to collect data: Experiences from the field*. Paper presented at the AMCIS Annual Conference, Boston.

Meadows, B., Bergal, J., Helling, S., Odell, J., Piligian, E., Howard, C. et al. (2005, March 21). The Web: The bully's new playground. *People*, pp. 152–155.

Nansel, T. R., Overpeck, M., Pilla, R. S., Ruan, W. J., Simons-Morton, B., & Scheidt, P. (2001). Bullying behaviors among US youth: Prevalence and association with psychosocial adjustment. *Journal of the American Medical Association, 285*, 2094–2100.

National Children's Home. (2002). *1 in 4 children are the victims of "on-line bullying" says children's charity*. Retrieved September 1, 2003, from http://www.nch.org.uk/news/news5.asp?auto=195

National Telecommunications and Information Administration. (2002). *A nation online: How Americans are expanding their use of the Internet*. Retrieved June 13, 2004, from http://www.ntia.doc.gov/ntiahome/dn/anationonline2.pdf

Neary, A., & Joseph, S. (1994). Peer victimization and its relationship to self-concept and depression among schoolgirls. *Personality and Individual Differences, 16*, 183–186.

NetRatings, N. (2002). *IM programs draw US kids and teens online*. Retrieved July 30, 2003, from http://www.nua.com/surveys/index.cgi?f=VS&art_id=905358261&rel=true

Network, M. A. (2001). *Canada's children in a wired world: The parents' view—Final report*. Retrieved July 30, 2003, from http://www.media-awareness.ca/english/resources/special_initiatives/survey_resources/parents_survey/loader.cfm?url=/commonspot/security/getfile.cfm&PageID=31576

ÓhAnluain, D. (2002). *When text messaging turns ugly*. Retrieved September 4, 2002, from http://www.wired.com/news/school/0,1383,54771,00.html

O'Leary, N. (2003). *Cell phone marketers tap teens as the next frontier*. Retrieved February 17, 2003, from http://www.adweek.com/aw/magazine/article_display.jsp?vnu_content_id=1818786

Olweus, D. (1978). *Aggression in the schools: Bullies and whipping boys*. Washington, DC: Hemisphere Press.

Olweus, D. (1993). *Bullying at school*. Oxford, UK: Blackwell.

Olweus, D. (Ed.). (1994). *Bullying at school: Long-term outcomes for victims and an effective school-based intervention program*. New York: Plenum.

Olweus, D. (1999). Norway. In P. K. Smith, Y. Morita, J. Junger-Tas, D. Olweus, R. Catalano, & P. Slee (Eds.), *Nature of school bullying: A cross-national perspective* (pp. 28–48). London: Routledge.

Olweus, D., Limber, S., & Mihalic, S. (1999). *Bullying prevention program*. Boulder, CO: Center for the Study and Prevention of Violence.

Patchin, J. (2002). Bullied youths lash out: Strain as an explanation of extreme school violence. *Caribbean Journal of Criminology and Social Psychology, 7*, 22–43.

Paulson, M. J., Coombs, R. H., & Landsverk, J. (1990). Youth who physically assault their parents. *Journal of Family Violence, 5*, 121–133.

Pew Internet and American Life Project. (2001). *Teenage life online: The rise of the instant-message generation and the Internet's impact on friendships and family relationships*. Retrieved July 13, 2004, from http://www.pewinternet.org/pdfs/PIP_Teens_Report.pdf

Preece, J., Rogers, Y., & Sharp, S. (2002). *Interaction design: Beyond human–computer interaction*. New York: John Wiley.

Quellet, R., & Joshi, P. (1986). Loneliness in relation to depression and self-esteem. *Psychological Reports, 58*, 821–822.

Richardson, T. (2003). *Bullying by text message*. Retrieved February 20, 2003, from http://www.theadvertiser.news.com.au/common/story_page/0,5936,6012025%5E2682,00.html

Rigby, K., & Slee, P. T. (1993). Dimensions of interpersonal relating among Australian school children and their implications for psychological well-being. *The Journal of Social Psychology, 133*, 33–42.

Rigby, K., & Slee, P. T. (1999). Australia. In P. Smith, Y. Morita, J. Junger-Tas, D. Olweus, R. Catalano, & P. Slee (Eds.), *The nature of school bullying: A cross-national perspective* (pp. 324–339). London: Routledge.

Roland, E. (1980). *Terror i skolen* [Terrorism in school]. Stavanger, Norway: Rogaland Research Institute.

Roland, E. (1989). Bullying: The Scandinavian research tradition. In D. P. Tattum & D. A. Lane (Eds.), *Bullying in schools* (pp. 21–32). Stroke-on-Trent, UK: Trentham.

Schwarz, N. (1999). Self-reports: How the questions shape the answers. *American Psychologist, 54*, 93–105.

Sheehan, K. B. (2001). E-mail survey response rates: A review. *Journal of Computer Mediated Communication, 6*. Retrieved January 18, 2006, from http://jcmc.indiana.edu/vol6/issue2/sheehan.html

Slee, P. T., & Rigby, K. (1993). The relationship of Eysenck's personality factors and self-esteem to bully/victim behaviour in Australian school boys. *Personality and Individual Differences, 14*, 371–373.

Smart, R., & Walsh, G. (1993). Predictors of depression in street youth. *Adolescence, 28*, 41–53.

Smith, C. B. (1997). Casting the net: Surveying an Internet population. *Journal of Computer Mediated Communication, 3*. Retrieved January 18, 2006, from http://jcmc.indiana.edu/vol3/issue1/smith.html

Stephenson, P., & Smith, D. (1989). Bullying in junior school. In D. P. Tattum & D. A. Lane (Ed.), *Bullying in schools* (pp. 45–58). Stroke-on-Trent, UK: Trentham.

Stewart, M. A. (1985). Aggressive conduct disorder: A brief review. 6th Biennial Meeting of the International Society for Research on Aggression (1984, Turku, Finland). *Aggressive Behavior, 11*, 323–331.

Striegel-Moore, R. H., Dohm, F.-A., Pike, K. M., Wilfley, D. E., & Fairburn, C. G. (2002). Abuse, bullying, and discrimination as risk factors for binge eating disorder. *The American Journal of Psychiatry, 159*, 1902–1907.

Tarde, G. (Ed.). (1903). *Gabriel Tarde's laws of imitation*. New York: Henry Holt.

Tattum, D. P. (1989). Violence and aggression in schools. In D. P. Tattum & D. A. Lane (Eds.), *Bullying in schools* (pp. 7–19). Stroke-on-Trent, UK: Trentham.

Turkle, S. (1995). *Life on the screen: Identity in the age of the Internet*. New York: Simon & Schuster.

Twenge, J. M., & Campbell, W. K. (2001). Age and birth cohort differences in self-esteem: A cross-temporal meta-analysis. *Personality and Social Psychology Review, 5*, 321–344.

UPOC. (2001). *Wireless stats*. Retrieved September 1, 2003, from http://www.genwireless.com/stats.html

Voss, L. D., & Mulligan, J. (2000). Bullying in school: Are short pupils at risk? Questionnaire study in a cohort. *British Medical Journal, 320*, 612–613.

Vossekuil, B., Fein, R. A., Reddy, M., Borum, R., & Modzeleski, W. (2002). *The final report and findings of the Safe School Initiative: Implications for* the prevention of school attacks in the United States. Retrieved August 29, 2003, from http://www.secretservice.gov/ntac/ssi_final_report.pdf

Walther, J. B. (2002). Research ethics in Internet enabled research: Human subjects issues and methodological myopia. *Ethics and Information Technology, 4*, 205.

Witmer, D. F., Colman, R. W., & Katzman, S. L. (1999). From paper-and-pencil to screen-and-keyboard. In S. Jones (Ed.), *Doing Internet research: Critical issues and methods for examining the Net* (pp. 145–161). Thousand Oaks, CA: Sage.

Witte, J. C., Amoroso, L. M., & Howard, P. E. N. (2000). Research methodology—Method and representation in Internet-based survey tools—Mobility, community, and cultural identity in Survey 2000. *Social Science Computer Review, 18*, 179–195.

Yammarino, F. J., Skinner, S., & Childers, T. L. (1991). Understanding mail survey response behavior. *Public Opinion Quarterly, 55*, 613–639.

Ybarra, M. L., & Mitchell, J. K. (2004). Online aggressor/targets, aggressors and targets: A comparison of associated youth characteristics. *Journal of Child Psychology and Psychiatry, 45*, 1308–1316.

Acknowledgments: We would like to thank the anonymous reviewers for helpful comments on an earlier draft.

Address correspondence to: Justin W. Patchin, Department of Political Science, University of Wisconsin, Eau Claire, 105 Garfield Avenue, Eau Claire, WI 54702-4004. E-mail: patchinj@uwec.edu

About the authors: *Justin W. Patchin* is an assistant professor of criminal justice at the University of Wisconsin, Eau Claire. His research areas focus on policy and program evaluation, juvenile delinquency prevention, and school violence. *Sameer Hinduja* is an assistant professor in the Department of Criminology and Criminal Justice at Florida Atlantic University. His research largely involves the integration of social science and computer science perspectives.

Exercise for Article 3

Factual Questions

1. The questionnaire was linked from what?

2. Did the researchers solicit demographic data at the "beginning" *or* at the "end" of the survey?

3. Were the majority of the respondents "male" *or* "female"?

4. Which ethnic/racial group constituted the vast majority of the respondents?

5. Are the results presented in Tables 2 through 6 based on the responses of "all respondents" *or* "only respondents younger than 18"?

6. What was the most frequent response to online bullying?

Questions for Discussion

7. The introduction and literature review in lines 1–552 are longer than most others in this book. In your opinion, is this lengthy review an important part of this research report? Would the report have been as effective with a shorter review?

8. What is your opinion on the importance of the researchers' inability to verify if participants under 18 years of age actually obtained permission from their parents and guardians? (See lines 593–600 and 876–888.)

9. The researchers used an incentive to encourage participation in the survey. What is your opinion on the particular incentive used in this research? (See lines 647–656.)

10. The researchers make a number of suggestions for future research in lines 889–951. In your opinion, are some of the suggestions more important than others? Are some more interesting than others? Explain.

11. The researchers conclude by stating that they hope this research will inspire additional interest in the etiology and consequences of cyberbullying. Do you think that it will? Explain. (See lines 982–985.)

Quality Ratings

Directions: Indicate your level of agreement with each of the following statements by circling a number from 5 for strongly agree (SA) to 1 for strongly disagree (SD). If you believe an item is not applicable to this research article, leave it blank. Be prepared to explain your ratings. When responding to criteria A and B below, keep in mind that brief titles and abstracts are conventional in published research.

A. The title of the article is appropriate.

   SA   5   4   3   2   1   SD

B. The abstract provides an effective overview of the research article.

   SA   5   4   3   2   1   SD

C. The introduction establishes the importance of the study.

   SA   5   4   3   2   1   SD

D. The literature review establishes the context for the study.

   SA   5   4   3   2   1   SD

E. The research purpose, question, or hypothesis is clearly stated.

   SA   5   4   3   2   1   SD

F. The method of sampling is sound.

   SA   5   4   3   2   1   SD

G. Relevant demographics (for example, age, gender, and ethnicity) are described.

   SA   5   4   3   2   1   SD

H. Measurement procedures are adequate.

SA   5   4   3   2   1   SD

I. All procedures have been described in sufficient detail to permit a replication of the study.

SA   5   4   3   2   1   SD

J. The participants have been adequately protected from potential harm.

SA   5   4   3   2   1   SD

K. The results are clearly described.

SA   5   4   3   2   1   SD

L. The discussion/conclusion is appropriate.

SA   5   4   3   2   1   SD

M. Despite any flaws, the report is worthy of publication.

SA   5   4   3   2   1   SD

Article 4

"I Missed the Bus": School Grade Transition, the Wilmington Truancy Center, and Reasons Youth Don't Go to School

ARTHUR H. GARRISON
Delaware Criminal Justice Planning Council

ABSTRACT. Data from a 3-year truancy reduction program operating in Wilmington, Delaware, are analyzed to assess the association of truancy and reasons for truancy with school grade transition points from elementary to middle school and from middle school to high school. Data showed that there was a 95% increase in the number of truants between fifth and sixth grade and a 76% increase in the number of truants between eighth and ninth grade. There was an 87% increase in truancy among youth between 10 and 11 years old and 68% increase in truancy among youth 13 and 14 years old. The study includes analysis of truancy by various demographic variables and makes policy suggestions on how truancy can be reduced by focusing on the two key school transition points, the fifth and eighth grades.

From *Youth Violence and Juvenile Justice*, *4*, 204–212. Copyright © 2006 by Sage Publications, Inc. Reprinted with permission.

Data from a truancy reduction center in Wilmington, Delaware, are used in this study to assess the association of truancy and reasons for truancy at school grade transition points. This research seeks to add to the literature on the relationship between the reasons youth give for why they are truant and school grade transition. Research that has been conducted on why youth are truant generally includes poor school performance, lack of interest in school, or that youth do not see any purpose or benefit in going to school (Ames & Archer, 1988; L. Anderman, Maehr, & Midfley, 1999; Chung, Elias, & Schneider, 1998).

One aspect of the newer research on truancy is how transition from one level of education to another (Akos, 2002; Alspaugh, 1998a, 1998b, 2000; Alspaugh & Harting, 1995; Arowosafe & Irvin, 1992; Mizelle & Mullins, 1997) can influence school performance and lead to truancy. School transition research has also examined the relationship between school grade transitions and various protective factors (Entwisle & Alexander, 1993; Gutman & Midgley, 2000; Newman, Myers, Newman, Lohman, & Smith, 2000). School level transition has also been used to explain why both dropout and truancy patterns increase when youth move from elementary to middle school and from middle school to high school (Alspaugh, 1998a, 1998b). Researchers have noted "potential dropouts from high school can be differentiated from graduates with 75% accuracy as early as third grade" (Phelan, 1992, p. 33; see also Lloyd, 1978). Robins and Ratcliff (1980) found that youth truants in elementary school were 3 times more truant in high school than were youth who were not truant in elementary school. Research presented shows that patterns of truancy start as early as 6 years old in the second grade.

Part of the difficulty students have transitioning from elementary to middle school is in the change in the learning environment they encounter. In elementary school, the educational environment is one of task-goal orientation in that students "engage in academic work in order to improve their competency or the intrinsic satisfaction that comes from learning" (E. Anderman & Midgley, 1997, p. 270). In addition to the change in the number of children in a class and the presence of multiple teachers for multiple subjects, middle schools have a performance-goal orientation learning environment. In a performance-goal orientation learning environment, students "engage in academic work to demonstrate or prove their competency, or to avoid the appearance of lack of ability relative to others" (E. Anderman & Midgley, 1997, p. 270).

In addition to the change in the educational environment, factors of puberty (Fenzel, 1989) and the students' perceptions about the transition and of being able to fit in (Hertzog & Morgan, 1999; Pintrich & Schunk, 1996) play a role in the ability of students to adapt to the new school environment. Other factors affecting the transition include increased peer pressure, cliquishness among students, fear of bullying, being the youngest in the new school, the need to fit in, and finding the right bus to go home (Akos, 2002; Schumacher, 1998). School transition research has shown that when youth transfer between school levels, a shift occurs in how the youth perceive and measure themselves. Farrington (1980) found that teacher labeling of elementary youth as "troublesome" was the best predictor of truancy in middle school.

The buildup of self-doubt or anxiety can develop while the youth is in the prior school transition grade (fifth grade—elementary before sixth grade—middle school) and continue into the school transition grade. Chung et al. (1998) concluded, "Students showing high levels of psychological distress prior to transition represent early adolescents at a greater risk than their peers for a continued stressful school transition" (p. 98). As the research by Midgley and Urban (1992) explained, after the "transition many students feel less positively about their academic potential and the value of schooling, they give up more quickly and put forth less effort, and their grades decline" (p. 5). Phelan (1992) concluded this alienation from school occurs when students "rightly or wrongly feel harassed or ignored by teachers [and] see no connection between school and their futures" (p. 33), and for "these children, this is the beginning of a downward trajectory that leads to school failure and school leaving" (Midgley & Urban, 1992, p. 5).

Method

In an effort to reduce truancy in the city of Wilmington, a truancy reduction center was established in a local community center, West End Neighborhood House, to provide services to youth who were found truant by the Wilmington Police Department. Wilmington police officers brought youth who were found not in school during school hours to the West End Neighborhood House. Truant youth were turned over to a police officer who was assigned to the program at the community center (to maintain legal custody of the youth and release the patrol officer) and were interviewed by a social worker also assigned to the truancy center. Truant youth were interviewed, parents were contacted, and the schools they attended were also contacted to determine why the youth were not in school and to establish plans to address the reasons for the truancy.

This study involves a nonrandomized group of 756 youth who were truant and brought to the truancy reduction center by the Wilmington Police Department during the 3-school-year period of the program operation (1999–2002). The majority of youth were black (79.5%) and between 12 and 16 years old. The majority of the youth were enrolled in school (66.5%). The majority of the truant youth were not on probation (56.3%) or suspension (62.4%). The majority of the truant youth were not attending alternative schools (57.4%).

Information was collected from each youth as he or she was brought to the truancy reduction center by staff of the truancy center. The social worker interviewing each truant used a one-page questionnaire in which the date and time a truant was brought to the center were recorded, and demographic, home school assignment,

age, race, sex, home address, the address where the youth was found truant, grade level, school district, whether the youth was suspended from school, and the stated reason the youth was truant were collected from each truant youth. Additional information including the number of days absent prior to being taken to the truancy center and whether the youth was on probation through the Delaware Family Court was collected through school contacts. This study provides results of cross-tabulation of age, race, sex, grade, and the reasons given for truancy.

Finding

Although the majority of youth were in the early pubescent through teenage years, truancy showed a progressive pattern even at the younger ages. As shown in Figure 1, from the ages of 7 to 15, each year showed a progressive increase in the number of youth who were truant. There was an 87% increase in truancy among youth between 10 and 11 years old and a 68% increase in truancy among youth 13 and 14 years old.

The same pattern of progressive truancy was demonstrated when viewing truancy by grade progression. As shown in Figure 2, the number of truant youth increased with each grade progression up until the 9th grade. After youth reached the 10th grade, the number of truant youth decreased. The majority of truant youth, 76%, were in the middle school grades (6th through 8th) and the first year of high school (9th grade). Truancy between 5th grade and 6th grade (transition from elementary to middle school) increased by 95% and by 76% between 8th and 9th grade (transition from middle school to high school).

As shown in Table 1, the reasons "missed the bus" and "didn't feel like going" accounted for the majority (53.0%) of explanations given when asked about not being in school. Whether the youth were on probation, enrolled in school, or enrolled in an alternative school, these two reasons dominated. A third of the males (31.3%) and 26.7% of the females claimed they missed the bus. Less than a quarter (23.6%) of the males and 21.4% of the females stated they did not feel like going to school. Of the youth who were on school behavior probation (*n* = 103), 27.2% stated that they did not feel like going, whereas 26.2% of them stated that they missed the bus. Of those enrolled in school (*n* = 503), 32.8% stated that they missed the bus, and 25.0% stated that they did not feel like going. The majority of youth attending alternative schools provided the same two explanations but differed from other youth in that the main excuse was that they did not feel like going. Although 16.3% of the youth stated that they missed the bus, 24% stated that they did not feel like going to school.

The reasons of "missed the bus" and "didn't feel like going" accounted for the greatest number among youth between 9 and 15 years old. Use of the excuse "missed the bus" increased each year with youth be-

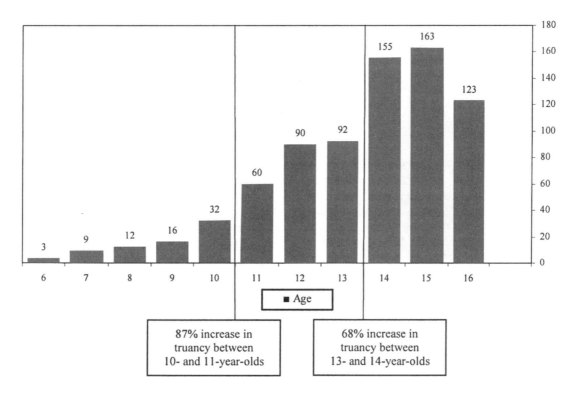

Figure 1. Number of youth truant by age.

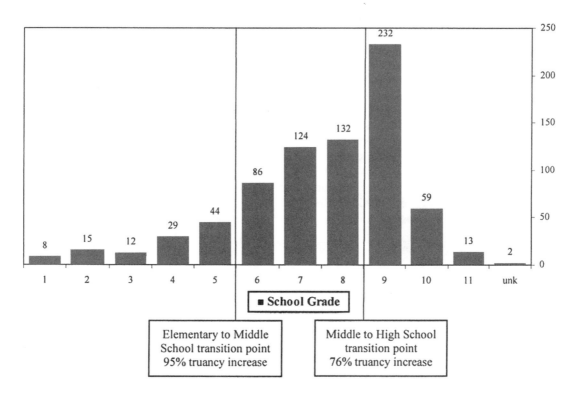

Figure 2. Number of youth truant by grade.

tween 9 and 14, after which use of the excuse decreased. The excuse "didn't feel like going" culminated with youth between 10 and 15, after which the excuse was used less often. The ages 9 through 15 and 10 through 15 are closely related to transition from elementary to middle school and from middle school to high school, respectively. As shown in Table 2, the two greatest increases in truancy are in the transfer grades (fifth to sixth and eighth to ninth).

The majority of youth who were truant were black (79.5%) and Hispanic (13.0%). Both Hispanic and black youth stated either to have "missed the bus" or that they "didn't feel like going" to school as explanations for truancy. Although 33.3% of Hispanic males stated they "didn't feel like going," only 22.0% of black males stated not wanting to go to school as an excuse. Overall, 53.0% of black youth stated that they either "missed the bus" or "didn't feel like going," and 54.0% of Hispanic youth provided the same two excuses. A greater majority of white youth (65.0%) provided the same two excuses.

The results of this study show that the majority of truant youth were in the transitional grades. The reason "didn't feel like going" increased consistently between the fifth and ninth grades. There was a 186% increase in the "didn't feel like going" explanation between the fifth and sixth grades and a 42% increase of the same excuse between the eighth and ninth grades. The number of youth truant increased by 95% between the fifth and sixth grades and 76% between the eighth and ninth grades. Use of the excuse "didn't feel like going" increased consistently between the fifth and ninth grades. Truancy occurred more with males than with females, and the age most vulnerable to truancy was between 11 and 15 years old. The most vulnerable grade to truancy was between the sixth and ninth grades.

The majority of truant youth were not "problem" youth (youth on school probation or attending alternative schools). In contrast to some research (Kee, 2001; McGiboney, 2001), youth have many reasons other than boredom and fear of other youth for not attending school. Only 2.8% of the youth stated they did not like school, and fear of other students was not reported as a reason for truancy.

A 186% increase in the "didn't feel like going" explanation between the fifth and sixth grade and a 42% increase of the same excuse between the eighth and ninth grade, as well as a 183% increase in the "missed the bus" explanation between the fifth and sixth grade and a 57% increase of the same excuse between the eighth and ninth grade, reflect the difficulty of school transition points. The use of the "missed the bus" explanation by elementary school youth (42%) and youth between 6 and 9 years old (50%) also demonstrates the problem of youth at very young ages being responsible for their own preparation and transportation to school. The use of the excuse "missed the bus" presupposes that they were responsible for catching the bus.

Policy Implications and Conclusion

Truancy is one of the early risk factors to future academic failure and one of the first delinquent behaviors that leads to more serious delinquent and criminal behaviors. As shown by this study, truancy increased 95% between fifth and sixth grade and increased 87% among youth between 10 and 11 years old. Antitruancy programs should be designed for youth who begin fifth grade and continue through the sixth grade. Such programs should focus on the fears of youth who are about to enter middle school and should acclimate them to life in middle school. Programs such as visiting the middle school and spending time with teachers and other students in middle school could help alleviate the fears and anxieties that youth feel about the transfer. Similar programs should be established for youth starting their eighth year through the start of the ninth year. Research has shown that "students showing a high level of psychological distress during transition tended to have more adaptive difficulties in middle school," and youth who show "high levels of psychological distress prior to transition represent early adolescents at a greater risk…for continued stressful school transition" (Chung et al., 1998, p. 98). This study found that truancy begins at a very early age and has a progressive development through the early life and grade development of youth through to the middle of high school. Research has shown that there are various reasons for youth disengagement from school; thus, antitruancy programs should be progressively both age and grade appropriate when designed and developed.

Research on school transition suggests that some students develop self-esteem problems after transition. The reduction in self-esteem and not fitting in can lead to other adjustment problems including declined academic achievement, difficulties in peer relationships (Chung et al., 1998), alienation from teachers, and negative views on the utility of school. Such negative views can lead to truancy and dropping out. Programs designed to match youth who are at risk of maladjustment to school after transition with one teacher throughout the first year of transition and with one upperclassman could be a solution. Together, the teacher and the upperclassman could shepherd the youth through the first year. The teacher would focus on keeping the youth on task with school and help deal with any problems the student may have with other teachers. The upperclassman could guide a desperate youth through some of the social pitfalls that await a youth who is not fitting in.

To conclude, it is proposed that truancy can be explained, in part, by the transition from one school level to another. This study found that truancy increases at the two main transfer points in a youth's education, between elementary and middle school and between middle school and high school. Programs designed to address the stress of these two points can have an effect on reducing truancy as a whole.

Table 1
Reasons Given for Not Going to School

Reason	n	%
Missed the bus	227	30.0
Didn't feel like going	174	23.0
Suspended	91	12.0
Not enrolled	67	8.9
No reason	46	6.1
Left early	29	3.8
Sick	28	3.7
Overslept	21	2.8
Doesn't like school	21	2.8
Medical appointment	17	2.2
Problems with other students	14	1.9
Court appointment	9	1.2
No transportation	6	0.8
Meeting parents	4	0.5
Lunch	2	0.3
Total	756	100.0

Table 2
Reason for Not Going to School, Cross-Tabulation to Grade of Truant

	Elementary					Middle			High				
	1	2	3	4	5	6	7	8	9	10	11	Unknown	Total
Missed the bus	4	6	6	11	12	34	42	37	58	14	3		227
Didn't feel like going	2	4		7	7	20	25	36	51	18	4		174
Suspended			2	3	5	14	17	15	30	4	1		91
Not enrolled	1			1	3	2	5	14	32	7	1	1	67
No reason	1	1	2	3	4	6	9	5	12	2	1		46
Left early					2		2	4	17	3	1		29
Sick		1		1	4	2	6	2	8	4	1		28
Overslept		1			4	2	5	5	3			1	21
Doesn't like school		1					4	4	8	4			21
Medical appointment		1		1			3	3	7	1			17
Problems with other students			1	1		2	1	3	3	2	1		14
Court appointment						2	2	3	2				9
No transportation			1	1	1		2		1				6
Meeting parents			1		1		1	1					4
Lunch						2							2
Total	8	15	12	29	44	86	124	132	232	59	13	2	756

References

Akos, P. (2002). Student perceptions of the transition from elementary to middle school. *Professional School Counseling Journal, 5*, 339–345.

Alspaugh, J. (1998a). Achievement loss associated with the transition to middle school and high school. *The Journal of Educational Research, 92*, 20–25.

Alspaugh, J. (1998b). The relationship of school-to-school transitions and school size to high school dropout rates. *The High School Journal, 81*, 154–160.

Alspaugh, J. (2000). The effect of transition grade to high school, gender, and grade level upon dropout rates. *American Secondary Education, 29*, 2–9.

Alspaugh, J., & Harting, R. (1995). Transition effects of school grade-level organization on student achievement. *Journal of Research and Development in Education, 28*, 145–149.

Ames, C., & Archer, J. (1988). Achievement goals in the classroom: Students' learning strategies and motivation process. *Journal of Educational Psychology, 80*, 260–270.

Anderman, E., & Midgley, C. (1997). Changes in achievement goal orientations, perceived academic competence, and grades across the transition to middle-level schools. *Contemporary Educational Psychology, 22*, 269–298.

Anderman, L., Maehr, M., & Midfley, C. (1999). Declining motivation after the transition to middle school: Schools can make a difference. *Journal of Research and Development in Education, 32*, 131–147.

Arowosafe, D., & Irvin, J. (1992). Transition to a middle level school: What kids say. *Middle School Journal, 24*, 15–19.

Chung, H., Elias, M., Schneider, K. (1998). Patterns of individual adjustment changes during middle school transition. *Journal of School Psychology, 36*, 83–101.

Entwisle, D., & Alexander, K. (1993). Entry into school: The beginning school transition and educational stratification in the United States. *Annual Review of Sociology, 19*, 401–423.

Farrington, D. (1980). Truancy, delinquency, the home and the school. In L. Hersov & I. Berg (Eds.), *Out of school: Modern perspectives in truancy and school refusal* (pp. 49–63). Chichester, UK: Wiley.

Fenzel, L. (1989). Role strains and the transition to middle school: Longitudinal trends and sex differences. *Journal of Early Adolescence, 9*, 211–226.

Gutman, L., & Midgley, C. (2000). The role of protective factors in supporting the academic achievement of poor African American students during the middle school transition. *Journal of Youth and Adolescence, 29*, 223–248.

Hertzog, C., & Morgan, P. (1999). Making the transition from middle level to high school. *High School Magazine, 6*, 26–30.

Kee, T. (2001). Attribution style and school truancy. *Early Child Development and Care, 169*, 21–38.

Lloyd, D. (1978). Prediction of school failure from third-grade data. *Educational and Psychological Measurement, 38*, 1193–1200.

McGiboney, G. (2001). Truants welcome here: An alternative school designed specially for truants is boosting student attendance. *American School Board Journal, 188*, 43–45.

Midgley, C., & Urban, T. (1992). The transition to middle level schools: Making it a good experience for all students. *Middle School Journal, 24*, 5–14.

Mizelle, N., & Mullins, E. (1997). Transition into and out of middle school. In J. Irvin (Ed.), *What current research says to the middle level practitioner* (pp. 303–313). Columbus, OH: National Middle School Association.

Newman, B., Myers, M., Newman, P., Lohman, B., & Smith, V. (2000). The transition to high school for academically promising, urban, low-income African American youth. *Adolescence, 35*, 45–66.

Phelan, W. (1992). Building bonds to high school graduation: Dropout intervention with seventh and eighth graders. *Middle School Journal, 24*, 33–35.

Pintrich, P., & Schunk, D. (1996). Motivation in education: Theory, research and applications. Englewood Cliffs, NJ: Prentice Hall.

Robins, L., & Ratcliff, K. (1980). The long-term outcome of truancy. In L. Hersov & I. Berg (Eds.), *Out of school: Modern perspectives in truancy and school refusal* (pp. 65–83). Chichester, UK: Wiley.

Schumacher, D. (1998). *The transition to middle school.* Retrieved February 24, 2004, from http://www.ericfacility.net/ericdigests/ed422119.html

About the author: Arthur H. Garrison, MS, is the director of criminal justice planning and senior researcher for the Delaware Criminal Justice Planning Council. He is also the project director for the Wilmington Hope Commission, which is a citywide initiative to design a strategy to reduce juvenile and adult violence in Wilmington, Delaware. He has written more than 20 program evaluations and has published more than 15 articles on a variety of juvenile and criminal justice issues. He has a master of science (1995) in criminal justice from West Chester University of Pennsylvania and a BA (1990) from Kutztown University of Pennsylvania.

Exercise for Article 4

Factual Questions

1. The youth were brought to the Neighborhood House by whom?

2. Who conducted the interviews?

3. Between what two ages was there the largest percentage increase in truancy?

4. What was the main excuse for truancy among students attending alternative schools?

5. How many of the truants were in fifth grade?

6. For all participants, how many indicated that they missed the bus?

Questions for Discussion

7. The researcher states that the participants were a "nonrandomized group." What is your understanding of the meaning of this term? (See lines 105–109.)

8. Only truants who were caught by police participated in this survey. Could valuable information also be obtained by questioning a sample of all students about their truancy behavior? Explain.

9. Are you surprised at the dramatic drop in truancy after grade 9? Explain. (See Figure 2.)

10. The findings of this survey focus on (a) reasons given for being truant and (b) patterns of truancy across grade and age levels. Do you regard one of these types of findings as more important than the other? Explain.

11. This survey was conducted at one program. In your opinion, does this limit the generalizability of the results? Explain.

12. In your opinion, how important are the implications of this study? (See lines 236–292.)

13. If you were to conduct a survey on the same topic, what changes in the research methodology, if any, would you make?

Quality Ratings

Directions: Indicate your level of agreement with each of the following statements by circling a number from 5 for strongly agree (SA) to 1 for strongly disagree (SD). If you believe an item is not applicable to this research article, leave it blank. Be prepared to explain your ratings. When responding to criteria A and B below, keep in mind that brief titles and abstracts are conventional in published research.

A. The title of the article is appropriate.

   SA   5   4   3   2   1   SD

B. The abstract provides an effective overview of the research article.

   SA   5   4   3   2   1   SD

C. The introduction establishes the importance of the study.

   SA   5   4   3   2   1   SD

D. The literature review establishes the context for the study.

   SA   5   4   3   2   1   SD

E. The research purpose, question, or hypothesis is clearly stated.

   SA   5   4   3   2   1   SD

F. The method of sampling is sound.

   SA   5   4   3   2   1   SD

G. Relevant demographics (for example, age, gender, and ethnicity) are described.

   SA   5   4   3   2   1   SD

H. Measurement procedures are adequate.

   SA   5   4   3   2   1   SD

I. All procedures have been described in sufficient detail to permit a replication of the study.

   SA   5   4   3   2   1   SD

J. The participants have been adequately protected from potential harm.

   SA   5   4   3   2   1   SD

K. The results are clearly described.

SA   5   4   3   2   1   SD

L. The discussion/conclusion is appropriate.

SA   5   4   3   2   1   SD

M. Despite any flaws, the report is worthy of publication.

SA   5   4   3   2   1   SD

Article 5

Homelessness in a Small Southern City

LINDA A. MOONEY
East Carolina University

KEVIN R. OUSLEY
East Carolina University

ABSTRACT. With recent predictions of the increase in the numbers of homeless, there has been a renewed interest in estimating homeless populations in a variety of locations. While a considerable amount of research has been conducted on homelessness in urban areas, less research has been directed toward estimating and describing the numbers of homeless in rural or nonurban areas. Further, several methodological issues surrounding the definitions of urban, nonurban, and rural (Toomey, First, Greenlee, & Cummins, 1993) have made comparisons between these locations difficult. Despite methodological confusion and the consensus that few comprehensive studies of nonurban and rural homelessness exist (Lawrence, 1995; Toomey et al., 1993; NCH, 1997a; Fitchen, 1992), researchers have been quick to conclude that rural and nonurban homelessness are demographically different from urban homelessness. The present research fills the gap in the homeless literature by collecting data on the homeless in a nonurban location, and comparing the results to representative urban and rural samples. A discussion of homelessness within the context of recent welfare reform follows the presentation of results.

From *Electronic Journal of Sociology*, 5, May 2000. Copyright © by Linda A. Mooney and Kevin R. Ousley. Reprinted with permission.

Introduction

The study of homelessness has become "old hat" (Hopper, 1998; Wright, Rubin, & Devine, 1998; Hambrick & Johnson, 1998). Once the target of a flurry of research activity, by the early 1990s the significance of

5   homelessness as a major social problem had considerably diminished. For example, in 1985, 32 separate bills relating to homelessness were introduced in the U.S. Congress; by 1992, politicians were all but silent on the topic—a topic soon to be dubbed as "last decade's is-

10   sue" (Wright et al., 1998:2). Further evidence is gleaned from the news media's coverage of "the homeless problem." In the fall of 1988, the *New York Times* carried over 50 articles on homelessness; in the fall of 1992, 25; and by the fall of 1998, 10 (Hsiao, 1999).

15   Of the many reasons homelessness has faded from the public's consciousness, one stands out—the tendency to view the problem as temporary (Hambrick & Johnson, 1998; Wright et al., 1998). Such a belief led to quick fixes in which the day-to-day needs of the

20   homeless became the focus of attention (e.g., food,

shelter) rather than addressing structural constraints (e.g., lack of affordable housing) or individual deficiencies (e.g., alcoholism) (*Priority Home!*, 1994; Wright et al., 1998; *America*, 1999).[1] Thus, few sig-

25   nificant changes in the causes of homelessness have been initiated and, with the signing of the 1996 welfare reform bill, the numbers of homeless are likely to increase dramatically over the next several years (NCH, 1997; Willis, 1997a; Applewhite, 1997; Stanfield,

30   1997; U.S. Conference of Mayors, 1998; Wright et al., 1998).

Such predictions have led to a renewed interest in homelessness and a return to empirical documentation of the numbers and characteristics of the homeless to

35   better develop policy directives. Estimates of the numbers of homeless and their characteristics have significantly changed over the years. Much of the variation in estimates is a result of definitional problems, that is, what constitutes homelessness (cf. Toomey et al.,

40   1993). Estimates also vary with the political persuasion of those involved—activist, for example, versus government official. It is not surprising that calculations vary considerably, from a low of 300,000 to a high of several million (Barak, 1991; National Law Center on

45   Homelessness and Poverty, 1996; NCH, 1998; Wright et al., 1998).

While there is little agreement over the number of homeless, there is some consensus that they are a heterogeneous population, at least in urban areas where

50   the bulk of research has been conducted (Rossi, 1989; Barak, 1991; Snow & Anderson, 1993; Jencks, 1994; NAEH, 1998; Reganick, 1997; NCH, 1999). There is also evidence that the rural homeless are different from their urban counterparts, more often female, intact

55   families, White, and currently working. They also have lower rates of chronic substance abuse and mental illness, and are disproportionately Native Americans and migrant workers (First, Rife & Toomey, 1994; NCH, 1999; NRHA, 1996; Vissing, 1996; U.S. Department of

60   Agriculture, 1996; Butler, 1997).

Considering the relatively few studies on rural homelessness, there is a remarkable lack of agreement as to what constitutes a "rural area" (Hewitt, 1989; Toomey et al., 1993). Despite the implied dichotomy of

65   a rural–urban designation, "the distribution of people and the density and form of living arrangements exist

on a continuum" (Toomey et al., 1998:25). The U.S. Census Bureau defines rural areas as incorporated locations that have a population of less than 2,500 residents, and unincorporated less densely populated areas. Urbanized areas are places with a population greater than 50,000. Any area with a population between 2,500 and 50,000 is simply considered a nonurban location (Hewitt, 1989; Toomey et al., 1993; *Statistical Abstract of The United States*, 1998).

Despite these relatively unambiguous definitions, in studies of rural homelessness the distinctions have become muddied. Butler defines small towns as *cities* which are "not incorporated...but have populations of more than 2,500" (1997:430); Vissing speaks of "urbanized rural areas" (1996:10); Segal investigates "two contiguous small towns" (1989:28); and Fitchen refers to "small towns and the open countryside" (1992:173).

Of even greater concern, many investigators appear willing to draw definitive conclusions about the differences between these ill-defined, inadequately researched areas. For example, Lawrence (1995:298) states that "...homelessness in the countryside is qualitatively different from homelessness in the city." Similarly, Vissing (1996:12) concludes that "[H]omeless people in small towns are much more like those in rural areas than those in cities...." Alternatively, Dahl, Harris, and Gladden comment that comparisons of rural data from North Dakota to several urban samples suggest that "...the origin of homelessness, demographics, and medical problems of urban and rural homeless are quite similar" (1992:2).

The present research thus fills a gap in the homeless literature by: 1) providing a picture of homelessness in a clearly defined nonurban location, and 2) comparing the results to both urban and rural samples of homeless. The two studies selected for comparison have each been hailed as the leading research in their respective locations. First, Toomey and Rice's (1990) *Homelessness in Rural Ohio* has been called the "largest and most comprehensive study of homelessness in rural America" (Dahl et al., 1992). Although almost a decade old, the results of this study still serve as the foundation for present-day discussions on rural homelessness (cf. Wright et al., 1998:182–184).

Similarly, Burt and Cohen's (1989, 1990) investigation of homelessness in a national sample of 20 urban areas with populations over 100,000 has been described as the "most comprehensive study of its kind" (Jencks, 1994:10) as well as the "most methodologically sound" (Toomey et al., 1993:23). As recently as 1998, the Urban Institute described this data set as the "most recent nationwide study of the urban homeless" available (Urban Institute, 1999).[2]

Methodological variations in sampling techniques, however, should be noted. Burt and Cohen's (1989, 1990) respondents were from homeless shelters and/or soup kitchens, while the rural data included people staying in shelters, inexpensive hotels and motels, or other unique transient locations (First et al., 1990, 1994). The use of nonshelter sources of the homeless is common in rural areas where there are fewer shelters and thus fewer visible homeless (Aron & Fitchen, 1996; NCH, 1997; Wright et al., 1998; NCH, 1998).

The present investigation uses shelter residences only—the common denominator between the two other data sets.[3] Although the rural data's inclusion of nonshelter residents may make data comparisons more difficult, Shlay and Rossi (1992) state that the majority of studies on the homeless use shelter residents as a criteria for inclusion, and Jencks (1993:13) concludes that "...the rate of shelter use is about the same in smaller communities as in big cities." Further, respondents were asked if they knew other homeless people who did not stay at the shelter. Ninety-seven percent of the respondents said no. Nonetheless, estimates of the homeless from shelter populations may *underestimate* the numbers of the homeless and, thus, skew the resulting demographics.

Methodology

Situated on the coastal plains of North Carolina,[4] Southern City had a population of 46,000 and a land area of 18.1 square miles at the time the survey was conducted. Serving as the regional center for commerce, health care, and education, Southern City is surrounded by several smaller communities with populations ranging from just over 5,000 to just less than 500. Dominated by agriculture in general, and tobacco and cotton production in particular, Southern City is the county seat—the county having a population of 108,000 with an unemployment rate of 5.5% in 1992.

Southern City's homeless shelter was established in 1988 as a response to citizen complaints of a number of people "hanging around in the streets." The shelter operates as a nonprofit organization, supported by a variety of church-affiliated groups and volunteers from the community. Although small grants through the Federal Emergency Management Agency and United Way provide the bulk of the over $100,000 operating budget, much of the food provided to the residents comes from contributions by the U.S. Department of Agriculture and donations from local churches, restaurants, and private individuals. Nonfood items such as bedding and clothes are exchanged with other facilities such as the County Family Violence Shelter.

The shelter is located in an abandoned elementary school, built in the 1950s and located in an inner-city Black residential neighborhood. The "gymtorium" serves as the center of the facility. It is here that residents sleep in a barracks-like setting with access to bathrooms and showers, and limited access to a cafeteria. There are no admitting restrictions, although "troublemakers" are required to leave the shelter for the night.[5] Facilities are sex-segregated with women and children sleeping on the stage behind a cloth barrier. The facility also contains an office and sleeping quar-

Table 1
Characteristics of Homeless by Location

Year of study:	URBAN Burt and Cohen 1987	SOUTHERN CITY 1992	RURAL First et al. 1990
Age			
Percent 18–30	30	34	52 (18–29)
Percent 31–50	51	57	40 (30–49)
Percent 51–65	16	9	5 (50–59)
Percent over 65	3	0	3 (60+)
Mean age	n/a	36	32
Marital status			
Percent never married	55	44	32
Percent married/living together	10	15	28
Percent divorced/separated/widowed	34	41	39
Education			
Percent 0–11 years	48	40	43
Percent H.S. graduate or equivalent	32	29	57 (H.S.+)
Percent some post H.S.	14	25	
Percent college graduate or more	6	6	
Percent H.S. graduate or more	52	60	57
Sex			
Percent male	81	75	49
Percent female	19	25	51
Race			
Percent Black	41	54	10
Percent White	46	29	85
Percent Hispanic	10	17	2
Percent Other	3	0	2
Percent non-White	54	71	14

Note. Numbers do not necessarily sum to 100 due to rounding error and/or missing data.

ters for the full-time director and two part-time assistants. The shelter is open from 6:00 p.m. to 6:00 a.m.

Interviews of shelter residents took place in February and March of 1992, and were conducted by senior
185 and graduate sociology students who had undergone several hours of faculty-led sessions on interviewing techniques. All interviews were conducted at the shelter between 7:00 and 10:00 in the evening and were, with the participants' permission, tape recorded. Each
190 of the seven students was assigned ten of the seventy beds (although not necessarily occupied) located in the shelter and were responsible for interviewing residents in those beds over the course of a six-week period. The days on which the interviews were conducted were
195 determined by shelter activities (i.e., no interviews took place on, for example, "clinic night" or "church night"). Hispanic residents were interviewed with the help of an interpreter. Forty-one residents were interviewed in total.
200 In addition to asking homeless-specific questions, standard demographic data were recorded (sex, race, age, number of children, marital status, education, and employment). Following Wright (1986: 228–229), percentage differences of ten or more were considered
205 meaningful.

Results

Table 1 reports demographic data from Southern City, as well as from the rural and urban samples. As in previous studies of the homeless, the majority of shelter residents were male—75%. The percentage of
210 males and females is significantly different from that of the rural sample, but varies little from the urban data.

Females have traditionally made up a larger proportion of the shelter population than other homeless populations, for example, the soup kitchen population.
215 Most research suggests that the overrepresentation of women in shelters is due to their need to care for dependent children (Vissing, 1996; Burt & Cohen, 1989, 1990; Butler, 1997). While just over half the respondents reported having children (57.1%), females
220 (77.8%) compared to males (52.0%) were more likely to report so and to have their children with them at the shelter.

Southern City homeless shelter residents were predominantly non-White (71%), a number significantly
225 higher than the percentage of non-Whites in the urban or rural samples. While approximately 34% of the county population is non-White, the disproportionately high rate of non-Whites in the Southern City sample may be an artifact of the time of year in which the in-

Table 2
Characteristics of Homeless by Location

	URBAN Burt and Cohen		SOUTHERN CITY	RURAL First et al.
Year of data collection:	1987		1992	1990
Time homeless?[a]				
Percent < 3 months	21		52	50 (49 days or less)
Percent 4–12 months	33		33	89 (1 year or less)
Percent over 1 year	46		15	6 (2 years or more)
Mean days	1170		141	221
Work for pay previous month?	25		34	31
Income maintenance				
Percent yes (any form)	20		48	n/a
Percent mentioning:				
SSI	4		13	11
GA	5		27	38
AFDC	12		n/a	n/a
SS/Pension	n/a		7	3
Causes of homelessness (self-report)?[b]				
Economics	75	(unemployed)	43	55
Chronic disability	13	(poor health)	21	7
Personal crisis	33	(alcohol/drugs)	26	36
	21	(suicide attempt)		
	43	(psychologically distressed)		
	66	(institutionalized)		
N =	1,704		41	919

[a] The urban and Southern City homeless were asked, "How long have you been homeless?" First et al. (1994) asked, "When was the last time you had a home or a permanent place to stay?"

[b] Burt and Cohen (1989) asked respondents a series of questions about: 1) employment for pay in the last month, 2) self-reported health as excellent, very good, good, fair, or poor, 3) suicide attempts: "Was there ever a time in your life when you felt so bad that you tried to kill yourself?" 4) alcohol and drug involvement, 5) psychological distress as measured by a score of 16 or above on the CES-D scale, and 6) whether or not respondents had ever been institutionalized in a prison/jail, detoxification center, or mental hospital. Answers to these questions, although not dealing directly with the causes of homelessness, are conditions that could "impair their ability to become self-sufficient" (Burt & Cohen, 1990, p. 31).

230 terviews were conducted—in the winter months. Of the 71% non-White residents, 54% were African American and 17% Hispanics. Hispanics were more likely than any other racial/ethnic group to report being "farm laborers" (83%). Farm labor, like construction, the sec-

235 ond most frequently reported work category, is seasonal and may have been responsible for the inflated number.

Consistent with both the urban and rural samples, the average age of shelter respondents was 36, with a

240 median value of 34. As Rossi (1990:957) states, "...today's homeless are surprisingly young; virtually all recent studies of the homeless report median ages in the low to middle 30s." Somewhat surprisingly, however, younger respondents were not more likely to re-

245 port being first-time shelter residents.

Southern City shelter residents were less likely to never be married (44%) than their urban counterparts (55%), but more likely than rural respondents (32%). As Barak (1991:36) notes, the percentage of married

250 people among the urban homeless is lower than that among the rural homeless. However, Southern City and

urban data in other marital categories are comparable. Respectively, Southern City and the urban data indicate that 15% and 10% of the respondents were married or

255 living together, and 41% and 34% of the respondents were divorced, separated, or widowed.

Over half the Southern City respondents reported graduating from high school or higher levels of education (60%), which is similar to the urban and rural

260 samples. Educational levels varied little by sex, but were substantively interesting by race/ethnicity. Forty percent of the non-White respondents reported having less than a high school degree compared to 67% of the White respondents. Thus, in the present sample, minor-

265 ity shelter residents were better educated than their White counterparts.

Of the variables of interest, length of time homeless was the most difficult to compare across samples given differences in measurement intervals. Some respon-

270 dents initially explained being unsure how long they had been homeless, reporting moving in and out of relatives' and friends' homes and abandoned houses. When asked how long he had been homeless, one 39-

year-old White male responded, "Off and on. I would
275 say approximately, you know, maybe a year and a
half...two years...maybe three." (#7)

Table 2 continues the analysis of characteristics of
urban, nonurban, and rural respondents. Southern City
residents most often reported being homeless three
280 months or less (52%), followed by 4 to 12 months
(33%), and more than 12 months (15%). Burt and
Cohen's (1989, 1990) research found that the modal
interval was over a year (46%) while 89% of the rural
respondents report being homeless for a year or less.
285 Mean days homeless indicate that time homeless is
significantly greater in urban areas (1,170 days), followed by rural (221 days) and nonurban areas (141
days).

Respondents in the rural and Southern City samples
290 were asked whether they had worked for pay in the
previous month. While rural and Southern City respondents varied little in the percent responding yes, 31%
and 34%, respectively, urban homeless respondents
reported that 25% were "presently working."

295 Income maintenance was measured by whether or
not a respondent, at the time of the survey, was receiving Aid to Families with Dependent Children (AFDC),
General Assistance (GA), Supplemental Security Income (SSI), or Social Security (SS)/pension. A slightly
300 higher than might be expected proportion of Southern
City shelter residents received income maintenance
benefits—48%—over twice the number receiving such
benefits in the urban sample. However, when asked the
type of benefit received, respondents in the nonurban
305 and rural samples were most likely to mention General
Assistance over any other type of benefit.

Finally, respondents were asked, "What do you
think caused your homelessness?"[6] Categories included
chronic disability (mental and physical illness, sub-
310 stance abuse, institutionalization); *personal crisis* (divorce, runaway/throwaway, family conflicts, death of
spouse); and *economic conditions* (loss of employment,
lack of sufficient funds, eviction, and/or no transportation). Consistent with other research (cf. Momeni,
315 1990:79), the modal category for the nonurban and
rural samples is economic conditions (43% and 55%,
respectively). As one 30-year-old Black female responded (#15):

The reason I'm in this place is because I do not have a
320 job. It is simply that. You have to have money to pay for
those things and most people are staying here because
they don't have a job. If you had a job you could stay and
save up money. No one wants to stay. The only people
who have to stay here, some of the people like, have al-
325 cohol problems or something like that, and they can't
work but I don't have any of those problems. There is no
reason why I should not be able to work and get out of
this shelter—none.

Chronic disability variables were the least likely to
330 be mentioned in both the nonurban and rural samples.
However, an examination of responses from the urban

sample indicates that a fairly high proportion of respondents reported being in poor health (13%) and
receiving some form of institutionalized treatment at
335 least once in their life (66%).

Discussion

The results, although reaffirming the heterogeneity
of the homeless population and the need for consistent
measurement techniques, also suggest that, contrary to
Vissing (1996), Lawrence (1995), and Dahl et al.
340 (1992), the characteristics of the nonurban homeless
reflect those of both comparison samples. The homeless in Southern City were predominantly non-White
males, with an average age of 36. Most were never
married; almost half did not graduate from high school
345 and, on the average, had been homeless for four to five
months. A third had worked for pay in the month prior
to the survey, and almost half were receiving some
kind of income maintenance.

The above portrait bears a remarkable similarity to
350 Burt and Cohen's (1989:36) description of urban respondents:

...homeless persons in cities with a population of 100,000
over...are male...the majority are non-White...between 30
and 51 years of age...[A]lmost half have not graduated
355 from high school....

Southern City homeless were also disproportionately Black, young, single males. However, similarities
between Southern City homeless and First et al.'s
(1990, 1994) rural sample also exist. Nonurban and
360 rural homeless were less likely to be homeless for over
a year, the mean days for rural and Southern City samples being 141 and 221, respectively. The mean number of days of homelessness for the urban sample was
1,170.

365 Further, the distribution of income maintenance between the rural and Southern City samples are similar—General Assistance being the most common form
of aid in both samples. While comparisons of self-
reported causes of homelessness are difficult given
370 differences in the interview formats, educational levels
appear analogous for all three groups with a range of
only 52% to 60% completing high school and/or with
some post-high school experience.

It is possible, however, that the variations in the
375 characteristics of the homeless may, in part, be an artifact of variations in the three sampling designs. For
example, Southern City homeless were exclusively
from shelters. Some research suggests that women are
more likely to seek refuge in shelters and, thus, the
380 Southern City estimates of the number of homeless
females may be exaggerated (Toomey et al., 1993). On
the other hand, Vissing (1996) and First et al. (1994)
suggest that homeless rural families, the highest proportion of which are headed by females, are more
385 likely to stay with friends and family than in shelters,
which would suggest that the Southern City sample
underestimated the number of homeless females. Given

that 75% of the sample were men, the second interpretation appears more likely.

390   Additionally, as noted earlier, the proportion of non-Whites was considerably higher than that in the urban or rural samples. It was suggested that the months in which the interviews took place—February and March—may have impacted the number of African

395 Americans and Hispanics who were disproportionately migrant workers. State statistics support this contention. North Carolina farm worker service providers estimate that between 15% and 50% of all migrant workers spend at least some time in a shelter, most

400 frequently in the winter months (North Carolina Consolidated Plan, 1996). Further, the number of the homeless in Southern City could be overestimated and/or "urbanized" as the homeless migrate south from the harsh winters of the northern states (Jencks, 1994:1).

405   The shelter has grown considerably since the data were collected. As if in preparation for what lies ahead, the staff has more than doubled. Consistent with national trends, there have been rumblings of funding cutbacks and moving the shelter to a different (i.e., less

410 visible) location. The National Law Center on Homelessness and Poverty recently published a report, *Out of Sight, Out of Mind?*, which documents similar efforts to conceal the homeless through the relocation of shelters, nightly "sweeps," and forcible removal from high

415 visibility areas (Nieves, 1998; Hsiao, 1998; *America*, 1999).

Such trends reflect a general movement toward what Hooper (1998) calls "remoralizing" the poor and, by extension, the homeless. The implication that the

420 poor and homeless are somehow accomplices in their own circumstances, that poverty is symptomatic of individual deficiency, is implicit in the Personal Responsibility and Work Opportunity Reconciliation Act of 1996, which subordinates need to merit. Ironically,

425 many of the same people who have been denied welfare assistance are now homeless and, once again, are being penalized for their poverty. For example, New York City officials have declared that shelters are a form of public assistance and, therefore, shelter resi-

430 dents must meet the requirements of all public assistance recipients including workfare (Bernstein, 1999:1).

The effects of welfare reform are, and will continue to be, disproportionately felt in rural areas where

435 homelessness is most closely linked to poverty and there are fewer shelters and other services to compensate for the loss of welfare benefits (Aron & Fitchen, 1996; Butler, 1997; NCH, 1998; Wright et al., 1998). In Wisconsin, a largely rural state, a 75% reduction in

440 welfare recipients has resulted in a three-fold increase in the homeless population (DeParle, 1999; Willis, 1997a; Stanfield, 1997); and in Maine, a five-year limit on welfare benefits has increased homelessness in a state "where welfare has kept many [of the respon-

445 dents] one step away from life on the streets" (Butler, 1997:432).

Thus, while government officials, as indicated by the policies they initiate, pursue the path of least resistance by blaming the victim, homeless advocates con-

450 tinue to call for structural alterations, most notably the reduction of poverty and an adequate supply of low-income housing (Wright et al., 1998:210). Ultimately, homelessness is a problem of poverty and in areas where poverty rates are the highest, often nonurban

455 areas, homelessness will continue to increase, particularly with the removal of the safety net of public assistance. The need to count and classify, describe and define, hence remains paramount in identifying the causes of homelessness in the hopes of developing

460 public policies that work.

References

America. 1999. "More Homeless, More Hungry." *America* 180 (3): 3.

Applewhite, Steven Lozano. 1997. "Homeless Veterans: Perspectives on Social Services Use." *Social Work* 42 (1): 19–31.

Aron, Laudan Y. and Janet M. Fitchen. 1996. "Rural Homelessness: A Synopsis" in *Homelessness in America* 1996. National Coalition for the Homeless. Washington, DC: Oryx Press.

Barak, Gregg. 1991. *Gimme Shelter*. NY: Praeger.

Bernstein, Nina. 1998. "New York City Plans to Extend Workfare to Homeless Shelters." *New York Times* (February 20): 1.

Burt, Martha and Barbara E. Cohen. 1989. *America's Homeless: Numbers, Characteristics, and Programs That Serve Them*. Washington, DC: The Urban Institute Press.

Burt, Martha and Barbara E. Cohen. 1990. "A Sociodemographic Profile of the Service-Using Homeless: Findings from a National Survey." Pp. 17–38 in *Homelessness in the United States—Data and Issues*, edited by Jamshid Momeni. NY: Praeger.

Butler, Sandra Sue. 1997. "Homelessness Among AFDC Families in a Rural State: It Is Bound to Get Worse." *Affilia* 12 (4): 427–441.

Dahl, Sherlyn, Helen Harris, and Joanne Gladden. 1992. "Homelessness: A Rural Perspective." *Prairie Rose* (August):1–6.

DeParle, Jason. 1999. "Wisconsin Welfare Overhaul Justifies Hope and Some Fear." *New York Times* (January 15): A1.

Department of Health and Human Services. 1998. "National Survey of Homeless Assistance Providers and Clients." HHS Homepage. http://www.dhhs.gov

First, Richard, John Rife, and Beverly Toomey. 1994. "Homelessness in Rural Areas: Causes, Patterns and Trends." *Social Work* 39 (1): 97–108.

First, Richard, Beverly Toomey, and J. Rife. 1990. *Homelessness in Rural Ohio*. Columbus, OH: Ohio State University.

Fitchen, Janet M. 1991. "On the Edge of Homelessness: Rural Poverty and Housing Insecurity." *Rural Sociology* 57 (2): 173–193.

Hambrick, Ralph S. and Gary Johnson. 1998. "The Future of Homelessness." *Society* 35 (6): 28–38.

Hewitt, M. 1989. "Defining 'Rural' Areas: Impact on Health Care Policy and Research." Washington, DC: Community for Creative Nonviolence.

Hopper, Kim. 1998. "Housing the Homeless." *Social Policy* 28 (3): 64–67.

Hsiao, Andrew. 1998. "The Disappeared." *The Village Voice* 43 (49): 32–33.

Jencks, Christopher. 1994. *The Homeless*. Cambridge, MA: Harvard University Press.

Lawrence, Mark. 1995. "Rural Homelessness: A Geography without a Geography." *Journal of Rural Studies* 11 (3): 297–301.

Momeni, Jamshid. 1990. "No Place to Go: A National Picture of Homelessness in America." Pp. 165–183 in *Homelessness in the United States—Data and Issues*, edited by Jamshid Momeni. NY: Praeger.

NAEH (National Alliance to End Homelessness). 1998. "Facts about Homelessness." National Alliance to End Homelessness, 1518 K Street, NW, Washington, DC, 20005 <http://www.naeh.org>

NCH (National Coalition for the Homeless). 1999. "Who is Homeless?: Fact Sheet No. 3." February. 1012 14th Street, NW. Suite 600. Washington, DC 20005. 202/73775-6444.

_____. 1998. "How Many Homeless: Fact Sheet No. 2." May. 1012 14th Street NW. Suite 600. Washington, DC. 20005. 202/73775-6444.

_____. 1997a. "Rural Homelessness: Fact Sheet Number 13." October. 1012 14th Street, NW. Suite 600. Washington, DC. 20005. 202/73775-6444.

_____. 1997b. "Homelessness in America: Unabated and Increasing." 1012 14th Street, NW. Suite 600. Washington, DC. 20005. 202/73775-6444.

National Law Center on Homelessness and Poverty. 1996. "Mean Sweeps: A Report on Anti-Homeless Laws, Litigation and Alternatives in 50 United

States Cities." National Law Center on Homelessness and Poverty. 918 F Street, NW, Washington, DC 20004. 202/638-2535.

National Rural Health Association. 1996. "The Rural Homeless: America's Lost Population." Kansas City: NRHA #PU0896-42.

Nieves, Evelyn. 1998. "Homelessness Tests San Francisco's Ideals." *New York Times* (November 13): A1.

North Carolina Consolidated Plan. 1996. "Housing Needs Assessment: Homeless Needs, Facilities and Services." November. Washington, DC: U.S. Department of Housing and Urban Development. Office of Community Planning and Development. <http:www.state.nc.us/commerce/commasst/plan>

Oreskes, Michael and Robin Toner. 1989. "The Homeless at the Heart of Poverty and Policy." *New York Times* (January 29).

Priority Home! 1994. "The Federal Plan to Break the Cycle of Homelessness." Interagency Council on the Homeless. Washington, DC: Government Printing Office.

Reganick, Karol A. 1997. "Prognosis for Homeless Children and Adolescents." *Childhood Education* 73 (3): 133–136.

Rossi, Peter H. 1989. *Down and Out in America: The Origins of Homelessness.* Chicago, Il.: University of Chicago Press.

Shinn, Marybeth. 1997. "Family Homelessness: State or Trait?" *American Journal of Community Psychology* 25(6): 755–770.

Shlay, Anne B. and Peter Rossi. 1992. "Social Science Research and Contemporary Studies on Homelessness." *Annual Review of Sociology* 18: 129–160.

Snow, David and Leon Anderson. 1993. *Down on Their Luck: A Study of Homeless Street People.* Berkeley: California University Press.

Snow, David, Susan Baker, Leon Anderson, and Michael Martin. 1986. "The Myth of Pervasive Mental Illness Among the Homeless." *Social Problems* 33 (5): 407–423.

Sosin, Michael. 1992. "Homeless and Vulnerable Meal Program Users: A Comparison Study." *Social Problems* 39 (2): 170–188.

Stanfield, Rochelle. 1997. "HUD Choice May Face Old Problems." *National Journal* 28 (3): 120–122.

Statistical Abstract of the United States, 118th edition. 1998. Washington, DC: Government Printing Office.

Toomey, Beverly, Richard First, Richard Greenlee, and Linda Cummings. 1993. "Counting the Rural Homeless Population: Methodological Dilemmas." *Social Work Research and Abstracts* 29 (4): 23–27.

U.S. Conference of Mayors. 1998. "A Status Report on Hunger and Homelessness in American Cities." U.S. Conference of Mayors. <http://www.usmayors.org/uscm/>

U.S. Department of Agriculture, Rural Economic and Community Development. 1996. "Rural Homelessness: Focusing on the Needs of the Rural Homeless." U. S. Department of Agriculture, Rural Housing Service, Rural Economic and Community Development, 14th St. and Independence Ave. SW. Washington, DC 20250-1533.

Urban Institute. 1998. "Homelessness: Ten Basic Questions Answered." <http://www.urban.org/news/ factsheet/homelessFS.html>

Vissing, Yvonne M. 1996. *Out of Sight, Out of Mind.* Lexington: University of Kentucky Press.

Willis, Laurie. 1997a. "Grim Forecast for Needy." *News and Observer.* December 5: B1.

Willis, Laurie. 1997b. "Conference to Focus on Homeless." *News and Observer.* December 4: B7.

Wright, James D., Beth A. Rubin, and Joel A. Devine. 1998. *Beside the Golden Door.* New York: Aldine.

Wright, S. E. 1986. *Social Science Statistics.* Newton, MA: Allyn and Bacon, Inc.

Note: This paper was presented at the annual meetings of the Southern Sociological Society in Chattanooga, TN, on April 2, 1993.

Acknowledgments: The authors gratefully acknowledge the valuable assistance of Jon Beckert, Brian Crisp, Michael Dalecki, Donna Evans, Bonnie Haswell, Michelle Hilhorst, Sarah Poulos, Christine Ransdell, Lisa Tripp, and Amy Whitcher.

Address correspondence to: Linda A. Mooney, Department of Sociology, East Carolina University, Greenville, NC 27858. E-mail: mooneyl@mail.ecu.edu

Endnotes

[1] Obviously, any given individual's homelessness has multiple causes. Nonetheless, the debate over causality most often has been framed as one between structural versus individualistic variables or what Shinn (1997) calls "states versus traits." Wright et al. (1998) proposes an intermediate and theoretically sound position: "defects and dislocations of structure...create a population at risk of homelessness; defects of persons determine who within the at-risk population actually becomes homeless" (p. 9).

[2] A more recent survey, the 1996 National Survey of Homeless Assistance Providers and Clients, was modeled after the Burt and Cohen (1989) study. Its emphasis, however, unlike its predecessor, is

on the providers of homeless assistance and the clients they serve (Department of Health and Human Services, 1998).

[3] Southern City does not have a soup kitchen or any other assisting services, with the exception of the Salvation Army, which, if called by the police, accompany the homeless person to the shelter.

[4] According to the North Carolina Consolidated Plan (1996), homelessness in the state varies by geographical region. The most populated area of the state, the Piedmont, has the highest rate of homeless, followed by the coastal plains and the mountains. Statistics from 1994, those that most closely approximate the study date, indicate that North Carolina had 187 emergency shelters with a sleeping capacity of 4,271 in 64 of the state's 100 counties. As in other states, homelessness in North Carolina is predicted to grow with a 1997 estimate of over 500,000 North Carolinians on the verge of homelessness (Willis, 1997b).

[5] Several city police were interviewed, as was the police attorney, in reference to police policy concerning the homeless. Police indicated that on any given night, the shelter was the location of an estimated 90 to 100 percent of the homeless in the city limits. Police, when coming upon a homeless person, drive the person to the shelter if so desired, or simply make sure that the person "moves along" since there is a policy of "no sleeping" in public parks at night, or in alleys, streets, or sidewalks. Additionally, the shelter director and staff members were interviewed concerning shelter policy and history.

[6] Burt and Cohen did not ask for self-reported causes of homelessness. They did, however, ask about employment, health concerns, institutionalization (prison/jail, mental hospital, drug/alcohol treatment facility), psychological distress, and attempted suicide.

Exercise for Article 5

Factual Questions

1. Estimates of the number of homeless nationally vary from a low of 300,000 to a high of how many?

2. Who conducted the interviews?

3. Were the interviews conducted in the shelter?

4. In Southern City, what percentage of the homeless were males?

5. According to the researchers, of the variables of interest, which one was the most difficult to compare across samples?

6. Did a higher percentage of "Southern City" *or* "urban" respondents receive income maintenance benefits?

Questions for Discussion

7. In your opinion, is it reasonably valid to compare the results of a study in which only respondents in shelters/soup kitchens were interviewed with results of a study in which other groups were also

included, such as respondents in inexpensive motels? Explain. (See lines 120–144.)

8. Would it be interesting to know why Southern
City and not some other city was chosen as the site
for the survey?

9. If you had been conducting this study, are there
any other questions you would have asked the
homeless? Explain.

10. The researchers are critical of "government officials." In your opinion, is it acceptable for researchers to voice such opinions? Explain. (See
lines 447–460.)

11. In light of the information in this article, do you
believe that more research on the homeless is
needed?

Quality Ratings

Directions: Indicate your level of agreement with each
of the following statements by circling a number from
5 for strongly agree (SA) to 1 for strongly disagree
(SD). If you believe an item is not applicable to this
research article, leave it blank. Be prepared to explain
your ratings. When responding to criteria A and B below, keep in mind that brief titles and abstracts are
conventional in published research.

A. The title of the article is appropriate.

    SA   5   4   3   2   1   SD

B. The abstract provides an effective overview of the
    research article.

    SA   5   4   3   2   1   SD

C. The introduction establishes the importance of the
    study.

    SA   5   4   3   2   1   SD

D. The literature review establishes the context for
    the study.

    SA   5   4   3   2   1   SD

E. The research purpose, question, or hypothesis is
    clearly stated.

    SA   5   4   3   2   1   SD

F. The method of sampling is sound.

    SA   5   4   3   2   1   SD

G. Relevant demographics (for example, age, gender,
    and ethnicity) are described.

    SA   5   4   3   2   1   SD

H. Measurement procedures are adequate.

    SA   5   4   3   2   1   SD

I. All procedures have been described in sufficient
    detail to permit a replication of the study.

    SA   5   4   3   2   1   SD

J. The participants have been adequately protected
    from potential harm.

    SA   5   4   3   2   1   SD

K. The results are clearly described.

    SA   5   4   3   2   1   SD

L. The discussion/conclusion is appropriate.

    SA   5   4   3   2   1   SD

M. Despite any flaws, the report is worthy of publica-
    tion.

    SA   5   4   3   2   1   SD

Article 6

Does Therapist Experience Influence Interruptions of Women Clients?

RONALD JAY WERNER-WILSON
Iowa State University

MEGAN J. MURPHY
Iowa State University

JENNIFER LYNN FITZHARRIS
Iowa State University

ABSTRACT. The feminist critique of marriage and family therapy and studies of interruptions in conversation influenced the topic of the present study. We replicated methodology from a study (Werner-Wilson, Price, Zimmerman, & Murphy, 1997) in which the researchers reported that student therapists interrupted women clients more frequently than male clients. Those results may have been related to therapist inexperience—since the therapists were students. In the present study, we compared interruptions from student therapists to those identified as "master" therapists who had extensive clinical experience. Analysis of Variance was used to compare videotaped sessions of therapists in marriage and family therapy training sessions to therapists from the American Association for Marriage and Family Therapy (AAMFT) Masters series. Results suggest that there is no statistically significant difference between the rate of interruptions used by students versus experienced therapists. Both groups interrupted women clients more often than men clients, a finding that replicates the earlier study by Werner-Wilson and colleagues (1997), which increases the generalizability about this pattern in marriage and family therapy.

From *Journal of Feminist Family Therapy, 16*, 39–49. Copyright © 2004 by The Haworth Press, Inc. Reprinted with permission.

One of the first empirical quantitative analyses of power in marriage and family therapy investigated interruptions, which were viewed as a sign of conversational power. That study reported that women clients
5 were interrupted three times more often than men clients regardless of therapist gender (Werner-Wilson et al., 1997). The study published in 1997 included only student therapists so the findings could have been the result of limited professional training because therapist
10 inexperience seems to be associated with a more directive interviewing style (Auerbach & Johnson, 1978). The present study represents a replication of the 1997 study with a sample of therapists that includes some who have significantly more experience so interrup-
15 tions could be compared between student therapists and those identified by the American Association for Marriage and Family Therapy as "master" therapists. This present study was influenced by two themes: language and therapeutic discourse as well as the feminist cri-
20 tique of marriage and family therapy.

Relevant Literature
The Feminist Critique

Feminists have brought to the forefront the importance of attending to social and political issues within the therapeutic context, such as examining the effects of race/ethnicity on client problems, openly discussing
25 power and privilege one may or may not have within the context of a relationship, and making gender a central component of case conceptualization and intervention (Silverstein, 2003). Embedded within these suggestions is a central issue of power: How does power
30 play out in relationships? Do therapists recognize power differences in the couples and families they treat? How do therapists attend to these power differences in the therapeutic context, that is, both between members of a couple and between themselves and their
35 clients? Although feminists have long called for therapists to examine power in relationships, only recently have concrete suggestions been given regarding how therapists can address abstract concepts like power in therapy (Blanton & Vandergriff-Avery, 2001; Had-
40 dock, Zimmerman, & MacPhee, 2000).

In addition to offering ways of conceptualizing and intervening in family therapy, feminists have highlighted the differential treatment of men and women in therapy by their therapists. One of the themes of the
45 feminist critique is associated with therapeutic process: women's voices are to be encouraged, heard, and validated in therapy. Feminist therapists actively encourage equal participation from women and men in therapy and in relationships (Cantor, 1990). From a feminist
50 perspective, therapists should attend to gender issues rather than ignore gender hierarchies in relationships. If "therapeutic talk is, of course, all about the politics of influence" (Goldner, 1989, p. 58), then how well do therapists negotiate power in therapy? Are therapists
55 replicating or challenging existing power inequalities in therapy? Furthermore, are therapists aware of their own stereotypes regarding gender and communication? One frequently heard stereotype is that women talk more than men (O'Donohue, 1996). Do therapists con-
60 sciously mitigate their own gender-related biases? These questions seem relevant in light of recent studies that show a negative relationship between marital satis-

faction and power inequality (Gray-Little, Baucom, & Hamby, 1996; Whisman & Jacobson, 1990).

65   Recent research seems to provide empirical support for this feminist critique of therapy. For example, Haddock and Lyness (2002) reported that male therapists frequently and negatively challenged female clients. The same pattern was not found for male clients. Other

70   research suggests that therapists scored low on taking a stance against client behaviors intended to control another (Haddock, MacPhee, & Zimmerman, 2001). Even though therapists may be aware of the importance of attention to power and gender issues in therapy, it

75   appears that they may not follow through in terms of how they communicate and/or intervene regarding conversational power. It could be argued that therapists have an ethical responsibility to challenge the hierarchies inherent in couples' relationships. Failure to do

80   so would be maintaining the status quo. Therefore, therapists' use of self seems particularly important given the power they have in relation to their clients to shape, end, or shift conversation (Avis, 1991).

Language and Therapeutic Discourse

    Given that therapists are responsible for monitoring

85   and perhaps intervening in the relational and communicational therapeutic context, it seems important to pay attention to interruptions—especially those employed by therapists—in therapeutic conversation. The language and communication literature is helpful in this

90   regard. In their pioneering investigation of interruptions as a power tactic in conversation, Zimmerman and West (1975) reported that males more frequently interrupt females in cross-sex pairs, whereas interruptions occur in equal numbers between same-sex con-

95   versational partners. Some studies have not found support for males interrupting more, regardless of partner sex (Hannah & Murachver, 1999; Turner, Dindia, & Pearson, 1995). Explanations of mixed results in studies of interruptions may result from different defini-

100   tions of "interruption," situational context, and whether activities are structured (Anderson & Leaper, 1998). In their meta-analysis of studies of interruption, Anderson and Leaper (1998) suggested that definitions of interruption may moderate gender differences, gender dif-

105   ferences are larger in unstructured activities, and situational factors may influence interruptions more than gender.

    In the language theory literature, two theories have been used to explain gender miscommunication: *two-*

110   *cultures theory* and *dominance theory*. The *two-cultures theory* of gender-linked language differences suggests that boys and girls grow up in different gender cultures, in which they learn different ways of communicating (Mulac, Erlandson, Farrar, Hallett, Molloy, &

115   Prescott, 1998). Boys use questions, for example, to control conversation, whereas girls use questions to sustain conversation. These cultural differences produce miscommunication when children grow up to be

120   adults, when they are interacting more with others from "different cultures." From this position, men do not view interruptions as a display of power; rather, men and women use language differently based on their previous experiences in their cultural sub-groups.

    The *dominance theory* of gender-linked language

125   differences suggests that men's domination of conversations via interruption and topic introduction is reflective of the power they hold in larger society. From this perspective, men use questions, interruptions, and other means of communication as a way to dominate conver-

130   sation and to keep women in a subordinate position. The result is that women speak less and men talk more, again isomorphic to patterns at a larger, societal level in which men have more power than women.

    Proponents of both theories seem to suggest that

135   there are communication differences between men and women, yet the theories posit different explanations for why these differences exist. Given that there have been few empirical investigations of interruptions in therapy, the first step should be to first examine whether there

140   are differences between rates of interruption in the therapeutic context. If gender differences related to interruption are discovered, then therapists may be compelled to address these differences, particularly if these differences impact power within the couple rela-

145   tionship.

    In recent years, researchers have begun to explore interruptions within the context of therapy. Although there are differences in results about the influence of therapist gender on use of interruptions, two different

150   studies (Stratford, 1988; Werner-Wilson et al., 1997) reported that women clients were much more likely than men clients to be interrupted by therapists. Stratford (1998) found that male therapists were more likely than female therapists to interrupt clients; Stratford also

155   reported that female clients were more likely than male clients to be interrupted. Werner-Wilson and his colleagues (1997) also reported that women clients were more likely than men clients to be interrupted in therapy but did not find a difference between women and

160   men therapists. Stratford (1988)—noting that therapist inexperience is associated with a more directive interviewing style (Auerbach & Johnson, 1978)—suggested that the difference in findings about therapist gender and interruptions might be due to differences in thera-

165   pist experience: Her study included experienced therapists while the Werner-Wilson et al. (1997) study included student therapists who have less experience. If Stratford's (1998) speculation is true, we might expect differences in interruption rates based on therapist ex-

170   perience level. The purpose of the present study is to investigate two related research questions:

1. Are women clients interrupted more than men clients?

2. Do student therapists interrupt women clients more

175   than experienced therapists?

Method

Participants

The sample for the present study included clients and therapists from two sources: (a) doctoral student therapists and clients at a nonprofit marriage and family therapy clinic at a major southern university that was accredited by the American Association for Marriage and Family Therapy, and (b) "master" therapists from the Master Series video collection distributed by the American Association for Marriage and Family Therapy. "The Master Series presents the world's most respected marriage and family therapists conducting live, unedited therapy sessions at AAMFT annual conferences" (AAMFT Catalog, 1993, p. 4). Including these master therapists provides an opportunity to compare therapy process between two levels of clinical experience: doctoral students versus master therapists. In each case, the session was the initial consultation with either the student therapist or the master therapist and it featured both an adult woman client and an adult man client who were romantic partners. Table 1 provides descriptive information about cases included in the study.

Procedures

We replicated the approach used by Werner-Wilson and colleagues (1997) to investigate interruptions in the therapy process. We examined the first therapy session to control for treatment duration. Therapy sessions have predictable stages (e.g., social, engagement, information collection, intervention, closure), so we examined multiple time points in the session. Three five-minute segments were coded for every client from early, middle, and later stages in the session: (a) 10:00 to 15:00 minute segment; (b) 25:00 to 30:00 minute segment; and (c) 40:00 to 45:00 minute segment. Two senior-level undergraduate students, who were unaware of the purpose of this research, coded videotapes from the first therapy session.

Table 1
Descriptive Information about Videotapes

	Student Therapists	Master Therapists	Total
Therapist gender			
Men	52	14	66
Women	22	14	36
Total	74	28	102
Modality			
Marital	60	16	76
Family	14	12	26
Total	74	28	102

Coder training. Coders learned the coding scheme by practicing on tapes not featured in the sample until they achieved 80 percent agreement. A graduate student, who was also unaware of the purpose of the present study, coded every sixth session; these tapes were used to calculate interrater reliability. The coders maintained an acceptable level of interrater reliability throughout the coding process: Intraclass correlations were .68.

Coding scheme. The transcripts were arranged with codes adjacent to each spoken turn to promote reliability by eliminating the need for coders to memorize codes: The coders viewed the video with the transcript and circled the appropriate code as they occurred during each speaking turn. A distinct set of codes was printed next to each speaker (e.g., therapist, woman client, man client) but each set of codes featured the same possible codes. For example, the therapist could interrupt either the woman or man client. Similarly, each client could interrupt either her/his partner or the therapist. In addition to enhancing reliability, this coding arrangement disguised the nature of the research project because coders identified conversational strategies used by each speaker, not just the therapist.

Dependent Measures

Interruptions. Interruptions—defined as a violation of a speaking turn, and operationalized as an overlap of speech that is disruptive or intrusive (West & Zimmerman, 1983; West & Zimmerman, 1977; Zimmerman & West, 1975)—were distinguished from other forms of overlap such as supportive statements that represent active listening skills. Statements that trailed off in tone or volume were not coded as interruptions because they represented invitations for reply. It is possible that people who talk more are interrupted more, so, following the procedure used by Werner-Wilson and colleagues (1997), we controlled for amount of client participation: A variable was constructed from the ratio of interruptions made by the therapist to number of speaking turns taken by the client. These ratios provided standardized measures to examine therapist interruptions.

Results

Based on our review of the literature, it seemed important to consider the influence of client gender, therapist gender, modality, and client experience since each variable has been found to have an influence on some dimension of therapy process. Analysis of Variance (ANOVA) was conducted to examine the following main effects on the dependent variable (ratio of therapist interruptions to number of client speaking turns): client gender (man, woman), therapist gender (man, woman), modality (couple, family), and therapist experience (student, AAMFT master therapist). Based on our review of the literature, it also seemed important to investigate the following interaction effects:

- Client gender × Therapist gender (Stratford, 1998; Werner-Wilson, Zimmerman, & Price, 1999);
- Client gender × Modality (Werner-Wilson, 1997; Werner-Wilson et al., 1999);

270 • Therapist gender × Modality (Werner-Wilson et al., 1999); Therapist gender × Therapist experience (Stratford, 1998); Client gender × Therapist gender × Modality (Werner-Wilson et al., 1999);
• Client gender × Therapist gender × Modality × Therapist experience (Stratford, 1998).

275 There was a statistically significant difference for gender of client on the dependent variable (see Table 2). Neither therapist gender, modality, therapist experience, nor the interaction of any variables was significant (see Table 2). On average, therapists in the present

280 study interrupted women clients ($M = 0.064$) almost two times more often than men clients ($M = 0.037$).

Table 2
Analysis of Variance for Therapist Behaviors: Interruption

Source	MS	F
Client Gender	0.014	4.780*
Therapist Gender	0.007	2.497
Modality	0.001	0.259
Therapist Experience	0.009	3.312
Client Gender × Therapist Gender	0.004	1.370
Client Gender × Modality	0.000	0.046
Therapist Gender × Modality	0.006	2.189
Therapist Gender × Therapist Experience	0.003	0.923
Client Gender × Therapist Gender × Modality	0.005	0.189
Client Gender × Therapist Gender × Modality × Therapist Experience	0.002	0.869

*$p < .05$, $n = 102$

Discussion

Gender As a Process Issue

285 Results from the present study continue to suggest that women clients are interrupted more often than men clients in conjoint couple and family therapy, although the rate was slightly lower in the present study than in the original study published in 1997. For some aspects

290 of the therapy process (e.g., therapy alliance, goal setting), there seems to be an interaction effect between client gender and therapy modality (Werner-Wilson et al., 1997; Werner-Wilson, Zimmerman, & Price, 1999) but this effect was not demonstrated in the present

295 study. Results from the present study also suggest that therapist experience—which was not measured in the 1997 study—does not significantly influence the number of interruptions directed toward women clients. In fact, master therapists interrupted women clients at a

300 higher rate than student therapists, although it was not statistically significant.

Our findings contribute to the literature in providing evidence that women clients are interrupted more frequently than men clients, regardless of therapist

305 gender or experience. Although the design of the current study could not directly test the validity of the two-cultures theory or the dominance theory (explain-

ing differences for men and women in language use), we tentatively suggest that these theories are too sim-

310 plistic to adequately capture the complexity of interactions and power dynamics at play in relationships. Both theories, for example, posit that women may be more likely to be interrupted than men, *and* suggest that men use language in a way that is different from how

315 women use language. One might hypothesize, from either theory of language use, that men therapists would be somehow different from women therapists in how often they interrupt clients, yet results from the current study do not support this view. Simply put, a

320 more comprehensive theory that incorporates therapist and client markers of social standing may be more helpful for future researchers seeking to expand on the repeated finding in the therapy literature that women clients are more frequently interrupted than men cli-

325 ents.

Findings from the present study suggest an ongoing need to consider the influence of gender as a process variable in marriage and family therapy. Most therapists would agree to the notion that men and women

330 should have relatively equal participation in therapy; it is likely that therapists are unaware that they tend to interrupt women far more frequently than men in therapy. The first step is for therapists to be aware of these patterns in therapy; the second step is for therapists to

335 use their positional power to assist men and women to equitably share the therapeutic floor.

References

Anderson, K. J., & Leaper, C. (1998). Meta-analyses of gender effects on conversational interruption: Who, what, when, where, and how. *Sex Roles*, *39*, 225–252.

Auerbach, A., & Johnson, M. (1978). Research on therapists' level of experience. In A. Gorman & A. Razin (Eds.), *The therapists' contribution to effective psychotherapy: An empirical assessment.* New York: Pergamon Press.

Avis, J. M. (1991). Power politics in therapy with women. In T. J. Goodrich (Ed.), *Women and power: Perspectives for family therapy* (pp. 183–200). New York: Norton.

Blanton, P. W., & Vandergriff-Avery, M. (2001). Marital therapy and marital power: Constructing narratives of sharing relational and positional power. *Contemporary Family Therapy*, *23*, 295–308.

Cantor, D. W. (1990). Women as therapists: What we already know. In D. W. Cantor (Ed.), *Women as therapists: A multitheoretical casebook* (pp. 3–19). Northvale, NJ: Aronson.

Goldner, V. (1989). Generation and gender: Normative and covert hierarchies. In M. McGoldrick, C. M. Anderson, & F. Walsh (Eds.), *Women in families: A framework for family therapy* (pp. 42–60). New York: Norton.

Gray-Little, B., Baucom, D. H., & Hamby, S. L. (1996). Marital power, marital adjustment, and therapy outcome. *Journal of Family Psychology*, *10*, 292–303.

Haddock, S., A., & Lyness, K. P. (2002). Three aspects of the therapeutic conversation in couples therapy: Does gender make a difference? *Journal of Couple & Relationship Therapy*, *1*, 5–23.

Haddock, S. A., MacPhee, D., & Zimmerman, T. S. (2001). AAMFT Master Series Tapes: An analysis of the inclusion of feminist principles into family therapy practice. *Journal of Marital and Family Therapy*, *27*, 487–500.

Haddock, S. A., Zimmerman, T. S., & MacPhee, D. (2000). The Power Equity Guide: Attending to gender in family therapy. *Journal of Marital and Family Therapy*, *26*, 153–170.

Hannah, A., & Murachver, T. (1999). Gender and conversational style as predictors of conversational behavior. *Journal of Language and Social Psychology*, *18*, 153–174.

Mulac, A., Erlandson, K. T., Farrar, W. J., Hallett, T. S., Molloy, J. L., & Prescott, M. E. (1998). "Uh-huh. What's that all about?" Differing interpretations of conversational backchannels and questions as sources of miscommunication across gender boundaries. *Communication Research*, *25*, 642–668.

O'Donohue, W. (1996). Marital therapy and gender-linked factors in communication. *Journal of Marital and Family Therapy, 22*, 87–101.

Silverstein, L. B. (2003). Classic texts and early critiques. In L. B. Silverstein & T. J. Goodrich (Eds.), *Feminist family therapy: Empowerment in social context* (pp. 17–35). Washington, DC: APA.

Stratford, J. (1998). Women and men in conversation: A consideration of therapists' interruptions in therapeutic discourse. *Journal of Family Therapy, 20*, 393–394.

Turner, L. H., Dindia, K., & Pearson, J. C. (1995). An investigation of female/male verbal behaviors in same-sex and mixed-sex conversations. *Communication Reports, 8*, 86–96.

Werner-Wilson, R. J. (1997). Is therapeutic alliance influenced by gender in marriage and family therapy? *Journal of Feminist Family Therapy, 9*, 3–16.

Werner-Wilson, R. J., Price, S. J., Zimmerman, T. S., & Murphy, M. J. (1997). Client gender as a process variable in marriage and family therapy: Are women clients interrupted more than men clients? *Journal of Family Psychology, 11*, 373–377.

Werner-Wilson, R. J., Zimmerman, T. S., & Price, S. J. (1999). Are goals and topics influenced by gender and modality in the initial marriage and family therapy session? *Journal of Marital and Family Therapy, 25*, 253–262.

West, C., & Zimmerman, D. H. (1977). Women's place in everyday talk: Reflections on parent-child interaction. *Social Problems, 24*, 521–529.

West, C. & Zimmerman, D. H. (1983). Small insults: A study of interruptions in cross-sex conversations between unacquainted persons. In B. Thorne, C. Kramarae, & N. Henley (Eds.), *Language, gender and society* (pp. 103–117). Rowley, MA: Newbury House.

Whisman, M. A., & Jacobson, N. S. (1990). Power, marital satisfaction, and response to marital therapy. *Journal of Family Psychology, 4*, 202–212.

Zimmerman, D. H., & West, C. (1975). Sex roles, interruptions, and silences in conversation. In B. Thorne & N. Henley (Eds.), *Language & sex: Difference & dominance* (pp. 105–129). Rowley, MA: Newbury House.

About the authors: *Ronald Jay Werner-Wilson*, PhD, associate professor and Marriage and Family Therapy Program and Clinic director; *Megan J. Murphy*, PhD, assistant professor, and *Jennifer Lynn Fitzharris*, MS, are all affiliated with the Department of Human Development and Family Studies, Iowa State University, Ames, IA.

Address correspondence to: Ronald Jay Werner-Wilson, PhD, Department of Human Development and Family Studies, 4380 Palmer Building, Suite 1321, Iowa State University, Ames, IA 50011-4380. E-mail: rwwilson@iastate.edu

Exercise for Article 6

Factual Questions

1. The researchers state that recent studies show what type of relationship between marital satisfaction and power inequality?

2. Dominance theory suggests that men use questions, interruptions, and other means of communication as a way to do what?

3. Coding for interruptions in each therapy session was done for three segments. How long was each segment?

4. The researchers defined "interruptions" as a violation of a speaking turn. How was "interruptions" operationalized?

5. Was the difference between women clients and men clients being interrupted statistically significant? If yes, at what probability level?

6. Was the difference between men therapists and women therapists statistically significant? If yes, at what probability level?

Questions for Discussion

7. The researchers discuss theories relating to their research in lines 108–145 and lines 302–325. In your opinion, is this discussion an important strength of this research report? Explain.

8. This study examined interruptions in only the initial consultation with a therapist. Would you be willing to generalize the results to subsequent sessions? Explain. (See lines 191–192.)

9. The researchers state that the undergraduate students who coded the videotapes were unaware of the purpose of this research. Speculate on why the researchers did not make them aware of the purpose. (See lines 207–210.)

10. In your opinion, is the "coder training" described in lines 211–219 an important part of this study? Explain.

11. The current study does not support the view that men therapists are different from women therapists in how often they interrupt clients. Does this result surprise you? Explain. (See lines 315–319.)

12. In your opinion, does this study make an important contribution to understanding how clients' gender *influences* therapists' behavior? Explain.

Quality Ratings

Directions: Indicate your level of agreement with each of the following statements by circling a number from 5 for strongly agree (SA) to 1 for strongly disagree (SD). If you believe an item is not applicable to this research article, leave it blank. Be prepared to explain your ratings. When responding to criteria A and B below, keep in mind that brief titles and abstracts are conventional in published research.

A. The title of the article is appropriate.

    SA   5   4   3   2   1   SD

B. The abstract provides an effective overview of the research article.

    SA   5   4   3   2   1   SD

C. The introduction establishes the importance of the study.

    SA   5   4   3   2   1   SD

D. The literature review establishes the context for the study.

SA   5   4   3   2   1   SD

E. The research purpose, question, or hypothesis is clearly stated.

SA   5   4   3   2   1   SD

F. The method of sampling is sound.

SA   5   4   3   2   1   SD

G. Relevant demographics (for example, age, gender, and ethnicity) are described.

SA   5   4   3   2   1   SD

H. Measurement procedures are adequate.

SA   5   4   3   2   1   SD

I. All procedures have been described in sufficient detail to permit a replication of the study.

SA   5   4   3   2   1   SD

J. The participants have been adequately protected from potential harm.

SA   5   4   3   2   1   SD

K. The results are clearly described.

SA   5   4   3   2   1   SD

L. The discussion/conclusion is appropriate.

SA   5   4   3   2   1   SD

M. Despite any flaws, the report is worthy of publication.

SA   5   4   3   2   1   SD

Article 7

An Unobtrusive Measure of Racial Behavior in a University Cafeteria

STEWART PAGE
University of Windsor
Windsor, Ontario, Canada

ABSTRACT. Observational data were gathered from a large university cafeteria for a period of 22 days, in 1-hour periods per day, over one semester. Observations were made of the frequency with which Black and White cashiers were selected. Chi-square analyses showed a significant association between a cashier's being Black and increased likelihood that she would not be selected. Some comments and comparisons are made with other research using similar measures.

Reprinted with permission from *Journal of Applied Social Psychology*, Vol. 27, No. 24, 2172–2176. Copyright © 1997 V. H. Winston & Son, Inc., 360 South Ocean Boulevard, Palm Beach, FL 33480. All rights reserved.

The study of interracial behavior has long-standing familiarity to social and community psychologists, as well described in the classic writings of Kenneth Clark, Gordon Allport, Thomas Pettigrew, and others. Allport's (1958) *The Nature of Prejudice,* for example, remains one of the most frequently cited books on the issue, both within and without the discipline of psychology (Pettigrew, 1988). The dramatic effects of race as a variable in research have been demonstrated, for example, in a variety of situations assessing social influence and stigmatization. Many such studies have used some form of Bogardus' (1931, 1959) notion of *social distance* (social intimacy) measures of racial acceptance.

Observational and experimental studies of race have undoubtedly declined somewhat in recent times, while more pragmatic and biopolitical aspects such as equal opportunity, affirmative action, ethnic and cultural diversity, and so on have become more prominent. These issues are important, yet many aspects of interracial behavior remain incompletely understood.

One such aspect involves behavior in open situations; that is, those without racial demand characteristics or obligations (Orne, 1962). Moreover, the factor of race may also function differently at varying levels of awareness and in accordance with the extent of reactivity in measures used to observe it (e.g., Webb, Campbell, Schwartz, & Sechrest, 1966). For example, in a study which has now become a classic, Weitz (1972) administered a questionnaire assessing White–Black racial attitudes to a university population. For many of her subjects who had expressed egalitarian attitudes, Weitz nevertheless found that these same individuals showed subtly rejecting nonverbal behaviors when later placed in a laboratory situation requiring cooperative work alongside a Black individual. From a psychoanalytic perspective, Weitz referred to these results as supporting a *repressed-affect model* of racial behavior. In this view, racial behavior assessed reactively, such as with questionnaires or interviews, is typically egalitarian, yet may show "leakage," that is, negative aspects, when assessed nonreactively and unobtrusively. Similarly, in a series of studies (e.g., Page, 1995; Page & Day, 1990), we have found frequently that publicly advertised rental accommodation is likely to be described privately (thus, unobservably) as "already rented" when landlords receive telephone inquiries from persons alleging to have some type of stigmatizing characteristic.

Although their study was not concerned directly with race, Hechtman and Rosenthal (1991) found, as another example of such leakage, that teachers showed more nonverbal warmth toward pupils for whom the teaching task was stereotypically gender appropriate (e.g., vocabulary items for girls; mechanical items for boys), as compared to when they taught a task which was gender inappropriate. Lott (1987), also in a nonracial context, similarly found that men did not show unfavorable attitudes toward women on paper-and-pencil measures. They did, however, in unobtrusively observed work situations, show subtle avoidance behaviors, more negative statements, and increased social distance specifically toward female co-workers. In a racial context, Taylor (1979) found that teachers' nonverbal behaviors varied subtly according to the race (White vs. Black) of their pupils in an unobtrusively observed teaching situation.

A long-standing difficulty in many studies remains that of generalization from laboratory-based research. The present study examined some aspects of racial behavior using a nonlaboratory (cafeteria) setting, whose essential functions are those of dining and so-

cialization. Such settings generally carry no outward prescriptions or expectations regarding race, based on
75 the tacit assumption that this factor indeed "does not exist." The cafeteria setting is also one in which many behaviors, performed with little awareness or at low levels of intensity, may be unobtrusively observed. The speculative hypothesis was explored that a pre-
80 dominantly White population of customers, consisting mostly of undergraduate students, might select a White cashier more frequently than a Black cashier.

Method

Participants

During a recent semester, observations were made of a university population in a large public cafeteria at
85 the University of Windsor over a period of 22 (nonconsecutive) weekdays, excluding Fridays. A daily 1-hour observation period, from approximately noon until approximately 1:00 p.m. each day, was used.

Procedure

The spatial arrangement of the cafeteria is such that
90 once food items are collected and before entering the main eating area, customers must select a cashier from (usually) three choices during peak lunchtime hours throughout the academic year. Cashiers for the current period of observation were three females, located at the
95 end of three separate pathways, one of which must be selected by exiting customers. Distances to each cashier, from locations occupied by customers after selecting all food items, are approximately equal. In the eating area directly beyond the cashiers is a counter area,
100 containing a straight row of individual seats. A vertical partition attached to the front edge of the counter partially obscures the occupants of these seats from view. From one end of the counter, the activities of each cashier can be observed reliably and unobtrusively.
105 Throughout the above time period, one of the three cashiers was Black; the remaining two were White. On the campus, as typical of Ontario universities generally, Black students form a distinct and visible minority group. A daily record was kept of the number of
110 (non-Black) customers paying for food at each cashier. For consistency, observations were made only when three cashiers, at separate locations, were on duty. Individual cashiers varied nonsystematically in their location from day to day. Cases in which a single person
115 paid for one or more companions' food were counted as representing only a single customer. Cases where individuals only requested change or approached a cashier for reasons other than paying for food were excluded. In general, therefore, a "unit" of observation
120 was recorded and signaled, in most cases, when a cashier was observed extending her hand to return change. No subjective judgments or ratings were thus required; data (Table 1) were gathered solely in the form of frequency counts.

Results and Discussion

125 Results, in terms of frequency of cashier selection, are shown in Table 1. A goodness-of-fit (χ^2) analysis of the frequency data showed a significant tendency for customers to select less frequently a cashier who was Black, $\chi^2(2, N = 9,713) = 6.57, p < .038$.

Table 1
Frequency of Cashier Selection by Race

Cashier	Frequency of selection
1 (White cashier)	3,320
2 (White cashier)	3,271
3 (Black cashier)	3,122
Cashier selection: Three White cashiers	
1	2,659
2	2,622
3	2,734

130 In order to evaluate further the possibility that a directional or spatial bias played some role in cashier selection, some additional data (covering 19 days; non-Fridays) were gathered, during a different semester. For these data, all three cashiers were White. There
135 was no significant location preference in selection, $\chi^2(2, N = 8,015) = 2.44, p < .296$.

In interpreting such results, one must exercise caution in view of certain limitations. One cannot know precisely what percentage of customers might have
140 been included more than once over the total time period, nor does one have complete information about other factors in a university population, which are germane to the issue of race. Moreover, populations such as the one observed in the present study consider them-
145 selves (and are considered) highly accepting, aware, and sensitive to matters concerning race, as congruent with commonly prevailing values and norms within a North American university campus.

Yet there remain other, more abstract issues, still
150 largely unresolved by social and community psychologists. One concerns Kelman's (1958) early distinctions between levels of attitude internalization and between the emotional, evaluative, and behavioral components of attitudes. Another concerns the unreliable, indeed
155 sometimes disturbing, relationship between racial attitudes and racial behavior (Pettigrew, 1988). Another concerns the related issue of congruence between behaviors elicited under reactive conditions, in which they may be detected, and those which may be ob-
160 served nonreactively and which may be performed at low levels of awareness. In this light, one is reminded of recent videotaped demonstrations on the ABC network program *Prime Time Live,* in which Black "pseudoclients" were given false information about job
165 availability, higher prices for used cars, and less accommodating service in stores. One is also reminded of LaPiere's (1934) classic study in which restaurateurs indicated by telephone that Chinese couples would not

170 be served, yet most such couples were served when they actually entered the restaurants.

Again, while the factor of race may become a conspicuous factor in research situations where reactive measures or manipulations are used, its presence and 175 effects in other situations may remain more insidious and ill-defined. Indeed, the present data reflect only frequency counts; that is, simple observations of human behavior. They seem sufficient, however, to illustrate the myth that race is irrelevant or does not exist in the context of everyday acts and social routines. Fur-180 ther research on the repressed affect model of racial behavior therefore seems clearly warranted.

References

Allport, G. (1958). *The nature of prejudice.* Garden City, NY: Doubleday Anchor Books.

Bogardus, E. (1931). *Fundamentals of social psychology.* New York, NY: Century Press.

Bogardus, E. (1959). *Social distance.* Yellow Springs, OH: Antioch.

Hechtman, S., & Rosenthal, R. (1991). Teacher gender and nonverbal behavior in the teaching of gender-stereotyped materials. *Journal of Applied Social Psychology, 21,* 446–459.

Kelman, H. (1958). Compliance, identification, and internalization: Three processes of attitude change. *Journal of Conflict Resolution, 2,* 51–60.

LaPiere, R. (1934). Attitudes versus actions. *Social Forces, 13,* 230–237.

Lott, B. (1987). Sexist discrimination as distancing behavior: A laboratory demonstration. *Psychology of Women Quarterly, 11,* 47–59.

Orne, M. (1962). On the social psychology of the psychological experiment: With particular reference to demand characteristics and their implications. *American Psychologist, 17,* 776–783.

Page, S. (1995). Effects of the mental illness label in 1993: Acceptance and rejection in the community. *Journal of Health and Social Behavior, 7,* 61–69.

Page, S., & Day, D. (1990). Acceptance of the "mentally ill" in Canadian society: Reality and illusion. *Canadian Journal of Community Mental Health, 9,* 51–61.

Pettigrew, T. (1988). The ultimate attribution error. In E. Aronson (Ed.), *The social animal* (pp. 325–344). New York, NY: W. H. Freeman.

Taylor, M. (1979). Race, sex, and the expression of self-fulfilling prophecies in a laboratory teaching situation. *Journal of Personality and Social Psychology, 37,* 897–912.

Webb, E., Campbell, D., Schwartz, R., & Sechrest, L. (1966). *Unobtrusive measures.* New York, NY: Rand-McNally.

Weitz, S. (1972). Attitude, voice, and behavior: A repressed affect model of interracial interaction. *Journal of Personality and Social Psychology, 24,* 14–21.

Address correspondence to: Stewart Page, Department of Psychology, University of Windsor, 401 Sunset, Windsor, Ontario N9B 3P4, Canada.

Exercise for Article 7

Factual Questions

1. What is the "speculative hypothesis" that was explored in this study?

2. The observations were made during which hour of the day?

3. Did the individual cashiers work in the same station (location) every day?

4. What was the "unit" of observation?

5. The Number 1 White cashier was selected how many more times than the Black cashier?

6. Was the first chi-square test statistically significant at the .05 level (i.e., with a probability of .05 *or less*)? Explain.

7. What is the first limitation mentioned by the researcher?

Questions for Discussion

8. The researcher suggests that questionnaires and interviews assess racial behavior *reactively*. What do you think this term means? Is it a good idea to use questionnaires and interviews for this purpose? Explain. (See lines 39–43.)

9. The researcher points out that this is a *nonlaboratory* study. In your opinion, is this important? Explain. (See lines 70–78.)

10. Would it be informative to have a larger number of White and Black cashiers in a future study on this topic? Explain.

11. In your opinion, does this study *prove* that there is racial discrimination? Explain.

Quality Ratings

Directions: Indicate your level of agreement with each of the following statements by circling a number from 5 for strongly agree (SA) to 1 for strongly disagree (SD). If you believe an item is not applicable to this research article, leave it blank. Be prepared to explain your ratings. When responding to criteria A and B below, keep in mind that brief titles and abstracts are conventional in published research.

A. The title of the article is appropriate.

    SA   5   4   3   2   1   SD

B. The abstract provides an effective overview of the research article.

    SA   5   4   3   2   1   SD

C. The introduction establishes the importance of the study.

    SA   5   4   3   2   1   SD

D. The literature review establishes the context for the study.

    SA   5   4   3   2   1   SD

E. The research purpose, question, or hypothesis is clearly stated.

    SA   5   4   3   2   1   SD

F. The method of sampling is sound.

        SA   5   4   3   2   1   SD

G. Relevant demographics (for example, age, gender, and ethnicity) are described.

        SA   5   4   3   2   1   SD

H. Measurement procedures are adequate.

        SA   5   4   3   2   1   SD

I. All procedures have been described in sufficient detail to permit a replication of the study.

        SA   5   4   3   2   1   SD

J. The participants have been adequately protected from potential harm.

        SA   5   4   3   2   1   SD

K. The results are clearly described.

        SA   5   4   3   2   1   SD

L. The discussion/conclusion is appropriate.

        SA   5   4   3   2   1   SD

M. Despite any flaws, the report is worthy of publication.

        SA   5   4   3   2   1   SD

Article 8

Shopping Center Fire Zone Parking Violators: An Informal Look

JOHN TRINKAUS
Baruch College (CUNY)

ABSTRACT. Data for 33 1-hr. observations at a shopping center in a suburban location showed about 700 violations of a traffic regulation prohibiting parking in a fire zone. Women driving vans were the least compliant—accounting for approximately 35% of the total.

From *Perceptual and Motor Skills*, 95, 1215–1216. Copyright © 2002 by Perceptual and Motor Skills. Reprinted with permission.

To glean some information about the profile of motorists who fail to comply with rules on parking in designated fire zones in shopping centers (5), an informal enquiry was conducted, June through August of 2001, at a shopping center located in a suburb of a large city in New York State. The center housed a bank, a large grocery food supermarket, three sit-down restaurants, and an assortment of 12 other shops and stores. The center was arranged in the form of a "U." The businesses—with sidewalks in front—lined the periphery, with parking (for about 450 vehicles) in the central area. Painted on the pavement in front of the establishments was a 6-ft.-wide continuous yellow zebra-striping, which, along with sign postings, delineated a no-parking fire zone.

Three shops were located in one corner of the center—a dry cleaner, a bakery, and a laundromat—all of which opened early in the morning and appeared to do a brisk business seemingly with folks on their way to work: people dropping off or picking up dry cleaning, those buying rolls, pastry, and coffee, and people leaving laundry to be done. It was the parking behavior of these people that was observed; in particular, those who pulled up in front of one of the three shops and parked their vehicles in the fire zone.

Convenience sampling of the number of parkers, the type of vehicles driven (car or van), and the gender of the driver was conducted. Hour-long observations were made on weekdays, between the hours of 0700 and 0900: none during inclement weather. No note was made of commercial vehicles or those in which the driver remained behind the wheel while a passenger exited the vehicle and entered the shop to conduct business. As counting was done early in the day, there were always many "legal" parking spaces available (but necessitated walking approximately 75 to 150 feet further).

Thirty-three 1-hr. observations were made. A total of 916 parkings were noted: 693 (76%) in the fire zone and 223 (24%) in designated lot spaces. Of the fire zone parkings, 396 (57%) were cars and 297 (43%) vans. Women were driving 222 (56%) of the cars, and men 174 (44%). Two hundred forty-one (81%) of the vans were driven by women, 56 (19%) by men. For every three motorists who parked in the fire zone, there was approximately one motorist who parked in a designated lot space.

Recognizing such methodological limitations as the use of a relatively small sample of convenience, the possibility of double counting, the lack of factoring for the intrinsic moral code of conduct of individual drivers, and the problem of verifiable replication of this enquiry, it seems that compliance with rules on parking in fire zones may leave something to be desired. As to the finding that women driving vans appeared to be the least compliant with the parking regulation, it should be cautiously interpreted. For example, it may well be that the pattern observed could simply reflect a sample of the population of drivers and their vehicle types in the geographical area or those normally frequenting the shopping center during the observation period. However, it does appear to track four other prior related informal enquiries by Trinkaus. Those who exceeded school zone limits (1), those who failed to observe stop signs (2), those who delayed moving out at left-turning traffic signals (3), and those who blocked road intersections (4) all tended to be women driving vans.

Epilogue: To assess whether the parking behavior of drivers frequenting this shopping center might have changed following the World Trade Center incident of September 11—more law abiding—five additional observations were made in late September. No note was made of vehicle type nor driver gender, but note was made of whether or not vehicles were adorned with American flags or other patriotic trappings. A total of 129 parkings were observed: 94 (73%) in the fire zone and 35 (27%) in designated lot spaces. Of those that were parked in the fire zone, 22 (23%) were

80 decorated, while in designated lot spaces there were 3 (9%).

References

1. Trinkaus, J. School-zone speed-limit dissenters: An informal look. *Perceptual and Motor Skills*, 1999, *88*, 1057–1058.
2. Trinkaus, J. Stop-sign dissenters: An informal look. *Perceptual and Motor Skills*, 1999, *89*, 193–194.
3. Trinkaus, J. Left-turning traffic procrastinators: An informal look. *Perceptual and Motor Skills*, 2000, *90*, 961–962.
4. Trinkaus, J. Blocking the box: An informal look. *Psychological Reports*, 2001, *89*, 315–316.
5. *Vehicle and traffic law.* (2000–2001) New York State, Stopping, standing, and parking. Article 32, Basic rules, Section 1200.

Address correspondence to: J. Trinkaus, One Linden Street, New Hyde Park, NY 11040.

Exercise for Article 8

Factual Questions

1. The observations were made in front of what types of shops?

2. How many one-hour observations were made?

3. What percentage of the fire zone parkings were made by individuals in vans?

4. The researcher mentions several "methodological limitations." What is the first one that is mentioned?

5. Five additional observations were made to assess what?

Questions for Discussion

6. In your opinion, how important is it to know that the observations were made between 7 AM and 9 AM (i.e., between 0700 and 0900)? (See lines 28–30.)

7. Speculate on why the researcher did not make observations during inclement weather. (See lines 28–30.)

8. Do any of the findings surprise you? Do you find any especially interesting? Explain.

9. If you were conducting a study on the same topic, what changes in the research methodology, if any, would you make?

Quality Ratings

Directions: Indicate your level of agreement with each of the following statements by circling a number from 5 for strongly agree (SA) to 1 for strongly disagree (SD). If you believe an item is not applicable to this research article, leave it blank. Be prepared to explain your ratings. When responding to criteria A and B below, keep in mind that brief titles and abstracts are conventional in published research.

A. The title of the article is appropriate.

SA 5 4 3 2 1 SD

B. The abstract provides an effective overview of the research article.

SA 5 4 3 2 1 SD

C. The introduction establishes the importance of the study.

SA 5 4 3 2 1 SD

D. The literature review establishes the context for the study.

SA 5 4 3 2 1 SD

E. The research purpose, question, or hypothesis is clearly stated.

SA 5 4 3 2 1 SD

F. The method of sampling is sound.

SA 5 4 3 2 1 SD

G. Relevant demographics (for example, age, gender, and ethnicity) are described.

SA 5 4 3 2 1 SD

H. Measurement procedures are adequate.

SA 5 4 3 2 1 SD

I. All procedures have been described in sufficient detail to permit a replication of the study.

SA 5 4 3 2 1 SD

J. The participants have been adequately protected from potential harm.

SA 5 4 3 2 1 SD

K. The results are clearly described.

SA 5 4 3 2 1 SD

L. The discussion/conclusion is appropriate.

SA 5 4 3 2 1 SD

M. Despite any flaws, the report is worthy of publication.

SA 5 4 3 2 1 SD

Article 9

Students' Ratings of Teaching Effectiveness: A Laughing Matter?

GARY ADAMSON
University of Ulster at Magee College

DAMIAN O'KANE
University of Ulster at Magee College

MARK SHEVLIN
University of Ulster at Magee College

ABSTRACT. Gump in 2004 identified a positive significant relationship between awareness of daily class objectives and ratings of the instructor's overall teaching effectiveness. The idea that rating of teaching effectiveness can be related to other nonteaching related attributes of the lecturer was further examined. Correlations based on ratings of teaching effectiveness from 453 undergraduate students ($M = 21$ yr., $SD = 5.5$; 73% women) showed that another nonteaching related variable, namely, how funny the instructor was perceived, was significantly related to indicators of teaching effectiveness.

From *Psychological Reports, 96*, 225–226. Copyright © 2005 by Psychological Reports. Reprinted with permission.

The practice of having students evaluate teaching in universities is widespread in the UK and the USA, and the information from such surveys can be a useful guide for potential changes in course material and method of delivery (QAA, 1997). For students' evaluation of teaching questionnaires to be used, there should be clear evidence that such measures are producing valid scores, that is, that such questionnaires are actually measuring teaching effectiveness.

Research suggests that ratings of teaching effectiveness are positively related to teaching and student-related variables such as awareness of daily class objectives (Gump, 2004), expected grades (Feldman, 1976; Marsh, 1987), the students' prior interest in the topic (Marsh & Roche, 1997), and grading leniency (Greenwald & Gillmore, 1997). More alarmingly, Shevlin, Banyard, Davies, and Griffiths (2000) tested a model that specified ratings of the lecturers' charisma, measured by a single item, as a predictor of teaching effectiveness, in particular "lecturer ability" and "module attributes." Using structural equation modeling, they found that the charisma ratings accounted for 69% of the variation of the lecturer ability factor and 37% of the module attributes factor.

The idea that ratings of teaching effectiveness can be related to other nonteaching related attributes of the lecturer was further examined. An additional item, "The lecturer was funny," was included in a larger questionnaire designed to measure teaching effectiveness. All items used a 5-point Likert response format with anchors of 1 (Strongly Disagree) and 5 (Strongly Agree). This questionnaire was administered at a UK university to a sample of 453 undergraduate students who were enrolled in full-time courses within a department of social sciences (M age = 21 yr., SD = 5.5; 73% women). In total, six lecturers were rated (four men and two women) in this study.

Analysis showed items designed to reflect aspects of effective teaching were positively correlated with rating how funny the lecturer was. Scores on the item "The lecturer was funny" were positively correlated with scores on the items "The lecturer helped me to develop an interest in the subject matter" ($r = .60$, $p < .01$), "I wanted to learn more about the topic" ($r = .49$, $p < .01$), "The lectures were well organized ($r = .40$, $p < .01$), and "The lecturer is successful in encouraging students to do supplementary reading on the subject matter of the module" ($r = .38$, $p < .01$).

The results suggest that students' perceptions of funniness were moderately and significantly associated with ratings of teaching-related activity.

Whereas previous research has focused mainly on the dimensionality of measures of teaching effectiveness (Abrami, d'Apollonia, & Rosenfield, 1997), it is suggested here that the validity of scores derived from any measure of teaching effectiveness ought to be ascertained prior to use of the measure.

References

Abrami, P. C., d'Apollonia, S., & Rosenfield, S. (1997). The dimensionality of student ratings of instruction: What we know and what we do not. In R. P. Perry & J. C. Smart (Eds.), *Effective teaching in higher education: Research and practice*. New York: Agathon Press. pp. 321–367.

Feldman, K. A. (1976). Grades and college students' evaluations of their courses and teachers. *Research in Higher Education, 18*, 3–124.

Greenwald, A. G., & Gillmore, G. M. (1997). Grading leniency is a removable contaminant of student ratings. *American Psychologist, 52*, 1209–1217.

Gump, S. E. (2004). Daily class objectives and instructor's effectiveness as perceived by students. *Psychological Reports, 94*, 1250–1252.

Marsh, H. W. (1987). Students' evaluations of university teaching: Research findings, methodological issues, and directions for future research. *International Journal of Educational Research, 11*, 253–388.

Marsh, H. W., & Roche, L. A. (1997). Making students' evaluations of teaching effectiveness effective. *American Psychologist, 52*, 1187–1197.

Quality Assurance Agency for Higher Education. (1997). *Subject review handbook: October 1998 to September 2000.* (QAA 1/97) London: Quality Assurance Agency for Higher Education.

Shevlin, M., Banyard, P., Davies, M. D., & Griffiths, M. (2000). The validity of student evaluation of teaching in higher education: Love me, love my lectures? *Assessment and Evaluation in Higher Education, 25*, 397–405.

Address correspondence to: Dr. Mark Shevlin, School of Psychology, University of Ulster at Magee Campus, Londonderry, BT48 7JL, UK.

Exercise for Article 9

Factual Questions

1. What were the anchors for the statement, "The lecturer was funny"?

2. How many students participated in this study?

3. What was the average age of the students in this study?

4. What is the value of the correlation coefficient for the relationship between "The lecturer was funny" and "I wanted to learn more about the topic"?

5. The strongest correlation was between the lecturer being funny and what other item?

6. Do all the correlation coefficients reported in this study indicate direct (positive) relationships?

Questions for Discussion

7. The researchers characterize being funny as a "nonteaching related" attribute. Do you agree with this characterization (i.e., that being funny is not a teaching attribute)? (See lines 25–30.)

8. Six lecturers were rated by the students. Would you recommend using a larger number of lecturers in a future study on this topic? Explain. (See lines 36–37.)

9. After each correlation coefficient, this information appears: $p < .01$. What does this tell you about the correlation coefficients? (See lines 43–48.)

10. Would you characterize any of the correlation coefficients in lines 43–48 as representing very strong relationships?

11. The relationships reported in this study are positive. If you had planned this study, would you have anticipated finding any inverse (negative) relationships among the variables studied? Explain.

12. Do you think that this study shows a *causal* relationship between being funny and perceptions of other teaching attributes (i.e., does it provide evidence that being funny causes higher ratings on other items)? Explain.

13. This research report is shorter than others in this book. In your opinion, is its brevity a defect of the report? A strength of the report? Explain.

Quality Ratings

Directions: Indicate your level of agreement with each of the following statements by circling a number from 5 for strongly agree (SA) to 1 for strongly disagree (SD). If you believe an item is not applicable to this research article, leave it blank. Be prepared to explain your ratings. When responding to criteria A and B below, keep in mind that brief titles and abstracts are conventional in published research.

A. The title of the article is appropriate.
   SA   5   4   3   2   1   SD

B. The abstract provides an effective overview of the research article.
   SA   5   4   3   2   1   SD

C. The introduction establishes the importance of the study.
   SA   5   4   3   2   1   SD

D. The literature review establishes the context for the study.
   SA   5   4   3   2   1   SD

E. The research purpose, question, or hypothesis is clearly stated.
   SA   5   4   3   2   1   SD

F. The method of sampling is sound.
   SA   5   4   3   2   1   SD

G. Relevant demographics (for example, age, gender, and ethnicity) are described.
   SA   5   4   3   2   1   SD

H. Measurement procedures are adequate.
   SA   5   4   3   2   1   SD

I. All procedures have been described in sufficient detail to permit a replication of the study.
   SA   5   4   3   2   1   SD

J. The participants have been adequately protected from potential harm.
   SA   5   4   3   2   1   SD

K. The results are clearly described.
   SA   5   4   3   2   1   SD

L.   The discussion/conclusion is appropriate.

SA   5   4   3   2   1   SD

M.   Despite any flaws, the report is worthy of publication.

SA   5   4   3   2   1   SD

Article 10

Relationships of Assertiveness, Depression, and Social Support Among Older Nursing Home Residents

DANIEL L. SEGAL
University of Colorado at Colorado Springs

ABSTRACT. This study assessed the relationships of assertiveness, depression, and social support among nursing home residents. The sample included 50 older nursing home residents (mean age = 75 years; 75% female; 92% Caucasian). There was a significant correlation between assertiveness and depression ($r = -.33$), but the correlations between social support and depression ($r = -.15$) and between social support and assertiveness ($r = -.03$) were small and nonsignificant. The correlation between overall physical health (a subjective self-rating) and depression was strong and negative ($r = -.50$), with lower levels of health associated with higher depression. An implication of this study is that an intervention for depression among nursing home residents that is targeted at increasing assertiveness and bolstering health status may be more effective than the one that solely targets social support.

From *Behavior Modification*, 29, 689–695. Copyright © 2005 by Sage Publications, Inc. Reprinted with permission.

Most older adults prefer and are successful at "aging in place"—that is, maintaining their independence in their own home. For the frailest and most debilitated older adults, however, nursing home placement is of-
5 tentimes necessary. About 5% of older adults live in a nursing home at any point in time, a figure that has remained stable since the early 1970s (National Center for Health Statistics, 2002). Depression is one of the most prevalent and serious psychological problems
10 among nursing home residents: About 15% to 50% of residents suffer from diagnosable depression (see review by Streim & Katz, 1996).

Social support is also an important factor in mental health among nursing home residents, and psychosocial
15 interventions often seek to bolster the resident's level of supportive relationships.

Assertiveness training plays an important role in traditional behavioral therapy with adults, and it has been recommended as a treatment component among
20 older adults with diverse psychological problems as well (Gambrill, 1986). Assertiveness may be defined as the ability to express one's thoughts, feelings, beliefs, and rights in an open, honest, and appropriate way. A

key component of assertiveness is that the communica-
25 tion does not violate the rights of others, as is the case in aggressive communications. It is logical that nursing home residents with good assertiveness skills would more often get what they want and need. Having basic needs met is a natural goal of all people, and failure to
30 do so could lead to depression or other psychological problems. Personal control has long been noted to improve mental health among nursing home residents (see Langer & Rodin, 1976), and assertiveness training would likely help residents express more clearly their
35 desires and needs.

Two studies have examined links between assertiveness, depression, and social support among older adult groups. Among 69 community-dwelling older adults, Kogan, Van Hasselt, Hersen, and Kabacoff
40 (1995) found that those who are less assertive and have less social support are at increased risk for depression. Among 100 visually impaired older adults, Hersen et al. (1995) reported that higher levels of social support and assertiveness were associated with lower levels of
45 depression. Assertiveness may rightly be an important skill among nursing home residents because workers at the institutional setting may not be as attuned to the emotional needs of a passive resident and the workers may respond poorly to the aggressive and acting-out
50 resident. However, little is known about the nature and impact of assertiveness in long-term care settings. The purpose of this study, therefore, was to assess relationships of assertiveness, social support, and depression among nursing home residents, thus extending the lit-
55 erature to a unique population.

Method

Participants were recruited at several local nursing homes. Staff identified potential volunteers who were ostensibly free of cognitive impairment. Participants completed anonymously the following self-report
60 measures: Wolpe-Lazarus Assertiveness Scale (WLAS) (Wolpe & Lazarus, 1966), Geriatric Depression Scale (GDS) (Yesavage et al., 1983), and the Social Support List of Interactions (SSL 12-I) (Kempen & van Eijk, 1995). The WLAS consists of 30 yes/no

65 items and measures levels of assertive behavior. Scores can range from 0 to 30, with higher scores reflecting higher levels of assertiveness. The GDS includes 30 yes/no items and evaluates depressive symptoms spe-
70 cifically among older adults. Scores can range from 0 to 30, with higher scores indicating higher levels of depression. The SSL12-I is a 12-item measure of received social support that has good psychometric properties among community-dwelling older adults. Re-
75 spondents indicate on a 4-point scale the extent to which they received a specific type of support from a member of their primary social network (1 = seldom or never, 2 = now and then, 3 = regularly, 4 = very often). Scores can range from 12 to 48 with higher scores corresponding to higher levels of support. The sample
80 included 50 older adult residents (mean age = 74.9 years, SD = 11.9, age range = 50–96 years; 75% female; 92% Caucasian).

Results and Discussion

The mean WLAS was 18.1 (SD = 4.1), the mean GDS was 9.0 (SD = 5.5), and the mean SSL12-I was
85 29.2 (SD = 7.3). The correlation between the WLAS and GDS was moderate and negative (r = −.33, p < .05), with lower levels of assertiveness associated with higher depression. The correlation between the SSL12-I and GDS was small and nonsignificant (r = −.15, ns),
90 indicating a slight negative relationship between overall support and depression. Similarly, the correlation between the SSL12-I and WLAS was small and nonsignificant (r = −.03, ns), indicating almost no relationship between overall support and assertiveness. Next,
95 correlations between a subjective self-rating of overall physical health status (0–100 scale, higher scores indicating better health) and the WLAS, GDS, and SSL12-I were calculated. As expected, the correlation between physical health and GDS was strong and negative
100 (r = −.50, p < .01), with poorer health associated with higher depression. The correlation between health and WLAS was positive in direction but small and nonsignificant (r = .17, ns), indicating little relationship between health and assertiveness. Similarly, the correla-
105 tion between health and SSL12-I was also small and nonsignificant (r = −.02, ns), indicating no relationship between health and overall support. The slight relationship between health and assertiveness is an encouraging sign because it suggests that assertiveness (which is
110 primarily achieved through effective verbalizations) is not limited to only the least physically impaired nursing home residents. Finally, gender differences on all dependent measures were examined (independent t tests) and no significant differences were found (all ps
115 > .05).

Notably, the mean assertion and depression scores among nursing home residents are consistent with means on identical measures in community-dwelling older adults (assertion M = 19.1; depression M = 7.9;
120 Kogan et al., 1995) and visually impaired older adults (assertion M = 18.3; depression M = 10.4; Hersen et al., 1995), suggesting that the higher functioning group of nursing home residents are no more depressed and no less assertive than other samples of older persons.
125 Regarding social support, our nursing home sample appeared to show somewhat higher levels of overall support than community older adults in the normative sample (N = 5,279, M = 25.5) in the SSL12-I validation study (Kempen & van Eijk, 1995). This may pos-
130 sibly be due to the nature of institutional living and the large numbers of support staff and health care personnel.

The correlational results regarding the moderate negative association between assertion and depression
135 are consistent with data from community-dwelling older adults (r = −.36; Kogan et al., 1995) and visually impaired older adults (r = −.29; Hersen et al., 1995), suggesting a pervasive relationship among the variables in diverse older adult samples and extending the
140 findings to nursing home residents. Contrary to the literature, the relationship between social support and depression among nursing home residents was weaker than the one reported in community-dwelling older adults (r = −.50; Kogan et al., 1995) and visually im-
145 paired older adults (r = −.48; Hersen et al., 1995). The relationship between assertiveness and overall support in this study was almost nonexistent, also contrary to earlier reports in which the relationship was moderate and positive in direction. Our results are consistent
150 with prior research showing no gender differences among older adults in assertiveness, depression, and social support using similar assessment tools (Hersen et al., 1995; Kogan et al., 1995). This study also suggests a strong negative relationship between health status and
155 depression among nursing home residents. An implication of this study is that an intervention for depression among nursing home residents that is targeted at increasing assertiveness and bolstering health status may be more effective than the one that solely targets social
160 support.

Several limitations are offered concerning this study. First, the sample size was modest and the sample was almost exclusively Caucasian. Future studies with more diverse nursing home residents would add to the
165 knowledge base in this area. All measures were self-report, and future studies with structured interviews and behavioral assessments would be stronger. We are also concerned somewhat about the extent to which the WLAS is content valid for older adults. Notably, a
170 measure of assertive behavior competence has been developed specifically for use with community-dwelling older adults (Northrop & Edelstein, 1998), and this measure appears to be a good choice for future research in the area. A final limitation was that partici-
175 pants were likely the highest functioning of residents because they were required to be able to complete the measures independently and were selected out if there was any overt cognitive impairment (although no for-

mal screening for cognitive impairment was done), thus limiting generalizability to more frail nursing home residents. Cognitive screening should be done in future studies. Nonetheless, results of this study suggest a potentially important relationship between assertiveness and depression among nursing home residents.

Finally, it is imperative to highlight that there are many types of interventions to combat depression among nursing home residents: behavioral interventions to increase exercise, participation in social activities, and other pleasurable activities; cognitive interventions to reduce depressogenic thoughts; and pharmacotherapy, to name a few. (The interested reader is referred to Molinari, 2000, for a comprehensive description of psychological issues and interventions unique to long-term care settings.) The present data suggest that training in assertiveness may be yet one additional option for psychosocial intervention in nursing homes. A controlled outcome study is warranted in which intensive assertiveness training is compared to a control group of nursing home residents who do not receive such training. Only with such a study can cause-and-effect statements be made about the role that assertiveness skills training may play in the reduction of depressive symptoms among nursing home residents.

References

Gambrill, E. B. (1986). Social skills training with the elderly. In C. R. Hollin & P. Trower (Eds.), *Handbook of social skills training: Applications across the lifespan* (pp. 211–238). New York: Pergamon.

Hersen, M., Kabacoff, R. L, Van Hasselt, V. B., Null, J. A., Ryan, C. F., Melton, M. A., et al. (1995). Assertiveness, depression, and social support in older visually impaired adults. *Journal of Visual Impairment and Blindness*, 7, 524–530.

Kempen, G. I. J. M., & van Eijk, L. M. (1995). The psychometric properties of the SSL12-I, a short scale for measuring social support in the elderly. *Social Indicators Research*, 35, 303–312.

Kogan, S. E., Van Hasselt, B. V., Hersen, M., & Kabacoff, I. R. (1995). Relationship of depression, assertiveness, and social support in community-dwelling older adults. *Journal of Clinical Geropsychology*, 1, 157–163.

Langer, E. J., & Rodin, J. (1976). The effects of choice and enhanced personal responsibility for the aged: A field experiment in an institutional setting. *Journal of Personality and Social Psychology*, 34, 191–198.

Molinari, V. (Ed.). (2000). *Professional psychology in long-term care: A comprehensive guide*. New York: Hatherleigh.

National Center for Health Statistics. (2002). *Health, United States, 2002*. Hyattsville, MD: Author.

Northrop, L. M. E., & Edelstein, B. A. (1998). An assertive-behavior competence inventory for older adults. *Journal of Clinical Geropsychology*, 4, 315–331.

Streim, J. E., & Katz, I. R. (1996). Clinical psychiatry in the nursing home. In E. W. Busse & D. G. Blazer (Eds.), *Textbook of geriatric psychiatry* (2nd ed., pp. 413–432). Washington, DC: American Psychiatric Press.

Wolpe, J., & Lazarus, A. A. (1966). *Behavior therapy techniques*. New York: Pergamon.

Yesavage, J. A., Brink, T. L., Rose, T. L., Lum, O., Huang, V, Adey, M., et al. (1983). Development and validation of a geriatric depression screening scale: A preliminary report. *Journal of Psychiatric Research*, 17, 314–317.

Acknowledgment: The author thanks Jessica Corcoran, M.A., for assistance with data collection and data entry.

About the author: Daniel L. Segal received his Ph.D. in clinical psychology from the University of Miami in 1992. He is an associate professor in the Department of Psychology at the University of Colorado at Colorado Springs. His research interests include diagnostic and assessment issues in geropsychology, suicide prevention and aging, bereavement, and personality disorders across the lifespan.

Exercise for Article 10

Factual Questions

1. Were the participants cognitively impaired?

   no

2. Was the mean score for the participants on the GDS near the highest possible score on this instrument? Explain. *— 9 — NO is on low score 0–30*

3. What is the value of the correlation coefficient for the relationship between the WLAS and the GDS? *Moderate to neg = more assert less depress*

4. Was the relationship between SSL12-I and GDS strong? *— Small not significant*

5. Was the correlation coefficient for the relationship between SSL12-I and GDS statistically significant? *Line 89 – Small & not sign.*

6. Was the relationship between physical health and GDS a "direct" relationship *or* an "inverse" relationship? *inverse*

Questions for Discussion

7. The researcher obtained participants from "several" nursing homes. Is this better than obtaining them from a single nursing home? Explain. (See lines 56–57.)

8. The researcher characterizes the *r* of −.33 in line 86 as "moderate." Do you agree with this characterization? Explain.

9. In lines 85–107, the researcher reports the values of six correlation coefficients. Which one of these indicates the strongest relationship? Explain the basis for your choice.

10. In lines 85–107, the researcher reports the values of six correlation coefficients. Which one of these indicates the weakest relationship? Explain the basis for your choice.

11. For the *r* of −.50 in line 100, the researcher indicates that "*p* < .01." What is your understanding of the meaning of the symbol "*p*"? What is your understanding of ".01"?

12. Do you agree with the researcher that a different type of study is needed in order to determine the role of assertiveness skills training in the reduction of depressive symptoms? Explain. (See lines 197–204.)

Quality Ratings

Directions: Indicate your level of agreement with each of the following statements by circling a number from 5 for strongly agree (SA) to 1 for strongly disagree (SD). If you believe an item is not applicable to this research article, leave it blank. Be prepared to explain your ratings. When responding to criteria A and B below, keep in mind that brief titles and abstracts are conventional in published research.

A. The title of the article is appropriate.

SA   5   4   3   2   1   SD

B. The abstract provides an effective overview of the research article.

SA   5   4   3   2   1   SD

C. The introduction establishes the importance of the study.

SA   5   4   3   2   1   SD

D. The literature review establishes the context for the study.

SA   5   4   3   2   1   SD

E. The research purpose, question, or hypothesis is clearly stated.

SA   5   4   3   2   1   SD

F. The method of sampling is sound.

SA   5   4   3   2   1   SD

G. Relevant demographics (for example, age, gender, and ethnicity) are described.

SA   5   4   3   2   1   SD

H. Measurement procedures are adequate.

SA   5   4   3   2   1   SD

I. All procedures have been described in sufficient detail to permit a replication of the study.

SA   5   4   3   2   1   SD

J. The participants have been adequately protected from potential harm.

SA   5   4   3   2   1   SD

K. The results are clearly described.

SA   5   4   3   2   1   SD

L. The discussion/conclusion is appropriate.

SA   5   4   3   2   1   SD

M. Despite any flaws, the report is worthy of publication.

SA   5   4   3   2   1   SD

Article 11

Correlations Between Humor Styles and Loneliness

WILLIAM P. HAMPES
Black Hawk College

ABSTRACT. In a previous study, a significant negative correlation between shyness with affiliative humor and a significant positive one with self-defeating humor were reported. Since shyness and loneliness share many of the same characteristics, poor social skills and negative affect, for example, significant negative correlations of loneliness with affiliative and self-enhancing humor and a significant positive one with self-defeating humor were hypothesized. 106 community college students (34 men, 72 women) ranging in age from 17 to 52 years ($M = 23.5$, $SD = 7.7$) were tested. The hypotheses were supported. Interrelationships among humor, shyness, and loneliness should be examined within one study.

From *Psychological Reports*, *96*, 747–750. Copyright © 2005 by Psychological Reports. Reprinted with permission.

Various studies, using self-report and rating scales, have yielded correlations of .40 or more between shyness and loneliness (Cheek & Busch, 1981; Jones, Freeman, & Goswick, 1981; Moore & Schultz, 1983; Anderson & Arnoult, 1985). Research studies have shown that those high in both variables tend to have poor social skills (Zahaki & Duran, 1982; Moore & Schultz, 1983; Wittenberg & Reis, 1986; Miller, 1995; Carducci, 2000; Segrin & Flora, 2000), poor interpersonal relationships (Jones, 1981; Jones, Rose, & Russell, 1990; Carducci, 2000), and low self-esteem (Jones et al., 1981; Olmstead, Guy, O'Malley, & Bentler, 1991; Kamath & Kanekar, 1993; Schmidt & Fox, 1995).

Hampes (in press) reported shyness negatively correlated with affiliative humor and positively correlated with self-defeating humor. Affiliative humor is an interpersonal form of humor that involves use of humor (telling jokes, saying funny things, or witty banter, for example), to put others at ease, amuse others, and to improve relationships (Martin, Puhlik-Doris, Larsen, Gray, & Weir, 2003). Since those high on affiliative humor tend to score high on extraversion and intimacy (Martin et al., 2003), and lonely people, like shy people, have poor social skills and relationships, it was hypothesized that loneliness would be negatively correlated with affiliative humor.

Self-defeating humor "involves excessively self-disparaging humor, attempts to amuse others by doing or saying funny things at one's expense as a means of ingratiating oneself or gaining approval, allowing oneself to be the 'butt' of others' humor, and laughing along with others when being ridiculed or disparaged" (Martin et al., 2003, p. 54). Since both lonely and shy people tend to have low self-esteem, and those high in self-defeating humor tend to score low on self-esteem (Martin et al., 2003), it was hypothesized that loneliness and self-defeating humor would be positively correlated.

Hampes (in press) did not find a significant correlation for his total group of 174 subjects between scores on shyness and self-enhancing humor, an adaptive intrapersonal dimension of humor that "involves a generally humorous outlook on life, a tendency to be frequently amused by the incongruities of life, and to maintain a humorous perspective even in the face of stress or of adversity" (Martin et al., 2003, p. 53). However, Martin et al. reported self-enhancing humor scores were positively correlated with those on self-esteem, social intimacy, and social support, just the opposite of the relationships between loneliness and self-esteem, social intimacy, and social support. Therefore, it was hypothesized that loneliness and self-enhancing humor would be negatively correlated.

Hampes (in press) did not find a significant correlation for his total group between scores on shyness and aggressive humor (a maladaptive interpersonal type of humor, involving sarcasm, teasing, ridicule, derision, hostility, or disparagement humor) for the total group. Therefore, it was hypothesized that there would be a nonsignificant correlation between loneliness and aggressive humor.

Method

The subjects were 106 students (34 men, 72 women) at a community college in the midwestern United States. These students ranged in age from 17 to 52 years ($M = 23.5$, $SD = 7.7$). Students in four psychology classes were asked to participate, and those who volunteered were included in the sample.

The UCLA Loneliness Scale (Version 3) measures loneliness as a unidimensional emotional response to a difference between desired and achieved social contact. It contains 20 items, each of which has four response options in a Likert-type format, anchored by 1 = Never and 4 = Always (e.g., "How often do you feel isolated from others?"). Coefficients alpha for the scale ranged from .89 to .94 (Russell & Cutrona, 1988). Russell, Kao, and Cutrona (1987) reported a 1-yr. test–retest correlation of .73 and estimated discriminant validity through significant negative correlations between scores on loneliness with those on social support and measures of positive mental health status.

In the Humor Styles Questionnaire, each of four scales has eight items. Each item has seven response options in a Likert-type format, anchored by 1 = Totally Disagree and 7 = Totally Agree. The Cronbach alpha for the four scales ranged from .77 to .81. The convergent validity for the Affiliative Humor Scale was indicated by significant correlations with scores on the Miller Social Intimacy Scale and Extraversion on the NEO PI–R. Discriminant validity for the Self-enhancing Humor Scale was estimated by a significant negative correlation with scores on Neuroticism of the NEO PI–R, and convergent validity was estimated with significant positive correlations with the Coping Humor Scale and the Humor Coping subscale of the Coping Orientations to Problems Experienced Scale. Convergent validity for the Aggressive Scale was supported by a significant correlation with scores on the Cook-Medley Hostility Scale. Discriminant validity for the Self-defeating Scale was based on significant negative correlations with ratings on the Rosenberg Self-esteem Scale and on the Index of Self-esteem (Martin et al., 2003).

Results and Discussion

Four Pearson product-moment correlations were computed for the scores on the UCLA Loneliness Scale-Version 3 ($M = 41.1$, $SD = 10.7$) and those on each of four humor scales: Affiliative ($M = 45.5$, $SD = 7.3$), Self-enhancing ($M = 37.4$, $SD = 8.4$), Aggressive ($M = 25.8$, $SD = 7.4$), and Self-defeating ($M = 26.0$, $SD = 8.9$). In each case, the hypotheses were supported, as correlations were significant for scores in Loneliness with Affiliative Humor ($r = -.47$, $p < .001$, $CI_{95} = -.28$ to $-.66$), Self-enhancing Humor ($r = -.39$, $p < .001$, $CI_{95} = -.20$ to $-.58$), and Self-defeating Humor ($r = .32$, $p < .001$, $CI_{95} = .13$ to $.51$). The correlation between scores on Loneliness and Aggressive Humor was not significant ($r = -.04$, $p > .05$, $CI_{95} = -.23$ to $.15$).

Dill and Anderson (1999) posited that shyness precedes loneliness. Given their social anxiety, shy people tend to be unsuccessful in social situations, and so they try to avoid these. Even if they do not avoid social relationships, they tend not to have satisfying personal relationships. As a result, they may report being lonely. The idea that shyness precedes loneliness is supported by the developmental research of Kagan (1994), who stated that shyness has a strong genetic component and

is manifested early in infancy, and Cheek and Busch (1981), who found shyness influenced loneliness reported by students in an introductory psychology course. If shyness does precede loneliness, it could be in part because shy individuals do not use affiliative humor and self-enhancing humor to help them be more successful in social situations and score high in self-defeating humor, which other people might not find appealing. Further studies are needed to evaluate the causal relationships among shyness, loneliness, and styles of humor.

References

Anderson, C. A., & Arnoult, L. H. (1985). Attributional style and everyday problems in living: Depression, loneliness, and shyness. *Social Cognition, 3,* 16–35.

Carducci, B. (2000). *Shyness: A bold new approach.* New York: Perennial.

Cheek, J. M., & Busch, C. M. (1981). The influence of shyness on loneliness in a new situation. *Personality and Social Psychology Bulletin, 7,* 572–577.

Dill, J. C., & Anderson, C. A. (1999). Loneliness, shyness, and depression: the etiology and interrelationships of everyday problems in living. In T. Joiner & J. C. Coyne (Eds.), *The interactional nature of depression* (pp. 93–125). Washington, DC: American Psychological Association.

Hampes, W. P. (in press). The relation between humor styles and shyness. *Humor: The International Journal of Humor Research.*

Jones, W. H. (1981) Loneliness and social contact. *Journal of Social Psychology, 113,* 295–296.

Jones, W. H., Freeman, J. A., & Goswick, R. A. (1981). The persistence of loneliness: Self and other determinants. *Journal of Personality, 49,* 27–48.

Jones, W. H., Rose, J., & Russell, D. (1990). Loneliness and social anxiety. In H. Leitenberg (Ed.), *Handbook of social evaluation anxiety* (pp. 247–266) New York: Plenum.

Kagan, J. (1994). *Galen's prophecy: Temperament in human nature.* New York: Basic Books.

Kamath, M., & Kanekar, S. (1993). Loneliness, shyness, self-esteem, and extraversion. *The Journal of Social Psychology, 133,* 855–857.

Martin, R. A., Puhlik-Doris, P., Larsen, G., Gray, J., & Weir, K. (2003). Individual differences in uses of humor and their relation to psychological well-being: Development of the Humor Styles Questionnaire. *Journal of Research in Personality, 37,* 48–75.

Miller, R. S. (1995). On the nature of embarassability, shyness, social evaluation, and social skill. *The Journal of Psychology, 63,* 315–339.

Moore, D., & Schultz, N. R. (1983). Loneliness at adolescence: Correlates, attributions and coping. *Journal of Youth and Adolescence, 12,* 95–100.

Olmstead, R. E., Guy, S. M., O'Malley, P. M., & Bentler, P. M. (1991). Longitudinal assessment of the relationship between self-esteem, fatalism, loneliness, and substance abuse. *Journal of Social Behavior and Personality, 6,* 749–770.

Russell, D. W., & Cutrona, C. E. (1988). Development and evolution of the UCLA Loneliness Scale. (Unpublished manuscript, Center for Health Services Research, College of Medicine, University of Iowa)

Russell, D. W., Kao, C., & Cutrona, C. E. (1987). Loneliness and social support: Same or different constructs? Paper presented at the Iowa Conference on Personal Relationships, Iowa City.

Schmidt, L. A., & Fox, N. A. (1995). Individual differences in young adults' shyness and sociability: Personality and health correlates. *Personality and Individual Differences, 19,* 455–462.

Segrin, C., & Flora, J. (2000). Poor social skills are a vulnerability factor in the development of psychosocial problems. *Human Communication Research, 26,* 489–514.

Wittenberg, M. T., & Reis, H. T. (1986). Loneliness, social skills, and social perception. *Personality and Social Psychology Bulletin, 12,* 121–130.

Zahaki, W. R., & Duran, R. L. (1982). All the lonely people: The relationship among loneliness, communicative competence, and communication anxiety. *Communication Quarterly, 30,* 202–209.

Address correspondence to: William Hampes, Department of Social, Behavioral, and Educational Studies, Black Hawk College, 6600 34th Avenue, Moline, IL 61265. E-mail: hampesw@bhc.edu

Exercise for Article 11

Factual Questions

1. In the introduction to the research article, the researcher hypothesizes a positive correlation between which two variables?

2. What was the mean age of the students in this study?

3. The correlation coefficient for the relationship between Loneliness with Affiliative Humor was −.47. This indicates that those who had high loneliness scores tended to have

   A. low Affiliative Humor scores.
   B. high Affiliative Humor scores.

4. In lines 111–117, the researcher reports four correlation coefficients. Which correlation coefficient indicates the strongest relationship?

5. Is the correlation coefficient for the relationship between Loneliness and Self-enhancing Humor statistically significant? If yes, at what probability level?

6. Is the correlation coefficient for the relationship between Loneliness and Aggressive Humor statistically significant? If yes, at what probability level?

Questions for Discussion

7. In your opinion, does the use of volunteers affect the quality of this study? (See lines 63–68.)

8. The correlation coefficient between Loneliness with Affiliative Humor equals −.47. The researcher also reports the 95% confidence interval (CI_{95}) for this correlation coefficient. What is your understanding of the meaning of the confidence interval? (See lines 111–113.)

9. Would you characterize any of the correlation coefficients reported in lines 111–117 as representing a "very strong" relationship? Explain.

10. Would you characterize any of the correlation coefficients reported in lines 111–117 as representing a "very weak" relationship? Explain.

11. The researcher mentions "causal relationships" in line 136. In your opinion, do the results of this study offer evidence regarding causal relationships? Explain.

Quality Ratings

Directions: Indicate your level of agreement with each of the following statements by circling a number from 5 for strongly agree (SA) to 1 for strongly disagree (SD). If you believe an item is not applicable to this research article, leave it blank. Be prepared to explain your ratings. When responding to criteria A and B below, keep in mind that brief titles and abstracts are conventional in published research.

A. The title of the article is appropriate.
   SA   5   4   3   2   1   SD

B. The abstract provides an effective overview of the research article.
   SA   5   4   3   2   1   SD

C. The introduction establishes the importance of the study.
   SA   5   4   3   2   1   SD

D. The literature review establishes the context for the study.
   SA   5   4   3   2   1   SD

E. The research purpose, question, or hypothesis is clearly stated.
   SA   5   4   3   2   1   SD

F. The method of sampling is sound.
   SA   5   4   3   2   1   SD

G. Relevant demographics (for example, age, gender, and ethnicity) are described.
   SA   5   4   3   2   1   SD

H. Measurement procedures are adequate.
   SA   5   4   3   2   1   SD

I. All procedures have been described in sufficient detail to permit a replication of the study.
   SA   5   4   3   2   1   SD

J. The participants have been adequately protected from potential harm.
   SA   5   4   3   2   1   SD

K. The results are clearly described.
   SA   5   4   3   2   1   SD

L. The discussion/conclusion is appropriate.
   SA   5   4   3   2   1   SD

M. Despite any flaws, the report is worthy of publication.
   SA   5   4   3   2   1   SD

Article 12

Counting Bones: Environmental Cues
That Decrease Food Intake

BRIAN WANSINK
Cornell University

COLLIN R. PAYNE
Cornell University

ABSTRACT. At an all-you-can eat buffet in a sports bar, it was tested whether people would eat less if they knew how much they had already eaten. Fifty-two graduate students were seated at 21 tables randomly assigned to be bussed (leftover wings removed) or unbussed (wings left on table). The 31 students at the bussed tables ate more than those at the unbussed tables (7 wings vs. 5.5 wings), with the effect being stronger for men than women. In distracting eating environments, environmental cues may provide an effective means of reducing consumption. Implications for controlling alcohol intake were also noted.

From *Perceptual and Motor Skills, 104*, 273–276. Copyright © 2007 by Perceptual and Motor Skills. Reprinted with permission.

While a wide range of environmental cues have been identified as contributing to overeating (Wansink, 2004), less attention has been given to the role of environmental cues that contribute to healthful eating. One environmental cue that may lead to healthful eating entails providing evidence of how much food (or of a beverage) has been consumed. For the most part, after food is eaten, there is no environmental cue—no evidence—of how much was consumed. This could be a reason why it is widely reported that people are poor at estimating how much food they have consumed (Polivy, Herman, Hackett, & Kuleshnyk, 1986). Such inaccuracies of estimation could also be further magnified in distracting eating environments, such as when eating with others or when watching television. In combination, the lack of evidence of food eaten and eating in distracting environments may contribute to mindless eating, which has been suggested to account for much of the variance in weight gain (Wansink, 2006).

Eating in distracting eating environments may lead people to over-rely on environmental cues to know when to stop eating (Wansink, Painter, & North, 2005). If this is the case, providing an appropriate environmental cue could help one monitor and modify intake better. Preliminary evidence for this comes from reports of alcohol consumption. Wait staff who are concerned about customers over-imbibing have been encouraged to leave bottles on the table (environmental cue) to make them more aware of how much they

have drunk (Wansink, Cordua, Blair, Payne, & Geiger, 2006). To examine this idea within the context of food consumption, it was necessary to find a food that could leave a visual reminder after it was consumed (such as bones from meat, seeds or pits from fruit, or wrappers from candy). In addition, it was necessary to find a distracting, low-inhibition environment in which this food was consumed.

Method

Fifty-two graduate students (17 men, 35 women whose mean age was 24.1 yr.) were invited to a Super Bowl party at a public sports bar in Urbana, Illinois. Super Bowl parties have been successfully used in past research (Wansink & Cheney, 2005) because eating and snacking are commonplace and because such parties increase the possibilities of distraction while eating.

A separate dining room was used so regular patrons of the sports bar were not disturbed. Big screen televisions were provided for viewing the football game, and during the party, chicken wings and soft drinks were furnished free-of-charge. At the beginning of the party, tables were randomly assigned to conditions wherein either people's plates would be regularly bussed or to a condition where people's plates would not be bussed. The students were seated at 21 different tables, and they were encouraged to help themselves to three different types of chicken wings centrally available to them in stem trays.

In the bussed condition (11 tables and 31 people), the residual bones from the chicken wings were removed continuously, and participants were encouraged to serve themselves additional wings. The bones were coded by the table, seating position, and sex of the participant, and they were then unobtrusively weighed. In the unbussed condition, bones were allowed to pile up on each plate, and participants were encouraged to serve themselves additional wings at the same frequency as those in the bussed condition. The bones were removed and recorded at half-time after which no more chicken wings were served to any participants. Following the game (approximately 80 minutes later), people were individually asked to report how many

Table 1
Salience of Chicken Wing Bones on Table

Measure	High intake salience unbussed table (n = 21)		Low intake salience bussed table (n = 31)		df	t	Cohen's d
	M	SD	M	SD			
Weight of chicken eaten, gm							
Total	192.0	85.1	244.2	82.2	50	2.2*	.62
Men	163.3	74.0	264.8	92.4	15	2.4*	1.21
Women	207.3	89.0	234.3	77.3	33	1.0	.32
No. of wing pieces eaten							
Total	5.5	2.4	7.0	2.3	50	2.2*	.64
Men	4.7	1.1	7.6	1.3	15	2.4*	2.40
Women	5.9	1.3	6.7	2.2	33	1.0	.44

*$p < .05$.

wing pieces they believed they had eaten. Their estimates were compared with the actual amount they had eaten.

Results

As expected, people whose leftover chicken wing bones were not bussed from their respective tables consumed significantly less than those whose chicken wing bones were bussed (cleared away). As Table 1 indicates, those eating from an unbussed table consumed an average of 5.5 wing pieces and those consuming from the bussed table consumed 7.0 pieces [t_{pieces} (50) = 2.2, p = .02; Cohen's d = .64]. As a percentage difference, those eating from a bussed table consumed 27.3% more pieces than those eating from an unbussed table.

The influence of this environmental cue was stronger for the men [t_{pieces} (15) = 2.4, p = .01; Cohen's d = 2.4] than for the women [t_{pieces} (33) = 1.0, p = .17; Cohen's d = .44]. This is consistent with prior work in a Super Bowl environment, which showed that women were less responsive to environmental cues in public areas (Wansink & Cheney, 2005). While this suggests higher self-monitoring (Wansink & Kim, 2005), women were generally no more accurate than men (Wansink, van Ittersum, & Painter, 2006). This might be explained, instead, by a tendency toward impression management.

Discussion

These results suggest that people restrict their consumption when an environmental cue (evidence of food consumed) signaled how much food was eaten. This is consistent with previous research that suggests people will report feeling sated not only when they are physiologically full, but when they *believe* they are full (Rolls, Bell, & Waugh, 2000). As an environmental cue, leftover chicken wing bones provided evidence of how much was eaten. As a consequence, knowing how much they had eaten might have helped people better calibrate how many more they cared to eat.

There are other possible reasons why such a decrease in consumption might have occurred in this study. Having the bones in the middle of the table might have suppressed some people's appetites, leading them to eat less. Or, embarrassment over showing others how much they had eaten might also have slowed consumption.

Regardless of the explanation, these results show that environmental cues of how much has been eaten effectively leads to reduced intake in a distracting social situation such as this. In situations where "counting bones" is not possible, other proxy environmental cues might be used to keep track of how much has been consumed. These might include the empty wrappers of Halloween candies, the pits or core of fruit, or the bottle caps of a beverage.

The use of environmental cues to help curb the overconsumption of alcohol has also been examined in field tests. In the distracting environments of college or fraternity parties, students could be encouraged (or required) to take a fresh plastic glass for each new drink and to stack these glasses within each other. Similarly, at a dinner party involving wine, providing fresh glasses for refills while leaving empty glasses sitting on the table was an effective curb. Another version would be to leave the empty bottles on the table. Efforts to provide an environmental cue of intake can help people better keep track of how much they have consumed. In a naturally distracting environment, such evidence seems an ally in the fight against mindless eating or drinking.

References

Polivy, J., Herman, C. P., Hackett, R., & Kuleshnyk, I. (1986). The effects of self-attention and public attention on eating in restrained and unrestrained subjects. *Journal of Personality and Social Psychology, 50*, 1203–1224.

Rolls, B. J., Bell, E. A., & Waugh, B. A. (2000). Increasing the volume of a food by incorporating air affects satiety in men. *American Journal of Clinical Nutrition, 72*, 361–368.

Wansink, B. (2004). Environmental factors that increase the food intake and consumption volume of unknowing consumers. *Annual Review of Nutrition, 24*, 455–479.

Wansink, B. (2006). *Mindless eating: Why we eat more than we think.* New York: Bantam-Dell. Wansink, B., & Cheney, M. M. (2005). Super bowls: Serving bowl size and food consumption. *Journal of the American Medical Association, 293*, 1727–1728.

Wansink, B., Cordua, G., Blair, E., Payne, C., & Geiger, S. (2006). Do promotions for new wines contribute to or cannibalize beverage sales? *Cornell Hotel and Restaurant Administration Quarterly, 47*, 1–10.

Wansink, B., & Kim, J.-Y. (2005). Bad popcorn in big buckets: Portion size can influence intake as much as taste. *Journal of Nutrition Education and Behavior, 37*, 242–245.

Wansink, B., Painter, J. E., & North, J. (2005). Bottomless bowls: Why visual cues of portion size may influence intake. *Obesity Research, 13*, 93–100.

Wansink, B., van Ittersum, K., & Painter, J. E. (2006). Ice cream illusions: Bowl size, spoon size, and self-served portion sizes. *American Journal of Preventive Medicine, 31*, 240–243.

Address correspondence to: Brian Wansink, 110 Warren Hall, Cornell University, Ithaca, NY. E-mail: Wansink@Cornell.edu

Exercise for Article 12

Factual Questions

1. Were there more "men" *or* more "women" participants in this study?

2. Were "students" *or* "tables" randomly assigned to the two conditions in this study?

3. What was the average number of wing pieces eaten by men in the bussed condition?

4. Was the difference between the average number of wing pieces eaten by men in the two conditions statistically significant? If yes, at what probability level?

5. In terms of weight of chicken eaten, was the value of *d* higher for "men" *or* "women"?

Questions for Discussion

6. This article is classified as an example of "Experimental Research" in the Contents of this book. Do you agree with this classification? Explain.

7. In your opinion, was the sample size adequate for a study of this type? Explain.

8. What is your understanding of the meaning of the statistic named Cohen's *d*? Does it help you understand the results of this study?

9. Do you agree with the authors that there might be more than one explanation for the results of this study? Explain. (See lines 110–116.)

10. Do you think the results of this study are sufficiently important to justify further research on this topic? Explain.

Quality Ratings

Directions: Indicate your level of agreement with each of the following statements by circling a number from 5 for strongly agree (SA) to 1 for strongly disagree (SD). If you believe an item is not applicable to this research article, leave it blank. Be prepared to explain your ratings. When responding to criteria A and B below, keep in mind that brief titles and abstracts are conventional in published research.

A. The title of the article is appropriate.

   SA   5   4   3   2   1   SD

B. The abstract provides an effective overview of the research article.

   SA   5   4   3   2   1   SD

C. The introduction establishes the importance of the study.

   SA   5   4   3   2   1   SD

D. The literature review establishes the context for the study.

   SA   5   4   3   2   1   SD

E. The research purpose, question, or hypothesis is clearly stated.

   SA   5   4   3   2   1   SD

F. The method of sampling is sound.

   SA   5   4   3   2   1   SD

G. Relevant demographics (for example, age, gender, and ethnicity) are described.

   SA   5   4   3   2   1   SD

H. Measurement procedures are adequate.

   SA   5   4   3   2   1   SD

I. All procedures have been described in sufficient detail to permit a replication of the study.

   SA   5   4   3   2   1   SD

J. The participants have been adequately protected from potential harm.

   SA   5   4   3   2   1   SD

K. The results are clearly described.

   SA   5   4   3   2   1   SD

L. The discussion/conclusion is appropriate.

   SA   5   4   3   2   1   SD

M. Despite any flaws, the report is worthy of publication.

   SA   5   4   3   2   1   SD

Article 13

Effects of Participants' Sex and Targets' Perceived Need on Supermarket Helping Behavior

PAMELA C. REGAN
California State University, Los Angeles

DELIA M. GUTIERREZ
California State University, Los Angeles

ABSTRACT. A field experiment was focused on whether participants' sex and targets' perceived need influenced helping behavior. Confederates approached 332 (166 women, 166 men) same-sex participants in a supermarket and asked for 25 cents to help purchase one of three randomly assigned food items: milk, which was defined as a high-need item; frozen cookie dough, which served as a low-need item; or alcohol, which was a low-need item with negative social connotations. The dependent variable was whether a participant provided help. Participants' sex was not associated with helping behavior as equal proportions of men and women provided assistance to the confederate; however, perceived need strongly influenced whether the confederate received help. Specifically, the high-need item produced more helping behavior than did either of the low-need items, and the socially acceptable low-need item of cookie dough produced more helping behavior than the socially unacceptable low-need item of alcohol. This may be interpreted as showing that what one buys and how deserving of help one appears to be influence whether one is helped by others.

From *Perceptual and Motor Skills*, *101*, 617–620. Copyright © 2005 by Perceptual and Motor Skills. Reprinted with permission.

Social psychologists have extensively documented the variables associated with prosocial or helping behavior (Batson, 1998). Much of this research has focused upon characteristics of the person in need. Physi-
5 cally attractive individuals, for example, are more likely to receive help than are their less attractive peers (Wilson, 1978; Regan & Llamas, 2002). Another perhaps equally important variable in helping behavior is the target's perceived need; that is, how deserving of
10 assistance the person appears to be. In general, targets in greater need of assistance tend to elicit more helping behavior from others (Enzle & Harvey, 1978; Sinha & Jain, 1986). For example, an early classic field experiment conducted by Bickman and Kamzan (1973) indi-
15 cated women shoppers were more likely to help a female confederate who asked for 10 cents when she was attempting to buy a high-need food item like milk, and thereby presumably appeared more deserving of help, than when she was purchasing a low-need food item
20 such as frozen cookie dough. The present field experiment was designed to replicate and extend this earlier work by investigating the extent to which two variables, participants' sex and targets' perceived need, would influence helping behavior. Perceived need was
25 manipulated by using three different food items: milk (a high-need item), frozen cookie dough (a low-need item), and alcohol (a low-need item with negative social connotations). Based upon earlier research, the high-need item was predicted to elicit greater helping
30 behavior than either of the low-need items. Because previous research exploring the association between participants' sex and helping behavior has yielded inconsistent results (Eagly & Crowley, 1986), there were no a priori predictions concerning this variable.

Methods

Participants

35 Participants were 332 adult (166 women, 166 men; estimated M age = 26 yr., SD = 4 yr.) shoppers at three large supermarkets located in Southern California. Participants were selected for inclusion in the experiment if they were the same sex as the confederate, appeared
40 to be over 21 years of age, were shopping alone as defined by being unaccompanied by friends or family members, and appeared to be somewhat relaxed and not in a hurry to find a particular item or finish their shopping.
45 Confederates were four university students, two men and two women, whose ages ranged from 24 to 31 years (M age = 27 yr., SD = 2.5 yr.). Each dressed in clean, informal attire (pants with a shirt or blouse). Two confederates were present for each experimental
50 session; one acted as an observer while the other approached the participant. Prior to entering the supermarket, each confederate team randomly selected the item they would use when soliciting help: a quart of milk, which served as a high-need item; a roll of frozen
55 cookie dough, which was defined as low need; or a large bottle of beer, which represented a low-need item with negative social connotations.

Procedure

Upon entering the store, Confederate 1 picked up the assigned food item and proceeded down the next
60 adjacent aisle. Confederate 2, masquerading as a shopper with a cart, followed at a discreet distance to observe the interaction, record the participant's response, and estimate the participant's age. The first shopper in the aisle who fulfilled the selection criteria was ap-
65 proached. Specifically, Confederate 1 approached the participant with two dollar bills and some change crumpled in one hand and with the selected food item held in the other. The confederate's statement was "Hi. I'm a little embarrassed, but I'm short 25 cents for this
70 [carton of milk/package of cookie dough/bottle of beer]. Can you spare a quarter?" If the participant questioned the confederate, he or she replied, "I thought I had enough money with me."

The participant's response of help or no help served
75 as the dependent variable. If the participant responded negatively to the confederate's request, the confederate said, "No problem, I understand" and proceeded to exit the aisle. If the participant responded affirmatively to the request and gave the confederate a quarter, the con-
80 federate accepted the quarter, thanked the participant, began to walk away, and then suddenly "found" a quarter in his or her own pocket. He or she immediately returned the participant's quarter, thanked the participant, and exited the aisle. Note that 23 participants
85 insisted that the confederate keep the quarter.

Results and Discussion

In Table 1 are the number and percentage of participants who provided help in each of the three conditions. There was no sex difference in rates of helping behavior; across conditions, roughly equal percentages
90 of men (51.2%) and women (56.6%) gave a quarter to the confederate when asked ($z = 0.99$, ns); however, perceived need clearly influenced helping behavior. As hypothesized, the high-need item produced greater helping behavior than both of the low-need items. Spe-
95 cifically, a series of z tests for proportions indicated that significantly more participants gave assistance to the confederate when he or she was trying to purchase milk than when he or she was trying to purchase frozen cookie dough (70.1 % vs 52.6%; $z = 2.85$, $p < .005$) or
100 alcohol (70.1% vs 29.3%; $z = 5.86$, $p < .0001$). Similarly, cookie dough, a low-need but nonetheless socially acceptable item, produced greater helping behavior than did alcohol, a low-need item with questionable social desirability (52.6% vs 29.3%; $z = 3.27$, $p <$
105 .001). In addition and in keeping with the lack of an overall sex difference in helping rates, the same result pattern was obtained when the responses of the men and women were examined separately.

These findings indicate that people in general are
110 fairly helpful. Over half of the participants and equal numbers of men and women gave assistance to the confederate when asked. They did not help indiscrimi-

115 nately, however, but based their decision to provide assistance, at least in part, on how deserving of help the confederate appeared to be. Although other researchers also have found high rates of helping behavior (North, Tarrant, & Hargreaves, 2003), it is important to recog-
120 nize that the scenario created here to elicit helping behavior from participants involved little risk of personal endangerment and low involvement with the target. It is possible that rates of helping behavior would be significantly lower in situations requiring greater personal involvement or risk.

Table 1
Helping Behavior As a Function of Targets' Perceived Need

Group		Milk	Cookie dough	Alcohol
Women	Total N	68	58	40
	Participants who helped			
	n	49	32	13
	%	72.0	55.2	32.5
Men	Total N	66	58	42
	Participants who helped			
	n	45	29	11
	%	68.2	50.0	26.2
Total	Total N	134	116	82
	Participants who helped			
	n	94	61	24
	%	70.1[ab]	52.6[ac]	29.3[bc]

Note. Percentages that share a superscript are significantly different. Z and p values are given in the text. Response patterns for men and women separately are identical with that of the total sample.

References

Batson, C. D. (1998). Altruism and prosocial behavior. In D. T. Gilbert, S. T. Fiske, & G. Lindzey (Eds.), *The handbook of social psychology*. (4th ed.) Vol. 2. Boston, MA: McGraw-Hill. Pp. 282–316.

Bickman, L., & Kamzan, M. (1973). The effect of race and need on helping behavior. *Journal of Social Psychology, 89*, 73–77.

Eagly, A. H., & Crowley, M. (1986). Gender and helping behavior: A meta-analytic review of the social psychological literature. *Psychological Bulletin, 100*, 283–308.

Enzle, M. E., & Harvey, M. D. (1978). Recipient vs. third-party requests, recipient need, and helping behavior. *Personality and Social Psychology Bulletin, 4*, 620–623.

North, A. C., Tarrant, M., & Hargreaves, D. J. (2003). The effects of music on helping behavior: A field study. *Environment and Behavior, 36*, 266–275.

Regan, P. C., & Llamas, V. (2002). Customer service as a function of shopper's attire. *Psychological Reports, 90*, 203–204.

Sinha, A. K., & Jain, A. (1986). The effects of benefactor and beneficiary characteristics on helping behavior. *Journal of Social Psychology, 126*, 361–368.

Wilson, D. W. (1978). Helping behavior and physical attractiveness. *Journal of Social Psychology, 104*, 313–314.

Acknowledgment: This research was supported in part by NIH MBRS-RISE Grant R25 GM61331.

Address correspondence to: Pamela Regan, Ph.D., Department of Psychology, California State University, 5151 State University Drive, Los Angeles, CA 90032-8227. E-mail: pregan@calstatela.edu

Exercise for Article 13

Factual Questions

1. According to the literature review, have high-need and low-need items been examined in an earlier experiment?

2. Confederate 2 masqueraded as what?

3. According to the researchers, what is the "dependent variable" in this experiment?

4. Was there a statistically significant sex difference in rates of helping behavior?

5. For the total sample, did cookie dough produce significantly greater helping behavior than alcohol?

6. Of the 66 men who were asked to help purchase milk, how many helped?

Questions for Discussion

7. This article is classified as an example of an experiment in the Contents of this book. In your opinion, is this classification correct? If yes, what feature of this study makes it an experiment?

8. In your opinion, are the criteria for inclusion of participants in this study reasonable? Explain. (See lines 37–44.)

9. Is the procedure in lines 58–85 sufficiently detailed so that you could conduct a replication of this study? Explain.

10. Do you agree with the researchers' concluding comment in lines 115–123? Explain.

11. This research article is shorter than most others in this book. In your opinion, is the article informative despite its brevity? Does it provide important results? Explain.

12. If you were on a funding board (e.g., on the board of a foundation that sponsors research), would you recommend funding for additional studies on this topic? Explain.

Quality Ratings

Directions: Indicate your level of agreement with each of the following statements by circling a number from 5 for strongly agree (SA) to 1 for strongly disagree (SD). If you believe an item is not applicable to this research article, leave it blank. Be prepared to explain your ratings. When responding to criteria A and B below, keep in mind that brief titles and abstracts are conventional in published research.

A. The title of the article is appropriate.

SA   5   4   3   2   1   SD

B. The abstract provides an effective overview of the research article.

SA   5   4   3   2   1   SD

C. The introduction establishes the importance of the study.

SA   5   4   3   2   1   SD

D. The literature review establishes the context for the study.

SA   5   4   3   2   1   SD

E. The research purpose, question, or hypothesis is clearly stated.

SA   5   4   3   2   1   SD

F. The method of sampling is sound.

SA   5   4   3   2   1   SD

G. Relevant demographics (for example, age, gender, and ethnicity) are described.

SA   5   4   3   2   1   SD

H. Measurement procedures are adequate.

SA   5   4   3   2   1   SD

I. All procedures have been described in sufficient detail to permit a replication of the study.

SA   5   4   3   2   1   SD

J. The participants have been adequately protected from potential harm.

SA   5   4   3   2   1   SD

K. The results are clearly described.

SA   5   4   3   2   1   SD

L. The discussion/conclusion is appropriate.

SA   5   4   3   2   1   SD

M. Despite any flaws, the report is worthy of publication.

SA   5   4   3   2   1   SD

Article 14

Baby Think It Over: Evaluation of an Infant Simulation Intervention for Adolescent Pregnancy Prevention

DIANE de ANDA
University of California

ABSTRACT. In an intervention aimed at showing students the amount of responsibility involved in caring for an infant, 353 predominantly ninth-grade and Latino students carried the Baby Think It Over simulation doll in an intervention and completed matched pre- and posttest measures. Statistically significant gains were found on the total score and the impact of having a baby on academics, social life, and other family members; emotional risks; understanding and handling an infant's crying; and apprehension of the amount of responsibility involved in infant care. On a posttest-only measure, 108 participants reported statistically significant differences before and after carrying the doll with regard to the age at which they wished to have a child, their career and education plans, and the perceived interference of an infant with those education and career plans and their social life.

From *Health & Social Work, 31*, 26–35. Copyright © 2006 by the National Association of Social Workers. Reprinted with permission.

To alter adolescents' perception of the effort involved in caring for a baby and successfully increase their intent to avoid pregnancy in adolescence, students at a Los Angeles County high school participated in an
5 intervention using a life-size infant simulation doll known as "Baby Think It Over" (BTIO). The participating high school is in one of the 10 poorest cities in the nation (United Way of Greater Los Angeles, 1998–1999) and has been designated one of the adolescent
10 pregnancy "hot spots" in California because of its high rates of adolescent pregnancy (California Department of Health Services, 2001). The intervention places the tangible consequences of pregnancy before adolescent participants rather than offering only the abstract mes-
15 sages about pregnancy risks often presented in other programs.

Adolescent Pregnancy in the United States

The steady rise in adolescent pregnancy rates became a significant concern among social service and health professionals, legislators, and the general public
20 during the 1970s and 1980s. The rates increased from 95.1 per 1,000 for 15- to 19-year-olds and 62.4 per 1,000 for 15- to 17-year-olds in 1972 to an all-time high of 117.1 (in 1990) and 74.4 (in 1989), respectively. Following a variety of intervention efforts, a
25 slow decline in the rates was noted in the first half of the 1990s, followed by a more rapid decrease to below the 1972 rate by 1997: 93.0 for 15- to 19-year-olds and 57.7 for 15- to 17-year-olds (Alan Guttmacher Institute, 1999a). This period included a 20% drop in the
30 pregnancy rate among African American adolescents and a 16% reduction among white adolescents. The pregnancy rate for Latina adolescents, however, increased between 1990 and 1992 and by 1996 decreased by only 6% (Alan Guttmacher Institute, 1999b), result-
35 ing in the birth rate of 149.2 per 1,000 for Latino adolescents—the highest among the total adolescent population (National Center for Health Statistics, 2000). Inasmuch as 54.1% of Latino high school youths report they have had sexual intercourse, and only slightly
40 more than half of those who are sexually active report using protection or birth control, Latino adolescents represent a population at high pregnancy risk (Kann et al., 2000).

As early as 1967, Elkind (1967) posited the impor-
45 tance of cognitive development in understanding adolescent risk-taking behavior, including pregnancy risks. Based on empirical research, the author and colleagues also proposed that adolescent pregnancy resulting from the risk taking of unprotected sexual intercourse might
50 be significantly related to cognitive development. Specifically, this behavior might reflect a lack of full attainment of formal operations and "the sense of invulnerability—described by Elkind as the 'personal fable'" (Becerra, Sabagh, & de Anda, 1986, p.136). For-
55 mal operations refer to the individual's ability to engage in abstract and hypothetical–deductive thinking (Piaget, 1972; Piaget & Inhelder, 1958) and, in this case, project the potential for pregnancy and ultimately becoming a parent. Adolescence typically includes a
60 period of transition from concrete to formal operations, at the beginning of which recognizing oneself as a sexual being is relatively easy because it is in the present and very concrete. By contrast, considering oneself

fertile can be a rather abstract concept for a young adolescent, and the consequences of fertility can be distant and hypothetical. Others have offered similar explanatory frameworks with regard to risk taking and adolescent pregnancy (e.g., Gordon, 1990; Kralewski & Stevens-Simon, 2000; Out & Lefreniere, 2001).

Interventions have been developed to accommodate these cognitive factors by creating simulated parenting experiences to provide a concrete learning situation that will make the hypothetical risks and consequences of adolescent pregnancy more real to the adolescent participants. Some past interventions have involved caregiving situations not directly analogous to caring for an infant, involving, for example, carrying a sack of flour or an egg. More recent interventions have used a simulation more directly analogous to caring for an infant—a computerized infant simulation doll that requires attention to its demands in the form of intermittent periods of crying.

BTIO: The Intervention

BTIO is an intervention using a computerized infant simulation doll to offer adolescents experiences similar to those involved in attending to an infant. The doll is programmed to cry at random intervals and to stop crying only when the adolescent "attends" to the doll by inserting a key into a slot in the doll's back until it stops crying. An examination of participant logs indicated that most crying periods ranged between 10 and 15 minutes, and the frequency between eight and 12 times in 24 hours (including the early A. M. hours). The key is attached to a hospital-style bracelet, which is worn by the participant 24 hours a day to ensure that the adolescent provides the caregiving responsibilities during an entire two-and-a-half-day study period. The bracelets are designed so that an attempt to remove the bracelet is detectable. "Babysitting" of the doll by another student with a key or by the health class teacher who has extra keys is permitted only in certain situations—to take an examination, for example. The doll records data, including the amount of time the adolescent takes to "attend" to the infant (insert the key) and any form of "rough handling," such as dropping or hitting the doll. The term "rough handling" is used rather than abuse because there is no way to determine intentionality. Students whose records indicate neglect and rough handling receive a private counseling session with the health class teacher and have mandatory participation in a parenting class.

The purpose of carrying the infant simulation doll is to provide the students with an understanding of the amount of time and effort involved in the care of an infant and how an infant's needs might affect their daily lives and the lives of their family and significant others. This experience is augmented by presentations and group discussions led by staff from a local social services agency, covering such topics as the high incidence of adolescent pregnancy in the community, the factors that increase risk of adolescent pregnancy, and the costs of adolescent pregnancy and parenthood, with particular emphasis on the limitation of education and career opportunities and achievement. The health class teacher also offers a pregnancy prevention education program in preparation for carrying the doll and a debriefing discussion period after everyone in the class has carried the doll.

BTIO in Previous Research

A relatively small amount of research has been conducted on the effectiveness of BTIO. A literature search produced eight published research articles evaluating BTIO interventions aimed at modifying attitudes, perceptions, and behaviors related to pregnancy risk. Six studies examined whether the program affected the adolescents' view of parenthood and child-rearing responsibilities: two found their objectives met in this respect, but four determined no change in perception. In a study conducted by Divine and Cobbs (2001) with 236 eighth-grade students in nine Catholic schools in a midwestern city, a greater number of BTIO students than control group students ($p < .05$) indicated a change on two of seven items: the amount of effort and cost involved in infant care, and the feeling that they have enough knowledge about what taking care of a baby entails. The majority (63% of the male adolescents, 75.5% of female adolescents) felt carrying the doll was effective in "helping me know the challenges of infant care" (p. 599). In Out and Lafreniere's (2001) sample of 114 Canadian students in the 11th grade, BTIO participants reported significantly ($p < .01$) more examples of child-rearing consequences and responsibilities than did control group students.

In contrast to these limited positive findings, Kralewski and Stevens-Simon's (2000) sample of 68 sixth-grade and 41 eighth-grade female Hispanic students from a middle school in a lower socioeconomic status Colorado neighborhood revealed no significant differences between anticipated difficulty and the actual difficulty in caring for the BTIO doll. In addition, BTIO did little to change the girls' desire to have a baby during adolescence, with 13 expressing this intent before BTIO and 16 after carrying the doll. Somers and Fahlman (2001) used a quasi-experimental design with a predominantly white, middle-class sample drawn from three high schools in the Midwest; MANCOVA performed on the posttest scores using the pretest scores as the covariate found no differences between the 151 students in the experiment group and 62 students in the control group on perceptions regarding childcare responsibilities. Somers, Gleason, Johnson, and Fahlman's (2001) study in two Midwest high schools found no change in participants' understanding of the responsibilities involved in child rearing. Strachan and Gorey (1997) did not find a change on their Parenting Attitude Scale measuring "realistic par-

175 enting expectations" (p. 175) in their sample of 48 African American and white youths ages 16 to 18.

Only one of the studies found any significant difference or change in attitudes or behavior related to sexuality. Out and Lafreniere (2001) found that "ado-
180 lescents in the intervention group...rated themselves as being significantly more susceptible to an unplanned pregnancy compared with adolescents in the comparison group" (p. 577). However, they found no differences between the groups in attitudes toward absti-
185 nence and contraceptive use. In studies conducted by Somers and Fahlman (2001) and Somers et al. (2001), no significant change from pretest to posttest in attitudes and behaviors related to sexual behavior, contraception, and pregnancy was detected. Out and La-
190 freniere found no changes from pretest to posttest in attitudes toward abstinence and contraceptive use. Finally, Divine and Cobbs (2001) found no differences between experimental and control groups in attitudes regarding contraception, abstinence, and sexuality.
195 Although no differences were found between their 245 BTIO participants and 186 control group participants, Tingle (2002) found the majority of parents reported that the intervention had increased both their children's perceptions of the difficulties involved in
200 caring for an infant and parent–child communication regarding sexuality and parenting. Moreover, the great majority (92%) indicated they would recommend the program to a friend; 82% for use in middle schools and 97% for use in high schools. Similarly, the majority of
205 the 89 parents in a rural Ohio sample felt that the program was successful in teaching their children that a baby was a considerable responsibility (85%), time consuming (79%), and a barrier to achieving their life goals (71%), and 90% indicated they would recom-
210 mend the BTIO program to friends (Price, Robinson, Thompson, & Schmalzried, 2000).

Of the 22 teachers in Tingle's (2002) study, 59% evaluated BTIO as "somewhat effective" in preventing pregnancies and 45% said it was effective in initiating
215 communication between parent and child. In Somers and colleagues' (2001) study, few of the 57 teachers felt that BTIO reduced sexual intercourse (5%) or the number of sexual partners (7%). However, the majority (91%) believed that students learned about the respon-
220 sibilities of parenthood and recommended that BTIO be continued in the school (86%) and be adopted in other schools (84%).

There were serious methodological limitations and flaws in the preceding studies. Many of the samples
225 were small and not random, thereby limiting generalizability. In addition, volunteers were also used in a number of the studies; for example, Out and Lafreniere's (2001) intervention group consisted of students from elective courses on parenting and the con-
230 trol group from geography and physical education classes at the same schools. Additional research with larger samples, greater control of confounds (especially

selection bias), and more rigorous research designs and methodology are needed, preferably with replication,
235 before any conclusions can be drawn regarding the effectiveness of this intervention as a model for reducing the risk of adolescent pregnancy.

Objectives

The present Baby Think It Over intervention had seven major objectives. The first four posited an in-
240 crease in the degree to which the adolescent recognized: (1) that caring for a baby affects an adolescent's academic and social life; (2) that other family members are affected by having an adolescent with a baby in the family; (3) that there are emotional risks for each par-
245 ent in having a baby during adolescence; and (4) that there are family and cultural values related to having a baby during adolescence. The remaining three proposed an increase in the number planning to postpone parenthood: (5) until a later age (for the majority until
250 graduation from high school); (6) until education and career goals were met; or (7) until marriage.

Research Design and Method

Program objectives and additional constructs were measured with two main instruments: BTIO-1 and BTIO-2. A repeated-measures design was used, with
255 the BTIO-1 measure as the pretest and posttest. To increase validity, participants were used as their own controls through paired pretest-posttest comparisons, with all data entered anonymously. Moreover, confounds related to history and maturation were elimi-
260 nated because the intervention was conducted sequentially and continuously across the academic year with multiple individuals as their own controls. A posttest-only evaluation measure (BTIO-2) also was used to obtain self-report data on the impact of the program.

Measures
265 *BTIO-1.* The four main program objectives were measured using a 25-item, closed-ended instrument with a four-point Likert-type scale, ranging from 4 = strongly agree to 1 = strongly disagree. Total score and scores for each of the first four objectives were created
270 by summing the scores of the relevant items. Two separate scores were also calculated for items pertaining to understanding and dealing with a crying infant and those related to overall infant care. A higher score indicated a higher level of agreement consonant with
275 the program objectives and greater accuracy in their evaluation of the statements. The measure demonstrated good internal consistency ($\alpha = .84$).

In addition, the youths were asked to indicate *when* they would "like to have children": (1) never, (2) right
280 now, (3) when I finish junior high school, (4) when I'm in high school, or (5) after I graduate from high school. Students also checked items they would like to do "before having a baby": (1) have a good paying job, (2) go to college, (3) graduate from a junior college, (4)
285 graduate from a four-year college, (5) go to a trade or

74

technical school, (6) get married, (7) have a career, and (8) "other" write-in responses. Multiple responses were possible.

BTIO-2. The Baby Think It Over-2 measure is a post hoc, self-report measure indicating whether the experience changed what participants thought it would be like to have a baby; when they thought they would like to have a baby in terms of age and educational and career achievements; beliefs regarding the use of birth control or protection; and how much time and work are involved in taking care of a baby. Perceptions before and after carrying the BTIO doll were indicated along Likert-type scales for use of birth control or protection, amount of effort involved in caring for a baby, and the interference of infant caregiving with education goals, career goals, and social life.

Data Analysis

Paired *t* tests were performed on the summated scores for the total number of items on the Likert-type scale, the summated scores for each of the first four objectives, and the scores for crying and overall care. ANCOVAs, using the pretest as the covariate, were also conducted to determine whether there were differences in responses based on gender. Chi-square analyses were performed on the nominal data for the last three objectives on postponing pregnancy and parenthood.

Findings

Demographic Data

A total of 353 of the students who carried the infant simulation doll completed matched pre- and posttest measures: 140 male participants and 204 female participants. Nine students did not report gender. The overwhelming majority (94.3%, $n = 333$) of the participants were in the ninth grade, with the remaining five (1.4%) in the 10th and three (.9%) in the 11th grade; 12 students (3.4%) did not indicate grade level. Correspondingly, most of the participants were 14 (48.2%, $n = 170$) to 15 (47.9%, $n = 169$) years old. Reflecting the demographics of the community, 92.9% of the participants in the sample were Latino (70.8% Mexican American, $n = 250$; 5.1% Central American, $n = 18$; 17.0% other Latino, $n = 60$). The remaining participants included one African American, five American Indian, three Asian/Pacific Islander, nine white, and two multiethnic youths; five students did not provide this information.

BTIO-1

On the BTIO-1 measure, statistically significant gains from pretest to posttest were found on all but one of the paired analyses (Table 1). The statistically significant increase in the means from pretest to posttest indicates that objective 1 was met: a greater recognition of the impact of caring for a baby on academic and social life. The posttest mean approached 20, equivalent to "agree" and edging closer to the "strongly agree" point on the scale. When items related to the students' academic and social life were summed separately, the gains were also found to be statistically significant: academics [$t(352) = 7.893$, $p < .001$]; social life [$t(352) = 9.862$, $p < .001$].

The gain from pretest to posttest for objective 2 was also statistically significant, indicating a greater recognition of the effect of adolescent parenthood on other family members. However, the gain was modest (from 10.8 to 11.24 in a range of possible scores from four to 16), and the mean at posttest did not quite reach the point of "agree" (12.0) on the scale. An examination of the responses to the various items provides clarification. Most participants "agreed" or "strongly agreed" on items that recognize how adolescent parenthood affects the adolescent's family: 93.8% that an infant's crying or illness might disturb other family members' sleep and 70.8% that a baby's needs would reduce money available for the needs of others in the family. The mean was reduced by the 25% to 30% who disagreed on two items that indicated that other family members would share care and responsibility for the baby.

On objective 3, a statistically significant increase in the recognition of emotional risks accompanying adolescent parenthood was found, with the posttest mean corresponding to "agree."

Objective 4—regarding family and cultural values on adolescent parenthood—was not met. The increase was minimal (.14); however, the mean of 8 (in a range of possible scores of three to 12) is equivalent to "agree" on the four-point scale. High pretest scores may have resulted in a ceiling effect, and it is likely that cultural and family values are relatively stable.

Responses to items related to understanding why a baby cries and what actions should be taken in response were calculated into a summated score. The gain from pretest ($M = 14.18$) to posttest ($M = 15.98$) achieved statistical significance [$t(352) = 12.266$, $p < .001$], moving the mean beyond a score of 15 (range five to 20) or "agree" on the scale. The individual items clearly reflect aspects of the experience of carrying the BTIO doll: 92.6% ($n = 327$) disagreed or strongly disagreed that it was "easy to ignore a fussy, crying baby"; 86.1% ($n = 304$) disagreed or strongly disagreed that babies would not cry if they were loved and loved the parent in return. Moreover, the majority appeared to understand why infants cry and refrained from making inaccurate and judgmental appraisals of both infant and parent behavior: 85.3% ($n = 301$) did not view a baby who "cries a lot" as "spoiled," 65.7% ($n = 232$) did not attribute the crying to insufficient care by parents, and 94.6% ($n = 334$) saw crying as a form of communication (trying "to tell you something").

Three questions ascertained the participants' views regarding overall care of an infant. The increase in the mean (from 9.24 to 10.28) was statistically significant [$t(352) = -9.471$, $p < .001$], indicating an increase in

Table 1
Paired t Test Results on Objectives 1 to 4 of the Baby Think It Over Program (N = 353)

	M	SD	df	t
Objective 1: Academic and social			252	−10.633***
Pretest	18.08	3.52		
Posttest	19.99	2.48		
Objective 2: Impact on family members			352	−3.935***
Pretest	10.80	1.65		
Posttest	11.24	1.59		
Objective 3: Emotional risks			352	−6.951***
Pretest	14.50	2.25		
Posttest	15.46	2.11		
Objective 4: Family and cultural values			352	−1.593***
Pretest	8.44	1.40		
Posttest	8.58	1.36		

***$p \leq .001$.

the recognition of the substantial time and effort involved in caring for an infant. A high percentage concurred regarding the 24-hour caregiving required for the BTIO doll: 89.8% ($n = 317$) agreed or strongly agreed that, for adolescent parents, taking care of a baby might be "too much for them to handle"; 88.7% ($n = 313$) disagreed or strongly disagreed that taking care of a baby was "fun and easy"; and 96.1% ($n = 339$) agreed or strongly agreed that "taking care of a baby takes a lot of time and hard work."

The difference between the pretest ($M = 72.2$) and posttest ($M = 78.27$) means for the total score on the 25 items was statistically significant [$t(352) = −12.655$, $p < .001$], demonstrating an increase in agreement with the objectives of the program. With a range of 25 to 100, the posttest mean is equivalent to beyond "agree" (75.0) on the four-point scale.

To determine whether there were any differences in outcomes based on gender, ANCOVA was conducted using the pretest as the covariate. Female participants demonstrated greater gains on the total score [$F(1, 352) = 6.446$, $p < .012$]; objective 1 (academic and social life) [$F(1, 352) = 4.411$, $p < .05$]; objective 3 (emotional risks) [$F(1, 352) = 10.619$, $p < .001$]; and crying [$F(1, 352) = 9.290$, $p < .01$]. Male participants showed greater gains on objective 4 (family and cultural values) [$F(1, 352) = 4.679$, $p < .05$], with gains negligible for both (males: 8.44 to 8.79; females: 8.42 to 8.43).

Objective 5 posited an increase in the length of time the adolescents planned to postpone parenthood. There was only a 1.4% increase (72.5% to 73.9%) in the number of those intending to wait until after graduating from high school to have children. However, the number of those wanting children before graduating from high school decreased dramatically, from 8.7% ($n = 31$) to 1.5% ($n = 5$). Perhaps the BTIO experience was extremely negative for some participants, as the number never wanting children increased from 15.9% ($n = 56$) to 23.8% ($n = 84$).

Objective 6 was met with a statistically significant increase on every item related to postponing pregnancy to achieve academic and career goals (Table 2). Financial stability was the highest priority, as job and career had the highest frequency at both pretest and posttest. For the majority of the youths, college aspirations took precedence over having a child. Although there was minimal increase in those who desired parenthood within a marital relationship after the BTIO experience—an additional 12 adolescents—the majority of the youths (71%; $n = 251$) had already indicated this preference at pretest.

BTIO-2

The BTIO-2 measure was completed by 108 participants, 60 female and 48 male, with most ages 14 to 15 (94.4%, $n = 102$), in the ninth grade (99.1%, $n = 107$), and Latino (92.6%, $n = 100$).

To obtain the adolescents' own view of the changes they experienced in perceptions and behavior as a result of carrying the BTIO doll, they were asked to indicate their thoughts, desires, or behavior "before BTIO" and "after BTIO/Now." Paired t test analyses found statistically significant differences in the desired direction on all items (Table 3).

Students reported that carrying the BTIO doll delayed the age at which they desired to have a child, from a mean of 23 to 25 years. A dramatic drop occurred in those indicating an age of 24 years or less (67% to 32.3%). Moreover, the majority (58.3%, $n = 63$) responded "yes," that carrying the BTIO doll had helped them change their mind regarding the age to have a child.

More than three-quarters of the BTIO-2 respondents indicated that they wanted to complete college and have a job or career before becoming parents. The already high "before" rate of 72.2% ($n = 78$) increased to 77.8% ($n = 84$) "after." There was an increase in those indicating that having a baby would interfere with their education (from 65.7%, $n = 71$ to 83.3%, $n = 90$); getting a good job or career (from 54.6%, $n = 59$ to 77.8%, $n = 84$); and their social life (from 58.3%, $n = 63$ to 73.1%, $n = 79$).

Table 2
Frequency of Response Selected by Participants in the Baby Think It Over Program

| | Pretest | | Posttest | | |
Factor	*f*	%	*f*	%	χ^2 (*df* = 1)
Good paying job	298	84.4	318	89.2	65.62***
Go to college	270	76.5	296	83.9	71.02***
Graduate from junior college	108	30.6	106	30.0	80.33***
Graduate from four-year college	173	49.0	183	51.8	89.17***
Technical school	102	28.9	112	31.7	59.75***
Career	288	81.6	303	85.8	92.95***
Married	251	71.1	263	74.5	61.02***

***p < .001.

Table 3
t Test Results BTIO-2: Before and After BTIO

	N	*M*	*SD*	*df*	*t*
Age want to have first baby				86	−7.210***
Before	87	23.16	3.55		
After	87	25.36	3.49		
School/job prior to having baby				91	−4.061***
Before	92	5.11	1.21		
After	92	5.51	1.08		
Amount of time it takes to care for baby				96	−5.821***
Before	97	3.24	.998		
After	97	3.78	.616		
How much baby interferes with education				102	−3.966***
Before	103	4.43	.986		
After	103	4.77	.675		
How much baby interferes with job/career				103	−4.984***
Before	104	4.16	1.18		
After	104	4.63	.827		
How much baby interferes with social life				100	−3.287***
Before	101	4.29	1.061		
After	101	4.60	.873		

Note. BTIO = Baby Think It Over
***p ≤ .001.

More than half of the respondents (55.6%, *n* = 60) answered affirmatively that BTIO changed their perceptions of what having a baby would be like. In the open-ended questions, the most frequently cited reason was that it was much harder work to care for a baby than they had previously thought (39.8%, *n* = 43). Many students chose not to respond to the open-ended questions.

Nearly two-thirds (58.3%) reported that BTIO helped change their minds about using birth control or protection to prevent unwanted pregnancies. Reported use of birth control or protection increased from 22.2% (*n* = 24) to 28.7% (*n* = 31). Few "never" used protection, and the number dropped slightly from 13.9% (*n* = 15) to 11.1% (*n* = 12). The remaining either indicated that they had never had sexual intercourse or left it blank, as the item was supposed to be skipped if not applicable.

Among the varied responses to the open-ended question regarding what they thought of the program in general, a few appeared with greater frequency including comments describing the program as "good" or "effective" (61.1%, *n* = 66), and that BTIO helped them learn how hard taking care of a baby actually was and that they did not want a child at this time (39.9 %, *n* = 43).

Discussion

The Baby Think It Over program appears to be a well-designed intervention that has multiple educational components, a well-controlled simulation experience, debriefing procedures, a stable position in the school's curriculum, support from the school faculty and administration, and a working collaboration with the staff from a local social services agency that funds the program through a state grant. Both the results of the data analyses and the adolescents' own evaluation confirm the effectiveness of the Baby Think It Over intervention in changing perceptions regarding the time and effort involved in caring for an infant and in recognizing the significant effect having a baby has on all major aspects of one's life. Participants increased their awareness of how caring for an infant would interfere with future plans and goals with regard to both education and career. The majority aspired to a college education, and the BTIO experience intensified this desire to further their education. Pregnancy prevention was increasingly recognized as important to ensure their future. Furthermore, the adolescents began to have a more realistic understanding of the demands of adolescent parenthood, acknowledging the loss to their social life along with loss of sleep and the freedom to use their time as they desired. The effect on other family members was also noted as well as the emotional stress created by the responsibility for an infant.

Most of the youths were surprised by how labor-intensive taking care of the BTIO doll was, by the frequency with which they had to attend to the doll's needs (crying), and the disruption this caused in their lives. For most, this ended their romanticized view of having a baby—for a few, to the point of never wanting to have a baby. In general, the youths appeared to be more realistic about how much time and work is involved in caring for a baby. The majority responded by adjusting the timeframe within which they desired to have a child, opting for parenthood at a later age and after important educational and career achievements. In summary, the program appears to have been eminently successful in achieving its immediate objectives.

It should be noted, however, that these are all changes in perceptions and intention rather than longitudinal measures of actual behavior. Nevertheless, perceptions and intentions are important antecedents of behavior. From a social learning theory perspective, perception and intention increase or decrease the probability that a behavior will occur. Moreover, the perceived consequences of behavior and one's perceived self-efficacy in determining the outcome of the behavior affect the likelihood that the behavior will occur (Bandura, 1995). In this case, the students appeared to have made a strong connection between unprotected sexual intercourse and what they now evaluate as a negative outcome: having to care for a demanding infant and the subsequent social, emotional, and academic costs. Most of the respondents wished to have financial stability, an established career, and a marital relationship before parenthood.

The quantitative analyses as well as the students' own comments testify to the importance of the "hands on," simulated experience. Given that most of these youths were 14 and 15 years old, still making the transition from concrete to formal operations, the use of a concrete mechanism that offers direct experiential learning appears to be extremely appropriate.

The program appears to be successful in changing perceptions and intentions; however, to increase the likelihood of its effectiveness in preventing adolescent pregnancy in the long term, an intervention that also provides the adolescents with methods for dealing with situations that involve pregnancy risk is needed. A comprehensive program that covers methods from abstinence to birth control methods and access would provide adolescents with the knowledge and skills needed to actualize their intentions and the opportunity for choice in the means to accomplish this.

Finally, a number of strengths in the design of the program should also be noted. First, the intervention was offered to both male and female adolescents. Second, the mechanism (BTIO) ensured that all participants received the same intervention experience. Third, the process was a mandatory part of a required class, so that all students participated, thereby eliminating selection bias within the school sample. Fourth, the intervention was used sequentially throughout the school year with different participants each time used as their own controls so that there was control of confounds, particularly related to history and maturation. Fifth, the program was not simply a two-day intervention, as the simulation is part of a complex educational program that involves both preparation for the experience, group and individual discussion of the experience, and additional intervention for those students who experienced difficulty during the simulation.

It would be ideal to assess the long-term effects of the program by obtaining data on the pregnancy rates of the participants over the subsequent three years. However, an accurate count is questionable as pregnancies are not necessarily reported to the school, and adolescents who become pregnant may drop out of school, transfer, or have a miscarriage or abortion without the school ever knowing they were pregnant. Moreover, because all students in a single grade receive the experience, no long-term control group will be available.

In the short term, students in the educational planning course, which runs parallel with the health course, can be used as controls to improve the validity of the evaluation because assignment to the courses is on a relatively random basis; that is, determined by fit within the student's schedule. Because the students switch classes the second semester, the controls will then also receive the intervention, thus eliminating any ethical questions regarding the withholding of the intervention. Furthermore, to ascertain the effects of the BTIO doll alone, a comparison group who receives all the educational components except the doll could be used.

The findings offer a number of implications for social work practice with adolescents, particularly regarding pregnancy prevention. It appears that an intensive, realistic experience can effect a rapid and significant amount of attitude change about sexual behavior and adolescent parenthood in a relatively short amount of time. Therefore, even if funds are limited, because the

630 experience is only two-and-a-half days long, a small number of the simulation dolls might suffice to bring about a change. However, it is important to note that the experiential intervention was supported by an educational component that included didactic instruction and peer discussion. It cannot be assumed that merely allowing an adolescent to carry the doll for a couple of

635 days will have the same effect. It is also possible that the memory of the experience may decrease in intensity over time, so that a repeated experience in the later grades might be necessary to reinforce and maintain the long-term effects of the intervention. Moreover, the

640 social worker needs to make sure that the experience is a balanced one, so that infants are not seen primarily as a source of annoyance and frustration. Finally, the findings suggest that an experiential learning component can alter perspectives and behavior, so that simulation,

645 because it makes the situation very concrete, might be a powerful intervention tool in general with youths who are transitioning to formal operations.

References

Alan Guttmacher Institute. (1999a). *Teenage pregnancy: Overall trends and state-by-state information.* New York: Author.

Alan Guttmacher Institute. (1999b). *U.S. teenage pregnancy statistics: With comparative statistics for women aged 20–24.* New York: Author.

Bandura, A. (Ed.) (1995). *Self-efficacy in changing societies.* New York: Cambridge University Press.

Becerra, R., Sabagh, G., & de Anda, D. (1986). *Sex and pregnancy among Mexican American adolescents: Final report to the Office of Adolescent Pregnancy Programs, Department of Health and Human Services.* Washington, DC: U.S. Department of Health and Human Services.

California Department of Health Services, Maternal and Child Health Branch, Epidemiology and Evaluation Section. (2001). *Teen birth rate hot spots in California, 1999–2000: A resource developed using a geographic information systems approach.* Sacramento: Author.

Divine, J. H., & Cobbs, G. (2001). The effects of infant simulators on early adolescents. *Adolescence, 36,* 593–600.

Elkind, D. (1967). Egocentrism in adolescence. *Child Development, 38,* 1025–1034.

Gordon, D. E. (1990). Formal operational thinking: The role of cognitive-developmental processes in adolescent decision-making about pregnancy and contraception. *American Journal of Orthopsychiatry, 60,* 346–356.

Kann, L., Kinchen, S. A., Williams, B. I., Ross, J. G., Lowry, R., Grunbaum, J., & Kolbe, L. J. (2000). Youth risk behavior surveillance—United States, 1999. *Morbidity and Mortality Weekly Report Surveillance Summaries, 49,* 1–96.

Kralewski, J., & Stevens-Simon, C. (2000). Does mothering a doll change teens' thoughts about pregnancy? [electronic edition], *Pediatrics, 105,* e. 30.

National Center for Health Statistics. (2000). *Health, United States, 2000.* Hyattsville, MD: Author.

Out, J. W., & Lafreniere, K. D. (2001). Baby Think It Over: Using role-play to prevent teen pregnancy. *Adolescence, 36,* 571–582.

Piaget, J. (1972). Intellectual evolution from adolescence to adulthood. *Human Development, 15,* 1–12.

Piaget, J., & Inhelder, B. (1958). *The growth of logical thinking from childhood to adolescence* (A. Parsons & S. Seagrin, Trans.). New York: Basic Books.

Price, J. H., Robinson, L. K., Thompson, C., & Schmalzried, H. (2000). Rural parents' perceptions of the Baby Think It Over Program—A pilot study. *American Journal of Health Studies, 16,* 34–40.

Somers, C. L., & Fahlman, M. M. (2001). Effectiveness of the "Baby Think It Over" teen pregnancy prevention program. *Journal of School Health, 71,* 188–195.

Somers, C. L., Gleason, J. H., Johnson, S.A., Fahlman, M. M. (2001). Adolescents' and teachers' perceptions of a teen pregnancy prevention program. *American Secondary Education, 29,* 51–66.

Strachan, W., & Gorey, K. (1997). Infant simulator lifespan intervention: Pilot investigation of an adolescent pregnancy prevention program. *Child Adolescent Social Work Journal, 14,* 1–5.

Tingle, L. R. (2002). Evaluation of North Carolina "Baby Think It Over" project. *Journal of School Health, 72,* 178–183.

United Way of Greater Los Angeles. (1998–1999). *State of the county report, 1999–1999.* Los Angeles: Author.

About the author: Diane de Anda, Ph.D., is associate professor, Department of Social Welfare, School of Public Affairs, University of California, 3250 Public Policy Building, Box 951656, Los Angeles, CA 90095. E-mail: ddeanda@ucla.edu

Exercise for Article 14

Factual Questions

1. According to the researcher, is the previous research on the effectiveness of the BTIO intervention extensive?

2. According to the researcher, do the previous studies have serious methodological limitations and flaws?

3. Was the BTIO-2 measure administered as both a pretest *and* as a posttest?

4. According to the researcher, was the gain from pretest to posttest for objective 2 very large?

5. For objective 3, was the increase from pretest to posttest statistically significant? If yes, at what probability level?

6. On the pretest, what percentage of the participants desired parenthood within a marital relationship? On the posttest, what percentage desired it?

Questions for Discussion

7. In your opinion, is the experimental intervention described in sufficient detail? Explain. (See lines 83–127.)

8. Is it important to know that the participants responded anonymously? Explain. (See line 258.)

9. In a future study of the intervention, would you recommend a longitudinal follow-up? Explain. (See lines 543–549 and 597–604.)

10. Is it important to know that participation was a mandatory part of a required class? Explain. (See lines 583–586.)

11. In a future experiment on this topic, would you recommend the use of a control group? Explain. (See lines 605–620.)

12. Based on this experiment, do you regard the intervention as promising? Would you recommend funding to extend the program to additional schools? Explain.

Quality Ratings

Directions: Indicate your level of agreement with each of the following statements by circling a number from 5 for strongly agree (SA) to 1 for strongly disagree (SD). If you believe an item is not applicable to this research article, leave it blank. Be prepared to explain your ratings. When responding to criteria A and B below, keep in mind that brief titles and abstracts are conventional in published research.

A. The title of the article is appropriate.

SA   5   4   3   2   1   SD

B. The abstract provides an effective overview of the research article.

SA   5   4   3   2   1   SD

C. The introduction establishes the importance of the study.

SA   5   4   3   2   1   SD

D. The literature review establishes the context for the study.

SA   5   4   3   2   1   SD

E. The research purpose, question, or hypothesis is clearly stated.

SA   5   4   3   2   1   SD

F. The method of sampling is sound.

SA   5   4   3   2   1   SD

G. Relevant demographics (for example, age, gender, and ethnicity) are described.

SA   5   4   3   2   1   SD

H. Measurement procedures are adequate.

SA   5   4   3   2   1   SD

I. All procedures have been described in sufficient detail to permit a replication of the study.

SA   5   4   3   2   1   SD

J. The participants have been adequately protected from potential harm.

SA   5   4   3   2   1   SD

K. The results are clearly described.

SA   5   4   3   2   1   SD

L. The discussion/conclusion is appropriate.

SA   5   4   3   2   1   SD

M. Despite any flaws, the report is worthy of publication.

SA   5   4   3   2   1   SD

Article 15

Project Trust: Breaking Down Barriers Between Middle School Children

MARY ELLEN BATIUK
Wilmington College

JAMES A. BOLAND
Wilmington College

NORMA WILCOX
Wright State University

ABSTRACT. This paper analyzes the success of a camp retreat weekend called Project Trust involving middle school students and teachers. The goal of the camp is to break down barriers between cliques identified as active in the school. The camp focuses on building team relationships across clique membership and incorporates elements of peace education and conflict resolution. A treatment group (campers) and comparison group (noncampers) were administered an adaptation of the Bogardus Social Distance Test and the Piers-Harris Children's Self-Concept Scale before and after the camp. Attendance was found to lower social distance scores for nine of the ten groups/cliques. Campers also had higher self-concept scores after the retreat.

From *Adolescence*, 39, 531–538. Copyright © 2004 by Libra Publishers, Inc. Reprinted with permission.

The *Final Report and Findings of the Safe School Initiative* indicates that from 1993 to 1997, the "odds that a child in grades 9–12 would be threatened or injured with a weapon in school were 8 percent, or 1 in 13 or 14; the odds of getting into a physical fight at school were 15 percent, or 1 in 7" (Vossekuil, Fein, Reddy, Borum, & Modzeleski, 2002, p. 12). Such widespread experiences of school violence have led to what McLaren, Leonardo, and Allen (2000) call a "bunker mentality" on many school campuses. As Tompkins (2000) points out, "increased levels of security suggest to students and teachers that they learn and teach in a violent environment where students cannot be trusted and are under suspicion" (p. 65). This is doubly unfortunate, not only because positive school climates promote learning, but that they have been found to be strong predictors of the absence of school violence (Welsh, 2000).

Further, one of the ten key findings of the analysis of the Safe School Initiative is that "many attackers felt bullied, persecuted or injured by others prior to the attack" (Vossekuil et al., 2002, p. 18). In a word, attackers felt excluded. Kramer (2000) has established that patterns of individual exclusion in school settings contribute to violence among students because exclusion separates them from the informal social control networks provided by parents, schools, and communities. This lack of informal social control has been linked to diminishing social and cultural capital (Hagen, 1985) and ultimately delinquency (Cullen, 1994; Currie, 1998; Sampson & Laub, 1993). Exclusion also preempts the kind of dialogue that can resolve conflicts (Aronowitz, 2003).

As a result, many educators have called for curricular changes incorporating programs in peace education (Caulfield, 2000; Harris, 1996; Pepinsky, 2000) and conflict resolution (Bretherton, 1996; Children's Defense Fund, 1998). For example, 10 years ago, Wilmington College collaborated with a local middle school to provide programming aimed at eliminating patterns of mistrust and exclusion fostered by student cliques. The collaboration was a natural one since Wilmington College offers extensive teacher education programs and maintains a strong tradition of conflict resolution and peacemaking tied to its Quaker heritage.

The training emphasized a mutual and reflexive process of problem solving and conflict resolution in which involved parties actively frame the understanding of both the problem and its solution. Teachers and students at the middle school overwhelmingly pointed to the ongoing problem of conflicts arising from student cliques. As a response, teachers and students designed activities that would help break down barriers among the cliques. From this collaboration emerged Project Trust—a weekend camp retreat in which student opinion/clique leaders engaged in discussions, role-playing, and noncompetitive risk-taking tasks.

The present paper focuses on a program for middle school children that incorporates principles of peace education and conflict resolution techniques to address the pervasive sources of these conflicts within networks of student cliques. It was hypothesized that by engaging student leaders in activities focused on cooperation and breaking down barriers, these same students would become more receptive to interacting with members of other cliques. It was also hypothesized that participation in the retreat weekend would lead to increased self-esteem in the participants.

Method

Project Trust

In the fall of 1990, middle school teachers and stu-

70 dents were asked to brainstorm about the kinds of cliques that were active in the school. A list of 24 groups, active within the school, emerged from these initial brainstorming sessions. Discussions with both students and teachers allowed project managers to hone 75 the list to eight, and these groups became the focal point for Project Trust. The groups included: (1) preps—smart and well dressed, well to do or at least giving the perception that they are, doing what they are told to do; (2) alternatives—baggy clothes, various 80 colors of hair, might be skaters, long hair; (3) jocks—athletes or individuals whose lives are dominated by sports interests, wearing NBA and NFL jerseys; (4) hoods/gangsters/thugs—rule-breakers, tough, like to fight, might be in a gang, wearing black; (5) dorks—85 geeks, socially awkward, nonathletic; (6) cheerleaders—attractive and active girls; (7) hicks/hillbillies—rural kids, possibly live in trailer parks, like country music; and (8) dirties—poor kids, dirty and cannot help it, poor hygiene.

90 The names of the cliques came directly from the students and teachers. Ethnic groups were not mentioned by the students but were added by the project managers after discussions with the teachers (i.e., whites and African Americans).

Treatment and Comparison Groups

95 Project Trust camp retreats include student opinion/clique leaders who are identified by teachers and invited to spend the weekend at a local camp that regularly provides team-building exercises to local civic groups and businesses. Middle school teachers receive 100 training from Wilmington College project managers in group process and team building. Both teachers and Wilmington College professors lead the retreats. Once at the camp, students and teachers are placed into Family Groups of 8–10 members designed to cut across 105 clique memberships. Students are encouraged to take ownership of the weekend agenda by developing contracts with retreat leaders. Contracting processes involve eliciting from students what they hope to "get" from the weekend (everything from food to fun activi-110 ties) and what they are willing to "give" to get those things. During the course of the weekend (Friday evening through Sunday afternoon), student family groups take part in discussions, cooperative tasks, and team building and survival exercises.

115 One team-building activity, titled Toxic Waste, involves blindfolded team members "dumping" a cupful of sludge into another cup inside a 4 × 4 square. Unsighted family team members cannot cross into the square, have access only to 4 bungee cords, the cup of 120 sludge and a rubber band, and are given directions by their sighted team members. Another activity, called Plane Crash, involves the completion of various tasks by team members who have received several handicaps (broken bones, loss of sight) and limited supplies 125 (food, water, blankets). Also included in the retreat are

an extended outdoor trust walk and a structured discussion about the harmful effects of put-downs and techniques for resolving conflicts around them. Students and teachers discuss the case study of a young girl who 130 committed suicide, leaving a note explaining the exclusion she felt because of being called a "fat hog" by her classmates.

Family groups are brought together regularly to assess how the retreat is progressing. Plenty of snacks, 135 pizza, and pop are provided to foster an environment of fun and relaxation during the time that students and teachers spend together.

In addition to this treatment group, fellow students who did not attend the camp were selected on the basis 140 of availability and assessed using the same instrument, for the purposes of comparison. Treatment group students were identified by teachers on the basis of being "opinion leaders."

Assessments

Assessment of Project Trust weekends relies pri-145 marily on an adaptation of the Bogardus (1933) Social Distance Scale to measure the social distances between the students and identified groups before and after the camp experience. The scale was chosen because of its ease of scoring and high reliability (Miller, 1991; 150 Owen et al., 1981). In addition, the scale has also been successfully and widely adapted for use with school-age children (Cover, 2001; Lee, Sapp, & Ray, 1996; Mielenz, 1979; Payne, 1976; Williams, 1992). On this modified scale, students were asked to rate all ten 155 groups on a scale of 0–7, with 7 representing the greatest degree of social distance: 0–be best friends with; 1–invite over to my house; 3–choose to eat lunch with; 4–say "hi" to only; 5–as a member of my homeroom only; 6–as a member of my school only; 7–exclude 160 them from my school. Both treatment and comparison groups completed this scale immediately before the retreat weekend and within one month after the camp.

In addition, treatment and nontreatment groups completed the Piers-Harris Children's Self-Concept 165 Scale (Piers, 1984). This self-report scale measures self-concept using 80 yes/no questions and is intended for use with youths aged 8–18. The scale was administered to the treatment group before and after the camp experience, and to the comparison group before the 170 camp experience.

Results

Camps have been held from 1998 through 2002 in both the fall and spring. An independent-samples t test (equal variances not assumed) comparing the pretest mean scores of the treatment group ($n = 298$) and com-175 parison group ($n = 215$) found significant differences between only two groups: preps ($t = 5.058$, $df = 405$, $p < .01$) and jocks ($t = 2.654$, $df = 378$, $p < .01$). In both cases, the means of the treatment group social distance scores were lower than for the comparison group: preps 180 ($M = 2.28$, $SD = 2.06$, for campers, vs. $M = 3.34$, $SD =$

2.24, for noncampers), jocks (*M* = 2.07, *SD* = 2.14, for campers, vs. *M* = 2.66, *SD* = 2.43, for noncampers). Thus, treatment and comparison students were roughly equivalent in their perceptions of social distance from
185 their classmates with the exception of the preps and the jocks. In these two instances, the campers reported statistically significant lower social distance scores when compared to noncampers.

A paired-samples *t* test was calculated for both the
190 treatment group (*n* = 216) and comparison group (*n* = 80). Table 1 reports the results for the treatment group. For all eight cliques, attendance at the camp significantly reduced perceptions of social distance. In addition, perceptions of social distance were significantly
195 reduced for African Americans but not whites. Mean scores for whites were already low (pretest *M* = .54, *SD* = 1.00) and did fall (posttest *M* = .47, *SD* = .86), though not to a statistically significant degree. The greatest change for campers was in their perceptions of
200 dirties, moving an average of 1.55 points on the 7-point scale (pretest *M* = 5.55, *SD* = 1.40; posttest *M* = 4.00, *SD* = 1.71); dorks, moving an average of 1.37 points (pretest *M* = 4.60, *SD* = 2.10; posttest *M* = 3.23, *SD* = 1.65); and hicks, moving an average of 1.23 points
205 (pretest *M* = 4.38, *SD* = 2.07; posttest *M* = 3.15, *SD* = 1.96).

Table 1

Paired-Samples Two-Tailed t Test for the Treatment Group (n = 216)

Campers	*t*	*df*	*p*
Preps	6.816	212	.000
Alternatives	5.254	196	.000
Jocks	6.532	207	.000
Hoods	6.709	205	.000
Dorks	10.810	206	.000
Cheerleaders	3.282	213	.001
Hicks	8.608	203	.000
Dirties	11.751	204	.000
African Americans	2.500	208	.013
Whites	1.141	206	.255

Table 2 reports the results for the comparison group (noncampers). The only statistically significant shift was for preps (pretest *M* = 3.18, *SD* = 2.23; posttest *M*
210 = 2.74, *SD* = 2.37). In all other instances, there were no statistically significant changes. However, there were two instances, for dorks and African Americans, in which social distance scores actually regressed.

On the Piers-Harris Children's Self-Concept Scale,
215 self-concept scores also shifted for the treatment (camper) group. The mean score on the pretest was 61.37 (*SD* = 12.6) and the mean on the posttest was 66.13 (*SD* = 11.32). The difference was statistically significant (*p* < .01).

Conclusions

220 The results suggest that educational programs for middle school children that incorporate peace education and conflict resolution hold potential for reducing divisive student cliques built around difference, mistrust, and exclusion, that often result in the violence
225 found in schools today. While this is only one study in a rural area of a mid-Atlantic state with a unique subculture, it does offer hope of greater validity and reliability with its longitudinal character. Obviously, the study needs to be replicated in a variety of cultural and
230 institutional contexts and across different age groups. However, there is much to be gained by such replication in a society struggling to understand the attitudes of the "other."

Table 2

Paired-Samples Two-Tailed t Test for the Comparison Group (n = 80)

Noncampers	*t*	*df*	*p*
Preps	2.035	72	.046
Alternatives	0.967	63	.337
Jocks	0.150	65	.881
Hoods	0.567	61	.573
Dorks	−0.068	68	.946
Cheerleaders	0.935	72	.353
Hicks	2.264	72	.353
Dirties	1.589	67	.117
African Americans	−0.271	74	.787
Whites	0.090	206	.928

References

Aronowitz, S. (2003). Essay on violence. In *Smoke and mirrors: The hidden context of violence in schools and society* (pp. 211–227). New York: Rowman and Littlefield.

Bogardus, E. S. (1933). A social distance scale. *Sociology and Social Research, 17*, 265–271.

Bretherton, D. (1996). Nonviolent conflict resolution in children. *Peabody Journal of Education, 71*, 111–127.

Caulfield, S. L. (2000). Creating peaceable schools. *ANNALS: The American Academy of Political and Social Science, 567*, 170–185.

Children's Defense Fund. (1998). *Keeping children safe in schools: A resource for states.* Available: http://www.childrensdefense.org.

Cover, J. D. (1995). The effects of social contact on prejudice. *The Journal of Social Psychology, 135*, 403–405.

Cullen, F. T. (1994). Social support as an organizing concept for criminology: Presidential address to the Academy of Criminal Justice Sciences. *Justice Quarterly, 11*, 527–559.

Currie, E. (1998). *Crime and punishment in America.* New York: Metropolitan Books.

Hagen, J. (1985). *Modern criminology: Crime, criminal behavior and its control.* New York: McGraw-Hill.

Harris, I. M. (1996). Peace education in an urban school district in the United States. *Peabody Journal of Education, 71*, 63–83.

Kramer, R. (2000). Poverty, inequality, and youth violence. *ANNALS: The American Academy of Political and Social Science, 567*, 123–139.

Lee, M. Y., Sapp, S. G., & Ray, M. C. (1996). The Reverse Social Distance Scale. *The Journal of Social Psychology, 136*, 17–24.

McLaren, P., Leonardo, Z., & Allen, R. L. (2000). Rated "cv" for cool violence. In S. U. Spina (Ed.), *Smoke and mirrors: The hidden context of violence in schools and society* (pp. 67–92). New York: Rowman and Littlefield.

Mielenz, C. C. (1979). Non-prejudiced Caucasian parents and attitudes of their children toward Negroes. *The Journal of Negro Education, 1979*, 12–21.

Miller, D. (1991). *Handbook of research design and social measurement.* Newbury Park, CA: Sage Publications.

Owen, C. A., Eisner, H. C., & McFaul, T. R. (1981). A half century of social distance research: National replication of the Bogardus studies. *Sociology and Social Research, 66*, 80–98.

Payne, W. J. (1976). Social class and social differentiation: A case for multidimensionality of social distance. *Sociology and Social Research, 61*, 54–67.

Pepinsky, H. (2000). Educating for peace. *ANNALS: The American Academy of Political and Social Science, 567*, 157–169.

Piers, E. V. (1984). *Piers-Harris Children's Self-Concept Scale revised manual 1984.* Los Angeles: Western Psychological Services.

Sampson, R. J., & Laub, J. H. (1993). *Crime in the making: Pathways and turning points through life.* Cambridge, MA: Harvard University Press.

Tompkins, D. E. (2000). School violence: Gangs and a culture of fear. *ANNALS: The American Academy of Political and Social Science, 567*, 54–71.

Vossekuil, B., Fein, R A., Reddy, M., Borum, R., & Modzeleski, W. (2002). *The final report and findings of the Safe School Initiative: Implications for the prevention of school attacks in the United States.* Washington, DC: U.S. Secret Service and U.S. Department of Education.

Welsh, W. N. (2000). The effects of school climate on school disorder. *ANNALS: The American Academy of Political and Social Science, 567*, 88–107.

Williams, C. (1992). The relationship between the affective and cognitive dimensions of prejudice. *College Student Journal, 26*, 50–54.

About the authors: *Mary Ellen Batiuk*, Department of Social and Political Studies, Wilmington College. *James A. Boland*, Department of Education, Wilmington College. *Norma Wilcox*, Department of Sociology, Wright State University.

Address correspondence to: Mary Ellen Batiuk, Department of Social and Political Studies, Wilmington College, Wilmington, OH 45177. E-mail: mebatiuk@wilmington.edu

Exercise for Article 15

Factual Questions

1. What resulted from the brainstorming sessions?

2. On the Social Distance Scale, what does a rating of "3" represent?

3. On the Social Distance Scale, does a high rating (e.g., "7") represent the "greatest degree" of social distance *or* does it represent the "least degree" of social distance?

4. In terms of social distance, the greatest change for campers from pretest to posttest was in their perceptions of what group?

5. In Table 1, all differences are statistically significant except for one group. Which group?

6. Was the treatment group's pretest to posttest difference on self-concept statistically significant? If yes, at what probability level?

Questions for Discussion

7. Keeping in mind that this is a research report and not an instructional guide, is the description of the treatment in lines 95–137 sufficiently detailed so that you have a clear picture of it? Explain.

8. For the comparison group, fellow students who did not attend the camp were selected on the basis of availability. How much stronger would this experiment have been if students had been randomly assigned to the treatment and comparison groups? Explain. (See lines 138–143.)

9. In your opinion, is the Piers-Harris Children's Self-Concept Scale described in sufficient detail? Explain. (See lines 163–170.)

10. The researchers state that "the study needs to be replicated in a variety of cultural and institutional contexts and across different age groups." (See lines 228–230.) In your opinion, are the results of this study sufficiently promising to warrant such replications? Explain.

11. What changes, if any, would you suggest making in the research methodology used in this study?

Quality Ratings

Directions: Indicate your level of agreement with each of the following statements by circling a number from 5 for strongly agree (SA) to 1 for strongly disagree (SD). If you believe an item is not applicable to this research article, leave it blank. Be prepared to explain your ratings. When responding to criteria A and B below, keep in mind that brief titles and abstracts are conventional in published research.

A. The title of the article is appropriate.

SA   5   4   3   2   1   SD

B. The abstract provides an effective overview of the research article.

SA   5   4   3   2   1   SD

C. The introduction establishes the importance of the study.

SA   5   4   3   2   1   SD

D. The literature review establishes the context for the study.

SA   5   4   3   2   1   SD

E. The research purpose, question, or hypothesis is clearly stated.

SA   5   4   3   2   1   SD

F. The method of sampling is sound.

SA   5   4   3   2   1   SD

G. Relevant demographics (for example, age, gender, and ethnicity) are described.

SA   5   4   3   2   1   SD

H. Measurement procedures are adequate.

SA   5   4   3   2   1   SD

I. All procedures have been described in sufficient detail to permit a replication of the study.

SA   5   4   3   2   1   SD

J.   The participants have been adequately protected
     from potential harm.

          SA   5   4   3   2   1   SD

K.   The results are clearly described.

          SA   5   4   3   2   1   SD

L.   The discussion/conclusion is appropriate.

          SA   5   4   3   2   1   SD

M.   Despite any flaws, the report is worthy of publica-
     tion.

          SA   5   4   3   2   1   SD

Article 16

Sex Differences on a Measure of Conformity in Automated Teller Machine Lines

STEPHEN REYSEN
California State University Fresno

MATTHEW B. REYSEN
Purdue University

ABSTRACT. Sex differences in conformity were examined as participants approached two ATMs, one of which was occupied by three confederates and the other immediately available. The number of men and women in the line in front of one of the ATMs was manipulated (3 men or 3 women), and an unobtrusive observer recorded the sex of each participant. The results indicated that women were more likely than men to wait in line to use the ATM regardless of the makeup of the line. Thus, the present study provides evidence in favor of the idea that sex differences in conformity are evident on a common task performed in a natural setting.

From *Psychological Reports, 95,* 443–446. Copyright © 2004 by Psychological Reports. Reprinted with permission.

In a highly influential series of experiments conducted in the 1950s, Solomon Asch (1952, 1955, 1956) examined conformity pressure in a group situation. Asch's classic conformity studies involved individuals making line-length judgments in the presence of others also making judgments about the same stimuli. Asch found that participants often agreed with incorrect confederate responses even though, presumably, they could easily discern which of three presented lines matched a target line. Based on Asch's results, it is clear that the behavior of others can influence an individual's own behavior.

Since Asch's experiments (1952, 1955, 1956), a great many studies have examined conformity in behavior (see McIlveen & Gross, 1999; Wren, 1999, for reviews). One important area of this research concerns whether women are more likely to conform than men. Sistrunk and McDavid (1971) reported that women conform more often than men on judgment tasks completed in the laboratory. They determined that the nature of the task plays a large role in contributing to sex differences in conformity and that a cultural role explanation is inadequate to explain the effect. A number of other studies have also demonstrated that women tend to conform more than men in laboratory situations (e.g., Krech, Crutchfield, & Ballachey, 1962; Aronson, 1972; Worschel & Cooper, 1976).

Based on the results of a meta-analysis, Eagly (1978) concluded that women may be conditioned to yield to men under certain circumstances. Eagly suggested that this tendency was the primary explanation for why women tend to conform more often than men. The current study was designed to analyze sex differences in conformity on a common task in a real world setting. Examining a situation in which participants complete a common task in their natural environment provides a much-needed test of the external validity of more artificial laboratory paradigms. A sex-neutral task was chosen in which men and women are likely to be equally competent.

In the present experiment, a line of two confederates was created behind another confederate using one of two adjacent ATMs. The three confederates were either all men or all women. The primary purpose of the study was to assess whether women would conform to the group more often than men. Conformity was operationally defined by number of times a participant stood in line behind the confederates for at least 5 sec. instead of using the vacant ATM. A participant who waited in line was assumed to accept implicitly the confederates' judgment that the available ATM was nonfunctional.

Method

Participants

Two hundred ATM users were observed at an outdoor shopping area in a small coastal town in California. This sample included 106 men and 94 women.

Design and Procedure

The purpose of the present experiment was to observe individuals' behavior while they used a public automated teller machine. To accomplish this, we located two ATMs at a local shopping area that met several specifications. The ATMs were less than 1 ft. apart and were not separated by a divider. There were no overt signs that either of the machines was nonfunctional. In fact, both of the machines were in perfect working order. The procedure used was straightforward. Two confederates stood behind another confederate using one of the two ATMs. On half of the trials, the left ATM was used and on the other half of the trials the right ATM was used. Thus, on every trial, the participant approached two ATMs, one vacant and the

70 other in use with two people waiting in line. In half of the trials, two men stood in line behind a man, while in the other half of the trials two women stood in line behind a woman.

75 A trial began when an individual approached the two ATMs. To constitute a usable trial, the person had to be alone and easily identifiable as being in line. An observer, sitting unobtrusively at a nearby table, recorded the sex of the participant and whether the participant stood in line or used the vacant ATM. "Wait-
80 ing in line" was operationally defined as standing in line behind the confederates for a period of at least 5 sec. Two hundred trials were recorded on weekday afternoons over the course of two weeks. Approximately 25 trials were recorded each day that observa-
85 tions were made.

Results and Discussion

The primary purpose of the present experiment was to examine whether men and women showed differential conformity on this common task. Our hypothesis, based on previous laboratory observations, was that
90 women would tend to conform more often than men. The data appear to support our hypothesis. The 89 women did, in fact, tend to wait in line more often than the 78 men (74%) for a period of at least 5 sec. This difference in distribution gave a statistically significant
95 chi-square (χ_1^2 ($N = 200$) = 16.09, $p < .001$).

Interestingly, the sex makeup of the line seemed to play little role in influencing the participants' behavior. Women tended to wait in line more often than men regardless of the sex of the confederates. With two
100 male confederates in line, 43 (91%) of the women waited in line, while only 35 (66%) of the men did so. This difference was statistically significant (χ_1^2 ($N = 100$) = 9.40, $p < .01$). In addition, when female confederates were in line, 46 (98%) of the women stood in
105 line, while only 43 (81%) of the men waited in line. This difference was also statistically significant (χ_1^2 ($N = 100$) = 7.13, $p < .01$). Thus, even when the sex composition of the line was manipulated, women were still more likely than men to wait in line.

110 The sex-role socialization explanation has been proposed to account for sex differences in conformity (Crutchfield, 1955; Tuddenham, 1958; Eagly, 1978). This account suggests that sex differences in conformity are a result of socialization. According to this
115 idea, women adopt a sex role that includes traits such as submissiveness and a tendency to rely on others. This idea could potentially explain why the women in our study may have been reluctant to challenge the judgment of others and instead chose to wait in line
120 rather than trying the vacant ATM. Whereas the present results seem to support the sex-role socialization theory, they are not consistent with several other prominent explanations for sex differences in conformity, namely, the information-deficit explanation (see
125 Allen, 1965; Endler, Wiesenthal, Coward, Edwards, & Geller, 1975), the verbal processing account (Eagly & Warren, 1976), and status allocation differences (Eagly, Wood, & Fishbaugh, 1981; Santee & Maslach, 1982; Eagly, 1987).

130 One limitation that must be considered with respect to the present results is the location in which the trials took place. The experiment was conducted in a small coastal town in California. It is unclear whether the results would remain consistent in a different setting. In
135 fact, this realization suggests other possible questions. For example, it would be interesting to evaluate whether manipulating the race, age, or status of the confederates would affect the outcome. It would also be informative to include a condition in which a line of
140 persons of mixed sex was used. In sum, the present data suggest that women conform more often than men when conducting a common task in a real world setting. This observation suggests that results obtained in laboratory paradigms using similar methods may not be
145 limited with respect to external validity.

References

Allen, V. L. (1965). Situational factors in conformity. In L. Berkowitz (Ed.), *Advances in experimental social psychology.* Vol. 2. (pp. 133–176). New York: Academic Press.

Aronson, E. (1972). *The social animal.* (2nd ed.) Oxford, UK: Freeman.

Asch, S. E. (1952). *Social psychology.* Englewood Cliffs, NJ: Prentice-Hall.

Asch, S. E. (1955). Opinions and social pressure. *Scientific American, 193,* 31–35.

Asch, S. E. (1956). Studies of independence and conformity: A minority of one against a unanimous majority. *Psychological Monographs, 70,* Whole No. 416.

Crutchfield, R. S. (1955). Conformity and character. *American Psychologist, 10,* 191–198.

Eagly, A. H. (1978). Sex differences in influenceability. *Psychological Bulletin, 85,* 86–116.

Eagly, A. H. (1987). *Sex differences in social behavior: A social-role interpretation.* Hillsdale, NJ: Erlbaum.

Eagly, A. H., & Warren, R. (1976). Intelligence, comprehension, and opinion change. *Journal of Personality, 44,* 226–242.

Eagly, A. H., Wood, W., & Fishbaugh, L. (1981). Sex differences in conformity: Surveillance by the group as a determinant of male nonconformity. *Journal of Personality and Social Psychology, 40,* 384–394.

Endler, N. S., Wiesenthal, D. L., Coward, T., Edwards, J., & Geller, S. H. (1975). Generalization of relative competence mediating conformity across differing tasks. *European Journal of Social Psychology, 5,* 281–287.

Krech, D., Crutchfield, R. S., & Ballachey, E. L. (1962). Individual in society: A textbook of social psychology. New York: McGraw-Hill.

McIlveen, R., & Gross, R. (1999). *Social influence.* London: Hodder & Stoughton.

Santee, R. T., & Maslach, C. (1982). To agree or not to agree: Personal dissent amid social pressure to conform. *Journal of Personality and Social Psychology, 42,* 690–700.

Sistrunk, F., & McDavid, J. (1971). Sex variable in conforming behavior. *Journal of Personality and Social Psychology, 17,* 200–207.

Tuddenham, R. D. (1958). The influences of a distorted group norm upon individual judgment. *Journal of Psychology, 46,* 227–241.

Worschel, S., & Cooper, J. (1976). *Understanding social psychology.* Oxford, UK: Dorsey.

Wren, K. (1999). *Social influences.* Florence, KY: Taylor & Francis/Routledge.

Acknowledgments: Thanks to Faye Crosby, Robert Levine, and Ellen Ganz for their helpful comments on previous versions of this article.

Address correspondence to: Stephen Reysen, Department of Psychology, California State University Fresno, Fresno, CA 93740-8019. E-mail: sreysen@jasnh.com

Matthew Reysen is now at University of Mississippi.

Exercise for Article 16

Factual Questions

1. How did the researchers operationally define "conformity"?

2. In half the trials, two men stood behind another man. Who stood in line in the other half?

3. With two male confederates in line, what percentage of the women waited in line? What percentage of the men did so?

4. Was the difference between the men and women in Question 3 above statistically significant? If yes, at what probability level?

5. When two female confederates were in line, what percentage of the men waited in line?

6. What is the limitation of the study that the researchers briefly discuss?

Questions for Discussion

7. This research report begins with a literature review with references to studies conducted in the 1950s. In your opinion, is it appropriate to cite older literature? Explain.

8. The researchers suggest that studying the variables of interest in their "natural environment" is needed. In your opinion, is this important? Explain. (See lines 33–38.)

9. Because the study was conducted in a natural environment, the researchers could not assign the individuals who approached the ATMs at random to the experimental conditions. In your opinion, is this an important issue? Explain.

10. In your opinion, is it important that the observer was unobtrusive? Explain. (See lines 76–79.)

11. Has this study convinced you that there are gender differences in conformity? Explain.

12. Do you agree with the researchers that it would be interesting to evaluate whether manipulating the race, age, or status of the confederates would affect the outcome? Explain. (See lines 136–138.)

Quality Ratings

Directions: Indicate your level of agreement with each of the following statements by circling a number from 5 for strongly agree (SA) to 1 for strongly disagree (SD). If you believe an item is not applicable to this research article, leave it blank. Be prepared to explain your ratings. When responding to criteria A and B below, keep in mind that brief titles and abstracts are conventional in published research.

A. The title of the article is appropriate.

    SA   5   4   3   2   1   SD

B. The abstract provides an effective overview of the research article.

    SA   5   4   3   2   1   SD

C. The introduction establishes the importance of the study.

    SA   5   4   3   2   1   SD

D. The literature review establishes the context for the study.

    SA   5   4   3   2   1   SD

E. The research purpose, question, or hypothesis is clearly stated.

    SA   5   4   3   2   1   SD

F. The method of sampling is sound.

    SA   5   4   3   2   1   SD

G. Relevant demographics (for example, age, gender, and ethnicity) are described.

    SA   5   4   3   2   1   SD

H. Measurement procedures are adequate.

    SA   5   4   3   2   1   SD

I. All procedures have been described in sufficient detail to permit a replication of the study.

    SA   5   4   3   2   1   SD

J. The participants have been adequately protected from potential harm.

    SA   5   4   3   2   1   SD

K. The results are clearly described.

    SA   5   4   3   2   1   SD

L. The discussion/conclusion is appropriate.

    SA   5   4   3   2   1   SD

M. Despite any flaws, the report is worthy of publication.

    SA   5   4   3   2   1   SD

Article 17

Benefits to Police Officers of Having a Spouse or Partner in the Profession of Police Officer

RONALD J. BURKE
York University

ASLAUG MIKKELSEN
Stavanger University College

ABSTRACT. This exploratory study of police officers examined potential effects of having a spouse or partner who is also in police work on levels of work–family conflict and spouse or partner concerns. Data were collected from 776 police officers in Norway using anonymously completed questionnaires. Police officers having spouses or partners also in police work reported significantly lower spouse or partner concerns but the same levels of work–family conflict. Possible explanations for these findings are offered.

From *Psychological Reports*, 95, 514–516. Copyright © 2004 by Psychological Reports. Reprinted with permission.

It has been observed that individuals sometimes follow the same occupation or profession as their parents and that individuals sometimes have a spouse or partner in the same occupation and profession (Hall, 1976).
5 It is not clear, however, how common this is, why this happens, and whether some professions are more likely to have couples working in them. In an earlier study of men and women in policing, it became clear that police officers' children often became police officers and the
10 possible benefits of this association were examined (Burke, 1997). In that research, we found that police officers with family in policing reported fewer job stressors, but the two groups were similar on measures of work outcomes and psychological health.
15 In the present study, the possible benefits are considered of having one's spouse or partner in the same profession: policing. Policing is seen as a demanding, highly stressful occupation, which may have potential negative effects on the psychological well-being and
20 physical health of police officers (Abdollahi, 2002). There is no doubt that police officers sometimes face high-risk, violent, and threatening situations. But police officers most often face the same demands as members of most other occupations, and there is no compelling
25 evidence that policing is in fact more stressful than other occupations (Abdollahi, 2002).
It is likely that having a spouse or partner in the same profession would increase the shared understanding of the experiences and challenges of that profes-
30 sion. The focus of this study is on the effect of the police officer's job on the family and, given the assump-

tion that policing can be dangerous and threatening, on the spouse's or partner's perceived concerns about the officer's safety. It was hypothesized that police officers
35 whose spouse or partner was also in policing would report lower work–family conflict and spouse's or partner's concerns about the respondent officer's safety and security.
Data were collected from a random sample of po-
40 lice officers in Norway ($N = 766$) using anonymous questionnaires that were mailed to respondents by the Police Union and returned to an independent research institute. The response rate was 62%. Most respondents were male (84%), married (82%), had children (88%),
45 held constable positions (62%), worked in urban areas (73%), worked in large departments (100 or more, 36%), worked between 36–39 hours per week (85%), worked 5 or fewer hours of overtime per week (75%), held fairly long police tenure (21 years or more, 39%),
50 and were born in 1960 or before (42%). A total of 623 police officers were married or partnered (538 men and 85 women). Ten percent of male officers and 44% of female officers had a spouse or partner in policing.
The two dependent variables, Work–Family Con-
55 flict and Spousal Concerns, were measured as did Torgen, Stenlund, Ahlberg, and Marklund (2001). Work–Family Conflict was measured by five items ($\alpha = .83$). One item was "My work has a negative impact on my family." Spousal Concerns was also measured
60 by five items ($\alpha = .81$); for example, "My spouse or partner worries about the health effects of my work." Respondents rated how frequently they experienced each item on a 5-point scale (1 = never, 5 = always).
Table 1 shows the comparisons of responses to the
65 Work–Family Conflict and Spouse Concerns scales, separating males' and females' spouses or partners in police work and those whose spouses or partners were not employed in police work. Mean values were compared using one-way analysis of variance. In the latter
70 group, some spouses or partners were employed in other jobs, while others were not employed outside the home for pay.
Both male and female officers reported the same mean values on Work–Family Conflict (nonsignificant
75 difference) whether the spouse or partner was em-

Table 1
Work–Family Conflict and Spouse Concerns by Sex of Respondent and Whether or Not Spouse or Partner Works in Policing

	Spouse/partner in policing			Spouse/partner not in policing			*p*
	M	*SD*	*n*	*M*	*SD*	*n*	
Male officers							
Work–family conflict	12.7	3.90	55	12.8	3.93	475	ns
Spouse concerns	9.6	4.07	48	11.0	3.76	419	.01
Female officers							
Work–family conflict	12.6	4.36	37	12.6	3.79	48	ns
Spouse concerns	9.2	3.62	37	11.1	3.79	48	.05

ployed in police work or not. But both male and female police officers reported lower scores on Spousal Concerns if the spouse or partner was also in policing than if they were not.

80   There are several possible reasons why having a spouse or partner in the law enforcement profession may have benefits. Such spouses or partners understand the realities of the job—the challenges, demands, rewards, and frustrations. They may share common

85   experiences and be better able to appreciate the experiences of their spouses or partners. They may also share more common attitudes, values, and aspects of personality. These common factors may diminish unrealistic thoughts on the realities of policing and the nature of

90   their spouse's or partner's job experiences.

It is not clear the extent to which these findings generalize to police officers in other countries or to other occupations. It should also be noted that all data were collected from police officers and not their

95   spouses. It would be informative to collect data from spouses or partners of police officers directly.

References

Abdollahi, M. K. (2002). Understanding police stress research. *Journal of Forensic Psychology Practice, 2*, 1–24.

Burke, R. J. (1997). On "inheriting" a career. *Psychological Reports, 80*, 1233–1234.

Hall, D. T. (1976). *Careers in organizations*. Pacific Palisades, CA: Goodyear.

Torgen, M., Stenlund, C., Ahlberg, G., & Marklund, S. (2001). *Ett hallbart arbetsliv foralla aldrar*. Stockholm: Arbetslivsinstitutet.

Acknowledgments: Preparation of this manuscript was supported in part by the Rogaland Institute, Stavanger, Norway, and the School of Business, York University. We acknowledge the support of the Police Union in conducting the study and collecting the data. Lisa Fiksenbaum assisted with data analysis.

Address correspondence to: R. J. Burke, Department of Organizational Behaviour, Schulich School of Business, York University, 4700 Keele Street, North York, ON, Canada M3J IP3. E-mail: rburke@schulich.yorku.ca

Exercise for Article 17

Factual Questions

1. What did the researchers hypothesize?

2. What percentage of the respondents were male?

3. For the female officers, was the difference between the means on Work–Family Conflict statistically significant?

4. What was the mean on Spouse Concerns for male officers who had a spouse/partner in policing?

5. What was the mean on Spouse Concerns for male officers who had a spouse/partner *not* in policing?

6. Was the difference between the two means in the answers to Questions 4 and 5 above statistically significant?

Questions for Discussion

7. Is it important to know that the researchers used a random sample? Explain. (See lines 39–40.)

8. In your opinion, was the response rate satisfactory? Explain. (See line 43.)

9. The researchers indicate that there were two dependent variables. What is your understanding of the meaning of this term? (See lines 54–55.)

10. Speculate on the meaning of "ns" in Table 1.

11. Do you think it would be important in future studies to collect information directly from the spouses (instead of from the police officers)? Why? Why not? (See lines 93–96.)

12. Does this article convince you that being married to a police officer results in less spousal concern? Explain.

13. This research article is shorter than most of the others in this book. Do you think that this article provides valuable information despite its length? Explain.

Quality Ratings

Directions: Indicate your level of agreement with each of the following statements by circling a number from 5 for strongly agree (SA) to 1 for strongly disagree (SD). If you believe an item is not applicable to this research article, leave it blank. Be prepared to explain your ratings. When responding to criteria A and B below, keep in mind that brief titles and abstracts are conventional in published research.

A. The title of the article is appropriate.

SA 5 4 3 2 1 SD

B. The abstract provides an effective overview of the research article.

SA 5 4 3 2 1 SD

C. The introduction establishes the importance of the study.

SA 5 4 3 2 1 SD

D. The literature review establishes the context for the study.

SA 5 4 3 2 1 SD

E. The research purpose, question, or hypothesis is clearly stated.

SA 5 4 3 2 1 SD

F. The method of sampling is sound.

SA 5 4 3 2 1 SD

G. Relevant demographics (for example, age, gender, and ethnicity) are described.

SA 5 4 3 2 1 SD

H. Measurement procedures are adequate.

SA 5 4 3 2 1 SD

I. All procedures have been described in sufficient detail to permit a replication of the study.

SA 5 4 3 2 1 SD

J. The participants have been adequately protected from potential harm.

SA 5 4 3 2 1 SD

K. The results are clearly described.

SA 5 4 3 2 1 SD

L. The discussion/conclusion is appropriate.

SA 5 4 3 2 1 SD

M. Despite any flaws, the report is worthy of publication.

SA 5 4 3 2 1 SD

Article 18

Relationship of Personalized Jerseys and Aggression in Women's Ice Hockey

JAMIE BLOME
University of Northern Iowa

JENNIFER J. WALDRON
University of Northern Iowa

MICK G. MACK
University of Northern Iowa

ABSTRACT. The present study examined the relationship between aggression and players' names on uniforms in collegiate women's ice hockey. Aggression was defined as mean penalty minutes per game. Information (i.e., win/loss record, penalties, and names on uniforms) about the 2002–2003 season women's ice hockey team was obtained via e-mail from 53 of 72 (74% return rate) sports information directors (Division I = 23, Division II = 2, Division III = 28). Analysis indicated that teams with personalized jerseys had significantly more penalty minutes per game than teams without personalized jerseys. However, as the majority of the teams with personalized jerseys were Division I teams and the majority of the teams without personalized jerseys were Division III teams, it is unclear whether results were due to personalized jerseys or competition level of play.

From *Perceptual and Motor Skills, 101,* 499–504. Copyright © 2005 by Perceptual and Motor Skills. Reprinted with permission.

Aggression has become a frequent topic of investigation in sport psychology, and several factors have been examined. For example, researchers have investigated the relationship between aggression and location

5 of games (Lefebvre & Passer, 1974), crowd size (Russell & Drewry, 1976), possible lunar influences (Russell & Dua, 1983), outcome of game (Worrell & Harris, 1986), frequency of competition (Widmeyer & McGuire, 1997), personality (Bushman & Wells,

10 1998), level of competition (Coulomb & Pfister, 1998), wearing personalized jerseys (Wann & Porcher, 1998), and type of sport (Huang, Cherek, & Lane, 1999). Because ice hockey offers a unique field setting in which aggression is tolerated and often encouraged, many

15 studies have focused on this sport. Not surprisingly, however, they have only examined male hockey teams.

Sex is one potential moderator of aggressive behaviors. For example, women are more likely to use indirect types of aggression (i.e., backbiting, spreading of

20 false rumors, gossiping, etc.), while men are more likely to engage in violence or acts of physical behavior (Bjorkqvist, Osterman, & Kaukiainen, 1992). Most of the previous studies examining sport aggression, however, have been conducted with male athletes so it

25 is not clear whether this relationship would occur in sports with women. With the substantial increase in the number of women participants in contact sports such as soccer, ice hockey, and football (Theberge, 1997), it is now possible to examine physical aggression during

30 women's athletic competitions.

Aggression in sports can be defined as a nonaccidental act that has the potential to cause psychological or physiological harm to another individual (Kirker, Tennebaum, & Mattson, 2000). Because penalty min-

35 utes are "acts of interpersonal aggression judged by highly trained and experienced referees to be in violation of the rules of competition" (Russell & Dua, 1983, p. 42), they are often used to measure aggression operationally in men's ice hockey (Russell & Dua, 1983;

40 Widmeyer & Birch, 1984; Widmeyer & McGuire, 1997; Bushman & Wells, 1998; Wann & Porcher, 1998). The use of penalty records has been a valid indicator of aggression in sports (Vokey & Russell, 1992), as more aggressive infractions require longer

45 periods of time of being restricted from participation. The same is true in women's ice hockey. However, it should be noted that there are slight differences in rules between the men's and women's games. The National Collegiate Athletic Association (NCAA) rules for

50 women's ice hockey do not allow body checking but do permit body contact (National Collegiate Athletic Association, 2002[1]). In other words, women's ice hockey has "rules that limit but by no means eliminate body contact" (Theberge, 1997, p. 71). Interestingly,

55 some of the women in Theberge's study believed that not permitting body checking actually caused more illegal contact during competition.

Understanding the triggers for aggression in sports is an important area of investigation and has been stud-

60 ied primarily in relation to men's sporting behaviors. The current study extends Wann and Porcher's study of men's ice hockey (1998) to women's ice hockey teams. Based on 86 Division I, II, and III ice hockey programs, Wann and Porcher found that the teams with

65 personalized jerseys showed more aggression, measured using penalties, than teams without identification

---

[1] Men's and women's ice hockey rules and interpretations. Retrieved November 6, 2003, from http://www.ncaa.org/library/rules/2003/ice_hockey_rules.pdf

on their jerseys and explained the findings using self-presentation theory.

Self-presentation theory predicts that individuals attempt to present themselves in a positive manner to others (Schlenker, 1980). For many male athletes, portraying a positive image to others requires them to be tough. Thus, especially in a sport such as ice hockey, which is known for its aggressive nature, participants may desire to present themselves as being aggressive (Wann & Porcher, 1998). Having one's name appear on the uniform would ensure that personal identity as an aggressor is known and would serve to enhance the "positive" image to their teammates, opponents, and fans.

Because self-presentation is a socially based concept, research examining sport aggression in women may yield different results. For example, researchers have reported that collegiate female athletes from a variety of sports were less violent on the playing field than their male counterparts (Tucker & Parks, 2001). Perhaps, as suggested by Bjorkqvist et al. (1992), women, following traditional norms of femininity, may desire to present themselves in a more socially desirable nonaggressive manner, which suggests that they would be more likely to engage in indirect acts of aggression that "mask" their behavior. This explanation would predict that wearing a jersey with one's name on the back would result in fewer acts of aggression for female athletes than for male athletes. Thus, it was hypothesized that there would be no significant difference between aggression of women's collegiate ice hockey teams, as measured by number of penalty minutes, with and without personalized names on their jerseys.

Method

A list of all colleges with women's ice hockey in Divisions I, II, and III was obtained from the NCAA Web site. E-mail addresses were obtained, and the sports information directors from each school were then contacted via e-mail. In the two cases where no sport information director was listed, the head coach was contacted. Two weeks following the initial e-mail, a follow-up was sent through e-mail to those who had not yet responded. The sports information directors or coaches of all NCAA women's ice hockey teams ($N = 72$) were contacted and 53 responded (Division I = 23, Division II = 2, Division III = 28). Therefore, the present sample represented approximately 74% of all NCAA women's hockey programs from the 2002–2003 season.

Each e-mail began with an introduction of the researchers' affiliation and an explanation of the research. This was followed by a request for the following information concerning the 2002–2003 women's ice hockey season: (1) What was your win/loss record? (2) What was the total number of penalty minutes? (3) Did your team have personalized names on their jer-

seys for home games? (4) Did your team have personalized names on their jerseys for away games? One of the sports information directors responded by telephone, while the rest of the directors replied using e-mail.

Aggression was operationally defined as the mean number of penalty minutes per game. This measure was calculated by dividing the total number of penalty minutes for the season by the total number of games. Because penalties for more aggression require more minutes in the penalty box (i.e., 2 min. for a minor penalty versus 5 min. for a major penalty), a larger number indicates more aggression.

Results

Of the 53 women's hockey teams for which responses were received, 21 had personalized names on both home and away jerseys (Division I = 19, Division II = 1, Division III = 1), 23 teams did not have personalized names on either home or away jerseys (Division I = 2, Division II = 1, Division III = 20), and 9 teams had names on either home or away jerseys, but not both (Division I = 2, Division III = 7). The mean number of penalties per game was 4.5 ($SD = 1.2$), and the mean for penalty minutes per game was 9.5 ($SD = 2.6$).

An independent-samples t test was used to compare penalty minutes per game between teams with and without personalized names on their jerseys. Teams whose jerseys had names for either their home or away games were not included in this analysis. Analysis indicated that the teams with personalized jerseys had significantly more penalty minutes per game ($M = 10.7$, $SD = 2.4$) than teams without personalized jerseys ($M = 8.4$, $SD = 2.2$; $t_{42} = 3.19$, $p < .01$, $d = 1.0$). Because the vast majority of teams having personalized jerseys were Division I ice hockey programs (90.5%), while most teams not having personalized jerseys were Division III programs (87.0%), an additional independent samples t test was performed to examine potential differences between the two divisions. Since data were received from only two Division II ice hockey programs, they were not included in this analysis. The analysis indicated that Division I teams had significantly more penalty minutes per game ($M = 10.7$, $SD = 2.3$) than Division III ($M = 8.2$, $SD = 2.3$; $t_{49} = 3.86$, $p < .01$, $d = 1.1$). For both of the independent samples t tests, the effect size (d) was large (Cohen, 1988). In other words, the magnitude or meaningfulness of the difference between the two groups was substantial.

Discussion

Contrary to what was predicted, results of the present study are similar to Wann and Porcher's findings (1998). The combined results from these two studies indicate that both samples of men's and women's ice hockey teams with personalized jerseys had more penalty minutes and thus more aggression than teams without personalized jerseys. The self-presentation explanation of desiring to be perceived as an aggres-

sive player might be appropriate for both men and women. Both male and female ice hockey players may
180 want an aggressive self-presentation to intimidate opponents, keep their position on the team, or maintain their self-identity (Widmeyer, Bray, Dorsch, & McGuire, 2002).

However, closer scrutiny of the demographic back-
185 ground of the teams involved raises doubts about the potential effectiveness of wearing personalized jerseys. When examining the data in the current study, it was noted that only one team in Division III had personalized jerseys, whereas only two teams in Division I did
190 not have names on their jerseys. Follow-up analyses comparing aggression between the divisions found that Division I teams had significantly higher aggression measured as penalties (min.) than Division III teams. A cursory examination of the demographic data provided
195 by Wann and Porcher (1998) raises similar questions. In their study, 95% of Division I teams had personalized jerseys, while 85% of Division III teams did not have personalized jerseys.

Wann and Porcher's attempt to provide evidence
200 that increased aggression could be attributed to personalized jerseys rather than competition level was also suspect. As noted in their results, small sample sizes precluded statistical analysis at the Division I level. Their analysis at the Division III level could similarly
205 be questioned given the unequal sample sizes (i.e., personalized jerseys = 28 and no personalized jerseys = 5). Unfortunately, the current study's design showed the same limitations, so additional t tests within each division could not be conducted given the small number of
210 teams without personalized jerseys in Division I and teams with personalized jerseys in Division III. Having only nine teams whose names were on jerseys worn during either their home or away games but not both was insufficient data on which to conduct statistical
215 analyses between the groups. Therefore, it is unclear whether differences in aggression were related to wearing personalized jerseys or to competition level.

In summary, research on the possible association of wearing personalized jerseys on aggression in men and
220 women's collegiate ice hockey appears inconclusive given the confounding variable of competition level. Significant differences in penalty minutes may have been a function of the competition level rather than wearing a personalized jersey. Researchers must fur-
225 ther delineate the various factors that may be associated with expression of aggression by both male and female participants in ice hockey and other sports.

References

Bjorkqvist, K., Osterman, K., & Kaukiainen, A. (1992). The development of direct and indirect aggressive strategies in males and females. In K. Bjorkqvist & P. Niemela (Eds.), *Of mice and women: Aspects of female aggression.* San Diego, CA: Academic Press. Pp. 51–64.

Bushman, B. J., & Wells, G. L. (1998). Trait aggressiveness and hockey penalties: Predicting hot tempers on the ice. *Journal of Applied Psychology, 83,* 969–974.

Cohen, J. (1998). *Statistical power analysis for the behavioral sciences.* (2nd ed.) Hillsdale, NJ: Erlbaum.

Coulomb, G., & Pfister, R. (1998). Aggressive behaviors in soccer as a function of competition level and time: A field study. *Journal of Sport Behavior, 21,* 222–231.

Huang, D. B., Cherek, D. R., & Lane, D. (1999). Laboratory measurement of aggression in high school age athletes: Provocation in a nonsporting context. *Psychological Reports, 85,* 1251–1262.

Kirker, B., Tennebaum, G., & Mattson, J. (2000). An investigation of the dynamics of aggression: Direct observations in ice hockey and basketball. *Research Quarterly for Exercise and Sport, 71,* 373–386.

Lefebvre, L., & Passer, M. W. (1974). The effects of game location and importance on aggression in team sport. *International Journal of Sport Psychology, 5,* 102–110.

Russell, G. W, & Drewry, B. R. (1976). Crowd size and competitive aspects of aggression in ice hockey: An archival study. *Human Relations, 29,* 723–735.

Russell, G. W, & Dua, M. (1983). Lunar influences on human aggression. *Social Behavior and Personality, 11,* 41–44.

Schlenker, B. R. (1980). *Impression management: The self-concept, social identity, and interpersonal relations.* Monterey, CA: Brooks/Cole.

Theberge, N. (1997). "It's a part of the game": Physicality and the production of gender in women's hockey. *Gender and Society, 11,* 69–87.

Tucker, L. W., & Parks, J. B. (2001). Effects of gender and sport types on intercollegiate athletes' perceptions of the legitimacy of aggressive behaviors in sport. *Sociology of Sport Journal, 18,* 403–413.

Vokey, J. R., & Russell, G. W. (1992). On penalties in sport as measures of aggression. *Social Behavior and Personality, 20,* 219–225.

Wann, D. L., & Porcher, B. J. (1998). The relationship between players' names on uniforms and athlete aggression. *International Sport Journal, 2,* 28–35.

Widmeyer, W. N., & Birch, J. S. (1984). Aggression in professional ice hockey: A strategy for success or a reaction to failure? *Journal of Psychology, 117,* 77–84.

Widmeyer, W. N., Bray, J. S., Dorsch, K. D., & McGuire, E. J. (2002). Explanations for the occurrence of aggression: Theories and research. In J. M. Silva & D. E. Stevens (Eds.), *Psychological foundations of sport.* Boston, MA: Allyn & Bacon. Pp. 352–379.

Widmeyer, W. N., & McGuire, E. J. (1997). Frequency of competition and aggression in professional ice hockey. *International Journal of Sport Psychology, 28,* 57–66.

Worrell, L. L., & Harris, D. V. (1986). The relationship of perceived and observed aggression of ice hockey players. *International Journal of Sport Psychology, 17,* 34–40.

Address correspondence to: Jennifer J. Waldron, Ph.D., School of Health, Physical Education, and Leisure Services, 203 Wellness/Recreation Center, Cedar Falls, IA 50614-0241. E-mail: jennifer.waldron@uni.edu

Exercise for Article 18

Factual Questions

1. Near the beginning of the article, the researchers provide a conceptual definition of "aggression." (See lines 31–33.) Later in the article, they provide an operational definition. What is the operational definition?

2. How were the participants contacted for this study?

3. Was there a significant difference between teams with personalized jerseys and teams without personalized jerseys? If yes, at what probability level was it significant?

4. What is the name of the significance test used in this research?

5. According to the researchers, were both effect sizes (d) "large"?

6. Are the results of this study consistent with what was predicted (i.e., consistent with the hypothesis)?

Questions for Discussion

7. Out of the 72 potential participants, 53 responded. In your opinion, does this affect the validity of the study? Explain.

8. If you had planned this study, would you have hypothesized that there would be no significant difference? Explain. (See lines 95–100.)

9. Do you agree with the researchers' statement that "…it is unclear whether differences in aggression were related to wearing personalized jerseys or to competition level."? (See lines 215–217.)

10. In your opinion, would a true experiment in which some women are randomly assigned to wear personalized jerseys while the remaining ones are not provide better information on this potential cause of aggression? Explain.

Quality Ratings

Directions: Indicate your level of agreement with each of the following statements by circling a number from 5 for strongly agree (SA) to 1 for strongly disagree (SD). If you believe an item is not applicable to this research article, leave it blank. Be prepared to explain your ratings. When responding to criteria A and B below, keep in mind that brief titles and abstracts are conventional in published research.

A. The title of the article is appropriate.

SA   5   4   3   2   1   SD

B. The abstract provides an effective overview of the research article.

SA   5   4   3   2   1   SD

C. The introduction establishes the importance of the study.

SA   5   4   3   2   1   SD

D. The literature review establishes the context for the study.

SA   5   4   3   2   1   SD

E. The research purpose, question, or hypothesis is clearly stated.

SA   5   4   3   2   1   SD

F. The method of sampling is sound.

SA   5   4   3   2   1   SD

G. Relevant demographics (for example, age, gender, and ethnicity) are described.

SA   5   4   3   2   1   SD

H. Measurement procedures are adequate.

SA   5   4   3   2   1   SD

I. All procedures have been described in sufficient detail to permit a replication of the study.

SA   5   4   3   2   1   SD

J. The participants have been adequately protected from potential harm.

SA   5   4   3   2   1   SD

K. The results are clearly described.

SA   5   4   3   2   1   SD

L. The discussion/conclusion is appropriate.

SA   5   4   3   2   1   SD

M. Despite any flaws, the report is worthy of publication.

SA   5   4   3   2   1   SD

Article 19

Significance of Gender and Age in African American Children's Response to Parental Victimization

CATHERINE N. DULMUS
University at Buffalo

CAROLYN HILARSKI
Buffalo State College

ABSTRACT. This study examined gender and age differences in children's psychological response to parental victimization in a convenience sample of African American children. Thirty youths, ages 6 to 12, whose parents had been victims of community violence (i.e., gunshot or stabbing), and a control group of 30 children matched on variables of race, age, gender, and neighborhood served as the sample for this study. Parents completed a demographics sheet and the Child Behavior Checklist (CBCL). Data were collected within six weeks of parental victimization. No significant difference was found in male and female youths' internalizing and externalizing behavior at ages 6 to 8. However, beginning at age 9 there was a significant difference in behavior. Youths exposed to parental victimization internalized and externalized to a greater degree than those children who were not exposed. Males externalized more than females, and females internalized more than males. Thus, the perceived trauma response may vary as a function of the child's gender and developmental level or age. These findings suggest that gender-specific response related to trauma exposure may begin as early as age 9.

From *Health & Social Work, 31*, 181–188. Copyright © 2006 by National Association of Social Workers. Reprinted with permission.

The United States is a violent country (Trickett & Schellenbach, 1998), and our children's exposure to this violence is a national public health issue (Glodich, 1998). Violence exposure, as either a witness or victim,
5 is rampant among inner-city youths (Hien & Bukszpan, 1999). Although violence has decreased in recent years, youths in poor urban areas continue to be disproportionately exposed (Gorman-Smith & Tolan, 1998; Gorman-Smith, Tolan, & Henry, 1999). Children
10 exposed to violence (either directly or indirectly) are vulnerable to serious long-term consequences, such as posttraumatic stress (Kilpatrick & Williams, 1997; McCloskey & Walker, 2000), delinquency (Farrell & Bruce, 1997; Gorman-Smith & Tolan, 1998; Miller,
15 Wasserman, Neugebauer, Gorman-Smith, & Kamboukos, 1999), depression (Gorman-Smith et al., 1999;

Kliewer, Lepore, Oskin, & Johnson, 1998), and impaired attention (Ford, Racusin, Ellis, & Daviss, 2000).

Trauma and posttrauma reactions have far-reaching
20 effects beyond the individual victim. Trauma can touch the victim's entire system (e.g., partner, professional helper, family members, and friends) (Figley, 1995a). In fact, the greater the degree of crisis (i.e., type of trauma event and length of stress reaction), the greater
25 the system stress (Peebles-Kleiger & Kleiger, 1994). Concern must be extended beyond the direct victims of violence to include those indirectly affected. Indirect victims include those children who have heard about violence occurring to members of their immediate and
30 extended family or acquaintances. Indirect victims are also those children who fear for their safety and that of their family and friends (Figley, 1995b).

Simply being in the presence of violence is harmful to children (Osofsky, 1995). Safety is an important
35 concept in childhood (Cicchetti & Aber, 1998). Learning to trust others, exploring the environment, developing confidence in oneself, and expanding social contacts outside of the family are important childhood challenges (Cicchetti & Aber, 1998; Dahlberg & Pot-
40 ter, 2001). In a predictable, safe, and secure environment, children are more likely to explore their surroundings to learn about themselves, their relationships with others, and the world (Cicchetti & Aber, 1998; Garbarino, 1995a). Violence exposure undermines feel-
45 ings of safety and restricts the range of experiences necessary for healthy development (Calvert, 1999).

Exposure to community violence affects children of all ages (Berman, Kurtines, Silverman, & Serafini, 1996; Ensink, Robertson, Zissis, & Leger, 1997;
50 Glodich & Allen, 1998; Gorman-Smith & Tolan, 1998). The response to a perceived violent event may actually overwhelm very young children. For example, they may become obsessed with the details of the event. They may reenact violent themes in play and
55 unconsciously in dreams (Eth, 2001). Younger children are also more likely to engage in bedwetting, thumb sucking, somatic complaints, social withdrawal, and high anxiety during caregiver separation (Eth, 2000).

School-age children exposed to violence display externalizing and internalizing behaviors and show declines in concentration, school performance, and overall functioning (Eth, 2001; Garbarino, 1993; Osofsky, 1999). These children have difficulty regulating their emotions, showing empathy, and integrating cognitions (Cicchetti & Rogosch, 1997). Such behaviors can interfere with the developmental challenges of adapting to the school environment and establishing positive peer relations. For example, traumatized children are often hypervigilant of their environment as a protective mechanism against additional traumatic events. This behavior can lead to environmental misinterpretations of hostile intent by others, thus, interfering with constructive social interactions (Dodge, Lochman, Harnish, Bates, & Pettit, 1997).

The effects of exposure to violence may differ from child to child. Following a similar exposure, children who internalize behave differently from those who externalize (Keane & Kaloupek, 1997; Keane, Taylor, & Penk, 1997). Moreover, there is an indication that gender influences traumatic response (Berton & Stabb, 1996; Miller et al., 1999; Singer, Anglin, Song, & Lunghofer, 1995). A study that examined the rates of depression and anxiety among bereaved children found that boys reported fewer depressive symptoms than girls did up to 18 months after the death of a parent (Raveis, Siegel, & Karus, 1999). Leadbeater, Kuperminc, Blatt, and Hertzog (1999) reported gender differences in the internalizing and externalizing of problems relative to stressful life events: Boys were at risk of externalizing their problems, and girls tended to internalize (Dulmus, Ely, & Wodarski, 2003). This study examined the effects of age and gender independently and conjointly on reactions to trauma.

Theoretical Model

The adverse effects of trauma on people other than the direct victim have been observed and documented (Terr, 1979, 1981). The actual manner of symptom transfer is not definitively established by empirical research. However, one explanation for externalizing behavior trauma response is the social interactional model of development in which children come to view what they are exposed to as normative and model these behaviors (Lorion & Saltzman, 1993). The cognitive processing theory attempts to explain internalizing response to trauma, suggesting that making sense of community violence can be distressing as it may conflict with the child's beliefs that home and neighborhood are safe (Finkelhor, 1997; Garbarino, 1995a; Marans & Adelman, 1997). The idea that the environment is not safe can challenge the child's basic need to trust and be part of a secure attachment, which is a fundamental developmental process for future health (Cicchetti & Rogosch, 1997; Pynoos et al., 1993). The struggle to cognitively assimilate violent events may lead to unwanted and uncontrolled thoughts resulting in anxiety and depressive symptomatology (Cicchetti & Toth, 1998). Violation of essential developmental processes can lead to internal dissonance and defensive behavioral and cognitive responses that are reminiscent of posttraumatic symptoms (Pynoos et al., 1993; Pynoos, Nader, Frederick, Gonda, & Stuber, 1987). Clinical observations and developmental research indicate that children's distress responses to trauma may manifest as a range of impaired symptomatology (Garbarino, 1995b).

From a developmental perspective, age-relevant achievements in cognition, social relationships, and emotional development provide children with specific vulnerabilities and unique strengths to interpret traumatic events and master violence-related stress and arousal (Apfel, 1996). Internal and external factors, therefore, interact to establish resiliency or risk. Trauma exposure may lead to traumatization or distress when fear, anger, or stress overwhelms the child's internal attributes and protective mechanisms (Finkelhor & Asdigian, 1996). A particular concern is that traumatic stress reactions may prevent young children from resolving stage-salient developmental challenges, which may then present as psychopathology (Cicchetti & Toth, 1998).

In sum, the primary victims of violence are not the only sufferers. Having a personal relationship with someone who has been a victim of violence can have long-term negative consequences. An understanding of the developmental circumstance (i.e., age) and gender-related response of children residing in a family where a parent has been victimized is vital to prevention and treatment efforts. Only by understanding the developmental effects of such exposure can we advance our remedial efforts.

Current Study

Internal Review Board (IRB) approval was obtained from the State University of New York at Buffalo before study implementation. Initial analysis of the data set used in this study reported that children in the exposure group were experiencing symptoms in the borderline clinical range (total score of 67–70) as indicated by scores on the Child Behavior Checklist (CBCL) (Achenbach, 1991), and children in the control group fell below this range (Dulmus & Wodarski, 2000). Direct and indirect exposure to community violence can negatively affect children (Dulmus & Wodarski, 2000), often resulting in children showing their distress by engaging in internalizing or externalizing behavior. However, research is unclear regarding the age-related influences of the trauma response, as only a few studies have examined the link between community violence exposure and negative outcomes in children younger than age 10. One study suggested that younger children engage in internalizing behavior more than older children (Schwab-Stone et al., 1999). Fitzpatrick and Boldizar (1993) suggested that younger

97

children indirectly exposed to violence are less likely to engage in internalizing behavior. Hence, there is no real understanding of how age may influence community violence exposure for young children.

175 Another factor that requires consideration is gender. Research has suggested that gender influences the behavioral outcome of violence exposure (Schwab-Stone et al., 1999; Song, Singer, & Anglin, 1998). Our research question thus was: Do children behaviorally
180 respond to perceived trauma differently according to age and gender?

Method

Sample and Procedures

A convenience sample of 30 children (exposure group), ages 6 to 12 years, whose parents had been admitted to Erie County Medical Center (ECMC)
185 trauma unit (December 1997 through May 1998) in Buffalo, New York, for treatment of injuries sustained as a result of community violence, were recruited for this study. The principal investigator daily reviewed the surgery list for those individuals who had surgery
190 because of a gunshot or stabbing wound. Such individuals were then approached to determine whether injuries had been sustained as a result of community violence. If so, they were asked whether they had a child between the ages of 6 and 12 who could partici-
195 pate in this study. One hundred percent of parents approached who met the criteria for the study and who had a child between the ages of 6 and 12 provided contact information on how to access their child's primary caregiver for study recruitment purposes. All primary
200 caregivers contacted agreed to allow themselves and their child to participate in this study. Mothers, who were the dominant primary caregivers in the exposure group, offered names of other parents in their neighborhood with a child of the same gender, race, and age as
205 their own child, but who had not had a parent who was a victim of community violence, to compose the control group. An exposure group (*n* = 30) and control group (*n* = 30) were matched on age, race, gender, and neighborhood. The sample size was adequate for a
210 large effect size, a .80 level of power, and an alpha of .05 (Cohen, 1992). Inclusion criteria for the exposure group were: (1) The child participant had to be the biological child of the victimized person admitted to the Buffalo trauma unit; (2) The victimized person had to
215 be a victim of community violence (thus, victims of domestic violence and self-inflicted wounds were excluded); (3) The victimized person had to be admitted to a medical floor for at least one night; (4) The child was not a witness to the parent's victimization; (5) The
220 child was not receiving mental health services; (6) The child had no documented history of mental retardation; and (7) Only one child per family could participate.

The exposure and control groups' female caregivers voluntarily provided, through interview and self-
225 administered instruments, demographic and behavioral descriptions of their child during a one-hour appointment with the principal investigator two to eight weeks following the parent's hospitalization. Confidentiality was discussed and ensured. Each parent received $20,
230 and each child $5, in addition to transportation, if needed.

Measures

A form was developed requesting social and demographic data. In addition, the parent with whom the child resided completed the CBCL. The CBCL can be
235 self-administered or administered by an interviewer and is designed to record in standardized format children's (ages 4 to 18) competencies and problems as reported by their parents or caregiver. The 118-item checklist allows parents to evaluate the behavior of
240 their children and provides a total score, as well as scores for internalizing and externalizing behaviors. It asks questions regarding a wide variety of symptoms and behaviors that children may have experienced in the past six months and asks parents to respond to each
245 question with three possible answers: "not true," "somewhat true or sometimes true," or "very or often true." The CBCL is widely used and accepted with good reliability (r = .87) and validity (Achenbach, 1991).

Results

Sample Characteristics

250 All children were African American, with 47% being females, and a mean age of nine years. Half of the sample was age 6 through 8. One child lived with an aunt, and the remaining children lived with their mother. The mean number of siblings in the home was
255 three, and the mean family gross income per month was $985. More than three-quarters of the victimized parents were men. Of those, 77% were shot and 23% had been stabbed. The average hospital stay was nine days, with a range of one to 24 nights. More than half
260 of the youths had visited their parent in the hospital. Sixty-one percent of the youths were in daily contact with their parent before the victimizing event. The remaining youths had a minimum of monthly contact.

Statistical Analysis of CBCL Internalizing and Externalizing Scores

Internalizing Scores. A 2 (gender: male and female)
265 × 2 (group: control or exposure) × 2 (agecode: 1 = 6 to 8 years, and 2 = 9 to 12 years) analysis of variance (ANOVA) was conducted on internalizing CBCL scores. There was a significant main effect for group, $F(1,52)$ = 9.27, p = .004 and agecode, $F(1,52)$ = 5.6, p =
270 .022. The control group had lower internalizing CBCL scores (M = 9.24, SE = 1.17) than the exposure group (M = 14.24, SE = 1.16). The youths age 9 to 12 had higher internalizing CBCL scores (M = 13.68, SE = 1.16) than the 6- to 8-year-olds (M = 9.8, SE = 1.16).

275 *Externalizing Scores.* A 2 (gender: male and female) × 2 (group: control or exposure) × 2 (agecode)

ANOVA was conducted on externalizing CBCL scores. There was a significant main effect for group, $F(1,52) = 12.73$, $p = .001$ and gender, $F(1,52) = 12.75$, $p = .001$. The control group had lower externalizing CBCL scores ($M = 6.27$, $SE = 1.31$) than the exposure group ($M = 12.86$, $SE = 1.30$). Males had higher externalizing CBCL scores ($M = 12.87$, $SE = 1.31$) than females ($M = 6.27$, $SE = 1.31$).

Younger Age Group. Male and female youths ages 6 to 8 years in the exposure group did not differ on their internalizing $t(13) = 1.550$, $p = .145$ and externalizing $t(13) = -0.186$, $p = .855$ CBCL scores according to independent t tests. Similarly, the independent t test was not significant for those 6- to 8-year-old male and female youths not exposed to parental victimization on internalizing $t(13) = .856$, $p = .408$ and externalizing $t(13) = 1.12$, $p = .284$ CBCL scores (see Table 1).

Older Age Group. The independent t test was significant for males and females ages 9 to 12 years in the exposure group on externalizing $t(13) = -2.57$, $p = .023$ and internalizing $t(13) = 5.09$, $p = .000$ CBCL scores. Youths ages 9 to 12 years in the control group showed no difference between male and female internalizing $t(13) = -.688$, $p = .503$ and externalizing $t(13) = .012$, $p = .990$ scores (see Table 1).

Table 1
Mean CBCL Internalizing and Externalizing Scores for Control and Exposure Groups, by Age and Gender

	6–8 year olds' internal/external mean scores	9–12 year olds' internal/external mean scores
Control		
Male	8.25/5.75	10.50/7.83
Female	6.00/3.71	12.22/7.78
Exposure		
Male	12.13/14.88	11.13/23.00
Female	12.86/8.00	20.86/5.57

Note. CBCL = Child Behavior Checklist

Discussion and Implications for Practice

Initial analysis of these data reported that children in the exposure group were experiencing symptoms in the borderline clinical range, and children in the control group fell below this range (Dulmus & Wodarski, 2000). The current analysis reports additional supportive findings in regard to gender and age-specific differences. No significant difference in male and female youths' internalizing and externalizing behavior at ages 6 to 8 in either the control or the exposure groups was found. In other words, male and female youths in early childhood engage in both internalizing and externalizing behavior. However, youths exposed to parental victimization internalized and externalized to a greater degree, according to caregiver report, than those children who were not exposed. At age 9, there was a significant difference in behavior. In the exposure group, males externalized more than females, and females internalized more than males. In the control group,

there was no significant difference in the internalizing and externalizing behavior of the male and female youths. Thus, the perceived trauma response may vary as a function of the child's gender and developmental level or age.

Research is beginning to suggest that internalizing and externalizing behavior is reciprocal (Hodges & Perry, 1999). For example, youths who engage in externalizing behaviors tend to be socially rejected, which can lead to internalizing behaviors (e.g., withdrawal). Conversely, youths who internalize can be perceived by parents and teachers as passive aggressive and noncooperative (e.g., externalizing) (Shaw et al., 1998). This internalizing and externalizing behavior is the child's defensive coping and is influenced by gender (Carter & Levy, 1991; Dubowitz et al., 2001). Indeed, females can be more reflective or passive, and males more antagonistic (Cramer, 1979; Erikson, 1964; Freud, 1933; Levit, 1991). Support for this premise was found in this study as well. However, the significance here is that both males and females internalize similarly in response to trauma according to age. This is pertinent information regarding assessment of an externalizing male. He may be externalizing because of internalizing a trauma exposure.

Young children respond to trauma by attempting to explain it. The cognitive level or age of the child influences the explanation. For example, a child in the pre-operational stage of cognitive development (two to seven years) (Piaget, 1973) is said to view the world egocentrically. Thus, the self is at the root of the explanation for the trauma event. A child in the concrete operations stage of cognitive development (7 to 11 years) is able to produce several explanations for the trauma event, such as blaming others, the self, or both. These distorted or dysfunctional schemas are born from stages of development not equipped to integrate traumatic circumstances. Moreover, the beliefs and attitudes formed during these stages are relatively stable and are the foundations for internalizing and externalizing behavior (Finkelhor, 1995), depending on gender (Levit, 1991). The traumagenic dynamic cites powerlessness as the fundamental dysfunctional cognition stemming from a trauma exposure (Finkelhor, 1997). Helplessness is a core belief for such disorders as anxiety, the need for control, and identification of self as either aggressor or victim, and is linked to depressive and aggressive behavior (Finkelhor, 1997).

Such knowledge has implications for practice as gender-specific assessment and intervention approaches must be used at younger ages than previously presumed. Moreover, feeling unsafe because of trauma exposure can lead to cognitive perceptions of chronic threat and feelings of powerlessness, which is associated with symptoms of psychological distress and maladaptive means of coping, including internalizing or externalizing behavior depending on gender. Failure to identify and intervene with children exposed to vio-

380 lence may result in a lifetime of social, emotional, and vocational difficulties. There is now a beginning understanding that gender and age are important influencing variables regarding a youth's behavioral response to trauma.

Limitations

This descriptive study of CBCL scores in a group of children recently exposed to parental trauma versus 385 a similar group of children not recently exposed to parental trauma had a number of limitations. First, the design lacked random assignment and the small sample limits the findings. Second, all participants in the study lived in the same area, which increased the risk of con- 390 founding variables and decreased generalizability. Third, all findings were based on self-reported data from primary caregivers (mothers); it is therefore possible that certain events and experiences were overestimated, underestimated, or otherwise distorted through 395 recall or gender influences. Also, the study did not take into account the amount of contact the child had with the parent before the victimization, which may have affected study results. Another limitation is that the sociodemographics of the sample limit the generalizability 400 bility of the findings because all children in this sample were African American. Finally, there is no historical information regarding the child's primary trauma exposure.

Future Research

Additional research needs to be conducted in other 405 locales, with a larger sample size, greater age range, and other racial backgrounds for results to be more conclusive. Studies need to be developed to examine the long-term effects of this type of perceived trauma and children. Although this study did control for the 410 specific trauma of parental victimization, future research may want to focus on children's responses in relation to the gender of the parent who is victimized, as well as the type of the parents' victimizations (i.e., beating, gunshot, stabbing) and circumstances sur- 415 rounding the incidents as to the impact on children. Last, the development of empirically based gender-sensitive assessment instruments and interventions that respond to individual gender differences in the expression of symptoms related to trauma are essential (Feir- 420 ing, Taska, & Lewis, 1999).

References

Achenbach, T. M. (1991). *Manual for the Child Behavior Checklist/4–18 and 1991*. Burlington: University of Vermont.

Apfel, R. J. (1996). "With a little help from my friends I get by": Self-help books and psychotherapy [Essay review]. *Psychiatry, 59*, 309–322.

Berman, S. L., Kurtines, W. M., Silverman, W. K., & Serafini, L. T. (1996). The impact of exposure to crime and violence on urban youth. *American Journal of Orthopsychiatry, 66*, 329–336.

Berton, M. W., & Stabb, S. D. (1996). Exposure to violence and post-traumatic stress disorder in urban adolescents. *Adolescence, 31*, 489–498.

Calvert, W. J. (1999). Integrated literature review on effects of exposure to violence upon adolescents. *ABNF Journal, 10*, 84–96.

Carter, D. B., & Levy, G. D. (1991). Gender schemas and the salience of gender: Individual differences in nonreversal discrimination learning. *Sex Roles, 25*, 555–567.

Cicchetti, D., & Aber, J. L. (1998). Contextualism and developmental psychopathology [Editorial]. *Development and Psychopathology, 10*, 137–141.

Cicchetti, D., & Rogosch, F. A. (1997). The role of self-organization in the promotion of resilience in maltreated children. *Development and Psychopathology, 9*, 797–815.

Cicchetti, D., & Toth, S. L. (1998). The development of depression in children and adolescents. *American Psychologist, 53*, 221–241.

Cohen, J. (1992). A power primer. *Psychological Bulletin, 112*, 155–159.

Cramer, P. (1979). Defense mechanisms in adolescence. *Developmental Psychology, 15*, 477–478.

Dahlberg, L. L., & Potter, L. B. (2001). Youth violence: Developmental pathways and prevention challenges. *American Journal of Preventive Medicine, 20* (Suppl. 1), 3–14.

Dodge, K. A., Lochman, J. E., Harnish, J. D., Bates, J. E., & Pettit, G. S. (1997). Reactive and proactive aggression in school children and psychiatrically impaired chronically assaultive youth. *Journal of Abnormal Psychology, 106*, 37–51.

Dubowitz, H., Black, M. M., Kerr, M. A., Hussey, J. M., Morrel, T. M., Everson, M. D., & Starr, R. H., Jr. (2001). Type and timing of mothers' victimization: Effects on mothers and children. *Pediatrics, 107*, 728–735.

Dulmus, C. N., Ely, G. E., & Wodarski, J. S. (2003). Children's psychological response to parental victimization: How do girls and boys differ? *Journal of Human Behavior in the Social Environment, 7*, 23–36.

Dulmus, C. N., & Wodarski, J. S. (2000). Trauma-related symptomatology among children of parents victimized by urban community violence. *American Journal of Orthopsychiatry, 70*, 272–277.

Ensink, K., Robertson, B. A., Zissis, C., & Leger, P. (1997). Post-traumatic stress disorder in children exposed to violence. *South African Medical Journal, 87*, 1526–1530.

Erikson, E. (Ed.). (1964). *Inner and outer space: Reflections on womanhood*. Boston: Beacon Press.

Eth, S. (2001). *PTSD in children and adolescents: A developmental-interactional model of child abuse*. Washington, DC: American Psychiatric Association.

Farrell, A. D., & Bruce, S. E. (1997). Impact of exposure to community violence on violent behavior and emotional distress among urban adolescents. *Journal of Clinical Child Psychology, 26*, 2–14.

Feiring, C., Taska, L., & Lewis, M. (1999). Age and gender differences in children's and adolescents' adaptation to sexual abuse. *Child Abuse & Neglect, 23*, 115–128.

Figley, C. R. (1995a). Compassion fatigue as secondary traumatic stress disorder: An overview. In R. E. Charles (Ed.), *Compassion fatigue: Coping with secondary traumatic stress disorder in those who treat the traumatized* (pp. 1–20). New York: Brunner/Mazel.

Figley, C. R. (Ed.). (1995b). *Compassion fatigue: Coping with secondary traumatic stress disorder in those who treat the traumatized*. New York: Brunner/Mazel.

Finkelhor, D. (1995). The victimization of children: A developmental perspective. *America Journal of Orthopsychiatry, 65*, 177–193.

Finkelhor, D. (Ed.). (1997). *The victimization of children and youth: Developmental victimology* (Vol. 2). Thousand Oaks, CA: Sage Publications.

Finkelhor, D., & Asdigian, N. L. (1996). Risk factors for youth victimization: Beyond a lifestyles/routine activities theory approach. *Violence Victims, 11*, 3–19.

Fitzpatrick, K. M., & Boldizar, J. P. (1993). The prevalence and consequences of exposure to violence among African-American youth. *Journal of the American Academy of Child & Adolescent Psychiatry, 32*, 424–430.

Ford, J. D., Racusin, R., Ellis, C. G., & Daviss, W. B. (2000). Child maltreatment, other trauma exposure, and posttraumatic symptomatology among children with oppositional defiant and attention deficit hyperactivity disorders. *Child Maltreatment, 5*, 205–217.

Freud, S. (1933). *The psychology of women* (J. Strachey, Trans. Vol. 22). London: Hogarth Press.

Garbarino, J. (1993). Children's response to community violence: What do we know? Irving Harris Symposium on Prevention and Intervention: The effects of violence on infants and young children: International perspectives on prevention (1992, Chicago, Illinois). *Infant Mental Health Journal, 14*, 103–115.

Garbarino, J. (1995a). The American war zone: What children can tell us about living with violence. *Journal of Developmental & Behavioral Pediatrics, 16*, 431–435.

Garbarino, J. (1995b). Growing up in a socially toxic environment: Life for children and families in the 1990s. In B. M. Gary (Ed.), *The individual, the family, and social good: Personal fulfillment in times of change. Nebraska Symposium on Motivation, Vol. 42* (pp. 1–20). Lincoln: University of Nebraska Press.

Glodich, A. (1998). Traumatic exposure to violence: A comprehensive review of the child and adolescent literature. *Smith College Studies in Social Work, 68*, 321–345.

Glodich, A., & Allen, J. G. (1998). Adolescents exposed to violence and abuse: A review of the group therapy literature with an emphasis on preventing trauma reenactment. *Journal of Child & Adolescent Group Therapy, 8*, 135–154.

Gorman-Smith, D., & Tolan, P. (1998). The role of exposure to community violence and development problems among inner-city youth. *Development and Psychopathology, 10*, 101–116.

Gorman-Smith, D., Tolan, P. H., & Henry, D. (1999). The relation of community and family to risk among urban-poor adolescents. In P. Cohen, L. Robins, & C. Slomkowski (Eds.), *Where and when: Influence of historical time and place on aspects of psychopathology* (pp. 349–367). Hillsdale, NJ: Lawrence Erlbaum Associates.

Hien, D., & Bukszpan, C. (1999). Interpersonal violence in a "normal" low-income control group. *Women & Health, 29*, 1–16.

Hodges, E. V., & Perry, D. G. (1999). Personal and interpersonal antecedents and consequences of victimization by peers. *Journal of Personality and Social Psychology, 76*, 677–685.

Keane, T. M., & Kaloupek, D. G. (1997). Comorbid psychiatric disorders in PTSD. Implications for research. *Annals of the New York Academy of Sciences, 821*, 24–34.

Keane, T. M., Taylor, K. L., & Penk, W. E. (1997). Differentiating post-traumatic stress disorder (PTSD) from major depression (MDD) and generalized anxiety disorder (GAD). *Journal of Anxiety Disorders, 11*, 317–328.

Kilpatrick, K. L., & Williams, L. M. (1997). Post-traumatic stress disorder in child witnesses to domestic violence. *American Journal of Orthopsychiatry, 67*, 639–644.

Kliewer, W., Lepore, S. J., Oskin, D., & Johnson, P. D. (1998). The role of social and cognitive processes in children's adjustment to community violence. *Journal of Consulting and Clinical Psychology, 66*, 199–209.

Leadbeater, B. J., Kuperminc, G. P., Blatt, S. J., & Hertzog, C. (1999). A multivariate model of gender differences in adolescents' internalizing and externalizing problems. *Developmental Psychology, 35*, 1268–1282.

Levit, D. B. (1991). Gender differences in ego defenses in adolescence: Sex roles as one way to understand the differences. *Journal of Personality and Social Psychology, 61*, 992–999.

Lorion, R. P., & Saltzman, W. (1993). Children's exposure to community violence: Following a path from concern to research to action. *Psychiatry, 56*, 55–65.

Marans, S., & Adelman, A. (Eds.). (1997). *Experiencing violence in a developmental context.* New York: Guilford Press.

McCloskey, L. A., & Walker, M. (2000). Posttraumatic stress in children exposed to family violence and single-event trauma. *Journal of the American Academy of Child & Adolescent Psychiatry, 39*, 108–115.

Miller, L. S., Wasserman, G. A., Neugebauer, R., Gorman-Smith, D., & Kamboukos, D. (1999). Witnessed community violence and antisocial behavior in high-risk, urban boys. *Journal of Clinical Child Psychology, 28*, 2–11.

Osofsky, J. D. (1995). The effect of exposure to violence on young children. *American Psychologist, 50*, 782–788.

Osofsky, J. D. (1999). The impact of violence on children. *Future of Children, 9*, 33–49.

Peebles-Kleiger, M. J., & Kleiger, J. H. (1994). Reintegration stress for Desert Storm families: Wartime deployments and family trauma. *Journal of Traumatic Stress, 7*, 173–194.

Piaget, J. (1973). The affective unconscious and the cognitive unconscious. *Journal of the American Psychoanalytic Association, 21*, 249–261.

Pynoos, R. S., Goenjian, A., Tashjian, M., Karakashian, M., Manjikian, R., Manoukian, G., Steinberg, A. M., & Fairbanks, L. A. (1993). Post-traumatic stress reactions in children after the 1988 Armenian earthquake. *British Journal of Psychiatry, 163*, 239–247.

Pynoos, R. S., Nader, K., Frederick, C., Gonda, L., & Stuber, M. (1987). Grief reactions in school-age children following a sniper attack at school. *Israel Journal of Psychiatry and Related Sciences, 24*, 53–63.

Raveis, V. H., Siegel, K., & Karus, D. (1999). Children's psychological distress following the death of a parent. *Journal of Youth and Adolescence, 28*, 165–180.

Schwab-Stone, M., Chen, C., Greenberger, E., Silver, D., Lichtman, J., & Voyce, C. (1999). No safe haven II: The effects of violence exposure on urban youth. *Journal of the American Academy of Child & Adolescent Psychiatry, 38*, 359–367.

Shaw, D. S., Winslow, E. B., Owens, E. B., Vondra, J. I., Cohn, J. F., & Bell, R. Q. (1998). The development of early externalizing problems among children from low-income families: A transformational perspective. *Journal of Abnormal Child Psychology, 26*, 95–107.

Singer, M. I., Anglin, T. M., Song, L. Y., & Lunghofer, L. (1995). Adolescents' exposure to violence and associated symptoms of psychological trauma. *JAMA, 273*, 477–482.

Song, L. Y., Singer, M. I., & Anglin, T. M. (1998). Violence exposure and emotional trauma as contributors to adolescents' violent behaviors. *Archive of Pediatric & Adolescent Medicine, 152*, 531–536.

Terr, L. C. (1979). Children of Chowchilla: A study of psychic trauma. *Psychoanalytical Study of Children, 34*, 547–623.

Terr, L. C. (1981). Psychic trauma in children: Observations following the Chowchilla school-bus kidnapping. *American Journal of Psychiatry, 138*, 14–19.

Trickett, P. K., & Schellenbach, C. J. (1998). *Violence against children in the family and the community.* Washington, DC: American Psychological Association.

About the authors: *Catherine N. Dulmus*, Ph.D., LCSW, ACSW, is associate professor and director, Buffalo Center for Social Research, University at Buffalo, 221 Parker Hall, Buffalo, NY 14214 (E-mail: cdulmus@buffalo.edu). *Carolyn Hilarski*, Ph.D., LCSW, ACSW, is associate professor, Social Work Department, Buffalo State College, New York.

Exercise for Article 19

Factual Questions

1. What is the explicitly stated research question?

2. What percentage of the parents approached who met the criteria provided contact information?

3. Who offered names of children who might serve in the control group?

4. Did the children in the exposure group witness the parents' victimization?

5. Were all the children in daily contact with their parents before the victimizing event?

6. Did the "9- to 12-year olds" *or* the "6- to 8-year olds" have higher internalizing scores on the CBCL?

Questions for Discussion

7. Is it important to know that review board approval to conduct this research was obtained? Explain. (See lines 150–152.)

8. The researchers state that they used a "convenience sample." Is it important to know this? Explain. (See lines 182–195.)

9. What is your opinion on the advisability of paying individuals for participation in research? (See lines 229–231.)

10. In your opinion, do the researchers make the meanings of the terms "internalizing" and "externalizing" behavior clear? (See lines 238–241 and 264–284.)

11. In your opinion, does the use of a control group make this study an "experiment"? Explain.

12. The researchers state this limitation: "…the study did not take into account the amount of contact the child had with the parent before the victimization, which may have affected study results." How important is this limitation? (See lines 395–398.)

Quality Ratings

Directions: Indicate your level of agreement with each of the following statements by circling a number from 5 for strongly agree (SA) to 1 for strongly disagree (SD). If you believe an item is not applicable to this research article, leave it blank. Be prepared to explain your ratings. When responding to criteria A and B below, keep in mind that brief titles and abstracts are conventional in published research.

A.   The title of the article is appropriate.

   SA   5   4   3   2   1   SD

B.   The abstract provides an effective overview of the research article.

   SA   5   4   3   2   1   SD

C.   The introduction establishes the importance of the study.

   SA   5   4   3   2   1   SD

D.   The literature review establishes the context for the study.

   SA   5   4   3   2   1   SD

E.   The research purpose, question, or hypothesis is clearly stated.

   SA   5   4   3   2   1   SD

F.   The method of sampling is sound.

   SA   5   4   3   2   1   SD

G.   Relevant demographics (for example, age, gender, and ethnicity) are described.

   SA   5   4   3   2   1   SD

H.   Measurement procedures are adequate.

   SA   5   4   3   2   1   SD

I.   All procedures have been described in sufficient detail to permit a replication of the study.

   SA   5   4   3   2   1   SD

J.   The participants have been adequately protected from potential harm.

   SA   5   4   3   2   1   SD

K.   The results are clearly described.

   SA   5   4   3   2   1   SD

L.   The discussion/conclusion is appropriate.

   SA   5   4   3   2   1   SD

M.   Despite any flaws, the report is worthy of publication.

   SA   5   4   3   2   1   SD

Article 20

Age Effects in Earwitness Recall
of a Novel Conversation

JONATHAN LING
University of Teesside, UK

ALLISON COOMBE
University of Teesside, UK

ABSTRACT. Recall of conversation is an important part of memory for events. Previous studies have focused predominantly on adults. In the present study, 195 participants ages 11 to 63 years listened to a novel audiotaped conversation. They were not informed they would later have to recall elements of this conversation. Recall was a week later. There were no age-related differences in the recall of children ages 11, 13, and 15; however, there was a difference between retention over 7 days of children and adults, with adults recalling more information correctly. No sex differences were observed. These results are evaluated in the context of research on eye and earwitness recall and suggestions for research are given.

From *Perceptual and Motor Skills, 100,* 774–776. Copyright © 2005 by Perceptual and Motor Skills. Reprinted with permission.

Most investigations of earwitness testimony have focused on identification (Roebuck & Wilding, 1993) rather than recall, although recall of conversation does appear to be a particularly poor aspect of memory
5 (Huss & Weaver, 1996). Researchers have yet to clarify whether there is a relationship between age and earwitness performance, as there may be confounds with other variables like knowledge (Chi, 1983). In a study of children ages 8, 11, and 15 yr., Saywitz (1987)
10 found few differences between 11- and 15-year-olds, which may be indicative of a plateau in auditory recall from mid to late childhood. It is unclear whether this plateau persists into adulthood.

The aim of this investigation was to compare the
15 recall of children and adults for a conversation heard as bystanders. No direct comparison has been made, so it is unclear how or whether earwitness recall changes across age groups. To control for knowledge, we presented information to participants about which they
20 would have little knowledge, daily life in rural Angola.

Method

Participants
A sample of 195 participants, including 95 females, was recruited. There were 93 children ages 11–16 years. Thirty-five were ages 11–12 ($M = 11.5$), 32 ages from 13–14 ($M = 13.4$), and 26 ages from 15–16 ($M =$
25 15.6). There were 98 adults ages 20–63 years. Adults were divided into four age groups: 20–29 yr. (45 participants; $M = 23.6$), 30–39 yr. (18 participants; $M = 34.5$), 40–49 (17 participants; $M = 44.7$), and 50–59 (18 participants; $M = 54.8$). Children came from one
30 school; adults were recruited from social clubs.

Materials
A 12-min. audiotape of a conversation between two females was produced. This contained information about one female's experiences in Angola, including information about the weather, the guerilla war, and
35 everyday life in the country.

Recall was assessed by questionnaire, which was checked by teachers from the participating school to ensure comprehension. The questionnaire had 17 questions that related to characteristics of Angola (e.g.,
40 "What was a katanger?").

Procedure
Children listened to the tape in class; adults listened in quiet areas of the clubs. Participants were not informed they had to recall the conversation; as a cover, adults rated the age-appropriateness of the conversa-
45 tion. A week later, they were read a set of instructions before completion of a questionnaire. There was no time limit. Participants were thanked and fully debriefed.

Results and Discussion

No age group had a high mean, and no group
50 scored higher than 10 out of a maximum of 17. Analysis of variance ($F_{6,190} = 47.01$, $p < .001$) indicated an age effect. Post hoc tests indicated that children of all ages differed from all age groups of adults (Tukey HSD, all $p < .01$), with children performing more
55 poorly (see Table 1).

There was no sex difference ($F_{1,190} = .330$, $p > .05$) or interaction between sex and age ($F_{6,190} = .665$, $p > .05$).

Overall, recall of conversation after a 1-wk. delay
60 was poor, with no group exceeding 60% correct. Although recall was generally inaccurate, adults showed no age group differences in performance, unlike those in recognition observed by Bull and Clifford (1984). The findings that children did not show good recall for
65 the content of the conversation and the absence of age

103

Table 1
Mean Proportion Correct and Raw Scores

Age (yr.)	n	Proportion correct	M	SD
11	35	.23	3.94	2.22
13	32	.24	4.00	2.22
15	26	.22	3.68	1.74
20–29	45	.51	8.69	2.05
30–39	18	.55	9.39	1.65
40–49	17	.51	8.59	1.87
50+	18	.53	9.06	2.04
Overall	191	.38	6.39	3.20

differences in recall by children of different ages replicate those of other researchers. Such results indicate children and adults appear to have particular difficulty in remembering conversations.

70   This study highlights that children's recall of conversation may be less reliable than adults', at least when recall occurs some time after the event. However, the reported age differences may be related to the way children were questioned—with a questionnaire—

75   unlike the more supportive methods employed by police and social workers. Although other research using interviews has also shown that children do not have good recall for conversations (Saywitz, 1987), researchers should explore whether such supportive

80   methods may reduce age differences.

References

Bull, R., & Clifford, B. R. (1984). Earwitness testimony. *Medicine, Science, and the Law, 39*, 120–127.

Chi, M. T. H. (Ed.) (1983). *Trends in memory development*. Basel: Karger.

Huss, M. T., & Weaver, K. A. (1996). Effect of modality in earwitness identification: Memory for verbal and nonverbal auditory stimuli presented in two contexts. *The Journal of General Psychology, 123*, 277–287.

Roebuck, R., & Wilding, J. (1993). Effects of vowel variety and sample length on identification of a speaker in a line-up. *Applied Cognitive Psychology, 7*, 475–481.

Saywitz, K. J. (1987). Children's testimony: Age-related patterns of memory errors. In S. J. Ceci, M. P. Toglia, & D. F. Ross (Eds.), *Children's eyewitness memory*. New York: Springer-Verlag. Pp. 36–52.

Address correspondence to: Dr. Jonathan Ling, School of Psychology, Keele University, Keele, Staffs ST5 5BG, UK. E-mail: j.r.ling@psy.keele.ac.uk

Exercise for Article 20

Factual Questions

1. The children who participated came from how many schools?

2. The adults were recruited from what?

3. Was the analysis of variance for the age effect statistically significant? Explain.

4. Was there a statistically significant sex difference? Explain.

5. Did the researchers regard the recall of the conversation after one week to be "good"?

6. Table 1 shows the proportion correct for various age groups. Proportions can be converted to percentages by multiplying by 100. What is the correct *percentage* for the 11-year-old group?

Questions for Discussion

7. The researchers state that to control for knowledge, they presented information to participants about which they would have little knowledge. In your opinion, is this important? Explain. (See lines 18–20.)

8. The questionnaire was checked by teachers to ensure comprehension. Was this a good idea? Explain. (See lines 36–38.)

9. The conversation used in this study concerned daily life in rural Angola. In your opinion, might a conversation on a different topic produce differences in recall? Explain. (See lines 18–20.)

10. Do you think that this study shows that increasing age is related to increased earwitness recall? Explain. (See lines 70–72.)

11. Do you agree with the researchers that measuring recall with a questionnaire might produce different results than more supportive methods (e.g., individual interviews) used by police and social workers? (See lines 72–76.)

Quality Ratings

Directions: Indicate your level of agreement with each of the following statements by circling a number from 5 for strongly agree (SA) to 1 for strongly disagree (SD). If you believe an item is not applicable to this research article, leave it blank. Be prepared to explain your ratings. When responding to criteria A and B below, keep in mind that brief titles and abstracts are conventional in published research.

A.   The title of the article is appropriate.

SA   5   4   3   2   1   SD

B.   The abstract provides an effective overview of the research article.

SA   5   4   3   2   1   SD

C.   The introduction establishes the importance of the study.

SA   5   4   3   2   1   SD

D.   The literature review establishes the context for the study.

SA   5   4   3   2   1   SD

E.   The research purpose, question, or hypothesis is clearly stated.

SA   5   4   3   2   1   SD

F.   The method of sampling is sound.

SA   5   4   3   2   1   SD

G.   Relevant demographics (for example, age, gender, and ethnicity) are described.

SA   5   4   3   2   1   SD

H.   Measurement procedures are adequate.

SA   5   4   3   2   1   SD

I.   All procedures have been described in sufficient detail to permit a replication of the study.

SA   5   4   3   2   1   SD

J.   The participants have been adequately protected from potential harm.

SA   5   4   3   2   1   SD

K.   The results are clearly described.

SA   5   4   3   2   1   SD

L.   The discussion/conclusion is appropriate.

SA   5   4   3   2   1   SD

M.   Despite any flaws, the report is worthy of publication.

SA   5   4   3   2   1   SD

Article 21

Using the Internet to Facilitate Positive Attitudes of College Students Toward Aging and Working with Older Adults

FRIEDA R. BUTLER
George Mason University

HEIBATOLLAH BAGHI
George Mason University

ABSTRACT. Published data suggest that a preponderance of negative attitudes toward the elderly and insufficient knowledge of aging may be the primary reasons that geriatrics is not the primary choice of employment for nurses. This study measured attitude changes toward the elderly as a result of participation by nursing, gerontology and health science students in an intergenerational reciprocal service-learning program. Using a pre- and posttest design, results revealed a significant improvement ($p < .001$) for the total group, with undergraduates showing a significantly greater mean increase in positive attitudes toward the elderly ($p < .001$). This study suggests that pairing students with well elderly and engaging in ongoing exposure, meaningful intergenerational exchanges and using Internet-based activities to communicate are effective strategies to improve attitudes of students toward the elderly.

From *Journal of Intergenerational Relationships*, 6, 175–189. Copyright © 2008 by The Haworth Press. Reprinted with permission.

Selection of geriatrics as a career specialization is a low priority among nursing students and other students in the health professions in the United States (Fusner & Staib, 2004; Happell & Brooker, 2001; Kotzabassaki,
5 2002). Of the total registered nurse population employed in the United States, only 6.3% currently work in nursing homes or extended care facilities—down from 6.9% in 2000 (U.S. Department of Health and Human Services, 2004). With a growing workforce
10 shortage, this lack of geriatric education will have a profound impact on health care delivery to the older population, particularly with the aging of the baby boomers (Mion, 2003). According to Wells et al. (2004), improving gerontological education most likely
15 would increase positive attitudes of nursing students and practitioners toward aging and would help to lessen the nursing shortage in long-term care.

The purpose of this study was to measure students' attitude changes toward the elderly and toward working
20 with the elderly as a result of their participation in an intergenerational service-learning project over a three-month period. It was hypothesized that student partici-

pation in a reciprocal service learning project would facilitate more positive attitudes toward aging. Specific
25 objectives were to explore the effectiveness of the Internet as a means of engagement between seniors and student partners and determine the effects of journaling and class reflections on student attitude change.

Angeles (2000) defines service-learning as struc-
30 tured activities that blend community service with academic learning. This reciprocal intergenerational service learning project was developed to provide gerontological education to nursing and other students in the health disciplines, while at the same time, meeting
35 health education needs of the well elderly. Mintz and Goodwin (1999) indicated that redesigning the gerontology curriculum by integrating innovative service-learning components increases learning opportunities for students and provides high-quality service to com-
40 munities.

Service learning has been utilized by various educational programs as a strategy to enhance learning and stimulate interest in working with the elderly. For example, Fusner and Staib (2004) provided service-
45 learning experiences for their nursing students and reported positive outcomes for seniors and students with additional exposure.

It is apparent from the existing literature that, with a few exceptions, prevailing perceptions of aging by
50 nursing students mirror those held by the general public and have shown little change over the past decade. While there is a preponderance of evidence that older adults in the U.S. are healthy and are valued, contributing members of society, much of the public still per-
55 ceive the elderly as weak, sickly, slow, immobile and senile. Unfortunately, the research literature indicates that undergraduate nursing students continue to believe these myths, which may significantly influence career choices (Moyle, 2003; Gething et al., 2004; Wells et
60 al., 2004).

In many instances, the first and only contact students have are with the institutionalized elderly, a setting which many students found heavily work intensive, routine, physical and nonstimulating. As a result,

65 this is their least preferred career choice (Bergland & Laerum, 2002; Fusner & Staib, 2004; Happell, 2002; Tovin, Nelms, & Taylor, 2002; McLafferty & Morrison, 2004). Employing focus groups, McLafferty and Morrison (2004) found that nurses employed in these

70 facilities tended to focus on the negative, thus doing little to improve the image of gerontological nursing.

Further, McKinlay and Cowan (2003) identified specific areas of curriculum improvement that focus on factors underlying the views of the nursing students.

75 Participants were asked about their beliefs concerning behavioral outcomes of working with the elderly. Examples of such beliefs or views were: *Making older people feel valued; viewing older persons as blocking beds; finding working with older people intellectually*

80 *stimulating; working with older people as uninteresting; and viewing older people as hard to please (p. 302).*

The dimensions and style of gerontological education are significant factors in selecting work with the

85 elderly (Avorti, 2004; Kotzabassaki, Vardaki, Andrea, & Parissopoulos, 2000). Avorti (2004) found a significant relationship between professional status, level of education, and attitude in a study conducted in Ghana; however, a large number of students lacked adequate

90 gerontological knowledge, which may account for their lack of interest in the field. To support the belief that feelings of nursing students and registered nurses toward older people may change when given more experience in caring for older adults, Soderhamn et al.

95 (2001) collected data on a convenience sample which included 151 undergraduate nursing students in Sweden using Kogan's Old People Scale (KOP). Results showed that limited experience of students who were less than 25 years of age was a significant factor in

100 holding less favorable attitudes toward the elderly.

Interestingly, findings of a study conducted with baccalaureate students in Hong Kong revealed no clear connection between attitudes toward care of the elderly and work with the elderly (Herdman, 2002). Perhaps

105 this distinction can be attributed to the Asian culture, since filial piety and respect toward elders are accepted cultural elements in many Asian countries. For example, Japan, whose aging population at this time is growing faster than any other country, implemented a suc-

110 cessful after-school program where frail elders and young children competed together in *Intergenerational Olympics* (Kaplan & Larkin, 2007). Although these studies are limited in geographical scope and lacking in representative samples, it is highly likely that career

115 choices by gerontology students are influenced by the care setting regarding initial exposure and type and extent of experiences with the elderly. Moreover, while many studies determined students' attitudes and reasons for not working with the elderly, only a few stud-

120 ies examined changes in attitudes following an intergenerational gerontological educational program that included early exposure to well elderly. With a few

exceptions, the literature focuses on student learning, companionship and meeting elder needs rather than

125 attitude change, positive student-elder interactions and *reciprocal* learning activities. Intergenerational reciprocity or shared learning is a concept which utilizes the theory that exchanges between older and younger generations help to dispel aging myths and stereotypes,

130 promote mutually beneficial experiences and foster positive attitudes toward the elderly (Butler, 2000).

Prior studies that were evaluated for attitude change as a result of service-learning, student-elder interactions, and/or nurse education presented both positive

135 and negative results (Achalu, 1999; Happell, 1999; Health Advisory Service, 1999; Johnson & Atkin, 2002; Lookinland & Anson, 1995; Roberts, Hearn, & Holman, 2003). On the plus side, several studies specifically provided evidence of positive attitude changes

140 in both old and young as a result of service-learning and satisfying intergenerational exchanges (Brosky, Deprey, Hopp, & Mayer, 2006; Doll, 2006; Jones, Herrick, & York, 2004). According to study participants, there is an overreliance on teaching the negative as-

145 pects of aging, rather than emphasizing the positive.

Method

An intergenerational service learning program was incorporated into two elective aging courses, "*Health Aspects of Aging*," an undergraduate introductory course, and "*Health Care of Aging Persons with*

150 *Chronic Illness*," a graduate introductory course. These courses were among the few health-related electives offered to students at convenient hours during the day; hence, the scheduled time of offering appeared to have been a strong selection factor for the undergraduate

155 students. Graduate students were enrolled in the gerontology major and had few elective aging courses from which to choose.

Health Aspects of Aging focused on the physiological, psychological, social and cultural factors that in-

160 fluence the health status of older adults. It identified assessment strategies and their corresponding interventions and techniques, which promote health and prevent deterioration in old age. *Health Care of Aging Persons with Chronic Illness* focused on the biological,

165 psychological and sociocultural factors in aging that influence the development, treatment and management of chronic illnesses. Emphasis was on examining the functional capacity of persons and the capacity for self-care. The courses were modified to incorporate effec-

170 tive intergenerational exchange and careful reflection in journal entries. It was hoped that this would facilitate more positive attitudes toward aging persons and increased understanding of aging health issues for both students and older adults.

175 Increasingly, older adults are using the computer and expanding their Internet skills. Because of this trend, we added a technology component to the traditional service-learning model and created a new model,

which we called George Mason University (GMU) *AgeNet*. Partnering with older adults and incorporating a technology component, we created an enthusiastic environment for both students and seniors. This model provided an effective reciprocal learning environment, in which seniors and students learned from each other in group sessions, email, social gatherings, face-to-face with one-on-one dialogue, and Web postings on health and wellness issues. An additional feature was that students and seniors learned new Internet skills in class together at the Learning in Retirement Institute (LRI).

This study examined changes in attitudes toward the elderly by college students enrolled in the two elective gerontology courses. Primarily, the investigators were interested in knowing if students exhibited any change in attitudes toward the aged and working with older adults as a result of participating in a reciprocal learning intergenerational project, GMU AgeNet. The program embraces the philosophy of intergenerational learning through regular intergenerational exchanges. GMU AgeNet addresses issues most relevant to successful aging through a reciprocal learning relationship.

The senior partners in this project used computers but had varying skill levels; therefore, the investigators seized this opportunity to present a joint class to students and their senior partners to improve their Internet communication skills. This technology was utilized in order for students to provide current health information to older adults. These seniors were in relative good health, sophisticated and well educated; therefore, students were challenged to present timely, in-depth and interesting health promotion and disease prevention information. In turn, older adults were encouraged to share their experiences, life stories, life events and knowledge concerning healthy living and/or their perspectives on aging with students through regular ongoing communication.

The specific aim of this paper is to present the effects of the GMU AgeNet project on the attitudes of students who participated in the project. This was indeed a challenge, since educators throughout the U.S. are struggling with the lack of student engagement with the elderly (Angeles, 2000) and are looking for ways to influence their decisions to choose gerontology as a career.

Student Participants

Eighteen undergraduate and 10 graduate students from nursing, social work and other programs, who were enrolled in the two introductory gerontology courses, partnered with 26 older adults in the LIR Center. Ages of the students ranged from twenty-three to sixty, with a mean age of 34.5. Two students were over 50, one of which was specifically requested as a partner by a senior participant. Seventy-five percent were female and 64.3 percent were undergraduate students. Student population consisted of seven males and 21 females, which included 20 Caucasians, two African

Americans, one nonwhite Hispanic and one Asian. This was the first gerontology class for 18 undergraduate students and the second gerontology class for the remaining 10 graduate students. In both courses, students were provided opportunities to examine current aging theories in relation to reality-based situations.

Older Adult Participants

Twenty-six older adults were recruited from the program's agency partner, a senior center for well elderly which promotes learning in retirement. Recruitment strategies included distribution of flyers, announcements in meetings and word of mouth. Criteria for inclusion were age 65 and over and membership and attendance at the center.

An initial welcoming event was held and included refreshments, a brief PowerPoint presentation, introductions, and orientation by the investigators and faculty. Following a *get acquainted* session, students and seniors paired up based upon mutual interests and other personal characteristics.

Instruments

The investigators administered a simple 20-item Aging IQ Quiz, designed by the National Institute on Aging, to the students at the beginning of the project to determine students' basic knowledge of aging. The *Geriatric Attitude Scale* developed by Reuben et al. (1998) was also administered to student participants at the beginning of the project and again at the conclusion of the project to measure any changes in attitudes as a result of participation in the project. This 14-item Likert scale, originally developed for primary care residents, was easy to administer and needed little modification for use with nursing and health science students. The internal consistency reliability of the scale measured by Cronbach's alpha has been reported to be .76 (Reuben et al., 1998). The instrument included questions such as "*Most old people are pleasant to be with*," and, "*If I have the choice, I would rather see younger patients than elderly ones*," which were for the students to answer.

Communication Strategies

Subsequent to the initial get acquainted meeting, interaction between students and their partners was primarily electronic, consisting of Town Hall Forums, personal emails and telephone calls between partners. Partners, on average, spent approximately 20 minutes per week in various electronic communication. Students were required to keep a journal of all contacts and interactions with their partners and record their reflections, indicating their impressions, knowledge gained and questions or concerns raised. With faculty as facilitators, students shared their reflections during class time each week. In addition to shared communications in class, there were several joint classroom sessions with senior partners, replete with an open discussion of aging, socializing and refreshments.

Results

Quantitative data were analyzed using descriptive and inferential statistical methods. Tests of signifi-
290 cance, including paired *t*-tests and Pearson Correlation, were used to determine differences in knowledge level between the undergraduate and graduate students, and changes in attitude at the conclusion of the project. Since the attitude scale was originally designed for
295 primary care residents, tests for internal consistency reliability using Cronbach's alpha (Cronbach, 1990) yielded a reliability coefficient of .66 on pretest and a coefficient of .84 on posttest for the total group.

Summary statistics (mean and standard deviation of
300 the scores) for pretest and posttest administration of the Aging IQ test and Attitude measures are presented in Table 1. Pretest and posttest assessments were com-pared using paired *t* tests to find evidence of statisti-cally significant improvement in the scores. Scores for
305 each item within the Aging IQ scores (k = 20) and atti-tude measures (k = 14) were added across participants' responses to derive summary statistics for the depend-ent variables, knowledge and attitude. Means and stan-dard deviations were computed using these scores for
310 the two test administrations for the entire group as well as the undergraduate and graduate students. The paired *t*-test results indicated that there was a statistically sig-nificant change ($p < .001$) from pretest to posttest ad-ministration of Aging IQ test in the total group, and for
315 each individual group of undergraduate and graduate students. The paired *t*-test results indicated that there was a statistically significant change ($p < .001$) from pretest to posttest administration of attitude measure in the total group, with the significance being attributed
320 primarily to undergraduate students. However, the changes in attitude measures were not statistically sig-nificant ($p > .05$) for graduate students alone.

Knowledge of aging posttest scores correlated sig-nificantly with scores on the Attitudes Toward Aging
325 Posttest. The correlation coefficient for scores on post aging IQ and scores on Attitudes Toward Aging Post-test for the total group was moderately high and statis-tically significant ($r = .75, p < 001$).

Qualitative Analyses

Qualitative data were analyzed using thematic
330 processes and contextual examination of student jour-nals, using rigorous review procedures. Three nursing faculty members facilitated class discussions, reviewed student journals, and identified themes and categories that emerged.

335 Six major themes emerged from review of student journals. These were: (1) immediate application of the-ory to real life situations, (2) a stronger connection to seniors, (3) a more positive image of aging, (4) in-creased sensitivity to the feelings, beliefs and values of
340 the elderly, (5) increased knowledge of the elderly, and (6) working with the elderly as a possible career choice.

Table 1

Score Changes in Pretest and Posttest Administration of the Aging IQ and Attitude Scales

Variables	Pretest		Posttest		Paired
	Mean	SD	Mean	SD	*t* test
Total group					
Aging IQ scores	12.18	1.98	19.82	.47	20.37***
Attitude scores	45.50	6.76	49.03	5.60	2.50**
Undergraduates					
Aging IQ scores	11.11	1.60	19.78	.55	21.44***
Attitude scores	42.89	4.17	47.28	6.08	2.87**
Graduates					
Aging IQ scores	14.10	.74	19.9	.32	29.00***
Attitude scores	50.00	.20	52.2	2.62	N.S.

***Significant at $p < .001$
**Significant at $p < .01$

Through interviews, analyses of journals and fac-ulty discussions, it was found that in general, signifi-
345 cantly more students and seniors were pleased with the interactions than were not. Seniors who were not pleased indicated that they expected to do more teach-ing of the students. A subsequent article will focus on senior outcomes. The following quotes illustrate stu-
350 dent responses to the project:

Examples of Student Written Reflections

Although most students provided positive comments, several comments indicated areas for improvement and refinement of the project.

355 *Undergraduate Students*:

Older adults increased my awareness about the phenome-non of aging as an opportunity for empowerment and the creation of positive images of aging. I feel that working with older individuals is the flame that heats my spirit
360 and kindles my desire for inner growth and self-expression. It was difficult setting up a discussion time with my partner. She seems to be very busy and commu-nication between us was sporadic.

Challenging/successful approaches included involving
365 senior adults in planning the project and carefully plan-ning for face-to-face group activities for maximum atten-dance.

My partner wanted to come back to the classroom for discussion and sharing and wanted to know when we
370 were going to do this.

He was more interested in teaching us than in receiving information from us.

Graduate Students:

My service learning experience has been a very success-
375 ful combination of academics and community service. Service learning provides a way of applying what is learned in class and through texts to the real world. It al-lows active student participation, the creation of connec-tions and the opportunity for reflection. Our project—
380 AgeNet—in conjunction with the Learning in Retirement Institute, became a gift to both senior and student. In so doing, it created a benefit, an outcome, a product and a connection of which to be proud.

Communicating with older persons has heightened the
385 creative perspective in my mind and resulted in my de-veloping a new attitude and understanding of the way

older people approach life experiences, relationships, and activities.

390 Unfortunately, my partner had symptoms which troubled her and it was difficult to get her to talk at times. She has to push herself to stay involved with whatever is going on.

Sometimes I did not know what to say to her when she refused to believe what her physician has told her. What
395 do you do for someone who has been told that tests show deterioration in the part of the brain that governs balance and she has to live with it for the rest of her life?

AgeNet couldn't be anything but a success. Generations need to come together and share. In these interactions, we
400 finally were able to begin breaking down the stereotypes and misconceptions of ageism. Certainly, differences exist between generations. Yet we start to realize that there are also many similarities. Age does not take away the interest to learn, socialize or attain future goals. It does
405 not eradicate ambition or desire, the need for love and affection. Possibly, greater understanding and communication through intergenerational interaction will make transitions into late adulthood easier, more rewarding. AgeNet may be one of the first steps toward this end.

Discussion

410 As expected, the study showed that the knowledge level of undergraduate nursing and gerontology students improved significantly ($p < .01$) when an innovative Intergenerational Reciprocal Service Learning Project using the Internet as a primary means of communi-
415 cation was added to the gerontology curriculum. The students, as a group, had a positive change in their attitudes toward aging at the completion of the project; however, more non-nursing students than nursing students showed a positive change.

420 Not surprisingly, scores were higher for graduate students than for undergraduates on pretesting; however, scores for both groups increased significantly on posttesting for both knowledge and attitude changes, with most of the changes being attributed to the under-
425 graduate students. Attitude scores for graduate students remained more or less the same. It was not surprising that the greatest variance was attributed to the undergraduate students, since graduate students most likely had a predetermined preference for work with older
430 patients. Since many of the graduate students enrolled in the course had chosen gerontology as a career, and had extensive work experience already, they were more likely to maintain a positive attitude toward working with the older population, resulting in little change in
435 attitudes toward aging measurements. Whereas younger students, who enrolled with preconceived stereotypical notions of the elderly, learned a great deal and appeared to have changed their attitudes toward working with the elderly.

440 Further, many of the undergraduates expressed enjoyment regarding working with the elderly on this project and would reconsider a career working with older adults. Most likely the setting (residential community) combined with the higher health status of the

445 senior partners had a positive influence on the attitudes of the students. This is consistent with the findings of Wells et al. (2004) and Avorti (2004) who reported that work setting is a strong influence on attitudes toward older adults and can influence the delivery of care.

450 As with Robinson and Cubit (2005), these investigators believed individual reflection and group discussions were critical in increasing knowledge and improving attitudes toward aging. It was observed that all students expressed a greater appreciation of the vast
455 knowledge this group of seniors possessed and expressed a new respect and understanding of aging.

In general, journal reflections and classroom discussions indicated that undergraduates as well as graduate students who are exposed to well older adults
460 and who engage in intergenerational reciprocal learning strategies appear to develop more positive attitudes toward aging and are more likely to consider working with older adults as a career choice.

Limitations

This study is not without limitations. The small
465 sample size and the fact that all elderly participants were Caucasian may limit the generalizability of these results. Also, it was not possible in this study to compare various components of the courses in order to ascertain the relative value of each component, including
470 the reciprocal intergenerational activities. In addition, two of the students were over fifty years of age, possibly introducing a slight bias to the study. All of the graduate students had taken a previous gerontology class, whereas this was the first gerontology class for
475 the undergraduate students. Most likely this had a significant influence on the outcomes of the Aging IQ pretest. However, during the course of the project, the instructors taught all of the material related to the aging IQ test to both groups, resulting in insignificant differ-
480 ences between the two groups on Aging IQ posttest. Self-selection was a limitation since all enrolled students participated as a class requirement.

The authors recognize that students' personal experiences, work experiences, and academic experiences
485 are intervening variables and most likely influenced knowledge and attitude scores. Further, the interaction of undergraduate and graduate students may have been a factor in the increase in knowledge and attitude scores of the undergraduates. Finally, the graduate stu-
490 dents, who were older, had specifically chosen gerontology as a career path and this may have influenced posttest scores on the attitude toward aging. Evidence of personal and intellectual growth and development was discerned from student journals and class discus-
495 sions. Rethinking career goals by students was an additional outcome of this unique project. However, it would be naive to assume that interesting and innovative educational strategies are the only means for changing attitudes toward working with the elderly.

Conclusions and Recommendations

500   Based on this research and other observations, it is possible to make several recommendations regarding gerontological and geriatric education programs at the undergraduate and graduate level. These recommendations include the need to: (1) improve gerontology cur-

505 ricula with meaningful service-learning components, (2) provide continuing education in various settings to change public perceptions, (3) encourage changes in media portrayals of the elderly, (4) improve work environments in facilities for the elderly, and (5) provide

510 adequate compensation to individuals working with older persons. These are real world challenges to increase a much needed work force for a growing population of culturally diverse aging clients.

Although findings cannot necessarily be general-

515 ized to students working with a more impaired population of elders, this study suggests that first exposure to well elderly in a reciprocal intergenerational service-learning project may influence decision-making regarding working with older adults. The investigators rec-

520 ommend further exploration with a larger and more culturally diverse sample, as well as the use of more in-depth measures of outcomes among the older adult participants.

References

Achalu, O. (1999). Attitudes of student nurses to older patients in Nigeria. *Elderly Care, 11*(2), 5–8.

Administration on Aging. (2002). *Profile of Older Americans: 2002.* Retrieved February 5, 2003, at www.aoa.gov/stats/profile/2002/default.htm

Angeles, J. (2000). Service Learning is the great connector. *Generations United, 5*(1), 1–26.

Avorti, G. S. (2004). Attitude of nurses towards the care of the elderly in Ghana. *West African Journal of Nursing, 15*(2), 81–86.

Bergland, A., & Laerum, H. (2002). Norwegian student nurses' attitudes towards pursuing a career in geriatric nursing after graduation. *Nursing Science and Research in the Nordic Countries, 22*(2), 21–26.

Brosky, J., Deprey, S., Hopp, J., & Mayer, E. (2006). Physical therapist student and community partner perspectives and attitudes regarding service-learning experiences. *Journal of Physical Therapy Education, 20*(3), 38–41.

Butler, F. R. (2000). Computer technology and intergenerational service learning. *Intergenerational Service Learning in Gerontology: A Compendium, 111*, 12–16.

Cooper, S. A., & Coleman, P. G. (2001). Caring for the older person: an exploration of perceptions using personal construct theory. *Age and Ageing, 30*(5), 399–402.

Cronbach, L. J. (1990). *Essentials of Psychological Testing* (5th Ed.). New York: Harper & Row.

Fusner, S. & Staib, S. (2004). Students and senior citizens learning from each other. *Journal of Gerontological Nursing, 30*(3), 40–45.

Gething, L., Fethy, J., McKee, K., Goff, M., Churchward, M., & Mathews, L. (2004). Knowledge, stereotyping and attitudes towards self-ageing. *Australian Journal of Ageing, 21*(20), 74–79.

Happell, B. (1999). When I grow up I want to be a.... Where undergraduate student nurses want to work after graduation. *Journal of Advanced Nursing, 29*(2), 499–505.

Happell, B. (2002). Nursing home employment for nursing students: Valuable experience or harsh deterrent? *Journal of Advanced Nursing, 39*(6), 529–536.

Happell, B., & Brooker, J. (2001). Global aging. Who will look after my grandmother? Attitudes of student nurses toward the care of older adults. *Journal of Gerontological Nursing, 27*(12), 12–17.

Health Advisory Service (1999). *Not because they are old: An independent inquiry into the care of older people on acute wards in general hospitals.* London, HAS.

Herdman, E. (2002). Challenging the discourses of nursing ageism. *International Journal of Nursing Studies, 39*(1), 105–114.

Hill, H. (2007). Research indicates: intergenerational interactions enhance creating relationships through dance and movements. *Together: The Generations United Magazine, 12*(1), 6.

Jones, E., Herrick, C., & York, R. (2004). An intergenerational group benefits from emotionally disturbed youth and older adults. *Issues in Mental Health Nursing, 25*(8), 753–757.

Kaplan, M., & Larkin, E. (2007). Japan and international partners host intergenerational conference. *Together: The Generations United Magazine, 12*(1), 7.

Kotzabasaaki, Vardaki, Z., Andrea, S., & Parissopoulos, S. (2002). Student nurses' attitudes towards the care of elderly persons: A pilot study. *ICU's & Nursing Web Journal, 12.* Retrieved March 27, 2006 from http://cinahl.com/cgi_bin/refscv?jid=837& accno=2003030388

Lohman, H., & Aitken, M. (2002). Occupational therapy students' attitudes toward service-learning. *Physical Occupational Therapy in Geriatrics, 20*(3/4), 155–164.

Lookinland, S., & Anson, K. (1995). Perpetuation of ageist attitudes among present and future health care personnel: Implications for elder care. *Journal of Advanced Nursing, 1*(1), 47–56.

McKinlay, A., & Cowan, S. (2003). Student nurses' attitudes towards working with older patients. *Journal of Advanced Nursing, 43*(3), 298–309.

McLafferty, I., & Morrison, F. (2004). Attitudes towards hospitalized older adults. *Journal of Advanced Nursing, 47*(4), 446–453.

Mintz, S., & Liu, G. (1999). Service learning: an overview. *Corporation for National and Community Resource Guide. The Corporation for Service Learning, 9*–16.

Mion, L. C. (2003). Care provision for older adults: Who will provide? *Online Journal of Issues in Nursing, 8*(2). Retrieved March 27, 2006 from http://www.cinahl.com/ cgi_bin/refsvc?jid= 1331&accno=2004010891

Moyle, W. (2003). Nursing students' perceptions of older people: Continuing society's myths. *Australian Journal of Advanced Nursing, 20*(4), 15–21.

Roberts, S., Hearn, J., & Holman, C. (2003). Picture this: Using drawing to explore student nurses' perceptions of older age. *Nursing Older People, 15*(5), 14–18.

Ruben, D. (1998). Development and validation of geriatric attitude scale for primary care physicians. *The Journal of the American Geriatrics Society, 46*(11), 1425–1430.

Soderhamn, O., Lindencrona, C., & Gustavsson, S.M. (2001). *Nurse Education Today, 21*(3), 225–229.

Tovin, M. M., Nelms, T., & Taylor, L. F. (2002). The experience of nursing home care: A strong influence on physical therapists students' work intentions. *Journal of Physical Therapy Education, 16*(1), 11–19.

U.S. Department of Health and Human Services. (2004). Preliminary findings: 2004 National Sample Survey of Registers. Retrieved March 27, 2006, from http://www.bhpr.hrsa.gov/healthworkforce/reports/rnpopulation/preliminaryfindings.htm

Wells, Y., Foreman, P., Gething, L, & Petralia, W. (2004). Multicultural Aging. Nurses' attitudes toward aging and older adults. examining attitudes and practices among health services providers in Australia. *Journal of Gerontological Nursing, 30*(9), 5–13.

About the authors: *Frieda R. Butler* is a professor and coordinator of the George Mason University Gerontology Programs, housed in the College of Health and Human Services, 4400 University Drive MS5B7, Fairfax, VA 22030-4444 (e-mail: fbutler@gmu.edu). *Heibatollah Baghi* is an associate professor and coordinator of the Master of Science in Epidemiology and Statistics Programs, George Mason University, College of Health and Human Services, 4400 University Drive MS5B7, Fairfax, VA 22030-4444 (e-mail: hbaghi@gmu.edu).

Address correspondence to: Frieda R. Butler, Ph.D., George Mason University, 4400 University Drive, MS5B7, Fairfax, VA 22030-4444.

Exercise for Article 21

Factual Questions

1. What was the hypothesis for this study?

2. What were the criteria for the inclusion of older adult participants?

3. For the total group, was the pretest-posttest difference on the Aging IQ test statistically significant?

4. What was the value of the correlation coefficient (r) for the relationship between Aging IQ posttest scores and Attitudes Toward Aging posttest scores?

5. Do the researchers believe that the results can clearly be generalized to students working with a more impaired population of elders?

Questions for Discussion

6. In your opinion, is the program that was evaluated in this study described in sufficient detail? Explain. (See lines 146–223 and 273–287.)

7. Is the initial welcoming event described in sufficient detail? Explain. (See lines 248–253.)

8. Are the quantitative results (lines 288–328) *or* the qualitative results (lines 329–409) more interesting? More informative? Explain.

9. If you were to evaluate the same program, would you use a control group? Why? Why not?

10. Overall, does this evaluation convince you that the program is effective? Explain.

Quality Ratings

Directions: Indicate your level of agreement with each of the following statements by circling a number from 5 for strongly agree (SA) to 1 for strongly disagree (SD). If you believe an item is not applicable to this research article, leave it blank. Be prepared to explain your ratings. When responding to criteria A and B below, keep in mind that brief titles and abstracts are conventional in published research.

A. The title of the article is appropriate.

   SA   5   4   3   2   1   SD

B. The abstract provides an effective overview of the research article.

   SA   5   4   3   2   1   SD

C. The introduction establishes the importance of the study.

   SA   5   4   3   2   1   SD

D. The literature review establishes the context for the study.

   SA   5   4   3   2   1   SD

E. The research purpose, question, or hypothesis is clearly stated.

   SA   5   4   3   2   1   SD

F. The method of sampling is sound.

   SA   5   4   3   2   1   SD

G. Relevant demographics (for example, age, gender, and ethnicity) are described.

   SA   5   4   3   2   1   SD

H. Measurement procedures are adequate.

   SA   5   4   3   2   1   SD

I. All procedures have been described in sufficient detail to permit a replication of the study.

   SA   5   4   3   2   1   SD

J. The participants have been adequately protected from potential harm.

   SA   5   4   3   2   1   SD

K. The results are clearly described.

   SA   5   4   3   2   1   SD

L. The discussion/conclusion is appropriate.

   SA   5   4   3   2   1   SD

M. Despite any flaws, the report is worthy of publication.

   SA   5   4   3   2   1   SD

Article 22

Reducing Adolescent Substance Abuse and Delinquency: Pilot Research of a Family-Oriented Psychoeducation Curriculum

THOMAS EDWARD SMITH
Florida State University

JEFFREY RODMAN
Here-4-You Consulting

SCOTT P. SELLS
Savannah Family Institute

LISA RENE REYNOLDS
Nova Southeastern University

ABSTRACT. Ninety-three parents and 102 adolescents were referred by juvenile court and treated for substance abuse and a co-morbid diagnosis of either oppositional defiant or conduct disorder using a parent education program over a six-week period. The goals of this study were to assess whether or not active parent involvement and the concurrent treatment of severe behavior problems would reduce teen substance abuse as measured by the adolescent SASSI scale. In addition, if the SASSI scale indicated a significant reduction in substance abuse, would these changes be maintained after a 12-month follow-up period as measured by re-arrest rates through juvenile court records? The results indicated that parents' participation in their teen's treatment of substance abuse and other severe behavioral problems did have a major positive impact. Even though the adolescent's attitudes and defensiveness toward drugs or alcohol did not significantly change, their substance abuse did. This was demonstrated by both the statistically significant changes on the adolescent's SASSI scores and the fact that 85% did not relapse over the course of an entire year after treatment was completed.

From *Journal of Child & Adolescent Substance Abuse*, *15*, 105–115. Copyright © 2006 by The Haworth Press, Inc. Reprinted with permission.

Introduction

There is a growing concern in our society about the dramatic increase of adolescent drug and alcohol abuse and dependence. There is no shortage of reports describing these alarming trends (e.g., Muck, Zempolich,
5   Titus, Fishman, Godley et al., 2001; Rowe & Liddle, 2003). Overall, drug abuse by teenagers has risen dramatically since 1996 while the overall use among adults has stayed the same or dropped (Department of Health and Human Services, 2002).
10   Increases in teen substance use have led to a greater need for theoretically based and empirically supported treatments (*The Brown University Digest*, 1999). Indeed the number of studies devoted to substance abuse and treatment in youth is continually growing (e.g.,
15   Coatsworth, Santisteran, McBride, & Szapocznik,

2001; Latimer & Newcomb, 2000; Liddle, Dakof, Parker, Diamond, Barrett et al., 2001). However, many agree that a gap still exists between research on adolescent substance abuse and the treatments currently being
20   provided (Liddle, Rowe, Quille, Mills et al., 2002; Robbins, Bachrach, & Szapocznik, 2002; Rowe & Liddle, 2003).

Recent studies have pointed to three critical gaps in adolescent substance-abuse research and treatment.
25   First, there is a growing body of evidence that links adolescent substance abuse to dysfunctional family dynamics (e.g., Carr, 1998; Friedman, Terras, & Glassman, 2000; Liddle & Schwartz, 2002; McGillicuddy, Rychtarik, Duquette, & Morsheimer, 2001; Public
30   Health Reports, 1997; Tuttle, 1995). Brown, Monti, Myers, Waldron, and Wagner (1999) reported that "family support" was often cited by teens as being most helpful in quitting drugs and maintaining sobriety. Despite the growing support for the incorporation
35   of family therapy into adolescent substance abuse treatment (e.g., Berlin, 2002; Lambie & Rokutani, 2002; Rowe, Parker-Sloat, Schwartz, & Liddle, 2003; Wallace & Estroff, 2001), many programs still do not involve the family as an intricate part of their ap-
40   proaches. Instead, the primary emphasis is still on the individual teen through traditional treatment approaches (e.g., Alcoholics Anonymous [AA] or Narcotics Anonymous [NA]), which are often designed for adults without taking into consideration the unique
45   needs of adolescents (Berlin, 2002). Deas and Thomas (2001) agree that many tenets of twelve-step programs may be overly abstract and distasteful for developing adolescents (p. 187).

Second, the majority of substance-abusing teens in
50   treatment also exhibit other problems such as truancy, fighting, and defiance (Fisher & Harrison, 2000), running away (Slesnick, Myers, Meade, & Segelken, 2000), or other problem behaviors (Schmidt, Liddle, & Dakof, 1996). In these cases, family-based treatments
55   were found to be highly effective not only in reducing

substance use, but also in alleviating associated symptomatic behaviors. In 1999, the National Assembly on Drug and Alcohol Abuse and the Criminal Offenders concluded that addressing "adolescent drug addiction or substance abuse without also treating, for example, behavioral problems such as truancy, running away, or threats of violence reduced the likelihood of success" (p. 2). Yet researchers at the National Assembly cited the failure of most treatment programs to address both substance abuse and severe behavioral problems concurrently.

Finally, researchers have found the psychoeducational component of family substance-abuse treatment to be successful in reducing the teen's drug use as well as heightening parents' functioning. Studies have highlighted the utility of psychoeducation in adolescent substance abuse treatment, including parent training (Bamberg et al., 2001; Schmidt et al., 1996) and skills training (McGillicuddy et al., 2001; Wagner, Brown, Monty, & Waldron, 1999). One problem with traditional parenting groups, however, is the significant dropout rate of parents and teens. Parents are often resistant to acceptability for their children's substance abuse. Not surprisingly, they state that adolescents are responsible for their own difficulties. Thus, they resent coming to a parent education group to learn new skills because their teen "got caught" abusing drugs or alcohol. As a result, parents are resistant to helping their teen overcome their substance abuse. However, a systemic approach to teen substance abuse treatment has been shown to result in a higher level of engagement in treatment and to lower dropout rates than other routine procedures (Cormack & Carr, 2000).

To address these deficits, a parent education program was used to treat teens that were diagnosed with substance abuse as well as oppositional defiant or conduct disorders (*DSM-IV*; American Psychiatric Association [APA], 1994) and the teens' parents. Ninety-three parents and 102 adolescents were referred by juvenile court and treated using the parent education program over a six-week period. Research studies have shown that teen substance abuse and conduct disorder relapse rates are typically extremely high, with some as high as 75% (Long, 1999; Sholevar & Schwoeri, 2003).

The goals of this study were to assess whether or not active parent involvement and the concurrent treatment of severe behavior problems would reduce teen substance abuse as measured by the adolescent SASSI scale and if these changes would be maintained over a 12-month period after treatment ended.

Research Questions

Three questions were examined in this study. First, would active parent involvement and the concurrent treatment of severe behavior problems reduce teen substance abuse as measured by the adolescent SASSI subscales? Second, would reductions in substance abuse behavior as measured by the SASSI subscales be maintained at the 12-month follow-up? Third, would adolescents relapse within a 12-month period as measured by re-arrest rates through juvenile court records?

Methods

The sample consisted of 102 adolescents and 93 parents who together attended a six-week *Parenting with Love and Limits*™ substance-abuse prevention program. The adolescents ranged in age from 9 to 18, with the average participant being 15 years old. Each participant was diagnosed with substance abuse and a co-morbid diagnosis of either oppositional defiant or conduct disorder. The study was conducted within an opportunistic window of opportunity. This required that the study be nonreactive in terms of measurement. As a result, we were unable to track demographic variables such as socioeconomic data and severity of offense.

The majority of the adolescents were white (82.4%). The remaining participants were African American (11.8%) and Mexican American (1.0%). Both males and females were present in the sample, with males accounting for the majority of the participants (56.9%). These adolescents committed a wide variety of offenses, with the most commonly occurring offense being shoplifting (22.5%). The next most frequent offense was possession of marijuana (14.7%). Each participant was court-ordered into treatment by the judge at juvenile court. Once those cases that were missing data related to the SASSI subscales were deleted, 93 adolescents remained in the sample.

Parenting with Love and Limits™

The six-week *Parenting with Love and Limits*™ psychoeducational program was developed from a three-year process-outcome research study (Sells, 1998; Sells, 2000; Sells, Smith, & Sprenkle, 1995) and integrated the best principles of a structural family therapy approach. Structural Family Therapy was rated a Model Program in the United States Department of Education's *Applying Effective Strategies to Prevent or Reduce Substance Abuse, Violence, and Disruptive Behavior Among Youth* (Scattergood, Dash, Epstein, & Adler, 1998). Programs using the framework of structural family therapy have consistently demonstrated success in reducing or eliminating substance abuse in adolescents (Lambie & Rokutani, 2002; Springer & Orsbon, 2002; Rowe, Parker-Sloat, Schwartz, & Liddle, 2003).

Two group facilitators led a small group of parents, caregivers, and their teenagers (no more than 4–6 families with no more than 15 people total in the group) in six classes, each two hours long. Two co-facilitators were needed because breakout groups were an essential piece of the program. Parents and teens met together collectively as a group but there were times in which each group met separately in breakout groups. The rationale for these breakouts was that oftentimes both parents and teens need to meet separately to address issues that collectively they cannot.

The *Parenting with Love and Limits*™ program provides parents with a detailed six-module treatment manual on curtailing their teenagers' substance abuse and other behavior problems. To assist in intervention delivery, workbooks were available for parents, their children, and group facilitators. In addition, a final workbook was available on how to train group facilitators to implement the program.

In the first module, parents learned reasons why teens engage in substance abuse, disrespect, running away, or violence as a form of "parent abuse." Presumably, parents are faced with adolescents whose normal rebellious stance is compounded by self-injurious behaviors such as substance abuse, extreme disrespectful behaviors, and so on. At the end of this module, parents and teens form respective breakout groups to vent their feelings and frustrations.

In the second module, presentations are made on how adolescents engage in provocative behavior (e.g., swearing, argumentative discussions). Presentations are also made on how parents engage in activities that are ineffective (e.g., lecturing, criticizing, acrimonious comments about past conflict).

In the third module, effective behavioral contracting methods are presented. Parents are taught to critique their contingency management contracts to ensure that adolescents will be apprised on the consequences of violating provisions of a behavioral contract. Parents and adolescents retire into separate breakout groups to critique and write new contracts.

In the fourth module, presentations are made on how adolescents creatively circumvent seemingly well-designed behavioral contracts.

In the fifth module, parents choose from a recipe menu of creative consequences to respond to adolescents' provocative behaviors. Such behaviors include skipping school, drug/alcohol abuse, sexual promiscuity, violence, and threats of suicide.

In the sixth module, parents and children are taught about the necessity to recreate a positive climate within a household and specific methods of doing so.

The rationale behind the use of this program is twofold. First, *Parenting with Love and Limits*™ is one of the first parent education programs of its kind to specifically address both substance abuse and oppositional and conduct disorder behaviors concurrently. Traditional psychoeducation group programs are not based on a lengthy period of process and qualitative research with adolescents and their families. Further, they are not designed to address a range of extreme behavior problems in adolescents. Finally, teens are not typically active participants in the parenting group process. Traditional groups are either for the parents only or the teens as passive observers and not active participants.

The high completion rate (i.e., 85% completion rate by adolescents and a 94% completion rate by parents of

all six weeks of the *Parenting with Love and Limits*™ program) ensured that the study was a credible investigation into the programmatic effects.

Measures

The Adolescent SASSI questionnaire was administered to the 93 adolescents before they began the first *Parenting with Love and Limits*™ class and again after the last parenting class was completed. It has five subscales: The FVA subscale measured self-perception of alcohol abuse. The FVOD subscale measured self-perception of other drug abuse (e.g., marijuana). The OAT (overt measure of attitudes toward drug use) and SAT (subtle measure of attitudes toward drug use) together measured adolescents' overt and covert willingness to admit that they have personality characteristics that are commonly and stereotypically associated with substance abusers (e.g., impatience, low frustration tolerance, grandiosity, etc). The fifth subscale was the DEF, which measured defensiveness toward drug use.

The Adolescent SASSI has a high reliability coefficient of .91 and high face validity for each of its five subscales (SASSI Manual, 2000). To assess for change following program participation, paired sample *t* tests were conducted for each subscale of the SASSI.

Recidivism or relapse rates for all 93 adolescents who completed the program were measured through juvenile court records for each adolescent. Re-arrest records for substance abuse or conduct related problems, such as shoplifting, were obtained for all 93 adolescents six months after the completion of the parenting program, and then again after twelve months of completing the program.

Results

Table 1 indicates both the FVA and FVOD subscale scores were significantly lower following their participation in the *Parenting with Love and Limits*™ six-week program. The pretest mean for the FVA was 2.06, whereas the posttest mean was .73. The pretest mean for the FVOD was 2.83, whereas the posttest mean was .95.

The adolescents' attitudes about their drug or alcohol use were measured through the OAT and SAT. On the OAT subscale, the average respondent changed only slightly. The pretest mean for the OAT subscale was 6.19, whereas the posttest mean was 5.85. A similar pattern is seen in the SAT subscale, with the exception of direction. The average respondent had a pretest SAT score of 1.90 and a posttest SAT score of 2.08. The difference between these scores was not statistically significant.

The last subscale (DEF) measured defensiveness concerning substance use. The primary purpose of the DEF scale is to identify defensive clients who are trying to conceal evidence of personal problems and limitations. Whether it is due to life events or to personality characteristics, excessive defensiveness can be prob-

Table 1
Paired Sample t-Test Results for the SASSI Subscales

Subscale	Pretest mean (standard deviation)	Posttest mean (standard deviation)	*t*-score	*p*-value
FVA	2.06 (2.79)	.73 (1.41)	4.532	< .001
FVOD	2.83 (4.94)	.95 (2.05)	3.732	< .001
OAT	6.19 (3.23)	5.85 (3.65)	1.176	.243
SAT	1.90 (1.76)	2.08 (1.80)	−1.038	.302
DEF	6.60 (2.46)	7.05 (2.90)	−1.830	.070

lematic and it must be taken into account in treatment planning.

On this subscale, the average respondent's score increased slightly (6.60–7.05). This indicates that the average program participant increased slightly in defensiveness. However, this change was very small and did not reach statistical significance. In addition, the average respondent was in the normal range at the time of pretest, so high levels of change were not expected on this subscale.

Only six (15%) of the 93 adolescents who completed the *Parenting with Love and Limits*[TM] program relapsed or re-offended over a 12-month period as indicated by juvenile court arrest records that tracked each of the 93 adolescents. Re-offenses included both substance abuse behaviors (e.g., illegal possession of alcohol or drugs like marijuana) and conduct disorder behaviors (e.g., shoplifting, violence, running away, etc.).

Discussion

The results indicate that parents' participation in adolescents' treatment of substance abuse and severe behavioral problems can have a major positive impact on program effectiveness. One key indicator was adolescents' self-reported substance use dropped significantly. This finding was juxtaposed by the finding that adolescents' attitudes and defensiveness toward drugs or alcohol did not significantly change. The significant change in subscales on perceived alcohol and drug use showed that adolescents believed that they misused these substances. This was demonstrated by both the statistically significant changes on the adolescents' SASSI scores and the fact that 85% did not relapse over the course of an entire year after treatment ended.

The low OAT and SAT scores among adolescents were not unexpected because while they may judge themselves as misusing or using drugs or alcohol, they do not see themselves as having a drug or alcohol problem. That is, adolescents often do not see themselves as chemically dependent or having personality characteristics that are associated with society's stereotypical alcoholic or drug abuser on skid row (SASSI Manual, 2000). Thus, a high score and level of change on these subscales was not wholly unexpected.

This evidence suggests that a group-oriented, family therapy informed psychoeducation is effective in helping parents reassert their authority and reduce, if not curtail, their teen's severe behavior problems and substance abuse. Additionally, attitudes toward alcohol and drug abuse may well change following behavioral changes. Notwithstanding this optimistic viewpoint, there are potential problems with the lack of congruence between attitudes and behavior. Without understanding why adolescents changed their behavior, the possibility of recidivism is elevated. The lack of recidivism in this study suggests that this process needs to be further studied.

One key ingredient in the current study may be parental involvement and providing them with the proper skills to address their adolescents' behavioral problems. The parental involvement may explain the 94% completion rate by parents and the 84% completion rate by adolescents of all six two-hour parenting classes. One intuitive explanation for adolescents' high rate of attendance was that they were ordered into treatment. However, that does not explain why parents' involvement was so elevated. High parent attendance in this six-week course contradicts research findings that this population of parents is resistant to treatment and shows a lack of participation in the overall therapeutic process. Therefore, the 94% completion rate shows promise that programs with the right curriculum can engage a population of parents who are traditionally highly resistant to participation.

Future studies that use qualitative research methods are needed to discover what particular concepts or techniques within the *Parenting with Love and Limits*[TM] program are reducing parental resistance and increasing their readiness to change. The identified key concepts can then be refined and modified to increase both parent and teen participation and readiness to change.

References

Bamberg, J., Toumbourou, J. W., Blyth, A., & Forer, D. (2001). Change for the BEST: Family changes for parents coping with youth substance abuse. *Australian and New Zealand Journal of Family Therapy, 22,* 189–198.

Berlin, M. (2002). Adolescent substance abuse treatment: A unified model. *Dissertation Abstracts International: Section B: The Sciences & Engineering, 63,* 2999.

Brown, S.A., Monti, P. M., Myers, M. G., Waldron, H. B., & Wagner, E. F. (1999). More resources, treatment needed for adolescent substance abuse. *The Brown University Digest of Addiction Theory and Application, 18,* 6–7.

Carr, A. (1998). The inclusion of fathers in family therapy: A research based perspective. *Contemporary Family Therapy, 20,* 371–383.

Coatsworth, J. D., Dsanisteban, D. A., McBride, C. K., & Szapocznik, J. (2001). Brief strategic family therapy versus community control: Engagement, retention, and an exploration of the moderating role of adolescent symptom severity. *Family Process, 40,* 313–333.

Cormack, C., & Carr, A. (2000). Drug abuse. In A. Carr (Ed.), *What works with children and adolescents? A critical review of psychological interventions with children, adolescents, and their families.*

Deas, D., & Thomas, S. E. (2001). An overview of controlled studies of adolescent substance abuse treatment. *The American Journal on Addictions, 10,* 178–189.

Fisher, G. L., & Harrison, T. C. (2000). *Substance abuse: Information for school counselors, social workers, therapists, and counselors.* Needham Heights, MA: Allyn & Bacon.

Friedman, A. S., Terras, A., & Glassman, K. (2000). Family structure versus family relationships for predicting substance use/abuse and illegal behavior. *Journal of Child & Adolescent Substance Abuse, 10,* 1–16.

Lambie, G. W., & Rokutani, J. (2002). A systems approach to substance abuse identification and intervention for school counselors. *Professional School Counseling, 5,* 353–360.

Latimer, W. W., & Newcomb, M. (2000). Adolescent substance abuse treatment outcome: The role of substance abuse problem severity. *Journal of Consulting and Clinical Psychology, 68,* 684–697.

Liddle, H. A., Dakof, G. A., Parker, K., Diamond, G. S., Barrett, K., & Tejeda, M. (2001). Multidimensional family therapy for adolescent drug abuse: Results of a randomized clinical trial. *American Journal of Drug and Alcohol Abuse, 27,* 651–688.

Liddle, H. A., Rowe, C. L., Quille, T. J., Dakof, G. A., Mills, D. S., Sakran, E., & Biaggi, H. (2002). Transporting a research-based adolescent drug treatment into practice. *Journal of Substance Abuse Treatment, 22,* 231–243.

Liddle, H. A., & Schwartz, S. J. (2002). Attachment and family therapy: The clinical utility of adolescent-family attachment research. *Family Process, 41,* 455–476.

Long, W. C. (1999). The dilemma of addiction and recovery during adolescence. *Dissertation Abstracts International Section A: Humanities and Social Sciences, 59,* 2440.

McGilliuddy, N. B., Rychtarik, R. G., Duquette, J. A., & Morsheimer, E. T. (2001). Development of a skill training program for parents of substance-abusing adolescents. *Journal of Substance Abuse Treatment, 20,* 59–68.

Muck, R., Zempolich, K. A., Titus, J. A., Fishman, M., Godley, M. D., & Schwebel, R. (2001). An overview of the effectiveness of adolescent substance abuse treatment models. *Youth and Society, 33,* 143–168.

Public Health Reports. (1997). Adolescent substance abuse tied to family structure. *Public Health Reports, 112,* 4–6.

Robbins, M. S., Bachrach, K., & Szapocznik, J. (2002). Bridging the research-practice gap in adolescent substance abuse treatment: The case of brief strategic family therapy. *Journal of Substance Abuse Treatment, 23,* 123–132.

Rowe, C. L., & Liddle, H. A. (2003). Substance abuse. *Journal of Marital and Family Therapy, 29,* 97–120.

Rowe, C. L., Parker-Sloat, E., Schwartz, S., & Liddle, H. (2003). Family therapy for early adolescent substance abuse. In S. J. Stevens & A. R. Morral (Eds.), *Adolescent substance abuse treatment in the United States: Exemplary models from a national evaluation study* (pp. 105–132). New York: The Haworth Press, Inc.

Schmidt, S. E., Liddle, H. A., & Dakof, G. A. (1996). Changes in parenting practices and adolescent drug abuse during multidimensional family therapy. *Journal of Family Psychology, 10,* 12–27.

Sholevar, G. P., & Schwoeri, L. D. (2003). Alcoholic and substance-abusing families. In G.P. Sholevar (Ed.), *Textbook of family and couples therapy: Clinical applications* (pp. 671–694). Washington, DC: American Psychiatric Publishing, Inc.

Slesnick, N., Meyers, R. J., Meade, M., & Segelken, D. H. (2000). Bleak and hopeless no more: Engagement of reluctant substance-abusing runaway youth and their families. *Journal of Substance Abuse Treatment, 19,* 215–222.

Springer, D. W., & Orsbon, S. H. (2002). Families helping families: Implementing a multifamily therapy group with substance-abusing adolescents. *Health and Social Work, 27,* 204–208.

Tuttle, J. (1995). Family support, adolescent individuation, and drug and alcohol involvement. *Journal of Family Nursing, 1,* 303–327.

Wagner, E. F., & Waldron, H. B. (1999). Innovations in adolescent substance abuse intervention. *Alcoholism: Clinical and Experimental Research, 23,* 236–249.

Wallace, S., & Estroff, T. W. (2001). Family treatment. In T. W. Estroff (Ed.), *Manual of adolescent substance abuse treatment* (pp. 235–252). Washington, DC: American Psychiatric Publishing, Inc.

About the authors: *Thomas Edward Smith*, PhD, is professor, Florida State University, School of Social Work, Tallahassee, FL (E-mail: tsmith@mailer.fsu.edu). *Scott P. Sells*, PhD, is director of the Savannah Family Institute, Savannah, GA (E-mail: spsells@difficult.net). *Jeffrey Rodman*, MA, is executive director, Here-4-You Consulting, LLC (E-mail: Jeffter46@hotmail.com). *Lisa Rene Reynolds*, PhD, is affiliated with the Nova Southeastern University (E-mail: lreynolds@norwalkreds.com).

Address correspondence to: Thomas Edward Smith, PhD, Florida State University, School of Social Work. Tallahassee, FL 32306. E-mail: tsmith@mailer.fsu.edu

Exercise for Article 22

Factual Questions

1. According to the researchers, there are how many "critical gaps" in adolescent substance abuse research and treatment?

2. The adolescents in this study committed a wide variety of offenses. What was the most commonly occurring offense?

3. The initial sample consisted of 102 adolescents. The researchers had complete data for how many?

4. What did the FVA subscale measure?

5. Was the "pretest mean" or the "posttest mean" on the FVA subscale higher?

6. Using .05 as the cutoff level for statistical significance, was the difference between the pretest and posttest means on the FVA subscale statistically significant? Explain.

Questions for Discussion

7. In your opinion, how important is the fact that a follow-up was conducted? Is 12 months an appropriate amount of follow-up for an evaluation of this type? (See the research questions in lines 107–115.)

8. How important is it to know that each participant was court-ordered into treatment by a judge? Would you be willing to generalize the results of this study to adolescents who volunteered to participate? (See lines 138–139 and 341–343.)

9. In your opinion, is the program that was evaluated in this study described in sufficient detail, keeping in mind that journal articles tend to be relatively short? Explain. (See lines 142–227.)

10. The researchers report a 15% relapse rate. Would it have been informative to have determined the relapse rate for a control group that did not receive the program? Explain. (See lines 289–297.)

11. In your opinion, might it be informative to ask the parents for their personal reactions to the program in a future evaluation of the program? Explain. Note that the completion rate for parents was 94%. (See lines 223–227 and 338–341.)

12. Do the data in this research article convince you that the *Parenting with Love and Limits*™ program is effective? Explain.

Quality Ratings

Directions: Indicate your level of agreement with each of the following statements by circling a number from 5 for strongly agree (SA) to 1 for strongly disagree (SD). If you believe an item is not applicable to this research article, leave it blank. Be prepared to explain your ratings. When responding to criteria A and B below, keep in mind that brief titles and abstracts are conventional in published research.

A. The title of the article is appropriate.

    SA   5   4   3   2   1   SD

B. The abstract provides an effective overview of the research article.

    SA   5   4   3   2   1   SD

C. The introduction establishes the importance of the study.

    SA   5   4   3   2   1   SD

D. The literature review establishes the context for the study.

    SA   5   4   3   2   1   SD

E. The research purpose, question, or hypothesis is clearly stated.

    SA   5   4   3   2   1   SD

F. The method of sampling is sound.

    SA   5   4   3   2   1   SD

G. Relevant demographics (for example, age, gender, and ethnicity) are described.

    SA   5   4   3   2   1   SD

H. Measurement procedures are adequate.

    SA   5   4   3   2   1   SD

I. All procedures have been described in sufficient detail to permit a replication of the study.

    SA   5   4   3   2   1   SD

J. The participants have been adequately protected from potential harm.

    SA   5   4   3   2   1   SD

K. The results are clearly described.

    SA   5   4   3   2   1   SD

L. The discussion/conclusion is appropriate.

    SA   5   4   3   2   1   SD

M. Despite any flaws, the report is worthy of publication.

    SA   5   4   3   2   1   SD

Article 23

Living with Severe Mental Illness—What Families and Friends Must Know: Evaluation of a One-Day Psychoeducation Workshop

DAVID E. POLLIO
Washington University

CAROL S. NORTH
University of Texas Southwestern
Medical Center

DONNA L. REID
Independence Center

MICHELLE M. MILETIC
Special School District of St. Louis County

JENNIFER R. McCLENDON
Washington University

ABSTRACT. One-day "family survival" psychoeducation workshops are a promising, convenient method of disseminating basic information to families with a relative who is diagnosed with a serious mental illness such as schizophrenia, major depression, or other affective disorders. At five separate psychoeducation workshops, 83 participating families completed the self-report North-Sachar Family Life Questionnaire and open-ended "problem lists" of issues facing the families both before and after the workshops. Outcomes consistently demonstrated positive change pre- to post-workshop. Issues reported by workshop participants included desire for education about illness, identification of resources, coping with the illness, and family relationships. The workshop model demonstrated consistent achievement of the outcomes measured, meeting short-term goals. Although models such as the family responsive approach reported in this article are not designed to create long-term gains for the family, they appear to benefit families and may help connect families with more intensive services to facilitate long-term change.

From *Social Work, 51*, 31–38. Copyright © 2006 by the National Association of Social Workers. Reprinted with permission.

Deinstitutionalization has shifted responsibility of care into community settings for even individuals with the most serious mental illnesses. Simultaneously, recent government policies have cut funding for intensive
5 psychosocial stabilization services in the community. As a result of these changes, overburdened families are finding themselves increasingly responsible for care of a family member with a serious mental illness. These families often struggle with this role because of their
10 lack of special training, knowledge, and sufficient professional support (McFarlane, 1991; North et al., 1998; Pollio, North, Osborne, Kap, & Foster, 2001; Solomon, 1996).

The stress of managing a family member's mental
15 illness can have a serious impact on families (Dixon & Lehman, 1995). The effects include not only problems interacting with the family member and the grief associated with the illness (Atkinson, 1994; Miller, Dworkin, Ward, & Barone, 1990), but also difficulties
20 in obtaining appropriate care and communicating effectively with service providers. Hanson (1993) found that families of people with mental illness were confused by their roles and felt helpless as these roles shifted over the course of treatment. Family stress can be asso-
25 ciated with physical and psychological problems in caregivers (Oldrige & Hughes, 1992; Vaddadi, 1996).

Families have critical needs for novel approaches to train them to assume their new responsibilities for care of their ill loved one. Psychoeducation models have
30 been developed to help families learn how to help their mentally ill member. Psychoeducation combines elements of education, support, and problem solving, generally within a standardized model (Pollio, Brower, & Galinsky, 2000). Psychoeducational goals for families
35 include obtaining relevant information, developing support within the group, learning to cope with the emotional aspects of care giving, recognizing the need for self-care, improving relationships with the care recipients and other family members, and using avail-
40 able formal services (Pollio et al., 2000; Smith, Majeski, & McClenny, 1996).

Multifamily psychoeducation group research for families coping with mental illness consistently demonstrates improved outcomes for the member with a
45 mental illness and the family. For the member with a mental illness, participation in psychoeducation and family treatment is associated with significantly decreased relapse rates (Anderson, Reiss, & Hogarty, 1986; Falloon et al., 1982; Leff, 1989; McFarlane,
50 Lukens, Link, & Dushay, 1995; North et al., 1998; Tarrier, Barrowclough, Vaughn, & Bamrah, 1989), reduced psychiatric symptoms (Leff; Leff, Kuipers, Berkowitz, Eberlein-Vries, & Sturgeon, 1982; Leff, Kuipers, Berkowitz, & Sturgeon, 1985; Tarrier et al.,
55 1988), and improved social adjustment (Anderson et

[handwritten note: 3 research Questions]

al., 1986; Leff et al., 1985; Falloon et al., 1985; Falloon, McGill, Boyd, & Pederson, 1987; Tarrier et al., 1988, 1989). Psychoeducation helps the caregiver by increasing social and family adjustment (Leff, 1989; Leff et al., 1982, 1985; Levene, Newman, & Jeffries, 1989; McFarlane, Dunne, Lukens, & Newmark, 1993; McFarlane et al., 1995), coping and well-being (Doane, Goldstein, Miklowitz, & Falloon, 1986; Zastowny, Lehman, Cole, & Kane, 1992), and by decreasing family burden and time spent worrying (Lam, 1991; McFarlane et al., 1995; Pollio, North, & Osborne, 2002; Solomon, 1996; Solomon & Draine, 1995; Solomon, Draine, Mannion, & Meisel, 1996, 1997).

A limitation of psychoeducation is its intensive time commitment for families participating in the groups (Smith & Birchwood, 1990). The chaos families experience trying to cope with mental illness in the family, along with multiple other factors (e.g., work and family commitments, difficulties gaining access to services), may make them reluctant to commit to long-term interventions.

Because of the substantial time commitment required by groups, brief psychoeducation workshops (Anderson et al., 1986) have become a popular forum. Few studies, however, have evaluated the outcomes of educational workshops for family members of individuals with mental illness. Reilly and colleagues (1988) examined the effects of a day-long workshop for families immediately before state hospital discharge and found no reduction in recidivism or engagement of families. It can be argued, however, that it may be unrealistic to expect long-term effects from this brief intervention. It is more appropriate to conceptualize such brief interventions as portals to more intensive services, providing hope and support, and offering ideas for coping with family concerns and problems related to the illness. Thus, an appropriate evaluation would focus on whether the family's perceived needs were met and skills or knowledge were acquired as part of the evaluation process. Establishing the effectiveness of a replicable model that meets these simple goals would contribute an important piece to the arsenal of systems of care seeking to support people with mental illness and their families.

The purpose of this study, therefore, was to measure the effectiveness of the "family survival" workshop, a one-day program developed collaboratively by researchers at Washington University and the National Alliance for the Mentally Ill (NAMI) of St. Louis. Its effectiveness was measured by answering the following three questions: (1) Did families report gains in family members' perceived ability to manage the illness and related crises, knowledge about the illness, feelings of control, guilt feelings, and knowledge of resources? (2) Which characteristics of families (age, race, gender, relationship to member with illness) and members with illness (primary diagnosis, length, and recent severity of illness) are associated with increased

likelihood of benefiting from the workshop? and (3) Did the topics presented match the reported needs of the participant families? We addressed these questions by comparing the families' responses to five questions before and after the workshop, modeling predictors of improvement in outcome variables, and qualitatively examining the families' responses to an open-ended question about their goals for attending the workshop.

Method

Setting

Five one-day "family survival" workshops in St. Louis provided the sources of data for this study between October 1999 and May 2001. Notices of the workshops were mailed to mental health services providers on a NAMI mailing list requesting them to disseminate information to their patients and clients, and to families on a NAMI mailing list. Staff at inpatient and outpatient mental health agencies in the St. Louis area were asked to post program announcements in their waiting areas. Workshop participants were also recruited directly through local newspaper and television announcements of the program. Family members paid $15 for the day per member (with scholarships available on request).

Workshop Format and Structure

The workshops were developed to serve families with a member suffering from a serious mental illness, primarily schizophrenia, bipolar disorder, major depression, and other affective disorders. The model is based on the authors' "family responsive" approach to services for these families (North et al., 1998; Pollio et al., 2002). This approach views family members (including the one with the illness) as capable partners in the intervention process. The philosophy of intervention includes a willingness to create services based on identifying and responding directly to family needs (rather than providing clinician or research-initiated information). In creating the workshop format, this philosophy influenced the workshop development process, choice of material presented, and structure of the program. For the workshop development process, the planning committee included family members and professionals working together. As part of the planning process, the team decided to present information to families at the same level of complexity as might be used for a professional audience. Anecdotally, this led to attendance by a number of students and professionals at these workshops (although this evaluation does not include data by this group). Finally, along with inclusion of rigorously developed materials produced for the workshops, material identified by participants uniquely for each workshop was included.

The workshops' programs included three opening plenary addresses: (1) "Mental Illness: What It Is and Is Not," which provided descriptive and diagnostic information on schizophrenia and mood disorders; (2) "The Brain," which described the biological basis of

mental illness, including neurochemistry and genetics;
and (3) "Treatment of Mental Disorders," which re-
170 viewed medication and other forms of treatment. These
sessions were standardized across all workshops, with
PowerPoint presentations and accompanying handouts
created by the second author. All lecturers were recruited by at least one of the authors to speak in their
175 area of expertise, and all presentations were monitored
to ensure that the general material was presented.

Before the initial plenary address, families were
asked to list problems they faced with having mental
illness in their family. During the workshops, these
180 lists were analyzed to identify issues of interest unique
to each group of attending families. The topics created
from these lists were used to organize informal discussion groups at a midday luncheon titled "Your Issues."
Placards announcing the topics created from the work-
185 shop problem lists were placed on luncheon tables seating eight to 12 participants each. Program participants
and staff were asked to sit at the table of the topic in
which they had the greatest interest. The topic generated a starting place for their lunchtime discussions.
190 Issues chosen were those that appeared on the participants' lists but were not specifically included in the
presentations.

The afternoon's program consisted of two sets of
hour-long breakout sessions. These sessions, chaired
195 by professionals with special expertise on the topic,
consisted of brief didactic presentations followed by
audience discussion. Although the content of these
sessions varied somewhat among the different workshops, the sessions generally included area resources;
200 success stories from families and their member with a
mental illness; "Ask the Doc," an informal question
and answer session with a psychiatrist; religion and
religious resources; and legal rights. As a part of these
workshops, families were asked permission to be con-
205 tacted to participate in a randomized clinical trial testing a year-long family-responsive psychoeducation
group model developed by the authors (North et al.,
1998; Pollio et al., 2002).

Data Collection

At the start of the program, one member from each
210 family was asked to complete the North-Sachar Family
Life Questionnaire (FLQ), consisting of 11 questions
that elicit information about family members' perceived ability to manage the illness and related crises,
knowledge about the illness, disruptions to family life,
215 communication with the ill member, success with behavioral expectations, guilt feelings, and hospitalization history (number of hospital days and episodes) (for
more details on this instrument, see North et al., 1998).
Workshop participants also completed a basic demo-
220 graphic form providing characteristics of both respondents and members with illness. Finally, families completed the list of "problems faced" to help provide the
content of sessions in response to their specific con-

cerns (Pollio, North, & Foster, 1998; Pollio et al.,
225 2001). Where more than one family member was present, we did not stipulate which family member completed the form, only requesting that the same family
member complete all forms and that family members
discuss responses where possible. At the workshop's
230 conclusion, one participant from each family completed a satisfaction questionnaire about the workshop.
This questionnaire, developed for the workshops, was
piloted and used in earlier research by this research
team (North et al., 1998; Pollio et al., 2002). Five ques-
235 tions provided postworkshop information using North-
Sachar FLQ items. The five items selected measured
separate concepts identified in earlier research, and
through workshop development procedures, as of interest to the workshop organizers. Of the 160 participating
240 families, 83 (52%) completed both pre- and posttests
and 77 (48%) completed only the pretest.

Variables in the Analysis

The outcome variables analyzed in the current report included the five items from the North-Sachar
FLQ completed both pre- and postworkshop: (1) family
245 members' perceived ability to manage the illness and
related crises, (2) knowledge about the illness, (3) feelings of control, (4) guilt feelings, and (5) knowledge of
resources. Each item was scored on a scale ranging
from 1 to 5, with higher scores being more positive. To
250 assess change, scores from the pretest were subtracted
from those from the posttest for each item. Demographic variables used in the analysis included respondents' age, race (white/not white), gender, and relationship to the person with a mental illness (parent, sibling,
255 or friend); primary diagnosis of the member with a
mental illness coded into three dichotomous variables
for schizophrenia, bipolar disorder, and depression (all
other diagnoses being the excluded categories); length
in years since first episode; number of days hospital-
260 ized; and number of hospital episodes for the previous
year. Scoring of the remaining items from the North-
Sachar FLQ collected only at baseline was similar to
that described previously.

Data Analysis

Quantitative data analyses were performed to iden-
265 tify systematic biases of posttest noncompletion for
variables of gender, race, age of respondent, primary
reported diagnosis, number of inpatient days and episodes, and all items in the pretest North-Sachar FLQ,
using chi-square and t test analyses; to determine
270 change (research question 1), using t tests to compare
pre- and posttest scores for the five paired variables;
and to identify predictors of change ($n = 83$: research
question 2). For this final analysis, we used simple
regression models to examine correlations between
275 single predictors and change scores for each outcome
variable. Once significant associations were identified
in simple regressions, multiple regressions were performed with all significant variables identified in sim-

ple models included in final regressions. For clarity, we
280   report only significant results from these final models.

Qualitative data analysis was used to describe reasons for attending the workshop. Although these data
did not provide information on outcomes, reasons identified by families provide evidence of the fit (or lack
285   thereof) between the family issues and the workshop
content (research question 3). These analyses followed
procedures we used previously to categorize data from
the "problem lists." All items in the analysis were examined by at least two authors who created categories
290   by consensus and placed items into categories. Earlier
use of this methodology yielded interrater reliabilities
of 85% to 91% for the categories (Pollio et al., 1998;
Pollio et al., 2000).

Results

Respondents

Participants completing both pre- and posttest were
295   female (78%) and predominantly white (97%). A majority of the family members were parents of the person
with illness (68%), with a mean age of 54 years (SD =
13). Families listed their member with illness' primary
diagnoses as bipolar disorder (51%), schizophrenia
300   (22%), major depression (6%), and other (22%). The
person with illness averaged 25 (SD = 57) inpatient
days in the previous year, and 47% had at least a single
episode of illness exacerbation (mean episodes = 1.0,
SD = 1.4). Families were experienced in care of their ill
305   members, who had been affected an average of 12.8
years (SD = 11.1). Finally, a majority of the families
attending the workshop (61%) agreed to consider an
invitation to participate in a multifamily psychoeducation clinical trial.
310   Across the entire sample, more than one-half (56%,
n = 90) of families attending the workshop reported
serious effects of the illness on other family members
for that item. Most families (63%, n = 101) reported at
least occasional yelling or violent episodes with their
315   ill member, and many of these families felt the violence was frequent or constant (27% overall, n = 43).
Families reported difficulties in behavioral expectations, with only 28% (n = 45) reporting being "usually"
or "always" successful at setting expectations and 25%
320   (n = 40) reporting the member as usually or always
successful at meeting expectations. Only a minority of
families (33%, n = 53) felt they communicated well
with their member with illness. However, respondents
generally reported that their family member with ill-
325   ness was usually or always medication compliant
(74%, n = 120).

No significant differences were found between
completers of pretest only and completers of both pre-
and posttest in any analysis.

Outcomes

330   All five questions asked in the North-Sachar FLQ
reflected significant improvements from workshop start
to finish. Paired responses indicated that families felt

more in control of their daily lives, more effective in
crisis situations, more knowledgeable in obtaining
335   community resources, more knowledgeable about mental illness and treatment, and decreased feelings of guilt
after the one-day psychoeducation workshop. Pre- and
posttest scores, t tests, and probabilities are displayed
in Table 1.
340   *Multivariate Analyses.* For the five variables reflecting change, three had significant predictors in a
final model, with two models as a whole providing
statistical significance. For prediction of change in
knowledge of community resources, although the equa-
345   tion as a whole was not significant, number of days
hospitalized for the ill member was negatively associated with change (ß = –.01, SE = .005, t = –2.02, p =
.05). Number of hospital episodes was significantly
predicted in the simple regression model, but not in the
350   multiple regression. The equation for prediction of
guilt feelings was significant [$F(4,58)$ = 4.6, p < .01],
with the diagnosis of major depression significantly
negatively associated with guilt reduction (ß = –.97, SE
= .36, t = –2.68, p = .01), and higher pretest ratings of
355   the member with a mental illness meeting behavioral
expectations were associated with reduction in guilt (ß
= .26, SE = .12, t = 2.13, p = .04). Two other variables,
medication compliance and number of episodes, were
not significantly associated with guilt reduction in sim-
360   ple regressions in this final model. The overall model
predicting families' ability to cope with crisis was statistically significant [$F(1,72)$ = 6.94, p = .01]. In it,
poor medication compliance was associated with increased feelings of ability to respond to crises (ß = –
365   .19, SE = .07, t = –2.63, p = .01).
Qualitative Analysis. A total of 360 items were tal-
lied from the families' problem lists, with 4.4 items per
family on average (range = 1 to 14). Five categories
identified by the analysis included 93% of the individ-
370   ual items (Table 2). The remaining 7% were either
unique or included in categories containing fewer than
nine items.

Discussion

Results from the workshop evaluation were overwhelmingly positive. Families consistently reported
375   significant gains from pre- to postworkshop. Limited
findings from multivariate analysis suggest the general
appropriateness of the model to accommodate the
range of families attending the workshop. Despite the
study's important limitations, all indications point to
380   the ability of the model to achieve its goals. The Family Skills Workshop not only appears to address identified needs of families coping with this significant challenge, but also may serve as a portal to more intensive
services.
385   The answer to the first research question (Did families report gains after the workshop?) appears to be
resoundingly positive. All items generated positive
change. Families reported gains in all areas specified

Table 1
Pre- and Posttest Scores on the North-Sachar FLQ for Families with a Member with a Mental Illness

Variable	Pre-score	Post-score	t test	p	N
Feelings of control	2.31	2.46	2.0	.05	80
Crisis intervention	2.47	2.70	3.2	.002	81
Knowledge of resources	2.27	2.62	3.5	.001	82
Knowledge of illness	2.53	2.79	3.1	.003	77
Feelings of guilt	3.86	4.17	3.3	.002	78

Notes. FLQ = Family Life Questionnaire. Higher scores indicate improvement. All items range from 1 to 5.

Table 2
Categories and Percentages from the Qualitative Problem List Analysis for Families with a Member with a Mental Illness

Category	% of items
Education about illness, including new information and advice on specific illnesses	36
Coping strategies, including problem solving and support skills and increasing personal effectiveness	21
Resources, including local and national information on getting help and legal resources	17
Social support and communication with the family member with illness, including the future for the person with illness, increasing communication and social support, and improving relationships	13
Increasing support from others in the community, including agency and informal support networks	4

Note. All items were placed in unique categories. Rounding errors and items not categorized caused differences in percentages.

for this research question. It may be the case that this response reflects a general positive appraisal of the workshop, rather than independent gains in each area. In either case, whether a generic positive response or a specific response to the items, it is clear that families reported an immediate positive experience to the workshop. Although the large percentage of families volunteering to be recruited for the longer-term intervention study suggests otherwise (and argues for the clinical impact of the findings), in making this interpretation, we would be remiss if we did not at least raise the possibility that this finding may represent a measurement artifact.

The paucity of findings from the second research question (Which characteristics of family and member with illness increased likelihood of benefiting from the workshop?) suggests that family and member-with-illness characteristics had little consistent association with gains. Higher functioning in the family member with a mental illness may allow family members to concentrate less on immediate needs and crises and more on acquiring new ways of coping. In addition, findings suggest that problems with medication compliance may encourage families to attend workshops in search of specific solutions, leading to greater gains when their needs are met. However, the few significant findings indicate need for a cautious approach to these speculations, as the potential for spurious significant "false positive" associations (Type II errors) may account for some or all of the apparent associations.

The third research question (Did the topics presented match the reported needs of the participant families?) is potentially confounded by the structure of the workshop. The "Your Issues" luncheon ensured

that each workshop was tailored to the audience's specific needs. However, examination of the categories emerging from the analysis and their relative emphasis with the structure described provides compelling evidence that the general structure of the workshops addressed the participants' expressed issues with some precision. The most frequently addressed category provided by preworkshop questionnaire data, desire for education about the illness, paralleled the focus of the plenary sessions of the morning's program. Thus, the material most frequently identified as family issues in qualitative analysis was provided to all participants. Similarly, content of the three next frequently identified categories was provided in the afternoon breakout sessions when families had opportunities to participate in two self-selected sessions. Finally, the smallest category, need for informal support, was addressed within the structure of the "Your Issues" luncheon.

Study Limitations

As an exploratory study, this research was not without significant limitations. The sample was neither random nor representative of all families affected by mental illness; therefore, the results may not be generalizable to families not participating in family psychoeducation workshops. This sampling bias also may limit the general applicability of success of the workshop to other settings. However, biases associated with self-selection to participate in educational workshops are inherent to these programs, as these programs are not for everyone. The sample also was demographically nonrepresentative, with low representation of African American and other racial and ethnic minority groups. Other researchers have identified the impor-

455 tance of racial differences in the experience of having a
family member with a mental illness (Stueve, Vine, &
Struening, 1997). Future research should focus on issues of generalizability and should include comparison
groups and more racial and ethnic diversity. In addi-
460 tion, although the statistical analyses did not indicate
any significant bias based on completers of both pre-
and posttest versus those completing pretest only, the
high attrition rates represent a limitation of the data and
an area for potential untested biases. Finally, the meth-
465 odology of a pre- and post-model does not strictly allow for assignment of causality.

Service Implications

Although this study had obvious limitations, the results clearly provide service implications. The ability to
conduct multiple workshops and recruit participants
470 from them for more intensive services suggests the
potential not only for the workshops, but also for this
model as a means to attract service-willing families to
services. The positive gains identified for the workshop
participants, combined with the willingness of families
475 to be contacted about potential participation in future
programs, suggest that these kinds of time-limited services have utility as a portal to more intensive and
powerful family interventions. Families willing to pay
for and commit to day-long attendance demonstrate
480 their readiness for more intensive services.

The results also provide directions for tailoring services for these families across locations. Although the
educational content is highly valued, it is clear that
families desire information relevant to finding and ef-
485 fectively using services within their specific communities. Agencies wishing to create a similar workshop
model would need to include presentations specific to
available treatment options and local systems of care.
Furthermore, workshops can be modified to focus on
490 more specific subpopulations. For example, workshops
might be developed to serve families whose member
with a mental illness has higher levels of functioning,
with greater attention paid to independence issues.

The promising evidence for the workshop presented
495 here also indicates the potential for this family responsive approach to creating and adapting interventions for
a range of families coping with a variety of mental illnesses. Multifamily psychoeducation groups already
have a broad history of generalizability to other popu-
500 lations (Pollio et al., 2000). Findings from the family
responsive workshop presented here suggest the utility
of models aimed at addressing, in a single setting,
families coping with multiple diagnoses and complex
challenges, rather than aiming interventions at specific
505 diagnostic groups or issues.

References

Anderson, C. M., Reiss, D. J., & Hogarty, G. E. (1986). *Schizophrenia and the family: A practitioner's guide to psychoeducation and management.* New York: Guilford Press.

Atkinson, S. D. (1994). Grieving and loss in parents with a schizophrenic child. *American Journal of Psychiatry, 151,* 1137–1139.

Dixon, L. B., & Lehman, A. F. (1995). Family interventions for schizophrenia. *Schizophrenia Bulletin, 21,* 631–643.

Doane, J. A., Goldstein, M. J., Miklowitz, D. J., & Falloon, I. R. (1986). The impact of individual and family treatment on the affective climate of families of schizophrenics. *British Journal of Psychiatry, 148,* 279–287.

Falloon, I. R., Boyd, J. L., McGill, C. W., Razani, J., Moss, H. B., & Gilderman, A. M. (1982). Family management in the prevention of exacerbations of schizophrenia: A controlled study. *New England Journal of Medicine, 306,* 1437–1440.

Falloon, I. R., Boyd, J. L., McGill, C. W., Williamson, M., Razani, J., Moss, H. B., Gilderman, A. M., & Simpson, G. M. (1985). Family management in the prevention of morbidity of schizophrenia: Clinical outcome of a two-year longitudinal study. *Archives of General Psychiatry, 42,* 887–896.

Falloon I. R., McGill, C. W., Boyd, J. L., & Pederson, J. (1987). Family management in the prevention of morbidity of schizophrenia: Social Outcome of a two-year longitudinal study. *Psychological Medicine, 17,* 59–66.

Hanson, J. G. (1993). Families of people with a severe mental illness: Role conflict, ambiguity, and family burden. *Journal of Sociology & Social Welfare, 20,* 105–118.

Lam, D. H. (1991). Psychosocial family intervention in schizophrenia: A review of empirical studies. *Psychological Medicine, 21,* 423–441.

Leff, J. (1989). Family factors in schizophrenia. *Psychiatric Annals, 19,* 542–547.

Leff, J., Kuipers, L., Berkowitz, R., Eberlein-Vries, R., & Sturgeon, D. (1982). A controlled trial of social intervention in the families of schizophrenic patients. *British Journal of Psychiatry, 141,* 121–134.

Leff, J., Kuipers, L., Berkowitz, R., & Sturgeon, D. (1985). A controlled trial of social intervention in the families of schizophrenic patients: Two-year follow-up. *British Journal of Psychiatry, 146,* 594–600.

Levene, J. E., Newman, F., & Jeffries, J. J. (1989). Focal family therapy outcome study I: Patient and family functioning. *Canadian Journal of Psychiatry, 34,* 641–647.

McFarlane, W. R. (1991). Family psychoeducational treatment. In A. S. Gurman, & D. P. Kniskern (Eds.), *Handbook of Family Therapy* (Vol. 2, pp. 363–395). Philadelphia: Brunner/Mazel.

McFarlane, W. R., Dunne, E., Lukens, E., & Newmark, M. (1993). From research to clinical practice: Dissemination of New York State's family psychoeducation project. *Hospital and Community Psychiatry, 44,* 265–270.

McFarlane, W. R., Lukens, E., Link, B., & Dushay, R. (1995). Multiple-family groups and psychoeducation in the treatment of schizophrenia. *Archives of General Psychiatry, 52,* 679–687.

Miller, F., Dworkin, J., Ward, M., & Barone, D. (1990). A preliminary study of unresolved grief in families of seriously mentally ill patients. *Hospital and Community Psychiatry, 41,* 1321–1325.

North, C. S., Pollio, D. E., Sachar, B., Hong, B., Isenberg, K., & Bufe, G. (1998). The family as caregiver for schizophrenia: A group psychoeducation model. *American Journal of Orthopsychiatry, 68,* 39–47.

Oldrige, M., & Hughes, I. (1992). Psychological well-being in families with a member suffering from schizophrenia. *British Journal of Psychiatry, 161,* 249–251.

Pollio, D. E., Brower, A., & Galinsky, M. J. (2000). Change in groups. In C. Garvin & P. Allen-Meares (Eds.), *Handbook of Social Work Direct Practice* (pp. 281–301). Thousand Oaks, CA: Sage Publications.

Pollio, D. E., North, C. S., & Foster, D. E. (1998). Content and curriculum in multifamily psychoeducation. *Psychiatric Services, 49,* 816–822.

Pollio, D. E., North C. S., & Osborne, V. (2002). Family-responsive psychoeducation groups for families with an adult member with mental illness: Pilot results. *Community Mental Health Journal, 38,* 413–421.

Pollio, D. E., North, C. S., Osborne, V., Kap, N., & Foster, D.A. (2001). The impact of psychiatric diagnosis and family system relationship on problems identified by families coping with a mentally ill member. *Family Process, 40,* 199–210.

Reilly, J. W., Rohrbaugh, M., & Lackner, J. M. (1988). A controlled evaluation of psychoeducation workshops for relatives of state hospital patients. *Journal of Marital & Family Therapy, 14,* 429–432.

Smith, J., & Birchwood, M. (1990). Relatives and patients as partners in the management of schizophrenia: The development of a service model. *British Journal of Psychiatry, 156,* 654–660.

Smith, G., Majeski, R. A., & McClenny, B. (1996). Psychoeducational support groups for aging parents: Development and preliminary outcomes. *Mental Retardation, 34,* 172–181.

Solomon, P. (1996). Moving from psychoeducation to family education for families of adults with serious mental illness. *Psychiatric Services, 47,* 1364–1370.

Solomon, P., & Draine, J. (1995). Subjective burden among family members of mentally ill adults: Relation to stress, coping, and adaptation. *American Journal of Orthopsychiatry, 65,* 419–427.

Solomon, P., Draine, J., Mannion, E., & Meisel, M. (1996). Impact of brief family therapy on self-efficacy. *Schizophrenia Bulletin, 22,* 41–50.

Solomon, P., Draine, J., Mannion, E., & Meisel, M. (1997). Effectiveness of two models of brief family education: Retention of gains by family members of adults with severe mental illness. *American Journal of Orthopsychiatry, 67,* 177–187.

Stueve, A., Vine, P., & Struening, E. L. (1997). Perceived burden among caregivers of adults with serious mental illness: Comparison of black, Hispanic, and white families. *American Journal of Orthopsychiatry, 67*, 199–209.

Tarrier, N., Barrowclough, C., Vaughn, C., & Bamrah, J. S., Porceddu, K., Watts, S., & Freeman, H. (1988). The community management of schizophrenia: A controlled trial of a behavioral intervention with families to reduce relapse. *British Journal of Psychiatry, 153*, 532–542.

Tarrier, N., Barrowclough, C., Vaughn, C., & Bamrah, J. S., Porceddu, K., Watts, S., & Freeman, H. (1989). Community management of schizophrenia: A two-year follow-up of a behavioural intervention with families. *British Journal of Psychiatry, 154*, 625–628.

Vaddadi, K. (1996). Stress of caregiving for the chronically mentally ill. *Psychiatric Annals, 26*, 766–771.

Zastowny, T. R., Lehman, A. F., Cole, R. E., & Kane, C. (1992). Family management of schizophrenia: A comparison of behavioral and supportive family treatment. *Psychiatric Quarterly, 63*, 159–186.

About the authors: *David E. Pollio*, Ph.D., LCSW, is associate professor, George Warren Brown School of Social Work, Washington University. *Carol S. North*, MD, is Ron & Nancy Hunt Professor of Psychiatry at University of Texas Southwestern Medical Center, Dallas. *Donna L. Reid*, MSW, is evaluation specialist, Independence Center, St. Louis. *Michelle M. Miletic*, MSW, is school social worker, Special School District of St. Louis County. *Jennifer R. McClendon*, MSW, is a doctoral student, George Warren Brown School of Social Work, Washington University, St. Louis.

Address correspondence to: David E. Pollio, George Warren Brown School of Social Work, Washington University, Campus Box 1196, One Brookings Drive, St. Louis, MO 63130-4899. E-mail: depollio@wustl.edu

Acknowledgments: The authors wish to thank staff and volunteers for the Family Survival Project and the National Alliance for the Mentally Ill of St. Louis, and Richard D. Stevenson and Marge Parrish for their participation in the research project. The project was funded by the National Institute of Mental Health, grant no. 22-1620-51320.

Exercise for Article 23

Factual Questions

1. Did the researchers recruit participants from a single source?

2. There were how many participating families?

3. What percentage of the families had a member with major depression?

4. What was the pretest mean for "knowledge of illness"? What was the posttest mean?

5. What is the value of p for the difference between the two means in Question 4 above?

6. What percentage of the responses to the open-ended question referred to "coping strategies"?

Questions for Discussion

7. Participants were paid to participate in the program. Is this important? Why? Why not? (See lines 133–135.)

8. Keeping in mind that journal articles tend to be relatively short, is the workshop described in sufficient detail? (See lines 163–208.)

9. Is it important to know that only 52% of the participants completed both the pre- and posttests? Explain. (See lines 239–241, 327–329, and 459–466.)

10. Do you agree that it would be desirable to have comparison groups in future evaluations of this program? Explain. (See lines 457–459.)

11. Do you believe that the program caused the changes from pretest to posttest? Explain. (See lines 464–466.)

12. Based on this evaluation, do you believe that the workshop deserves further investigation in the future? Explain.

Quality Ratings

Directions: Indicate your level of agreement with each of the following statements by circling a number from 5 for strongly agree (SA) to 1 for strongly disagree (SD). If you believe an item is not applicable to this research article, leave it blank. Be prepared to explain your ratings. When responding to criteria A and B below, keep in mind that brief titles and abstracts are conventional in published research.

A. The title of the article is appropriate.

SA 5 4 3 2 1 SD

B. The abstract provides an effective overview of the research article.

SA 5 4 3 2 1 SD

C. The introduction establishes the importance of the study.

SA 5 4 3 2 1 SD

D. The literature review establishes the context for the study.

SA 5 4 3 2 1 SD

E. The research purpose, question, or hypothesis is clearly stated.

SA 5 4 3 2 1 SD

F. The method of sampling is sound.

       SA   5   4   3   2   1   SD

G. Relevant demographics (for example, age, gender, and ethnicity) are described.

       SA   5   4   3   2   1   SD

H. Measurement procedures are adequate.

       SA   5   4   3   2   1   SD

I. All procedures have been described in sufficient detail to permit a replication of the study.

       SA   5   4   3   2   1   SD

J. The participants have been adequately protected from potential harm.

       SA   5   4   3   2   1   SD

K. The results are clearly described.

       SA   5   4   3   2   1   SD

L. The discussion/conclusion is appropriate.

       SA   5   4   3   2   1   SD

M. Despite any flaws, the report is worthy of publication.

       SA   5   4   3   2   1   SD

Article 24

Evaluation of a Program Designed to Reduce Relational Aggression in Middle School Girls

CHERYL DELLASEGA
Penn State College of Medicine

PAMELA ADAMSHICK
Moravian College

ABSTRACT. Physical and verbal aggression is an increasing problem in both middle and high schools across the United States. While physical forms of aggression are targeted in traditional "bullying" programs, relational aggression (RA), or the use of relationships to hurt another, is often not detected or addressed. For girls in the stage of identity formation, RA can impact negatively on self-concept, peer relationships, school performance, and mental and physical health. An innovative program designed specifically to help middle school girls confront and cope with issues related to RA was developed, implemented, and evaluated in two school systems. Attitudes and self-reported behaviors were measured before and after the program. Results show an improvement in relationship skills after participation in the program. Most noticeable improvements were in a girl's stated willingness to become involved when witnessing another girl being hurt and girls benefiting from the mentoring they received from high school juniors and seniors.

From *Journal of School Violence*, 4, 63–76. Copyright © 2005 by The Haworth Press, Inc. Reprinted with permission.

Introduction

Aggression in Youth

Since Columbine, the issue of aggression in youth has been at the forefront of the nation's consciousness. Across the country, administrators, guidance counselors, school nurses, and teachers witness violence between young people in the classroom, often on a daily basis. In a recent survey of high school students, more than one-third of respondents reported being in a physical fight in the past twelve months (CDC, 2002). A report commissioned by former President Clinton showed that 30 to 40 percent of male youths and 15 to 30 percent of female youths admit to having committed a serious violent offense by age 17. The violent offenses included in this group are homicides, robberies, aggravated assaults, and forcible rapes (U.S. Department of Health and Human Services, 2001).

Statistics on adolescent female violence show that the self-reported rate of violent acts by female adolescents is closing the gender gap. In 1998, the prevalence rates for male and female violence were similar to 1993, but the incidence rate for violent acts by females rose (U.S. Department of Health and Human Services, 2001). In addition, the arrest of girls for assault and weapons charges has increased and exceeds that for boys (Smith & Thomas, 2000). According to U.S. Department of Justice statistics from 1991, 54% of reported violent crimes against 12–15-year-old girls were committed by other girls or women (Whitaker & Bastian, 1991). In response to these troubling data, one of the national goals designated in *Healthy People 2010* is to decrease physical fighting among adolescents (U.S. Department of Health and Human Services, 2000).

Bullying and School Violence

Bullying is a form of violence that may include behaviors that are verbally and/or physically aggressive. While many different definitions of bullying are used, consensus has been reached on these characteristics: the bully's intent to inflict harm, his or her perceived or real power over the victim, repeated nature of the aggression, nonprovoking behavior by the victim, and the occurrence of the bullying within familiar social groups (Griffin & Gross, in press; Olweus, 1994; Greene, 2000).

The bullying dynamic is a complex interrelational process that relies on and is fueled by behaviors and responses of more than one participant. Typical roles are the aggressor, the victim, and bystanders (also referred to as "witnesses" or "in-betweeners"). Victims may or may not provoke their aggressors, and many victims become retaliatory aggressors. As observers or passive participants, bystanders can deliberately or inadvertently facilitate bullying (Hazler, 1996).

Relational Aggression

In studies on styles of aggression, interesting gender-specific findings have emerged. Researchers Lagerspetz, Bjorkqvist, and Peltonen (1988) studied 167 children aged 11–12 years and found that girls engaged in more indirect aggression, a circuitous type of attack on another that amounted to social manipulation. Boys tended to use direct means of aggression. The term "social aggression" is sometimes applied to these behaviors because they occur within the context of groups and because the participants have some de-

127

gree of relationship with one another (Underwood, Galen, & Paquette, 2001).

Some behaviors that can be involved in this type of nonphysical aggression can be found in Figure 1.

Gossip
Manipulation
Intimidation
Exclusion
Gestures
Ridicule
Saying something mean then pretending you were "joking"
Name calling
Teasing
Cliques
Campaigns
"On again–off again" friendships
Betrayal of confidence
Sending hurtful messages via cell phone or computer
Other subtle or not-so-subtle forms of harassment

Figure 1. Examples of Relational Aggression.

65   Crick and Grotpeter (1995) also found that girls were significantly more relationally aggressive than boys. They chose the term "relational aggression" rather than "indirect aggression" to describe the type of aggression displayed by females because the behaviors
70   they found were aimed at harming others through purposeful manipulation and damage of peer relationships. Their research, done with 491 third- through sixth-grade children in a Midwestern town in the United States, included children of varying ethnic backgrounds
75   (60% European American), thus supporting cross-cultural validity of gender differences in style of aggression. Their study added greater refinement to terms by using an instrument that did not confound relational aggression with nonverbal aggression.
80   The notion that girls can be bullies too is a phenomenon of great interest, as demonstrated by the recent movie *Mean Girls*. While physical aggression is an obvious cause for concern and intervention, the types of social aggression portrayed in the movie and
85   played out in classrooms, sports, and online every day are harder to detect and measure. These behaviors are sometimes dismissed as a female rite of passage, perhaps because RA seems to be most problematic in adolescent girls in middle and secondary school (Ahmad &
90   Smith, 1994).
RA may be more threatening to girls than physical forms of violence. In an online survey of over 2,000 girls ages 8–17, 41% of preteen girls and 22% of teen girls listed being teased or made fun of as their top
95   safety concern, remarkable when choices such as "terrorism" and "kidnapping" were other alternatives offered (Girl Scout Research Institute, 2003).
The developmental needs of adolescent girls who are struggling with identity formation through forging
100   connections with others may explain many RA behaviors (Gilligan, 1982). For example, exclusionary tactics

whereby a girl distances herself from peers she identifies as being "not like me," allows her to perceive a sense of status and being part of a select group (Hazler,
105   1996). There is also evidence that RA occurs within a girl's friendship circle, whereas males tend to aggress outside their circle of friends (Dellasega & Nixon, 2003). Relational aggression can impair normal development in that girls who consistently use RA behaviors
110   to interact with others begin to believe that their indirect bullying is not only acceptable, but also normal (Dellasega & Nixon, 2003).
Research by Galen and Underwood (1997) added another dimension to understanding nonphysical aggression in youth. They defined social aggression to include not only verbal rejection or social exclusion, but also negative facial expressions or body movements. Their use of vignette measures that included nonverbal examples of social aggression had high internal consistency. The importance of nonverbals in aggression was further supported in a study by Paquette and Underwood (1999) with pre-adolescents. Findings showed that nonverbal forms of social aggression are experienced most frequently in that age group.
125   Cillessen and Mayeux (2004) followed a group of 905 students from fifth to ninth grade and examined the interplay between popularity and aggression during this developmental period. They found that as participants moved from middle childhood into early adolescence
130   relational aggression increasingly predicted high popularity, but low levels of liking. However, the concept of popularity itself changed during this span of time. "Popular" evolved from being well liked as a fifth grader to being influential and powerful in the ninth
135   grade. The researchers conclude that adolescents use relational aggression to maintain their dominant, influential position in the peer group. The results suggest that intervention studies to reduce bullying should take into account the status enhancing and rewarding quali-
140   ties of relationally aggressive behaviors for this developmental period.
While the old adage of "names will never hurt you" (as opposed to sticks and stones, which will break bones) is often cited, the reality is that RA can have
145   serious outcomes for both aggressors and victims (Crick & Grotpeter, 1995; Dellasega & Nixon, 2003; Nansel et al. 2001; Paquette & Underwood, 1999). These include risk for substance abuse, bulimic behaviors, delinquency, and development of low self-esteem
150   and adjustment problems in victims (Crick, Casas, & Nelson, 2002). In one tragic case, repeated RA led a Canadian girl to suicide, and others have observed that in girls, RA often precedes physical forms of violence (Dellasega, in preparation). Some negative impacts
155   specifically reported by aggressors include a sense of loneliness and depression (Tomada & Schneider, 1997). Crick and Grotpeter (1995) found that relationally aggressive youth were significantly more rejected than their nonrelationally aggressive peers and reported

160 higher levels of isolation, depression, and loneliness. Young women often replicate these roles into adulthood, adopting a "victim" or "bully" stance in their relationships with men (Dellasega, in press).

Risk for relationally victimized females is sup-
165 ported by the research of Crick and Grotpeter (1995), which showed females had a stronger relationship between relational aggression and social–psychological maladjustment than males. Paquette and Underwood's (1999) study of gender differences in the experience of
170 peer victimization found that girls were more distressed by social aggression than boys were. Their findings showed that frequency of social aggression was more strongly related to girls' self-concepts than to boys'.

Studies on factors that motivate young females to
175 use relational aggression in their relationships have also been conducted. One qualitative study using focus groups was completed with adolescent females in Australia to determine their perspectives on the causes of relational aggression. Some explanations for the behav-
180 ior included boredom and desire for excitement (Owens, Shute, & Slee, 2000). Further studies are needed to determine factors that underlie relational aggression in girls of nonwhite cultures and disadvantaged economic groups. By illuminating the experience
185 of peer-to-peer aggression in diverse groups of adolescent females, a more comprehensive view of etiological factors in relational aggression will emerge.

Interventions

Empirical studies of antibullying interventions in general suggest that school-based interventions
190 (Olweus, 1994), strategies aimed at peer involvement ("befriending") (Menesini, Codecasa, Benelli, & Cowie, 2003) and peer support processes (Stevens, De Bourdeaudhuij, & van Oost, 2000) may be effective. The most efficacious treatments for bullying appear to
195 be those that utilize the peer group in a supportive way to assist the bully or victims.

Few interventions to specifically address RA have been developed, and often teachers admit they feel illprepared to handle these behaviors (Smith, personal
200 communication, 2003). While empirical studies are lacking, innovative approaches to mediate relational aggression seem to be achieving success. Camp Ophelia™ and Club Ophelia™ are two initiatives that function in a preventive mode for middle school girls.
205 These programs are designed to create safe environments for middle school girls to learn positive relational skills. The programs use an arts-based curriculum and mentoring by high school girls in an ERI model: educate, relate, and integrate. Girls first are
210 taught about RA and how it hurts others. They then relate RA to their everyday lives and develop alternative behaviors. Finally, they integrate the new healthy relationship behaviors they have identified as feasible for them into their everyday life. For example, not
215 every girl who is a bystander or witness of RA is brave

enough to speak out. One realistic alternative some girls felt they could use was to move away from the aggressor and stand next to the victim.

The Study

This study involved a program evaluation of Club
220 Ophelia™, which was offered at two middle schools serving a diverse population of girls during the 2003–2004 academic year. Each program lasted throughout a semester (twelve weeks) and utilized the same ERI model.

Methods

225 In both locations, the director of Club Ophelia (CD) implemented the program with a school faculty as codirector. Middle school girls could self-select or be referred into the program. Junior and senior girls from the same school system served as mentors for the mid-
230 dle school girls with a 1:5 ratio. Each session of the program was supervised by the director and at least one other adult director with counseling skills.

Evaluation

A basic demographic sheet, which also measured relationship-oriented behaviors, was the first part of the
235 evaluation. These questions asked girls what they thought their "RA role" was and how often they suffered from the consequences of RA in a week's time.

To assess the impact of the program on relationship skills of the participants, The Girls Relationship Scale
240 (GRS) was administered. This scale was developed using a previous evaluation tool from camp and club as well as input from participants. It contains 20 items in a four-point Likert-type format that measures Knowledge About Relationships (4 items), Beliefs About Self (4
245 items) and Beliefs About Relationships with Others (10 items). A higher score represents better relational skills. To prevent response-set bias, some items are reverse coded. After establishing content validity, to assess the reliability of the scale, a test–retest Pearson's
250 correlation coefficient was calculated and revealed a coefficient of .74.

Procedures

Forty-two girls (*M* age 13.2 yrs.) participated in the program. In addition to a face sheet that collected demographic and relationship information, the GRS
255 was given before beginning and upon completion of the program. Girls responded anonymously by using birth date rather than name so confidentiality was preserved. In the closing session, girls were also given the opportunity to share what, if anything, they had learned
260 during the program in small and large group discussions.

Analysis

Data were coded and entered using Minitab, Release 14 (2003). Summary statistics on demographic data at baseline were performed first. Although re-
265 sponses were matched from pre- to post-program for

those girls who completed two evaluation forms, only 26 girls (62%) did so. The data here, therefore, use group averages to estimate changes in behavior.

Characteristics of participants are presented in Table 1. Due to the preliminary nature of the program evaluation, details such as self-referral vs. referral by others, history of delinquency, and other variables which would be relevant in an empirical study were not collected.

Table 1
Demographic Characteristics of Participants

Variable	N	(%)
Ethnicity		
Caucasian	16	(66)
Black	3	(3)
Bi- or Multiracial	5	(20)
No response	18	
Your role in RA in the last week		
Bully	1	(2)
Bystander	10	(23)
Victim	9	(21)
All three	12	(28)
None	10	(23)
Difficulty concentrating in school because of RA		
Very often	4	(10)
Often	5	(12)
Not sure	19	(45)
Not often	3	(7)
Never	11	(26)
Think of staying home from school due to RA		
Very often	4	(10)
Often	5	(12)
Not sure	19	(45)
Not often	6	(23)
Never	3	(12)

The next series of analyses focused on RA behaviors. First, girls were asked to identify how many times in the previous week relationships with other girls had influenced their behavior. A separate series of *t*-tests were used to compare before and after program responses. These results are in Table 2.

Table 2
RA Behaviors

Variable	Pre	Post
# of times hurt by RA	5.2	3.04
# of times seen others hurt by RA	6.3	4.8
# of times girl used RA	2.4	2.4
# of times RA message sent via computer	1.1	.76
# of times felt physically sick or depressed because of RA	.90	.88

Note. All questions within context of week immediately before.

Next, the subscales and total scores of the GRS were compared using *t*-test and ANOVA to check for significant differences (Table 3).

Table 3
Means for Responses on the Girls Relationship Scale

Item	Time one	Time two	Change	*p*
Feelings about self	2.8	2.9	+.1	NS
Believe girls are nice	2.1	2.4	+.3	NS
Trust other girls	1.2	1.5	+.3	NS
Want more friends	2.0	2.0		NS
Okay to be mean back	1.5	1.4	−.1	NS
Enjoy being with girls	2.2	2.1	−.1	NS
Girls in my school are nicer	1.2	1.2		NS
I know what RA is	1.4	1.6	+.2	NS
Okay to defend physically	2.3	2.0	−.3	NS
Want to change behavior	1.7	1.9	+.2	NS
Relationships make me afraid to come to school	3.1	3.0	−.1	NS
I know where to get help	2.8	2.8		NS
I know what to do when hurt	2.7	2.8	+.1	NS
Feel confident of friend-ability	2.7	2.9	+.2	NS
Mentoring helps	2.2	2.7	+.5	NS
Feeling safe is important	2.4	2.3	−.1	NS
Ability to communicate	2.4	2.5	+.1	NS
Okay to hurt back	1.8	1.9	−.1	NS
Don't get involved when other girl hurt	1.8	2.4	+.6	NS
Total score	45.2	47.1	+1.9	NS

Results

Nearly a quarter of this diverse group of middle school girls experienced an impact of RA on their behavior, either in thinking of staying home from school, being unable to concentrate, or actually feeling physically sick or depressed because of relationship issues with girls. Girls recognized that they could play all three RA roles at some time or another in an average week.

Actual behaviors were reported to change in a favorable direction, although, again, not statistically significant. Girls were hurt less by RA, did not see others hurt by RA as much (perhaps because they intervened), and sent fewer hurtful messages on the computer. Although none of the change scores on the GRS or the total score reached significance, relationship skills improved in the expected dimension for all items except "Feeling safe with other girls is important to me," which girls indicated was slightly less important. The most noticeable improvement (but still nonsignificant) in relationship skills was demonstrated for two items that related to getting involved when you saw another girl being hurt and benefiting from mentoring.

Limitations of the Study

Obviously, this was a very preliminary study with a small sample and new evaluation tool. Since the two middle schools used were very different in demographic and ethnic composition, specific comparisons across sites with a larger sample would enhance the findings of the study. Since the evaluation was focused on the program, more sophisticated data collection which could assess variables connected with RA did not occur.

Discussion

315 This study shows that the everyday life of many middle school girls is profoundly influenced by the negative consequences of RA, whether it arrives face-to-face or online. The degree to which girls could not concentrate in school or thought of staying home from 320 school because of relationship issues with other girls suggests that verbal aggression is as intimidating and distressing as physical forms of violence. However, after completing a program specifically targeted at RA, girls developed a sense of confidence about them-325 selves, their friend-ability, and what to do when hurt and where to go for help.

Implications for Practice

Although many excellent programs exist for addressing overt physical bullying, this study suggests that strategies for overcoming relational aggression are 330 equally important. Perhaps more significant than the statistics contained here is the observation of a guidance counselor in one of the participating schools that the frequency of certain girls' visits to her office decreased during the program. One administrator calcu-335 lated (roughly) that delinquent episodes decreased 33% in girls participating in the program.

Girls in middle school need to feel safe in relationships. Initiatives such as Club Ophelia™ address the core safety issues in girls' relationships through a plat-340 form of mentoring that allows girls to experience a positive and safe relationship with an older peer. Research on bullying has confirmed that processes using befriending and peer support are the most efficacious (Menesini, Codecasa, Benelli, & Cowie, 2003; Stevens, 345 De Bourdeaudhuij, & van Oost, 2000).

Teachers, school nurses, administrators, guidance counselors, and school social workers are in a front line position to facilitate use of the ERI model to educate, relate, and integrate principles of RA for girls. The 350 addition of the arts-based curriculum and mentoring from senior girls as occurs in Club Ophelia™ can enhance effectiveness of this intervention.

Girls in this study responded that they have awareness of where and how to get help when hurt in their 355 relationships, which is another important strategy that can be promoted by school personnel. Asking each girl to identify a "safe place, safe person" empowers her to have a response ready when RA occurs.

School personnel need to be alert to aggressive sub-360 tleties that are the hallmark of relational aggression. Early and appropriate recognition of these behaviors as well as an understanding of the damage they can inflict is a key first step in combating RA. Ground rules for classroom RA behaviors and student-generated conse-365 quences for infringement can be a powerful experiential activity that accomplishes both of these purposes. To address RA on a school-wide basis, one middle school administrator chose to have all girls participate in a brief intervention which used the ERI model.

370 Middle school is the learning laboratory for relationship skills that can last a lifetime. In this study, an intervention with concrete skills for "helping rather than hurting" demonstrated that girls really do want to be kind.

References

Centers for Disease Control. (2002). Youth risk behavior surveillance—United States, 2001. *MMWR, 51* (SS-04) 1–64.

Cillessen, A. H. N., & Mayeux, L. (2004). From censure to reinforcement: Developmental changes in the association between aggression and social status. *Child Development, 75.*

Club Ophelia a safe place for girls. (n.d.). *What's Club Ophelia? You are!* Retrieved March 8, 2004, from http://www.clubophelia.com/index.htm

Crick, N. R., Casas, J. F., & Nelson, D. A. (2002). Toward a more comprehensive understanding of peer maltreatment: Studies of relational victimization. *Current Directions in Psychological Science, 11*, 98–101.

Crick, N. R., & Grotpeter, J. (1995). Relational aggression, gender, and social–psychological adjustment. *Child Development, 66*, 710–722.

Dellasega, C. (In preparation). *The impact of mentoring.*

Dellasega, C. (In press). *Two faced: Adult women who aggress.* John Wiley: 2005.

Dellasega, C., & Nixon, C. (2003). *Girl wars: Twelve strategies that will end female bullying.* New York: Fireside.

Galen, B. R., & Underwood, M. K. (1997). A developmental investigation of social aggression among children. *Developmental Psychology, 33*, 589–600.

Gilligan, C. (1982). *In a different voice: Psychological theory and women's development.* Cambridge, MA: Harvard University Press.

Girl Scout Research Institute. (2003). *Feeling safe: What girls say.* New York: Girl Scouts of the USA.

Greene, M. B. (2000). Bullying and harassment in schools. In R. S. Moser, & C. E. Franz (Eds.), *Shocking violence: Youth perpetrators and victims—A multi-disciplinary perspective* (pp. 72–101). Springfield, IL: Charles C. Thomas.

Griffin, R. S. & Gross, A. M. (in press). Childhood bullying: Current empirical findings and future directions for research. *Aggression and Violent Behavior.*

Hazler, R. J. (1996). *Breaking the cycle of violence: Interventions for bullying and victimization.* Washington, DC: Taylor & Francis.

Lagerspetz, K. M., Bjorkqvist, K., & Peltonen, T. (1988). Is indirect aggression typical of females? Gender differences in aggressiveness in 11 to 12 year old children. *Aggressive Behavior, 14*, 403–414.

Menesini, E., Codecasa, E., Benelli, B., & Cowie, H. (2003). Enhancing children's responsibility to take action against bullying: Evaluation of a befriending intervention in Italian middle schools. *Aggressive Behavior, 29*, 1–14.

Nansel, T. R., Overpeck, M., Ramani, S. P., Pilla, R. S., Ruan, W. J., Simons-Morton, B. et al. (2001). Bullying behaviors among U.S. youth: Prevalence and association with psychosocial adjustment. *Journal of the American Medical Association, 285*, 2094–2100.

Olweus, D. (1994). Annotation: Bullying at school: Basic facts and effects of a school-based intervention program. *Journal of Child Psychology and Psychiatry, 35*, 1171–1190.

Owens, L., Shute, R., & Slee, P. (2000). "I'm in and you're out...." Explanations for teenage girls' indirect aggression. *Psychology, Revolution, and Gender, 2.1*, 19–46.

Paquette, J. A., & Underwood, M. K. (1999). Gender differences in young adolescents' experiences of peer victimization: Social and physical aggression. *Merrill-Palmer Quarterly, 45*, 242–266.

Smith, H., & Thomas, S. P. (2000). Violent and nonviolent girls: Contrasting perceptions of anger experiences, school, and relationships. *Issues in Mental Health Nursing, 21*, 547–575.

Stevens, V., De Bourdeaudhuij, I., & van Oost, P. (2000). Bullying in Flemish schools: An evaluation of anti-bullying intervention in primary and secondary schools. *British Journal of Educational Psychology, 70*, 195–210.

Tomada, G., & Schneider, B. H. (1997). Relational aggression, gender, and peer acceptance: Invariance across culture, stability over time, and concordance among informants. *Developmental Psychology, 33*, 601–609.

Underwood, M. K., Galen, B. R., & Paquette, J. A. (2001). Top ten challenges for understanding gender and aggression in children: Why can't we all just get along? *Social Development, 10*, 248–266.

U.S. Department of Health and Human Services. (2000). *Healthy people 2010.* (Conference Edition, in Two Volumes). Washington, DC: U.S. Government Printing Office.

U.S. Department of Health and Human Services. (2001). *Youth violence: A report of the surgeon general.* Washington, DC: U.S. Government Printing Office.

Whitaker, C., & Bastian, L. (1991). *Teenage victims: A national crime survey report*. Washington, DC: U.S. Department of Justice, Bureau of Justice Statistics.

About the authors: *Cheryl Dellasega* is professor, Penn State College of Medicine, Hershey, PA. *Pamela Adamshick* is assistant professor of nursing, Moravian College, 1200 Main Street, Bethlehem, PA 18018.

Address correspondence to: Dr. Dellasega, Department of Humanities, H134, 500 University Drive, P.O. Box 850, Hershey, PA 17033-0850. E-mail: cdellasega@psu.edu

Exercise for Article 24

Factual Questions

1. For the GRS, what is the value of the test–retest Pearson correlation coefficient?

2. Did the girls respond anonymously?

3. What percentage of the girls completed two evaluation forms (pre and post)?

4. What was the mean total score at time one on the GRS?

5. Was the difference between the time one and time two means on the GRS statistically significant?

Questions for Discussion

6. In your opinion, is the program described in sufficient detail? (See lines 197–232.)

7. This evaluation used a one-group, pretest-posttest design. In future studies, would you recommend using a control group? Explain.

8. The researchers describe the limitations of the evaluation in lines 306–314. In your opinion, are there any additional limitations that are not mentioned here?

9. Do you agree with the statement in the last sentence of the article? (See lines 371–374.)

10. Based on this evaluation, would you recommend funding for widespread implementation of this program? Would you want to see the results of additional evaluations before making such a recommendation? Explain.

Quality Ratings

Directions: Indicate your level of agreement with each of the following statements by circling a number from 5 for strongly agree (SA) to 1 for strongly disagree (SD). If you believe an item is not applicable to this research article, leave it blank. Be prepared to explain your ratings. When responding to criteria A and B below, keep in mind that brief titles and abstracts are conventional in published research.

A. The title of the article is appropriate.

    SA   5   4   3   2   1   SD

B. The abstract provides an effective overview of the research article.

    SA   5   4   3   2   1   SD

C. The introduction establishes the importance of the study.

    SA   5   4   3   2   1   SD

D. The literature review establishes the context for the study.

    SA   5   4   3   2   1   SD

E. The research purpose, question, or hypothesis is clearly stated.

    SA   5   4   3   2   1   SD

F. The method of sampling is sound.

    SA   5   4   3   2   1   SD

G. Relevant demographics (for example, age, gender, and ethnicity) are described.

    SA   5   4   3   2   1   SD

H. Measurement procedures are adequate.

    SA   5   4   3   2   1   SD

I. All procedures have been described in sufficient detail to permit a replication of the study.

    SA   5   4   3   2   1   SD

J. The participants have been adequately protected from potential harm.

    SA   5   4   3   2   1   SD

K. The results are clearly described.

    SA   5   4   3   2   1   SD

L. The discussion/conclusion is appropriate.

    SA   5   4   3   2   1   SD

M. Despite any flaws, the report is worthy of publication.

    SA   5   4   3   2   1   SD

Article 25

An Application of Fear Appeal Messages to Enhance the Benefits of a Jail Encounter Program for Youthful Offenders

JAMES O. WINDELL
Oakland County Circuit Court
Family Division Psychological Clinic

J. SCOTT ALLEN, JR.
Oakland County Circuit Court
Family Division Psychological Clinic

ABSTRACT. Research has consistently shown that so-called Scared Straight types of jail encounter programs do not have positive benefits for youthful offenders. However, few, if any, inmate–youth encounter programs have utilized the results of fear appeals message research. Results of the present study suggest that an inmate–youth encounter program may lead to attitude change in youthful offenders if components of successful fear appeals are incorporated into the program.

From *Youth Violence and Juvenile Justice, 3*, 388–394. Copyright © 2005 by Sage Publications, Inc. Reprinted with permission.

After almost 20 years of researching and studying aversion programs for juveniles, Finckenauer and other criminologists have concluded that Scared Straight and similar programs are failures (Finckenauer, Gavin, Hovland, & Storvoll, 1999; Sherman et al., 1998). Nonetheless, such programs persist, usually with public and governmental approval. The underlying theory of all such programs is criminal deterrence. Program advocates believe that the realistic depiction of adult prison will deter juvenile delinquents or children at risk from becoming delinquent and from further involvement with crime (Finckenauer, 1982; Szymanski & Fleming, 1971).

However, no matter how often researchers review programs that provide juveniles with scary messages about crime and delinquency, the results are at best disheartening. Most recently, Petrosino, Turpin-Petrosino, and Finckenauer (2000) reviewed nine randomized evaluations of Scared Straight prison programs conducted between 1967 and 1992. Data from this review indicate that such programs likely have harmful effects leading to increased crime and delinquency. The authors concluded that given the harmful effects of these kinds of interventions, governments have an ethical responsibility to rigorously evaluate the policies, practices, and programs they implement (Petrosino et al., 2000).

Although Scared Straight types of programs have a dubious theoretical and research history, there is a considerable body of research related to persuasive messages that arouse fears. The psychology of using fear to influence people has been studied during the past 50 years, but this research has not been applied to Scared Straight types of programs. Because the purpose of jail tours and youth–inmate confrontations is to evoke fear of consequences, the psychology of fear appeals is particularly relevant. Witte and Allen (2000) indicate that the nearly 5 decades of research on fear appeals show that certain fear appeals are successful. Recent research (Witte & Allen, 2000) suggests that the stronger the fear appeal, the greater the potential influence over attitudes toward relevant behaviors, intentions to change, and actual behavior changes.

Witte (1992) proposed a model known as the extended parallel process model (EPPM) that postulates that threat and corresponding fear motivates a response and that the efficacy of the threat determines the nature of that response. The possible responses to the perceived threat include either danger-control or fear-control actions. In this model, if the perceived threat is low, then the individual does no further cognitive processing of the fear because of a lack of motivation. If the perceived threat is high and there is also a high perception of one's ability (efficacy) to perform the recommended action (for instance, avoid further criminal behavior), the individual will be more inclined to follow the danger control recommendations. On the other hand, if the threat is high but the individual's perceived ability to deal with the danger is low or the individual believes the recommended action might not work (e.g., an individual might believe that he or she has no power to avoid criminal behavior), then the individual will be more likely to take some action to control his or her fear. A possible way of dealing with the fear is to become defensive or deny that the threat is real or that it applies to him or her.

Pratkanis and Aronson (1991) claim that a fear appeal is most effective when (a) it genuinely scares people, (b) it offers a specific recommendation for overcoming the fear-aroused threat, (c) the recommended

action is perceived as effective for reducing the threat, and (d) the message recipient believes he or she can perform the recommended action. These four criteria for an effective fear appeal may help explain why pre-
75   vious research on Scared Straight types of programs shows negative results.

It is suggested that the EPPM theoretical model is useful for understanding adolescent juvenile offenders who participate in any fear-arousing jail tour program
80   or any modified Scared Straight type of program. The Jail Tour Program (JTP) in the present study involved scheduling a group of adolescent offenders to go to an adult jail, view the facilities, hear lectures from police officers, and have a series of face-to-face confronta-
85   tions and encounters with inmates. Inaugurated in 1992 and run continuously since then, the program has had several hundred adolescent participants. To date, there has been no evaluation or assessment of its effective- ness, even though it continues to be included as a stan-
90   dard part of the probation requirements for many young people in the juvenile court selected for this study.

Most fear-inducing inmate–youth encounter pro- grams do not couple the induced fear with either an
95   underlying theoretical approach or specific components that have been found to bring about effective results in the fear appeals literature. In comparing the JTP of the present study to previous Scared Straight types of pro- grams, it was the addition of a segment incorporating
100   support for positive choices and recommendations to avoid future delinquency that differentiated it from others. The authors recognized that this fit with a fear appeals model and suggested the approach may hold greater potential for success than those previously stud-
105   ied. The program herein studied was unique in that it does use components that lead to more efficacious fear appeals.

The jail exposure program in the present study in- corporated fear, followed by useful recommendations
110   and efforts to heighten participants' efficacy—all com- ponents outlined by the EPPM model. Therefore, it was hypothesized that adolescent offenders participating in the program would report less favorable attitudes to- ward jail following the jail tour. Second, research has
115   shown that fear appeals do not affect males and fe- males in a differential manner. Therefore, it was hy- pothesized that adolescent offenders in the present study would develop less favorable attitudes toward jail regardless of their gender.

Method

JTP Description

120   The data collection for the present study took place in the county jail of a suburb of a large midwestern city. Corrections officers in the county jail developed a program for juvenile offenders, referred to as the JTP. The 2-hour JTP, in brief, utilizes a fear appeal coupled
125   with encouragement and recommendations for avoid-

ing future criminal activity. The evening JTP begins shortly after juveniles, who were court-ordered to par- ticipate, arrive with their parents. Three deputies (often three males but sometimes two males and one female)
130   experienced in running this program start by treating the adolescents as if they are new inmates of the jail. They are asked to store coats, hats, and belts in a locker and to stand in a line. They are led into the jail (without their parents, as parents are discouraged from going on
135   the tour) and in the succeeding hour and a half are in- troduced to how adult inmates are expected to adhere to a concrete, limited behavioral repertoire. In addition, the juveniles are given harsh messages about the mag- nitude of reduced individuality and restrictions on free-
140   dom in jails and the likelihood of experiencing un- pleasantness or harm. Vivid and personal language is used by the officers to emphasize the similarities be- tween the participants and the adult inmates. Messages, commands, and remarks that heighten the seriousness
145   of incarceration and even the likelihood that the juve- niles are highly susceptible to being incarcerated are repeated. The juveniles are allowed to see various sec- tions of the jail and to get a firsthand view of how in- mates are housed. Along the way they are given infor-
150   mation about recidivism, jailhouse management, and typical treatment of prisoners. When they reach group cells housing several prisoners, they are told to stand outside of these cells and ask any questions of the in- mates they choose. There is a give-and-take with in-
155   mates, with some inmates trying to intimidate the juve- niles. Some inmates reiterate the themes that were de- livered by the corrections officers, whereas others offer useful and well-intentioned advice.

In the last half hour of the JTP, the tone of the tour
160   changes, and the corrections officers soften their ap- proach. They ask more questions and try to relate more with the juveniles. The officers focus more on efficacy messages (e.g., "You can make the choice to avoid high-risk situations") and offer recommendations.
165   Based on Witte and Allen (2000), how individuals think about the threat and their assessment of their own power in dealing with that threat leads to adaptive or maladaptive attitudes and behaviors. The juveniles are finally taken to a cafeteria where they are encouraged
170   to talk about their goals and aspirations along with how they can avoid becoming jail inmates in the future. The officers give encouragement about how the juveniles will be able to implement their goals, stay in school, and avoid troublesome peers. The officers provide rein-
175   forcing statements that suggest they believe the juve- niles have it within their abilities to avoid further criminal behavior.

Participants

Juvenile Court hearing officers routinely order ado- lescents between the ages of 16 and 17 who have been
180   adjudicated for a criminal offense to go through the JTP. Overall, 327 adolescents participated in this study.

Table 1
Means and Standard Deviations for Scores on a Measure of Impressions of Jail for Juvenile Offenders

| | Pretest | | Posttest | |
Group	M	SD	M	SD
Male	25.7	6.17	20.1	3.03
Female	25.6	5.69	19.9	6.19
Violent	27.8	5.32	22.3	5.07
Nonviolent	25.2	5.90	20.0	6.61

Note. The maximum possible score was 65, and the minimum possible score was 13.

Of these, 282 were males and 45 were females. A planned exploratory analysis necessitated identifying the nature of the offenses committed by the females in the sample. Of the females, 32 had committed nonviolent crimes, whereas 13 had been convicted of violent offenses.

Instrument

An instrument, termed the Jail Tour Adolescent Questionnaire (JTAQ), was developed for use in the present study. The JTAQ was constructed with the assistance of psychologists who work with adolescent offenders, and it was reviewed by juvenile probation officers and corrections officers. The JTAQ has 13 self-report items with a 5-point Likert-type scale (the points include strongly disagree, disagree, not sure, agree, and strongly agree). Each question asks the respondent to evaluate certain behaviors that occur in jail. The JTAQ items address favorable or unfavorable attitudes toward incarceration held by the respondent. Examples of items include, "Prisoners these days are treated very nicely by prison staff," "While in prison, prisoners get along and support each other," and "I think living in jail would be fun sometimes." The instrument was completed just prior to the program and again following the JTP.

Results

This study looked at the overall effect of the JTP on participants' responses on a self-report questionnaire. A one-way analysis of variance was used to assess the degree to which there were changes in adolescent offenders' scores on a questionnaire designed to reflect favorable and unfavorable evaluations of certain behaviors in jail. It was anticipated that participants would report a less favorable impression of jail after the JTP relative to their reported attitude before the JTP. A significant time effect was found, $F(1, 327) = 139.9$, $p < .001$, indicating that significant changes on the measure of attitude were associated with the JTP. Means for the pre-JTP versus post-JTP groups were 25.7 ($SD = 6.11$) and 20.1 ($SD = 6.06$), respectively.

This study also examined if significant differences existed between male and female participants on the instrument before and after the program. Previous research found no differential effect of fear appeals on boys and girls. No studies have examined the differential effect of a Scared Straight type of program on boys' and girls' evaluations of jail. Therefore, a subsequent focus of the current project was to identify if the sex of the participant mattered in whether or not they responded to the JTP as measured by changes in their attitudes as measured by the JTAQ. It was expected that male and female participants would develop a more critical attitude toward incarceration.

Based on these predictions, the data were analyzed using two-tailed paired samples t tests with a 95% confidence interval computed for the true differences between each pair of group means. All assumptions were met to allow for a parametric test. First, boys' pre-JTP and post-JTP mean standard scores on the JTAQ were compared. The boys' perspectives decreased significantly from pre-JTP to post-JTP: $t(281) = 14.6$, $p < .001$. Second, girls' mean pre-JTP and post-JTP standard scores on the JTAQ were compared using a paired t test. The girls' perspectives also decreased significantly from pre-JTP to post-JTP: $t(44) = 14.6$, $p < .001$. Both boys and girls were influenced by the JTP as reflected in the changes on the JTAQ (see Table 1 for means and standard deviations).

Discussion

The present study integrated fear appeal theory (the EPPM in particular) with a naturalistic inmate–juvenile encounter program. It was hypothesized that participants would report differences in their attitudes and impressions of jail after the JTP and that there would be no difference between the attitude of boys and the attitude of girls.

Consistent with the first hypothesis, it was found that participants did report a less favorable impression of jail after experiencing the JTP. Boys and girls were analyzed separately, and it was found that both groups had less favorable impressions of jail.

Although other studies found no difference or a negative influence from Scared Straight and juvenile–inmate encounter programs, this study found, on a questionnaire administered both before and after the encounter, that there was a significant and positive difference. One reason for this finding may be that this study used a pre-JTP and post-JTP self-report survey that was designed to measure attitudes toward jail and incarceration. Other research projects have used recidivism and various other indicators of attitude change as a measurement (Finckenauer, 1982; Petrosino, Turpin-Petrosino, & Buehler, 2003). The JTAQ was developed for this research project to gauge adolescent respon-

dents' attitudes toward jail. However, no psychometric properties were established for the JTAQ. Neverthe-
275 less, the results from the use of the JTAQ suggest that going through the JTP may have had a significant effect on the participants' impressions of jail. In particular, their attitudes toward being incarcerated became less favorable following the JTP.

280 Although the theory underlying the JTP is criminal deterrence, the mechanism for change in this type of intervention is through fear appeal. Because the purpose of jail tours and youth–inmate confrontations is to invoke fear, the psychology of fear appeals is particu-
285 larly relevant. That is, the JTP offers solutions that may be viewed by the juveniles as within their ability. In the EPPM explanation of fear appeals, messages that fail to offer solutions that the participants believe they can implement are less likely to lead to attitude and behav-
290 ior change. This theory suggests that for any jail tour program to be effective, it should incorporate the elements necessary for a fear appeals program to be successful. It should not only deliver a strong and scary message, but it should also tell adolescents very clearly
295 how they can avoid the scary outcome (going to jail). Then, participants need to come away convinced that they can apply the strategy successfully in their own life. The JTP may satisfy the conditions of a successful fear appeal.

300 A strength of this study is that it was conducted in a naturalistic setting. Most previous research into the effectiveness of fear appeals has studied participants in artificial settings (Witte & Allen, 2000). However, a limitation of this study is that multiple independent *t*
305 tests were conducted with no correction for chance significant findings. At least one significant finding may be because of chance. Furthermore, the questionnaire used in this study may not be a measurement of attitude but a measure of fear or some other construct.
310 Therefore, normed and standardized instruments need to be employed to better understand the effectiveness of the JTP. Also, this study did not have a follow-up phase, nor did it take into account recidivism or post-JTP behavior.

315 Finally, this research needs to be extended with the addition of other measures (such as recidivism) to determine effectiveness. A future direction for research could include development of an instrument that is based on the EPPM model to determine more precisely
320 if this model does explain positive changes. Determining this can help in the development of a paradigm for Scared Straight types of programs with a greater potential for bringing about the expected results.

References

Finckenauer, J. O. (1982). *Scared straight! And the panacea phenomenon.* Englewood Cliffs, NJ: Prentice Hall.
Finckenauer, J. O., Gavin, P. W., Hovland, A., & Storvoll, E. (1999). *Scared straight: The panacea phenomenon revisited.* Prospect Heights, IL: Waveland Press.
Petrosino, A., Turpin-Petrosino, C., & Buehler, J. (2003). Scared straight and other juvenile awareness programs for preventing juvenile delinquency: A systematic review of the randomized experimental evidence. The *Annals of the American Academy of Political and Social Science, 589,* 41–62.
Petrosino, A., Turpin-Petrosino, C., & Finckenauer, J. O. (2000). Well-meaning programs can have harmful effects! Lessons from experiments of such programs as scared straight. *Crime & Delinquency, 46,* 354–379.
Pratkanis, A., & Aronson, E. (1991). *Age of propaganda.* New York: Freeman.
Sherman, L. W., Gottfredson, D. C., MacKenzie, D. L., Eck, J., Reuter, P., & Bushway, S. D. (1998). *Preventing crime: What works, what doesn't, what's promising* (NCJ 171676). Rockville, MD: National Institute of Justice, U.S. Department of Justice.
Szymanski, L., & Fleming, A. (1971). Juvenile delinquency and an adult prisoner—A therapeutic encounter? *Journal of the American Academy of Child Psychiatry, 10,* 308–320.
Witte, K. (1992). Putting the fear back into fear appeals: The extended parallel process model. *Communication Monographs, 59,* 329–349.
Witte, K., & Allen, M. (2000). A meta-analysis of fear appeals: Implications for effective public health campaigns. *Health Education & Behavior, 27,* 591–615.

About the authors: James O. Windell, M.A., is a court psychologist at the Oakland County Court Clinic, where he runs adolescent treatment groups and conducts high-conflict, postdivorce treatment groups. He is also an instructor in the Criminal Justice Department of Wayne State University. His major interests include parenting, juvenile delinquency, social skills training of adolescents, and treatment of high-conflict divorces. *J. Scott Allen, Jr.,* Ph.D., works as a senior psychologist at the Oakland County Court Clinic, where he primarily conducts court-ordered psychological evaluations for children, adolescents, and adults and supervises doctoral candidate students. His private practice focuses on family issues (e.g., child behavior management, challenges of adolescence) and mood and anxiety disorders.

Exercise for Article 25

Factual Questions

1. The letters "JTP" stand for what three words?

2. The researchers state two hypotheses. What is the first one that they state?

3. How many of the females had committed nonviolent crimes?

4. What was the mean pretest score for the females? What was the mean posttest score for the females?

5. Was the difference between the two means in your answer to Question 4 above statistically significant? If yes, at what probability level?

6. According to the researchers, what is cited as a "strength" of this study?

Questions for Discussion

7. In your opinion, is the program described in sufficient detail? Explain. (See lines 120–177.)

8. The researchers provide examples of the JTAQ self-report items in lines 200–203. To what extent do these examples help you understand what the instrument measures?

9. In this evaluation, the researchers used a self-report instrument. An alternative is to use recidivism as an outcome measure for judging the effectiveness of such a program. In your opinion, is self-report or recidivism a better measure? Are they equal? (See lines 265–271 and 312–314.)

10. For a future study on the effectiveness of this program, would you recommend using a control group? Why? Why not?

11. If you were on a panel considering the possibility of major funding to permit widespread use of the JTP, what recommendation would you make? Would you recommend major funding? Limited funding until additional evaluations are made? No funding? Explain.

Quality Ratings

Directions: Indicate your level of agreement with each of the following statements by circling a number from 5 for strongly agree (SA) to 1 for strongly disagree (SD). If you believe an item is not applicable to this research article, leave it blank. Be prepared to explain your ratings. When responding to criteria A and B below, keep in mind that brief titles and abstracts are conventional in published research.

A. The title of the article is appropriate.

   SA   5   4   3   2   1   SD

B. The abstract provides an effective overview of the research article.

   SA   5   4   3   2   1   SD

C. The introduction establishes the importance of the study.

   SA   5   4   3   2   1   SD

D. The literature review establishes the context for the study.

   SA   5   4   3   2   1   SD

E. The research purpose, question, or hypothesis is clearly stated.

   SA   5   4   3   2   1   SD

F. The method of sampling is sound.

   SA   5   4   3   2   1   SD

G. Relevant demographics (for example, age, gender, and ethnicity) are described.

   SA   5   4   3   2   1   SD

H. Measurement procedures are adequate.

   SA   5   4   3   2   1   SD

I. All procedures have been described in sufficient detail to permit a replication of the study.

   SA   5   4   3   2   1   SD

J. The participants have been adequately protected from potential harm.

   SA   5   4   3   2   1   SD

K. The results are clearly described.

   SA   5   4   3   2   1   SD

L. The discussion/conclusion is appropriate.

   SA   5   4   3   2   1   SD

M. Despite any flaws, the report is worthy of publication.

   SA   5   4   3   2   1   SD

Article 26

A Review of Online Social Networking Profiles By Adolescents: Implications for Future Research and Intervention

AMANDA L. WILLIAMS
Oklahoma State University

MICHAEL J. MERTEN
Oklahoma State University

ABSTRACT. This study explored content posted and interactions taking place on adolescent online social networking profiles. Although "blogging" continues to soar in popularity, with over half of teenagers online participating in some form, little research has comprehensively explored blog communication within the context of adolescent development. Content was qualitatively coded from 100 randomly selected profiles authored by adolescents between the ages of 16 and 18. Rich thematic elements were identified, including family and social issues, risk behaviors, disclosure of personally identifiable information, and frequent peer interaction. Results indicate adolescent blogs frequently contain appropriate images, positive comments about parents and peers, athletics, a variety of risk behaviors, and sexual and profane language. In addition, school type was examined (public versus private, religious) as a potential factor in understanding the differences in content posted by adolescents; however, no significant differences were found. Implications for parental monitoring and intervention are discussed as well as direction for future research. Adolescents' online profiles contain a wealth of intimate, candid, and publicly available information on a wide range of social issues pertinent to adolescence that contribute to the understanding of adolescent development and well-being.

From *Adolescence*, 43, 253–274. Copyright © 2008 by Libra Publishers, Inc. Reprinted with permission.

The Internet has earned its own niche in social research (Greenfield & Yan, 2006) and the newest phenomena of online social networking is rapidly developing its own field of inquiry in the social sciences (Herring, Scheidt, Wright, & Bonus, 2005; Mee, 2006). In fact, researchers are scrambling to understand the phenomenon almost as quickly as the technology advances. Mazur (2005) defined blogs as updateable public records of private thoughts. As our knowledge of this new social forum advances, research is beginning to differentiate between social networking sites and blogs. However, for the purposes of this study, blogs, Web journals, and social networking profiles are considered synonymous as they all involve individuals creating and maintaining personal Internet sites allowing authors and other users to post content, thus creating a personal network.

Lenhart and Madden (2007), senior researchers for the Pew Internet and American Life Project, said that in the past five years social networking has "rocketed from a niche activity into a phenomenon that engages tens of millions of Internet users" (p. 3). Previous studies have examined surface content found in various Web journal forums, such as demographic information, communication styles, thematic content, purposes for blogging, and disclosure of personally identifiable information—also referred to by Huffaker (2006) as identity vulnerability (Lenhart & Fox, 2006; Fox & Madden, 2005; Subrahmanyam, Smahel, & Greenfield, 2006; Huffaker & Calvert, 2005; Mazur, 2005; Herring et al., 2005; Mee, 2006). However, to date there has been very little research on dynamic social and emotional content provided in blogs and how such content relates to adolescent development, peer relationships, and indicators of emotional well-being. The present study proposes that online social networking profiles posted by adolescents contain intimate, candid, and observable self-disclosure and peer interaction that can be analyzed, creating an overall picture of adolescent behavior, highlighting specific areas needing additional research and addressing implications for parental monitoring and intervention.

Adolescent Social Networking

Fifty-five percent of teenagers online use and create online social networking profiles (Lenhart & Madden, 2007). With more than half of teenage Internet users interacting online, the concept of blogging is a salient research topic investigating what adolescents are blogging about, how they are socially interacting, and what potential effects this phenomena may have on other dimensions of their lives.

Social networking profiles present a unique research opportunity as the process of blogging involves individuals voluntarily posting information about themselves—personal thoughts, feelings, beliefs, activities—in a public arena with unlimited access for anyone with an Internet connection. The amount of

personal information contained in a blog is completely dependent on the author's judgment. This situation is ideal for social scientists as it allows unobtrusive ob-
60 servations of authentic human behaviors and interactions with no "real" contact or interference. Adolescent blogs are full of information about their daily lives (Mazur, 2005) documenting whatever they choose to disclose about themselves and any subsequent written
65 interaction by individuals posting comments to the blog. A recent study involving adolescents and the Internet sums up the communication medium's impact and potential:

> The Internet is more exciting and challenging as a re-
70 search environment than earlier media because it is a complex, virtual, social, and physical world that children and adolescents participate in and co-construct, rather than something that is merely watched or used such as television or personal computers. It becomes a complex
75 virtual universe behind a small screen on which developmental issues play out...offering new views into the thoughts, feelings, and behaviors of children and adolescents (Greenfield & Yan, 2006, p. 393).

Themes often permeating adolescent blogs include
80 romantic relationships, friends, parents, substance use, sexuality, popular culture, eating disorders, school, depression, conflicts, self-expression, and self-harm (Mazur, 2005; Whitlock, Powers, & Eckenrode, 2006). Blogs have become a standard form of teenage com-
85 munication comparable to cell phones, email, or instant messaging (Mee, 2006). The differences between blogging and other forms of communication are: (1) they are accessible at any time, from any location, (2) they leave a trail of observable dialogue that can be printed
90 or stored, and (3) they incorporate advanced multimedia components. Adolescents have the ability to construct a personal profile or online environment, depicting how they view themselves or how they want others to view them.
95 It is unwise to write off Internet communication as superficial or unconnected to real life. Symbolic interactionists would argue that blogging is as meaningful to adolescents as they believe it to be and plays as large a role in their life as they allow. White and Klein
100 (2002) proposed that "the more individuals put into something, the more they get out of it [sic]" (p. 68). The more adolescents participate in blogging activities, the more importance they are likely to associate with it. The words on the screen have as much power as they
105 are assigned by both the author and the reader—thus developing co-constructed meanings. An ecological perspective makes this method of communication even more complex by appreciating that while teens are unique individuals sitting at a computer typing their
110 thoughts, they are also students, children, employees, and citizens, with various rules, regulations, codes of ethics, and standards of behavior attached to each identity. Online communication has the potential to interact

with, affect, or be influenced by all other spheres of
115 life.

According to Lenhart and Fox (2006), as reported in the Pew Internet and American Life Project, the top two reasons individuals create blogs are for creative self-expression and to document and share personal
120 experiences. These reasons are even more significant for adolescents as they actively explore new forms of self-expression, identity development, and social interaction (Kidwell, Dunham, Bacho, & Pastorino, 1995). Some researchers attribute the popularity of reality
125 television shows with adolescents' comfort in sharing intimate details of their lives with a global audience in real time (Mee, 2006). Perhaps online social networking tempers the Eriksonian concept of antagonism between adolescents and their environment. Nearly two
130 decades ago, he acknowledged that new forums for growth and formation would arise, thus necessitating adaptable and progressive traditions to maintain a normative, expectable developmental environment. In 1968, he said, "Today, when rapid technological
135 changes have taken the lead the world over, the matter of establishing and preserving...an 'average expectable' continuity for child rearing and education everywhere has, in fact, become a matter of human survival" (p. 222). In order to develop and maintain the ego, ado-
140 lescents seek "conflict-free energy in a mutually supportive psychosocial equilibrium" (Erikson, 1968, p. 223)—a desire online social interaction has great potential to fulfill.

The Internet provides an unrestricted laboratory set-
145 ting for adolescent identity experimentation as they seek to understand how they fit into the world around them. Concurrently, the Internet is a functioning community involving personal morals and regulatory processes. However, these processes are stunted if adoles-
150 cents do not see their online activities as subject to any ethical code. In day-to-day "real-life" interactions, adolescents are in a constant state of checks and balances with parents, teachers and school administrators, peers, and societal norms. Their actions generate perceivable
155 reactions that they use to gauge future decisions and behaviors. The Internet, specifically blogging, does not provide this type of "real" reinforcement or punishment. Internet standards for behavior are established via text communication normalizing or encouraging
160 various activities or attitudes. These "invisible cyberfriendships" (Mee, 2006, p. 1) allow adolescents to coconstruct the environments that will shape their psychosocial development (Greenfield & Yan, 2006).

Identity formation is a primary task in adolescence
165 (Erikson, 1968) and young people who actively explore their identities are more likely to experience mood swings, self-doubt, confusion, disturbed thinking, impulsivity, conflict with parents, reduced ego strength, and increased physical symptoms (Kidwell et al.,
170 1995). These indicators of identity exploration are generally observable in adolescent self-disclosure and peer

139

relationships. As adolescents explore their identity, they will go through behavioral patterns that on the surface may appear to be cause for concern, but are actually developmentally appropriate and healthy. This may explain why certain risky behaviors and discussions observed online look like "an adult's worst nightmare" (Mazur, 2005, p. 9), but may be a positive and safe outlet for self-expression and experimentation. Adolescents who feel they have lost their voice or are unheard by authority figures in their personal lives can channel their energy and need for attention into their online journal, versus feeling confused, worried, negative, misunderstood, or physically acting out (Kidwell et al., 1995).

Prior research has identified specific behaviors associated with adolescence and identity exploration, and researchers have observed such behaviors in various Internet forums. For example, adolescents use blogs to communicate information via Web text that would be obvious in face-to-face interaction, such as gender, ethnicity, and physical appearance. Adolescents also use Internet communication to explore their sexuality. Subrahmanyam, Smahel, and Greenfield (2006) observed teenagers' chat rooms and recorded one sexual comment per minute and one obscenity every two minutes, elevating sexual content and adult language high in the ranks of what teens talk about online. Through systematic review of adolescents' online profile content, researchers hope to achieve a comprehensive understanding of how adolescents use online social networking sites and what role such sites play in teenagers' ontogenetic and social development.

Method

Sample

Social network profiles were randomly collected from a major hosting site with more than one-fourth of users registered as teenagers (Anonymous, 2006). Utilizing random multistage cluster sampling, 100 adolescent blog authors were selected between the ages of 16 and 18 years who maintained active networks. "Active" status was determined by frequency of profile updates and/or comment posts that had to have occurred within the 60 days prior to date of analysis. Though the term "participants" is used to refer to profile authors, there was no contact, interaction, intervention, or interference between researcher and subjects as all content studied was publicly available without any special knowledge, fee-based subscription or membership, or authorization. Per regulations outlined in the host site's terms of use and privacy agreement, all Web site participants were required to acknowledge and consent to unlimited public access of any information posted to their profile by themselves or by anyone else.

The participants were selected based on region, school affiliation, gender, and age. Five nationally representative locations were selected, equally distributed throughout the country, representing each coast as well as central, north-, and south-central regions of the U.S. Two schools were randomly selected from each state—one public and one parochial. From each school, five male- and five female-authored profiles were randomly selected for review. The age distribution within the sample was purposively organized as follows: two 16-year-olds, one 17-year-old, and two 18-year-olds. Participants were also equally distributed between public and parochial high schools to determine if any content or online behaviors differed based on type of school attended. As parochial schools are founded in religious doctrine, it is reasonable to speculate that behaviors and peer relationships would differ based on school environment.

Content posted by participants was systematically coded based on various demographic, behavioral, and thematic elements. Themes were assigned based on content alone, without applying any intent or inference to the text or imagery. For example, if a comment said, "I think I would really kill myself without you," it was coded as violent—regardless of the spirit in which it was intended by the author. Similarly, sexual comments were coded based on text alone and categorized by their reference to sexual activity versus sexual language. Precodes were created prior to data collection for anticipated content such as gender, last log-on date (to ensure recent activity), and presence of personally identifiable information. While reviewing each profile, open codes were created to record unexpected, exploratory data such as differentiation between types of risk behaviors discussed and other unanticipated behaviors requiring unique coding strategies. Scales were in the form of questions "asked" of the profile. For example, "Is there an image of the author posted to the blog?" (0 = no; 1 = yes). The majority of categories were dichotomous based on presence of any specific variables (0 = not present, 1 = present); several categories implemented multiple nominal response options.

Measures

Demographic content. The demographic characteristics of participants were classified into five categories: gender, school affiliation, relationship status, religious affiliation, and sexual orientation. Location was also coded but was omitted from results to preserve participant anonymity. Once demographic information was obtained, each profile was reviewed for additional precoded content pertaining to preselected categories and unexpected themes encompassing an array of attitudes and behaviors.

Social content. Each unique profile was reviewed for text-based and pictorial content and captions. The 50 most recent comments posted to the authors' profiles within the preceding 60 days were reviewed for the same qualifying variables. Social variables included image (did the author post an image and was it appropriate?), family issues (positive/negative comments about parents/siblings), school issues (skipping school,

collegiate aspirations, and athletics), social issues (positive/negative comments about peers), discussion
285 of special interests such as reading, music, movies, and sports, and discussions of "parties," which were indicated by comments about prior social gatherings or specifically referenced attended "parties."

Image appropriateness. This was assessed based on
290 a number of factors. Images labeled "appropriate" would generally include photos of an individual (assumed to be the owner of the blog) fully clothed, and not participating in any risky or suggestive behaviors. Inappropriate images generally included photos in
295 which an individual was not wearing a shirt, pants, or was wearing provocative swimwear, underwear, or other suggestive attire. Swimsuit photos were not deemed inappropriate unless they were accompanied by sexual body position, explicit captions, or swimwear
300 that was generally inappropriate for the age of the sample. Inappropriate activities included sexual body language or positioning usually accompanied by suggestive captions or risk behaviors, such as holding weapons, fighting, or using substances. Overtly conservative
305 images were deemed inappropriate if they were accompanied by suggestive, profane, or otherwise inappropriate captions.

Family issues encompassed comments about parents and/or siblings. Positive parent/sibling comments:
310 make positive statements about one or both parents or any sibling. Negative comments: make negative or derogatory statements about one or both parents or any sibling. Coded "issues" ranged from simple statements such as "I love my dad," to detailed stories retelling
315 positive, negative, or neutral experiences with family. Again, no comments were coded based on assumed intent, perceptions, or feelings of the author. Positive, negative, or neutral attitudes were scaled based on descriptive content alone and any obvious relationship
320 with family cohesion or conflict.

School issues dealt with attendance, school participation, and future academic goals. A comment was coded if it referenced skipping school or a desire to skip school. College attendance was coded if a com-
325 ment or survey was posted that specifically addressed wanting to attend college (generally with a "yes" or "no" response). If a comment was posted about wanting to be a lawyer, for example, it was assumed they also wanted to attend college. Discussion of athletics,
330 including participation in sports, was also coded.

Social issues consisted of comments relating to peers' interactions, special interests, and socialization. Peer comments were evaluated based on text provided. Positive comments: made a friendly or positive state-
335 ment about a peer. Negative comments were overtly negative, derogatory, or confrontational. Each category, positive and negative, was coded based on presence which often resulted in each blog having multiple responses because both types of comments were made.
340 Special interests included references to hobbies or en-

joyable activities such as reading books, listening to or playing music, and watching movies. Discussions of social gatherings, or "parties," were coded if a comment directly referenced a previously attended "party"
345 or other social gathering such as homecoming dance, birthday event, and club or bar attendance. The type of gathering was not discerned in coding, only the presence of the discussion.

Risk behaviors were addressed in regard to sub-
350 stance use, criminal activity, sexual content, profanity, and physical violence. Substance use was recorded if the profile or comment section included discussion or images of alcohol and/or drugs. Most blogs contained a survey-type question asking if participants smoked and
355 their response was coded as either "smokes" or "doesn't smoke." Profiles that did not contain a "do you smoke?" survey question were listed as "no response." Criminal activity was merely assessed as present or not present and qualitative details pertaining to
360 type of crime was attached to the coded data.

Sexual content is a rather abstract umbrella for adolescent behavior, so responses were split into two categories: explicit/graphic language and comments referencing sexual activity. Responses that were sexual in
365 nature but did not fit into one of these categories were coded as general sexual content. Profanity includes standard curse words as well as slang and sexual profanity. Because of the tendency for profane language and sexual language to overlap, certain terms and
370 phrases were coded under both headings. Physical harm was recorded regardless of victim/perpetrator status. Violence was noted as present or not present if physical harm was discussed toward self or others, by self or others.

375 *Identity vulnerability* (Huffaker, 2006) is the term developed to reference personally identifiable information posted on the Internet. Such data include adolescent's full name (first, last), phone number, business name, online contact information (e-mail, instant mes-
380 sage user name), or other type of identifiable data. An "other" category was necessary as some personally identifiable data were not easily categorized, such as school schedule with room numbers, general directions to home, scanned image of driver's license, etc. As
385 blogs frequently included at least one image of the author, any information providing location or contact information could make the teenager an easy target for Internet predators. "Many (students) don't grasp that not only their friends and classmates are reading their
390 sites, but also complete strangers who may have the worst intentions" (Anonymous, 2006, p. 25).

Peer interaction included size of personal network, frequency of interaction among "friends" within the network, and prior/past or proposed/future "real-life"
395 encounters. The networks consisted of anyone the participant registered as a "friend"—whether they knew that person in their day-to-day lives or exclusively online. Frequency of comments was determined based

on the first 50 available comments that display in chronological order, summing the time distance between posts, and then dividing by number of entries. This information is important to determine how frequently adolescents use their online social network to communicate. Finally, prior or proposed meetings reference comments that specifically state whether the participant and "friend" had met in person, a.k.a. "real-life," or whether they had made specific plans to meet. This information can be positive, indicating that online socialization includes and/or facilitates live interaction between adolescents who are physically involved in each other's lives. However, it can also be negative if data infers adolescents are meeting people they have known only online or people who are not appropriate to interact with (i.e., older adults, unknown adults from out of town, proponents of risk behaviors).

Procedure

Once a sample of 100 profiles had been accumulated, each profile was reviewed following the same "script" of variables and presence of specific content recorded in an Excel database. The original HTML profiles were saved on a separate electronic storage device and numerically coded so that any identifiable information was detached from the profile data. After reviewing all profiles and posting all variable responses to the database, information was transferred to SPSS statistical software for further evaluation and analysis.

Based on thematically coded categories of adolescent blog data, a systematic review was conducted to account for behaviors, identify any patterns between observed behaviors, and infer any possible association with type of school attended. Such data were also explored for indicators of potential dysfunction or questionable emotional states. As no significant variations were found between adolescents attending public vs. parochial school, results were consolidated to present an overview of online social networking content based on the total sample size and organized by gender. Based on the overall picture of adolescent Web content, implications for future research are discussed as well as potential intervention needs/strategies for parents and educators.

Results

Available demographics contained in the sample blogs indicate that the majority of adolescent profile authors reported being single (61%) or in a serious relationship (32%). The majority of these authors did not reference their religious affiliation (39%); 26% stated a Catholic affiliation; 22% stated other Christian affiliations. A substantial 75% of blog authors reported being heterosexual, 3% declared homosexuality, another 3% claimed to be bisexual, and 2% said they were unsure about their sexual orientation. Of the entire sample, 17% did not include any information pertaining to their sexual preferences (see Table 1).

Table 1

Profile Demographic Content Posted by Adolescents Listed by Gender

	Males (n = 50)	Females (n = 50)	Total (n = 100)
Relationship status			
Single	33%	28%	61%
Married	2%	2%	4%
Divorced	1%	1%	2%
In relationship	14%	18%	32%
No response	- - -	1%	1%
Religious affiliation			
Catholic	13%	13%	26%
Christian-other	11%	11%	22%
Other	8%	5%	13%
No response	18%	21%	39%
Sexual orientation			
Heterosexual	41%	34%	75%
Homosexual	2%	1%	3%
Bisexual	1%	2%	3%
Unsure	1%	1%	2%
No response	5%	12%	17%

All profiles contained images posted by the author (n = 100), 83% of which were deemed appropriate while 17% were inappropriate. Examples of inappropriate images included an individual urinating, shirtless females dancing on tables with shirtless males, photos of a homemade device captioned as a "working bomb," individuals drinking alcohol as well as pictures of alcohol bottles/cans. There were also photos taken from mirror reflections of nude males with the image stopping just above the genitals, often referred to by authors and friends as their "V" because of the V-shaped abdominal muscles just above male genitalia. These "V" images typically excluded part or all of the face of the individual photographed. Some pictures were conservative in content, but were accompanied by inappropriate captions containing references to alcohol or substance use and intoxication, profanity, obscene gestures, or suggestive/sexual body postures.

Of comments made about family, 37% were positive about parents and 22% were positive about siblings; 16% of participants made negative comments about parents with negative sibling comments accounting for 2% of responses. Regarding school issues, male profiles did not contain content related to skipping school while 4% of female profiles contained the topic. Fourteen percent of males' and 13% of females' profiles referenced a plan or desire to attend college. Of all blogs reviewed, 58% referenced athletics in some capacity—either making participatory comments or discussing a general interest (males 34%; females 24%).

Social issues included comments about peers with 97% of the entire sample making positive statements about or to their friends; 100% of female profiles contained positive peer comments compared to 94% of male profiles. Most blogs included special interest topics such as movies, music, books, and hobbies (71%), and 40% of all blogs reviewed referenced prior social gatherings or attended "parties"—some with revealing details of participants' activities, such as this comment posted about a new club in town: "Very loose 18 ID to enter; You know how the rest goes..." (see Table 2).

Table 2
Social Content Observed in Adolescent Profiles Listed by Gender

	Males (*n* = 50)	Females (*n* = 50)	Total (*n* = 100)
Image			
Appropriate	40%	43%	83%
Inappropriate	10%	7%	17%
Family issues			
Positive parental comment	16%	21%[1]	37%
Negative parental comment	5%	11%[1]	16%
Positive sibling comment	11%	11%	22%
Negative sibling comment	1%	1%	2%
School issues			
Skipping school	- - -	4%	4%
Aspires to attend college	14%	13%	27%
Athletics	34%[1]	24%	58%
Social issues			
Positive peer comments	47%	50%	97%
Negative peer comments	19%	17%	36%
Special interests	33%	38%	71%
Discussion of "parties"	18%	22%	40%

[1]Indicates significant difference at .05 between males and females

Risk behaviors made up a significant portion of content observed from the sample, with 84% of profiles and blog discussions containing some type of risk-taking behaviors; 83% of profiles included discussion or referencing of substances, 81% referenced alcohol, and 27% discussed illegal drugs. Fifty-six percent of authors stated that they did not smoke. Across-sample rates of criminal activity content were near-equal with 15% of blogs discussing some type of crime; 9% of blogs referenced shoplifting or stealing, while others referenced rape, selling drugs, gambling, vandalism, and automobile infractions.

Nearly half of all blogs contained some form of sexual content, with 44% using explicit or graphic language and 16% referencing sexual activity. Some of the sexual content was extremely explicit in nature, as represented in text and imagery. Certain references were also made about specific types of sexual activity, including individuals' virginity statuses. Naturally, profanity is intimately intermingled with sexual content, and the overall frequency of any type of profane language among all profiles was 81%, almost evenly distributed within the sample. Twenty-seven percent of profiles include statements relating to physical harm of self or others such as gang references, suicidal ideation, discussion of fights, or images of weapons implying violence.

Regarding personally identifiable information disclosed by adolescents, 43% listed their full name; 10% listed their phone number; 11% disclosed their place of employment, and 20% revealed their online contact information (i.e., e-mail address). Overall, nearly half the sites analyzed contained information that could

potentially jeopardize the identity security of the adolescent participants (see Table 3).

Table 3
Risk Behaviors Observed in Adolescent Online Social Networking Profiles Listed by Gender

	Males (*n* = 50)	Females (*n* = 50)	Total (*n* = 100)
Risk behaviors	44%	40%	84%
Substance use	44%[1]	39%	83%
Alcohol discussion/ comments	42%	39%	81%
Author smokes	9%	9%	18%
Author doesn't smoke	31%	25%	56%
Illegal drugs discussion/ comments	15%	12%	27%
Criminal activity	8%	7%	15%
Stealing/shoplifting	5%	4%	9%
Sexual content	29%	20%	49%
Explicit/graphic language	25%	19%	44%
Sexual activity comment	10%	6%	16%
Profanity	42%	39%	81%
Physical harm–self/others	18%	9%	27%
Included full name (first, last)	23%	20%	43%
Included phone number	2%	8%	10%
Included employer name	2%	9%	11%
Provided online contact information	10%	10%	20%

[1]Indicates significant difference at .05 between males and females

In an effort to tie the virtual world of adolescent bloggers to their "real" day-to-day lives, their frequency of interaction with other users was collected. Comments about physical meetings and frequency of comment postings were indicative of "real" relationships; 83% of the sample referenced previous in-person contact as well as proposed future in-person encounters and such "real" contact was evenly distributed across the sample. Profiles had an average network size of 194 "friends" with a standard deviation of 162.28. This figure not only represents the number of contacts made and maintained online but also highlights the diversity in network sizes. The average frequency of interaction was 2.79 days, with a standard deviation of 3.10 days. Such a short time lapse between postings indicates that adolescents frequently use online social networks to communicate and maintain relationships on a regular basis. With a standard deviation of less than a week, it is safe to assume that adolescents use these networks as a major method of interpersonal communication (see Table 4).

Discussion

Process

This study brought to light two aspects of online social networking research: process and content. The process function of the analysis was to determine if content from adolescent social networking profiles could be systematically and scientifically studied. Though broad and randomly led with diverse content, social networking profiles successfully fit into a coding scheme that allowed for exploratory collection of qualitative themes relating to adolescent thought, behavior, and socialization. The proposition that such content could be successfully researched was strongly supported. The information adolescents post online does contain intimate and candid personal information as well as peer interaction that can be randomized, sorted, and systematically coded, creating a comprehensive overview of online social behavior. The process of reviewing profiles was time-consuming and detail-oriented, thus requiring intense focus on accuracy and unbiased recording. With that said, and considering the variety and amount of data collected in this study, it is concluded that adolescent blogs are an ideal research opportunity with many diverse avenues for analysis.

Table 4
Peer Interaction: Frequencies and Means of Adolescents By Gender

	Males ($n = 50$)	Females ($n = 50$)	Total ($n = 100$)
In-person contact (not online)			
Prior	42%	41%	83%
Future/proposed	40%	43%	83%
Length of "friend" list (number of users)			
Mean	218.00	170.00	194.00
Standard deviation	196.30	133.36	168.73
Frequency of comment posts (in days)			
Mean	2.97	2.61	2.79
Standard deviation	4.17	2.23	3.33

Content

The second aspect of the study relating to blog content resulted in concurrent findings with prior literature as profiles included personal demographic details, comments relating to family well-being and functioning, peer interactions, substance use, sexual activity, body-image issues, identity vulnerability, and frequency of contact among bloggers. Findings of sexual and profane content strongly supported prior research by Subrahmanyam, Smahel, and Greenfield (2006) in that adolescents use online forums to explore their sexuality. Because of the vastness and richness of content available, it is recommended and strongly encouraged that future studies focus on specific aspects of adolescence (e.g., body image), and collect only data pertinent to such focus. It is not feasible to address a broad array of variables with extreme depth or comprehension. However, unlike prior research, this study thoroughly assessed for thematic, overarching variables adolescents frequently include in their online discussions providing direction for future, more contemplative analyses. During the course of this investigation, many salient research topics presented themselves (adolescent alcohol use, parent-child relationships, gender differences in body image, adolescent sexual

expression) as ideal future research themes related to adolescent development. This study was successful in demonstrating the diverse information that is literally at the research world's fingertips and freely available for analysis.

Future studies must address the concept of "freely available" information, and clear lines must be drawn regarding how ethical it is to observe controversial and disturbing material posted by minors. Prior to embarking on a study of this kind, researchers must outline what information they will collect, and what they will report to site administrators or authorities as inappropriate or dangerous. Though social network participants must waive any rights to the content, one cannot assume users—specifically adolescents—thoroughly review hosting sites' terms of use, privacy policies, or register with sites using accurate demographic information.

Identity Exploration

Through observation of adolescents' online interactions and behaviors, it is evident that identity exploration is facilitated by online social networking. Topics that have been associated with adolescence and individuation were present in online profiles—especially in the areas of self-disclosure, peer relations, risk behaviors, and sexual exploration. The content posted to adolescent blogs followed expected paths of identity and role experimentation as originally understood by Erikson's developmental stages (1968). It is an advantage to understand that adolescents use social networking sites to quasi-publicly experiment with their identity, trying out different roles. However, it is much more beneficial for researchers, parents, and educators to have firsthand knowledge of the specific ways adolescents communicate with their peers and social networks and to view blogging as a relatively safe method of role exploration. Understanding *how* teenagers communicate with one another potentially facilitates better communication between authority figures and adolescents and enables adults to be more aware of adolescent emotional health and well-being.

School Environment

Through the lens of school environment, results did not highlight any demonstrative trends associated with attendance at any type of school but provided enough interesting data to warrant additional research. Faith, or attendance at a faith-based school, was not observed either as a risk or protective factor. However, in light of the expectations that accompany parochial school attendance, it is possible that a lack of difference between public and private-religious school is, in itself, a significant finding—especially considering the provocative topics that were equally present among all students.

Intervention

Findings from this review highlight several areas

where adolescent social networking profiles could be useful in educating parents about adolescents' attitudes and behaviors, as well as indicate several areas where intervention may be needed, primarily in the areas of risk-taking behavior and personal identity disclosure. Based on results from this study, adolescents are blogging about a considerable amount of risk behaviors such as substance use, crime, and promiscuity. The infinite and unguarded nature of the Internet may require parents to revisit their philosophy on adolescent privacy expectations and parent-child communication about such behaviors. Not only can parents benefit from observing their child's uncensored disclosure and behavior by gaining a greater understanding of their attitudes and motivations, they can also learn more about the Internet world, their child's level of participation within it, and how their parental role as monitor fits into the scheme of virtual reality.

If parents are able to observe their adolescents' peer communications, they may be able to embrace a more realistic perspective of their attitudes, values, and motivations and be able to adapt their parenting styles appropriately. In other words, parents will be able to know their children better. Adolescents view their parents as more permissive or more authoritarian than parents often see themselves, which significantly affects emotional autonomy and parent-child conflict (Smetana, 1995). Instead of perceiving online content as a form of personal diary that adolescents are entitled to keep private, parents should view the medium as an invaluable tool for helping them understand their teenagers better—their hopes, challenges, opinions, communication styles, activities, and social networks.

"The explosive growth in the popularity of (social networking sites) has generated concerns among some parents, school officials, and government leaders about the potential risks posed to young people when personal information is made available in such a public setting" (Lenhart & Madden, 2007, 3). Parents and educators could take an appreciation of online social networking, and its role in adolescent life, a step further by incorporating it into routine discussion and curriculum. By transforming computer-mediated communication (CMC) from a contemporary phenomenon, where parents have no presence and limited understanding, to common knowledge incorporated into everyday language, CMC loses its power and stigma as a technology that only adolescents use or comprehend. Alienating the Internet from the academic environment would only succeed in creating a greater divide between young people and authority figures. It is also essential that school administrators stay abreast of online networking within their institution to monitor the social climate of their school community. It is imperative that teachers, school administrators, and most certainly parents familiarize themselves with the Internet well enough to at least monitor who students are talking to and about what.

By addressing online activities with teens, in relation to ethics, propriety, safety, and language, all parties involved learn more about one another and create a safer environment in which this modern method of communication will continue to grow. As demonstrated in the current study, online social networks can be a positive form of communication within the school system. Several sites were created to maintain friendships after students had relocated to another state or, in one instance, when a foreign-exchange student returned to his home country. A series of comments were found on a male's profile welcoming him to his new school and initiating new friendships. Within parameters guided by parents, schools, and other invested authorities, online social networking could be a positive outlet for peer interaction and appropriate self-disclosure.

Limitations

The findings of this study should be understood solely as indicators of the need for more focused research. The most obvious limiting factor of the analysis is the inability to verify any of the information collected or understand it from the participants' perspectives. Everything included in online social networking profiles, or on the Internet for that matter, is completely subjective and limited by what the authors choose to disclose or their subjective depiction of themselves. However, these limitations are not so different from the challenges encountered with any type of self-report data collection that is dependent on honest disclosure of participants.

A second limitation affecting generalizability is the small sample size. But each of the 100 profiles reviewed contained extensive detail that provides insight into adolescents' online social networking. The amount of detail in this analysis mandated a smaller, more manageable sample size with limited scope, but resulted in more complex and salient recordings. Social networking sites are, as Mazur (2005, p. 180) noted, "mines of adolescent data." The information is out there and is rich in substance and meaning; it just needs to be systematically collected and coded for generalizable analysis.

Conclusion

This study certainly begs more questions than it answers; however, that was the purpose. The intention of reviewing adolescent blogs was not to learn more about the Internet, but to learn how online social networking sites could benefit and give direction for future research on adolescent behavior and development. The question of what topics teenagers discuss online was answered and content ranged from families and friends, hobbies and athletics, to drug use, profanity, and promiscuity. Observing adolescent behavior within an online network supported the notion that profiles are rich in behavioral data as related to development and individuation. Researchers continually strive to understand the teenage mind better, especially as society advances and new modes of communication and exploration develop. Blogging could be viewed as more authentic behavior compared to cross-sectional methods asking

765   adolescents how often they participate in or feel about certain aspects of life. The inconsistencies found within the 100 blogs observed in this analysis demonstrate that what a teenager marks on a survey form may be very different from how they actually feel or behave

770   with their peers.

In this sample, few patterns were evident, though some phenomena appeared promising, such as communication style, self-image, sexual behavior, or violence. More research that explores readily available informa-

775   tion to create a more comprehensive analysis from which stronger inferences and generalizations can be made is needed. Even though no patterns were established based on school environment, that does not mean no associations are to be found. This review

780   highlighted a dire need for more data collection addressing adolescent behaviors—both positive and risky—to see if and how they are affected by the school environment. The content analyzed from the profiles in this study indicate the importance of adoles-

785   cent behavior and peer interaction as it relates to social relationships, risk behaviors, special interests, extracurricular activities, and family dynamics. The overall goal of this study was achieved—an overview has been developed outlining what adolescents are communicat-

790   ing online. Future studies should take this research further by investigating the specific behaviors observed in order to understand what they mean within the context of the adolescent's "real life."

References

Erikson, E. (1968). *Identity: Youth and crisis.* New York: Norton.

Fox, S., & Madden, M. (2005, December). Generations online (Memo). *Pew Internet and American Life Project.* Retrieved October 22, 2006, from: www.pewInternet.org

Greenfield, P., & Yan, Z. (2006). Children, adolescents, and the Internet: A new field of inquiry in developmental psychology. *Developmental Psychology, 42*(3), 391–394.

Herring, S., Scheidt, L., Wright, E., & Bonus, S. (2005). Weblogs as a bridging genre. *Information Technology and People, 18*(2), 142–171.

Huffaker, D. (2006). *Teen blogs exposed: The private lives of teens made public.* Presented at the American Association for the Advancement of Science in St. Louis, MO., February 16–19.

Huffaker, D., & Calvert, S. (2005). Gender, identity, and language use in teenage blogs. *Journal of Computer-Mediated Communication, 10*(2), article 1. http://jcmc.indiana.edu/vol10/issue2/huffaker.html

Kidwell, J., Dunham, R., Bacho, R., & Pastorino, E. (1995). Adolescent identity exploration: A test of Erikson's theory of transitional crisis. *Adolescence, 30*(120), 785–794.

Lenhart, A., & Fox, S. (2006, July 19). A portrait of the Internet's new storytellers. *Pew Internet and American Life Project.* Retrieved October 22, 2006, from: www.pewInternet.org

Lenhart, A., & Madden, M. (2007, January 7). Social networking websites and terms: An overview (Memo). *Pew Internet and American Life Project.* Retrieved January 26, 2007, from: www.pewInternet.org

Mazur, E. (2005). Teen blogs as mines of adolescent data. *Teaching of Psychology, 32*(3), 180–182.

Mee, C. (2006). To blog or not to blog. *On Target, 2*(1), 30–31.

"MySpace" cadets are up for sudden death. (2006, September). *The Education Digest, 72*(1), 25.

Smetana, J. (1995). Parenting styles and conceptions of parental authority during adolescence. *Child Development, 66*, 299–316.

Subrahmanyam, K., Smahel, D., & Greenfield, P. (2006). Connecting developmental constructs to the Internet: Identity presentation and sexual exploration in online teen chatrooms. *Developmental Psychology, 42*(3), 395–406.

White, J., & Klein, D. (2002). *Family Theories* (2nd ed.). Thousand Oaks, London, New Delhi: Sage Publications.

Whitlock, J., Powers, J., & Eckenrode, J. (2006). The virtual cutting edge: The Internet and adolescent self-injury. *Developmental Psychology, 42*(3), 1–11.

About the authors: *Amanda L. Williams* and *Michael J. Merten,* Department of Human Development and Family Science, Oklahoma State University.

Address correspondence to: Michael J. Merten, Department of Human Development and Family Science, Oklahoma State University, 1111 Main Hall, Tulsa, Oklahoma 74106. E-mail: michael.merten@okstate.edu

Exercise for Article 26

Factual Questions

1. Was random selection used in this study?

2. In addition to substance abuse and criminal activity, what other "risk behaviors" were addressed?

3. Were significant differences (i.e., variations) found between adolescents attending public versus parochial schools?

4. Was there a statistically significant difference between the percentage of males and females mentioning athletics in their profiles?

5. According to the researchers, what is the "most obvious limiting factor" of the analysis?

6. According to the researchers, what is the "second limitation" of this study?

Questions for Discussion

7. The researchers examined profiles on "a major hosting site," but did not name the site. Speculate on why they did not name it. (See lines 204–206.)

8. The researchers identified themes based on "content alone." If you had conducted this study, would you also have done this *or* would you have made inferences about the intent of the participants? (See lines 243–248.)

9. In your opinion, would it be difficult to make judgments on image appropriateness? Explain. (See lines 289–307.)

10. What is your opinion on the researchers' suggestion that future studies should address the concept of "freely available information"? Is this an important issue? Explain. (See lines 601–613.)

11. Do you agree that the researchers achieved their "overall goal"? Explain. (See lines 198–203 and 787–790.)

12. If you were to conduct a study on this topic, what changes in research methodology, if any, would you make?

Quality Ratings

Directions: Indicate your level of agreement with each of the following statements by circling a number from 5 for strongly agree (SA) to 1 for strongly disagree (SD). If you believe an item is not applicable to this research article, leave it blank. Be prepared to explain your ratings. When responding to criteria A and B below, keep in mind that brief titles and abstracts are conventional in published research.

A. The title of the article is appropriate.
    SA   5   4   3   2   1   SD

B. The abstract provides an effective overview of the research article.
    SA   5   4   3   2   1   SD

C. The introduction establishes the importance of the study.
    SA   5   4   3   2   1   SD

D. The literature review establishes the context for the study.
    SA   5   4   3   2   1   SD

E. The research purpose, question, or hypothesis is clearly stated.
    SA   5   4   3   2   1   SD

F. The method of sampling is sound.
    SA   5   4   3   2   1   SD

G. Relevant demographics (for example, age, gender, and ethnicity) are described.
    SA   5   4   3   2   1   SD

H. Measurement procedures are adequate.
    SA   5   4   3   2   1   SD

I. All procedures have been described in sufficient detail to permit a replication of the study.
    SA   5   4   3   2   1   SD

J. The participants have been adequately protected from potential harm.
    SA   5   4   3   2   1   SD

K. The results are clearly described.
    SA   5   4   3   2   1   SD

L. The discussion/conclusion is appropriate.
    SA   5   4   3   2   1   SD

M. Despite any flaws, the report is worthy of publication.
    SA   5   4   3   2   1   SD

Article 27

Diabetes Portrayals in North American Print Media: A Qualitative and Quantitative Analysis

MELANIE ROCK

University of Calgary, Alberta, and Université de Montréal, Quebec

Objectives. This study investigated how media coverage has portrayed diabetes as newsworthy.

Methods. The quantitative component involved tabulating diabetes coverage in two major Canadian newspapers, 1988–2001 and 1991–2001. The qualitative component focused on high-profile coverage in two major U.S. magazines and two major Canadian newspapers, 1998–2000.

Results. Although coverage did not consistently increase, the quantitative results suggest an emphasis on linking diabetes with heart disease and mortality to convey its seriousness. The qualitative component identified three main ways of portraying type 2 diabetes: as an insidious problem, as a problem associated with particular populations, and as a medical problem.

Conclusions. Overall, the results suggest that when communicating with journalists, researchers and advocates have stressed that diabetes maims and kills. Yet even when media coverage acknowledged societal forces and circumstances as causes, the proposed remedies did not always include or stress modifications to social contexts. Neither the societal causes of public health problems nor possible societal remedies automatically received attention from researchers or from journalists. Skilled advocacy is needed to put societal causes and solutions on public agendas.

Type 2 diabetes mellitus is a serious public health problem in developed countries and increasingly in developing countries too.[1] Yet only a handful of peer-reviewed articles have examined mass media coverage
5 of type 1 or type 2 diabetes.[2-5] This study examined how print media coverage portrayed diabetes as a newsworthy problem. The results suggest that public health advocacy needs to take into account the roles played by journalists but also by expert sources in in-
10 fluencing portrayals of health problems in the mass media and thereby influencing how members of the public understand health problems.

The premise underlying this mixed-method study is that discourses highlight some diseases, health risks,
15 and approaches to intervention—while obscuring others—by influencing how people think, express themselves, and act.[6-11] Problem framing can be understood as a social process that involves the selection of some aspects of a perceived reality and making them seem
20 more apparent or salient so as to promote particular definitions, causal interpretations, moral evaluations, or possible remedies.[12] This article's emphasis on media portrayals resonates with the "public arenas" model of how problems achieve social recognition.[13] Unlike the
25 "natural history" model of problem recognition, which emphasizes how bona fide harms achieve visibility, the public arenas model does not assume that objective harms become socially recognized problems. Instead, the public arenas model underscores that the mass me-
30 dia, public policy, scientific publications, and other discursive domains interact with one another to confer recognition or to obscure harm.

Methods

Quantitative Methods

The quantitative component aimed to establish the extent to which mass media coverage has portrayed
35 diabetes as problematic. To do so, the amount and select key features of diabetes coverage were tabulated longitudinally in two newspapers: *The Toronto Star* and *The Globe and Mail*. *The Toronto Star* is the largest-circulation newspaper in Canada, and *The Globe*
40 *and Mail* was the only newspaper distributed across Canada throughout the 1990s. LexisNexis was used to access the full-text electronic archives of *The Toronto Star* for all available years: 1988–2001. The data for *The Globe and Mail* were obtained from InfoGlobe for
45 all available years: 1991–2001.

The search term "diabet!" (the "!" denotes a wildcard search; in the case of "diabet!" items with the word "diabetic" and "diabetics" would be included, as well as those using the word "diabetes") was used to
50 identify references dealing with diabetes, and the search strategy "heart disease, heart attack, heart association, heart failure, cardiac OR cardiol!" was used to identify references dealing with heart disease.[2] Combining these two sets yielded the number of references

55 related to both diabetes and heart disease. The combined set was searched for mentions of death ("death, dead, dies, dying OR obit!"). To establish how often coverage focused attention on diabetes, rather than merely mentioning this condition, the search term
60 "diabet!" was used to retrieve items mentioning diabetes in obituaries, headlines, or lead paragraphs. All items found were tabulated.

Qualitative Methods

The qualitative component focused on identifying the framing devices[12] used in recent print media cover-
65 age of type 2 diabetes. First and foremost, the analysis examined how the print media portrayed type 2 diabetes as a problem by asking, "What is it about this condition that is made to seem problematic?" Related questions included, "Which dimensions and causes of
70 the problem are highlighted?" "Who or what is blamed?" and "What remedies are endorsed?"

Two large-circulation U.S. magazines (*Time* and *Newsweek*), *The Globe and Mail*, and *The Toronto Star* were monitored prospectively, 1998–2000. (Both *Time*
75 and *Newsweek* are sold on Canadian newsstands.) Only stories profiling type 2 diabetes in the first section of the newspaper or magazine cover stories were selected for analysis. To identify any items fitting these criteria that had been missed during prospective monitoring, I
80 searched the following databases: InfoGlobe (for *The Globe and Mail*), Canadian Newsstand (for the *Toronto Star*), and Business Source Premier (for *Newsweek* and *Time*).

Results

Quantitative Results

The number of *Globe and Mail* references mention-
85 ing diabetes increased nearly fivefold between 1991 and 2000 and then dropped off in 2001. Meanwhile, the number of articles mentioning diabetes in *The Toronto Star* did not increase overall from 1988 through 2001 but spiked dramatically in 1995, and again in 1998
90 (Figure 1). I hypothesized that these spikes might correlate to the publication in 1993 and 1995 of landmark clinical trial results showing that tight blood glucose control can curb the incidence of microvascular and macrovascular complications.[14,15] The University of
95 Toronto is home to Bernard Zinman, one of the investigators in these trials, so this international story would have a strong local "angle." Three articles published in 1993 that contained interviews with Zinman focused attention on these results, but searching the 1995 and
100 1998 diabetes coverage for mentions of Zinman did not retrieve any items.

The number of *Toronto Star* articles mentioning diabetes as well as heart disease and death spiked in 1995 and again in 1998 (Figure 2), and the number of
105 articles in *The Globe and Mail* mentioning both of these health problems increased most from 1991 through 2001 (Figure 3). The number of times that diabetes was mentioned in *Toronto Star* obituaries, head-

lines, and lead paragraphs did not increase overall from
110 1988 (75) through 2001 (55), but the number of times that diabetes appeared in *Globe and Mail* obituaries, headlines, and lead paragraphs more than tripled from 1991 (19) to 2001 (61).

Qualitative Results

In the time period studied, *The Globe and Mail*
115 published 14 items that met the inclusion criteria, *The Toronto Star* published nine items, *Newsweek* published two, and *Time* published none. All 25 articles that met the inclusion criteria were found to exhibit at least one of three frames, and six exhibited more than
120 one (Table 1).

Type 2 diabetes is an insidious problem. Each article in the sample that portrayed type 2 diabetes as an insidious problem provided at least one of the following two reasons: (1) modern comforts and conven-
125 iences contribute to this public health problem and (2) individual cases often escape detection for years; meanwhile, complications such as impaired vision, loss of sensation in the limbs, kidney damage, and heart disease often set in. These articles listed the following
130 as possible remedies for preventing complications or for reducing the incidence of type 2 diabetes (or both): intensive clinical treatment, lifestyle changes, improved disease surveillance, increased public awareness, and more public funding.

135 This frame was particularly prominent in two lengthy feature articles that appeared in 2000 and whose titles included the phrase *silent killer*. A September 4, 2000, *Newsweek* cover story (Table 1: NW2. For the remainder of the article, news and news maga-
140 zine articles will be followed by a bracketed referent to allow easy location in Table 1) bore the title "An American epidemic: Diabetes, the silent killer," whereas "Forgotten communities stalked by silent killer: Lost People" was the front-page headline of an
145 April 30, 2000, *Toronto Star* feature article (TS7). It is difficult to imagine that a contemporary report might bear a title like "Cancer: A serious disease," or "AIDS: A public health problem." But in 2000, the Centers for Disease Control and Prevention released "Diabetes: A
150 serious public health problem,"[16] which sparked the *Newsweek* cover story. Note that diabetes was called "serious" in the Centers for Disease Control and Prevention report title, and then *Newsweek* reframed it for a broader public as insidious or sinister. It is also useful
155 to compare the September 4, 2000, *Newsweek* "silent killer" cover story on type 2 diabetes (NW2) with an issue from a year earlier (September 27, 1999 [NW1]), whose cover featured the title, "Where health begins," placed over a photograph of a fetus. The subtitle for the
160 earlier cover story announced, "Obesity, cancer and heart attacks: How your odds are set in the womb." The lead paragraph of that story profiled a 73-year-old man who was diagnosed with type 2 diabetes as well as hypertension in his early 50s. Although diabetes figures

149

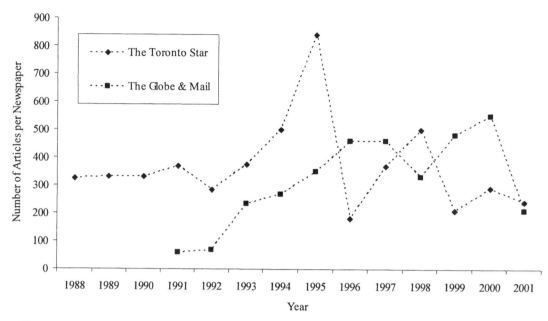

Figure 1. Mention of diabetes in Canadian newspapers.

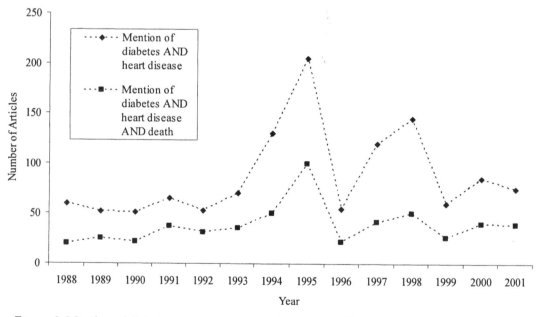

Figure 2. Mention of diabetes, heart disease, and death in *The Toronto Star*.

165 in the "typical case" mobilized in the lead paragraph to personify the lifelong impact of embryonic and fetal development, the editorial board apparently did not consider type 2 diabetes sufficiently dramatic for the cover page. But within a year, *Newsweek* dramatized

170 type 2 diabetes as a cover story by portraying it as an insidious problem whose human costs are unevenly distributed across different social groups and whose financial costs burden American society as a whole.

Type 2 diabetes is associated with certain groups.
175 This frame emphasized that type 2 diabetes and related complications are not randomly or evenly distributed. Articles deploying this frame emphasized one or more of the following: (1) type 2 diabetes is more prevalent in some groups than others; (2) type 2 diabetes has
180 spread to hitherto unaffected groups; (3) type 2 diabetes is more prevalent overall than it used to be across the United States or Canada; (4) type 2 diabetes incidence is expected to increase further; and (5) type 2

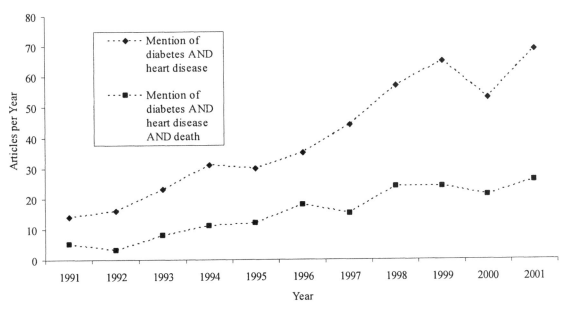

Figure 3. Mention of diabetes, heart disease, and death in *The Globe Mail.*

diabetes is costly—in human and financial terms. Arti-
185 cles using this frame portrayed modern lifestyles as the
main cause. Proposed remedies included intensive
clinical management, community-level interventions,
lifestyle changes, increased public funding for health
and social programs, improved disease surveillance,
190 and further medical research. In articles rooting causa-
tion in the societal conditioning of lifestyle, the proposed remedies sometimes stressed informed individual choice (e.g., *The Toronto Star*, October 20, 1999
[TS4]).
195   This frame emerged as the most common in the
sample. All the articles that portrayed type 2 diabetes
as an insidious problem also used the group association
frame. The disproportionate impact of type 2 diabetes
on Aboriginal people across Canada was the most
200 common topic. Other groups associated with type 2
diabetes in the sample included people older than 40
years (*The Toronto Star*, October 20, 1999 [TS4], and
August 25, 2000 [TS5]), people of African or Latin
American descent (*The Globe and Mail*, May 3, 2000
205 [GM13]; *The Toronto Star*, August 25, 2000 [TS5];
Newsweek, September 4, 2000 [NW2]) and—an alarming new development—youths (*The Globe and Mail*,
June 28, 1999 [GM4]; *The Toronto Star*, August 25,
2000 [TS5]; *Newsweek*, September 4, 2000 [NW2]).
210   *Type 2 diabetes is a medical problem.* This frame
presents type 2 diabetes as a problem requiring medical
treatment rather than a problem stemming mainly from
societal forces and circumstances. Portraying type 2
diabetes as a medical problem underscores that type 2
215 diabetes is truly a serious disease mainly because of its
complications. For instance, one article in *The Toronto
Star* (March 5, 1999 [TS2]) noted that "the disease
remains a major factor in blindness, kidney disease and

heart disease." The remedies to reduce complication
220 among people who already have type 2 diabetes explicitly endorsed in this portrayal included pharmaceuticals
(e.g., *The Globe and Mail*, March 26, 1998 [GM1]) or
lifestyle changes (e.g., *The Globe and Mail*, September
11, 1998 [GM2]), and articles employing this frame all
225 explicitly or implicitly endorsed further medical research.
One article featuring the insidious problem and associated group frames made clear reference to a competing medical problem frame in quoting an expert
230 source as saying, "The question is: Is diabetes a problem of biology or a problem of sociology?" (*The Globe
and Mail*, June 28, 1999 [GM4]). Yet the distinction
between framing type 2 diabetes as a problem rooted in
society or a medical problem could be subtle. Consider
235 the article titled "Couch potatoes more likely to get
diabetes" (*The Globe and Mail*, June 28, 1999 [GM5]).
Although the article stressed that type 2 diabetes is
common today because of sedentary lifestyles, it did
not report on the social distribution of TV watching,
240 physical activity, or type 2 diabetes, and it did not present lifestyle change as a process mediated by social
norms and circumstances. By comparison, another article in the sample (*The Toronto Star*, October 20, 1999
[TS4]), reporting on a similar study led by the same
245 investigator, framed type 2 diabetes as a problem associated with particular groups. It did so in two ways: by
noting that type 2 diabetes is mainly found in people
aged more than 40 years and by noting that the research focused on whether walking can reduce type 2
250 diabetes risk because walking is the most common
form of physical activity among people middle-aged
and older.

Table 1
Frames Deployed by Coverage Included in the Qualitative Analysis

Periodical	References	Insidious problem	Associated groups	Medical problem
The Globe and Mail	**GM1.** Diabetes drugs work together. *Globe and Mail.* March 26, 1998:A19.			√
	GM2. Fat cited as villain in diabetes. *Globe and Mail.* September 11, 1998: A19.			√
	GM3. Let's make a DNA deal. Sandy Lake has the third-highest diabetes rate in the world. The gene hunters pay to find out why. *Globe and Mail.* December 7, 1998:A1.		√	√
	GM4. "Adult" version of diabetes afflicting children. *Globe and Mail.* June 28, 1999:A8.		√	
	GM5. Couch potatoes more likely to get diabetes. *Globe and Mail.* June 28, 1999:A8.			√
	GM6. Diabetes outbreak hits Quebec Crees. *Globe and Mail.* May 5, 1999:A2.	√	√	
	GM7. Genetic link found to natives' diabetes. *Globe and Mail.* March 11, 1999:A10.		√	
	GM8. Genetic trait for diabetes uncovered. *Globe and Mail.* March 9, 1999:A11.		√	
	GM9. Ottawa to target diabetes. *Globe and Mail.* May 18, 1999:A5.		√	
	GM10. Ottawa to spend $115 million to fight diabetes. *Globe and Mail.* November 20, 1999:A12.	√	√	
	GM11. Pharmaceuticals: diabetes drug approved. *Globe and Mail.* October 14, 1999:A8.			√
	GM12. Research traces gene for obesity, diabetes. *Globe and Mail.* March 5, 1999:A12.			√
	GM13. Diabetes hits black women worst: study. *Globe and Mail.* May 3, 1999:A6.		√	
	GM14. Heart disease on increase for natives. Smoking, obesity and epidemic of diabetes in Aboriginal community contributing. *Globe and Mail.* June 26, 2000:A2.		√	
The Toronto Star	**TS1.** Hot tub therapy helps diabetics, study suggests. *Toronto Star.* September 16, 1999:1.			√
	TS2. Mice tests offer hope in the war on diabetes; crucial enzyme discovery made by Montreal team. *Toronto Star.* March 5, 1999:1.			√
	TS3. Mutated gene behind diabetes rate; Ontario doctor finds why Ojibwa-Cree are at a much higher risk. *Toronto Star.* March 10, 1999:1.		√	
	TS4. Walking cuts risk of diabetes: research; Harvard study followed health of 70,000 women. *Toronto Star.* October 20, 1999:1.		√	
	TS5. Diabetes "epidemic" looming; no exercise, bad diet blamed for expected doubling of cases. *Toronto Star.* August 25, 2000:A02.	√	√	
	TS6. First nations need help to fight diabetes. *Toronto Star.* May 15, 2000:A19.		√	
	TS7. Forgotten communities stalked by silent killer: Lost People. *Toronto Star.* April 30, 2001:1.	√	√	
	TS8. The Lost People Natives' plight sparks outrage; readers react to *Star* series on reserve conditions. *Toronto Star.* May 1, 2000:A01.		√	
	TS9. Natives to get update on diabetes. *Toronto Star.* June 1, 2000:A23.		√	
Newsweek	**NW1.** Shaped by life in the womb. *Newsweek;* September 27, 1999:50–53.			√
	NW2. An American epidemic: diabetes, the silent killer. *Newsweek.* September 4, 2000:40–47.	√	√	

Discussion

As is common among studies of the popular press in public health,[17,18] previous studies of diabetes media coverage[2-5] assessed reporting accuracy. The evaluation of reporting accuracy presumes that there is a correct way for the media to convey health information to the public: Not only should accurate information be provided about diseases and health risks, but the allocation of coverage should reflect (presumably accurate) epidemiological survey data. Indeed, the contrasting conclusions reached in previous studies of diabetes mass media coverage—with two studies concluding that the coverage generally reflects mortality rates[2,5] and two studies concluding that coverage tends to distort its impact on mortality[3,4]—stem largely from differences in the epidemiological data used as the standard against which to evaluate reporting accuracy. Public health researchers and advocates certainly have an interest in ensuring that the health information transmitted to the public is accurate. But it is also important to understand why some health issues receive more attention than do others and to understand how these issues are defined as socially significant. In adopting a framing analysis, this study did not disregard accuracy, but it focused on meaning.

The status of the terms *diabetes* and *type 2 diabetes* differs when emphasizing meaning rather than content accuracy. When emphasizing content accuracy, the question is whether the terms are used correctly in describing health problems and risks. Emphasizing meaning presumes that such terms and their definitions constitute part of the framing process.[9,11,19] Naming is part of framing, and that brings into view some limitations and strengths of this study. Because the term *diabetes* is commonly used to refer to all types of diabetes mellitus, searching LexisNexis and InfoGlobe to tabulate references to diabetes likely retrieved references dealing with type 1 diabetes or type 2 diabetes, or both. Yet the qualitative results suggest that even with a detailed analysis of each and every instance of mass media coverage included in a study such as this, completely isolating type 2 diabetes coverage from type 1 diabetes coverage would be impossible because the high-profile newspaper items analyzed qualitatively for this study sometimes explicitly discussed how type 2 diabetes differs from type 1 diabetes (e.g., *Newsweek*, September 4, 2000 [NW2]).

Moreover, the qualitative results show that portraying type 2 diabetes as insidious or unevenly distributed, or both, brought into focus the societal nature of this health problem. Through these framing processes, the term *type 2 diabetes* acquired fresh significance beyond that connoted by the medical problem frame. Yet even when societal forces and circumstances were acknowledged as causes, the proposed remedies did not always include or stress social interventions, and that may reflect media interviews with expert sources: health professionals and researchers.[8] In other words, by conducting a framing analysis, this study highlights that mass media coverage reflects careful packaging, not only of facts but of interpretations. This study also underscores the role played by a journalist's expert sources in packaging interpretations and transmitting meaning.

When I adopted a framing analysis, I designed the qualitative and quantitative components to detect whether mass media coverage attended to links between diabetes and related complications, notably heart disease. In other words, the analysis sought to reveal whether these links were "framed in" or "framed out" in problem naming and definition. *The Toronto Star* and *The Globe and Mail* quantitative results each provide some support for increased emphasis on a link between diabetes and heart disease. The qualitative results, meanwhile, included several instances of heart disease and other complications being evoked to portray type 2 diabetes either as a serious medical problem or as a serious problem rooted in societal organization and norms. These results are particularly noteworthy because prevalence and mortality data often underestimate the overall impact of diabetes for two main reasons. First, about one-third of all type 2 diabetes cases in Canada and the United States remain undiagnosed and untreated.[20-23] Undiagnosed type 2 diabetes surely tends to hasten death, but other causes will be recorded, usually cardiovascular disease. In addition, surveys based on self-report data cannot capture undiagnosed cases. Second, even when diabetes is diagnosed, physicians often do not record diabetes on death certificates. Instead, the deaths of people diagnosed with diabetes are often attributed to cardiovascular disease.[24,25] Using frame analysis to investigate meaning rather than a conventional content analysis to assess reporting accuracy did not presume that available national or international statistics fully capture the impact of diabetes.[2-5]

Indeed, for the insidious problem frame, undiagnosed cases emerged as pivotal. Nevertheless, consistent with the current medical definition of diabetes, which pivots on hyperglycemia but not necessarily with how members of disadvantaged populations in particular develop and perceive hyperglycemia,[26] high-profile type 2 diabetes media coverage did not consider community mental health as a possible etiologic factor and intervention target. Overall, the qualitative and quantitative results suggest that when communicating with journalists, researchers and advocates have lobbied for greater recognition of diabetes by stressing that diabetes maims and kills.

The results therefore fit the public arenas model better than the natural history model of how health problems achieve media coverage and other forms of social recognition. Although the natural history model uses individualistic biological metaphors (birth, development, maturation, death) and often stresses correspondence with population trends,[2] the public arenas model argues that the definition and relative status of social problems never mirror objective harms, so this model proposes evolutionary metaphors (carrying capacity, competition, selection) to help explain why some problems and problem dimensions receive more recognition than others.[13] The key point is that newspapers and other public arenas have only limited space or time available, so public recognition is a scarce resource for which problems and their advocates compete—through social selection processes that often hinge on framing.[27,28] Although the present study suggests that the amount and emphasis of recent media coverage have taken into account the changing socioeconomic distribution of type 2 diabetes, neither increased prevalence nor the related impact on mortality has translated directly into media coverage; instead, garnering media coverage for public health issues always requires careful thought and organized effort.[27] Understanding how the mass media continually frame and reframe health-related phenomena can enhance public health's capacity to advocate for due attention to societal causes and possible societal solutions.

References

1. Screening for Type 2 Diabetes. Report of a World Health Organization and International Diabetes Federation Meeting. Geneva, Switzerland: World Health Organization: 2003. Available at: http://www.who.int/diabetes/publications/en/screening_mnc03.pdf. Accessed June 9, 2005.
2. Adelman RC, Verbrugge LM. Death makes news: The social impact of disease on newspaper coverage. *J Health Soc Behav*. 2000;4:347–367.
3. Frost K, Frank E, Maibach E. Relative risk in the news media: A quantification of misrepresentation. *Am J Public Health*. 1997;87:842–845.
4. Mercado-Martinez FJ, Robles-Silva L, Moreno-Leal N, Franco-Almazan C. Inconsistent journalism: The coverage of chronic diseases in the Mexican press. *J Health Community*. 2001;6:235–247.
5. Van der Wardt EM, Taal E, Rasker JJ, Wiegman O. Media coverage of chronic diseases in the Netherlands. *Semin Arthritis Rheum*. 1999;28:333–341.
6. Foucault M. *L'Ordre du discours*. Paris, France: Gallimard: 1970.
7. Foucault M. Governmentality. In: Burchell G, Gordon C, Miller P, eds. *The Foucault Effect: Studies in Governmentality With Two Lectures by and an interview With Michel Foucault*. Chicago, Ill: University of Chicago Press; 1991 [1978]:87–104.

153

8. Lloyd B, Hawe P. Solutions forgone? How health professionals frame the problem of postnatal depression. *Soc Sci Med.* 2003:57:1783–1795.

9. Rosenberg CE. Disease in history: Frames and framers. *Milbank Q.* 1989;67(suppl 1):1–15.

10. Sontag S. *Illness as Metaphor and AIDS and Its Metaphors.* New York, NY: Anchor Books: 1990 [1988].

11. Young A. The anthropologies of illness and sickness. *Annu Rev Anthropol.* 1982;11:257–285.

12. Entman RM. Framing: Toward clarification of a fractured paradigm. *J Community.* 1993;43(4):51–59.

13. Hiltgartner S, Bosk CL. The rise and fall of social problems: A public arenas model. *Am J Sociol.* 1988;84(1):53–78.

14. Diabetes Control and Complications Trial Research Group. Effects of intensive diabetes management on macrovascular events and risk factors in the Diabetes Control and Complications Trial. *Am J Cardiol.* 1995;75:894–903.

15. Diabetes Control and Complications Trial Research Group. Effects of intensive diabetes management on the development and progression of long-term complications in insulin-dependent diabetes mellitus. *N Engl J Med.* 1993;329:977–986.

16. Centers for Disease Control and Prevention. Diabetes Public Health Resource Web site Diabetes: A Serious Public Health Problem Available at: http//www.medhelp.org/NIHlib/GF-558.html. Accessed November 15, 2004.

17. Wenger L, Malone R, Bero L. The cigar revival and the popular press: A content analysis, 1987–1997. *Am J Public Health.* 2001;91:288–291.

18. Bartlett C, Sterne J, Egger M. What is newsworthy? Longitudinal study of the reporting of medical research in two British newspapers. *BMJ.* 2002;325:81–84.

19. Lock M. *Encounters With Aging: Myths of Menopause in Japan and North America.* Berkeley, Calif: University of California Press; 1993.

20. Harris MI, Eastman RC, Cowie CC, Flegal KM, Eberhardt MS. Comparison of diabetes diagnostic categories in the U.S. population according to the 1997 American Diabetes Association and 1980–1985 World Health Organization diagnostic criteria. *Diabetes Care.* 1997;20:1859–1862.

21. Harris MI. Undiagnosed NIDDM: Clinical and public health issues. *Diabetes Care.* 1993;16:642–652.

22. Meltzer S, Leiter L, Daneman D, et al. 1998 Clinical practice guidelines for the management of diabetes in Canada. *CMAJ.* 1998;159(suppl 8):S1–S29.

23. Leiter LA, Barr A, Belanger A, et al. Diabetes Screening in Canada (DIASCAN) Study: Prevalence of undiagnosed diabetes and glucose intolerance in family physician offices. *Diabetes Care.* 2001;24:1038–1043.

24. Balkau B, Papal L. Certification of cause of death in French diabetic patients. *J Epidemiol Community Health.* 1992;46(1):63–65.

25. Tan M-H, Wornell C. Diabetes mellitus in Canada. *Diabetes Res Clin Pract.* 1991;14:S3–S8.

26. Rock M. Sweet blood and social suffering: Rethinking cause–effect relationships in diabetes distress and duress. *Med Anthropol.* 2003;22(2):131–174.

27. Finnegan JR Jr., Viswanath K, Hertog J. Mass media, secular trends, and the future of cardiovascular disease health promotion: An interpretive analysis. *Prev Med.* Dec 1999;29(6 pt 2):S50–S58.

28. Randolph W, Viswanath K. Lessons learned from public health mass media campaigns: Marketing health in a crowded media world. *Annu Rev Public Health.* 2004;25:419–437.

Acknowledgments: This study was made possible by a doctoral fellowship from the Social Sciences and Humanities Research Council of Canada (award 753-91-0166), a postdoctoral fellowship jointly funded by the Canadian Health Services Research Foundation and the Canadian Institutes of Health Research (award PDA-0800-05), and a research grant from the Groupe de recherche interdisciplinaire en santé (Interdisciplinary Health Research Group) at the Université de Montréal. Jean-Michel Billette assisted with collecting and organizing the quantitative data. Drs. Jennifer Godley, Penelope Hawe, Pascale Lehoux, Lindsay McLaren, and Louise Potvin provided helpful feedback on previous versions. Dr. Mary E. Northridge and three anonymous reviewers also provided helpful feedback while this paper was under review with the Journal. No protocol approval was needed for this study.

About the author: Melanie Rock, Ph.D., MSW, is with the Department of Community Health Sciences, the Faculty of Social Work, and the Department of Anthropology at the University of Calgary, Alberta, and the Université de Montréal, Quebec.

Address correspondence to: Melanie Rock, University of Calgary, Department of Community Health Sciences, Health Sciences Centre, 3330 Hospital Drive NW, Calgary, AB, Canada T2N 4N1. E-Mail: mrock@ucalgary.ca

Exercise for Article 27

Factual Questions

1. Which newspaper is the largest circulation newspaper in Canada?

2. In the quantitative methods, the researcher searched in three areas for mention of diabetes. One of the areas was in obituaries. What were the other two?

3. For the qualitative methods, did the researcher select stories appearing in all sections of the newspapers? Explain.

4. Which "frame" emerged as the most common?

5. In the Discussion section, the researcher states that portraying diabetes as insidious or unevenly distributed brings what into focus?

6. The research states that while the natural history model uses individualistic biological metaphors, the public arenas model proposes what type of metaphors?

Questions for Discussion

7. In your opinion, is it important to know the search terms used to locate the articles used in this research? Explain. (See lines 46–62.)

8. The material in Figure 1 is summarized in lines 84–90. In your opinion, how important is the figure? Would the article be as effective without it? Explain.

9. To what extent does the information in Table 1 add to your understanding of the results of this study? Explain.

10. Do you think the quantitative *or* qualitative results are more interesting? Are they equally interesting? Explain. (See lines 84–252.)

11. Would you recommend replication of this study using samples of other newspapers and magazines? Explain.

12. This article illustrates how documents (e.g., newspapers) can be analyzed to obtain information. Does this article convince you that the analysis of documents is an important scientific method? Explain.

Quality Ratings

Directions: Indicate your level of agreement with each of the following statements by circling a number from 5 for strongly agree (SA) to 1 for strongly disagree (SD). If you believe an item is not applicable to this research article, leave it blank. Be prepared to explain your ratings. When responding to criteria A and B below, keep in mind that brief titles and abstracts are conventional in published research.

A. The title of the article is appropriate.

    SA   5   4   3   2   1   SD

B. The abstract provides an effective overview of the research article.

    SA   5   4   3   2   1   SD

C. The introduction establishes the importance of the study.

    SA   5   4   3   2   1   SD

D. The literature review establishes the context for the study.

    SA   5   4   3   2   1   SD

E. The research purpose, question, or hypothesis is clearly stated.

    SA   5   4   3   2   1   SD

F. The method of sampling is sound.

    SA   5   4   3   2   1   SD

G. Relevant demographics (for example, age, gender, and ethnicity) are described.

    SA   5   4   3   2   1   SD

H. Measurement procedures are adequate.

    SA   5   4   3   2   1   SD

I. All procedures have been described in sufficient detail to permit a replication of the study.

    SA   5   4   3   2   1   SD

J. The participants have been adequately protected from potential harm.

    SA   5   4   3   2   1   SD

K. The results are clearly described.

    SA   5   4   3   2   1   SD

L. The discussion/conclusion is appropriate.

    SA   5   4   3   2   1   SD

M. Despite any flaws, the report is worthy of publication.

    SA   5   4   3   2   1   SD

Article 28

Perceptions and Beliefs About Body Size, Weight, and Weight Loss Among Obese African American Women: A Qualitative Inquiry

CHRISTIE A. BEFORT
University of Kansas Medical Center

JANET L. THOMAS
University of Kansas Medical Center

CHRISTINE M. DALEY
University of Kansas Medical Center

PAULA C. RHODE
University of Kansas Medical Center

JASJIT S. AHLUWALIA
University of Minnesota

ABSTRACT. The purpose of this qualitative study was to explore perceptions and beliefs about body size, weight, and weight loss among obese African American women in order to form a design of weight loss intervention with this target population. Six focus groups were conducted at a community health clinic. Participants were predominantly middle-aged with a mean Body Mass Index of 40.3 ± 9.2 kg/m^2. Findings suggest that participants (a) believe that people can be attractive and healthy at larger sizes; (b) still feel dissatisfied with their weight and self-conscious about their bodies; (c) emphasize eating behavior as the primary cause for weight gain; (d) view pregnancy, motherhood, and caregiving as major precursors to weight gain; (e) view health as the most important reason to lose weight; (f) have mixed experiences and expectations for social support for weight loss; and (g) prefer treatments that incorporate long-term lifestyle modification rather than fad diets or medication.

From *Health Education & Behavior, 35,* 410–426. Copyright © 2008 by Sage Publications, Inc. Reprinted with permission.

African American (AA) women are 60% more likely to become obese (Lewis et al., 1997) and 50% more likely to be moderately to severely obese than Caucasian women in the United States (Flegal, Carroll, 5 Ogden, & Johnson, 2002). Congruent with their higher rates of obesity, AA women are less likely to engage in regular physical activity (Centers for Disease Control, 2004) or to consume healthy diets (Arab, Carriquiry, Steck-Scott, & Gaudet, 2003). Likewise, obesity 10 among AA women has been linked to their higher mortality and incidence rates of coronary heart disease, hypertension, diabetes mellitus, cerebral vascular disease, and certain cancers (American Cancer Society, 2005; Harris, 1998; Must et al., 1999).

15 Although nearly two-thirds of obese AA women report that they want to lose weight and are attempting to do so (Clark et al., 2001), their weight loss efforts tend to be shorter in duration (Tyler, Allan, & Alcozer, 1997) and less successful compared to Caucasian 20 women (Kumanyika, Obarzanek, Stevens, Hebert, & Whelton, 1991; Wing & Anglin, 1996; Wing et al., 2004). In a number of controlled clinical trials, AA participants lost on average only half as much weight as Caucasian participants (Kumanyika et al., 1991; 25 Wing & Anglin, 1996). As Kumanyika, Morssink, and Agurs (1992) have articulated, mainstream weight loss programs may not be effective for AA women because they are based on assumptions and values of the dominant culture, for example, personal autonomy and self-30 management, whereas AA culture is more oriented toward interconnectedness and group support. In response to this, several lifestyle intervention trials have been culturally tailored to promote weight loss among AA women; however, the results of these trials have 35 been mixed, with many reporting only minimal weight loss and high attrition among participants (Agurs-Collins, Kumanyika, Ten Have, & Adams-Campbell, 1997; Kanders et al., 1994; Karanja, Stevens, Hollis, & Kumanyika, 2002; Kennedy et al., 2005; Kumanyika & 40 Charleston, 1992; Kumanyika et al., 2005; McNabb, Quinn, Kerver, Cook, & Karrison, 1997; Walcott-McQuigg et al., 2002; Yanek, Becker, Moy, Gittelsohn, & Koffman, 2001). More work is needed to better understand how to maximize the potential for AA women 45 to be successful in weight loss interventions.

Several researchers have suggested that greater acceptance of larger body sizes among AA women contributes to their higher risk for obesity (Flynn & Fitzgibbon, 1998; Wolfe, 2000). Body image studies comparing African Americans and Caucasians have used 50 questionnaires and figure drawings of graduated sizes to quantify preferences for, and satisfaction with, body sizes. Many studies have found that AA women have a larger ideal body size, are less likely to perceive themselves as overweight, are more satisfied with their bodies at heavier weights, and are more likely to report 55 feeling attractive even when they are dissatisfied with their weight (DiLillo, Gore, Jones, Balentine, & West, 2004; Fitzgibbon, Blackman, & Avellone, 2000; Flynn

60 & Fitzgibbon, 1998; Stevens, Kumanyika, & Keil, 1994). However, this research has been limited by a lack of culturally relevant and racially neutral figure rating scales, which only recently have been developed (Pulvers et al., 2004). Furthermore, some research has
65 found that after controlling for age, education, and body weight, racial/ethnic differences in body image perceptions are diminished (Cachelin, Rebeck, Chung, & Pelayo, 2002). Indeed, data show that many overweight and obese AA women are largely dissatisfied
70 with their weight and experience fluctuating levels of negative body image (Baturka, Hornsby, & Schorling, 2000; Davis, Clark, Carrese, Gary, & Cooper, 2005).

Qualitative research is well suited to provide indepth answers to complex questions and to suggest
75 ways of developing successful interventions with specific target groups (Bernard, 2002). In recent years, focus groups have been used to gain a better understanding of how AA culture may contribute to dietary patterns, physical activity, and weight loss behavior.
80 Barriers to physical activity viewed as central to AA culture include the perception that occupational and daily activities provide sufficient exercise and the high value placed on rest and relaxation after work. Other barriers commonly reported by AAs include lack of
85 motivation, time constraints because of family responsibilities (especially for AA women), child care and monetary costs, and concerns about neighborhood safety (Airhihenbuwa, Kumanyika, Agurs, & Lowe, 1995; Richter, Wilcox, Greaney, Henderson, & Ains
90 worth, 2002; Wilcox, Richter, Henderson, Greaney, & Ainsworth, 2002). Young, Gittelsohn, Charleston, Felix-Aaron, and Appel (2001) conducted focus groups with AA women older than 40 to assess motivation for exercise and found that women who were already exer
95 cising were more likely to report being motivated by health, weight control, and stress reduction, whereas sedentary women reported they would be motivated by social support and enjoyment of physical activities (Young et al., 2001).
100 Focus group studies have also provided insight into various cultural aspects of eating and food patterns among AAs. For example, AAs from differing socioeconomic groups have associated healthy eating with giving up their traditions of large family meals, fried or
105 roasted meats as the centerpiece of the meal, and preferences for high-fat foods and sweets (Hargreaves, Schlundt, & Buchowski, 2002; James, 2004). AA food traditions have often been passed down across generations from mothers to daughters (Wilson, Musham, &
110 McLellan, 2004), and efforts to change eating patterns may therefore be hindered by sociocultural influences, such as family tradition and church socials (Hargreaves et al., 2002). These sociocultural influences may vary depending on level of acculturation to mainstream val
115 ues (Beech et al., 2004).

Although each of these previous qualitative studies offers important insights, none of the studies included

solely obese AA women; none classified participants according to measured height and weight; and none
120 specifically addressed perceptions and beliefs about body size, weight, and weight loss per se. Within the context of AA culture, obese women may have unique perceptions regarding body image and weight loss that influence their weight-related behaviors. Given that
125 weight loss interventions are typically targeted for obese participants, it is important to have an in-depth understanding of the relevant perceptions and beliefs of this subgroup of AA women. Therefore, the purpose of this study was to explore perceptions and beliefs re
130 lated to body size, weight, and weight loss among this target group in order to inform the design of appropriate interventions with an obese AA female population.

Method

Participants

Participants were recruited with flyers posted throughout an urban, predominantly low-income, AA
135 community in a midwestern state. Flyers were posted in churches, shopping centers, work sites, gyms, health centers, and neighborhoods. In addition, a research assistant sat at a booth and handed out flyers to interested participants in the lobby of a community health
140 clinic that serves under- and uninsured, predominantly AA patients. This health clinic was also the site where the focus groups were held. The one-page recruitment flyer was designed to recruit AA women who "thought they might be overweight" and "were interested in par
145 ticipating in a discussion about weight and weight loss." Eligible participants were 18 years or older, AA, female, and had self-reported height and weight that classified them as obese according to the National Institutes of Health clinical guidelines (calculated as
150 body mass index [BMI] = 30 kg/m^2). Exclusion criteria included obvious intoxication or current in-patient substance abuse treatment, marked inappropriate affect or behavior, acute illness, or impaired cognition that would hinder participation in a group discussion.
155 Of 93 women who responded to the study flyers, 83 were eligible. Reasons for exclusion were BMI < 30 (n = 7), impaired cognition (n = 1), acute illness (n = 1), and younger than 18 years (n = 1). Of those eligible, 10 were unable to attend a focus group because of sched
160 uling conflicts, and another 11 did not show up for their scheduled appointment. Thus, the final sample included 62 women.

Procedure

Women who responded to the flyer were screened for eligibility by phone or in the health clinic lobby.
165 Eligible participants provided contact information and available times and were contacted by phone within 2 weeks to be scheduled for a group. We had anticipated a 50% attendance rate based on our previous experience conducting focus groups in the same setting using
170 a similar recruitment strategy. Therefore, we scheduled 12 to 16 participants per group, expecting to have at

157

Table 1
Outline of Focus Group Topics and Questions

Topic	Questions
Beliefs about body size and attractiveness	How do you feel about your current body shape?
	How does your body size affect how attractive you feel?
	What does it mean to have a healthy body size?
Attributions for weight	What do you think caused you to become overweight?
Reasons to lose weight	Why might you want to lose weight?
	Of all the reasons to lose weight, which one is most important?
Social support for weight loss	How do you think your family and friends feel about your weight?
	How do you feel about discussing your weight concerns with your family or friends?
	What kind of support would you like from your family and friends?
Experiences with weight loss	What have you done to try to lose weight?
	What has been most helpful?
	What has been least helpful?
Treatment preferences	What would you like to see in a weight loss program?

least six to eight women attend each group. The actual attendance rate was 85% and ranged from 62% to 100% per group. In response to the high attendance, we
175 recruited two additional research staff during the study and divided the last group into two smaller groups. The group sizes ranged from 6 to 16 participants.

Six focus groups were conducted in a 2-week period. Two clinical psychologists with training in group
180 facilitation moderated the focus groups, alternating between serving as the moderator and assistant moderator. In addition, two research assistants with training in the study protocol, focus group facilitation, and protection of human subjects helped by welcoming par-
185 ticipants, offering them healthy snacks, completing forms, video- and audiorecording, and distributing incentives. One research assistant was an AA woman from the local community who was employed by the research team for more than 1 year and whose primary
190 task was to assist with focus group studies. Prior to data collection, all participants provided informed consent and permission to audio- and videorecord. Participants then completed a 15- to 20-minute pre-focus group survey on demographic information, medical
195 diagnoses, and weight history. The assistant moderator read all questions aloud while a research assistant circulated to assist individual participants as needed.

The focus groups followed a semistructured format with a standard guide of open-ended questions to
200 stimulate discussion about perceptions and experiences with body size and weight. Researchers with experience in weight loss treatment and focus group methodology developed the guide according to published methodological suggestions (Fern, 2001). Table 1 dis-
205 plays questions from the focus group guide.

During each focus group meeting, the moderator probed participants' responses and encouraged all

members to participate. The assistant moderator took detailed notes and provided a summary at the end of
210 the meeting. The group discussions lasted approximately 90 to 100 minutes. After the meetings ended, the research assistants measured each participant's height and weight behind a privacy partition to corroborate their self-reported data. Measurements were
215 taken without shoes and heavy clothing using a balance beam scale and height rod and were rounded to the nearest 0.1 inch and 0.1 pound. After being weighed, participants received a $40 Wal-Mart gift card as compensation for their travel cost, time, and effort. We
220 stopped data collection after we felt that data saturation had occurred for the majority of our topic areas (i.e., no new data would be found by conducting further focus groups [Bernard, 2002]). The research protocol was approved by the University of Kansas Medical Center's
225 Human Subjects Committee prior to implementation.

Data Analysis

Survey data were double-data entered into a database, and descriptive statistics were computed using SPSS Version 13.0. Audiorecordings of the focus groups were transcribed verbatim by a contracted pro-
230 fessional transcription service. The focus group moderators proofread each transcript and compared them to the videorecordings to check for completeness and accuracy. A medical anthropologist with 10 years of experience using qualitative methodology led the
235 analysis and trained the additional coders. Three independent coders first deductively categorized verbatim transcripts by hand into six major topic areas using initial codes developed by the research team based on the focus group moderator's guide. Coders then induc-
240 tively open-coded by hand within each major topic area using a grounded theory approach whereby categories

Table 2
Participant Demographics, Weight History, and Comorbid Conditions

Characteristic	%
Age, years	
≤ 35	17.7
36–45	22.6
45–55	35.5
≥ 56	24.2
Education	
Some high school	14.5
High school graduate	21.0
Some college	62.9
College graduate	1.6
Partner status	
Married/living with partner	25.8
Divorced	37.1
Single	35.5
Caretaker/parent status	
One or more children living in home	52.6
Employment	
Employed full-time	50.0
Employed part-time	8.1
Unemployed	41.9
Body mass index (BMI), kg/m^2	
Class 1 obesity, BMI = 30–34.9	38.7
Class 2 obesity, BMI = 35–39.9	16.1
Class 3 obesity, BMI ≥ 40	45.2
Weight perceptions and history	
Classify self as overweight	88.6
Currently trying to lose weight	83.6
No. lifetime weight loss attempts	5.0 (median)
No. times lost ≥ 10 lbs.	3.0 (median)
Comorbid conditions	
Smoker	19.6
Diabetes	25.8
Hypertension	48.4
Heart disease	11.3
Asthma or emphysema	36.1
No. of comorbid diseases	
0	24.2
1	30.6
2	16.1
≥ 3	29.1

and concepts emerge from the text and are then linked together (Bernard, 2002). This approach allows the data to speak for themselves. A fourth independent
245 researcher cross-checked inductive codes and identified minor discrepancies in the coding and different terminology used by each coder to describe the same content. Cross-checking codes provides a measure of how well the data are indexed and, thus, gives a qualitative
250 measure of intercoder reliability (Stewart, 1998). Overall, the independent researcher found high intercoder reliability and identified major themes within the codes. The research team then met as a group to discuss the major themes and reach a consensus. Specifi-
255 cally, the fourth investigator presented her interpretation of each coder's inductive work and the coder clari-

fied as necessary. The seven major saturated themes were identical across coders. An additional six unsaturated themes were identified and will be used for the
260 development of further research.

Results

Participant Characteristics

Table 2 displays participant characteristics. The women were on average middle-aged ($M = 46.6 \pm 10.9$ years), had a high school level education plus some college ($M = 12.7 \pm 1.4$ years of education), and were
265 divorced or single. Participants' mean BMI was 40.3 kg/m^2, with 49% of the women being classified as having Class 3 extreme obesity (BMI ≥ 40 kg/m^2). Nearly 20% were current smokers, and 75.8% had at least one

Table 3
Focus Group Themes

1. Belief that people can be attractive and healthy at larger sizes
2. Dissatisfaction with weight and self-consciousness about body
3. Recognition of eating behavior as the primary cause for weight gain
4. Pregnancy, motherhood, and family caregiving as precursors to weight gain
5. Health and functional status as motivators to lose weight
6. Mixed social support for weight loss
7. Preference for lifestyle modification and distrust of medication for weight loss

comorbid chronic disease, including 25.8% with diabetes and 48.4% with hypertension. Most participants classified themselves as either a little overweight (23.0%) or very overweight (65.6%), and the vast majority was interested in losing weight.

Thematic Analysis

Seven themes emerged across focus groups and reached saturation (see Table 3).

Belief That People Can Be Attractive and Healthy at Larger Sizes

Participants expressed a sense of acceptance of larger body sizes, both in terms of attractiveness and perceived health. They stated that attractiveness does not depend on being a particular size and that people of many sizes can look good. "The [size] 10 is in your mind," one 40-year-old woman said, "it doesn't have to be a 10. You could be a 20 and look good." Rather than associating attractiveness with body size, attractiveness was described as having self-esteem and feeling beautiful as a person, and to a lesser extent with dress, makeup, and hair. Many women reported that even though they knew they were overweight, they could still feel attractive and positive about themselves. A 27-year-old woman stated,

> I think I look good even though I'm overweight. I feel like I'm not the ugliest person in the world. To myself, I'm an attractive black female. That's the way I feel about myself. Might feel even better about myself if I did lose an extra 100 pounds or so.

Often, their feelings of attractiveness were amplified by nice clothing. "As long as I'm happy about myself inside, it will show on the outside," a 34-year-old woman said, "but I have always tried to wear great clothes...I feel good about myself inside, so I feel I'm just beautiful."

Participants also expressed the view that being healthy does not depend on being a certain size and that a person can be just as unhealthy if they are underweight, as one 35-year-old woman stated, "You can be too small and be unhealthy as well as being too big." Some women expressed the belief that height and weight charts are unrealistic and AA women naturally have larger body frames. "I think a healthy body size could be almost any size," a 41-year-old woman said, "as long as it's not too much weight for that person.

Because, you know, there's all sizes and shapes of people."

Dissatisfaction with Weight and Self-Consciousness About Body

Although participants expressed tolerance of larger body sizes, most also acknowledged that they were overweight and were largely dissatisfied with their weight. In fact, most women reported that losing weight was the number one thing they wanted to change about themselves. Many reported feeling self-conscious about their bodies, and they described a sense of discomfort when unclothed or when seeing themselves in a mirror. "When I'm dressed up and got my hair together and makeup, you can't touch me," one 57-year-old woman said, "but when these clothes come off, that's when I have a problem." Another 53-year-old woman stated,

> I've got a mirror by the side of [my bed] on my closet...and I sit there by accident if I'm watching something on TV and then I look around at the mirror and see myself, I look and I just can't believe it. I am, my body is so ugly.

Several women expressed a sense of surprise when seeing a picture or reflection of their bodies. "I didn't know that I looked like I did until someone took a picture of me and I said, 'Oh, is that me?'" They noted specific likes and dislikes about body parts, with many women describing a specific dislike of their waist. As one 46-year-old woman stated,

> I feel conscious about my size because around my waistline, my belt don't fit in my pants. I have a hard time trying to get my belt to buckle, and most of my pants I have to get Spandex...my stomach is my most, well that's my guilt...I change in my closet and hide from my fiancé because my stomach is so big.

Again, the extent to which participants felt uncomfortable with their bodies was often related to how they felt in their clothes. They spoke about coping with feeling self-conscious by covering up the body parts that they disliked or avoiding looking at themselves, especially when unclothed. "I just don't show my arms," a 49-year-old woman said, "but I feel good. I just don't show my arms. I cover them up." Other women indicated that they do not dwell on their weight dissatisfaction or let it affect their mood. "I'm not content [with my body size], but I don't dwell on it. When you dwell

355 on things, everything seems to go backwards." Another 41-year-old woman stated, "I want to wear a bikini once in my life and look good in it, but overall, I'm not unhappy with myself because if I did, I would be in a depression. I'd be a sad person."

Recognition of Eating Behavior as the Primary Cause for Weight Gain

360 When asked what led them to become overweight, participants were much more likely to name behavioral reasons as opposed to medical and genetic causes. The most common attribution was related to eating behavior. They spoke about their love for cooking and eating,
365 as one 54-year-old women stated, "Oh goodness, I'm a good cook and I love my food. I do. I love my food. I really do." They also spoke about how taste preferences are woven into their culture. "I love to eat, and for my ethnic group, you know, we like to eat those
370 Southern stuff. I enjoy cooking that, and I enjoy eating that, so it's very difficult for me to stop it." Another 33-year-old woman echoed this sentiment, stating that "once you already tasted fried foods, you get a taste for it…you want the neck bones and all the good soul
375 food." Participants also spoke about their childhood experiences with family meals, as a 57-year-old woman stated,

> All of my aunts were heavy, you know, they stayed in the kitchen. They would feel offended if when we came to
380 > their house, we didn't sit down to macaroni and cheese, potatoes and gravy, fried chicken, homemade rolls, and Kool-Aid.

Many of these women themselves prepared meals for large family gatherings and enjoyed bringing family
385 together with food.

> The whole family comes over to our house on Sundays to eat, and I'm the one that cooks, and all the nephews and sisters and brothers and nieces, they all come over and eat, and I love to see them eat, but I'll lose those 5
390 > pounds, and on Sunday I'll gain them all back.

For many women, enjoyment of eating with family and friends often took precedence over eating healthy. As one 57-year-old woman from another group stated, "We have family gatherings, and they all come over to
395 my house eating, and then they talk about me losing weight…but they like for me to cook so I can't have it both ways."

Many participants named specific eating behaviors as contributors to their weight gain, including eating
400 late, eating excessive portions, consuming too much soda and junk food, and eating at fast food and all-you-can-eat restaurants. Lack of physical activity was also named as a cause of weight gain, although less frequently and typically in the context of eating behavior.
405 For example, one woman stated, "I was at a job where I sat all day, and I would have the nerve to go to an all-you-can-eat for lunch."

Pregnancy, Motherhood, and Family Caregiving as Precursors to Weight Gain

Motherhood was commonly reported as a precursor to weight gain. Many women reported that they never
410 lost the weight they gained during pregnancy, and then they gained even more because of lifestyle changes associated with motherhood, for example, snacking more often, cooking larger meals, and being less active outside the house. Although participants recognized
415 changes in their behavior as contributing to their post-pregnancy weight gain, pregnancy was named as a primary antecedent. Many women across groups echoed the following statement from a 57-year-old woman:

420 > I was never overweight until I had my first child. When I got pregnant with her, I weighed 110, and I never, she's 34, and I never went back. It's overeating during [pregnancy]…and then after I had them, I was home with them until they were all in school, so they ate breakfast, I ate
425 > breakfast. They ate lunch, I ate lunch. They had snacks, I had snacks. So you just ate with them, and when they slept, I slept. So it's just the way your lifestyle changes.

In addition, several women either had been or were currently caretakers for older family members. Similar
430 to motherhood, they reported that caretaking responsibilities and the added stress they caused resulted in weight gain. One 40-year-old woman recalled,

> My aunt passed, it will be a year…and I was her caretaker for about 2-1/2 years. During that time your activ-
435 > ity, your lifestyle, your everything just tends to change. You know, so stress has a lot to do with it.

Health and Functional Status as Motivators to Lose Weight

Participants unanimously reported that health was their number one reason for wanting to lose weight. Many participants had chronic medical conditions (e.g.,
440 diabetes, hypertension, heart disease, pain) and had received advice from their physicians to lose weight. They wanted to avoid further medical complications, as one 62-year-old women indicated: "For me, it's just health because they told me my cholesterol will go
445 down, definitely the high blood pressure, and I'll get my diabetes within normal range."

Participants who did not have chronic conditions often spoke about their families' medical histories and acknowledged the association of health problems with
450 excess weight. Many had a strong desire to prevent the weight-related diseases that they had witnessed in their family members.

> I'm getting fairly close to 60, so I'm trying to improve my health to, you know, keep my blood pressure down,
455 > because there are a lot of health problems that run in my family, and I'm trying to keep, I'm going to try to keep from developing those problems myself.

Participants also spoke about wanting to lose weight to improve their daily functioning. They com-
460 plained about low energy, feeling tired, and having

difficulty breathing with only minimal exertion. Many wanted to lose weight so they would have more energy to play with their children or grandchildren, whereas others were functionally limited because of their weight (e.g., not fitting in seats, not being able to bend over easily, or having difficulty walking up several flights of stairs).

> I think a healthy size for me would mean, it wouldn't really be a size as much as it would be a freedom to just do whatever I want to do. Just anything because so much, so many things I just don't do because I'm tired.

Mixed Social Support for Weight Loss

Participants reported very mixed experiences regarding social support for weight loss. About half of the women indicated that their families were supportive, either of their weight status or their efforts to lose weight. The most common forms of perceived support were acceptance regardless of body size, assistance with weight loss through tangible tools such as diet books and exercise videos, and simply not saying anything about their weight. One 30-year-old woman stated,

> I've never felt judged and probably because most of the women in my family are overweight...I think their acceptance of me for all that I am and not just for how much I weigh has always been just sort of something I could count on.

A 54-year-old woman in another group stated,

> I have a bunch of sisters, and I guess you could say we're real supportive of one another in that we don't say anything to each other. We've all been fat, and we all understand. When one is thin, they visit more. And when one's fat, they don't visit as much. They don't talk about it.

Many women also reported a lack of support for weight loss and negative social experiences, such as teasing from family members, criticism regarding food choices (e.g., "Are you going to eat that?"), disapproval of their weight loss efforts, and sabotaging their weight loss by bringing home unhealthy food. "I wish my family would support me a lot more on my weight as far as compliments or something like that," one 66-year-old woman said. "They were kind of harsh when I was younger." Likewise, some women reported experiences in which partners or family members discouraged them from losing weight.

> I have people tell me, what are you trying to lose weight for?...I said, "Well, I'm trying to lose weight for me and my health," and I leave it at that. I don't discuss it with people because I don't feel like I have to answer to anybody to lose weight.

When asked what kind of support they wanted, participants again responded in mixed ways. On one hand, they indicated that the only support they need is to not be "nagged." "I wouldn't mind being supported but just don't get to the nagging point." Some women indicated they wanted to lose weight on their own.

> I'd rather not have no support. I'd rather be able to do it on my own. Because without that support, I don't have to worry about, oh, if I don't do it, will they be mad, or if I do it, will they be mad or something...doing it on my own, it's just better for me.

On the other hand, participants said they wanted more constructive support, typically in the form of a partner or buddy who is also attempting to lose weight and who would hold them accountable and help motivate them. Typically, they indicated that this person would ideally be outside their common social network.

> I think [you have to] go outside to get support through other ways. So it's not necessarily going to be coming from your family or your friends, but say, if you join Weight Watchers or some other weight loss [program] or if you had another friend and you did a buddy system, get support that way.

Preference for Lifestyle Modification and Distrust of Medication for Weight Loss

Participants expressed a strong interest in group-based weight loss programs, where they could meet with "like-minded" women and learn skills for healthy cooking and eating, increasing regular physical activity, and changing their lifestyle. They also spoke about a need for tailored exercise plans that were appropriate for their level of fitness. They were generally opposed to fad diets and understood that weight loss takes a great deal of time and effort. Thus, their preference was for a long-term (i.e., 1 year) weight loss program. Again, they frequently mentioned a need for ongoing social support, both during the structured components of the program and afterwards.

The vast majority of participants held negative views about weight loss medications. They spoke about medication as being "unnatural" or "putting a band-aid on the real problem." They were distrustful about potential side effects and unforeseen interactions with other medications. Many women were also concerned about becoming dependent on medications.

> I'm leaning more toward wanting to do it naturally without pills. Anything that would make you psychologically dependent upon it, because if you lose the weight on it, then you kind of become dependent, if you start gaining weight back then you go, oh, I need to get those pills again.

Discussion

This study examined the perceptions and beliefs about body size, weight, and weight loss among a community sample of obese AA women, and the findings offer insights for understanding and treating obesity in this target population. Consistent with prior research, the women in this study expressed an acceptance of larger body sizes and believed that body size should not influence a person's feelings of attractiveness, self-esteem, or happiness. At the same time, they were concerned about their weight and largely self-conscious of their bodies. They described various

570 strategies to cope with these self-conscious feelings and perhaps reconcile them with a culturally embedded acceptance of larger body sizes. For example, clothing was emphasized as a way to feel attractive despite feeling self-conscious about body size, and many partici-
575 pants avoided thinking about their weight or looking at themselves in the mirror as a way to ward off negative feelings. These strategies provide insight into how AA women are able to preserve feelings of attractiveness even when they are dissatisfied with their weight (Ku-
580 manyika, 1998).

Although participants expressed body image concerns, their interest in weight loss was largely driven by a desire to improve their health, a finding that is underscored by the fact that more than three-fourths of
585 the participants reported having at least one comorbid chronic disease. This comorbidity rate is similar to the report of Hope, Kumanyika, Whitt, and Shults (2005), where 76% of obese AAs in a weight loss program had at least one obesity-related chronic disease. Women in
590 the current study were knowledgeable about the health benefits of weight loss and the behavioral causes of weight gain; however, they spoke about poor dietary behavior much more than lack of physical activity, suggesting less awareness or importance placed on
595 physical activity. Further research is needed to understand how cultural differences may influence the use of physical activity specifically for controlling weight. For example, the "rest ethic" of AA culture, or the belief that rest is important after a "busy" day (Airhihen-
600 buwa et al., 1995; Wilcox et al., 2002), may conflict with recommendations to increase leisure-time activity to manage weight.

Participants spoke frequently and in-depth about sociocultural influences on food choices, such as their
605 preference for traditional AA foods, including high-fat meats and sweets (Kumanyika & Odoms, 2003), and the strong connection between food and social affiliation (Airhihenbuwa et al., 1996). The family centeredness of their culture was evident as they spoke about
610 food as a way to bring family members together, and many women enjoyed cooking large meals for this reason. They also revealed a connection between family responsibility and weight gain; many seemed to prioritize family caretaking over their own health behavior
615 change. This observation is consistent with the work of Kumanyika et al. (1992) and others suggesting that AA women have a limited inclination to assume the self-centered posture that is typically the focus of health behavior programs. AA women may be reluctant to
620 focus on themselves, often considering their own health as secondary to that of their children, or prioritizing caretaking responsibilities over self-care (Ahye, Devine, & Odoms-Young, 2006; Samuel-Hodge et al., 2000). Consistent with this, the women in the current
625 study described pregnancy as a critical time when they gained weight and after which they struggled to lose weight, largely because of lifestyle changes associated

with caretaking responsibilities of motherhood. Several longitudinal studies indicate that AA women struggle
630 with childbearing-associated weight gain more so than Caucasian women (Rosenberg et al., 2003).

Our findings and those of others are consistent with the extant literature examining *collectivism* as an important cultural construct that distinguishes AAs from
635 dominant culture, most markedly for AA women (Baldwin & Hopkins, 1990). Collectivism is the belief that the central unit of society is social groups, most commonly the extended family, and not the individual. Collectivism prioritizes group goals over individual
640 goals and thus emphasizes cooperation, responsibility for others, loyalty, helpfulness, forgiveness, family security, and respect for traditions (Nobles, 1991). The women in the current study conveyed a collectivist orientation toward mutual support among family and
645 peers, but they reported a need for more social support specific to weight loss.

Indeed, one of the most challenging findings was the mixed responses to questions about social support for weight loss. Participants were uncertain about how
650 to obtain and integrate social support for weight loss from their existing social networks, perhaps because of lack of guidance from common individualistically oriented weight loss treatments. They largely perceived weight-related feedback as critical and an absence of
655 feedback as accepting, and they preferred support from overweight peers who were also attempting to lose weight over support from family. One interpretation of these findings may be that within a collectivistic value system, mutual support (i.e., two or more women sup-
660 porting one another toward the same goal) is value congruent more so than individual support (e.g., one spouse supporting the other spouse toward her individual goal). In addition, other interactions surrounding weight issues may be perceived as more supportive if
665 they are congruent with deep-rooted values. For example, the participants derived social support from large family gatherings centered on cooking and eating and from their family members' acceptance of their body sizes, and both of these sources of social support may
670 be rooted in collectivistic values such as loyalty and respect for traditions. Although this interpretation is speculative, further research along these lines is warranted given the accumulating evidence indicating that social support is a crucial factor affecting obese AA
675 women's weight loss (Wolfe, 2004).

The results of this study should be viewed in the context of the methodology and the characteristics of the sample. Because qualitative research is designed to provide in-depth understanding of a specific group or
680 topic, the results from this study may not generalize across groups but rather may be transferred to similar groups and settings (Fern, 2001). However, as noted above, the findings of this study are consistent with other focus group results with AA women from other
685 regions of the United States and provide useful infor-

mation for generating testable hypotheses. As this area of scientific inquiry progresses, the emerging themes should be validated with larger and more representative samples.

690   In the context of focus group methodology, the current study was limited in that it was not designed as a nested sampling frame that would help to parcel out differences between subgroups of AA women (e.g., age group, educational level, or obesity class) or subcul-

695   tures within the larger AA group. In addition, the large number of participants (greater than 10 participants) in three of the six focus groups may have limited the depth of response among some participants. However, we did not detect any systematic differences in re-

700   sponses across groups, and we observed that the participants quickly developed rapport with one another and all women participated, even in the larger groups. Strengths of this study are that the community recruitment attracted women who were candid in discussing

705   weight-related issues, had a long history of weight loss attempts, and desired to lose weight. In addition, the objective measurement of height and weight established that on average, participants were morbidly obese. Thus, the findings reflect the perspectives and

710   experiences of obese AA women who could not only greatly benefit from weight loss but who would likely agree to participate in a weight loss intervention. The rapid response to recruitment flyers and the high attendance rate further indicate a need for weight loss pro-

715   grams in the community.

Implications

This study indicates that among a community sample of obese AA women, many will be interested in weight loss, experienced in weight loss attempts, knowledgeable regarding dietary causes of weight gain,

720   and motivated to lose weight for health reasons. The findings corroborate existing recommendations for tailoring weight loss programs for AA women, such as the importance of involving social networks and adapting materials and recipes to be culturally relevant

725   (Bronner & Boyington, 2002). The findings also provide several new suggestions for future programs. First, results indicate that obese AA women in a weight loss program may feel self-conscious about their bodies and actively engage in behaviors to maintain feelings of

730   attractiveness. Although appearance concerns are not as important as health concerns for motivating weight loss in this population, negative body image may still play a role in weight-control behaviors and should therefore not be overlooked. For example, some evi-

735   dence suggests that women with negative body image are more likely to be chronic dieters (Gingras, Fitzpatrick, & McCargar, 2004) and are less successful in losing weight (Teixeira et al., 2002). Second, obese AA women may be less knowledgeable and/or ready to

740   increase energy expenditure compared to decreasing caloric intake, thus interventions may need to pay spe-

cial attention to knowledge, perceived barriers, and benefits related to physical activity. Third, pharmacotherapy for weight loss may not be well received with

745   this population. Finally, given that participants may have varying levels, experiences, and preferences for social support for weight loss, the provision of support should be rooted in a clear understanding of the perceived needs and values of each participant. As others

750   have suggested (Kreuter et al., 2002), by building on existing values and practices, such as mutual responsibility and caretaking, AA women may become more involved in weight loss and other health-related programs.

References

Agurs-Collins, T. D., Kumanyika, S. K., Ten Have, T. R., & Adams-Campbell, L. L. (1997). A randomized controlled trial of weight reduction and exercise for diabetes management in older African-American subjects. *Diabetes Care, 20*(10), 1503–1511.

Ahye, B. A., Devine, C. M., & Odoms-Young, A. M. (2006). Values expressed through intergenerational family food and nutrition management systems among African American women. *Family & Community Health, 29*(1), 5–16.

Airhihenbuwa, C. O., Kumanyika, S., Agurs, T. D., & Lowe, A., (1995). Perceptions and beliefs about exercise, rest, and health among African-Americans. *American Journal of Health Promotion, 9*(6), 426–429.

Airhihenbuwa, C. O., Kumanyika, S., Agurs, T. D., Lowe, A., Saunders, D., & Morssink, C. B. (1996). Cultural aspects of African American eating patterns. *Ethnicity & Health, 1*(3), 245–260.

American Cancer Society. (2005). *Cancer facts and figures for African Americans 2005-2006.* Atlanta: Author.

Arab, L., Carriquiry, A., Steck-Scott, S., & Gaudet, M. M. (2003). Ethnic differences in the nutrient intake adequacy of premenopausal US women: Results from the Third National Health Examination Survey. *Journal of the American Dietetic Association, 103*(8), 1008–1014.

Baldwin, J. A., & Hopkins, R. (1990). African-American and European-American cultural differences as assessed by the worldviews paradigm: An empirical analysis. *Western Journal of Black Studies, 14*, 38–52.

Baturka, N., Hornsby, P. P., & Schorling, J. B. (2000). Clinical implications of body image among rural African-American women. *Journal of General Internal Medicine, 15*(4), 235–241.

Beech, B. M., Kumanyika, S. K., Baranowski, T., Davis, M., Robinson, T. N., Sherwood, N. E., et al. (2004). Parental cultural perspectives in relation to weight-related behaviors and concerns of African-American girls. *Obesity Research, 12*(Suppl.), 7S–19S.

Bernard, H. R. (2002). *Research methods in anthropology: Qualitative and quantitative approaches* (3rd ed.). Walnut Creek, CA: AltaMira Press.

Bronner, Y., & Boyington, J. E. (2002). Developing weight loss interventions for African-American women: Elements of successful models. *Journal of the National Medical Association, 94*(4), 224–235.

Cachelin, F. M., Rebeck, R. M., Chung, G. H., & Pelayo, E. (2002). Does ethnicity influence body-size preference? A comparison of body image and body size. *Obesity Research, 10*(3), 158–166.

Centers for Disease Control. (2004). Prevalence of no leisure-time physical activity—35 states and the District of Columbia, 1988–2002. *Morbidity and Mortality Weekly Report, 53*(4), 82–86.

Clark, J. M., Bone, L. R., Stallings, R., Gelber, A. C., Barker, A., Zeger, S., et al. (2001). Obesity and approaches to weight in an urban African-American community. *Ethnicity & Disease, 11*(4), 676–686.

Davis, E. M., Clark, J. M., Carrese, J. A., Gary, T. L., & Cooper, L. A. (2005). Racial and socioeconomic differences in the weight-loss experiences of obese women. *American Journal of Public Health, 95*(9), 1539–1543.

DiLillo, V., Gore, S., Jones, J., Balentine, C., & West, D. S. (2004). Body image dissatisfaction among Black and White women enrolled in a weight loss program. *Annals of Behavioral Medicine, 27*(Suppl.), S83.

Fern, E. (2001). *Advanced focus group research.* Thousand Oaks, CA: Sage.

Fitzgibbon, M. L., Blackman, L. R., & Avellone, M. E. (2000). The relationship between body image discrepancy and body mass index across ethnic groups. *Obesity Research, 8*(8), 582–589.

Flegal, K. M., Carroll, M. D., Ogden, C. L., & Johnson, C. L. (2002). Prevalence and trends in obesity among US adults, 1999–2000. *Journal of the American Medical Association, 288*(14), 1723–1727.

Flynn, K. J., & Fitzgibbon, M. (1998). Body images and obesity risk among Black females: A review of the literature. *Annals of Behavioral Medicine, 20*(1), 13–24.

Gingras, J., Fitzpatrick, J., & McCargar, L. (2004). Body image of chronic dieters: Lowered appearance evaluation and body satisfaction. *Journal of the American Dietetic Association, 104*(10), 1589–1592.

Hargreaves, M. K., Schlundt, D. G., & Buchowski, M. S. (2002). Contextual factors influencing the eating behaviours of African American women: A focus group investigation. *Ethnicity & Health, 7*(3), 133–147.

Harris, M. I. (1998). Diabetes in America: Epidemiology and scope of the problem. *Diabetes Care, 21*(Suppl. 3), C11–C14.

Hope, A. A., Kumanyika, S. K., Whitt, M. C., & Shults, J. (2005), Obesity-related comorbidities in obese African Americans in an outpatient weight loss program. *Obesity Research, 13*(4), 772–779.

James, D. C. (2004). Factors influencing food choices, dietary intake, and nutrition-related attitudes among African Americans: Application of a culturally sensitive model. *Ethnicity & Health, 9*(4), 349–367.

Kanders, B. S., Ullmann-Joy, P., Foreyt, J. P., Heymsfield, S. B., Heber, D., Elashoff, R. M., et al. (1994). The Black American Lifestyle Intervention (BALI): The design of a weight loss program for working-class African-American women. *Journal of the American Dietetic Association, 94*(3), 310–312.

Karanja, N., Stevens, V. J., Hollis, J. F., & Kumanyika, S. K. (2002). Steps to Soulful Living (STEPS): A weight loss program for African-American women. *Ethnicity & Disease, 12*(3), 363–371.

Kennedy, B. M., Paeratakul, S., Champagne, C. M., Ryan, D. H., Harsha, D. W., McGee, B., et al. (2005). A pilot church-based weight loss program for African-American adults using church members as health educators: A comparison of individual and group intervention. *Ethnicity & Disease, 15*(3), 373–378.

Kreuter, M. W., Lukwago, S. N., Buchholtz, D. C., Clark, E. M., & Sanders-Thompson, V. (2002). Achieving cultural appropriateness in health promotion programs: Targeted and tailored approaches. *Health Education & Behavior, 30*(2), 133–146.

Kumanyika, S. K. (1998). Obesity in African Americans: Biobehavioral consequences of culture. *Ethnicity & Disease, 8*(1), 93–96.

Kumanyika, S. K., & Charleston, J. B. (1992). Lose weight and win: A church-based weight loss program for blood pressure control among Black women. *Patient Education and Counseling, 19*(1), 19–32.

Kumanyika, S. K., Morssink, C., & Agurs, T. (1992). Models for dietary and weight change in African-American women: Identifying cultural components. *Ethnicity & Disease, 2*(2), 166–175.

Kumanyika, S. K., Obarzanek, E., Stevens, V. J., Hebert, P. R., & Whelton, P. K. (1991). Weight-loss experience of Black and White participants in NHLBI-sponsored clinical trials. *American Journal of Clinical Nutrition, 53*(6 Suppl.), 1631S–1638S.

Kumanyika, S. K., & Odoms, A. (2003). Nutrition. In R. L. Braithwaite & A. J. Taylor (Eds.), *Health issues in the Black community* (pp. 419–447). San Francisco: Jossey-Bass.

Kumanyika, S. K., Shults, J., Fassbender, J., Whitt, M. C., Brake, Y., Kallan, M. J., et al. (2005). Outpatient weight management in African-Americans: The Healthy Eating and Lifestyle Program (HELP) study. *Preventive Medicine, 41*(2), 488–502.

Lewis, C. E., Smith, D. E., Wallace, D. D., Williams, O. D., Bild, D. E., & Jacobs, D. R., Jr. (1997). Seven-year trends in body weight and associations with lifestyle and behavioral characteristics in Black and White young adults: The CARDIA study. *American Journal of Public Health, 87*(4), 635–642.

McNabb, W., Quinn, M., Kerver, J., Cook, S., & Karrison, T. (1997). The pathways church-based weight loss program for urban African-American women at risk for diabetes. *Diabetes Care, 20*(10), 1518–1523.

Must, A., Spadano, J., Coakley, E. H., Field, A. E., Colditz, G., & Dietz, W. H. (1999). The disease burden associated with overweight and obesity. *Journal of the American Medical Association, 282*(16), 1523–1529.

Nobles, W. (1991). African philosophy: Foundations for Black psychology. In R. Jones (Ed.), *Black psychology* (3rd ed.). Berkeley, CA: Cobb & Henry.

Pulvers, K. M., Lee, R., E., Kaur, H., Mayo, M. S., Fitzgibbon, M. L., Jeffries, S. K., et al. (2004). Development of a culturally relevant body image instrument among urban African Americans. *Obesity Research, 12*(10), 1641–1651.

Richter, D. L., Wilcox, S., Greaney, M. L., Henderson, K. A., & Ainsworth, B. E. (2002). Environmental, policy, and cultural factors related to physical activity in African American women. *Women & Health, 36*(2), 91–109.

Rosenberg, L., Palmer, J. R., Wise, L. A., Horton, N. J., Kumanyika, S. K., & Adams-Campbell, L. L. (2003). A prospective study of the effect of childbearing on weight gain in African-American women. *Obesity Research, 11*(12), 1526–1535.

Samuel-Hodge, C. D., Headen, S. W., Skelly, A. H., Ingram, A. F., Keyserling, T. C., Jackson, E. J., et al. (2000). Influences on day-to-day self-management of Type 2 diabetes among African-American women: Spirituality, the multi-caregiver role, and other social context factors. *Diabetes Care, 23*(7), 928–933.

Stevens, J., Kumanyika, S. K., & Keil, J. E. (1994). Attitudes toward body size and dieting: Differences between elderly Black and White women. *American Journal of Public Health, 84*(8), 1322–1325.

Stewart, A. (1998). *The ethnographer's method.* Thousand Oaks, CA: Sage.

Teixeira, P. J., Going, S. B., Houtkooper, L. B., Cussler, E. C., Martin, C. J., Metcalfe, L. L., et al. (2002). Weight loss readiness in middle-aged women: Psychosocial predictors of success for behavioral weight reduction. *Journal of Behavioral Medicine, 25*(6), 499–523.

Tyler, D. O., Allan, J. D., & Alcozer, F. R. (1997). Weight loss methods used by African American and Euro-American women. *Research in Nursing & Health, 20*(5), 413–423.

Walcott-McQuigg, J. A., Chen, S. P., Davis, K., Stevenson, E., Choi, A., & Wangsrikhun, S. (2002). Weight loss and weight loss maintenance in African-American women. *Journal of the National Medical Association, 94*(8), 686–694.

Wilcox, S., Richter, D. L., Henderson, K. A., Greaney, M. L., & Ainsworth, B. E. (2002). Perceptions of physical activity and personal barriers and enablers in African-American women. *Ethnicity & Disease, 12*(3), 353–362.

Wilson, D., Musham, C., & McLellan, M. S. (2004). From mothers to daughters: Transgenerational food and diet communication in an underserved group. *Journal of Cultural Diversity, 11*(1), 12–17.

Wing, R. R., & Anglin, K. (1996). Effectiveness of a behavioral weight control program for Blacks and Whites with NIDDM. *Diabetes Care, 19*(5), 409–413.

Wing, R. R., Hamman, R. F., Bray, G. A., Delahanty, L., Edelstein, S. L., Hill, J. O., et al. (2004). Achieving weight and activity goals among diabetes prevention program lifestyle participants. *Obesity Research, 12*(9), 1426–1434.

Wolfe, W. A. (2000). Obesity and the African-American woman: A cultural tolerance of fatness or other neglected factors. *Ethnicity & Disease, 10*(3), 446–453.

Wolfe, W. A. (2004). A review: Maximizing social support—A neglected strategy for improving weight management with African-American women. *Ethnicity & Disease, 14*(2), 212–218.

Yanek, L. R., Becker, D. M., Moy, T. F., Gittelsohn, J., & Koffman, D. M. (2001). Project joy: Faith based cardiovascular health promotion for African American women. *Public Health Reports, 116*(Suppl. 1), 68–81.

Young, D. R., Gittelsohn, J., Charleston, J., Felix-Aaron, K., & Appel, L. J. (2001). Motivations for exercise and weight loss among African-American women: Focus group results and their contribution towards program development. *Ethnicity & Health, 6*(3–4), 227–245.

About the authors: *Christie A. Befort, Janet L. Thomas, Christine M. Daley,* and *Paula C. Rhode,* University of Kansas Medical Center, Kansas City. *Jasjit S. Ahluwalia,* Office of Clinical Research, University of Minnesota, Minneapolis.

Address correspondence to: Christie A. Befort, University of Kansas Medical Center, 3901 Rainbow Blvd., MS 1008, Kansas City, KS 66160. E-mail: cbefort@mc.edu

Exercise for Article 28

Factual Questions

1. Was the setting for this study "urban," "suburban," *or* "rural"?

2. How many women were in the final sample?

3. What question was asked about attributions for weight?

4. What did the participants receive as compensation?

5. What percentage of the participants were between 45 and 55 years of age?

6. Are the results of this study consistent with previous focus group results?

Questions for Discussion

7. Eleven of the potential participants did not show up for their appointments for the focus groups. Could this have affected the results of this study? (See lines 155–161.)

8. Is the fact that six focus groups were conducted (instead of only one) an important strength of this study? Explain. (See lines 178–179.)

9. Is the method of data analysis described in sufficient detail? Explain. (See lines 226–260.)

10. What is your understanding of the meaning of the term "independent coders"? (See lines 235–239.)

11. To what extent do the quotations in the Results section of this report help you understand the results? (See lines 274–558.)

12. If you were to conduct a study on a similar topic in the future, would you use "qualitative" *or* "quantitative" methodology? Why?

Quality Ratings

Directions: Indicate your level of agreement with each of the following statements by circling a number from 5 for strongly agree (SA) to 1 for strongly disagree (SD). If you believe an item is not applicable to this research article, leave it blank. Be prepared to explain your ratings. When responding to criteria A and B below, keep in mind that brief titles and abstracts are conventional in published research.

A. The title of the article is appropriate.

    SA   5   4   3   2   1   SD

B. The abstract provides an effective overview of the research article.

    SA   5   4   3   2   1   SD

C. The introduction establishes the importance of the study.

    SA   5   4   3   2   1   SD

D. The literature review establishes the context for the study.

    SA   5   4   3   2   1   SD

E. The research purpose, question, or hypothesis is clearly stated.

    SA   5   4   3   2   1   SD

F. The method of sampling is sound.

    SA   5   4   3   2   1   SD

G. Relevant demographics (for example, age, gender, and ethnicity) are described.

    SA   5   4   3   2   1   SD

H. Measurement procedures are adequate.

    SA   5   4   3   2   1   SD

I. All procedures have been described in sufficient detail to permit a replication of the study.

    SA   5   4   3   2   1   SD

J. The participants have been adequately protected from potential harm.

    SA   5   4   3   2   1   SD

K. The results are clearly described.

    SA   5   4   3   2   1   SD

L. The discussion/conclusion is appropriate.

    SA   5   4   3   2   1   SD

M. Despite any flaws, the report is worthy of publication.

    SA   5   4   3   2   1   SD

Article 29

Getting Children with Attention Deficit Hyperactivity Disorder to School on Time: Mothers' Perspectives

MYRA TAYLOR
The University of Western Australia,
Crawley

STEPHEN HOUGHTON
The University of Western Australia,
Crawley

KEVIN DURKIN
University of Strathclyde,
United Kingdom

ABSTRACT. This article details the school-readying routines Western Australian mothers employ in their efforts to dispatch children diagnosed with attention deficit hyperactivity disorder off to school in a timely manner. A grounded theory of instilling an awareness of time emerged from the data. In seeking to instill an awareness of time, mothers reveal their experiences of dealing with the chaos that arises out of their children's untimely actions from the point of waking them to the point of getting them out of the house and off to school. In an attempt to eliminate sources of stress contributing to the chaos, mothers reflect on their children's idiosyncratic concept of time and analyze the mismatch between their and their child's attitude toward time management. The article concludes by detailing strategies mothers put in place to instill in their child an awareness of time and to establish a workable school-readying routine.

From *Journal of Family Issues, 29*, 918–943. Copyright © 2008 by Sage Publications, Inc. Reprinted with permission.

Attention deficit hyperactivity disorder (ADHD) is a seemingly heterogeneous group of behavioral disorders affecting between 2% and 12% of school-age children (American Academy of Pediatrics, 2000;
5 Daley, 2005) and approximately 50% of the child psychiatric population (Pocklington & Maybery, 2006). The past two decades have witnessed changes in diagnostic criteria for ADHD, along with a shift from a unidimensional conceptualization of the disorder to a
10 model comprising two factors: hyperactivity/impulsivity and inattention (Sagvolden, Johansen, Aase, & Russell, 2005). These behavioral markers of the disorder are believed to stem from frontal lobe-mediated executive and self-monitoring functions (Rubia, Over-
15 meyer, et al., 1998). Structural and neuroimaging suggest a dysfunction in fronto-strio-thalamocortical and fronto-cerebellar circuitries as the neural correlate of the disorder (Rubia & Smith, 2001).

According to one comprehensive theory of ADHD
20 (Barkley, 1997), the regulatory deficits arising weaken the ability of the brain's executive functions to effectively control time-related aspects of working memory (temporal continuity and temporal order), reconstitution (learning from past experience), self-regulation
25 (future motivation and arousal), and nonverbal working memory (sense of time) (Barkley, 1997; Barkley, Koplowitz, Anderson, & McMurray, 1997; Meaux & Chelonis, 2005). Of these four, the sense-of-time function remains underinvestigated. This is not to say that evi-
30 dence supporting the sense-of-time deficit hypothesis does not exist. Recent neuropsychological research, for example, shows that children with ADHD demonstrate deficits in motor timing (but not in temporal perception; Rubia, Sergeant, Taylor, & Taylor, 1999) and
35 poor ability to associate events that are separated by time (see Rubia, Noorloos, Smith, Gunning, & Sergeant, 2003). At the neuroanatomical and neurophysiological levels, fMRI has shown reduced mesial prefrontal activation in adolescents with ADHD during
40 motor timing tasks (Rubia et al., 1999; Rubia, Oosterlaan, Sergeant, Brandeis, & Leeuwen, 1998). Furthermore, the most widely used and effective treatment for ADHD symptoms (methylphenidate via dopaminergic pathways) increases the metabolism in the dorsolateral
45 prefrontal cortex, the cerebellum, and the basal ganglia (Volkow et al., 1997), all brain areas implicated in motor timing functions and compromised in ADHD (see Rubia, Oosterlaan, et al., 1998; Rubia & Smith, 2001).

Extensive information also exists about children
50 with ADHD and their executive performance on laboratory-based timing tasks. For example, children with ADHD (undifferentiated by subtype) tend to be more impaired in their ability to gauge time (Cappella, Gentile, & Juliano, 1977); they have a developmental delay
55 in their gross sense of time; and they more frequently manifest disorganized patterns of memory recall and planning than do their non-ADHD peers (Barkley, 1997). Furthermore, their naturalistic time perceptions can be distorted (McGee, Brodeur, Symons, Andrade,
60 & Fahie, 2004). Children with the predominantly hyperactive subtype have been found to make larger time estimation errors, grossly overestimate time duration, and have greater difficulty with tasks that involve time

duration discrimination (Cappella et al., 1977; Fleck,
65 Bischoff, & O'Laughlin, 2001; Toplak, Rucklidge,
Hetherington, John, & Tannock, 2003).

Although such research is laudatory, it tells us little
about the problems that these children experience in
the course of activities conducted in real-world envi-
70 ronments (Rapport, Chung, Shore, Denney, & Isaacs,
2000). This is somewhat puzzling because in their everyday lives, these children are likely to be confronted
with a range of tasks involving time management that
affect not only them but also their families. Thus,
75 Barkley and associates' assertion (1997) that "time is
the ultimate yet nearly invisible disability affecting
those with ADHD" (p. 337) remains to be tested in
relation to a range of everyday tasks.

Research has shown that mothers shoulder the ma-
80 jority of the parental task of ensuring that children diagnosed with ADHD establish workable time-related
routines (e.g., complete chores and arrive at or be collected from school, church, extracurricular activities,
sporting, and social events on time; Bianchi, 2000;
85 Gager, Cooney, & Call, 1999; Kellner, Houghton, &
Douglas, 2003; Milkie, Mattingly, Nomaguchi, Bianchi, & Robinson, 2004). In light of this, the present
study examined the real-life issue that mothers with
children diagnosed with ADHD commonly experi-
90 ence—namely, that of establishing and maintaining a
time-regulated school-readying routine. By engaging in
the practice of establishing a time-regulated routine,
mothers (in anthropological terms) demonstrate an adherence to what Graham (1981) defined as the linear-
95 separable model of time perception. This model operates from a premise that people who view time in a
linear-separable manner perceive the past, present, and
future as distinct entities. This tripartite conceptualization allows such persons to quantify and separate time
100 into discrete compartments, which can in turn be displayed and managed through the use of clocks and cal-
endars (Owen, 1991). The way in which people with
linear-separable perceptions of time manage themselves and others, however, is not fully understood
105 (Covic, Adamson, Lincoln, & Kench, 2003; Daly,
2001). This article provides insights into one such
facet, namely, early-morning routines, which mothers
who are manifesting a linear-separable orientation toward time and time management instigate within their
110 family units to ready themselves and their children
(those with and without ADHD) to leave the home by a
specified deadline. The article is presented in three
parts and a conclusion: As already presented, the first
part contextualizes the study; the second outlines the
115 design of the study; the third details the findings; and
the article concludes with a brief discussion.

Design of the Study

The aim of the study was to generate a substantive
theory that would broaden understanding of how mothers of children with ADHD get their children ready for

120 school from the point of waking them to the point of
getting them out of the house. To focus on how they do
so is to be concerned with the process. Thus, it seemed
appropriate to design the study within the symbolic
interactionist tradition within social theory. Symbolic
125 interactionism has been described by Charmaz (2006)
as a theoretical perspective derived from pragmatism
that assumes that people construct and mediate meaning of selves, society, and reality through their interaction with others. This tradition emphasizes the need to
130 explore participants' perspectives on issues, how they
act in light of such perspectives, and the patterns that
emerge through the interaction of their perspectives
and actions over time (O'Donoghue, 2007). It is also a
tradition that accommodates grounded theory as a re-
135 search approach (Punch, 2005) because one stream of
this methodology derives its theoretical underpinnings
from the related positions of pragmatism, symbolic
interactionism, and social constructionism (Blumer,
1969; Crotty, 2003; Hughes, 1971). Accordingly,
140 grounded theory approaches to data gathering and
analysis were selected as an appropriate method for the
study. Such approaches allow for an in-depth understanding of social phenomena (McLeod, 2003; Piantanida, Tananis, & Grubs, 2004; Strauss & Corbin,
145 1990).

Participants

Participants were selected in the first instance on
the basis of sampling for variation, rather than the more
"pure" approach of starting with one and successfully
sampling for difference and thus ensuring theoretical
150 sampling. The participants consisted of 18 Caucasian
mothers residing in the capital city of Perth, Western
Australia. Twenty-two percent ($n = 4$) were located in
low socioeconomic suburbs, 17% ($n = 3$) in high socioeconomic suburbs, and the remaining 61% ($n = 11$) in
155 medium socioeconomic suburbs, as determined by an
index defined at the postcode level from the *Census of
Population and Housing* (Australian Bureau of Statistics, 1996). Eighty-three percent ($n = 15$) were in either
an ongoing relationship with their Caucasian spouse or
160 a long-term Caucasian partner (i.e., more than 6 years),
and the remaining 17% ($n = 3$) were single parents. All
3 single mothers, plus 3 mothers in ongoing relationships, indicated that they had been diagnosed with
ADHD. None of the mothers, however, indicated that
165 they had been diagnosed with a comorbid condition,
such as anxiety disorder or depression. Mothers were
aged between 33 and 51 years. Nine mothers who participated in the study were recruited from the University of Western Australia's Centre for Attention and
170 Related Disorders database. The other 9 participants
were recruited through the Western Australian Learning and Attentional Disorder Society support group.

All 18 of the children reported in this study had
been diagnosed by their primary care physician as hav-
175 ing either the predominantly inattentive subtype of

ADHD (n = 9) or the combined predominantly hyperactive subtype of ADHD (n = 9). All but one 16-year-old girl had been prescribed stimulant medication. None of the children were engaged in a behavior modification program. Of the 18 children, 10 (9 males and 1 female) were attending secondary school. The remaining 8 children (7 boys and 1 girl) attended primary school. The children ranged in age between 8 and 17 years (M = 14.0). Twelve of the children had one sibling, whereas the other 6 children had two siblings.

Data Collection

In the initial stages, the study was open-ended. It started with general conversations with each participant and aimed at identifying time-management parenting issues. It soon became apparent that for mothers who were raising a child diagnosed with ADHD, a central time-related concern lay in the difficulty that they faced in readying their families for school. The study then became more focused on this maternal concern. As such, the aim of the study, from this point of refocusing, was to develop an understanding of how mothers of children with ADHD deal with getting their children ready for school from the point of waking them in the morning to the point of getting them out of the house. The next step taken was to translate this aim into a number of guiding questions. The following eventuated:

Question 1: How do mothers set about readying their families for school in the mornings?

Question 2: What sort of daily occurrences disrupt maternal school-readying plans, and how do mothers cope with such disturbances?

Question 3: Different people have different attitudes toward the notion of being on time. What does the term *being on time* mean in the family context?

These guiding questions acted as a guide for the generation of 15 interview questions (see Table 1). It was these interview questions that produced the data for analysis from which the substantive theory was generated.

Procedure

Semistructured interviews were conducted with each of the participants at a time of their choosing. No time limit was placed on the interviews, but they generally varied between 25 and 50 minutes. All interviews were audiorecorded, and all recordings were transcribed verbatim. All but two of the interviews were conducted by telephone to accommodate the participants' work schedules (Dinhan, 1994). The remaining two face-to-face interviews were conducted in a room put aside for this purpose at the University of Western Australia.

Permission to conduct the research was obtained from the Human Research Ethics Committee of the University of Western Australia. Information letters and consent forms were mailed to the respondents. On receipt of the returned signed consent form, respondents were contacted by telephone and offered the choice of a face-to-face or telephone interview. Once the participants made their choice, a mutually convenient time for the interview was arranged. A week before the interview date, participants were mailed a list of 15 interview questions as an aide mémoire. Before the commencement of the interview, the requirements of participants were outlined, and participants were given the option to withdraw from the study at this time without prejudice; none chose to do so. All participants were informed before the start of the interview that if they did not feel comfortable in answering any of the questions, they could opt to pass to the next. Mothers were not confined to answering the list of questions in the aide mémoire order. If, for example, during the course of answering Question 3, a mother provided the answer to Question 9, then Question 9 was not asked later in the interview. Or, if during the course of the interview, a mother raised an issue that was not included on the original aide mémoire but was deemed by the interviewer to be an issue of potential importance to the study, then this question was in turn raised with subsequent interviewees.

Data Analysis

Transcribed interviews formed the raw data of the study. The initial interview provided the first set of data and was analyzed to detect patterns and salient features (O'Donoghue & Haynes, 1997). These patterns were explored in subsequent interviews, where further emerging trends were identified. This process of simultaneous data collection, coding, and analysis continued until theoretical saturation was achieved—that is, until the new data collected were not displaying any new categories but rather confirming those already found (Strauss & Corbin, 1990).

The constant comparative method, which forms the basis of grounded theory analysis, was utilized to analyze the data. This process requires the employment of two analytic procedures: the constant making of comparisons and the constant asking of questions (Glaser & Strauss, 1967; Tesch, 1990). Each piece of data was interrogated by asking such questions as "What is this piece of data an example of?" and "What property does this piece of data represent?" These properties were compared constantly and thus resulted in the formation of categories (Strauss & Corbin, 1990). This data-scrutinizing process utilizes theoretical sensitivity to recognize what is important in data and to apportion meaning (Strauss & Corbin, 1990). Accordingly, the open-coding process of fracturing, examining, comparing, conceptualizing, and categorizing data was employed (O'Donoghue, 2007; Punch, 2005). Following these coding procedures, the process of analytic induction was employed. Analytic induction analysis is con-

Table 1
Interview Questions

1. Some children are able to wake up at the same time every morning while other children seem to need an alarm clock or family member to wake them up. How would you describe your child's ability to wake in the morning at a set time?
2. Does your child wake up at the same time on school holidays as she or he does during term time?
3. From the time that your child gets up in the morning to the moment when she or he leaves for school, what is your child like at getting ready?
4. Talk me through what usually happens. What is your usual routine?
5. What sorts of things does your son or daughter do that disrupt your morning routine?
6. How do you deal with these disruptions?
7. What sorts of things do you do to help your child get ready for school on time?
8. Children have to take different things to school on different days. What is the routine in your family for ensuring that everything your child needs is packed in her or his school bag?
9. How important is being on time to you?
10. How important is being on time to your child?
11. How important is it to be on time for the rest of your family?
12. If you were to warn your child that she or he needs to be ready to leave for school in 15 minutes, what would be your child's response and would your child be ready on time?
13. Can you talk me through what happens from the moment that you issue the warning to the moment when your child has to leave for school?
14. How does your child keep track of time? Does she or he wear a watch?
15. Does your child understand the language of time?

285 sidered by Punch (2005) to be not only compatible with the qualitative grounded theory method of data analysis but also appropriate for the systematic examination of similarities contained in the data.

290 The reliability of the initial coding was determined by having a second independent rater listen to 10% of each audiotaped interview and then by comparing the transcriptions with those of the principal author. In addition, an independent rater reviewed the transcripts and coded themes. Intercoder reliability was calculated 295 by dividing the number of instances of agreement by the number of instances of agreement plus the number of instances of disagreement between the two raters. This figure was in turn multiplied by 100 to convert the intercoder reliability to a percentage (Merrett & 300 Wheldall, 1986). The range of agreement was 99% to 100%, with an overall mean for intercoder reliability being 99.5%.

Outcomes of the Study: The Substantive Theory of Instilling an Awareness of Time

Recall that a central sociopsychological problem for mothers of children diagnosed with ADHD is how 305 to deal with their children from the point of waking them to the point of getting them out of the door and off to school. The substantive theory of instilling an awareness of time was generated with regard to how mothers deal with this problem. This theory is now 310 outlined in four parts. Part 1 describes the daily experience of mothers in dealing with the chaos arising out of the actions and inactions of their children from the moment of their waking to the moment of their leaving for school. Part 2 outlines the initial blaming process 315 that mothers go through as they attempt to eliminate stress arising out of the chaos. Part 3 details the manner in which mothers attempt to reach an understanding of their own concept of time management and that of their children. Part 4 presents the strategies that mothers 320 employ in light of these attempts.

Part 1: Daily Experience of Mothers in Dealing with Chaos

From the first day that mothers attempt to ready their children diagnosed with ADHD for school, their early-morning experience is generally one of chaos. This chaos mainly arises out of the untimely actions 325 and inactions of their children from the moment of waking to the moment of leaving for school. Consequently, mothers are challenged to establish an early-morning school-readying routine because of the chaos that reigns. Furthermore, this chaos prevails regardless 330 of their children's diagnostic ADHD subtype. As such, children are classified according to the fourth edition of the American Psychiatric Association's *Diagnostic and Statistical Manual of Mental Disorders* (2000). The manual differentiates ADHD subtypes on the basis of 335 the number of hyperactive-impulsive and inattentive symptoms manifest in the child at the time of diagnosis. Thus, in the context of school readying, mothers refer to children with the combined type ADHD diagnostic subtype as being hyperactive early risers and to 340 children with the predominantly inattentive ADHD diagnostic subtype as being laidback hypoactive reluctant risers. Regardless of whether children are early or reluctant risers, mothers insist that their children's hyperactive actions or hypoactive inactions always have 345 the potential to initiate chaos within the family unit. The unique and common experiences of mothers with hyperactive early-rising and hypoactive reluctant-rising children are presented in turn.

Maternal Experiences Unique to Dealing with Hyperactive Early-Rising Children

Mothers commented that the high-spirited and

170

noisy actions of their hyperactive early-rising children frequently disturbed the sleep patterns of other family members and, as such, disrupted the harmonic balance within the family unit. One mother explained,

He wakes up very early in the mornings long before anyone else in the house is up. Long before even my husband and I are up. He gets out of bed straight away. He can't lie in bed or read or do anything like that. He is instantly hungry so as soon as his feet hit the carpet he is in the kitchen rattling around for breakfast or whatever else he can get his hands on. He is mad keen on snooker at the moment so after he has eaten he will go to the pool table and play that. The rest of us wake up *every* morning to the sound of balls being played on the table. The moment he knows that someone else is awake, and then he has to be there, and be in your face.

This "in your face" attitude was seen by mothers to be the chief provocation for early-morning conflicts that arose between their offspring with and without ADHD. One mother reflected,

His brothers are very good at getting ready quietly in the morning. They are just not interested in any of A's hi-jinks. They tend to be a bit quiet and grumpy, whereas A is full of energy and wants to be alive. A, though, is usually quiet and reasonable until his brothers appear. Then he is apt to being a bit silly and making a bit of a racket. There aren't many mornings when we don't have to say: "A, don't make such a racket!" Every morning he makes stupid noises and every morning we have to say: "STOP IT, A."

Whereas mothers of hyperactive early risers related accounts of highly disruptive early-morning activity, mothers of hypoactive reluctant risers revealed that it was their children's lack of action that provoked their experience of early-morning chaos.

Maternal Experiences Unique to Dealing with Hypoactive Reluctant Risers

Mothers of hypoactive early risers revealed that it was their children's laidback, absentminded, no-worries approach to life that created early-morning tensions within the family unit. The mothers stated that the frustration that they experienced arose out of the realization that despite their best endeavors to ready the family for school, their hypoactive children's general slowness and total inaction cast their school-readying efforts into disarray. One mother explained,

There is usually a lot of shouting involved in the mornings just to get him out of bed and when he does get up and, if it is a good day, he will come down dressed. If it is not a good day he'll drag himself down the stairs, still in his jammies, and start arguing with whoever is there.

Mothers additionally surmised that their children's disruptive inactions stemmed from their inability to remain focused on any one task for a sufficiently long enough period to enable the task to be carried through to completion. They cited as a case in point their children's inability to dress in a timely manner. For example, one mother recounted,

She'll get up, but then she'll be off with the fairies. Then she'll come back to earth and then she'll dawdle and be off with the fairies again. She is really disorganized. It can take an hour for her to get dressed in the mornings. By the time she's dressed and everything else is done like the dishes and the dog poo, it is time to walk out the door. And then at the very last minute she'll say: "But I haven't got this or I haven't got my water bottle" and then I really lose it and I'll say: "Hang on a minute, you have had all this time to get your stuff ready. You are old enough to realize that you have got to go to the toilet, or you've got to get your water bottle or whatever."

Maternal Experiences Common to Hyperactive Early and Hypoactive Reluctant Risers

Regardless of whether children were hyperactive or hypoactive, mothers asserted that the disruptions that their children's actions and inactions caused to the harmonic balance within the family unit not only thwarted their maternal efforts to ready the family for school but also slowed the morning preparations of other family members. One mother explained,

In the morning there is generally a lot of friction because M knows how to push all of our buttons and then his brother C often intentionally distracts M to get back at him. Then I have to drag C aside and say: "I really want to get you all to school on time so can you please stop distracting M?" There is always just a lot of fighting and friction before school.

Another mother similarly disclosed, "There is quite a bit of stress involved in getting off to school on time." A third mother summed up the feelings of many when she somewhat apologetically admitted, "It is always chaotic until M like goes to school and then I'll breathe a big sigh of relief when he goes out the door. I know that sounds like a horrible thing to say, but it's true." A fourth mother, who drove her child with ADHD to school, explained that she achieved this sense only when her child alighted from the car at the school gates:

It usually ends up with the rest of us sitting in the car and me honking the horn. The dog hasn't been fed or put away and C, well, he is still running around the house grabbing at everything! He'll get in the car and he'll start eating his lunch on the way to school because he hasn't had any breakfast yet. Then I just know he is going to be hungry at lunchtime. By now, we are usually running about five minutes late and C is worrying whether he is going to get a detention. So you see there is usually quite a bit of stress involved in getting him off to school.

It appeared that the elimination of time-related sources of school-readying stress was an ongoing problem for mothers and one that left them feeling mentally drained and physically exhausted. Over time, mothers became so worn down by the process that they either gave in or gave up, with the result being that their offspring with ADHD gained an inappropriate level of

460 control. Indeed, such levels of child control may be an early sign of family dysfunction.

Part 2: Assigning Blame

Mothers of hyper- and hypoactive children blamed the disturbances that their children's morning antics cause to the harmonic balance within the family unit on
465 their children's ambivalent approach to time and time management. They claimed that time truly resonated with their children only when it related to an activity that they valued. School was generally not one of these activities. Mothers typically commented as such:

470 It depends on what type of day he has planned. Like, if we are going somewhere special then he will get up at six o'clock in the morning and get himself dressed without me having any input whatsoever. His interest isn't so enthusiastic though for going to school. If it is just an ordi-
475 nary school boring type of day, then he will take a long time. It can take him half an hour to eat a piece of toast and it will take him another 10 minutes to swallow his tablets. He is just not task focused. But, if he's got something planned that he wants to do, he'll be ready in 15
480 minutes.

In this regard, mothers perceived their children with ADHD to have a self-serving selective awareness of time.

Mothers of children with the predominantly inatten-
485 tive (hypoactive) subtype of ADHD apportion blamed the disturbances to the harmonic balance within the family unit on their children's inability to retain focus and their tendency to procrastinate. One mother explained,

490 I am on his back the whole time because otherwise he'll just sit there and not do anything. I will say: "R, we are leaving in 15 minutes" and he'll say: "Yes, yes, yes, fine." He might even get up and do one thing to get himself ready, but then he will sit himself down again and I
495 will say: "Look, R, we have only got five minutes left!" Then he might get up and do a few more things but normally by the time that 15 minutes has come around he still has more things to do. He is basically just never ready on time.

500 Such mothers considered children with ADHD to be adept at wasting time.

Mothers confided that at times they became so ex-
asperated by their children's actions and inactions that they resorted to desperate measures. One mother, for
505 example, having reached the end of her tether, admit-
ted, "I have even gone as far as taking him to school in his pajamas!" Her desperation was not an isolated occurrence. Other mothers who reached a similar point of feeling overwhelmed confessed that they had at times
510 just given up because the effort of trying to deal with the chaotic aftermath of their children's actions and inactions all seemed just too hard. One mother confided,

He sleeps through his alarm clock and I have to go in and
515 wake him up several times. His ability to wake up in the mornings is pretty terrible. He likes to stay up late at night. He doesn't like to go to bed and go to sleep. He plays in his room. He does all sorts of things including making his room look like a bomb has hit it. He says he
520 feels comfortable with it like that. In the end I just give in and let him do whatever it is that he wants to do.

Overwhelmed mothers indicated that it was this type of low-ebb experience that initiated the realization that if they were ever going to restore harmony within the
525 family unit, they needed to move out of the blaming stage and into a mindset that would allow them to come to terms with the differences between their and their children's concept of time management.

Part 3: Understanding Their Children's Concept of Time Management

Time management is crucial to the smooth schedul-
530 ing of routine family events. Any variation to or disruption of the family schedule has the potential to pro-
voke chaos in quasi-stable family units. According to one mother, a descent into chaos is more likely to occur if the parenting partners do not share an underlying
535 philosophical approach to time management:

Time is a huge thing in our house. We have this constant argument in the mornings. I like to be 5 minutes early or on time for things, never more than 5 minutes late. My husband on the other hand thinks that time is wasted if
540 you get somewhere early.

Philosophical differences on time management were not just an adult phenomenon. Many mothers recognized that children with ADHD have a markedly different concept of time management. Moreover, in
545 their attempts to lessen the potential for early-morning chaos, mothers indicated their need to understand the difference between their and their child's concept of time management. They achieved this understanding through progressively engaging in the substages of
550 self-reflection and analyzing attitudes.

Self-Reflection

Coming to terms with their and their children's concept of time management was for many mothers a lengthy procedure that started with a period of self-
reflection. Mothers eventually concluded that their
555 children diagnosed with ADHD have concepts of time and time management different from their own and that their children's understanding was frequently different from that of their family members. One mother, for example, who had reflected on her son's inactivity,
560 stated, "It has taken me a long while to recognize that he has a laissez-faire attitude to time." She continued that unlike his brother, "He just sits there. He has no real concept of time." Another asserted, "He is very literal. He has no concept of the language of time and
565 that kind of thing. It took us over a year to learn that he has no idea how long 15 minutes actually is." Once mothers passed through this self-reflection substage, they generally moved into the substage of analyzing attitudes.

Analyzing Attitudes

570 The first attitude toward time management that mothers analyzed was their own. They attested to having a measured, punctual, and orderly attitude toward time management. Typical comments included the following:

575 I think I am very, very organized. I just have to have things done by a certain time. I have in my head an idea of what I need to do, and what amount of time I need to do it in. Sometimes I'll use a planner. I like to have my day planned meticulously, especially when I have to or-
580 ganize my husband and my son.

Being on time is incredibly important. I understand how society works. Society is very performance based and value orientated so punctuality is one of those things like a person's word being their bond. I have to live by a work
585 timetable. I have to be on time to drop kids off at school. So in that way time is very important to me.

Once mothers developed an understanding of their own attitude toward time management, they then turned to analyzing their child's.

590 In general, mothers perceived children with ADHD to have either an overly anxious or a laissez-faire attitude toward time management. In both instances, they conceded that their children's attitudes contrasted sharply with their own. For instance, mothers of time-
595 anxious children commonly commented,

He really does keep a very close eye on the clock. He hates to be late for school and school activities. He doesn't have a fear of being late but rather a need to be on time. He doesn't want to be late for school. He doesn't
600 like to be late for lessons. He doesn't want to be late. He likes to be on time because his teacher doesn't like late-comers. He doesn't want to have the finger pointed at him. He relies on us to keep the time for him. He tries to get himself organized but more often than not I have to
605 go in and give him a helping hand.

The comments of mothers of time-anxious children contrast sharply with the following observation, which involves a mother whose child with ADHD manifested a laissez-faire attitude toward time management:

610 He is anxious about lots of other things but not time. Not being on time doesn't worry A at all. If you send him off to do something, he'll get distracted by something else and then he'll spend his time like watching parrots out of the window. He'll get totally distracted and when you
615 complain he'll look at you as if to say: "What are you fussing about?" He has a very laissez-faire attitude to time.

Regardless of whether children are time anxious or have a relaxed, laissez-faire attitude toward time man-
620 agement, mothers concluded that learning how to organize time was vital to their and their children's school-readying success. One mother, for example, stated, "If you are a person like M, who has difficulties with organization, then the last thing that you need is to
625 be late as well: People don't care why you are late. It is just the fact that you are late that is noticed." The de-

velopment of strategies that instilled an awareness of time management thus became the final stage in the process of eliminating time-related sources of stress
630 within the family unit. This strategizing stage is the subject of Part 4.

Part 4: Developing Strategies That Instill an Awareness of Time Management

Parents typically receive a plethora of advice on how to deal with their children's inappropriate actions and inactions from a variety of well-intentioned indi-
635 viduals, such as doctors, psychologists, counselors, social workers, teachers, friends, extended family members, politicians, work acquaintances, and neighbors. In addition to citing these avenues of advice, mothers revealed that they frequently sourced
640 parenting directives from media reports, books, and the Internet. The sheer volume and diversity of this collective advice is, at times, overwhelming (M. F. Taylor, O'Donoghue, & Houghton, 2006). Mothers stated that although they sometimes struggled to filter out extra-
645 neous parenting directives, their partners often became totally overpowered by the enormity of the problem and the sheer volume of advice. Several mothers revealed that their partners had just given up and had abdicated all school-readying responsibilities because
650 they found "the whole ADHD thing to be just too damn hard."

Regardless of whether mothers chose or were forced into a position of assuming full responsibility for instigating their families' school-readying regime,
655 they stated that the best way of dealing with the matter was to examine the available "expert" parenting directives and then, on the basis of their intuitive, gut feeling, decide which directive or cluster of directives will work best in their own family situation. Having se-
660 lected what they considered to be the most promising, mothers embarked on a trial-and-error process of eradicating those directives that did not work and moulding those that did. In this way, they formulated a set of strategies for dealing with the problem of readying
665 their children with ADHD for school. Over time, these refined strategies became their modus operandi, their early-morning school-readying routine.

Mothers indicated that although their initial selection of parenting directives and subsequent meld of
670 strategies were based largely on a desire to eliminate or ameliorate the stressful conditions within the family unit that delayed and disrupted their early-morning school-readying routine, their selection was often influenced by the nature of the directive. Mothers re-
675 vealed, for example, that certain preemptive directives had immediate appeal because they tended to be easier to implement and because they left the onus of control with them. Such directives clustered into a set of what can be termed controlling strategies, which in turn seg-
680 regate into four distinct categories—namely, manipulative, organizational, directive, and pharmacological.

173

Manipulative Controlling Strategies

Mothers who implemented manipulative strategies confided a need to be personally in control of every aspect of their children's early-morning school-readying routine. In this regard, mothers indicated that they would go to great lengths to manipulate the family environment to accommodate their means of time management, as exemplified in the following account:

> My watch is always 10 minutes early. To me time is elastic. I have no stress because the time on my watch is a different time to the time on my house clock, which is like halfway to the real time on my car clock. Stretching time is okay because the time in the car is the reality of time to everyone else.

Such mothers indicated that they could deal with their children's disruption to the early-morning school-readying routine only if they were in total control of the physical environment. However, for overtly less controlling mothers, the focus of control appeared to be centered on maintaining a chaos-free home environment rather than on the manipulation of the home environment to accommodate their personal concept of time management.

Organizational Controlling Strategies

Mothers who implemented organizational strategies stated that they felt equipped to deal with the pressures of readying their child for school only when they were able to assume organizational control over their children's every movement, from the moment that the children woke to the moment that they left for school. The mothers explained their organizational control in the following terms:

> I leave his uniform out the night before so that he doesn't have to think too much about what he has got to put on. I will actually put everything out for him, his socks, his shoes, his underwear, everything. Then in the mornings, he gets up and gets his uniform on for school and comes downstairs and waits for his breakfast to be made. I will make his lunch and put it in his bag. I will pack everything for him.

> I'll get breakfast ready and everything and then I will go and wake T up. T is really disorganized. She is like so carefree. She'll get up but then she'll dawdle around. It gets to the point where I have to go in and like dress her. I have to go into her room and get her dressed. By this stage it is getting late. I'll get her into the bathroom and stand over her while she does her hair and washes her teeth and her face. By the time that that has happened it is just about time to walk out the door.

For such mothers, the attainment of organizational control over their children's actions mainly occurred through the imposition of their physical presence next to their children at moments that they deemed essential to their children's school-readying routine. Other control-oriented mothers adopted directive strategies.

Directive Controlling Strategies

For some mothers, situational control was achieved through the constant use of nagging and screaming types of verbal directives. One mother, for example, who described herself as "the nag from hell," confided, "What usually happens is that I nag and nag and nag." Another mother commented,

> You have to tell him step-by-step you know. Tell him, "Have your breakfast." Tell him, "Get your clothes on." Tell him, "Brush your hair" and tell him, "Clean your teeth." I have to be very specific, I have to say: "Get your socks. Put your socks on. Go get your shoes. Put your shoes on. Now go and clean your teeth." It is all very staged.

Whereas directive and organizational strategies were the most commonly applied strategies, some mothers revealed that when nothing else worked, they resorted to the pharmacological strategy.

Pharmacological Controlling Strategy

Mothers who tried nonpharmacological treatment options (e.g., behavior management) for remediating their children's inappropriate school-readying actions and inactions with little to no success stated that they on occasion resorted to using the administration of their children's medication as a last-resort means of maintaining control. One mother explained,

> With B, well, what happens is that I will go in and wake him and tell him that it is time to get up. With B it is like, "Yep, I'm getting up" and he will walk around and like go to the toilet but then he'll go back to bed again. So I'll have his tablets ready so that when he comes out of the toilet I can make sure that he takes his tablets right there and then.

Another mother who resorted to the pharmacological means of control conceded that she had come to realize, after receiving several midmorning telephone complaints from her child's school, that her "pill the moment he arises" strategy was counterproductive. She explained, "It doesn't work because by the time he actually gets to school the effect has gone and so he has lost all the benefit." It is this realization that eventually motivated this mother and mothers like her to not only review their use of the pharmacological strategy but reconsider their original selection of parenting directives. At this point, mothers indicated that they generally selected a new set of directives to trial. The difference between their previous strategies and their second set of strategies was that the more recent ones were oriented toward shifting the balance of control away from themselves and onto their children. Moreover, the implementation of this set of less autocratic, less judgmental self-governing strategies was born out of a realization that mothers cannot always do for their children. As such, the mothers acknowledged that they needed to prepare their children to assume greater responsibility for their own actions and for control over their own lives. As with the preemptive strategy clus-

790 ter, the self-governing strategy cluster segregates out into four distinct categories—namely, teaching, negotiation, prompting, and discrete supervision.

Self-Governing Teaching Strategies

Maternal teaching strategies initially involved the mothers' purchase of an analog watch or bedroom
795 clock for their children. Mothers indicated that the act of teaching their children how to tell time was not only vital to the successful implementation of their early-morning school-readying routines but also essential to every aspect of their children's lives. The following
800 comment was typical:

> Every morning for years it has been all about getting M programmed. The best way to get him ready on time for school is to make time visible. I point to his clock and say: "This is the time that you have got to get this or that
805 done by." Or, when he has friends over we explain on the watch how long before they will be here and how long they will stay. We do try to speak in units of time and explain and show him how long things are. We help him that way.

810 Providing a timepiece as a visual reminder of the passage of time and teaching children how to tell time became the primary self-governing strategies that mothers employed when attempting to instill an awareness of time in their children. It was only after mothers
815 believed that their children mastered the basic skill of time telling that they moved into the second self-governing strategy: negotiation.

Self-Governing Negotiation Strategies

Only after their children mastered the rudiments of time telling did mothers deem it appropriate to teach
820 them the more advanced skill of time management. As a mastery incentive, they provided a selection of negotiated rewards, such as preschool use of the computer or preschool television viewing. The key point of negotiation from the mothers' perspective was that their
825 children had to be completely ready for school before they could be granted free time and thus be eligible to select a reward activity. One mother justified her use of negotiated incentives by saying, "I feel that it is important that M learns to do things for himself and to be
830 independent rather than me like doing everything for him." Mothers were aware that their children's adherence to these negotiated strategies was not an easy or automatic occurrence; therefore, they augmented the strategies with time-related visual, auditory, and verbal
835 prompts.

Self-Governing Prompting Strategies

The most basic prompt employed by mothers was the visual pictorial reminder chart, detailing every step that their children needed to take to ready themselves for school. Mothers instructed their children that if they
840 followed the chart in the order set out, there would be enough free time for them to engage in a negotiated activity. For example, one mother, who was contem-

plating the use of an incentive chart as part of her child's school-readying routine, commented,

845 > It is a real struggle, I am trying to give him a bit more independence and yet still remind him of what he needs to do to prepare himself for school. He needs to start to do more things on his own. We are working on this at the moment. I am thinking of drawing up a chart so that
850 > when he gets up in the morning there is a list of things that he has to do to get himself organized for the morning. It will help him work out what he has to do next. I have been trying to deal with T on a more positive level than just growling at him all of the time.

855 Although the practice of providing a pictorial reminder was appealing, the majority of mothers who employed this strategy indicated that its effectiveness was short-lived because their children tended to become so accustomed to the presence of the chart that
860 they failed to see it after a while.

By far, the most commonly employed maternal visual prompt was the constant arm-gesturing type of point toward the family clock when endeavoring to reinforce the notion of time's passing. One mother, for
865 example, remarked that every morning, 10 minutes before the family's scheduled departure time, she would point to the kitchen clock and say, "We have got to leave in 10 minutes." In a further attempt to reinforce the passage of time, she would open the garage
870 door 3 minutes before the family's scheduled departure time and then point again to the clock and say, "We are leaving in 3 minutes."

Yet other mothers revealed their use of auditory time prompts (e.g., countdown timing devices on ovens
875 and microwaves), which they set to beep at what they considered to be critical stages in their children's school-readying routine. The following comment was typical:

> Even though we have clocks all over the house and he
880 > has a clock in his bedroom, quite a large one, I still do have to remind him of the time. I will talk him through so he knows exactly what it is that he needs to do to be ready. I put a countdown timer on for him. I actually put it in his hand or somewhere where he is going to hear it
885 > or we'll use the timer on our oven. He will hear it go off and he'll know that he has to finish off doing whatever it is he should be doing.

The end plan for mothers was to reduce the number and frequency of their promptings and to instigate a set
890 of discrete strategies that allowed them to maintain supervisory control from afar.

Discrete Self-Governing Supervisory Strategies

Mothers believed that they reached their goal of instilling an awareness of time in their children when their children were able to make the shift to assuming
895 total or near-total responsibility for their own school-readying activities. According to mothers, this shift normally occurred within a year or two of starting high school:

900 Time has become quite important to him now that he is at high school. There are consequences if he is not on time. If he is late to school the consequence is a detention at lunchtime. Now, he is the kid that wants things to be quantified. He likes to know where he is at. I think that 905 now he has got the same sense of time as me he wants to be at places on time.

Mothers revealed that once their children assumed responsibility for their own school-readying routine, the shift sometimes opened up new sets of problems. For example, mothers observed that their children with 910 ADHD, who were inherently anxious, tended to become obsessed with time and to react adversely if their school-readying routines were altered. One mother remarked,

Being punctual to her is being at least 10 minutes early. 915 She gets quite upset if things aren't punctual. If her father is even 5 minutes late leaving the house she gets quite upset as she is now very conscientious in her time allocation and things.

Finally, mothers indicated that their children's time 920 anxiety tended to dissipate to a certain extent as they matured and entered into adolescence. It was at this stage that mothers reported having enough confidence in their children's ability to manage themselves in relation to time that they were able to make the final shift 925 and allow their children to assume total or near-total management of their school-readying routine. However, mothers admitted that even though they relinquished the preponderance of their control, they did remain vigilant and ready to resume control if things 930 began to go awry.

Discussion

Understanding individual and collective perspectives on a topic and detecting relationship patterns contained within data is fundamental to interpretive research because the process allows a picture of the in-935 ternal and external worlds of the respondents to emerge (Lemma, 2003). Accordingly, this article employs grounded theory methods of data analysis to report on the maternal practice of instilling an awareness of time in response to the central research question—namely, 940 how do mothers deal with their children from the point of waking them to the point of getting them out of the door and off to school? This response reveals that mothers of children diagnosed with ADHD experience a need to instill an awareness of time to reduce or ame-945 liorate the chaotic and stressful conditions that arise out of their children's inappropriate early-morning school-readying actions and inactions. These inappropriate forms of activity not only thwart maternal efforts to establish workable early-morning school-readying rou-950 tines but also upset the harmonic balance within family units. Such balance, attained through collaboration, is recognized as being necessary for inter- and intrafamily growth, whereas imbalance in relationships is thought to result in unequal or inappropriate distributions of

955 power between family members (Breulin, Schwartz, & Kune-Karrer, 1992; Flynn, 2005). Therefore, it is reasonable to conclude that disharmony occurs when a child with ADHD consciously or unconsciously exerts an inappropriate level of control over the family's 960 school-readying activities. Mothers who reached this realization revealed their need to arrest the onus of control back from their children.

Mothers indicated that their attempts at regaining control of their families' school-readying procedures, 965 for the most part, were structured around their personal attitudes toward time and time management. In this regard, they stated that time for them was a scarce commodity that needed to be rationalized and operationalized if they were to establish a workable early-970 morning school-readying routine. The way in which they set about establishing such a routine involved dividing the time available for school readying into blocks of minutes and then assigning a task to each block (e.g., 15 minutes for dressing, 20 minutes for 975 preparing and eating breakfast, 25 minutes for readying children, 15 minutes for completing chores, and 5 minutes for exiting the house). Such a conceptualization is consistent with Graham's linear-separable model of time perception (1981). Mothers concluded, however, 980 that their children with ADHD lacked this fundamental linear sequential conceptualization of time. They contended that their hyper- or hypoactive children operated at an accelerated tempo (i.e., completed their school-readying activities in a haphazard rush) or at a much 985 reduced tempo. Either way, mothers perceived the disparity between their and their children's operating tempo as an underlying reason explaining why their children's actions and inactions disrupted their families' harmonic balance.

990 This concept of balance within families is considered by Kramer (1985) to be vital to understanding family interface. In regard to the present study, mothers revealed that the way in which they dealt with harmonic imbalance was to instill in their children an 995 awareness of time. Having taught the rudiments of time telling to their children, mothers sourced some basic "expert" recommended strategies to assist them in instilling time management skills in their children. In the main, mothers selected strategies that left the onus of 1000 control with them. Mothers admitted that after instigating these control-orientated strategies, they discovered that such strategies were for the most part counterproductive because they caused their children with ADHD to become reliant on them or other family members for 1005 the management of their early-morning school-readying activities.

Whereas the notion of being in control is recognized as being instrumental in reducing stress levels within individuals (Jex & Elacqua, 1999; Macan, 1010 1994), it has also been determined that in instances where a prolonged or extreme imbalance exists within a family unit, adverse parenting and learning outcomes will occur (Kramer, 1985). In the context of this study, mothers acknowledged the long-term impracticality of trying to maintain control over their children's school-readying activities. Consequently, they moved to implement a set of self-governing strategies, which shifted the onus of control back onto the child. Although realizing the necessity for the shift, mothers attested to their wariness of a rapid transition and generally engaged in a form of power balancing (A. Taylor, 2002) as they adopted a measured approach to relinquishing their onus of control.

The maternal process of instilling an awareness of time is a lengthy and arduous one. It is not possible to categorically state that all mothers achieved their end goal. Neither is it possible to categorically state that all mothers moved through the process of instilling an awareness of time in exactly the same order or with the same intensity. It is clear, however, from the findings that all mothers engaged to some degree in the process. In addition, whereas it is not possible to claim generalizability based on these findings, they are transferable insofar as they allow others to gain an understanding of the time-related experiences of mothers parenting children with ADHD.

These findings have particular implications for teachers of children diagnosed with ADHD. For example, that students with ADHD appear to have an inappropriate understanding of the concept of time and time management is instructive to teachers. Furthermore, the study raises awareness that although some students with ADHD are able to master the mechanics of time (i.e., they can tell time), many have little to no understanding well into adolescence of either the language of time or the more abstract aspects of time (e.g., the duration of 2 weeks, a month, a term). This knowledge can inform teachers when issuing classroom instructions or when planning classroom assignments, as can the knowledge that the use of time generalities (e.g., "finish that later" or "the bell will be ringing soon") can be problematic for children with ADHD. Thus, if teachers wish to convey time-orientated instructions to pupils with ADHD, the most effective strategy is to augment the delivery of the instruction with a verbal, visual, or auditory prompt.

The study's findings are also applicable to those outside the field of education. For instance, pediatricians, child psychologists, counselors, and social workers may benefit from the knowledge that marked differences exist between adult and child perceptions of time and time management. Moreover, such differences may underpin some of the time-related conflicts that arise in families where one or more of the children have been diagnosed with ADHD.

Finally, the present study provides a basis for future research. In particular, empirical studies are needed to determine whether the time-related responses of children diagnosed with the predominantly inattentive and predominantly hyperactive subtypes of ADHD differ significantly from each other and whether such differences occur in both clinical and real-life settings. Such studies would provide greater understanding of how time and time management differences in children with ADHD affect home and school relationships.

References

American Academy of Pediatrics. (2000). Clinical practice guideline: Diagnosis and evaluation of the child with attention-deficit/hyperactivity disorder. *Pediatrics, 105*(5), 1158–1170.

American Psychiatric Association. (2000). *Diagnostic and statistical manual of mental disorders* (4th ed., text rev.). Washington, DC: Author.

Australian Bureau of Statistics. (1996). *Census of population and housing, information paper, socioeconomic indexes for areas.* Retrieved August 14, 2006, from http://www.dest.gov.au/sectors/higher_education/publications_resources/statistics/outcomes/

Barkley, R. A. (1997). Behavioral inhibition, sustained attention, and executive functions: Constructing a unifying theory of ADHD. *Psychological Bulletin, 121,* 65–94.

Barkley, R. A., Koplowitz, S., Anderson, T., & McMurray, M. (1997). Sense of time in children with ADHD: Effects of duration, distraction, and stimulant medication. *Journal of the International Neuropsychological Society, 3,* 359–369.

Bianchi, S. M. (2000). Maternal employment and time with children: Dramatic change or surprising continuity? *Demography, 37,* 401–414.

Blumer, H. (1969). *Symbolic interactionism: Perspective and method.* Englewood Cliffs, NJ: Prentice Hall.

Breulin, D., Schwartz, R., & Kune-Karrer, B. (1992). *Metaframeworks: Transcending the models of family therapy.* San Francisco: Jossey-Bass.

Cappella, B., Gentile, J., & Juliano, D. B. (1977). Time estimation by hyperactive and normal children. *Perceptual and Motor Skills, 44,* 787–790.

Charmaz, K. (2006). *Constructing grounded theory: A practical guide through qualitative analysis.* Thousand Oaks, CA: Sage.

Covic, T., Adamson, B. J., Lincoln, M., & Kench; P. L. (2003). Health science students' time organization and management skills: A cross-disciplinary investigation. *Medical Teacher, 25,* 47–53.

Crotty, M. (2003). *The foundations of social research: Meaning and perspectives in the research process.* Thousand Oaks, CA: Sage.

Daley, D. (2005). Attention deficit hyperactivity disorder: A review of the essential facts. *Child: Care, Health and Development, 32,* 193–204.

Daly, K. J. (2001). Deconstructing family time: From ideology to livid experience. *Journal of Marriage and Family, 63,* 283–294.

Dinhan, S. (1994). The use of the telephone interview in educational research. *Education Research Perspectives, 21,* 17–27.

Fleck, S. L., Bischoff, L., & O'Laughlin, E. (2001). Time perception in children with attention deficit hyperactivity disorder. *The ADHD Report, 9,* 7–10.

Flynn, D. (2005). The social worker as family mediator: Balancing power in cases involving family violence. *Australian Social Work, 58,* 407–418.

Gager, C. T., Cooney, T. M., & Call, K. T. (1999). The effects of family characteristics and time use on teenagers' household labor. *Journal of Marriage and Family, 61,* 982–994.

Glaser, B. G., & Strauss, A. L. (1967). *The discovery of grounded theory: Strategies for qualitative research.* Chicago: Aldine.

Graham, R. (1981). The role of perception of time in consumer research. *Journal of Consumer Research, 7,* 335–342.

Hughes, E. C. (1971). *The sociological eye.* Chicago: Aldine.

Jex, S. M., & Elacqua, T. C. (1999). Time management as a moderator of relations between stressors and employee strain. *Work & Stress, 13,* 182–191.

Kellner, R., Houghton, S., & Douglas, G. (2003). Peer-related personal experiences of children with attention-deficit/hyperactivity disorder with and without comorbid learning disabilities. *International Journal of Disability, Development and Education, 50,* 119–136.

Kramer, J. R. (1985). *Family interfaces: Trans-generational patterns.* New York: Brunner/Mazel.

Lemma, A. (2003). *Introduction to the practice of psychoanalytic psychotherapy.* Chichester, UK: Wiley.

Macan, T. H. (1994). Time management: Test of a process model. *Journal of Applied Psychology, 79,* 381–391.

McGee, R., Brodeur, D., Symons, D., Andrade, B., & Fahie, C. (2004). Time perception: Does it distinguish ADHD and RD children in a clinical sample? *Journal of Abnormal Child Psychology, 32,* 481–490.

McLeod, J. (2003). *An introduction to counseling* (3rd ed.). New York: Open University Press.

Meaux, J. B., & Chelonis, J. J. (2005). The relationship between behavioural inhibition and time perception in children. *Journal of Child and Adolescent Psychiatric Nursing, 18*(4), 148–160.

Merrett, F., & Wheldall, K. (1986). Observing Pupils and Teachers in Classrooms (OPTIC): A behavioural observation schedule for use in schools. *Educational Psychology, 6*(1), 57–70.

Milkie, M. A., Mattingly, M. J., Nomaguchi, K. M., Bianchi, S. M., & Robinson, J. P. (2004). The time squeeze: Parental statuses and feelings about time with children. *Journal of Marriage and Family, 66,* 739–761.

O'Donoghue, T. (2007). *Planning your qualitative research project: An introduction to interpretivist research in education.* New York: Routledge.

O'Donoghue, T., & Haynes, F. (1997). *Preparing your thesis/dissertation in education.* Katoomba, New South Wales, Australia: Social Sciences Press.

Owen, A. J. (1991). Time and time again: Implications of time perception theory. *Lifestyles: Family and Economic Issues, 12,* 345–359.

Piantanida, M., Tananis, C. A, & Grubs, R. E. (2004). Generating grounded theory of/for educational practice: The journey of three epistemorphs. *International Journal of Qualitative Studies in Education, 17,* 325–346.

Pocklington, B., & Maybery, M. (2006). Proportional slowing or disinhibition in ADHD? A Brinley plot meta-analysis of Stroop Color and Word Test performance. *International Journal of Disability, Development and Education, 53,* 67–92.

Punch, K. (2005). *Introduction to social research: Quantitative and qualitative approaches.* Thousand Oaks, CA: Sage.

Rapport, M. D., Chung, K. M., Shore, G., Denney, C. B., & Isaacs, P. (2000): Upgrading the science and technology of assessment and diagnosis: Laboratory and clinic-based assessment of children with ADHD. *Journal of Clinical Child Psychology, 29,* 555–568.

Rubia, K., Noorloos, J., Smith, A., Gunning, B., & Sergeant, J. (2003). Motor timing deficits in community and clinical boys with hyperactive behaviour: The effect of methylphenidate on motor timing. *Journal of Abnormal Child Psychology, 3,* 301–313.

Rubia, K., Oosterlaan, J., Sergeant, J. A., Brandeis, D., & Leeuwen, T. V. (1998). Inhibitory dysfunction in hyperactive boys. *Behavioural Brain Research, 94,* 25–32.

Rubia, K., Overmeyer, S., Taylor, E., Brammer, M., Williams, S., Simmons, A., et al. (1998). Prefrontal involvement in "temporal bridging" and timing movement. *Neuropsychologia, 36,* 1283–1293.

Rubia, K., Sergeant, J., Taylor, A., & Taylor, E. (1999). Synchronization, anticipation and consistency of motor timing in dimensionally defined children with attention deficit hyperactivity disorder. *Perceptual and Motor Skills, 89,* 1237–1258.

Rubia, K., & Smith, A. (2001). Attention deficit-hyperactivity disorder: Current findings and treatment. *Current Opinion of Psychiatry, 4,* 309–316.

Sagvolden, T., Johansen, E. B., Aase, H., & Russell, V. A. (2005). A dynamic developmental theory of attention-deficit/hyperactivity disorder (ADHD) predominantly hyperactive/impulsive and combined subtypes. *Behavioral and Brain Sciences, 28,* 397–419.

Strauss, A., & Corbin, J. (1990). *Basics of qualitative research: Grounded theory procedures and techniques.* Thousand Oaks, CA: Sage.

Taylor, A. (2002). *The handbook of family dispute resolution: Mediation theory and practice.* San Francisco: Jossey-Bass.

Taylor, M. F., O'Donoghue, T., & Houghton, S. (2006). To medicate or not to medicate? The decision-making process of Western Australian parents following their child's diagnosis with attention deficit hyperactivity disorder. *International Journal of Disability, Development and Education, 53,* 111–128.

Tesch, R. (1990). *Qualitative research: Analysis types and software.* London: Falmer Press.

Toplak, M. E., Rucklidge, J. J., Hetherington, R., John, S. C. F., & Tannock, R. (2003). Time perception deficits in attention-deficit/hyperactivity disorder and comorbid reading difficulties in child and adolescent samples. *Journal of Child Psychology and Psychiatry, 44,* 88–104.

Volkow, N. D., Wang, G. J., Fowler, J. S., Logan, J., Angrist, B., Hitzemann, R., et al. (1997). Effects of methylphenidate on regional brain glucose metabolism in humans: Relationship to dopamine D2 receptors. *American Journal of Psychiatry, 154,* 50–55.

Note: This research was funded by a grant from the Australian Research Council.

Acknowledgments: The authors extend gratitude to Professor Tom O'Donoghue, University of Western Australia, for his assistance with the data analysis.

Address correspondence to: Dr. Myra Taylor, Centre for Attention and Related Disorders, Graduate School of Education, University of Western Australia, 35 Stirling Highway, Crawley, WA 6009 Australia. E-mail: myra.taylor@uwa.edu.au

Exercise for Article 29

Factual Questions

1. What is the explicitly stated "aim of the study"?

2. What was the age range of the mothers who were interviewed?

3. What was the average age of the children?

4. Were the participants provided with the questions prior to being interviewed?

5. What formed the "raw data" for this study?

6. What was the overall mean for intercoder reliability?

Questions for Discussion

7. If you had planned this study, would you have used a diverse socioeconomic sample? Explain. (See lines 152–158.)

8. Most of the interviews were conducted by telephone. In your opinion, is this as desirable as conducting face-to-face interviews? Explain. (See lines 221–226 and 230–233.)

9. What is your understanding of the meaning of the term "consent forms"? Are they important? Explain. (See lines 229–231.)

10. Is Table 1 an important part of this report? Would the report be as effective without the table? Explain.

11. Are any of the results surprising? Are any especially interesting? Explain. (See lines 303–930.)

12. In your opinion, would it be worthwhile to replicate this study with a sample from the United States? Explain.

Quality Ratings

Directions: Indicate your level of agreement with each of the following statements by circling a number from 5 for strongly agree (SA) to 1 for strongly disagree (SD). If you believe an item is not applicable to this research article, leave it blank. Be prepared to explain your ratings. When responding to criteria A and B below, keep in mind that brief titles and abstracts are conventional in published research.

A. The title of the article is appropriate.

     SA   5   4   3   2   1   SD

B. The abstract provides an effective overview of the research article.

     SA   5   4   3   2   1   SD

C. The introduction establishes the importance of the study.

     SA   5   4   3   2   1   SD

D. The literature review establishes the context for the study.

     SA   5   4   3   2   1   SD

E. The research purpose, question, or hypothesis is clearly stated.

     SA   5   4   3   2   1   SD

F. The method of sampling is sound.

     SA   5   4   3   2   1   SD

G. Relevant demographics (for example, age, gender, and ethnicity) are described.

     SA   5   4   3   2   1   SD

H. Measurement procedures are adequate.

     SA   5   4   3   2   1   SD

I. All procedures have been described in sufficient detail to permit a replication of the study.

     SA   5   4   3   2   1   SD

J. The participants have been adequately protected from potential harm.

     SA   5   4   3   2   1   SD

K. The results are clearly described.

     SA   5   4   3   2   1   SD

L. The discussion/conclusion is appropriate.

     SA   5   4   3   2   1   SD

M. Despite any flaws, the report is worthy of publication.

     SA   5   4   3   2   1   SD

Article 30

Contributions to Family and Household Activities by the Husbands of Midlife Professional Women

JUDITH R. GORDON
Boston College

KAREN S. WHELAN-BERRY
Utah Valley State College

ABSTRACT. This article presents an exploratory study that furthers our understanding of the functioning of two-career couples at midlife and, in particular, our understanding of the husband's contributions to family and household activities. More specifically, it addresses the following questions regarding dual-career couples: (a) Whose career has precedence? (b) What is the nature of the husband's contributions to the family and household? and (c) What types of support result? This study is part of a larger research project that focuses on the professional and personal lives of a group of midlife professional women who were married, had children, and had enduring careers. The results presented here describe the women's perceptions of support (or lack of support) provided by their spouses in their family and household. It discusses the implications of such support for family functioning and for the ability of midlife women to pursue full-time careers.

From *Journal of Family Issues, 26*, 899–923. Copyright © 2005 by Sage Publications, Inc. Reprinted with permission.

Recent research has suggested that between one-third and one-half of women in top executive and professional positions at midlife do not have children. They remain childless as a result of a "creeping 'non-choice'" because they cannot successfully combine employment and family responsibilities and still rise to high-level positions (Hewlett, 2002). Although organizations have instituted family-friendly programs as one way of supporting women employees, most of these programs address concerns of women early in their careers. Husbands are another potential source of support for midlife professional women; in fact, such support has been shown to result in greater well-being for the women (Cutrona & Russell, 1990; Greenglass, 1993). Although research has recognized the contributions of men in two-career families, their involvement has been studied primarily for families with young children (Barnett & Rivers, 1996; Deutsch, 1999; Deutsch, Lussier, & Servis, 1993; Ehrensraft, 1987; Gilbert, 1993). Are these contributions the same for the families of midlife professional women? As more

women have moved into higher positions at midlife, have the contributions of their spouses changed?

The study reported here examines the contributions of husbands of midlife women in helping them balance employment and family demands. More specifically, it addresses the following questions: (a) Whose career has precedence? (b) What is the nature of the husband's contributions to the family and household? and (c) What types of support result?

A great deal has been written about women who work outside the home and the special challenges women with children face in balancing employment and family. During the past 20 years most of this work has focused on women in early career stages, although some of the more recent research has examined women at midlife (e.g., Apter, 1995; Borysenko, 1996; Gordon & Whelan, 1998; James & Liewkowicz, 1997; Levinson, 1996; J. Marshall, 1994). We have been particularly interested in studying professional women at midlife who are married, have children, but also have had enduring careers because they have likely experienced the potential conflict between employment and family. Because they have had enduring careers, they most likely have established a workable division of responsibilities with their husbands and have found ways to either overcome or minimize this conflict.

Women who reached midlife in the mid-1980s to early 1990s were among the first who attempted to work full-time throughout their adult lives while still marrying and having children without significant time away from the workforce as a result of childbearing. As pioneers, they faced special challenges in dealing with employment and home in ways that professional men had never considered. Some of these professional women achieved a degree of success previously unknown for women who were married and had children. This particular group of women, one that has been able to meld the responsibilities of employment and family, provides insight into the broader array of challenges women who work outside the home face and the ways their partners help or hinder their balancing act.

This article describes a group of midlife professional women with enduring careers and their perceptions of the role their husbands played in sustaining and supporting their careers. As an exploratory study, it attempts to delineate the participation by the husbands of professional midlife women in the family and household arena. Although these contributions represent only part of the potential support that husbands can provide (e.g., they can also offer emotional or financial support), they represent areas that appear to be important for balancing employment and family. Subsequent research examines other areas of support.

We first present some background about the functioning of two-career families. Next we describe the research method, including data collection, analysis procedures, and an overview of the sample. Then we consider the results of the analysis, looking specifically at the midlife women's perceptions of their husband's involvement and support in employment and family domains. Finally, we discuss the implications of the results, as well as limitations to the study and directions for future research.

Background

As the baby boomers reach midlife and beyond, they have swelled the ranks of workers between the ages of 40 and 50 years. For example, the percentage of the labor force between the ages of 35 and 54 years increased from 42% in 1990 to 47% in 2004 (U.S. Bureau of Labor Statistics, 2004). The number of women between the ages of 35 and 44 years was 16.6 million in 2004, as compared to 11.7 million in 1985 (U.S. Bureau of Labor Statistics, 2004). Understanding the issues faced by these workers at midlife and beyond can facilitate the development of appropriate policies and practices.

Although some research has addressed the issues of midlife workers (A. Kruger, 1994; Levinson, 1978; O'Connor & Wolfe, 1991) and now midlife women (Apter, 1995; Gordon & Whelan, 1998; Grambs, 1989; L. Jacobson, 1995; Levinson, 1996; J. Marshall, 1995), little of this work has looked at women with enduring careers at midlife and similarly at the roles their spouses play in their lives. Women at midlife typically have established their careers and home and family life (Gordon & Whelan, 1998; Reid & Willis, 1999; White, 1995). They often have school-age or young-adult children, although they can still have preschool children at home. Other published data from this study of married midlife women with enduring professional careers and families (Gordon & Whelan, 1998) indicated that these women had needs for renewed work-family balance, more personal time, and continued achievement, accomplishment, and perceived value to the organization. They also perceived a need for assistance in preparing for the next decade's challenges, which included good mothering, especially of adolescents; building their career path and continuing to advance in their organization; maintaining balance in their lives; developing career competencies; and dealing with their aging parents. Most of these women developed personal coping strategies as ways of meeting these needs. Yet Gordon and Whelan's (1998) study did not address the role that husbands played in the midlife of these professional women. As the number of dual-career couples continues to increase and the workforce continues to age, a significant number of dual-career couples at midlife and beyond will continue to face the challenge of balancing employment and family responsibilities.

Support Provided by Wives and Husbands in Two-Career Families

Prior research indicates that many women significantly support their husband's careers. Women provide support by taking primary responsibility for family and household (Beck, 1998; Bonney, Kelley, & Levant, 1999; P. Kruger, 1998; Manke, Seery, Crouter, & McHale, 1994; Shelton & John, 1993). Historically, employed women have done a greater share of family work than their husbands (Biernat & Wortman, 1991; Coverman, 1989). Even when women jointly own family companies with their husbands, they have assumed more family and household responsibilities (Marshack, 1994). Wives have also been viewed as partners in their husband's careers. Recruitment for executive positions, for example, has often included the husband and wife in interviews and on-site visits, even investigating the wife's character, personality, and marital relations (Murray, 1986). Women with careers may relinquish them or reduce their career advancement as a result of their spouse's career moves, thus becoming the trailing spouse.

Women have rarely experienced the same type of support from their spouse, even if they have equal or primary careers, although husbands contributed more to household labor in a younger cohort of spouses (Pleck, 1997; Robinson & Godbey, 1997; Rogers & Amato, 2000). A study, for example, indicated that husbands' participation in childcare increases as mothers have extended work hours (Bonney et al., 1999). Traditionally, however, men have worked outside the home and women worked inside the home. Employed women merely added job-related responsibilities to their home responsibilities (Potuchek, 1997). In large part, this lack of support results from the competing career obligations that the husbands have because their participation in dual-career families has personal and professional consequences (Rosin, 1990). The amount and sharing of household, childcare, and family work evolves, increasing and decreasing, as children and parents age or are ill. At midlife, women and men may find themselves sandwiched between generational responsibilities, placing additional burdens on them.

Outcomes in Two-Career Couples

Satisfaction with the division of household labor influences marital happiness (Suitor, 1991). A larger percentage of wives than husbands restructured their work for family reasons (Karambayya & Reilly, 1992). Even though the men were equally involved with their families, they did not restructure their employment as much as the women to meet family obligations, instead making so-called special arrangements instead of more consistent adjustments. Some men felt stuck in what has been called the "daddy trap" (Hammonds & Palmer, 1998), where they face significant work demands that conflict with their (and their wife's) desire for them to be equal participants in dealing with family and household responsibilities (Hertz, 1999). Women were more satisfied when their husbands shared the chores they had traditionally performed rather than spent more time performing household chores in general (Benin & Agostinelli, 1988). Clearly, the intertwining of their careers and lives can create problems for the advancement of one member of the couple if relocation is required (Cohen, 1994; Taylor & Lounsbury, 1988). Yet their relationship and support for each other can overcome some of these negative outcomes (Gilbert, 1985, 1993). Special cases exist when husband and wife work in the same business, altering and increasing the requirements for support (Marshack, 1994). Decision making and responsibilities in these careers are not equal, with women primarily responsible for the home arena and husbands for the work arena (Marshack, 1994; Ponthieu & Caudill, 1993; Wicker & Burley, 1991).

In addition to the impact of the actual attitudes and behaviors on the wives' outcomes, the wives' perceptions can also influence their attitudes and behaviors. Wives' perceptions of their husbands' attitudes toward the wives working influenced the wives' attitudes about their own work (Spitze & Waite, 1981). The impact of perceptions is further illustrated in a study where perceptions of unfairness in household chores and spending money were significantly related to husbands' and wives' assessment of marital quality (Blair, 1993). Perceptions of equity play a key role in marital satisfaction and quality (Gager, 1998; Gilbert, 1993).

Summary and Unanswered Questions

As more women have entered the workforce, their husbands have contributed to the family by helping with household and child care tasks. Most of the research so far has focused on men and women at early career stages with young children. Husbands' contributions to two-career families have been chronicled in numerous studies, although most have not specifically considered the nature of participation in couples at midlife (Aldous, Mulligan, & Bjarnasin, 1998; Barnett & Baruch, 1987; Barnett & Rivers, 1996; Deutsch, 1999; Gilbert, 1993). This stage of career and life offers new complexities and poses special challenges that make understanding the role of husbands important. Does one person's career take precedence, or does true

equality exist in the careers of husbands and wives at midlife? What happens at midcareer to career precedence and sharing of home and family responsibilities, for example, when both partners are highly successful in their careers? Furthermore, what do these pioneering women have to say about their husbands' contributions to family life? To what extent do the husbands share in the work of the family? What happens when the husband and wife have career aspirations that call for spending significant time on job-related activities and also have children who require attention?

The current exploratory study attempted to take a first step in addressing these unanswered questions by looking at the husbands' involvement in employment and family in midlife dual-career couples. We focus on three questions (a) Whose career has precedence? (b) What is the nature of the husbands' contributions to the family and household? and (c) What types of support result? In the current study, we report the results in the women's voice as a way of better identifying, describing, and understanding the subtleties, complexities, and common issues of the families of midlife professional women.

Method

We used a qualitative methodology in the current exploratory study because it provides a richness of data that helps identify key themes that can form the basis of subsequent quantitative studies (Denzin & Lincoln, 1998; C. Marshall & Rossman, 1999; Strauss & Corbin, 1990). We interviewed 36 professional women between the ages of 36 and 50 years. These women were part of a pioneering group who combined marriage and parenting with enduring and relatively uninterrupted full-time work throughout their adult lives. They are an unusual group because of the degree of their career accomplishments—each woman had attained significant professional stature; the sample included top business executives, well-regarded physicians, partners in major legal firms, and successful self-employed consultants and businesswomen. Their husbands were equally accomplished, holding high-level business, not-for-profit, legal, and medical positions. Most of the women and men in the sample were at the pinnacle of demanding careers that required large amounts of time and energy and gave no indication of diminishing in importance during the next 10 years.

Data Collection and Analysis

Although the current study was part of a larger one that involved an extensive interview protocol, the results of the current study were based primarily on the women's responses to the following questions, which allowed us to delineate the contributions made by the husbands of the midlife professional women: "What role has your husband played in helping you manage family and career?" "How do you interface with your husband's career and vice versa?" We also coded comments about the woman's spouse in other parts of the interview, which included questions about the nature of their employment and family responsibilities, the way they manage these responsibilities now and in the past, their key challenges, the major issues they faced at various times in their lives, the nature of the transition between life stages, the impact and contributions of their organization in handling their employment and family responsibilities, and their satisfaction with their job, career, and life.

We used a nonrandom sample of Boston-area professionals; securing a random sample or a complete sample of the population would have been desirable but was unrealistic because of difficulty in locating married, professional women with children and enduring careers. The first author contacted a small group of women who could help identify women in professional-level jobs who had worked full-time throughout their adult lives, were married, and had at least one child. The women identified in this way were contacted by telephone and asked to participate in the current study. All but two of the women contacted agreed to be interviewed; these two women declined to participate, not because of lack of interest, but because of significant time demands on their lives at that time. The women who participated were then asked to suggest additional women. This snowball technique resulted in a convenience sample, which is appropriate for an exploratory study. The interviews lasted between 1 and 3 hours and were audiotaped. The first author conducted all interviews to ensure relative consistency in their content.

Each interview was transcribed. We analyzed the transcripts using the qualitative analysis approach suggested by Miles and Huberman (1994) as follows. We created a data set with the responses to questions that related directly to the husband, household and family management, and career interfaces between the husband's and wife's career. We then searched the full interview transcript and included any interviewee comments that related to the spouses of the women interviewed. We first coded the responses according to the broad, thematic areas of the interview questions related to spouse, for example, the role the husband played in helping manage family and career and the nature of the two careers. During this coding, we focused on and identified the themes that related to the involvement of the spouses in helping the women handle career and family responsibilities, although the larger research project addressed multiple themes and issues. Next, we reviewed each transcript to identify any additional thematic areas not yet specified and to ensure that all relevant themes were identified. For this article, we focused on career precedence and the husband's contribution to family and household. A second coder then coded the nature of career precedence and the husband's contribution to family and household based on comments about the husband previously extracted from the interviews. The interrater agreement

(Miles & Huberman, 1994) between the two coders initially was 83% for career precedence and 69% for husband's contributions. When the second coder read the entire transcript of the interviews of the women where coding differences existed, and after discussing discrepancies between the two sets of codes and trying to reconcile them, the agreement rose to 97% and 81%, respectively. In cases where no agreement could be reached, the codings by the first coder are reported in this article.

Sample

The women in the sample were all White, and the majority were between the ages of 40 and 45 years, although younger and older women were included in the sample to capture the breadth of experiences at midlife. The length of their marriage varied from fewer than 5 years to more than 20 years, with most of the women having marriages of 15 to 20 years, followed in frequency by 11 to 15 and 6 to 10 years, respectively. Some women had been divorced previously; however, all were married at the time of the interview. More than one-half of the sample had two children, and one-third had only one child; having three or more children was less common. These children ranged in age from preschool to adult. Table 1 provides more specific information about the sample.

Table 1

Age, Marital Status, and Children of the Women in the Sample (N =36)

	Number of women
Age of the women (*M*)	(41)
36 to 39 years	8
40 to 45 years	26
46 to 50 years	2
Length of marriage (*M*)	(15)
0 to 5 years	1
6 to 10 years	8
11 to 15 years	10
15 to 20 years	12
More than 20 years	5
Number of children (*M*)	(2)
1	12
2	20
3 or more	4
Age of youngest child	
Preschool	9
Elementary school	20
Secondary school	6
College or older	1
Age of oldest child	
Preschool	4
Elementary school	19
Secondary school	5
College or older	8

The women in our sample were quite successful and worked in an array of professions, as shown in the left-hand column of Table 2. Many held high-level positions in major Boston-area organizations; they

Table 2
Occupations of the Women and Their Husbands (N = 36)

Woman's occupation	Number of women with this occupation	Woman's description of husband's occupation			
Account manager	1	Self-employed			
Attorney	3	Attorney (2)	Bank executive		
Bank executive	4	Consultant	Development officer	Higher education executive	High technology manager
Chief financial officer	1	Psychologist			
Consultant	3	Administrative judge	Consultant	Medical researcher	
Development officer[a]	1	N/A			
Film producer	2	Media executive	Television reporter		
Financial manager	1	Attorney			
Human resource manager[a]	5	Development director	Executive chef	Human resource manager	Psychoanalyst N/A
Information systems manager	2	Attorney	Professor		
Investment banker	1	Consultant			
Physician	4	Physician (4)			
Professor	1	Hotel administrator			
Psychologist	1	Hospital administrator			
Real estate developer	1	Real estate developer			
Senior administrator	2	Attorney	Politician		
Social worker	1	Physician			
Systems engineer	1	Architect			
Systems planning manager	1	Physician			

[a]The data from the interviews of one of the women with this occupation did not include the husband's occupation, shown in the table as N/A.

were partners in law firms, well-regarded physicians, top human resources executives, senior vice presidents in financial services organizations, and top managers in the nonprofit sector. The husbands of these women also
375 held professional-level positions, as shown in Table 2; the right-hand column lists the professions of the husband of each woman with the specified occupation. One-fourth held the same type of job as their wives; for example, the sample included couples who were attor-
380 neys, physicians, media-related professionals, or human resources managers. This sample was unusual because in most of the couples the husband and wife had achieved a high, relatively equal level of success in their careers.

Results

385   We present the results as they answer our three research questions. First, we analyze whose career has precedence. Next, we present the data regarding the husband's contribution to the family and household. Finally, we combine these data into a typology of four
390 types of husbands to describe the overall type of support they offer.

Career Precedence

Career precedence was reflected either in whose career was the primary focus of career decisions or in who assumed the burden of balancing employment and
395 family. The women in the current study described whose career took precedence in one of three ways: their husband's, their own, or equal.

Husband's career had precedence. The husband's
430 career took precedence for 22% of the couples. The

400 women explained this precedence as occurring for four reasons. First, the salaries associated with the two careers may have resulted in the husband's career having precedence. A social worker reported, for example, that her husband's career took precedence because he made
405 a higher salary: "I still did most of the daytime stuff, I mean, that was an economic reality." Second, decisions about job location, such as whether the wife trailed the husband in job relocations, reflected the type of career precedence. A husband's career took precedence, for
410 example, because job mobility for the wife was easier. Third, the husband may have had ego needs, such as providing security for his family or having status or power, that were met by his having the dominant career. The wife in a physician couple noted this motiva-
415 tion:

His career is skyrocketing and all that, and I've come to realize that that's important to him. Because of his needs and deprivations and so on as a child [his career] is something he just had to keep working at until he feels com-
420 fortable.

Finally, this traditional attitude toward career precedence may be a function of many men's socialization to expect to be the family's breadwinner.
One attorney noted this influence when she de-
425 scribed her husband's career having precedence:

Oh, definitely if there has to be any give it seems to be mine.... Men have a fascinating way of forgetting that they had to be home at six.... I think they just naturally assume they're primo. I think women are by nature more
430 accommodating.

Wife's career had precedence. For a slightly smaller percentage of couples, 19%, the wife's career had precedence. For these couples, only two of the factors—salary and job mobility—seemed to play a major role in the decision. For a human resources manager, for example, her higher salary resulted in her career having precedence. She believed that her husband also felt comfortable limiting his career achievement:

It just sort of happened gradually because of my advancement. It wasn't a choice, do you take this promotion or not? And the fact that he also was someone who has a lot of interests around the home, is very interested in the computer, and is project oriented. [He] didn't feel like he had to prove himself professionally. And we just felt for the total family, this was the best thing to do.

A physician described the lesser mobility of her career because of job vacancies or the special nature of her work: "In many ways, he has a more common and saleable job…. So when we've talked about moving, it's always been with an eye to what academic jobs are out there for me that he could find a job around."

The careers had equal precedence. The largest group of the women interviewed, 58%, either stated or implied that the two careers held equal precedence, as captured in one attorney's comment about her husband, also an attorney: "Every time I go to give up mine, he says he'll retire too." Yet the equality is not without some tension and trade-offs. As one physician noted, "We're even. If anything, I got to be an associate professor a year ahead…[however,] I would have left several times for good job offers, but [my husband] does not want to leave Boston." A human resource manager commented,

We both sacrifice somewhat in our career. My husband is an executive chef, and in that business if you're really going to get ahead, you have to be willing to put in the 60, 70, 80 hours per week. You have to be willing to relocate with some of the bigger chains or work in Boston and make the long commute, put in the hours. He has sacrificed that to help maintain the family life at home. So in that respect he sacrificed, and I have sacrificed also.

Another woman described the trade-offs in her family:

Now I'm reaching another sort of crossroads where I'm feeling maybe the business isn't really going to bring in enough money in the next few years to pay all those bills easily. The other dilemma is that my husband has been working at his job for so many years…and he's got a great job but he's also in midlife crisis. I mean, he doesn't want to do that forever. And I'm feeling a bit more pressure to pull a little more weight so he can slack off a little and try something new in a couple of years. So there's always a dilemma, there's always a trade-off. You know, things change.

Trade-offs have a lot to do with managing the logistics of the two careers. They also relate to personal issues about growing older, accomplishing desired goals, and an equal commitment to ensuring that family needs are met. It is a dynamic process, with adjustments occurring continuously.

Contributions to Family and Household

No midlife woman did all of the family and child care herself. Most husbands made some contributions to the family and household activities, although some contributions were extremely limited. The husbands' contributions ranged from doing a small part, to sharing relatively equally, to the husbands having primary responsibility. Our thematic analysis indicated that many of the husbands played specific supportive roles, as well as offered general support. This support helped the wife handle the challenges created by the requirements of a professional career and a demanding family. For example, an information systems manager noted that "I think having a supportive husband and a supportive daughter have always been important." A business executive noted,

I think that [my husband] has always been real supportive around my career and very supportive around the intellectual challenges that I find associated with my work. Not that it doesn't create stress, when there's not enough clean underwear, but I think that's [support's] the key.

Without this basic type of support, managing employment and family likely would be even more stressful for the midlife women.

Although most families purchased extensive child care and household services (depending, of course, on the ages of their children), significant responsibilities for managing and implementing family-related activities remained. Of the wives, 42% explicitly characterized their husband's involvement using the language of "managing" and "doing." In the remainder of the cases, this distinction was based on women's description of the tasks and responsibilities performed by themselves and their husbands. *Managing* refers to the planning, coordinating, and initiating of all household and family-related activities. The person or persons who manage carry the emotional burden or psychological responsibility for making sure that the household runs smoothly and that children receive appropriate care. The manager often initiates and delegates various family and household activities to other family members or paid caregivers or household service providers. One woman, for example, described herself as the "domestic coordinator" of her family. Another noted about her husband, "On a day-to-day basis, he does more of the planning part of it."

Doing refers to the carrying out, performing, or implementing of a sequence of household activities. Typically these activities occur in response to initiatives or requests by the person who manages the household and family-related activities. The same person can manage and do, or one person can manage while the other person does the family and household work. Often the women describe their husbands as helping in the household. As one woman noted, "He

Table 3
Types of Support Provided by Husbands (N = 36)

		Managing	
		Low	High
Doing	Low	Uninvolved (*n* = 5) The *au pair* does it…. Oh, he couldn't plan [household responsibilities] if his life depended on it…. We have to send somebody to do the grocery shopping…. The major need is for carpooling, baseball. I mean [the nanny] doesn't really take care of the kids.	Coordinator (*n* = 3) [Husband] probably [makes greater contributions]. It's changing. Right now, it's about 60–40, but until recently, it's probably been 90–10…. [My husband] always has the higher percentage. He would do drop off and pick up. He would do teacher conferences. He would do whatever.
	High	Helpmate (*n* = 18) [He's] a great husband. He'll do anything I ask him to do. He doesn't necessarily think of things on his own. And there were a number of years when that bothered me, but then I realized that…I ought to be thankful that he does these things, and all I have to do is say, "Would you do this?" and he says, "Sure, fine."	Egalitarian (*n* = 10) But he was always very good about [my traveling] on short notice. He certainly did more than half, pitching in, running errands, and taking kids to the doctor and making sure that there was food in the house and that kind of thing…. It's always been shared. I think I did more of some things than he did all along, even when my career was maybe even busier than his.

545 couldn't plan it if his life depended on it." Another woman described doing as follows: "Sometimes you just have to ask him. He knows the basics. He cooks, he cleans, he grocery shops, he does errands. It's just part of the routine. He's there to help out."

Categories of Support

550 Based on the wives' perceptions as expressed during our interviews, we identified the extent to which husbands manage or do most activities regarding family and household as high or low. We characterized (not counted) the content of the wives' comments to 555 determine the level of each type of support by their husbands. We categorized a husband as high on managing if the wife reported that he consistently and of his own initiative performed numerous tasks related to the planning, coordinating, and initiating of activities; 560 we categorized a husband as low on managing if the wife described him as rarely performing such activities. Similarly, we categorized a husband as high on doing if his wife described him as implementing household-related activities, typically after she specified that they 565 needed to be done; we categorized a husband as low on doing if he rarely performed any household-related activities.

This results in four possible combinations. Table 3 illustrates the combinations and offers an example of a 570 woman's comments about husbands who fall into each category. We have chosen descriptive names— uninvolved, helpmate, egalitarian, and coordinator—to reflect the underlying approach of these husbands to the sharing of household and family responsibilities. 575 The labels are intended solely to differentiate about possibilities rather than definitively characterize each husband.

Uninvolved husbands. Of the husbands, 14% were low on managing and doing household and family ac- 580 tivities and so were perceived as making very limited contributions in these areas. Some men lack the time because of extensive career commitments. As one physician commented, "If I ever had any question about where my focus would be, knowing that he's so busy 585 means that somebody has to be home running the show."

Other men remain uninvolved because they believe that they can completely enjoy their family in less time than their wives need. Still, others have retained a 590 view, often based on early socialization, that women should assume primary responsibilities for their family and household. These husbands can serve as a source of security by providing the financial backing that allows their wife the freedom to work at any career, re- 595 gardless of its compensation: "His doing all of the things he's doing gives us a lot of security." The husband can also give his wife the opportunity to opt out of working because the family does not need her salary to maintain its standard of living: "My husband refers 600 to it as 'women have this net.' They can always say 'I'll just stop working.'"

Helpmate husbands. One-half of the husbands are low on managing and high on doing. They help with family and household either by doing the chores men 605 typically do or by willingly doing whatever their wives ask them to do. One woman described her husband's contribution as follows:

I went and I did laundry, and I had a laundry basket, and I carried it and put it at the foot of the stairs. And all the 610 clothes were folded and the laundry basket sat there for a day. And so the next day I put a second laundry basket next to it. And the next day I had like three laundry baskets sitting at the bottom of the stairs. Everybody stepped over them. The kids took out what they needed. After the third or fourth day, I said to [my husband], "Could you take these upstairs?" "Oh, sure dear. No problem."…. I probably do more than he does…but I probably could get him to do more by asking him to do more.

Helpmate husbands can also serve as a personal lifeline. In this role, the husband acts as a stabilizing force by being a calm center or reminding his wife about the importance of her personal health and well-being:

My husband, who has just been the most consistent center of my life, [is] a very calm, tranquil being that I've kind of run around for 20 years. I think that to the extent that that has been a center of my life, it's been a quiet center, and it's been an extremely important one in that we've always kind of figured out how to get things done together.

In some families, the wives preferred to retain responsibility for, control of, and psychological oversight of the family and child care. Perhaps because many of the women care more about the details of home life, they spend more energy than their husbands in this regard. As one senior executive noted,

I probably have always done more of that [managing the household]. I think that's pretty classic, too. And that's by choice…I can't stand a messy house. So if nobody else in the house is going to do it, I'm going to do it. And I feel guilty if my kids don't have sort of a square meal at the end of the day…. But I clearly impose on myself a level of responsibility that's ridiculous.

Even if husbands share child care, the couple may take a more traditional approach to household management, resulting in the husbands acting as helpmates rather than truly egalitarian:

I'd say [we divide up] the child care responsibilities 50-50. With the running of the house and making decisions for the house and all that kind of thing, 90/10, with me taking 90% and him taking 10%. Because no matter what I do, no matter how many agreements we make, no matter how we sit down and write it down on paper, after 3 weeks it just goes back to me taking responsibility for it. It doesn't get done. He says that, although he thinks that he is very liberated and that he thinks I have every much a right to a career as he does, when it comes right down to it, he thinks he has old-fashioned values about who is going to be in charge of the house and he just won't help with it.

Helpmate husbands can also act as team players, playing the role of facilitator or partner. One woman noted, "He's a facilitator because when he's home he's a 50-50 participant." Another commented,

He's been very, very much a partner. He really encouraged me to take advantage of the work opportunities [to be self-employed] and convinced me that whatever support I needed at home to make that work out would be, we'd make it.

Egalitarian husbands. Of the husbands, 28% shared responsibilities for managing and doing family and household responsibilities relatively equally. As one woman commented, "Absolutely [he still does half]. More if I can get him to." Such sharing results in more positive balance between employment and family responsibilities, although the negotiations involved in allocating responsibilities and ensuring that either the husband or wife has the so-called big picture can sometimes be associated with more stress and reduced life satisfaction in the short run.

Our strategy has been that I do mornings and my husband does the evenings and afternoon type thing. So whatever I do workwise, I am always going to be late for work [in comparison to other employees] in the morning…. We use chores actually as trade-offs because I hate to clean the bathroom; he hates to iron. So this Sunday I ironed 10 shirts so he's cleaned the bathroom; I had to sort of learn to not want the housework done as I would do it, but just, you know, done.

Although a number of the women say that their husbands share the responsibilities relatively equally, the men do not assume quite as much responsibility for organizing or managing as their wives. If they straddle the helpmate and egalitarian categories, they likely spend more time in doing than managing family and household activities than the typical helpmate. Yet a number of the wives justify this less-than-equal contribution by acknowledging that their husbands do more than most husbands do. This seems particularly the case in household work as opposed to childcare.

Coordinator husbands. Of the husbands, 8% were perceived to have the primary responsibility for managing the family and household responsibilities and rely on their wives' help in doing the related activities. This type of activity by the husband as manager and wife as doer is analogous to the helpmate type; however, the roles are reversed. The coordinator husbands may make it possible for some women to work at all and for others to have high-level, high-profile, extremely demanding careers. As one woman noted,

But over the years…because of what was happening in my career in terms of advancement and because he had flexibility…we decided that we didn't need more money. We needed more time, and we needed to have some semblance of sanity in our life. He has continued to cut back…. Realistically, I could never have done this if my husband had a career that required him to be gone from 7:00 in the morning till 7:00 at night or traveling.

One woman described her husband's attitude in assuming the coordinator role that she should "do what you need to do." Another husband felt that he was missing important times with his children, so he changed his priorities and schedule to take responsibility for them.

Coordinator husbands can serve as the family manager, such as by organizing family activities. One woman described her husband's role: "[My husband]

organizes field trips for us all the time, which we joke about, [calling him] Mr. Field Trip." It is also possible
730 for the husband to take charge of all household and family activities. The wife of one husband who had this role estimated that she had only 10% of the responsibility in the household or family.

Discussion

Families with both spouses employed are the major
735 pattern in the United States (Elloy & Flynn, 1998); however, most of the research attention has been paid to young couples early in their careers. By midlife, such couples have likely established workable patterns of sharing responsibilities. The current study was a first
740 step in documenting the nature of this pattern and, more specifically, the husband's contribution to the family and household in which the wife held a high-level professional job. This article presented preliminary results regarding the career precedence of spouses
745 in the families of midlife professional women, the contributions to family and household by husbands in those families, and the pattern of overall support offered by the husbands to the midlife women. In this section, we discuss the results in each of these areas.

Career Precedence

750 Our results suggest that equal career precedence is more common than either the husband's or the wife's career having precedence. Yet even when the wives report equal career precedence, creating truly equal careers often requires trade-offs and sacrifices from
755 one or both partners that may be extremely difficult, often testing their commitment to their careers and sometimes to their families. In almost all cases, precedence is economically driven; however, equal economic contributions do not necessarily translate into
760 equal precedence because other factors, such as logistics, early socialization, or personal ego needs may moderate the impact of the economic contributions. At the same time, organizations need to better appreciate the movement toward greater equality in career prece-
765 dence. For example, managers are more likely to assume that female employees who are mothers would handle any household or family emergencies that occur (Hammonds & Palmer, 1998). Such assumptions may be inaccurate and negatively affect the wife's career
770 advancement, increase stress for male employees who have assumed such responsibilities, or undermine the arrangements made by spouses for handling the challenges posed by the interaction of employment and family.

775 We captured these couples at one time in their careers. Over time, shifts in career precedence to ensure a sense of open fairness in the marriage occurred for many couples, as either the husband or wife wished to change his or her level of involvement with family or
780 as job opportunities opened or closed. This dynamic, somewhat free-form texture reflects the value partners placed on ensuring their husband's or wife's happiness

and fulfillment. The couples continually renegotiated priorities as a way of making the family situation work
785 and the partners feel happy and successful.

Contributions to Family and Household

Not unexpectedly, the contributions by husbands of midlife women vary significantly. When we categorized the contributions as managing and doing, we noted that some midlife professional women character-
790 ized their husbands as contributing in neither, one, or both ways. Regardless of their relative contributions, men still spend more time doing than managing in the household. This pattern of contribution continues to put the psychological burden on women, causing them to
795 face the necessity of either acting as so-called superwomen or finding other ways of handling the overload at work or home. Because of their relatively high income, many of the professional women we interviewed bought household services as a way of handling this
800 potential conflict, a solution available only to those women or families with sufficient discretionary income. Still, the nature of the husband's contribution likely has a psychological impact and hence consequences for the life satisfaction, career commitment,
805 and job satisfaction of the midlife professional women (and their husbands).

Some husbands may complement or substitute for their performance of household or family responsibilities by providing support in other ways. For example,
810 some act as career advisors to their working wives. As sounding boards, the husbands may offer advice about career-related issues that range from decisions about returning to work after a maternity leave to how to handle specific personnel problems. In this role, they
815 might also serve as mentors or role models in which they demonstrate desirable professional behavior.

A number of the women described their relationships with their husbands as ones of "independence and dependence." The analysis we presented about hus-
820 band's contributions highlights this tension. By midlife, however, the couples have developed the mechanisms, such as hiring household staff, alternating whose job requirements receive priority, or developing responsive scheduling patterns, for resolving conflict-
825 ing demands.

Support Provided by the Husbands

We presented the beginnings of a four-cell typology of support provided by the husbands of midlife professional women. Such a typology highlights the critical role that husbands play in supporting the individual
830 work–life balance of professional midlife women. The typology provides a way for husbands and wives to consider all the tasks necessary to support effective, functional home and family life. Such intentional consideration may provide a more satisfactory division of
835 these responsibilities and related work than a division based on family-of-origin patterns or traditional gender roles and responsibilities.

Where the husband falls in the typology could provide insight into the amount and type of support needed from the husband's and the wife's employer. For example, the woman with a helpmate may need less flexibility and more referral services; the woman with a coordinator husband may need the reverse. This highlights the need for use of benefits to be equally accepted for men and women. Until recently, it was more acceptable for women than men to take advantage of various benefits, such as leave following the birth of a child or flextime to attend children's activities.

Just as career precedence and contributions to household and family may change during an individual's life span, so may a husband's place in the typology. Although a husband may act as a helpmate early in his and his wife's career, later he may shift to a coordinator as the demands of his work lessen and his wife's increase. Organizations, too, must be flexible in responding to such changes. They must offer an array of benefits so that professional women and their spouses can tailor their choices to their specific needs.

Limitations and Future Research

Although the current study has taken a first step in trying to understand the contributions and support that the husbands of midlife professional women provide, future research should involve a larger study that would verify our results. The work on career precedence could be extended, such as by measuring career precedence on a 100% scale, where husbands and wives are asked to divide the percentage according to the contribution of each spouse. How career precedence changes during the course of the marriage would also provide interesting insights into husbands' support in dual-career families. Future research might also involve obtaining data about career precedence and family and household contributions from the husbands and comparing the two sets of perceptions. In addition, the typology proposed here should be tested and expanded to describe the wife's role as perceived by the husband and the relationship as perceived by the husband and wife.

Future research should also test specific hypotheses about the impact of perceived or actual behaviors and attitudes on both spouses' job, family, life satisfaction, employment and family balance, and stress. Additional research should compare perceptions to actual attitudes and behavior to determine which has the greater impact on these outcomes. Replicating this research with younger and older workers will also provide insight into whether this support is a unique midlife phenomenon or a general set of behaviors and attitudes in dual-career couples. This research should also be extended to different racial and ethnic groups, occupational categories, and geographical locations. In addition, the role of children in performing household chores and supporting their parents' careers should be considered.

Conclusion

Personal, relationship, and societal factors affect the way partners combine occupational and family roles (Gilbert, 1988, 1993). The extent of the husbands' contributions depends on factors such as the husbands' egos, the relative salaries of the spouses, their job mobility, the flexibility of their work situations, and the early socialization of husband and wife regarding the appropriate roles for each spouse. The current study suggested that wives' perceptions of their husbands' attitudes and behaviors about employment and family are important. It represents a next step in understanding the complex dynamics of dual-career families at midlife. The midlife professional women whom we interviewed were almost uniformly enthusiastic about the support they received from their husbands. This support facilitated their management of employment and family obligations. Although the nature of support varied, knowing that their husbands valued them and their careers helped them deal with the challenges of balancing the many facets of their lives.

References

Aldous, J., Mulligan, G. M., & Bjarnasin, R. (1998). Fathering over time: What makes the difference? *Journal of Marriage and the Family, 60,* 809–820.

Apter, T. (1995). *Secret paths: Women in the new midlife.* New York: Norton.

Barnett, R. C., & Baruch, G. K. (1987). Determinants of fathers' participation in the family work. *Journal of Marriage and the Family, 49,* 29–40.

Barnett, R. C., & Rivers, C. (1996). *She works/he works: How two-income families are happier, healthier, and better-off.* San Francisco: Harper San-Francisco.

Beck, B. (1998). Women and work: At the double. *Economist, 348,* S12–S16.

Benin, M. H., & Agostinelli, J. (1988). Husbands' and wives' satisfaction with the division of labor. *Journal of Marriage and the Family, 50,* 349–361.

Biernat, M., & Wortman, C. (1991). Sharing of home responsibilities between professionally employed women and their husbands. *Journal of Personality and Social Psychology, 60,* 844–860.

Blair, S. L. (1993). Employment, family, and perceptions of marital quality among husbands and wives. *Journal of Family Issues, 14,* 189–212.

Bonney, J. F., Kelley, M. L., & Levant, R. F. (1999). A model of fathers' behavioral involvement in child care in dual-earner families. *Journal of Family Psychology, 13,* 401–415.

Borysenko, J. (1996). *A woman's book of life: The biology, psychology, and spirituality of the feminine life cycle.* New York: Riverhead Books.

Cohen, C. E. (1994). The trailing-spouse dilemma. *Working Woman, 19,* 69–70.

Coverman, S. (1989). Women's work is never done: The division of domestic labor. In J. Freeman (Ed.), *Women: A feminist perspective* (pp. 356–368). Palo Alto, CA: Mayfield.

Cutrona, C., & Russell, D. (1990). Type of social support and specific stress: Toward a theory of optimal matching. In B. Sarason, I. Sarason, & G. Pierce (Eds.), *Social support: An Interactional View* (pp. 319–366). New York: John Wiley.

Denzin, N. K., & Lincoln, Y. S. (1998). Introduction: Entering the field of qualitative research. In N. K. Denzin & Y. S. Lincoln (Eds.), *Strategies of qualitative inquiry* (pp. 1–17). Thousand Oaks, CA: Sage.

Deutsch, F. M. (1999). *Halving it all: How equally shared parenting works.* Cambridge, MA: Harvard University Press.

Deutsch, F. M., Lussier, J. B., & Servis, L. J. (1993). Husbands at home: Predictors of paternal participation in childcare and housework. *Journal of Personality and Social Psychology, 65,* 1154–1166.

Ehrensaft, D. (1987). *Parenting together: Men and women sharing the care of children.* New York: Free Press.

Elloy, D. F., & Flynn, W. R. (1998). Job involvement and organization commitment among dual-income and single-income families: A multiple-site study. *Journal of Social Psychology, 138,* 93–101.

Gager, C. T. (1998). The role of valued outcomes, justifications, and comparison referents in perceptions of fairness among dual-earner couples. *Journal of Family Issues, 19,* 622–648.

Gilbert, L. A. (1985). *Men in dual-career families: Current realities and future prospects.* Hillsdale, NJ: Lawrence Erlbaum.

Gilbert, L. A. (1988). *Sharing it all: The rewards and struggles of two-career families.* New York: Plenum.

Gilbert, L. A. (1993). *Two careers/one family: The promise of gender equality.* Newbury Park, CA: Sage.

Gordon, J. R., & Whelan, K. S. (1998). Successful professional women in midlife: How organizations can more effectively understand and respond to the challenges. *Academy of Management Executive, 12,* 8–24.

Grambs, J. D. (1989). *Women over forty: Visions and realities.* New York: Springer.

Greenglass, E. R. (1993). Social support and coping of employed women. In B. C. Long & S. E. Kahn (Eds.), *Women, work and copying: A multidisciplinary approach to workplace stress* (pp. 215–239). Montreal, Canada: McGill-Queen's University Press.

Hammonds, K. H., & Palmer, A. T. (1998, September 21). The daddy trap. *Business Week, 3596,* 56–60.

Hertz, R. (1999). Working to place family at the center of life: Dual-earner and single-parent strategies. *Annals of the American Academy of Political and Social Science, 562,* 16–31.

Hewlett, S. A. (2002). Executive women and the myth of having it all. *Harvard Business Review, 80,* 66–72.

Jacobson, J. M. (1995). *Midlife women: Contemporary issues.* Boston: Jones and Bartlett.

James, J. B., & Liewkowicz, C. (1997). Themes of power and affiliation across time. In M. E. Lachman & J. B. James (Eds.), *Multiple paths of mid life development* (pp. 109–144). Chicago: University of Chicago Press.

Karambayya, R., & Reilly, A. H. (1992). Dual earner couples: Attitudes and actions in restructuring work for family. *Journal of Organizational Behavior, 13,* 585–601.

Kruger, A. (1994). The midlife transition: Crisis or chimera? *Psychological Reports, 75,* 1299–1305.

Kruger, P. (1998). The good news about working couples. *Parenting, 12,* 69.

Levinson, D. J. (1978). *The seasons of a man's life.* New York: Knopf.

Levinson, D. J. (1996). *The seasons of a woman's life.* New York: Knopf.

Manke, B., Seery, B. L., Crouter, A. C., & McHale, S. M. (1994). The three corners of domestic labor: Mothers, fathers, and children's weekday and weekend housework. *Journal of Marriage and the Family, 56,* 657–668.

Marshack, K. J. (1994). Copreneurs and dual-career couples: Are they different? *Entrepreneurship Theory and Practice, 19,* 49–69.

Marshall, C., & Rossman, G. B. (1999). *Designing qualitative research* (3rd ed.). Thousand Oaks, CA: Sage.

Marshall, J. (1994). Why women leave senior management jobs. In M. Tanton (Ed.), *Women in management: A developing presence* (pp. 185–201). London: Routledge.

Marshall, J. (1995). Working at senior management and board levels: Some of the issues for women. *Women in Management Review, 10,* 21–25.

Miles, M. B., & Huberman, A. M. (1994). *Qualitative data analysis.* Thousand Oaks, CA: Sage.

Murray, T. J. (1986). Checking out the new corporate wife. *Dun's Business Month, 128,* 50–51.

O'Connor, D., & Wolfe, D. M. (1991). From crisis to growth at midlife: Changes in personal paradigm. *Journal of Organizational Behavior, 12,* 323–340.

Pleck, J. (1997). Paternal involvement: Levels, sources, and consequences. In M. E. Lamb (Ed.), *The role of the father in child development* (3rd ed., pp. 66–103). New York: John Wiley.

Ponthieu, L., & Caudill, H. (1993). Who's the boss? Responsibility and decision making in copreneurial ventures. *Family Business Review, 6,* 3–17.

Potuchek, J. L. (1997). *Who supports the family? Gender and breadwinning in dual-earner marriages.* Stanford, CA: Stanford University Press.

Reid, J. D., & Willis, S. L. (1999). Middle age: New thoughts, new directions. In S. L. Willis & J. D. Reid (Eds.), *Life in the middle: Psychological and social development in middle age* (pp. 276–280). San Diego, CA: Academic Press.

Robinson, J. P., & Godbey, G. (1997). *Time for life: The surprising ways Americans use their time.* State College: Pennsylvania State University Press.

Rogers, S. J., & Amato, P. R. (2000). Have changes in gender relations affected marital quality? *Social Forces, 79,* 731–754.

Rosin, H. M. (1990). Consequences for men of dual career marriages: Implications for organizations. *Journal of Managerial Psychology, 5,* 3–8.

Shelton, B. A., & John, D. (1993). Does marital status make a difference? Housework among married and cohabiting men and women. *Journal of Family Issues, 14,* 401–423.

Spitze, G. D., & Waite, L. J. (1981). Wives' employment: The role of husbands' perceived attitudes. *Journal of Marriage and the Family, 45,* 117–124.

Strauss, A., & Corbin, J. (1990). *Basics of qualitative research: Grounded theory procedures and techniques.* Newbury Park, CA: Sage.

Suitor, J. J. (1991). Marital quality and satisfaction with the division of household labor across the family life cycle. *Journal of Marriage and the Family, 53,* 221–230.

Taylor, A. S., & Lounsbury, J. W. (1988). Dual-career couples and geographic transfer: Executives' reactions to commuter marriage and attitude toward the move. *Human Relations, 41,* 407–424.

U.S. Bureau of Labor Statistics. (2004). *Employment status of the population by sex and age.* Available at www.bls.gov/cps/home.htm

White, B. (1995). The career development of successful women. *Women in Management Review, 10,* 4–15.

Wicker, A., & Burley, K. (1991). Close coupling in work–family relationships: Making and implementing decisions in a new family business and at home. *Human Relations, 44,* 77–92.

Acknowledgment: We thank Mary Dunn and Peter Rivard for their assistance with the data analysis for this article.

Exercise for Article 30

Factual Questions

1. The researchers state that they are "particularly interested in studying professional women at midlife who are married, have children, but also have had enduring careers." What reason do they give for this interest?

2. The results of this study are based primarily on the women's responses to two questions. What is the first question?

3. The researchers indicate that securing a random sample would have been desirable but was unrealistic for what reason?

4. Why were all interviews conducted by only one of the authors (i.e., researchers)?

5. According to the researchers, why were younger and older women included in the sample?

6. What was the mean (average) age of the women in the sample?

7. In their conclusion, do the researchers conclude that the women were enthusiastic about the support they received from their husbands?

Questions for Discussion

8. The researchers provide "Background" for this study in lines 85–251. How helpful is this background in establishing the context for this study? Would the report of the study be as effective without the background material? Explain.

9. The researchers indicate that this study is an "exploratory study." Do you agree with this characterization? If yes, what could be done in future studies on this topic to make them more definitive? (See lines 66, 240, 253, and 310–311.)

10. In your opinion, is the process of coding the participants' responses described in sufficient detail? (See lines 315–351.)

11. The researchers describe interrater reliability in lines 337–351. In your opinion, how important is this information? Would it be a weakness of the report if this information were not given? Explain.

12. The women in this study had diverse occupations. Is this a strength of this study? Explain. (See Table 2.)

13. How helpful are the direct quotations of the words of the women in this study in helping you understand the results? Are there a sufficient number of quotations? Are there too many? Explain. (See lines 403–733.)

14. The researchers make suggestions for future research in lines 859–892. Do some of these seem more important than others? Explain.

Quality Ratings

Directions: Indicate your level of agreement with each of the following statements by circling a number from 5 for strongly agree (SA) to 1 for strongly disagree (SD). If you believe an item is not applicable to this research article, leave it blank. Be prepared to explain your ratings. When responding to criteria A and B below, keep in mind that brief titles and abstracts are conventional in published research.

A. The title of the article is appropriate.

    SA   5   4   3   2   1   SD

B. The abstract provides an effective overview of the research article.

    SA   5   4   3   2   1   SD

C. The introduction establishes the importance of the study.

    SA   5   4   3   2   1   SD

D. The literature review establishes the context for the study.

    SA   5   4   3   2   1   SD

E. The research purpose, question, or hypothesis is clearly stated.

    SA   5   4   3   2   1   SD

F. The method of sampling is sound.

    SA   5   4   3   2   1   SD

G. Relevant demographics (for example, age, gender, and ethnicity) are described.

    SA   5   4   3   2   1   SD

H. Measurement procedures are adequate.

    SA   5   4   3   2   1   SD

I. All procedures have been described in sufficient detail to permit a replication of the study.

    SA   5   4   3   2   1   SD

J. The participants have been adequately protected from potential harm.

    SA   5   4   3   2   1   SD

K. The results are clearly described.

    SA   5   4   3   2   1   SD

L. The discussion/conclusion is appropriate.

    SA   5   4   3   2   1   SD

M. Despite any flaws, the report is worthy of publication.

    SA   5   4   3   2   1   SD

Article 31

Exploring Young Adults' Perspectives
on Communication with Aunts

LAURA L. ELLINGSON
Santa Clara University

PATRICIA J. SOTIRIN
Michigan Technological University

ABSTRACT. Women are typically studied as daughters, sisters, mothers, or grandmothers. However, many, if not most, women are also aunts. In this study, we offer a preliminary exploration of the meaning of aunts as familial figures. We collected 70 nieces' and nephews' written accounts of their aunts. Thematic analysis of these accounts revealed nine themes, which were divided into two categories. The first category represented the role of the aunt as a teacher, role model, confidante, savvy peer, and second mother. The second category represented the practices of aunting: gifts/treats, maintaining family connections, encouragement, and nonengagement. Our analysis illuminates important aspects of aunts in family schema and kin keeping.

From *Journal of Social and Personal Relationships*, 23, 483–501.

Despite the tremendous proliferation in family forms, the popular image associated with "the family" is still overwhelmingly a heterosexual nuclear family with a husband, wife, and children (Garey & Hansen, 5 1998). Many family communication researchers, particularly feminists, are committed to honoring a plurality of family forms and relationships, for both ideological and pragmatic reasons because families that deviate from the idealized nuclear norm outnumber supposedly 10 normative families (Coontz, 2000). Kinship resources are important to many families, yet these resources have been understudied by family researchers (Johnson, 2000). Anecdotal evidence of the significance of kin exists, but modern studies demonstrate a decline 15 both in families' involvement with, and scholarly interest in, kinship ties (Johnson, 2000). We know little about the relationship between aunts and their nieces/nephews. Aunts are not nuclear family members, but neither are they obscure, distant relations. 20 They are typically a sibling from a parent's immediate family of origin. Traeder and Bennett (1998), in their popular tribute, claim that aunts are a crucial resource for maintaining and enriching family and community life, and provide anecdotal evidence of the importance 25 of aunts in family relations in family stories and everyday conversation.

Women are typically studied by family communication researchers as daughters, sisters, mothers, or grandmothers. Yet many, if not most, women in these 30 roles are also aunts. In this study, we explore the meaning of aunts as extended kin. We contend that the meanings of aunting have been ignored in favor of framing motherhood as women's essential role (e.g., O'Reilly & Abbey, 2000; Peington, 2004). As feminist 35 researchers, we seek not to idealize aunts or to essentialize them within a single, fixed identity. Instead, we intend to recognize the complexities of the roles aunts may play in their nieces' and nephews' lives. Our goal is to uncover patterns among nieces' and nephews' 40 experiences of relating to their aunts. We frame our thematic analysis by first offering a theoretical perspective on family communication and reviewing literature on kinship and kin keeping.

Theoretical Perspective
The traditional nuclear family model of family communication is "losing its ecological validity" due to 45 the proliferation of alternative family forms in modern society (Koerner & Fitzpatrick, 2002, p. 71). Koerner and Fitzpatrick suggest that theories of family communication "increasingly define family as a group of intimates who generate a sense of home and group identity 50 and who experience a shared history and a shared future" (p. 71). Transactional definitions are useful because they expand the boundaries of the family and therefore better reflect the tremendous variation in how families define themselves (Noller & Fitzpatrick, 55 1993). Jorgenson (1989) positions the family "as a system of relations that comes about as individuals define those relations in their everyday communication with another" (p. 28). Boundaries between households in 60 extended kin networks are porous and negotiable, rather than fixed or rule bound (Wellman, 1998). Hence, extended families may be understood as constituted through their communication as they mutually negotiate relationship norms. Our intention in this 65 study was to delineate the organized knowledge structures, or schemas, that nieces and nephews have for aunts. Koerner and Fitzpatrick (2002) proposed a theory of family communication that identified a hierarchy of relational schemas used by family members to inter-

70 pret their communication with other family members. Relational schemas consist of declarative and procedural knowledge and interpersonal scripts. Such schemas include information and beliefs concerning: "Intimacy, individuality, affection, external factors, conver-
75 sation orientation, and conformity orientation" (p. 88). Individuals cognitively process interactions with other family members by drawing upon relationship-specific schemas first (e.g., a sister's relationship to her younger brother). If a schema does not provide the in-
80 formation or insights necessary to interpret or address the family member's behavior or to form an appropriate response, the person then draws upon more general family relationship schemas. If family relationship schemas also prove insufficient, then an individual
85 family member draws upon general social schemas regarding relationships for information. It follows, then, that when nieces and nephews communicate with aunts and with others about aunts, they both rely on and construct schemas for who aunts are and how they
90 behave. These schemas develop through communication and, in turn, influence subsequent communication. Because knowledge contained in family relationship schemas influences family communication, it is imperative to understand such knowledge (Koerner &
95 Fitzpatrick, 2002).

Researchers suggested that the concept of family scripts also is helpful in exploring understanding of kinship roles and relationships. Family scripts "are mental representations that guide the role performance
100 of family members within and across contexts" (Stack & Burton, 1998, p. 408). In extended kin relationships, "kin-scripts" designate who is obligated or entitled within a particular network to perform types of kin-work tasks, when such tasks should be performed (kin-
105 time), and how the process of assigning kin-work should be handled (kin-scription) (Stack & Burton, 1998). We posit that underlying their extended family's kin-scripts, people have relationship schemas regarding the norms and expectations of aunts, as well as rela-
110 tionship-specific schema for particular aunts. Moreover, there are social level messages in the dominant U.S. culture about what it means to be or have an aunt (Sotirin & Ellingson, in press). Hence, perceived cultural norms will influence aunts' and nieces'/nephews'
115 schema for family communication (Koerner & Fitzpatrick, 2002).

Aunts and Kinship

Kinship and Kin Keeping

Garey and Hansen (1998) define kinship as a "system of rights and responsibilities between particular categories of people...'kinship' refers not only to bio-
120 logical or legal connections between people but also to particular positions in a network of relationships" (p. xviii). Cultures vary in the norms for determining who counts as kin, in the rights and responsibilities accorded to various types of kin, and in the degree to

125 which kinship association is voluntary (Wellman, 1998). Kinship networks may also change over time (Garey & Hansen, 1998). Aunts are part of the extended kinship network. Aunts can be either "consanguineal" kin (related biologically) or "affinal" (related
130 through marriage). In some families "fictive" kin are created by inducting people not biologically related into a network of kinship, such as calling one's mother's best friend "aunt" (Stack, 1974).

Researchers have demonstrated that women are the
135 primary "kin keepers" in extended families (Dill, 1998). This suggests the importance of aunts in establishing and maintaining relational bonds with nieces and nephews (Arliss, 1994) and implies that kin keeping is likely part of relationship-type schemas for aunts.
140 Kin keeping has been traditionally associated with feminine roles and remains largely the province of women, despite changing gender roles (Garey & Hansen, 1998). Feminist scholars rendered visible the unpaid work of women—including kin keeping—and
145 acknowledged its importance within a capitalist society that values only paid labor (di Leonardo, 1998). Moreover, feminists have reclaimed women's focus on kin networks as potential sources of personal satisfaction, empowerment, and, at times, vital material and emo-
150 tional resources (Gerstel & Gallagher, 1993). Juggled beside paid employment, housework, and child care, *kin work* involves "the collective labor expected of family centered networks across households and within them" (Stack & Burton, 1998, p. 408). Kin work in-
155 cludes such activities as child and dependent care, wage and nonwage labor, and relationship-maintaining communication, and tasks such as "visits, letters, telephone calls, presents, and cards to kin; the organization of holiday gatherings; the creation and maintenance of
160 quasi-kin relations" (di Leonardo, 1998, p. 420). Leach and Braithwaite (1996) found that kin keeping communication has five primary outcomes: providing information, facilitating rituals, providing assistance, maintaining family relationships, and continuing a previous kin
165 keeper's work.

Kin keepers are most likely to be mothers, aunts, or grandmothers (Leach & Braithwaite, 1996); and of course, mothers and grandmothers are also likely to be aunts within kinship networks. Many kinship studies
170 discuss mothers, grandmothers, and sisters without considering aunting. Rather, kin work is framed in terms of sisterhood or motherhood (e.g., di Leonardo, 1998). Thus the experience and meaning of an aunt's role is implied more than specified in research. Re-
175 search on communication among adult siblings and their spouses implicitly addresses communication with aunts when they focus on women's roles and sister relations (e.g., Cicirelli & Nussbaum, 1989). Given that sibling relationships among parents affect children's
180 perceptions of their relatives, aunts who are emotionally close to a child's parents are likely to be perceived as more integral in the child's experiences of family

life. At the same time, Troll (1985, as cited in Arliss, 1994) points out that conflicts among adult siblings obligate husbands and wives to distance themselves from their siblings, and such "family feuds" negatively impact relationships within the extended family including aunts, nieces, and nephews. Further, adult sisters who may have gone separate ways often become closer as they begin to follow parallel paths in life (marriage, children), providing material and emotional support for each other and renewing familial bonds (Arliss, 1994). Cicirelli and Nussbaum (1989) suggest that the association of women with feminine nurturing and expressiveness leads family members to turn to their sisters for support and aid as adults. This observation implies both the likelihood that aunts will be closer to their nieces and nephews if aunts and mothers find themselves on parallel life paths and that aunts may provide emotional and material support not only for their sisters and other adult family members but for their nieces and nephews as well. Sisters may work to make their respective children close to each other as cousins (di Leonardo, 1998).

Moreover, aunting schemas are likely to reflect other culturally significant female figures. The significance of "othermothers" (Collins, 2000) and "godmothers" in Black, Latino, and Native American child-rearing practices has been recognized and even celebrated and promoted as a model for White, mainstream American culture (see Clinton, 1996). Godmothers also are particularly important in Catholic communities (e.g., Italian-Americans, see di Leonardo, 1984; Mexican-Americans, see Falicov & Karrer, 1980), whose members choose godparents for their child as a crucial aspect of religious and cultural practice (Sault, 2001). Of course, "othermothers" and "godmothers" may or may not overlap the aunt, so despite the increased, often feminist-inspired, attention to such practices, there is not an explicit focus on aunts and aunting per se in this research. So although we may know where aunts are and that they are important within extended family configurations, we do not know much about how they communicatively enact those locations.

One topic in family communication where aunts are explicitly identified are studies of extended family configurations. Studies of extended family roles and practices generally focus on the following three themes: the extended family as a historically, racially, or ethnically identified familial form (the African American urban family, the traditional Latino family, or the immigrant Asian family; e.g., Stack, 1974); mapping extended family configurations (e.g., Galvin, Bylund, & Brommel, 2003) or family histories (e.g., Halsted, 1993); and the extended family as threatened by contemporary patterns of mobility, divorce, and nonfamilial commitments and identifications (Stone, 2000). These themes overshadow the particular communication characteristics and functions (as they constitute relationship-type schemas) of aunt–niece/nephew relationships.

Other types of kinship studies in which aunts appear are kinship foster care, kinship networks for immigrants, and family histories, all of which constitute kin keeping and thus are likely to be reflected in students' relationship schema for aunts. Studies of kinship foster care show that aunts are second only to grandmothers in numbers of kin who function voluntarily (although increasingly regulated and, in some states, compensated) as foster caregivers for children removed from their parents' custody (Davidson, 1997; Thorton, 1991). Research also explores the importance of kinship networks for new immigrants needing financial and social support. For instance, aunts featured prominently in the accounts of Mexican migrant women as they relocated, found work, and established households (Bastida, 2001). Finally, aunts often figure prominently in family stories (Wilmot, 1995), perhaps because family culture and lore are preserved and promulgated primarily by women (Stone, 2000). Stone holds that family stories define the family, providing rules for its enactment, identities for its members, and a shared memory and view of family and the world. For example, women report learning "commonplace" wisdom about relating to men from older women relatives, including aunts (Romberger, 1986).

Our goal in this project is to follow up on the allusions to the aunt in family scholarship by describing nieces' and nephews' family relational schemas for aunts. If kinship is constituted through communication rather than through biological and legal ties (Koerner & Fitzpatrick, 2002), then exploring how aunts are constructed in nieces' and nephews' communication is a good starting point for understanding the meaning of aunts in families. Further, this inquiry may shed light on the issue of choice and voluntary association with extended kin of various types: "Because the American kinship networks are flexible in their expectations, personal preferences can play a key role" in how the meaning of kin ties is negotiated (Johnson, 2000, p. 626). To these ends, we posed our research question: How do nieces and nephews describe communication with their aunts?

Method

Participants

Participants in this study were 70 undergraduate students enrolled in communication courses in a private university in the western U.S., a public university in the northern U.S., Midwest, and a public university in the southeast U.S. Our sample ranged in age from 18 to 27, with the vast majority being between 20 and 22 years of age (median age = 21, $M = 21.07$). Most participants self-identified as European American or White ($n = 51$), 4 as Latino/a, 4 as African American, 7 as Asian American, and 1 each as: from Kurdistan, biracial African American and White, Guyanese East Indian, and Ecuadorian Romanian. Most participants ($n = 52$) were female and 18 were male.

Data Collection and Analysis

Students in four courses were offered extra credit points to write a brief (typed) narrative in response to the statement, "Please describe communicating with one or more of your aunts." We consciously left the parameters of the response open by phrasing the prompt broadly. Participants were also asked to provide their age, sex, and ethnic/racial group. Responses were written outside of class over a 1- to 2-week span and returned to the course instructor.

We collected 70 responses that ranged in length from less than one double-spaced page to four pages, with an average of about two pages (154 pages of data). We used Owen's (1984) criteria for inductively deriving themes in our qualitative data: repetition, recurrence, and forcefulness. Repetition exists when the precise word or phrase is present across the data. Recurrence is present when different wording is used to express similar ideas. The third criterion, forcefulness, includes nonverbal cues that stress words or phrases (e.g., underlining, bolding, or italicizing text, one or more exclamation points, or all-caps for a word or phrase).

Thematic analysis began with the two authors independently reading the narrative data. We noted key words that repeated, recurrent ideas, and forceful words and phrases. We then independently inductively grouped repeated, recurrent, and forceful phrases into a set of preliminary themes. At that point, we discussed our themes and continually refined our inductive categorization until we were confident that our themes were coherent, inclusive, and saturated in data (Fitch, 1994). Finally, because our sample was predominantly female and European American, the first author inspected the responses from males and people of color and reviewed them to determine whether all themes were present and whether other critical ideas emerged within this subset of the data. After careful consideration, we judged that the male responses and person of color responses did not vary collectively from the larger sample, and there were no differences that could be attributed to gender or race. There was as much variation within these groups as there was between groups.

Results

We derived nine content themes from the data and divided them into two groups. The first group of themes focused on aunting roles, such as teacher, role model, confidante, savvy peer, and second mother. The second group focused on aunting practices, such as gifts/treats, maintaining family connections, encouragement, and nonengagement. We contend that these roles and practices collectively reflect nieces' and nephews' relationship-type schema for aunts.

Aunting Roles

Teacher. Participants indicated that their aunts taught them many skills. Aunts taught their niece/nephew everything from how to ride a bike, knit, and cook special meals, to running a successful business and the meaning of religion. Nieces/nephews depicted learning from an aunt as fun, particularly in comparison to school and to learning from parents. An Asian American woman wrote: "The reason why [my aunt] and I became more communicative was because she'd show me how to bake cakes and cookies. And I loved cooking, so this was a fun and good thing for us both." At times, an aunt may teach an appreciation or understanding of something rather than a specific skill or technique, for example, a European American male student reported, "[My aunt] got me started being a fan of Duke basketball, which I still am today." Or it may be appreciation of a serious topic, such as religious faith. As one European American woman student explained: "When I was confused about the Lord and my beliefs, [my aunt] took the time to explain things to me, and why faith is important." Other nieces/nephews described their aunts as preparing them for life by guiding them to become competent adults. One European American woman noted that her aunts "have helped me with a million lessons.... They have taken me college hunting, apartment searching, as well as [on] trips across the country so I could learn and live and see what this big world was made of." We understand teaching as conscious efforts by aunts to instill skills or attitudes in a niece/nephew. The next theme, role model, places more emphasis on nieces'/nephews' agency.

Role model. Aunts function as role models to their nieces/nephews when they serve as examples of how to be in the world. Participants reported that they looked to their aunts as models of proper behavior, religious devotion, wives, mothers, and successful career women. Aunts may embody appropriate or ideal actions, roles, and identities for their nieces and nephews. One European American woman wrote:

> She has been one of my greatest role models. Her work has taken her to many exciting places, and she is now the CEO of a nonprofit charity that offers services to families and children. She has accomplished so much in her life...and she has set a great example for women.

Clearly, this niece will benefit from her aunt's example when she begins her career. Aunts also provide role models for how to be aunts, of course. A European American woman explains how her aunt inspired her to be a good aunt to her niece. In this case, her sister "asked me to be [niece's] godmother...I am going to be the best aunt to that little girl. I hope that I can be as good an aunt to her as [my aunt] was to me." This niece considers her aunt to embody the standard for aunting that the niece wants to reach. The participant's sister's designation of her as a godmother adds a sense of formality and responsibility to the aunt role.

Several participants also noted that aunts can serve as negative role models, reinforcing to nieces/nephews what they do not want to be. One European American woman poignantly explained that she did not want to be like one of her aunts in whom there was

> 410 just always something missing—like she lacked a spirit, or vitality, that I seek in others. My uncle is hilarious— we get along great…but I think he kind of pushes her around. Not literally, but it is very clear who wears the pants in that relationship. I guess I always knew that, even when young, and I have always preferred strong, in-
> 415 dependent women.

This niece perceives her aunt's submissiveness to a dominating husband as a barrier to her connection with her aunt. The niece does not indicate disapproval of her uncle's behavior, and instead frames her lack of close-
420 ness with her aunt as due to her aunt's personality. While we found her placement of blame problematic, clearly the niece believes her aunt has nonetheless served a vital role in her life. That is, watching her aunt's life inspired the niece to think about the kind of
425 woman she wants to be and the type of relationships she wants to have. Another European American woman explains how her aunt went from being a posi- tive to a negative role model: "My aunt was my idol. As a young girl…she represented everything I thought
430 a woman should: Beauty and femininity. In my eyes— she was perfect…[Now] I truly have lost all respect for [her]…." As an adult, this niece understood that femi- nine behavior she found charming in her aunt as a small child—obsessive attention to hairstyling,
435 makeup, and other beauty regimes at the expense of being fiscally responsible, holding down a job, or maintaining healthy relationships—was irresponsible and reflected consistently poor judgment by her aunt. Clearly, aunts were powerful figures—both positive
440 and negative—to nieces and nephews.

Confidante/advisor. Many participants reported that the aunts with whom they were closest were those to whom they could talk easily, who listened carefully and sympathetically, and were trustworthy. One Euro-
445 pean American man was confident of his aunt's will- ingness to listen: "I know that if I ever need advice or financial help or just wanted someone to talk to for fun, my aunt would be absolutely thrilled that I chose her to call." These aunts functioned as important confidantes
450 and sources of good advice. The terms "nonjudgmen- tal" and "open minded" were repeated. The aunt func- tioned as a safe person to turn to when a mistake had been made or a tough decision needed to be faced, and advice was needed.
455 A key component of this theme is that nieces/nephews discussed with their aunts topics that they felt they could not approach with their parents. Participants reported that aunts were not as closely tied to them as were their parents, and that this differing
460 relational dynamic enabled aunts to help the niece/nephew without the emotional upheaval expected from their parents. In this sense, the aunt's third-party perspective enabled them to become ideal confidantes. The aunt knew both the niece/nephew and the parent,

465 and hence was in a good position to understand the nature of the problem, the personalities involved, and what steps would best address the problem. This "third- party" perspective was articulated by a European American man who offered an analysis of why he
470 could confide in his aunt:

> I have one small theory on why I'm so close to my aunt. She wasn't immediate family, so when I was introduced to her when I was 11 or so…I got to choose just how much I wanted to accept my aunt. It sort of took the fam-
> 475 ily part out of the equation…I don't trust a lot of people, and I don't really have that many close friends…I men- tion this because what I share with my aunt is really spe- cial.

Likewise, another European American man explained
480 that with his aunt, "Its [sic] almost like talking to a long-distance friend, your [sic] not afraid to really tell them anything because they are not present in your life, yet you still feel comfortable with them when they are around."
485 Sometimes the problem actually involved one or more parents. "When there is a huge family fight be- tween my mother and I, I would call [my aunt]," ex- plained one Asian American man. Other times, the issues involved sensitive topics. One European Ameri-
490 can woman explained: "If I need someone to talk to about taboo issues that my mom would slip into cardiac arrest over, I call [my aunt]." Confidante aunts can also be trusted to have integrity. A Latina described her aunt: "I can trust her with my problems— that she'll be
495 empathetic, loving, kind, nonjudgmental…not only will she be wonderful at providing wisdom…she'll also call it like she sees it, whether she thinks I'll like hear- ing it or not." For this niece, her aunt's willingness to express an unpopular opinion was taken as a sign of
500 her aunt's love and respect for her. While not all aunts fulfilled the role of confidante and advisor, aunts con- sidered by nieces/nephews to be "favorite," "the best," or "the aunt I am closest to" shared this role.

Savvy peer. This theme involves references to an
505 aunt who is closer in age to the respondent than other relatives. This youngest aunt is often the "coolest." That is, the aunt who is closest in age to her nieces/nephews is most often the one who was de- scribed as being able to identify with the niece/nephew,
510 being the most fun, giving the best gifts, and being the most able to understand the experiences of the niece/nephew. Age was frequently mentioned as the primary reason why the aunt shared many common interests. A European American man described the
515 nature of his conversations with his young aunt: "[My aunt] is quite a bit younger than my mother is and it seems like our conversations are more about the 'cooler' stuff in my life…she understands the vernacu- lar of kids in their early 20s." For this nephew, his aunt
520 speaks a language that his mother is unable or unwill- ing to speak. He perceived that he was comprehensible to his aunt because of her biological age. For a Guy-

anese/East Indian niece, her favorite aunt is much like herself:

525 The reason why I think my aunt is the coolest, is because she is not old fashion[ed] at all: she is outgoing, loves shopping, likes to be in style with the young girls and she fits in well. I also like that she has a lot of energy to keep up with me, we would often go out on Friday and Satur-
530 day night every week, and we don't get home until 5 a.m.

The ability to share common activities brings nieces/nephews closer to younger aunts. Of course, commonalities could also bring nieces and nephews together with older aunts, but participants' descriptions
535 strongly associated age similarity of an aunt with shared views and interests. An Asian American woman contrasted aunts who "are very old and very traditional and so they do not understand some of the things I do" to the youngest of her mother's sisters who "dresses
540 very fashionably and loves to party...I refer to her as my cool aunt who loves to have fun." Such aunts are seen as more like slightly older peers than like parents, and that perception appears to be critical to nieces'/nephews' views of their aunts. Aunts who were
545 kind and nurturing but who did not understand youth culture fit into the next theme, second mother.

Second mother. Participants described their nurturing aunts as a "second mother" and "like another mother to me," and described themselves as like an
550 aunt's child: "I'm her other daughter." A Kurdistan man stated that he often stayed at his aunts' homes where his aunts "were parents to me." An African American male said of one aunt, "I believe she looks at me as another son of her own," and of another aunt,
555 "We spent so much time together that she developed a 'mother's sense' (the sense that a mom 'just knows') and helped me through those tough times." Sometimes the second mother title was literal: the aunt had been instrumental in raising the niece/nephew. For example,
560 one European American woman related that her mother had been an unwed mother and was expected to give up her baby. A week before giving birth, her mother went to her sister's home to stay with her. She says of her mother's sisters: "My mom's sisters are my closest
565 aunts. They had a hand in raising me. They were my second mothers." Other aunts provided childcare for young nieces/nephews. A European American woman recalled that her aunt regularly provided childcare: "[My aunt] is my Godmother, and in a lot of ways, my
570 mother. She took very good care of me when I was a little girl and my mom was at work."

For other nieces/nephews, aunts provided a temporary home in times of trouble during their teen years. A Latina described her aunt's kindness in inviting her
575 niece to live with her "for a short period in high school when I wasn't getting along with my parents.... This was an important time in our relationship...a whole lot of bonding went on." This aunt allowed breathing room for her niece and the niece's parents until their differ-

580 ences could be resolved. For those months, she served as a mother to her niece. An Asian American niece has lived with her aunt throughout high school and college: "She acts on behalf of my mother who lives overseas; she is my guardian.... Basically, I treat her like another
585 mother." One European American male reported that he turned to his aunt for comfort during college:

I am closest to her because she was there for me when I first went away to college. I was homesick and she would pick me up and I would stay weekends at her house....
590 *Every* time I go to her house she makes a gourmet meal.... Whenever I go over to her house that room is "my room," and I love it, I feel like I have a home away from home.

In some ways, the second mother has an easier role
595 than the mother. As one European American woman succinctly put it: "To me, an aunt is like a mom, only they don't have to enforce the rules. They just give you guidance and direction but never have to punish you, so they always stay on your good side." Like the confi-
600 dante, the second mother has the benefit of a third-party perspective. From her position outside the parent–child relationship, she is able to nurture without having to be responsible for many parents' duties, particularly discipline.

Aunting Practices

605 Having explored the roles aunts play in their nieces'/nephews' lives, we now turn to specific practices that emerged in our data as central to participants' perceptions of aunts.

Gifts/treats. Nieces/nephews reported that gifts of-
610 fered tangible evidence of the quality of their relationships with aunts. Participants considered the receiving of holiday and birthday gifts that were appropriate to their age and interests to be signs of a caring aunt. Spontaneous gift giving and/or taking them for special
615 meals, trips, movies, or other activities that parents did not provide often were especially valued. Sometimes, the treat involves special foods; a Latina enthusiastically stated: "Every time I go to visit, she cooks for me—anything I want. She spoils me rotten!" An Asian
620 American male shared this memory of his aunt: "My greatest memory of [my aunt] was when I was still a little boy was when we went to [a local] park.... We would all bike around the park and then go to the museum." Other aunts allowed indulgences that parents
625 presumably did not. One European American female stated that her favorite aunt "often took us out to the movies or out to dinner...and shopping for toys. We went to Lake Tahoe every summer together. She would cook for us every night and let us eat junk food on the
630 beach."

Allowing such tame but "naughty" behavior was seen as a sign of affection and indulgence. Other aunts were prized because they indicated their understanding of a child's point of view, as in this example from a
635 European American man: "I remember going to a fam-

197

ily Christmas party and [aunt] was so cool, she was the only relative that got my brother and I completely separate gifts." As a little boy, having his own gift was meaningful, and the aunt who provided separate gifts was "cool" because she understood her nephews' desires. Conversely, receiving no gifts or gifts that reflected a lack of understanding of the niece's or nephew's personality (e.g., a doll given to a 16-year-old) were seen as signs of an aunt not caring enough to find out what the child likes.

Maintaining family connections. Aunts were key hubs in the networks of extended family kin. We were intrigued by the fact that virtually all participants—with no prompting—volunteered explanations of how their aunts were related to them through their mother's or father's family and the aunt's position in that family (e.g., younger or older than the participant's parent). For example, one European American man explained that he would discuss "my mother's sister...[my aunt] is the second oldest child in a family of seven. [My aunt] has two female children." Locating the aunt within the constellation of relationships was critical to understanding the relationship to the aunt. That is, as a nonnuclear family member, the aunt had to be accounted for. This is in contrast to participants' mentioning of their parents or siblings, who evidently needed no such kinship contextualization before they could be described.

Family gatherings also helped to maintain relationships. Nieces/nephews described family celebrations (e.g., Christmas, birthdays, Thanksgiving) as primary times for seeing aunts, particularly those who did not live nearby. The sharing of family rituals influenced the relationships of some nieces/nephews to their aunts. A Latina explained: "Tia [Spanish for 'aunt'] is the aunt that I know the best. Our family spent numerous holidays with her family." For others, family gatherings were the only occasions in which they interacted with aunts. Another Latina said of her mother's sister, "While all the other siblings moved on...[my aunt] stayed behind to take care of my grandparents.... I get to see her most because...when I go [to] visit my grandparents, [my aunt] is there." An Asian American woman explained how a family gathering provided her with an opportunity to converse with an aunt: "I went to a family gathering for my grandma's birthday. This was the first one I had gone to in a few years.... I got to talk to my aunt again and amazingly, we had a great conversation." Aunts were often strongly associated with family gatherings, whether as primary organizers of such events or as key participants. One Asian American woman explained that in Hawaii, women in the community, such as neighbors and parents' friends, are addressed as "aunty." She describes one aunty who has been her neighbor "since the day I was brought home from the hospital" as instrumental to organizing gatherings:

[My aunty] maintains very close relationships with all the kids in the cul-de-sac and is known as the "Party Coordinator." Ever since I can remember, Aunty has planned the neighborhood parties for Christmas, Easter, and summer.... So, if someone asked me how many people were in my family, I would not be able to give them an exact number because my family extends beyond my Mom and Dad, it consists of other special people...and aunties like my Aunty [name].

Finally, an African American woman told of attending her great-grandmother's 90th birthday party in a distant state and assumed she was invited to stay with her aunt. Upon her arrival, "I realized that my grandmother and uncle were staying with my great-grandparents, and I had just invited myself to [my aunt's] home.... She just laughed and said it was ok because I'm young and I'm family." Thus, family connections are facilitated by aunts whose presence, cooperation, and (often) hospitality fosters interaction and ritual celebrations among extended kin.

Encouragement. Participants described the aunts they liked as those who were very encouraging to them in school, sports, work, and other activities. Aunts' verbal encouragement appeared to significantly and positively influence nieces'/nephews' self-esteem. Sometimes this encouragement was a sense of being cherished. A Latina participant described her affectionate aunt: "My aunt is also demonstrative with her love for me. Not only does she make herself available when I need her but she lets me know how much she cares with her tender hugs and kisses." An African American nephew characterized aunts as increasing his self-worth: "I think that is the great thing about aunts: They make you feel good about yourself." A European American woman reported how much her aunt increased her self-confidence. She explained: "[My aunt] made me feel like queen of the world. I remember when she gave birth to my cousin Katie. I was only 8 and she let me hold her." By trusting in her niece to behave competently, this aunt demonstrated her faith in her young niece and made her feel special.

At the same time as making nieces/nephews feel good about themselves, aunts provide encouragement to do and be more. An African American man explained that: "My aunts love to 'push' all of their nephews and nieces toward success by any means necessary.... They are also big advocates of higher education. They have pushed my whole life." This participant attributed his educational success in part to his aunts' "pushing," and he valued their role in his success. Likewise, an African American woman explained that "when no one [in] the family thought I should leave home and got [sic] to college, [my aunt] supported the idea of me leaving and recommended it.... She [talked] with the rest of [my] family," and eventually the aunt persuaded her niece's parents to support her plan to attend college. Participants felt inspired by

750 their aunts' belief in them and appreciated their efforts to encourage them in their goals.

Nonengagement. Perhaps one of the most intriguing findings was the unapologetic way in which nieces/nephews expressed a lack of closeness with
755 some aunts. While examples of nonengagement were numerous, participants rarely stated that they perceived the lack of closeness as regrettable or problematic. We propose that this is an important difference between aunting and mothering: in the dominant U.S. culture,
760 reporting that one is not close to one's mother would seem to require some explanation, and perhaps be accompanied by an expression of regret, sadness, or anger. No such feelings are needed for lack of closeness to an aunt. For example, a European American woman
765 stated: "I'm not as close to [my aunts] as I am with my friends or cousins. They just kind of exist as relatives." A Latina described her communication with an aunt as fairly impersonal: "We tend to discuss more general, 'safe' topics rather than anything deeply per-
770 sonal...because I don't feel all that close to her." An Asian American woman reported that "I am not particularly close to any of my aunts, and do not look forward to talking to them. When I do, it is mostly for practical reasons or to be sociable.... This is not be-
775 cause I have a bad relationship with them, but that tends to be how [it is]."

The lack of closeness is just something to be accepted and not worried over. The matter-of-fact attitude toward lack of closeness with some aunts was
780 explained as due to lack of proximity that precluded frequent interaction. A European American man's explanation is representative: "As I was growing up I did not get many opportunities to see her, as I [was]...raised in [another state]. So as a result of this
785 distance, my relationship with [aunt] is not a very close one." Living close to an aunt did not necessarily entail great emotional attachment. However, more frequent interactions with their aunts did seem to relate to perceptions of them as meaningful figures in participants'
790 lives. While geographic distance recurred, no other consistent or cohesive reason was given for not being close to an aunt. Nieces and nephews listed personality traits they disliked, unfortunate events, and family patterns that led to or perpetuated nonengagement, but
795 such justifications were diverse, and we found no pattern among them.

Discussion

The themes reported here illustrate the roles (teacher, role model, confidante, savvy peer, and second mother) and practices (gifts/treats, family gather-
800 ings, encouragement, and nonengagement) of aunts as perceived by their nieces and nephews. Participants described how communication (or the lack thereof) with aunts is integral to their self-development and has significant impacts on their relationships and their
805 lives. While the relationship-specific schemas (Koerner & Fitzpatrick's first level of cognitive processing) necessarily varied among the nieces and nephews and the relationships with each of their aunts, central characteristics of a relationship-type schema (second level of
810 Koerner & Fitzpatrick's model) emerged. Taken together, the themes in our data point to four core aspects of a relational schema for aunts.

First, aunts are defined within the kin network but outside of the nuclear family. The biological, marital,
815 and/or fictive relationships that create both connection and "third-party" perspectives for aunts and their nieces/nephews are part of what made aunts powerful in their lives. That is, whether an aunt was wonderful, weird, dull, absent, or unpleasant, her position as non-
820 parent and nonsibling is an integral part of her identity *as an aunt.* Occupying a niche outside the nuclear family enables the aunt to avoid the deep identification, responsibility, and vulnerability of the parent–child bond that (ideally) leads both to closeness and to chil-
825 dren's need to rebel to establish their own identity. Perceived vulnerability is a critical factor in an individual's decisions over what information to disclose to others (Petronio, 2002). Thus, it follows that nieces and nephews are likely to feel less vulnerable with aunts
830 than with parents.

Aunts usually are free from the burden of imposing everyday rules, and nieces and nephews need not separate themselves from their aunt in order to establish their independence. Hence, aunts may make ideal con-
835 fidantes for nieces and nephews who do not wish to discuss sensitive issues with their parents, and fun and indulgent time spent with aunts does not threaten a child's sense of having a stable and secure home. Likewise, lack of attention from an aunt generally is
840 unlikely to wound a child, certainly not to the degree that rejection by a parent would, and a niece's or nephew's choice to not engage with a particular aunt was generally not problematic. Thus to be structurally apart from the nuclear family was to enjoy a greater
845 degree of flexibility in determining the relationship-specific schema for each aunt-niece/nephew relationship. Multiple ways of enacting roles and practices fit within the boundaries of aunt schemas. Unlike motherhood, the successful performance of which generally is
850 circumscribed within the boundaries of a full-time nurturer of children (e.g., Rich, 1977; Trebilcot, 1984), the aunt can be successful as an aunt in a multiplicity of ways. Enacting the role of nurturer (second mother) is acceptable, but so is visiting just once a year, mailing
855 cards or gifts without regular visits, briefly interacting at family gatherings, or engaging in a fun, peer relationship.

Second, the benefits of the relationship are almost entirely unidirectional, focusing on the aunt as fulfill-
860 ing the needs and desires of the niece or nephew, with no implicit or explicit reciprocity. Nieces and nephews told of learning skills from their aunts but not teaching their aunts, confiding in their aunts but not of being

confidantes for them, receiving gifts and encouragement from aunts, but not of giving to them, and so on.
From college-age nieces' and nephews' perspective,
the role of aunt is that of a giver rather than a receiver
of care and support. This phenomenon is likely related
to the age difference between nieces and nephews who
participated in this study and their aunts; reciprocity
may increase over time as nieces and nephews leave
college, assume adult responsibilities (e.g., full-time
work), and grow older.

Third, the aunt relationship-type schema included
passing on of a wide range of knowledge from aunts to
nieces and nephews. This knowledge included specific
skills, religious beliefs, family lore and traditions, and
broader knowledge of the world. Knowledge was
transmitted through direct instruction and interpersonal
conversations, but also more diffusely through role
modeling, such as when nieces/nephews sought to
emulate aunts' career paths.

Fourth, when the previous two conditions were met
(i.e., aunts focused on the nieces'/nephews' needs,
knowledge was passed on), the communication involved in the aunt–niece/nephew relationship fostered
(and in turn was fostered by) a sense of closeness to the
aunt. The word "close" was invoked again and again to
describe participants' feelings toward their aunts. Many
emphasized that a close relationship was maintained
despite geographical distance, busy schedules, and
other obstacles. Aunts with whom the niece or nephew
was not engaged (whether by conscious choice or circumstances) were labeled "not close" relationships and
accepted as such. The nonengagement of (some) aunts
in their nieces' and nephews' lives should not be dismissed as a failure or an unacknowledged kinship tie.
Limited, infrequent, or even no contact between aunts,
nieces, and nephews is not necessarily negative or a
violation of the aunt schema. Nieces and nephews
stated their lack of involvement matter of factly, expressing no discomfort about revealing the lack of a
close tie with a given aunt.

We posit that these four aspects constitute an exploratory relationship-type schema that may be useful
in understanding how nieces and nephews engage in
cognitive processing regarding interactions with (and
about) their aunts (Koerner & Fitzpatrick, 2002). While
there is variation among our participants, there were
also several prominent themes that suggest that U.S.
culture reflects some shared commonalities in the understandings of and enactment of aunting.

Limitations

This study was limited in several ways. Our participants included a convenience sample of undergraduate
students. Families whose members are enrolled in college may have different expectations for aunts than
those whose members have not attended college, particularly poor and immigrant communities. Also, the
age range of participants reflects one life stage: young
adulthood. In some ways, this is an ideal group to
study, for whom childhood was recent enough to be
easily recalled and for whom going to college made
shifts in familial relationships and roles more immediate and evident. However, future research should explore niece/nephew perspectives on aunts across the
lifespan. Our findings also reflect predominantly European Americans and females. Clearly, more research is
required to locate potential gender and ethnic/racial
group understandings of aunts. Finally, the study focused on communication with aunts solely from the
perspective of nieces and nephews. Of course, aunts'
perspectives must be incorporated into our understanding of aunting in order to construct a more complex
rendering of these roles and relationships. Ideally,
matched pairs of aunts and nieces or nephews could
shed light on how the perceptions of aunts reflect
and/or vary from those of their nieces/nephews.

Implications and Conclusion

Several implications of our findings are relevant to
research on communication within family and kin networks. First, aunts embody a great deal of flexibility in
their enactment of acceptable roles and practices, and
we recognize and celebrate flexibility within this gen-
dered construct. Despite changing social gender roles,
women's roles in the home and family too often are
circumscribed within narrow parameters of appropriate
(feminine) behavior (e.g., Coontz, 2000; Wood, 2002).
Aunts, nieces, and nephews are making choices of how
to communicate together, and we suggest that the range
of behavior reported here reflects openness to privileg-
ing the needs and desires of each niece/nephew and
aunt dyad over those of a perceived social standard.
While most of the communication and behavior reported here is hardly radical or unusual, the ability for
nieces and aunts to choose a variety of ways of interacting with a variety of aunts reflects a truly transactional definition of a family relationship constituted in
interaction rather than dictated by legal or biological
ties (Noller & Fitzpatrick, 1993). Such a pseudo-aunt
model of flexibility could be instructive or even inspi-
rational to those adapting to new family forms, such as
blended families (e.g., Braithwaite, Olson, Golish,
Soukup, & Turman, 2001).

Our study also contributes to studies of extended
families and kinship. Aunts' kin-keeping work reported
here is consistent with previous studies' findings that
many women put significant effort into kin keeping
(e.g., Dill, 1998). It also suggests that while the recent
trend away from studying extended kin may reflect
declining interest in maintaining kinship relationships,
that also may not be the case. Johnson (2000) proposed
that studies that find declining instances of kin keeping
may suffer from methodological flaws that focus on
sustained interaction and thus fail to consider contemporary means of maintaining close ties over large geographical distances and within increased nuclear family

mobility. Our findings support that critique, as our participants clearly recognized and valued aunts' kinkeeping work and participation in rituals, gatherings, and long-distance communication.

980   Our third implication concerns the lack of reciprocity of nieces/nephews toward meeting aunts' needs or desires. We believe that the almost complete lack of reciprocity reported is a function of the age of our participants. As college students, they appear to have not
985   yet assumed the role expectations of adults, and remain self-focused, as is characteristic of children. Preliminary data analysis of interviews with aunts, nieces, and nephews indicates that at least some adult nieces and nephews feel an obligation and/or take pleasure in ma-
990   terially and emotionally giving to their aunts (Sotirin & Ellingson, 2006). Some research has shown cultural differences in this area of kinship; in African American families, for example, nieces and nephews were considered by their elderly aunts and uncles to be impor-
995   tant family members and the latter reported receiving assistance from them, while elderly Whites reported no expectations of assistance from siblings' children (Johnson & Barer, 1995). Clearly, more research is needed on how aunt–niece/nephew relationships
1000   change over time.

    Finally, we note that none of the participants mentioned popular culture images of aunts. Given Koerner and Fitzpatrick's (2002) position that cultural messages about relationships influence the formation and main-
1005   tenance of family relationship schemas, we anticipated that nieces and nephews might compare their aunts to popular figures, perhaps claiming that an aunt was cruel like *Harry Potter*'s Aunt Petunia or very kind and maternal, like *Andy Griffith*'s Aunt Bea. Such was not
1010   the case, indicating that at least in this exploratory study nieces and nephews made no conscious associations between their own experiences with aunts and those in the media. Future research should seek to determine what, if any, relationships exist between rela-
1015   tionship-type schemas for aunts and cultural messages about aunts.

    Our findings support the value of inquiry into aunts, family relationship schemas, and kin keeping. While the practices and functions of family communication
1020   and kinship may be changing, extended family such as aunts remain vital aspects of many people's lives. As Gerstel and Gallagher (1993) suggest, "contemporary extended family does not simply persist. Someone expends a great deal of time and energy to maintain it"
1025   (p. 598). That many aunts, nieces, and nephews are expending time and energy with each other is significant to our scholarly understanding of contemporary extended family networks and certainly warrants further study.

References

Arliss, L. P. (1994). *Contemporary family communication: Meanings and messages*. New York: St. Martin's Press.

Bastida, E. (2001). Kinship ties of Mexican migrant women on the United States/Mexico border. *Journal of Comparative Family Studies, 32*, 549–569.

Braithwaite, D. O., Olson, L. N., Golish, T. D., Soukup, C., & Turman, P. (2001). "Becoming a family": Developmental processes represented in blended family discourse. *Journal of Applied Communication Research, 29*, 221–247.

Cicirelli, V., & Nussbaum, J. (1989). Relationships with siblings in later life. In J. Nussbaum (Ed.), *Life-span communication: Normative processes* (pp. 283–299). Hillsdale, NJ: Lawrence Erlbaum.

Clinton, H. (1996). *It takes a village: And other lessons children teach us*. New York: Simon & Schuster.

Collins, P. H. (2000). *Black feminist thought: Knowledge, consciousness and the politics of empowerment*. New York: Routledge.

Coontz, S. (2000). *The way we never were: American families and the nostalgia trap* (revised ed.). New York: Basic Books.

Davidson, B. (1997). Service needs of relative caregivers: A qualitative analysis. *Families in Society, 78*, 502–510.

di Leonardo, M. (1984). *The varieties of ethnic experience: Kinship, class, and gender among California Italian-Americans*. Ithaca, NY: Cornell University Press.

di Leonardo, M. (1998). The female world of cards and holidays: Women, families, and the work of kinship. In K. V. Hansen & A. I. Garey (Eds.), *Families in the U.S.: Kinship and domestic politics*. Philadelphia: Temple University Press.

Dill, B. T. (1998). Fictive kin, paper sons, compadrazgo: Women of color and the struggle for family survival. In K. V. Hansen & A. I. Garey, (Eds.), *Families in the U.S.: Kinship and domestic politics* (pp. 431–445). Philadelphia, PA: Temple University Press.

Falicov, C. J., & Karrer, B. M. (1980). Cultural variations in the family life cycle: The Mexican-American family. In E. A. Carter & M. McGoldrick (Eds.), *The family life cycle: A framework for family therapy* (pp. 383–425). New York: Gardner Press.

Fitch, K. L. (1994). Criteria for evidence in qualitative research. *Western Journal of Communication, 58*, 32–38.

Fitzpatrick, M. A., & Vangelisti, A. L. (Eds.). (1995). *Explaining family interactions*. Thousand Oaks, CA: Sage Publications.

Galvin, K. M., Bylund, C. L., & Brommel, B. J. (2003). *Family communication: Cohesion and change*. Boston, MA: Allyn & Bacon.

Galvin, P. J., & Cooper, P. J. (2000). *Making connections: Readings in relational communication*. Los Angeles: Roxbury.

Garey, A. I., & Hansen, K. V. (1998). Introduction: Analyzing families with a feminist sociological imagination. In K. V. Hansen & A. I. Garey (Eds.), *Families in the U.S.: Kinship and domestic politics* (pp. xv–xxi). Philadelphia, PA: Temple University Press.

Gerstel, N., & Gallagher, S. K. (1993). Kin keeping and distress: Gender, recipients of care, and work–family conflict. *Journal of Marriage and the Family, 55*, 598–607.

Halsted, I. (1993). *The aunts*. Boston, MA: Sharksmouth Press.

Hansen, K. V., & Garey, A. I. (1998). *Families in the U. S.: Kinship and domestic politics*. Philadelphia, PA: Temple University Press.

Johnson, C. L. (2000). Perspectives on American kinship in the later 1990s. *Journal of Marriage and the Family, 62*, 623–639.

Johnson, C. L., & Barer, B. M. (1995). Childlessness in late life: Comparisons by race. *Journal of Cross Cultural Gerontology, 9*, 289–306.

Jorgenson, J. (1989). Where is the "family" in family communication?: Exploring families' self-definitions. *Journal of Applied Communication Research, 17*, 27–41.

Koerner, A. F., & Fitzpatrick, M. A. (2002). Toward a theory of family communication. *Communication Theory, 12*, 70–91.

Leach, M. S., & Braithwaite, D. O. (1996). A binding tie: Supportive communication of family kin keepers. *Journal of Applied Communication Research, 24*, 200–216.

Noller, P., & Fitzpatrick, M. A. (1993). *Communication in family relationships*. Englewood Cliffs, NJ: Prentice Hall.

O'Reilly, A., & Abbey, S. (Eds.). (2000). *Mothers and daughters*. Lanham, MD: Rowman & Littlefield.

Owen, W. F. (1984). Interpretive themes in relational communication. *Quarterly Journal of Speech, 70*, 274–287.

Peington, B. A. (2004). The communicative management of connection and autonomy in African American and European American mother-daughter relationships. *Journal of Family Communication, 4*, 3–34.

Petronio, S. (2002). *The boundaries of privacy: Dialectics of disclosure*. New York: SUNY Press.

Rich, A. (1977). *Of woman born: Motherhood as experience and institution*. New York: Bantam Books.

Romberger, B. V. (1986). "Aunt Sophie always said....": Oral histories of the commonplaces women learned about relating to men. *American Behavioral Scientist, 29*, 342–367.

Rosenthal, C. S. (1985). Kin keeping in the familial division of labor. *Journal of Marriage and the Family, 47*, 965–974.

Sault, N. L. (2001). Godparenthood ties among Zapotec women and the effects of Protestant conversion. In J. W. Dow & A. R. Sandstrom (Eds.), *Holy saints and fiery preachers: The anthropology of Protestantism in Mexico and Central America* (pp. 117–146). Westport, CT: Praeger.

Sotirin, P., & Ellingson, L. L. (2006). The "other" woman in family life: Aunt/niece/nephew communication. In K. Floyd & M. Morman (Eds.), *Under-studied family relationships* (pp. 81–99). Thousand Oaks, CA: Sage Publications.

Sotirin, P., & Ellingson, L. L. (in press). Rearticulating the aunt in popular culture. *Cultural Studies.*

Stack, C. (1974). *All our kin.* New York: BasicBooks.

Stack, C. B., & Burton, L. M. (1998). Kinscripts. In K. V. Hansen & A. I. Garey (Eds.), *Families in the U.S.: Kinship and domestic politics* (pp. 405–415). Philadelphia, PA: Temple University Press.

Stone, L. (2000). *Kinship and gender: An introduction.* Boulder, CO: Westview Press.

Thorton, J. (1991). Permanency planning for children in kinship foster homes. *Child Welfare, 5,* 593–601.

Traeder, T., & Bennett, J. (1998). *Aunties: Our older, cooler, wiser friends.* Berkeley, CA: Wildcat Canyon Press.

Trebilcot, J. (Ed.). (1984). *Mothering: Essays in feminist theory.* Lanham, MD: Rowman & Littlefield.

Troll, L. E. (1985). *Early and middle adulthood.* Pacific Grove, CA: Brooks/Cole.

Wellman, B. (1998). The place of kinfolk in personal community networks. In K. V. Hansen & A. I. Garey (Eds.), *Families in the U.S.: Kinship and domestic politics* (pp. 231–239). Philadelphia, PA: Temple University Press.

Wilmot, W. (1995). The relational perspective. In *The relational communication reader* (pp.1–12). New York: McGraw-Hill.

Wood, J. T. (2002). "What's a family, anyway?" In J. Stewart (Ed.), *Bridges not walls: A book about interpersonal communication* (pp. 375–383). New York: McGraw-Hill.

Address correspondence to: Laura L. Ellingson, Communication Department, Santa Clara University, Santa Clara, CA 95053. E-mail: lellingson@scu.edu

Exercise for Article 31

Factual Questions

1. According to the literature review, how is the term "kinship" defined?

2. What is the research question posed by the researchers?

3. What was the median age of the participants?

4. Of the 70 participants, how many were female?

5. In analyzing the data, the researchers used Owen's (1984) criteria. What were the criteria?

6. What is a key component of the theme of "confidante/advisor"?

Questions for Discussion

7. The researchers refer to themselves as "feminist researchers." Speculate on the meaning of this term. (See lines 34–35.)

8. The sample was heterogeneous in terms of racial and ethnic background. If you had conducted this study would you have used a heterogeneous sample or a homogeneous one (e.g., only European Americans)? (See lines 289–294, 327–337, and 926–929.)

9. Is it important to know that the researchers *independently* read and *independently* grouped responses into themes? Explain. (See lines 318–323.)

10. The researchers used a "convenience sample." What is your understanding of the meaning of this term? Could the fact that it was a convenience sample affect the validity of the results? Explain. (See lines 913–915.)

11. What is your opinion on the researchers' suggestion for using matched pairs of aunts and nieces or nephews in future research on this topic? (See lines 934–937.)

12. If you had planned this study, would you have opted to use qualitative *or* quantitative methodology (*or* both)? Explain.

Quality Ratings

Directions: Indicate your level of agreement with each of the following statements by circling a number from 5 for strongly agree (SA) to 1 for strongly disagree (SD). If you believe an item is not applicable to this research article, leave it blank. Be prepared to explain your ratings. When responding to criteria A and B below, keep in mind that brief titles and abstracts are conventional in published research.

A. The title of the article is appropriate.

SA   5   4   3   2   1   SD

B. The abstract provides an effective overview of the research article.

SA   5   4   3   2   1   SD

C. The introduction establishes the importance of the study.

SA   5   4   3   2   1   SD

D. The literature review establishes the context for the study.

SA   5   4   3   2   1   SD

E. The research purpose, question, or hypothesis is clearly stated.

SA   5   4   3   2   1   SD

F. The method of sampling is sound.

SA   5   4   3   2   1   SD

G. Relevant demographics (for example, age, gender, and ethnicity) are described.

SA   5   4   3   2   1   SD

H. Measurement procedures are adequate.

SA   5   4   3   2   1   SD

I. All procedures have been described in sufficient detail to permit a replication of the study.

SA   5   4   3   2   1   SD

J. The participants have been adequately protected from potential harm.

SA   5   4   3   2   1   SD

K. The results are clearly described.

SA   5   4   3   2   1   SD

L. The discussion/conclusion is appropriate.

SA   5   4   3   2   1   SD

M. Despite any flaws, the report is worthy of publication.

SA   5   4   3   2   1   SD

Article 32

The Voices of Black and White Rural Battered Women in Domestic Violence Shelters

APRIL L. FEW
Virginia Polytechnic Institute and State University

ABSTRACT. Very little research has examined the experiences of black and white rural battered women. In this exploratory study of 88 participants, 30 rural battered women who sought assistance from domestic violence shelters in southwest Virginia were interviewed. Black and white rural women's experiences in the shelters, help-seeking, and perceived social support during and after their stay in the shelter were compared. Future research directions and suggestions to improve services are presented.

From *Family Relations, 54,* 488–500. Copyright © 2005 by the National Council on Family Relations. Reprinted with permission.

Background and Significance: Rurality and Domestic Violence

According to the U.S. Census Bureau (2000), more than 24% of U.S. residents live in rural areas. However, despite an increasing body of research on domestic violence, few research studies focus on domestic
5 violence in rural settings (Van Hightower, Gorton, & DeMoss, 2000). Much of the research on battered women is conducted with samples from urban and college populations, rendering the experiences of rural battered women practically invisible (Van Hightower
10 & Gorton, 2002; Van Hightower, Gorton, & DeMoss, 2000; Websdale, 1995, 1998). This lack of attention to domestic violence in rural communities may result, in part, from existing perceptions and myths about the "idyllic, tranquil, and nonviolent life in rural communi-
15 ties" (Krishnan, Hilbert, & Pase, 2001, p. 2). Yet research debunks this myth and has consistently found that domestic violence is as prevalent in rural areas as it is in urban areas (Websdale, 1995).

Scholarship on domestic violence in rural areas is
20 necessary as there is some evidence that women in rural contexts face unique barriers in terms of accessing help. Beliefs and values are elements of the rural culture that impact women's experience with violence as well as their helpseeking practices. For example,
25 domestic violence research in rural Kentucky (Websdale, 1995, 1998) and rural Appalachia (Gagne, 1992) indicates that residents of rural communities generally hold patriarchal views of the family, tradi-
30 tional sex-role ideologies, strong religious values, and conventional beliefs about privacy. These beliefs, rules, and values, in turn, promote gender inequality, failure to report incidents to police, and potentially undermine intervention when it does occur (Websdale, 1998; Wendt, Taylor, & Kennedy, 2002).

35 In addition to challenges in rural life with regard to values and beliefs that make it difficult for rural battered women to seek help, rural battered women also often face logistic barriers. Rural residence is an isolating factor that can reduce access to domestic violence
40 services and contribute to the perpetuation of battering (Van Hightower et al., 2000). Physical isolation can allow battering to go on without neighbors being aware of the violence, and access to services can be challenging in rural areas where shelters may be located many
45 miles away from the battered wife who seeks services.

The overall inattention given to domestic violence in rural settings extends to minority women. This is a particularly glaring omission, given that blacks are the largest minority group (i.e., 4.1 million) living in rural
50 areas, and rural counties with high concentrations of blacks frequently are characterized by a greater degree of economic disadvantage, higher rates of family violence, and lower availability of and access to community services than white rural counties (Whitener, Jen,
55 & Kassel, 2004).

For black women in rural communities, racial status in and of itself can be an isolating factor contributing to their victimization and further compromising intervention. For example, McNair and Neville (1996) sug-
60 gested that institutional racism and blacks' historical distrust of social services and mental health facilities were reasons for blacks' underuse of the domestic violence shelters. In addition, Wilson, Cobb, and Dolan (1987) found that rural black women were often un-
65 aware that domestic violence shelters even existed in their community. They conducted a study to assess a domestic violence shelter's success in reaching black clients in rural Virginia communities. They surveyed black workshop participants and found that 70% of the
70 respondents reported that they did not know about the existence of a local domestic violence shelter, yet 95%

reported either having experienced or knowing someone who had experienced domestic violence.

The Importance of Domestic Violence Shelters

75　Research indicates that shelters are beneficial for many women and shelter stays dramatically reduce the likelihood of new violence (Berk, Newton, & Berk, 1986; Davis & Srinivasan, 1995; Roberts & Lewis, 2000). Battered women have also credited shelters for helping them secure employment, further their educa-
80　tion, and lead healthier lives (Brown, Reedy, Fountain, Johnson, & Dichiser, 2000; Gordon, 1996). Shelter staff is credited for providing a safe environment, effectively manning crisis telephone lines, maintaining emotional ties to and community resources for former
85　residents, and training other professionals who service battered women (Davis, Hagan, & Early, 1994; Johnson, Crowley, & Sigler, 1992; Tutty, Weaver, & Rothery, 1999).

　For many women and their children, shelters pro-
90　vide a reprieve from the violence in their lives. Domestic violence shelters seem to be a primary resource for women seeking safety from violent intimate partners (Tutty et al., 1999), yet very few studies examine the efficacy of domestic violence shelters in assisting rural
95　battered women to make the transition back into their communities and families (Van Hightower & Gorton, 2002; Websdale, 1998). Further, as previously noted, very little is known about black battered women in rural communities who seek shelter. There is some
100　evidence that abused black women may seek help more frequently from their social support networks (i.e., family and friends) before seeking help from police or shelters (Few & Bell-Scott, 2002; West, 2003). Thus, it seems that the nuances of rural social life are linked to
105　the underuse of shelters (Websdale, 1995, 1998). There is also concern that for black rural women, racism can be an additional isolating factor contributing to this underuse (McNair & Neville, 1996). In their effort to increase the participation of black clients in domestic
110　violence shelters, Wilson et al. (1987) reported that culturally specific training and community volunteers were key in bridging the gap between shelters and black communities. Respondents described the shelter staff and community volunteers as credible transmitters
115　of information about alternatives to domestic violence and positive role models because they shared similar (e.g., racial/ethnic, rurality) background and personal experiences. These studies highlight how race/ethnicity matters in the rural context in terms of accessibility to
120　community resources and personal empowerment.

Study Purpose: Using a Feminist Lens

　Feminist scholars have underlined the importance of linking the personal with the political in research and advocacy (Jackson, 1998; Young, 1997). From a feminist perspective, the choices made by abused
125　women are political acts, and their personal narratives are political testimonies. Both Harding (1987) and Thompson (1992) have suggested that feminist research is done for women and "acknowledges women as active agents in their own lives, even if not within
130　the conditions of their own making" (Thompson, p. 6). Harding also asserted that our research questions need to come out of women's experiences; thus, using the experiences of women within research should allow women to understand themselves and provide them
135　with the explanations and insights that they need to become more self-empowered.

　Feminist theory is particularly applicable to the present study because it emphasizes how structural and cultural contexts inform the social construction of gen-
140　der and advocate for policies and programs that are responsive to women's needs and interests (Thompson & Walker, 1995). A feminist framework informs our understanding of the rural context in which abused women have to negotiate and the barriers to receiving
145　help that are inherent in such a context. Further, feminism contextualizes women's helpseeking and shelter experiences. Helpseeking can be viewed as a dimension of coping used to deal with personal and emotional crises, buffering the negative effects of traumatic
150　life events (Kaukinen, 2002). It may include talking to family, friends, police, and shelter hotlines to process a crisis.

　One aim of the present study was to learn more about how women seek help, reflect back on their ex-
155　periences, and generate ideas that can help abused women facing similar challenges to transition more successfully out of the shelter. A second aim of the present study was to explore "shelter culture" in greater depth. Shelter culture encompasses the extent to which
160　shelter staff followed standard operating procedures and helped the women feel safe, and also includes cultural differences that might have emerged and caused conflict among the staff and residents. For example, I wondered if rural ethnic women felt isolated in the
165　shelter because other ethnic women were not present in the shelter, if resource materials offered reflected ethnic women and their social networks, or if ethnic women experienced overt or covert racism by staff or other residents. I was also curious as to whether ethnic
170　women had difficulty negotiating the politics of intersectionality (i.e., race, class, gender, region, age) while existing in a vulnerable state—healing from the violence in their lives. In this descriptive study, a forum is provided for women to share their interpretations of
175　experiences in shelters and in their communities and to provide suggestions to improve shelter services for future patrons. It is in this sense, by sharing parts of their lives, that study participants are indeed activists.

Research Questions

　The present study explores domestic violence and
180　shelter culture through descriptions of black and white rural women's helpseeking practices and experiences in shelters in hopes of assisting human service provid-

ers in constructing and augmenting intervention programs to better accommodate the needs of diverse, rural, battered women. Through a feminist lens, the personal narratives of 30 women were interpreted to discern similarities and differences in two contexts—outside and within the shelter environment.

The following research questions guided the study:

1. Are there differences in how black and white battered rural women seek and receive help from their social networks and community?
2. How do battered rural women describe their experiences in domestic violence shelters?
3. What are battered rural women's perceptions of the efficacy of shelter staff and services?

Method

Procedures

Eighteen shelters in southwest Virginia were contacted to request their assistance with this project. Fourteen of 18 domestic violence shelters agreed to participate and to have caseworkers or other staff personnel solicit current and former residents to participate in our project.

Interview procedures. Shelter caseworkers were given a brief description of the study and instructions to read to women who might be interested in participating in this study. The caseworkers notified the research team when women agreed to be interviewed and scheduled the interviews with the women to take place at the shelter. In this way, the caseworkers were able to control our access to women and any disruption to the daily routines of staff and residents. Thirty women were interviewed for at least 2 hr. A semistructured list of questions guided the interview. The questions addressed helpseeking behaviors, experiences in the shelter environment, and suggestions to improve the efficacy of shelters in assisting the women to transition back into the community and their families.

The research team, which consisted of the author and trained graduate students, interviewed women only after they signed a consent form and completed a survey that assessed the types of violence the women received from their abusive partners, social support they received, coping (included helpseeking) strategies used, and their shelter experiences. This particular paper focuses only on women's interview narratives and the qualitative findings regarding helpseeking strategies and shelter experiences. For the safety of the researchers and the women, all but one of the interviews were held in a private room at the shelter (we interviewed one woman who was bedridden at her home). Shelter staff were not present in the room during interviews. Most of the women preferred to be interviewed alone. However, in keeping with a feminist epistemology that was responsive to the needs of our participants (e.g., Ramazanoglu & Holland, 2002), we also interviewed women in three focus groups that were composed of three or four women. The women interviewed in groups tended to have transportation issues, mandated appointments, or work that would prevent participation longer than 2 hr. The same interview protocol was followed for the focus groups. We limited the size of focus groups with the intention of facilitating the transcription process and being respectful of time constraints of the women. The women reported comfort in being interviewed in groups because the experience was similar in format to their resident support groups.

The interview protocol consisted of questions that asked the participants to recall (a) their family of origin, current family, and intimate partner histories; (b) substance abuse or mental health histories; (c) incidences of intimate partner violence; (d) helpseeking strategies; (e) community response; (f) shelter experiences; (g) and their own suggestions for how shelters could improve their transition back into the community. Examples of questions are "How did you make the decision to go to the shelter?" "From whom did you seek help while you were in the relationship with your partner?" "What things hindered your decision to go to the shelter?" "What things do you think the shelter could do that would help you adjust (get back on your feet) once you leave the shelter?"

All women who completed an interview received a stipend of $20.00. Directly after each interview, the researcher's reactions to the dynamics of participant–researcher interactions and salient issues were audio-taped and later integrated into the researcher's journal. Each interview was transcribed by students in the office of the author and reviewed by the author for accuracy.

We asked participants to complete the survey before the interview so that they could begin thinking about helpseeking, shelter culture, and messages family and friends communicated to them about shelters before participating in the interview.

Study Design and Qualitative Data Analysis

The overall approach of the study was exploratory and qualitative. As mentioned above, a survey was administered to residents and former residents of 14 shelters during a 16-month time period in order to compare the shelter experiences and helpseeking strategies of black and white rural women. Women were solicited and identified by shelter staff to participate, and those women would often recommend other residents to participate while we were at the interview site. Interviewing ceased upon saturation (i.e., nothing really new was being introduced in response to the interview questions) (Glaser & Strauss, 1967). The strengths of qualitative research are derived from its inductive approach, its focus on specific context and people, and its emphasis on personal narratives (Maxwell, 1996). Although the emphasis on context limits generalization, a major goal of quantitative research, the qualitative approach provides thick, rich descriptions of the participant's interpretations of the phenomenon being studied in specific contexts or social settings (Janesick, 1994).

With the greater acceptance of postmodern research methods, personal narratives are now seen as a valid means of knowledge production (Reissman, 1993). Narratives are integral to understanding culture because culture is constituted through the "ensemble of stories we tell about ourselves" (Plummer, 1995, p. 5). Whether it is in the community, marketplace, or home, culture shapes how individuals interpret their world and talk about their "places" in it (Berg, 1998; Fraser, 2004).

The present study appropriately utilizes personal narrative, via interview, as cultural representation in an attempt to understand the context of woman abuse within rural culture and shelter life. Indeed, methodologists note the importance of telling and listening to stories through narrative interviews as a means of understanding culture and experience (Narayan & George, 2001). Additionally, interviews are critical tools for "the developing of new frameworks and theories based on women's lives and women's formulations" (Anderson & Jack, 1991, p. 18). By entering into dialogue with others, narrative interviewers may unearth hidden or subordinated ideas (Borland, 1991). Thus, the findings produced may lead to the development of new theories that relate more with people's lives (Hyden, 1994).

Interviews were analyzed using a form of modified analytic induction (Gilgun, 1995; Patton, 2002). Inductive, rather than deductive, reasoning is involved, allowing for modification of concepts and relationships between concepts to occur throughout the process of doing research, with the goal of most accurately representing the reality of the situation. There are basically six steps to analytic induction. These are:

1. A research topic is defined in a tentative manner.
2. A hypothesis is developed about it.
3. A single instance is considered to determine if the hypothesis is confirmed.
4. If the hypothesis fails to be confirmed, either themes are redefined or the hypothesis is revised so as to include the instance examined.
5. Additional cases are examined and, if the new hypothesis is repeatedly confirmed, some degree of certainty about the hypothesis results.
6. Each negative case requires that the hypothesis be reformulated until there are no exceptions to identified themes.

Analyses are tentative and provisional throughout the study and only become comprehensive once the data are completely collected.

A list of markers to sensitize us to indicators of helpseeking and shelter experiences (featuring our preselected concepts) was developed from a review of the literature. Each transcript was read four times and coded independently by the research team using NVivo qualitative software. Interview transcripts, interviewer notes, coding lists, and entries from the author's journal were triangulated in order to identify and confirm inconsistencies, salient issues, and patterns. Participant's statements for inconsistencies, contradictions, and omissions were scrutinized by a line-by-line process in NVivo. Independent coding allowed for the isolation of subcategories and the reintegration or creation of density in the data by focusing on relationships between categories (Strauss, 1987). If, for example, participants' narratives about their experiences were incongruent with markers identified in the literature, we would have made a revision of the major categories.

Findings

Participants

The interview sample. Ten black women and 20 white women agreed to be interviewed at their local shelters. Eight of the 10 black women interviewed came from a town with a higher black population than many counties in southwest Virginia (U.S. Census Bureau, 2000). With the exception of one, all participants' income fell under $10,000. Only one of the women had a bachelor's degree. The majority of women ($n = 26$, $M = 2.16$, $SD = 1.17$) had at least one child. Eight women were married, 13 women were divorced or in the process of divorcing, and 9 women were never-married cohabitants.

Women's Ways of Helpseeking

Only 5 of 30 women interviewed ($n = 3$ black, $n = 2$ white) reported that they had prior knowledge that a shelter existed in their community at the time of deciding to leave their abusive partners. Women sought community assistance in leaving their abusive partners mainly from the police, family, friends, and from a doctor in the emergency room. Many of the women were sidetracked from seeking help from the local shelter by abusive partners feeding them misinformation about who used shelters and what shelter life would be like.

The police. The majority of white women interviewed ($n = 12$) reported that the police recommended the local shelter to them after responding to their domestic violence calls. In contrast, only 2 black women reported being told about a local shelter at the time of police response. Several black and white women reported that they did not initially telephone the police themselves for help. As one woman stated, "I was ashamed. Who wants to admit your ass is being kicked by your husband?" Rather, it seemed that for those women who were not surrounded by extended kin, unrelated neighbors were most likely to call the police.

Some women found that the police could be helpful in providing a temporary respite from their abusive partners. Half of the women ($n = 15$), all white, reported using the police to threaten their partner. None of the black women reported that the police could be

405 used as a vehicle for temporary safety or as a kind of "weapon" against their abusive partner.

It was not surprising that black and white women did discuss how geographic isolation may have contributed to poor police response. For instance, Char-
410 lotte, a 26-year-old white woman, talked about how the geographic isolation gave her a feeling that her community had a lawless quality:

> [My town] is way out. It's maddening to me. It's out far
> enough so that the law doesn't bother you. I can tell a
415 > dozen people driving around with no license, drunk half
> the time and fighting with each other—men, women.
> There's no patrolling. There's nothing.... Help comes too
> late or not at all.

White women were more likely than black women
420 to live outside city limits. However, black women reported feeling isolated in predominantly black neighborhoods because those areas were not regularly policed.

When speaking of the police as a source for help,
425 most of the women, black and white, reported that the perpetrator was either told to "walk away" or was arrested at the scene but later released after the women failed to file charges. Only 8 women spoke in positive terms about the police. Three white women mentioned
430 that they were given brochures about domestic violence and a local shelter by the police. Two women's stories particularly emphasized their negative experiences with the police. Tamara, a 48-year-old, bedridden white woman whose ex-husband was a police officer, shared:

435 > None of the police round here are any good. They all
> abusers themselves like my ex-husband. There's no use
> in calling them because nobody takes those calls seri-
> ously. Especially when the call is made from the house of
> one of their own.

440 Yvette, a 43-year-old black woman, shared her harrowing experience of waiting for police response:

> I was beaten until my head swoll the size of a water-
> melon. I was unrecognizable. I knew I was gonna die.
> The Devil blinked and I was able to get to a phone. I di-
445 > aled 911.... I left the phone off the hook so they had eve-
> rything on tape from the last 20, 30 minutes, and they
> stayed outside of my mobile home for 20 minutes.... This
> man only got a knife, and they had to wait until four, five
> carloads of police to come.... And that's when I lost trust
450 > in the police department because I almost died. My own
> child couldn't recognize me. And they were just sitting
> out there. Now I see that they're ready to solve a murder
> case. Yeah, but not a domestic violence thing.

Yvette stated that the police finally arrested the
455 abusive partner after she managed to crawl out of the mobile home herself. She also believed that poor police response to abused black rural women was a common thing in her area. Black women in her focus group all nodded their heads in agreement. Black women talked
460 about feeling like victims of racial discrimination by white police officers. White participants in the study more commonly discussed gender discrimination when describing their perceptions of sexist attitudes on the part of police officers.

465 *Support from family and friends.* Black women were more likely than white women to report that family and friends were more helpful than the police. Black women were also more likely to learn of local shelters through family and friends than through the
470 police. Nine of the 10 black participants in the study reported that family members were likely to provide temporary shelter before recommending that they go to the police station for more help. Only 5 white women reported that family and friends were primary sources
475 of help. For the most part, white women were more likely to be geographically separated from their families and surrounded by the extended kin of the abusive partner. The majority of white women reported being estranged from their own families because either their
480 families did not like the abusive partner or the women had previously left their families of origin to escape family violence (e.g., incest, physical and psychological abuse) or multigenerational alcoholism. Many white women spoke of being ostracized by the com-
485 munity if they left their abusive partners. Lauren, a 24-year-old white woman, reported:

> The Bible says we's supposed to stay together and for a
> long time. I had no place else to go. His kin surrounded
> me in the hollow. I would run to them when he beat me
490 > and they acted like nothin' was wrong. People in church
> knew I was being beaten. No one said a thing but for us
> to stay together. Stay. I felt if I left, I'd be letting every-
> body down.

Those women who described themselves as reli-
495 gious seemed to have difficulty leaving a marital partner. Leaving was a difficult decision because they were raised to believe that marriages were supposed to last forever. Some thought that leaving their marital partners was "almost sacrilegious" and that their actions of
500 breaking up the family would be viewed that way by their close-knit communities. It is not surprising that some of the more religious women, particularly white women, felt isolated even within their church communities.

Misled by Partners

505 Women in the study were asked about their initial thoughts regarding domestic violence shelters as a primary help-seeking strategy. Many of the women reported feeling a little anxious about using a shelter because of the stories they were told about shelters. Nine
510 white women and 1 black woman stated that they were misled, usually by their abusive partners, family members, and in-laws, about what to expect in the environment and the kind of women who resided in domestic violence shelters. For instance, Katie, a 26-year-old
515 white woman, said:

> My husband just told me lies. He knew I wasn't well-
> educated and stuff.... He said that you wouldn't have

your privacy. They'd be constantly going through your things. They could walk right in on you through the night. They'd rape me and my daughter. He would tell me these things to keep me with him. I understand that now.

Joan, a 37-year-old white woman, told a similar story of how her partner kept her from seeking help from a shelter: "When my boyfriend found out that I was coming here, he said 'the women that stay there are whores and there are men...men hang out over there at the park waiting for [the women] to come out.'"

Like Katie and Joan, all of the women interviewed reported that they did not know exactly what to expect when they first entered the shelter. Black women were more likely to state that shelters were not discussed by family and that domestic violence was considered "unsuitable conversation" or "dirty laundry." For these black women, the shelter was "the last resort" as long as there was family present and willing to get involved.

The Shelter Experience

Interviews revealed five main themes about participants' shelter experiences: (a) the shelter was a safe haven from intimate violence; (b) racial or cultural differences were not significant detractors from a satisfactory experience; (c) shelter residents and staff became a new family in this stressful time; (d) shelter residents experienced a positive, supportive relationship with shelter staff; and (e) shelter residents were highly satisfied with shelter service efficacy.

A safe haven. The women were asked to talk about their experience in the shelter. White women reported staying at the shelter longer and requesting extensions more often than black women. All but two women stated that they immediately felt safe once they entered the shelter. One middle-aged white woman revealed, "They showed me my room and once my head hit the pillow, I slept hard and long for the first time in years." All of the women felt that the shelter was a safe haven for themselves and their children. Four of 10 black women reported noticing the absence of ethnic staff and feeling somewhat isolated. These four women were located in counties where the black population was less than 5% (U.S. Census Bureau, 2000). These four women spoke of the racism that they and other blacks experienced outside the shelter. They came to the shelter very mindful about their minority status in their communities. These four black women stated that overall they were more concerned about the racial attitudes of the staff rather than their fellow residents. The black women watched the staff to see whether racism would be a factor in receiving the best assistance and resources available during this vulnerable time. They developed relationships with white residents that did not directly confront issues of ethnicity or race or the more complex systems of intersecting multiple oppressions. Despite the potential for ethnic women's cultural

isolation, narrative material suggested that black women still felt like they were a part of the group on the basis that all residents were survivors of male violence and were most likely poor. Conversations between black and white women in the hallways and support group meetings focused on abuse and transitioning out of that experience. The other six black women interviewed were in the only shelter in southwest Virginia, where all staff and residents were black and did not report cultural isolation.

Once arriving in the shelter, the majority of participants (17 white women and five black women) reported in the interviews that they trusted other women in the shelter. For instance, Rhonda, a 38-year-old black woman, stated, "I trust the women that are here. Basically, what it all comes down to is each has a unique, original story, but the rope that ties us all together...we've been bound by abuse."

Cultural differences muted by violence. Rhonda's attitude reflected the sisterhood that black and white rural women reported feeling in the shelters that offered them a safe haven from the violence in their lives. It seemed that the common experience of domestic violence and shelter life united the women. Yet racial differences, although muted by their shared experiences, were an issue. For example, in mandatory support group meetings, black women revealed that they did not discuss with white women how it felt to be abused by black men or challenges they may have faced with different social services. However, in speaking with the author, a black researcher, black women reported that they believed racism in their interactions with community resources employees may have contributed to their receiving fewer services or less information than their white counterparts. Black study participants avoided talking about these types of challenges because they believed that fellow white residents "just wouldn't understand" racism or what they perceived as differential treatment by an occasional shelter staff member or resident. Still, it is important to note that, although black women seemed less likely to "culturally identify" with others (i.e., perceived themselves as sharing a common history of racial and institutional discrimination or common religious background) in the shelter, they were not less likely to feel comfortable in the shelter environment or among most white staff.

My new family. The majority of women reported that they felt that for the time they were there in the shelter, the other residents were their family. When they were asked if racial discrimination was felt by anyone, black women reported that they did not feel racially discriminated against by the other women or the staff. One 32-year-old black woman laughed when she answered our question: "We're all just the same here. We see past the skin color and the bruises." Ruth, a 25-year-old white woman who only had an eighth-grade education and was in the process of getting a divorce, said that the other women were a comfort to her: "Yes, I trust the women here...they knew the Lord, and we had a lot in common, so it was like a little, happy family...what I always dreamed a family would be like."

The women expressed a bond in the shelter because they all had a common experience: abuse. The result of this bond was the formation of a kind of temporary family and contained "fictive kin network."

For instance, many of the older women revealed that they took on a caretaking role over younger women and children in the shelter. Two particular women, 1 black and 1 white, both older than 40 years of age, were proud to list their caretaking activities in their shelter. They reported that they prepared meals, taught younger women how to prepare certain meals, acted as emotional counselors to younger women, made younger women complete their chores, and actively took care of other women's children. "We keep each other in line whenever we feel crazy." Barbara, a 48-year-old black woman, felt such "motherly responsibility" to abused women that after she made the transition back into the community, she has returned to the shelter as a volunteer and activist.

Relationship with shelter staff. The women were asked about their interactions with the shelter staff. All of the women, with the exception of 1 white woman, positively evaluated the emotional support and extensive caregiving given by staff members. Pamela, a middle-aged black woman, shared her observation of the staff's emotional support and accessibility: "They spoil us really. If you need somebody to talk to, somebody will make time. Some ladies like myself come in here and do have very low self-esteem."

Pamela's comments were echoed by the majority of the women in the shelter. None of the women felt that the staff were ever too busy to help them process their abusive experience. In fact, only 1 participant, Terry (a 40-year-old white woman), complained that she felt her confidence by shelter staff had been violated. In this case, the participant learned that a staff member gossiped about her with a social services employee, a close friend of the staff member.

Shelter efficacy. The last research question asked women to specifically discuss which shelter services were the most useful to them. We prompted them by querying, "What is this shelter doing really well for you and other women?" All but Terry reported that the staff performed their responsibilities effectively with "all their heart and soul," and, with the exception of Terry, all the women in the study reported that staff helped them recognize their inner strength and build up their self-esteem. For example, Mary, a 45-year-old white woman, outlined the many services that the shelter provided her and her family:

I took advantage of every service that was offered to me. They helped me find a job and a lawyer.... Actually a week and a half after I moved in here, I got my kids back.

She got somebody to go to court with me. I came here with no clothes. She took care of that for me. Helped me to get an apartment. They helped me to get a welfare check and food stamps. Every program the shelter had, I took full advantage. When I got here, I wanted for nothing.

Like Mary, the majority of women praised staff members in their roles as primary liaisons and advocates for dealing with social services, the workforce, housing, and the legal system. The women also emphasized the importance of taking full responsibility for actively pursuing opportunities that shelter staff provided them. No one framed these opportunities as "easy handouts" but saw them as "opportunities for real change."

Finally, the women talked about the staff monitoring their attendance at drug and alcohol rehabilitation programs and psychiatric services. One white woman, 32-year-old Betty, stated, "I'm in AA because if I stop going, I won't qualify for an extension if I need it. I'm sober because these women [staff] make sure I'm there and they support me all the way." All but one white woman, Terry, felt empowered that the staff quickly arranged for these wellness services and incorporated some issues related to addiction or depression into group counseling sessions. Overall, these rural battered women found the shelters to be safe and supportive.

Discussion

The results from this study are supported by two bodies of literature—research on rural abused women and on domestic violence among black couples and families. Using qualitative methods, a picture of the experiences of black and white women in domestic violence shelters in rural communities was constructed. Narrative material revealed interesting similarities and differences found between white and black rural women.

White and black rural women experienced different interactions with law-enforcement officers that have important implications with regard to helpseeking behaviors within the context of domestic violence. Study findings provide confirmation of previous research on barriers to seeking help from the police as a result of a violent incident at the hands of an intimate partner. Similar to other research (e.g., U.S. Department of Justice, 1998), both white and black women in this study reported being too ashamed to call the police. Important differences also emerged with regard to how forthcoming shelter information was from the police for victims. It seemed that white women were better informed than black women in terms of the availability and use of shelters, and this is likely due in part to police apparently discussing shelters more often with white participants than with minority women. Even so, the extent of shelter information given to any woman in the study, white or black, was "thin." For example, although several police officers reportedly did tell the participants about the shelter, only 2 participants reported that police officers gave them written material about the shelter. Further, less than a third of the women spoke enthusiastically or in positive terms about their experience with the police.

Both white and black women felt discriminated against by police, although the nature of the discrimination differed in that black women talked about feelings of racial discrimination by white police officers and white women mostly discussed sexist attitudes of some police officers. It is interesting that some white participants saw the police as a potential resource, even threatening their batterers with calling the police. Although it appears that the police certainly could have done a better job overall, the fact that white battered women could consider the police as a potential resource, whereas black battered women did not seem to consider the police as a resource, is perhaps a result of white privilege. This difference between the experiences of black and white battered women suggests how privilege mediates the experience of gender and geographic location for rural battered women. Also, it is possible that black women were likely not to see the police as a resource because of the traditionally hostile relationship law enforcement has had with black communities (Richie, 1996). This finding supports our earlier suggestion that racism can be an additional isolating factor.

These findings suggest that more training needs to be offered to rural police officers dealing with domestic violence. Ongoing training of police officers should be conducted to address gender and cultural sensitivity relative to racial/ethnic minorities. Policy should provide law-enforcement officers with a structured format for addressing domestic violence cases, including the expectation that written material about community services for domestic violence victims be delivered to all possible victims of domestic violence. Community policing, a philosophy that includes all efforts of the police to achieve the goal of a closer relationship with the public, may also help victims see the police and criminal justice system as supportive (Robinson & Chandek, 2000).

There were also differences in how black and white survivors experienced shelters. All of the black women revealed being ashamed of being in a shelter and that within their families, discussion about shelters was considered airing "dirty laundry." This attitude may reflect the internalization of the Superwoman stereotype of black women. Few (1999) has noted that for some black women who internalize the Superwoman myth, "disclosure to and helpseeking from those outside of the abusive relationship may be perceived as a sign of vulnerability and weakness" (p. 70). Similarly, Asbury (1987) observed that black women may be more reluctant to call attention to the abuse because they feel they should be able to find the strength to handle their own relationship problems. The findings in

this study seem to confirm black women's reluctance to discuss help seeking, and shelter assistance was not deemed as appropriate conversation among family or friends.

Black women also described experiencing the shelter culture differently, and several felt that the lack of racial diversity in the shelter sometimes affected what they would share with others. The remaining black women were in a shelter in a predominantly black community; they talked about having access to black shelter staff and other resources (e.g., counselors), pointing to the importance of black shelter staff and community volunteers as credible role models because of shared background and personal experiences (e.g., Wilson et al., 1987). Indeed, Collins (1991) has written about the positive effects of black community "othermothers" who take part in caring for vulnerable groups within the community. Despite differences between black and white participants that may center around race, it is important to recognize that the majority of black participants emphasized bonding within the shelter based on the common experience of victimization.

Perhaps one of the reasons that white women strongly identified with and trusted other shelter residents is because the shelter residents were, in a sense, a new social support network to combat isolation. White women in this study particularly highlighted the impact of geographic and social isolation on their ability to seek help, whereas black women seemed to rely on social support of family outside the shelter as a means to provide a reprieve from an abusive partner. Scott and Black (1999) discussed the importance of kinship networks for black women as obligatory resources that are basic to the economic, emotional, and community survival among black poor and near-poor. Blacks have survived crises and violence by the strength of family ties. Compared to white women, fellow shelter residents were not the major source of emotional support for black women. Thus, isolation and an inability to access shelters may, in fact, have more profound implications for white women, given their heavier reliance on such services for assistance and emotional support.

The issue of isolation seems to be of great significance with respect to domestic violence and women's victimization. Both Gagne (1992) and Websdale (1995) note that rural women are more likely to be isolated from health care, social services, transportation, housing, educational opportunities, and child care. Geographic, social, and economic isolation amplified the extent of control by abusive partners and was the major constraint that all of the women had to negotiate effectively in order to walk in the door of a shelter. In this study, white women were more likely to be surrounded by their partner's kinship network, and thus their social support networks were quite limited as they were often defined by their abusive partners' affiliation. White women also told more stories of marrying early to escape the "normalcy" of family of origin violence and openly talked about multigenerational substance abuse fueling family violence.

865   In contrast, all of the black women lived close to their own extended family and had alternate venues of social support. Black families, although not as likely to suggest a domestic violence shelter as a primary option for leaving abusive relationships, were more likely to offer their homes as temporary sanctuary. Conse-

870 quently, the duration of shelter stay was often shorter for black women. Black women did not have to rely on transitional housing solely because there were relatives in the area to take them in once they left the shelter. However, this finding should not be misinterpreted to

875 suggest that shelters are not an important service for abused black rural women. In fact, studies suggest that black women are satisfied with their shelter stay (Thomas, 2000) and report a high quality of life at follow-up (Sullivan & Rumptz, 1994). These findings may

880 suggest that black rural women bring into the shelter potential resources such as a stronger or existing social support system that can be tapped into by the women and shelter staff for child care, housing, and employment, or to assist the survivor in relocation plans. Since

885 white rural women were more likely to be in need of reconnecting or building new social support systems that are independent of their abusive partners, transitional housing and extended shelter stays may be more pertinent to or instrumental to their success in leaving

890 abusive relationships and making the transition from the shelter back into the community.

    The significance of social support networks for women in transition cannot be overlooked. Tan, Basta, Sullivan, and Davidson (1995) examined the impor-

895 tance of social support networks and their connection to self-esteem and psychological well-being among 141 participants. They found that 79% of shelter residents identified social support as one of the areas they would most like to work on after leaving the shelter.

900 Within 10 weeks after shelter exit, 41% of the women reported working on increasing their social support networks. Further, abused women who had closer ties to family and friends were more likely to be pleased with their lives and less depressed.

Implications for Practice

905   It should be noted that, overall, the women were satisfied with the services offered by the shelters. Both black and white rural women reported that shelter staff did a good job of caring for residents with sincerity and honesty, creating a safe, structured environment, and

910 providing assistance with resources such as legal aid and social services. However, participants did make suggestions as to how shelters could improve their services for rural battered women. Feminist research centers on the everyday experiences of participants with

915 the intention of learning how coproduced knowledge in the research process can inform personal, institutional, or social change (DeReus, Few, & Blume, 2005). In

this study, the participants became "advocates" who provided practical suggestions to help women who

920 would come to the shelter after they had long left.

    1. *Provide greater visibility of services.* All of the women suggested that shelters located in rural communities needed greater visibility. They sug-

925 gested placing more pamphlets in faith-based organizations, grocery stores, and places women frequent the most (e.g., beauty parlors, women's restrooms). The results of this study indicated that the majority of women (especially black women)

930 did not know that a local domestic violence shelter existed in their community. Clearly, greater collaboration with local law enforcement is needed because the police are important liaisons between shelters and victims of domestic vio-

935 lence. Shelters were "invisible" to many black women because the police simply did not appear to discuss shelters as a viable reprieve from domestic violence to black women. Community outreach on the part of shelter staff may achieve

940 stronger collaborations. For example, shelter staff may be able to incorporate law-enforcement, community, and legislative representatives into workshops or training sessions to create mutually beneficial relationships aimed at providing ser-

945 vices to rural women.

    2. *Include employment training.* Women expressed a need for state and local job bulletins to be accessible or posted in the shelters. They suggested that computers and computer training be made avail-

950 able in shelters to search for jobs and to improve clerical skills to increase their probability of getting higher-paid jobs. A need for a separate phone service or line with which they could communicate with possible employers quickly was re-

955 quested. In sum, these women realized that part of what kept them in abusive homes was a lack of employment opportunities.

    3. *Offer shelter exit aftercare.* Women felt they needed to be in touch with shelter staff and resources for longer than 90 days to get their lives

960 back on track. Some women felt that once they left the shelter, they were "cast away." Their suggestion was that shelters have transitional housing with longer stay periods.

    4. *Consider inspirational resources.* Black and Ap-

965 palachian women specifically requested more interaction with the faith-based organizations and space to nurture their spirituality. The majority of white women and all black women were primarily raised participating in rural faith-based organiza-

970 tions. They identified spirituality as one of the main coping strategies that allowed them to reconnect to themselves positively and to have hope for a better future. Although researchers have identified the church and fundamentalism in rural

975 regions as institutional foundations of rural patri-archy (Navin, Stockum, & Campbell-Ruggaard, 1993), it is important to note that these women recommended working on their spiritual selves rather than focusing on religious passages that re-
980 quired the submission of women to men. Additionally, faith-based organizations may be particularly important sources of support for black women (Eugene, 1995).

5. *Diversify shelter staff.* Black women specifically
985 requested that more racial/ethnic women be recruited as shelter directors and staff to create a more diverse shelter culture. Only black women suggested that a staff person with foreign language proficiency be on call for rural migrant
990 women. It is noteworthy that the majority of black women were less likely to believe that they could say what they felt in the shelter environment and wished they had access to black resources. Black community leaders and othermothers could work
995 in collaboration with shelters to depathologize shelters and other health services.

Conclusion

Black and white rural women in this exploratory study experienced domestic violence differently in terms of helpseeking access, behaviors, and social sup-
1000 port, but shared many commonalities once they were in the shelter environment. Our findings invite researchers and practitioners to consider the recommendations proposed by women who have lived and are living in transition from the shelter back into their communities and
1005 families. Longitudinal studies with rural women, especially black women, who have sought assistance from battered women's shelters are needed to further track the barriers or successes of transitioning from the shelter.

References

Anderson, K., & Jack, D. C. (1991). Learning to listen: Interview techniques and analyses. In S. Berger Gluck & D. Patai (Eds.), *Women's words: The feminist practice of oral history* (pp. 11–26). New York: Routledge.

Asbury, J. (1987). African-American women in violent relationships: An exploration of cultural differences. In R. Hampton (Ed.), *Violence in the black family: Correlates and consequences* (pp. 89–119). Lexington, MA: Lexington Books.

Berg, B. (1998). *Qualitative research methods for the social sciences.* Boston: Allyn & Bacon.

Berk, R. A., Newton, P. J., & Berk, S. F. (1986). What a difference a day makes: An empirical study of the impact of shelters for battered women. *Journal of Marriage and the Family, 48,* 481–490.

Borland, K. (1991). "That's not what I said": Interpretive conflict in oral narrative research. In S. Berger Gluck & D. Patai (Eds.), *Women's words: The feminist practice of oral history* (pp. 63–76). New York: Routledge.

Brown, C., Reedy, D., Fountain, J., Johnson, A., & Dichiser, T. (2000). Battered women's career decision-making self-efficacy: Further insights and contributing factors. *Journal of Career Assessment, 8,* 251–265.

Collins, P. H. (1991). *Black feminist thought: Knowledge, consciousness, and the politics of empowerment.* New York: Routledge.

Davis. L. V., Hagan. J. L., & Early, T. J. (1994). Social services for battered women: Are they adequate, accessible, and appropriate? *Social Work, 39,* 695–704.

Davis, L. V., & Srinivasan, M. (1995). Listening to the voices of battered women: What helps them escape violence? *Affilia, 10,* 49–69.

DeReus, L., Few, A. L., & Blume, L. B. (2005). Multicultural and critical race feminisms: Theorizing families in the third wave. In V. L. Bergtson, A. C. Acock, K. R. Allen, P. Dilworth-Anderson, & D. M. Klein (Eds.), *Source-*

book of family theory and research (pp. 447–468). Thousand Oaks. CA: Sage.

Eugene, T. M. (1995). There is a balm in Gilead: Black women and the Black Church as agents of a therapeutic community. *Women & Therapy, 16,* 55–71.

Few, A. L. (1999). The (un)making of martyrs: Black mothers, daughters, and intimate violence. *Journal for the Association of Research on Mothering, 1,* 68–75.

Few, A. L., & Bell-Scott. P. (2002). Grounding our feet and hearts: Black women's coping strategies and the decision to leave. *Women & Therapy, 25,* 59–77.

Fraser, H. (2004). Doing narrative research: Analyzing personal stories line by line. *Qualitative Social Work, 3,* 179–201.

Gagne, P. L. (1992). Appalachian women: Violence and social control. *Journal of Contemporary Ethnography, 20,* 387–415.

Gilgun, J. F. (1995). We shared something special: The moral discourse of incest perpetrators. *Journal of Marriage and the Family, 51,* 265–281.

Glaser, B. G., & Strauss, A. L. (1967). *The discovery of grounded theory: Strategies for qualitative research.* Hawthorne, NY: Aldine deGruyter.

Gordon, J. S. (1996). Community services for abused women: A review of perceived usefulness and efficacy. *Journal of Family Violence, 11,* 315–329.

Harding, S. (Ed.). (1987). *Feminism and methodology.* Bloomington: Indiana University Press.

Hyden, M. (1994). Women battering as a marital act: Interviewing and analysis in context. In C. K. Riessman (Ed.), *Qualitative studies in social work research* (pp. 95–112). Thousand Oaks, CA: Sage.

Jackson, S. (1998). Telling stories: Memory, narrative, and experience in feminist research and theory. In K. Henwood, C. Griffin, & A. Phoenix (Eds.), *Standpoints and differences: Essays in the practice of feminist psychology* (pp. 45–64). London: Sage.

Janesick, V. (1994). Dance of qualitative research design: Metaphor, methodology, and meaning. In L. Denzin & Y. Lincoln (Eds.), Handbook of qualitative research (pp. 209–219). Newbury Park, CA: Sage.

Johnson, I., Crowley, J., & Sigler, R. (1992). Agency response to domestic violence: Services provided to battered women. In E. Viano (Ed.), *Intimate violence: Interdisciplinary perspectives* (pp. 191–202). Washington, DC: Hemisphere.

Kaukinen, C. (2002). The help-seeking decisions of violent crime victims: An examination of the direct and conditional effects of gender and the victim–offender relationship. *Journal of Interpersonal Violence, 17,* 432–456.

Krishnan, S. P., Hilbert, J. C., & Pase, M. (2001). An examination of intimate partner violence in rural communities: Results from a hospital emergency department study from Southwest United States. *Family and Community Health, 24,* 1–16.

Maxwell, J. (1996). *Qualitative research design: An interactive approach.* Thousand Oaks, CA: Sage.

McNair, L., & Neville, H. (1996). African American women survivors of sexual assault: The intersection of race and class. *Women & Therapy, 18,* 107–118.

Narayan, K., & George, K. (2001). Personal and folk narrative as cultural representation. In J. Gubrium & J. Holstein (Eds.), *Handbook of interview research: Context & method* (pp. 815–831). Thousand Oaks, CA: Sage.

Navin, S., Stockum, R., & Campbell-Ruggaard, J. (1993). Battered women in rural America. *Journal of Humanistic Education and Development, 32,* 9–16.

Patton, M. Q. (2002). *Qualitative research and evaluation methods* (3rd ed.). Thousand Oaks, CA: Sage.

Plummer, K. (1995). *Telling sexual stories: Power, change, and social worlds.* London: Routledge.

Ramazanoglu, C., & Holland, J. (2002). *Feminist methodology: Challenges and choices.* London: Sage.

Reissman, C. (1993). *Narrative analysis.* Newbury Park, CA: Sage.

Richie, B. (1996). *Compelled to crime: The gender entrapment of battered black women.* New York: Routledge.

Roberts, A. R., & Lewis, S. J. (2000). Giving them shelter: National organizational survey of shelters for battered women and their children. *Journal of Community Psychology, 28,* 669–681.

Robinson, A. L., & Chandek, M. S. (2000). Philosophy into practice? Community policing units and domestic violence victim participation. *Policing: An International Journal of Police Strategies and Management, 23,* 280–302.

Scott, J. W., & Black, A. (1999). Deep structures of African American family life: Female and male kin networks. In R. Staples (Ed.), *The black family* (pp. 232–240). New York: Wadsworth.

Strauss, A. (1987). *Qualitative analysis far social scientists.* Cambridge. NY: Cambridge University Press.

Sullivan, C., & Rumptz, M. (1994). Adjustment and needs of African American women who utilize a domestic violence shelter. *Violence and Victims, 9,* 275–285.

Tan, C., Basta. J., Sullivan. C. M., & Davidson, W. S. (1995). The role of social support in the lives of women exiting domestic violence shelters: An experimental study. *Journal of Interpersonal Violence, 10,* 437–451.

Thomas, E. K. (2000). Domestic violence in African American and Asian American communities: A comparative analysis of two racial/ethnic minority cultures and implications for mental health service provision for women of color. *Psychology: A Journal of Human Behavior, 37*, 32–43.

Thompson, L. (1992). Feminist methodology for family studies. *Journal of Marriage and the Family, 54*, 3–18.

Thompson, L., & Walker, A. (1995). The place of feminism in family studies. *Journal of Marriage and the Family, 57*, 847–856.

Tutty, L. M., Weaver, G., & Rothery, M. A. (1999). Resident's views of efficacy of shelter services for assaulted women. *Violence Against Women, 5*, 898–925.

U.S. Census Bureau. (2000). *American fact finder database.* Retrieved March 2, 2005, from http://factfinder.census.gov/

U.S. Department of Justice. (1998). *Violence by intimates: Analysis of data on crimes by current or former spouses, boyfriends, and girlfriends.* Washington, DC: Bureau of Justice Statistics.

Van Hightower, N. R., & Gorton, J. (2002). A case study of community-based responses to rural woman battering. *Violence Against Women, 8*, 845–872.

Van Hightower, N. R., Gorton, J., & DeMoss, C. L. (2000). Predictive models of domestic violence and fear of intimate partners among immigrant and seasonal farm worker women. *Journal of Family Violence, 15*, 137–154.

Websdale, N. (1998). Rural woman abuse: The voices of Kentucky women. *Violence Against Women, 1*, 309–338.

Websdale, N. (1998). *Rural woman battering and the justice system: An ethnography.* Thousand Oaks. CA: Sage.

Wendt, S., Taylor, J., & Kennedy, M. (2002). Rural domestic violence: Moving towards feminist poststructural understandings. *Rural Social Work, 2*, 25–35.

West, C. M. (Ed.). (2003). *Violence in the lives of black women.* New York: Haworth.

Whitener, L., Jen, J., & Kassel, K. (2004. February). *Programs and partnership in a dynamic rural America.* U.S. Department of Agriculture, Economic Research Service. Retrieved November 8, 2004, from http://www.ers.usda.gov/Amberwaves/February04

Wilson, M. N., Cobb, D. D., & Dolan, R. T. (1987). Raising the awareness of wife battering in rural black areas of central Virginia: A community outreach approach. In R. L. Hampton (Ed.). Violence in the black family: Correlates and consequences (pp. 121–131). Lexington. MA: Lexington Books.

Young, I. M. (1997). *Intersecting voices: Dilemmas of gender, political philosophy, and policy.* Princeton, NJ: Princeton University Press.

Acknowledgments: I wish to acknowledge Dr. Sandra Stith for her review of previous drafts; the Support Program for Innovative Research Strategies (ASPIRES), which is sponsored by the Office of the Provost; and the Office of the Vice President for Research at Virginia Polytechnic Institute and State University for funding this research. I also humbly thank the participating domestic violence shelters in southwest Virginia for their generous assistance.

About the author: April L. Few is an assistant professor in the Department of Human Development, Virginia Polytechnic Institute and State University, 401-A Wallace Hall, Blacksburg, VA 24061. E-mail: alfew@vt.edu

Exercise for Article 32

Factual Questions

1. The researcher states two "aims" of the study. What is the second aim?

2. How many women were interviewed?

3. What was done for the safety of the researchers and the women?

4. Were all the participants interviewed in private one-on-one interviews? Explain.

5. How many of the black women came from a single town?

6. How many of the women spoke in positive terms about the police?

Questions for Discussion

7. In your opinion, is it important to know that this study was conducted through a "feminist lens"? Explain. (See lines 121–196.)

8. Is it important to know that the participants were drawn from 14 different shelters? Explain. (See lines 199–202.)

9. While the researcher indicates that 30 women were interviewed, she does not state how many women were approached but declined to be interviewed. Would you be interested in knowing the number who declined? Why? Why not?

10. The researcher states that this research was "exploratory." Do you agree with this characterization of the research? Explain. (See lines 276–277 and 997–998.)

11. In your opinion, does the researcher make a strong argument for using qualitative research to explore the research problem? (See lines 287–322.)

12. In your opinion, is the method of analysis described in sufficient detail? (See lines 323–364.)

13. If you had planned a study on this topic, would you have used interviews (as in this study) or structured questionnaires? Explain.

Quality Ratings

Directions: Indicate your level of agreement with each of the following statements by circling a number from 5 for strongly agree (SA) to 1 for strongly disagree (SD). If you believe an item is not applicable to this research article, leave it blank. Be prepared to explain your ratings. When responding to criteria A and B below, keep in mind that brief titles and abstracts are conventional in published research.

A. The title of the article is appropriate.

   SA   5   4   3   2   1   SD

B. The abstract provides an effective overview of the research article.

   SA   5   4   3   2   1   SD

C. The introduction establishes the importance of the study.

   SA   5   4   3   2   1   SD

D. The literature review establishes the context for the study.

   SA   5   4   3   2   1   SD

E. The research purpose, question, or hypothesis is clearly stated.

   SA   5   4   3   2   1   SD

F. The method of sampling is sound.

   SA   5   4   3   2   1   SD

G. Relevant demographics (for example, age, gender, and ethnicity) are described.

   SA   5   4   3   2   1   SD

H. Measurement procedures are adequate.

   SA   5   4   3   2   1   SD

I. All procedures have been described in sufficient detail to permit a replication of the study.

   SA   5   4   3   2   1   SD

J. The participants have been adequately protected from potential harm.

   SA   5   4   3   2   1   SD

K. The results are clearly described.

   SA   5   4   3   2   1   SD

L. The discussion/conclusion is appropriate.

   SA   5   4   3   2   1   SD

M. Despite any flaws, the report is worthy of publication.

   SA   5   4   3   2   1   SD

Article 33

Generational Differences and Similarities Among Puerto Rican and Mexican Mothers' Experiences with Familial Ethnic Socialization

ADRIANA J. UMAÑA-TAYLOR
Arizona State University

ANI YAZEDJIAN
Texas State University

ABSTRACT. We used focus group methodology to explore differences and similarities in the process of familial ethnic socialization among first- and second-generation Mexican and Puerto Rican mothers ($N = 75$). Across all groups, mothers communicated the importance and purposefulness of familial ethnic socialization practices that took place in their homes. A number of similarities emerged across national origin and generational groups, indicating that there were numerous shared experiences that did not change with greater time in the U.S. and did not vary by national origin. Nevertheless, origin groups were also discovered. Findings are discussed within the context of Bronfenbrenner's ecological theory and an acculturative framework.

From *Journal of Social and Personal Relationships*, 23, 445–464.

The United States population is undergoing a rapid demographic shift, with Latinos contributing greatly to this change. Given high fertility rates and high levels of continuing immigration, Latinos represent the largest ethnic minority group in the U.S., outnumbering both Black and Asian populations (U.S. Census Bureau, 2004). Despite this rapid growth, current theoretical and empirical knowledge regarding the experiences of Latino youth and families in the United States is relatively limited. Nevertheless, existing work suggests that Latino parents play a critical role in the important developmental process of ethnic identity formation (Knight, Bernal, Garza, Cota, & Ocampo, 1993; Umaña-Taylor & Fine, 2004). Although parents' ethnic socialization has emerged as a significant factor that predicts healthy ethnic identity formation, we have limited knowledge concerning parents' experiences in this process.

Furthermore, many studies continue to treat Latinos as a homogenous population and do not account for the variation that exists among them (Umaña-Taylor & Fine, 2001). Latinos in the U.S. represent over 20 distinct national origins, with Mexicans and Puerto Ricans being the two largest groups. The varied histories of Latino national origin groups distinguish them from each other on a number of significant demographic variables (Baca Zinn & Wells, 2000). The two largest Latino groups, for example, differ with regard to immigration status (i.e., Puerto Ricans are U.S. citizens by birth, whereas Mexicans must apply for entry into the U.S.), are concentrated in different regions of the U.S. (i.e., 55% of Mexicans live in the West, while 61% of Puerto Ricans live in the Northeast [Guzman, 2001]), and differ significantly with regard to household composition (i.e., 31% of Mexican households vs. 17% of Puerto Rican households contain five or more people [Ramirez & de la Cruz, 2002]). These demographic differences can differentially affect family life and therefore provide an important context within which to examine the family experiences of Latino groups (Baca Zinn & Wells, 2000). As such, the current study examined generational differences in parental practices and experiences regarding familial ethnic socialization among Mexican and Puerto Rican parents.

Guiding Theoretical Frameworks

Although the current study was primarily of an exploratory nature, two theoretical frameworks (i.e., ecological and acculturation) guided our interpretation of the results. Bronfenbrenner's (1989) ecological theory suggests that processes and outcomes of human development are a joint function of individuals and the environments in which their lives are embedded. Furthermore, ecological theory posits that proximal (e.g., family) and distal (e.g., societal ideologies) settings influence human development. Given that familial ethnic socialization is a process that involves adolescents, their families, and society, ecological theory fittingly provides a framework from which to understand the interface of immediate settings and broader social contexts. Thus, we used ecological theory as a framework from which to understand the interconnectedness of mothers' and adolescents' lives as well as to understand how familial experiences were informed by broader social contexts, such as children's schools, neighborhoods, and societal ideologies.

65 While ecological theory provides an understanding of how individuals' lives are influenced by (and influence) their environments, an acculturation framework helps us to understand how experiences within cultural groups may vary based on individuals' degree of ad-
70 herence to mainstream and native cultures. Past theoretical work on acculturation asserted that in the process of adapting to the ways of the dominant culture, individuals will lose their identification with their ethnic group; however, current empirical and theoretical
75 work indicates that such dichotomous thinking is no longer relevant in today's increasingly heterogeneous society (Cortes, Rogler, & Malgady, 1994). Individuals are clearly demonstrating that they can maintain strong ties with their ethnic group, while also becoming adept
80 at surviving in the dominant culture (Rosenthal, Whittle, & Bell, 1989; Saylor & Aries, 1999). Furthermore, research reveals that while immigrants do bring with them a series of cultural patterns and traditions, which have a strong influence on family functioning and indi-
85 vidual behavior, the nature of these cultural patterns may change in the process of adaptation to the new culture (Foner, 1997; Garcia Coll, Meyer, & Brillon, 1995). The redefined culture becomes a hybrid of the native culture in order to allow ethnic group members
90 the opportunity to continue to maintain the ethnic experience within the broader framework of the dominant culture. Thus, ethnicity is redefined and is experienced in a new way in response to the circumstances that immigrants encounter in their new culture. Accord-
95 ingly, we were interested in exploring how the process of familial ethnic socialization remained unchanged across generational cohorts, as well as possible adaptations that emerged over time as families adapted to U.S. culture.

Familial Ethnic Socialization

100 Familial ethnic socialization has been defined as the degree to which family members (e.g., grandparents, parents, siblings, and other kin) expose, discuss, and possibly directly teach children about their ethnic background. Although children gain information about
105 their ethnicity from various sources (e.g., peers, media, etc.), scholars agree that the family plays a central role in this process (Harrison, Wilson, Pine, Chan, & Buriel, 1995; Knight, Bernal, et al., 1993; Phinney & Rosenthal, 1992). On a broader level, Erikson (1968)
110 also discusses familial influences on identity, suggesting that individuals define themselves partly through their relationships and interactions with family members. In line with these ideas, and consistent with an ecological framework, theoretical models of ethnic
115 identity formation (e.g., Knight, Bernal et al., 1993; Umaña-Taylor & Fine, 2004) present familial ethnic socialization as a central construct.

Although familial ethnic socialization has been considered a central component in theoretical models
120 of ethnic identity, little empirical work has been con-

ducted on this construct. In studies that have explored familial ethnic socialization, it has been described as both covert and overt (see Umaña-Taylor & Fine, 2004). With covert familial ethnic socialization, par-
125 ents are not intentionally trying to teach their children about ethnicity but may be inadvertently doing so with their choice of decor and everyday activities (e.g., decorating the home with objects from their native country). Overt familial ethnic socialization refers to
130 family members purposefully and directly attempting to teach adolescents about their ethnicity (e.g., buying books about the native country and requiring adolescents to read them). Research with ethnic minority parents indicates that families report a need to pass on
135 their ethnic culture via language (Sridhar, 1988), beliefs, and customs (Dasgupta, 1998). Furthermore, scholars suggest that a major goal of socialization for ethnic minority families is to foster a positive orientation toward one's ethnic group and promote bicultural-
140 ism (Harrison et al., 1995). Thus, whether ethnic socialization is occurring in an overt or covert manner, it appears to be an important parenting goal for ethnic minority families.

Ethnic socialization appears to have beneficial out-
145 comes for ethnic minority youth. Research conducted with children and adolescents suggests that familial ethnic socialization has positive implications for ethnic identity development. A study of Mexican-origin adolescents found that familial ethnic socialization was
150 positively related to ethnic identity achievement. That is, the more adolescents reported that their families were socializing them about their ethnicity, the higher their reports of exploration, commitment, and affirmation regarding their ethnic identity (Umaña-Taylor &
155 Fine, 2004). This same relationship was found in other studies conducted with Asian, Black, and Latino adolescents (Phinney & Nakayama, 1991; Umaña-Taylor, Bhanot, & Shin, 2006). Furthermore, research conducted with Mexican-origin children has found a simi-
160 lar relationship, in that mothers who reported teaching their children about their ethnic culture tended to have children who were more ethnically identified (Knight, Cota, & Bernal, 1993; Knight, Bernal et al., 1993).

Although families appear to be an important me-
165 dium through which adolescents learn about their cultural background, researchers have not directly explored the ways in which parents transmit their culture to their children, nor have they examined parents' beliefs regarding the factors that assist them in the proc-
170 ess of ethnic socialization. Because previous research indicates that familial ethnic socialization is strongly related to Latino adolescents' ethnic identity, and ethnic identity is positively associated with adolescents' self-esteem (Umaña-Taylor, Diversi, & Fine, 2002), it
175 is critical to understand how Latino parents are negotiating this process.

Familial ethnic socialization and generational status. An important variable that may be associated

with variation in familial ethnic socialization practices
180 is generational status. Research reveals that while immigrants do bring with them a series of cultural patterns and traditions, these may change in the process of
adaptation to the new culture. These changes may in
turn have a significant influence on both family func-
185 tioning and individual behavior (Foner, 1997).

The relation between language loss and generational status has been well documented by Portes and
Schauffter (1994) who showed that knowledge of and
fluency in the native tongue often disappear by the
190 third generation. Similarly, Alba (1990) found that
greater separation from the immigrant generation corresponds with a decline of salient ethnic markers, such
as language, which serve to maintain boundaries between the majority group and the ethnic group. Finally,
195 researchers also found that generational status was related to individuals' ethnic identification, such that
knowledge of and adherence to ethnic values, and engagement in ethnic behaviors tended to diminish with
greater removal from the immigrant generation (Lay &
200 Verkuyten, 1999; Rosenthal & Feldman, 1992). Thus,
it is plausible that as families gain more experience in
mainstream culture and perhaps become more accul-
turated, the ways in which they teach their children
about ethnic group membership may also change over
205 time.

Research also reveals that value systems change
both as ecological contexts change and as individuals
move into new ecological niches. As a result, even
within ethnic groups, values can vary due to length of
210 exposure to another culture (Roosa, Dumka, Gonzales,
& Knight, 2002). For example, Sabogal, Marin, Otero-
Sabogal, Marin, and Perez-Stable (1987) examined
changes in three dimensions of familism among Latinos and Whites. When compared with second-
215 generation respondents, first-generation and foreign-
born respondents differed on two of the three dimensions of familism. This suggests that adherence to practices and values varies by generational status. Given
that values appear to change within a specified popula-
220 tion as a result of generational status, it is plausible that
not only the content but also the process of the transmission of culture may change from one generation to
the next. This idea is consistent with research reporting
a negative relationship between generation and familial
225 ethnic socialization among Mexican-origin adolescents; that is, adolescents who reported fewer family
members born in the U.S. tended to report high levels
of familial ethnic socialization (Umaña-Taylor & Fine,
2004). Thus, it is critical to explore not only the proc-
230 ess of familial ethnic socialization, but also the factors
by which it varies across families.

Familial ethnic socialization and national origin.
Another potential source of variation to consider is
families' national origin. Unfortunately, variation in
235 familial ethnic socialization practices among Latino
national-origin groups has not received scholarly atten-

tion. The limited research that exists focuses on parent
socialization strategies, in general, and emphasizes the
focus on familism among Mexican-origin families
240 (Baca Zinn & Wells, 2000; Buriel & DeMent, 1997)
and respect for elders among Puerto Rican families
(Garcia-Preto, 1996b; Gonzales-Ramos, Zayas, &
Cohen, 1998). One important difference between
Puerto Rican and Mexican families, which may con-
245 tribute to variability in familial ethnic socialization, is
the facility with which families can travel to the country of origin. In fact, the facility of migration between
the island and the mainland has been shown to exert a
strong influence on family life by facilitating the links
250 that families maintain to Puerto Rican culture (Garcia-
Preto, 1996a). In contrast, migration between Mexico
and the U.S. is more complicated, as individuals must
obtain visas to travel between countries. The current
study explored this potential source of variability by
255 examining the individual experiences of these two
groups.

Goals of the Present Study

Few studies have explored the ethnic socialization
practices of either foreign-born or U.S.-born Latino
parents, and knowledge is further limited with regard to
260 possible variations in familial ethnic socialization that
exist within ethnic groups. Although our purpose was
exploratory, the following research questions guided
our inquiry: (a) Are families socializing their children
about ethnicity? (b) If so, how is this socialization oc-
265 curring? (c) What resources and/or barriers are families
encountering, if any, to ethnic socialization? (d) What
are the commonalities among Mexican and Puerto Rican mothers with regard to the process of ethnic socialization? (e) Is familial ethnic socialization similar
270 and/or different for Mexico-born mothers versus their
U.S.-born counterparts? (f) Is familial ethnic socialization similar and/or different for Puerto Rico-born
mothers versus their mainland-born counterparts?

Method

Participants

Participants included 75 mothers who were of
275 Puerto Rican (*n* = 39) or Mexican (*n* = 36) descent, had
a child between the ages of 10 and 20, and lived within
the city limits of one large midwestern city. Twelve
focus groups were conducted, with group composition
determined by mothers' country of origin and genera-
280 tional status. Generational status was assigned based on
the location where mothers were born and/or raised
(i.e., Puerto Rico, Mexico, or U.S. mainland). For example, a mother who was born in the U.S. (mainland)
but taken to Puerto Rico as an infant and raised in
285 Puerto Rico participated in the focus group with mothers who were born in Puerto Rico; for ease of presentation, these mothers are referred to as Puerto Rico born.
In the entire sample, mothers' ages ranged from 26 to
66 (*M* = 38.13, *SD* = 7.15), and educational levels
290 ranged from no formal schooling to a masters degree.

A detailed description of each focus group is available from the first author.

Procedure

To facilitate recruitment, we developed relationships with county organizations (e.g., recreational centers, organizations serving Latino populations, neighborhood associations, and consulates). The first author visited these locations with members of the research team and actively recruited mothers for participation. Based on mothers' availability, focus group dates were set and participants were given several reminder calls. We provided participants with a $5 gift certificate to a local store for each referral that resulted in active participation.

We conducted separate focus groups for Puerto Rico-born mothers, mainland-born Puerto Rican mothers, Mexico-born mothers, and U.S.-born Mexican mothers. Thus, our study involved four cases with multiple examples within each case (Miles & Huberman, 1994). Focus groups lasted between 90 and 120 minutes, were conducted in participants' language of preference, and were audiotaped. All mothers who were born outside the U.S. preferred Spanish and all U.S.-born mothers preferred English. Thus, groups with Mexico-born and Puerto Rico-born mothers were all conducted in Spanish and focus groups with U.S. (mainland)-born mothers were conducted in English. Focus groups took place in a recreational center that was near participants' homes and on a bus route. Complimentary transportation, onsite childcare, and refreshments were provided. Furthermore, mothers received a $20 gift certificate to a local store for their participation.

Focus groups were conducted with moderators and note takers fluent in both Spanish and English. After brief introductions, the moderator explained the purpose of the project and began the focus group by stating, "Some people believe that teaching their children about their ethnic background is very important, while others feel that this is not so important and that there are other things that are more important. We are here to find out your ideas about this topic. There is no right or wrong answer; we would just like to hear your thoughts on this issue."

Design

Given the limited research on ethnic socialization practices, we felt it necessary to first understand the process by which parents teach children about their ethnic backgrounds. We attempted to eliminate our presuppositions regarding the process of ethnic socialization by adopting an emic, or insider, approach. Our aim was to gather rich data from mothers describing *their* views on ethnic socialization (Rubin & Rubin, 1995).

We chose focus group methodology because of its usefulness when researchers may be unfamiliar with issues specific to a particular context or population

(Patton, 1990). Specifically, we adopted a "bottom-up" approach, which enabled us to understand the practices, attitudes, and values within the framework of Latina mothers' national culture of origin (Zayas & Rojas-Flores, 2002). While we wanted to allow mothers' experiences to be clearly heard through the interviews, our stance as researchers who view socialization from an ecological perspective led us to establish basic parameters for the study. Thus, focus group moderators followed a semistructured protocol in which parents were asked about both proximal and distal sources of socialization. Specifically, three general areas were introduced in all focus groups: (1) the ways in which families socialized their children about ethnicity, (2) the ways in which children learned about ethnicity outside the home, and (3) the resources and/or barriers that facilitated/hindered the process of socialization. The same protocol was followed for all focus groups, and moderators were trained to probe until mothers could provide no more examples for the particular topic under discussion. Nevertheless, we did not presume that mothers engaged in ethnic socialization and therefore began each focus group with a question regarding whether or not mothers socialized their children regarding their ethnicity.

Results

Preparing the Data

Because our data were analyzed by Spanish-speaking *and* non-Spanish-speaking researchers, tapes were transcribed and also translated for meaning. Interviews conducted in Spanish were transcribed and translated by one staff member and checked for accuracy by a second staff member. For focus groups with Mexican-origin parents, a Mexican-origin research team member was always involved in at least one of the steps above; this was also the case for focus groups with Puerto Rican mothers.

Analyzing the Data

Given the exploratory nature of the study, data analysis was guided by Hill, Thompson, and Williams's (1997) Consensual Qualitative Research (CQR) approach. This study collected data using a uniform protocol in order to ensure the consistency of responses. Further, this study incorporated a team of individuals to arrive at consensus in coding judgments. Finally, data were compared across the four cases to determine whether themes were relevant.

The first author and a research team worked together in analyzing the transcripts. After discussion of the guiding questions of the study, all team members independently read one transcript and developed codes. Coding discrepancies were then discussed until consensus was reached regarding the best representation of the data. Individual team members then coded a second focus group, creating new codes as necessary. The research then discussed the second focus group and,

400 again, the process of coding via consensus ensued. We repeated this process until all focus groups were coded.

The authors reexamined the coding sheets to determine the most salient codes. To formulate categories or themes, both authors independently summarized the 405 core idea of each code for each focus group (Hill et al., 1997). The themes discussed below were deemed typical because mothers in all focus groups in a particular case (e.g., island-born Puerto Rican mothers) described them as a component of ethnic socialization. We begin our discussion with the similarities that transcended 410 national origin and generational status. We follow that with similarities by generational status and conclude with an exploration of within-group differences and similarities.

Similarities Across All Groups

Nine themes were applicable across all groups re-415 garding how familial ethnic socialization took place. First, when asked how they taught their children about their culture, mothers often emphasized the importance of *traveling to their country of origin*. Although Puerto Rico is a territory of the U.S., for ease of discussion we 420 refer to Puerto Rico as a "country of origin." Dolores (all names presented are pseudonyms), a U.S.-born Mexican mother, said, "You can always talk to your kids about it, but it's not the same as being there and actually seeing it." Thus, parents indicated that their 425 children experienced a connection to the culture by visiting the native country that was more valuable than anything that parents could provide in the U.S. Parents felt that visiting their country of origin exposed children to a way of life that was absent in the U.S. For 430 immigrant parents, there was an additional component of having children experience firsthand some of the same things parents had experienced when they were growing up. Mothers indicated that visiting the country of origin enriched children's understanding of their 435 heritage and promoted a degree of internalization that could not be achieved through discussion alone.

A second mechanism involved *books, videos, and the Internet*. These tools facilitated parents' efforts to expose children to their cultures. One immigrant Mexi-440 can mother explained, "And, like, one can teach the history of Mexican[s]. Buy yourself a book of the history of Mexico and, well, help them read it. Then they can understand what each date signifies, why it is being celebrated, because it could be the Battle of Puebla, the 445 Mexican Independence.... I believe that one has to teach the history."

Third, parents in all groups mentioned the importance of *food as a mechanism* to expose their children to their background. For example, Ana, a mainland-450 born Puerto Rican mother, expressed the importance of daily rice and beans, while Raquel, a Mexico-born mother, discussed the availability of traditional foods in the U.S. All mothers discussed traditional food as a

455 part of daily life, interwoven throughout their daily routines.

Beyond specific practices and behaviors, a fourth commonality among mothers involved a more abstract discussion of instilling a sense of ethnic identification in their children. There was a general sentiment that 460 *instilling their roots* would facilitate cultural transmission to future generations. For example, Elsa, a mainland-born Puerto Rican, stated,

> I think every kid should know where you're coming from, their parents are coming from. I mean, it's nice to 465 know where you come from...from your ancestors and sometimes, you get a good sense and a strong sense from where your, you know, you've been, where your parents come from. So that way, you can teach your children also.

470 There appeared to be a hope that if parents taught their children about their heritage, they would be equipped to continue this with their own children.

Fifth, children also learned about their respective cultures from their *extended family* (particularly grand-475 parents). A number of U.S.-born mothers stated that their children were able to speak Spanish because their children's grandparents were around to expose them to the native language. Similarly, a Puerto Rico-born mother stated, "Taking them to their grandparents to 480 have them talk to them [children], because sometimes the grandparents know more than we do." Thus, because of their life experiences, grandparents appeared to supplement mothers' efforts by providing a more direct link to the homeland.

485 Mothers reported that children often raised *questions* about ethnicity covering a range of topics including group history, traditions, ways of celebrating holidays, and ways of life in the country of origin. Broadly, questions appeared from children's experiences in their 490 immediate environments. Mothers shared instances where children asked questions because of something they saw on Spanish television, or when a family member was cooking a traditional meal using a plantain leaf, or during a visit to the island. Parents ap-495 peared to use children's questions to initiate a dialogue about culture. One mother explained, "Well, I won't actually just tell my Ashley, 'come on let's sit down and talk about Puerto Rico', no, it just happens. There's something in, all over, my house that will ex-500 plain about Puerto Rico, so if she asks me, 'where did this come from?' then we'll get down into the questions" [another mother agrees].

Mothers discussed the importance of the Spanish language. *Teaching children how to speak Spanish* 505 served a dual purpose: first, passing on the language skills themselves, and second, as a method of passing on the ethnic culture. In addition, teaching the native language allowed parents to reinforce their children's unique identities and distinguish them from the domi-510 nant culture. Mothers across all groups discussed the importance of being fluent in *both* English and Spanish and the benefits one gained in the workplace as a result of being bilingual. The following conversation illustrates this sentiment:

515 *Patricia*: Especially nowadays, you know you need that, that Spanish to get a good job. So you, so they need to know it.

Yolanda: Yeah, and it's very important. As a matter of fact, you have a lot of different people going to school to
520 learn Spanish [many agree]. Yeah, so that's very important and here at home we can teach it to them without having to pay for it.

Many mothers felt that teaching English wasn't a concern. Generally, mothers indicated that they could as-
525 sume that their children would learn English, but not Spanish, through their school and community environments.

In addition to maintaining culture via language, mothers also continued their respective native *tradi-*
530 *tions* in the U.S. Mothers described that these traditions brought their children closer to the culture and, in some cases, children valued the traditions because they represented their native culture. As described by one Mexican U.S.-born mother, "I mean, we went through
535 this whole…she [daughter] just had a quinceañera [traditional Mexican 15th birthday party for girls]…a little while ago, and it was very important to her. And, I think it was because, not because it was a party, or because she was gonna dress up. For her, it was because
540 this was a Mexican tradition." Although mothers introduced children to familial traditions, children elicited the continuation of these practices. In addition, how traditions were practiced changed over time as they adapted to the U.S.

545 Although these eight themes all pertain to aspects of active familial ethnic socialization, mothers also mentioned that the process was facilitated via the *school curriculum*. For example, Mexico-born mothers mentioned that the curriculum exposed their children to
550 Mexican culture via textbooks and homework assignments that required them to research Mexican culture (e.g., *Cinco de Mayo*, Day of the Dead, and Day of the *Puebla* Battle). Similarly, Puerto Rico-born mothers mentioned that they specifically chose their children's
555 schools based on whether dual language or bilingual programs were available. As Estella put it, "That is why we have our children here, because here in this school they speak both English and Spanish."

Differences by Generational Status

Our analysis revealed differences by generational
560 status. Specifically, foreign-born mothers reported three themes that were not reported by their U.S.-born counterparts. The first theme unique to the experiences of Mexico- and Puerto Rico-born mothers involved the importance of instilling in their children a sense of
565 *pride in being Latino* generally, and Mexican or Puerto Rican specifically. For example, one mother stated, "I think that more than anything instilling in them the

pride of being…of being Hispanic, of being Mexican…the respect, the family, to feel proud of, of being,
570 of being Mexican. Because unfortunately racism exists here and, well, we like to prepare them a little." Both Mexico- and Puerto Rico-born mothers mentioned the importance of instilling this sense of pride as a buffer for potential encounters with racism.

575 Another difference across generational status was the notion that traditional *religious foods* were an important component of celebrating religious holidays and provided an opportunity for mothers to socialize their children. For example, Mexico-born mothers dis-
580 cussed the importance of the Christmas *posadas* (a reenactment of Mary and Joseph's search for shelter to await the birth of Christ, which culminates in a celebration at a community member's home) and how it was important to carry on this tradition in the U.S. Further-
585 more, they went into detail about the special meals that were prepared during this occasion. Generally, mothers discussed with their children the traditional ways of celebrating Christmas in their country of origin, and those conversations often revolved around the tradi-
590 tional meals that were served.

Foreign-born mothers also introduced the importance of instilling in their children the value of *respect*, not only toward elders, but toward humankind. As one mother stated, "I think that since they are young, one
595 has to teach them the respect for people, and for one [i.e., herself], and for themselves." Thus, there was a common sentiment across foreign-born groups that children should be taught to respect people, in general. Furthermore, mothers implied that this value was a
600 unique representation of their culture.

Analysis of Mexican-Origin Mothers

Similarities by generation. Mexican-origin mothers shared one common theme across generations: the idea that identity transcends birthplace or place of residence. Their discussions emphasized the idea that their
605 children's identity as Mexican would not change regardless of place of residence or birth. For example, the statements below illustrate this sentiment:

Tina: Because he is never going to stop being Mexican no matter where he is, or where he was born.

610 *Cecilia*: He is Mexican, despite that they can give him a legal citizenship, yes, he can be a resident…but his parents are Mexican and he has to…follow.

Differences by generational status. There were also differences in the process of ethnic socialization that
615 emerged between Mexican mothers born in Mexico and those born in the U.S. Specifically, seven themes emerged in the focus groups of Mexico-born mothers, which did not emerge in the focus groups of Mexican mothers born in the U.S. In contrast, one theme
620 emerged in the focus groups of U.S.-born mothers but did not emerge in the focus groups of Mexico-born mothers. Finally, while teaching cultural differences emerged in the groups of both U.S.-born and Mexico-

born mothers, the types of cultural differences that were discussed were different.

First, Mexico-born mothers often discussed *family get-togethers* as a method of socializing their children about their Mexican heritage. Specifically, events such as birthdays, baptisms, Christmas, and New Year's were critical to the process of familial ethnic socialization. In these events, family members could pass on their heritage and their traditions. Yet it was not necessarily through the activities that children learned, but through the family unity that the gatherings provided. Furthermore, family gatherings were mentioned as an important aspect of Mexican culture that should be continued throughout generations.

Mothers also socialized their children about their Mexican heritage by *exposing them to Mexican music, dances, and traditional costumes*. Specifically, Mexico-born mothers indicated that music symbolized culture and that by teaching their children how to distinguish the music and dances from various regions, they were teaching them about the Mexican culture.

Mexico-born mothers also explained that part of the process of ethnic socialization involved *instilling* the value of a *strong* work ethic. For many mothers, this idea was discussed in the context of discriminatory experiences or the lower status that they felt that Mexicans, in general, experienced. The following statement illustrates this idea: "But we are never at the top, we are always at the bottom. We are always the worst. And I think that I sometimes talk to my son about that, that there are a lot of negative things out there about us, and that we should try to excel, that we should try to show them that we are not what they show we are."

Mexico-born mothers also emphasized the role of *religion* in the process of familial ethnic socialization. They discussed the value of teaching their children about God and taking them to church. In fact, mothers seemed in agreement that religion was not separate from culture.

When asked where and how their children learned about their culture from outside the home, Mexico-born mothers indicated that community museums provided an opportunity to teach their children about their Mexican heritage. As Tina explained, "once a month, ah, we go to the, the museum where there is everything about...we usually go as a family...where there is everything about Mexico.... And who better [to explain] than us who truly know or who studied a little bit of that."

Watching *Spanish television* or listening to *Spanish radio stations* were other important ways in which children of Mexico-born mothers learned about their background. Specifically, Mexico-born mothers discussed the value of having their children learn about the culture and maintain the Spanish language by watching Spanish television.

Finally, Mexico-born mothers discussed how their children learned about their ethnic culture by attending *celebrations, festivals, and dances in their schools*. This was not discussed by U.S.-born Mexican mothers, although, as described earlier, all Mexican-origin groups discussed the school curriculum as a facilitator of the process of familial ethnic socialization.

One theme that emerged among U.S.-born mothers but did not emerge among Mexico-born mothers involved using home decor as an opportunity for ethnic socialization. Specifically, they discussed decorating their homes with objects such as pottery, posters, and Mexican flags, which taught their children about their background.

Interestingly, while *teaching cultural differences* emerged in the focus groups of both U.S.-born and Mexico-born mothers, the types of cultural differences that were discussed were very different for the two groups. Both U.S.- and Mexico-born Mexican mothers discussed teaching their children cultural differences as a method of exposing them to their ethnic background. For U.S.-born mothers, however, the focus was on teaching children about diversity in general. For example, mothers discussed teaching their children about the diversity in customs and language that exists within cultures. On the other hand, Mexico-born mothers emphasized the importance of teaching their children the specific differences between U.S. and Mexican cultures. These discussions usually emerged from their children's interest in doing something that their friends were doing, and something that Mexico-born parents felt was inappropriate. Ricarda's statement nicely illustrates the sentiment expressed by various mothers:

For example, my daughter says to me, "Mom, can I go with my friend?" I say to her, "yes." She says, "what is my curfew?" I say to her, "seven in the evening." She says, "that is too early." I tell her, "no," I say, "you have to obey the rules and you can...." For example, we are Mexicans, our culture is Mexican and, for example, we have to emphasize that they understand that. They are not Americans. They ask why I am not very liberal. They say I am very strict. I tell them that we are here in the United States, but I want for them to have the Mexican customs. Like I was raised.

Analysis of Puerto Rican Mothers

Similarities across generations. Four themes appeared salient in the narratives of all Puerto Rican mothers. First, mothers discussed regularly *getting together with family members* and spending time with one another as a part of their culture. They viewed this as an integral practice for maintaining family unity and described the ways in which their children were socialized regarding this value. Two island-born mothers discussed how holidays provided opportunities for families to get together:

Zoraida: Yes, but every holiday, well, one, the family gets together and everyone, everyone brings something. But all traditional food.

Veronica: Yeah, that's something already in us as Hispanics. Like, it already is a given that we have to get together and....

740 *Nancy*: ...and celebrate.

Mothers often *reminisced* by comparing childhood experiences in Puerto Rico with their children's experiences growing up in the United States. Specifically, island-born mothers like Stella used their own child-
745 hood experiences in Puerto Rico as a way of reminding their children of their ethnic roots, saying, "And it's a dialogue all the time in, or how we, remember, 'Oh, oh, ok, look, this is done in Puerto Rico.' In other words, we bring, bring up 'in Puerto Rico, we do that', 'Oh,
750 yes, look, I learned this in Puerto Rico'." While island-born mothers discussed their own childhood experiences, mainland-born mothers relayed stories of others' experiences in Puerto Rico. Although whose stories were being recounted varied by generational status,
755 both groups of mothers discussed instances of contrasting life in Puerto Rico with life in the U.S.

In addition to reminiscing, mothers in both groups also discussed how *music and dancing* were ways of getting their children interested in their ethnic heritage.
760 Ethnic music and dances provided mothers with opportunities to talk to their children about their ethnic heritage because these were topics in which their children were already interested. Mothers capitalized on their children's interest and used it as a starting point for
765 explaining Puerto Rican culture. What was unique to this discussion of music and dance was that it was cited as something that children learned about both in the family and in the community. Beyond what happened in their homes, mothers stated that children also
770 learned about their culture through community events such as parades, dances, and concerts. Although the communities provided these events, mothers often discussed instances where they attended the events with their children. Their statements illustrated a tacit un-
775 derstanding regarding the interplay between community and familial ethnic socialization. Although mothers were lucky to live in an area where such events were readily available, if they did not choose to attend with their children, these events would probably no
780 longer occur.

Finally, mothers discussed the importance of teaching their children how to *prepare traditional meals*. Similar to their sentiments regarding teaching Spanish, a number of mothers stressed that if they did not teach
785 these skills, their children would have no way of learning about traditional Puerto Rican cuisine. The following exchange illustrates this point:

Lisa: And the thing is, if we don't teach it to our kids, you're not going to find books on it. There ain't no books
790 on it. So we have to make sure, that we teach *our* kids, when our kids grow up, they teach *their* kids and it keeps going.

Mary: It continues throughout the generations.

795 *Blanca*: Put it this way, you know what, you don't learn that from books...it's like you learn it from watching your parents cooking it.

Thus, while there are obvious practical benefits to teaching children how to cook, mothers' discussions also conveyed the importance of food as a connection
800 to the ethnic culture.

Differences by generational status. Although both generations of Puerto Rican mothers shared similar views regarding ethnic socialization, one theme appeared unique to the experiences of island-born moth-
805 ers. While both generations of mothers agreed on the importance of fluency in Spanish, island-born mothers also discussed the importance of rhetoric. For example, Stella's statement illustrates the responsibility she felt about ensuring not only that her children could speak
810 Spanish, but also were able to write it properly:

Ah, when I taught my daughter, it's repetition. One doesn't say "..." one repeats. Repeating a lot so that they can and they catch it more easily because they already come with, they have their, they are descendants of....
815 Yeah, but repetition. Afterwards, there's writing. Because writing is very important, because yes, they probably know how to speak it but sometimes they don't know how to write it, and it's very important to me that we sit down to teach them how to write it.

Discussion

820 Our study aimed to discern how Mexican and Puerto Rican-origin mothers were socializing their adolescent children about ethnicity. Across all groups, mothers communicated the importance and purposefulness of familial ethnic socialization practices that took
825 place in their homes. A number of these practices did not change with greater time in the U.S. For example, mothers in all groups emphasized the importance of exposing their children to their country of origin and utilizing extended family as a resource to facilitate eth-
830 nic socialization. The narratives also support previous findings with Latinos suggesting that parents try to instill a sense of one's ethnic roots by exposing children to the culture, history, and heritage (Hughes, 2003). The prevalence of this finding suggests that
835 ethnic socialization is a normative component of child rearing and undercuts national origin or generational status (Garcia Coll et al., 1995; Hughes, 2003). Perhaps parents recognized that although group membership would not change, the connection to the culture might
840 lose its meaningfulness from one generation to the next.

Another factor discussed across all groups was the importance of teaching the Spanish language. These findings support Padilla's (1999) argument that the
845 native language is a tool that allows individuals to transmit information about the culture from one generation to the next. Mothers' reported fears about the loss of the native tongue are not unfounded. Portes and Schauffter's (1994) study of Latino youth in southern

223

850 Florida revealed that Spanish language use was greater among second-generation youth in a city with a larger Latino population than in one with a more diverse population. The mothers' statements indicate that they recognize the influence of the community on their chil-
855 dren's language proficiency.

Finally, although the family is viewed as the earliest and most influential context for ethnic socialization (Phinney & Rosenthal, 1992), our findings also supported the idea that children's ethnic socialization is a
860 product of the interactions among family, school, and community (e.g., Phinney, 1996). Mothers viewed schools as participating in the ethnic socialization process of their *specific* ethnic origin (e.g., Puerto Rican), as opposed to a panethnic (e.g., Latino) culture.
865 This may be a result of Latino segregation in the city where data were gathered: Puerto Ricans are found predominantly in the northern part of the city, while Mexicans are found predominantly in the south-central part of the city. Given that backdrop, it is easier to un-
870 derstand how parents can find schools that focus on their specific Latino population.

An analysis of similarities by generation provided support for the influence of acculturation on socialization behaviors. Regardless of national origin, foreign-
875 born mothers' statements reflected an awareness of their immigrant (or immigrant-like) status in society that are absent in U.S.-born mothers' statements. First, foreign-born mothers focused on ethnic practices and their authenticity as they were performed in the U.S.
880 For example, they were able to discuss, from firsthand experience, practices of religious celebrations, which appeared to revolve around traditional meals. This is consistent with previous research that finds that religion is a central component of cultural identity and
885 serves as a bridge between the family and the community (Maldonado, 2000; Garcia Coll et al., 1995).

Second, mothers' discussions of values also appeared to serve as a mechanism for preparing their children for stigmatization, an experience that previous
890 research found to be common among Latino groups (Garcia Coll et al., 1995). Regardless of what factors (e.g., discrimination) prompt these discussions, previous research has identified instilling ethnic pride as important among Latinos (Hughes, 2003; Phinney &
895 Chavira, 1995). Finally, mothers' statements regarding the importance of showing respect to *all* individuals support previous research indicating that Asians and Latinos report placing a higher value on respecting others in general and authority figures in particular
900 than do those of European origin (Fuligni, 1998; Fuligni, Tseng, & Lam, 1999; Garcia Coll et al., 1995; Garcia-Preto, 1996a; Harwood, 1992). In addition, Fuligni's (1998) findings with adolescent populations suggested generational differences in that those born
905 and raised in the U.S. were more likely to maintain beliefs and values consistent with the norms of U.S. society. The fact that we did not hear similar discus-

sions among U.S.-born mothers may be a reflection of the acculturation process occurring within the family
910 system, a finding documented in previous work (Rodriguez, Ramirez, & Korman, 1999).

Our findings indicate a number of differences by generation in the narratives of Mexican-origin mothers. These differences in practices could be a reflection of
915 the effects of chronosystem and macrosystem influences on family life. Specifically, as U.S. society becomes more diverse, parents have increased opportunities to expose their children to their ethnic heritage. Given that we found a number of differences by gen-
920 erational status, our findings appear consistent with an acculturation framework, which suggests that families discontinue certain practices as a result of their adaptation to the host culture. The redefined traditions reflect the transactional nature of the acculturative process
925 whereby the interactions between parents, children, and community contribute to the evolution of cultural traditions in both meaning and practice (Foner, 1997; Martinez, 1986). Thus, it is possible that U.S.-born mothers' biculturalism leads them to acknowledge greater
930 complexities in their own group identification, which in turn is reflected in their discussions with their children (Rodriguez et al., 1999).

Puerto Rican mothers revealed more agreement than difference. Specifically, mothers' narratives
935 stressed the importance of connectedness between family members, reflecting the sociocentric (interconnected) orientation of Puerto Rican culture (Harwood, 1992). For example, Harwood, Schoelmerich, Schulze, and Gonzalez (1999) found that when compared to
940 White mothers, Puerto Rican mothers tended to emphasize values and behaviors that reinforced their children's obligations and connections to others.

Our findings regarding the importance of family get-togethers also support this interconnected orienta-
945 tion. These gatherings served the purpose of instilling a cultural value of family unity (Garcia-Preto, 1996b) and allowed mothers to convey their culture to their children by maintaining practices that were common on the island. Given that these gatherings were discussed
950 across generational groups may imply that, in contrast to Mexican mothers, such a practice, with all else that may go along with it (e.g., food), may be more feasible for Puerto Rican mothers because of the close proximity to the island.

955 In addition to differences by generational status, a salient difference that emerged when comparing the experiences of Mexican and Puerto Rican mothers was that Puerto Ricans were more similar across generational groups than were Mexicans. That is, Puerto Ri-
960 can mothers cited similar practices associated with ethnic socialization regardless of whether they were born on the island or the mainland, whereas greater variation existed in the themes raised by Mexican-origin mothers based on their place of birth. The rela-
965 tionship between the country of origin and the U.S.

224

likely plays a significant role in the practices and behaviors that families maintain after migrating to the
U.S. For Puerto Ricans, families can travel with ease
between the U.S. and the island because Puerto Rico is
970 a territory of the U.S., and those born on the island
automatically gain U.S. citizenship. For Mexican-
origin families, on the other hand, travel is encumbered
by federal policies that restrict movement between the
two countries. These regulations at the macrosystem
975 level may be influencing familial ethnic socialization
(i.e., the microsystem level); thus, the differences that
are found between generations among Mexicans but
not Puerto Ricans may be a result of the differing governmental policies. Nevertheless, it appears that there
980 are more similarities in the process of ethnic socialization between these national origin groups than there are
differences, and differences that do exist may be attributed to generational status.

Strengths and Limitations

985 This study represents an important first step in understanding familial ethnic socialization as experienced
by Latina mothers. Our work moves beyond past research that sought to understand minority parents' experiences using a comparative framework, whereby
their practices are interpreted according to the tradi-
990 tional paradigm of the dominant population. Further,
few studies have explored ethnic socialization practices
of either foreign-born or U.S.-born Latino parents. Our
study allowed the mothers' voices to be heard through
the data that enabled us to highlight unique experiences
995 by both national origin and generational status.

Given the exploratory nature of our study, there
remain questions about generalizability. We examined
only two national origin groups and therefore our findings do not represent the vast diversity that exists
1000 among Latinos with regard to national origin. Further,
given our recruitment strategies, our findings do not
represent the views of those who are not at least minimally involved in the community. It is possible that
mothers who maintain involvement in their community
1005 are more likely to consider and value issues surrounding the process of familial ethnic socialization.

One of the strengths of qualitative research is that it
allows for the collection of rich and detailed data. For
example, the differences in themes between Puerto
1010 Rican and Mexican mothers suggest the importance of
viewing the acculturative process as an experience
unique to specific ethnic groups rather than a uniform
process occurring within broad ethnic categories. Our
findings are consistent with the claim that heterogene-
1015 ity can be found both within and between cultural
groups (Garcia Coll et al., 1995). Thus, our findings
can serve as a foundation with which to develop a more
comprehensive understanding of the impact of the acculturative process and the complex interface between
1020 ecological systems on socialization practices.

Directions for Future Research

Future studies should explore the experiences of
other cultural groups, explore nonfamilial socialization
agents, and investigate how ecological factors influ-
1025 ence adolescents' conceptions and understanding of
their ethnicity. For instance, immediate environmental
factors (e.g., representation of ethnic group in one's
neighborhood) may influence salience of ethnicity.
Furthermore, the impact of macroecological factors
1030 (i.e., broader and more distal influences such as SES
and race relations) should be examined as they can
have a considerable impact on adolescents' and families' experiences.

It is also important to decipher whether differences
1035 between foreign-born and U.S.-born mothers are related to the acculturation process or are a function of
life experiences. For example, due to their relatively
recent arrival in the U.S., immigrant mothers may have
greater familiarity with the cultural practices from the
country of origin, which can lead to more diverse
1040 strategies than are available to their U.S.-born counterparts. This is not because the U.S.-born are any less
attached to or engaged in their native culture but because they cannot draw from the recent experiences.

Finally, our findings underscore the need for future
1045 studies to incorporate a more comprehensive and multi-
faceted theoretical framework when studying familial
processes among ethnic groups. For example, we saw
the influence of acculturation in how mothers taught
their children the Spanish language; however, we also
1050 saw the relevance of ecological theory, as mothers re-
lied heavily on their communities to supplement their
efforts. As future studies are conceptualized, there
should be an increased emphasis on the unique role that
these perspectives provide as well as attention to their
1055 interactive influence on relational practices and outcomes.

References

Alba, R. D. (1990). *Ethnic identity: The transformation of white America.* New Haven, Yale University Press.

Baca Zinn, M., & Wells, B. (2000). Diversity within Latino families: New lessons for family social science. In D. H. Demo, K. R. Allen, & M. A. Fine (Eds.), *Handbook of family diversity* (pp. 252–273). Oxford: Oxford University Press.

Bronfenbrenner, U. (1989). Ecological systems theory. *Annals of Child Development, 6*, 187–249.

Buriel, R., & DeMent, T. (1997). Immigration and sociocultural changes in Mexican, Chinese, and Vietnamese American families. In A. Booth, A. C. Crouter, & Landale (Eds.), *Immigration and the family: Research policy on U.S. immigrants* (pp. 165–200). Mahwah, NJ: Erlbaum.

Cortes, D. E., Rogler, L. H., & Malgady, R. G. (1994). Biculturality among Puerto Rican adults in the United States. *American Journal of Community Psychology, 22*, 707–721.

Dasgupta, S. D. (1998). Gender roles and cultural continuity in the Asian Indian immigrant community in the U.S. *Sex Roles: A Journal of Research, 38*, 953–974.

Erikson, E. H. (1968). *Identity: Youth and crisis.* New York: W. W. Norton and Company.

Foner, N. (1997). The immigrant family: Cultural legacies and cultural changes. *International Migration Review, 31*, 961–974.

Fuligni, A. J. (1998). Authority, autonomy, and parent-adolescent conflict and cohesion: A study of adolescents from Mexican, Chinese, Filipino, and European backgrounds. *Developmental Psychology, 34*, 782–792.

Fuligni, A. J., Tseng, V., & Lam, M. (1999) Attitudes toward family obligations among American adolescents with Asian, Latin American, and European backgrounds. *Child Development, 70,* 1030–1044.

Garcia Coll, C. T., Meyer, E. C., & Brillon, L. (1995). Ethnic and minority parenting. In M. H. Bornstein (Ed.), *Handbook of parenting* (pp. 189–209). Mahwah, NJ: Erlbaum.

Garcia-Preto, N. (1996a). Latino families: An overview. In M. McGoldrick, J. Giordano, & J. K. Pearce (Eds.), *Ethnicity and family therapy* (pp. 141–154). New York: Guilford.

Garcia-Preto, N. (1996b). Puerto Rican families. In M. McGoldrick, J. Giordano, & J. K. Pearce (Eds.), *Ethnicity and family therapy* (pp. 183–189). New York: Guilford.

Gonzalez-Ramos, G., Zayas, L. H., & Cohen, E. V. (1998). Child-rearing values of low-income, urban Puerto Rican mothers of preschool children. *Professional Psychology: Research and Practice, 29,* 377–382.

Guzman, B. (2001). The Hispanic population: Census 2000 Brief. *Current Population Reports,* C2KBR/01-3. Washington, DC: U.S. Census Bureau.

Harrison, A. O., Wilson, M. N., Pine, C. J., Chan, S. Q., & Buriel, R. (1995). Family ecologies of ethnic minority children. In N. R. Goldberger & J. B. Veroff (Eds.), *The culture and psychology reader* (pp. 292–320). New York: New York University Press.

Harwood, R. L. (1992). The influence of culturally derived values on Anglo and Puerto Rican mothers' perceptions of attachment behavior. *Child Development, 63,* 822–839.

Harwood, R. L., Schoelmerich, A., Schulze, P. A., & Gonzalez, Z. (1999). Cultural differences in maternal beliefs and behaviors: A study of middle-class Anglo and Puerto Rican mother-infant pairs in four everyday situations. *Child Development, 70,* 1005–1016.

Hill, C. E., Thompson, B. J., & Williams, E. N. (1997). A guide to conducting consensual qualitative research. *Counseling Psychologist, 25,* 517–72.

Hughes, D. (2003). Correlates of African American and Latino parents' messages to children about ethnicity and race: A comparative study of racial socialization. *American Journal of Community Psychology, 31,* 15–33.

Knight, G. P., Bernal, M. E. Garza, C. A., Cota, M. K., & Ocampo, K. A. (1993). Family socialization and the ethnic identity of Mexican-American children. *Journal of Cross-Cultural Psychology, 24,* 99–114.

Knight, G. P., Cota, M. K., & Bernal, M. E. (1993). The socialization of cooperative, competitive, and individualistic preferences among Mexican American children: The mediating role of ethnic identity. *Hispanic Journal of Behavioral Sciences, 15,* 291–309.

Lay, C., & Verkuyten, M. (1999). Ethnic identity and its relation to personal self esteem: A comparison of Canadian-born and foreign-born Chinese adolescents. *The Journal of Social Psychology, 139,* 288–299.

Maldonado, D., Jr. (2000). The changing religious practice of Hispanics. In P. S. J. Cafferty & D. W. Engstrom (Eds.), *An agenda for the 21st century: Hispanics in the United States* (pp. 97–121). New Brunswick, NJ: Transaction.

Martinez, M. A. (1986). Family socialization among Mexican Americans. *Human Development, 29,* 264–279.

Miles, M., & Huberman, M. A. (1994) *Qualitative data analysis.* Thousand Oaks, CA: Sage Publications.

Morgan, D. L. (1997). *Focus groups as qualitative research.* Thousand Oaks, CA: Sage Publications.

Padilla, A. (1999). Psychology. In J. A. Fishman (Ed.), *Handbook of language and ethnic identity* (pp. 109–121). New York: Oxford University Press.

Patton, M. Q. (1990). *Qualitative evaluation and research methods.* Newbury Park, CA: Sage Publications.

Phinney, J. S. (1996). Understanding ethnic diversity: The role of ethnic identity. *American Behavioral Scientist, 40,* 143–152.

Phinney, J. S., & Chavira, V. (1995). Parental ethnic socialization and adolescent coping with problems related to ethnicity. *Journal of Research on Adolescence, 5,* 31–53.

Phinney, J. S., & Nakayama, S. (1991, April). Parental influences on ethnic identity formation in adolescents. Paper presented at the Biennial Meeting of the Society for Research in Child Development, Seattle, WA.

Phinney, J. S., & Rosenthal, D. A. (1992). Ethnic identity in adolescence: Process, context, and outcome. In G. R. Adams, T. P. Gullota, & R. Montemayor (Eds.), *Adolescent identity formation* (pp. 145–172). Newbury Park, CA: Sage Publications.

Portes, A., & Schauffter, R. (1994). Language and the second generation: Bilingualism yesterday and today. *International Migration Review, 28,* 640–661.

Ramirez, R. R., & de la Cruz, G. P. (2002). The Hispanic population in the United States: March 2002. *Current Population Reports,* 520–545. Washington, DC: U.S. Census Bureau.

Rodriguez, N., Ramirez III, M., & Korman, M. (1999). The transmission of family values across generations of Mexican, Mexican American, and Anglo American families: Implications for mental health. In R. H. Sheets et al. (Eds.), *Racial and ethnic identity in school practices: Aspects of human development* (pp. 7–28). Mahwah, NJ: Erlbaum.

Roosa, M. W., Dumka, L. E., Gonzales, N. A., & Knight, G. P. (2002). Cultural/ethnic issues and the prevention scientist in the 21st century. *Prevention and Treatment, 5,* Article 5.

Rosenthal, D. A., & Feldman, S. S. (1992). The nature and stability of ethnic identity in Chinese youth. *Journal of Cross-Cultural Psychology, 23,* 214–227.

Rosenthal, D., Whittle, J., & Bell, R. (1989). The dynamic nature of ethnic identity among Greek-Australian adolescents. *Journal of Social Psychology, 129,* 249–258.

Rubin, H. J., & Rubin, I. S. (1995). *Qualitative interviewing: The art of hearing data.* Thousand Oaks, CA: Sage Publications.

Sabogal, F., Marin, G., Otero-Sabogal, R., Marin, B. V., & Perez-Stable, E. J. (1987). Hispanic familism and acculturation: What changes and what doesn't. *Hispanic Journal of Behavioral Sciences, 9,* 397–412.

Saylor, E. S., & Aries, E. (1999). Ethnic identity and change in social context. *The Journal of Social Psychology, 139,* 549–566.

Sridhar, K. K. (1988). Language maintenance and language shift among Asian-Indians: Kannadigas in the New York area. *International Journal of Sociology of Language, 69,* 73–87.

Umaña-Taylor, A. J., Bhanot, R., & Shin, N. (2006). Ethnic identity formation during adolescence: The critical role of families. *Journal of Family Issues, 27,* 390–414.

Umaña-Taylor, A. J., Diversi, M., & Fine, M. A. (2002). Ethnic identity and self-esteem among Latino adolescents: Making distinctions among the Latino populations. *Journal of Adolescent Research, 17,* 303–327.

Umaña-Taylor, A. J., & Fine, M. A. (2001). Methodological implications of grouping Latino adolescents into one collective ethnic group. *Hispanic Journal of Behavioral Sciences, 23,* 347–362.

Umaña-Taylor, A. J., & Fine, M. A. (2004). Examining a model of ethnic identity development among Mexican-origin adolescents living in the U.S. *Hispanic Journal of Behavioral Sciences, 26,* 36–59.

U.S. Census Bureau. (2004). 2004 Fact Sheet for U.S. Retrieved December 1, 2005, from http://factfinder.census.gov/servlet/ACSSAFFFacts

Zayas, L. H., & Rojas-Flores, L. (2002). Learning from Latino parents: Combining etic and emic approaches to designing interventions. In J. M. Contreras, K. A. Kerns, & A. M. Neal-Barnett (Eds.), *Latino children and families in the United States* (pp. 233–249). Westport, CT: Greenwood/Praeger.

Acknowledgments: The authors would like to thank Jennifer Hardesty for her comments on a previous version of this article. Stanley O. Gaines, Jr., was the action editor on this article.

Address correspondence to: Adriana J. Umaña-Taylor, Arizona State University, Department of Family and Human Development, P.O. Box 872502, Tempe, AZ 85287-2502. E-mail: adriana.umana-taylor@asu.edu

Exercise for Article 33

Factual Questions

1. According to the literature review, does *current* theoretical work on acculturation indicate that in the process of adapting to the ways of the dominant culture, individuals will lose their identification with their ethnic group?

2. How is "familial ethnic socialization" defined?

3. The researchers state how many research questions?

4. To facilitate recruitment, the researchers developed relationships with what?

5. Did the researchers *independently* summarize the core idea of each code?

6. In the Results section, the researchers indicate that nine themes were applicable across all groups. What is the first theme the researchers discuss?

Questions for Discussion

7. The researchers used a sample that was heterogeneous in age (ranging from 26 years to 66 years old). If you had planned this study, would you have used a sample this heterogeneous in age? Explain. (See lines 288–289.)

8. In your opinion, did the researchers use a convenience sample? Explain. (See lines 293–303 and 1000–1006.)

9. The researchers show the exact words used to introduce the purpose of the research project to the focus groups. How helpful is it to know these words? (See lines 324–333.)

10. The researchers present quotations from participants in the Results section. How helpful are these quotations in helping you understand the results of this study? Could the presentation of the results be improved by adding more quotations? By reducing the number of quotations? Explain. (See lines 371–819.)

11. The Results section in lines 371–819 and the Discussion section in lines 820–1056 are longer than corresponding sections in most of the articles in this book. Is the length of these sections a strength of this research report? Explain.

12. If you had planned this research, would you have opted to use a qualitative approach or a quantitative approach? Explain.

Quality Ratings

Directions: Indicate your level of agreement with each of the following statements by circling a number from 5 for strongly agree (SA) to 1 for strongly disagree (SD). If you believe an item is not applicable to this research article, leave it blank. Be prepared to explain your ratings. When responding to criteria A and B below, keep in mind that brief titles and abstracts are conventional in published research.

A. The title of the article is appropriate.

SA 5 4 3 2 1 SD

B. The abstract provides an effective overview of the research article.

SA 5 4 3 2 1 SD

C. The introduction establishes the importance of the study.

SA 5 4 3 2 1 SD

D. The literature review establishes the context for the study.

SA 5 4 3 2 1 SD

E. The research purpose, question, or hypothesis is clearly stated.

SA 5 4 3 2 1 SD

F. The method of sampling is sound.

SA 5 4 3 2 1 SD

G. Relevant demographics (for example, age, gender, and ethnicity) are described.

SA 5 4 3 2 1 SD

H. Measurement procedures are adequate.

SA 5 4 3 2 1 SD

I. All procedures have been described in sufficient detail to permit a replication of the study.

SA 5 4 3 2 1 SD

J. The participants have been adequately protected from potential harm.

SA 5 4 3 2 1 SD

K. The results are clearly described.

SA 5 4 3 2 1 SD

L. The discussion/conclusion is appropriate.

SA 5 4 3 2 1 SD

M. Despite any flaws, the report is worthy of publication.

SA 5 4 3 2 1 SD

Article 34

Help-Seeking Behaviors and Depression Among African American Adolescent Boys

MICHAEL A. LINDSEY
University of Maryland

WYNNE S. KORR
University of Illinois

MARINA BROITMAN
National Institute of Mental Health

LEE BONE
Johns Hopkins University

ALAN GREEN
Johns Hopkins University

PHILIP J. LEAF
Johns Hopkins University

ABSTRACT. This study examined the help-seeking behaviors of depressed, African American adolescents. Qualitative interviews were conducted with 18 urban, African American boys, ages 14 to 18, who were recruited from community-based mental health centers and after-school programs for youths. Interviews covered sociodemographic information, questions regarding depressive symptomatology, and open-ended questions derived from the Network-Episode Model—including knowledge, attitudes and behaviors related to problem recognition, help seeking, and perceptions of mental health services. Most often adolescents discussed their problems with their family and often received divergent messages about problem resolution; absent informal network resolution of their problems, professional help would be sought, and those receiving treatment were more likely to get support from friends but were less likely to tell friends that they were actually receiving care. Implications for social work research and practice are discussed.

Childhood depression is a serious public health concern for families, schools, social workers, and other mental health practitioners. Annual estimates in the general population indicate that 8.3% of adolescents
5 suffer from depression (Birmaher et al., 1996). Although research indicates that depression is highly amenable to treatment (Petersen et al., 1993), the *Surgeon General's Report on Mental Health* (U.S. Department of Health and Human Services [HHS], 2001)
10 indicated that few children and adolescents with a depressive disorder receive care.

African American adolescents who reside in urban, high-risk communities may be among the most underserved populations. African American adolescents ex-
15 perience depression more than adolescents from other racial and ethnic groups (Garrison, Jackson, Marsteller, McKeown, & Addy, 1990; Roberts, Roberts, & Chen, 1997; Wu et al., 1999). Because African American adolescents are more likely than other groups to live in
20 low-income households, they may be at particularly

high risk of depression. Depression among African American adolescent boys, in particular, has been linked to having fewer perceived future opportunities (Hawkins, Hawkins, Sabatino, & Ley, 1998); low
25 neighborhood social capital and kinship social support (Stevenson, 1998); and violent behavior in African American adolescent boys living in an urban, high-risk setting (DuRant, Getts, Cadenhead, Emans, & Woods, 1995). Furthermore, African American adolescents
30 may experience barriers to identifying and using effective treatments.

Although African American adolescent boys have been recognized as a group having multiple needs, few of these discussions address their mental health needs.
35 High rates of substance abuse, academic failure (i.e., dropout rates), and high arrest and incarceration rates are problems disproportionately experienced by urban African American adolescent boys (Gibbs, 1990; Hutchinson, 1996; Majors & Billson, 1992). Unrecognized
40 and untreated mental illness may underlie these problems. Although researchers have recognized that few African American children and adolescents in need of mental health services receive them (Angold et al., 2002; HHS, 2001), there has been little discussion of
45 the attitudes and beliefs of the youths, their families, and their peers that might contribute to their underutilization of mental health services.

It is unlikely that access to services will increase unless we achieve a better understanding of how these
50 youths view their symptoms and service options and how their networks influence these views. For example, studies indicate African American adolescents and adults are less likely than white adolescents and adults to acknowledge the need for mental health services and
55 to be skeptical of using mental health services, especially when they believe they may be stigmatized by their social networks because of their service use (McKay, Nudelman, McCadam, & Gonzales, 1996; Richardson, 2001). African American adolescents and
60 their families are therefore likely to have many negative perceptions (and experiences) of mental health

care that reduce the likelihood of their seeking care even when it is available.

Social networks (peers and families) play an impor-
65 tant role regarding help-seeking behaviors and responses to ill health (Pescosolido & Boyer, 1999;
Pescosolido, Wright, Alegria, & Vera, 1998; Rogler &
Cortes, 1993). Studies regarding access to care indicate
that pathways to care are shaped by the type of prob-
70 lem experienced, as well as the social support provided
by network members (Bussing et al., 2003;
Pescosolido, Gardner, & Lubell, 1998). Social networks may attempt to provide care or are used as a
resource for identifying pathways to formal help,
75 sometimes coercing the affected individual into care
(Pescosolido, Gardner, & Lubell; Pescosolido &
Boyer). Social networks also monitor the care received
and provide assistance with maintenance of care (i.e.,
offer transportation to care, give appointment remind-
80 ers), or network members may perpetuate stigma regarding formal service use.

Earlier studies examining the use of mental health
services have tended to ignore the social processes related to seeking care and advice (Pescosolido, 1991),
85 but these processes may be particularly cogent in considering service seeking among African American adolescent boys. A majority of African American adults
use informal help sources exclusively or in combination with professional help in response to psychological
90 distress (Chatters, Taylor, & Neighbors, 1989). These
processes are particularly important to consider when
discussing adolescents because adolescents turn first to
family members and friends when experiencing a mental health problem (Boldero & Fallon, 1995; Offer,
95 Howard, Schonert, & Ostrov, 1991; Saunders, Resnick,
Hobermann, & Blum, 1994).

It is important to improve access to care for African
American adolescent boys in mental health treatment.
Therefore, the purpose of this study was to explore the
100 help-seeking behaviors and mental health attitudes of
depressed African American adolescent boys. To better
control for variability in disorder type, the study focused on depression in youths. To better understand the
factors that facilitate or hinder entrée into treatment,
105 participants included both youths receiving mental
health services and youths not in treatment. Findings
from this study can inform social work practitioners
and other mental health providers in their efforts to
facilitate this group's use of services through better
110 understanding of the role that network members play in
facilitating or inhibiting service use and increase the
number of services perceived as acceptable and effective to this underserved group through the design of
more culturally appropriate interventions and engage-
115 ment strategies.

Method

Participants and Data Collection

Eighteen respondents ages 14 to 18 who were already participating in a broader study titled "Social
Network Influences on African American Adolescents'
Mental Health Service Use" (Lindsey, 2002) were re-
120 cruited for this study. Participants (*n* = 10) were recruited from community-based mental health treatment
centers and a mental health practitioner in private practice and from community-based, nonclinical programs
for high-risk youths (i.e., a violence prevention pro-
125 gram, truancy abatement center, and homeless shelter)
(*n* = 8). In each setting, all potential participants were
individually approached by a therapist or program staff
member who explained the study and assessed their
participation interest. Flyers were posted in each re-
130 cruitment site describing the study. Informed consent
for participation was obtained from parents or guardians, and informed assent was obtained from participants.

Participants in this study were selected on the basis
135 of elevated depressive symptoms as assessed by the
Center for Epidemiologic Studies Depression Scale
(CES-D) (Radloff, 1977). Of the 69 who participated in
the original study, 18 met this criterion and agreed to
participate. This study received Institutional Review
140 Board (IRB) approval at the University of Pittsburgh
(IRB Approval: #001132).

Data were collected through a semi-structured interview schedule. Questions were derived from the
Network-Episode Model (NEM) (Pescosolido, 1991);
145 in particular, the NEM concept *network content* (i.e.,
degree of support, attitudes, and beliefs toward mental
illness and mental health care). In addition to network
content, questions were derived from the literature on
help-seeking behaviors among adolescents (i.e., help-
150 seeking pathways engaged in by youths), as well as the
literature on mental health service utilization among
African Americans. (See Table 1 for examples of the
questions and follow-up probes used in the protocol.)
Most of the interviews were conducted in the respon-
155 dents' homes and a few in community sites: mental
health centers or community-based organizations. All
interviews were conducted in private areas and lasted
between 45 min and 1 hr and 45 min.

The interview covered processes and help-seeking
160 patterns, network influences, and attitudes toward mental health care and race or ethnicity of the provider. The
first author and a trained research assistant conducted
the interviews. Participants were encouraged to talk at
length about their help-seeking behaviors in relation to
165 their depressive symptoms, with detailed accounts regarding the ways their network influenced their behaviors. They were also asked how they conceptualized
and defined mental health and associated emotional
and psychological struggles (described in the protocol
170 as "feeling sad or hurt inside").

Interviews were tape-recorded, transcribed, and
analyzed using inductive coding techniques (Miles &
Huberman, 1994). Three readers, including the first
author and two research assistants, independently re-

Table 1

Sample Interview Questions and Follow-Up Probes Regarding the Help-Seeking Behaviors Among African American Adolescent Boys

Question	Probe
When you start feeling like something makes you feel sad or hurt inside, what do you do?	How did you know that you needed to talk with somebody?
	Was there anyone who helped you to recognize or identify the feelings that you were having?
	Whom did you turn to first for help?
	Are there other things you tried to do to help you feel better beyond talking with other people?
	How did these other things work?
If you felt you just couldn't handle things going on in your life, where would you prefer to go for help? Why?	(If therapist/counselor not mentioned) Why wouldn't you go to a therapist/counselor?
	What would your friends think if you went to a therapist/counselor?
	What about your family?

175 viewed and coded transcripts to identify patterns and themes emerging from the data. After the review and designation of codes, the readers convened consensus sessions to determine the categories and subcategories of themes. A final coding matrix was developed by the 180 first author to indicate the category and subcategory of themes, a definition clarifying the meaning for each category and subcategory, and corresponding sample quotes that best captured the theme.

Findings

Themes emerged in the following areas: type of 185 problems experienced, descriptions of help-seeking behaviors, dealing with emotional pain, influence of the social network on help seeking, and perceptions of mental illness and mental health care. Within these themes, differences emerged between respondents in 190 treatment for their depressive symptoms and those not in treatment (see Table 2).

Influences of Social Network on Experiences of Depression

Family members played an important role as sources for help and support as the respondents discussed how they actively sought out family members 195 for help when dealing with depressive symptoms—that is, feeling sad or hurt inside. In many cases, respondents from both groups reported that their mother was the family member they talked to most frequently:

When problems are too bad where I just can't, I can't like 200 stop them, I can't do nothing, can't control it or nothing. I try to go out and play, but for some reason it pops back up in my head, and I can't get it out so I go to her [referring to his mother]. (*Participant not in treatment.*)

(*Referring to what prompts him to talk to his mother.*) 205 Like, I mean if something happened like with me or my friends that we couldn't handle as friends, we couldn't handle as minors, but something that my mother should know…. I mean I'm thankful that I have an understanding mom and all that. (*Participant in treatment.*)

210 Family members were equally important for both groups regarding advice or counsel received when feeling sad or hurt inside. However, those in treatment typically received advice and counsel from friends as well, whereas those not in treatment typically sought 215 the advice and counsel of only their family members.

As a way to deal with feeling sad or hurt inside, some respondents talked about how they would spend time alone or isolate themselves before or in place of talking with someone in their network:

220 Just deal with it. There's nothing—I mean it's just life. I go through. I mean, I don't know. I don't seek no help. I don't talk to nobody or nothing. I just go on with whatever I'm doing. (*Participant in treatment.*)

I try to go within myself, so I pretty much get the an- 225 swers. It's like a self-conscious. (*Participant in treatment.*)

Adolescent boys in treatment typically identified their emotional and psychological struggles on their own, first, with eventual assistance from family mem- 230 bers:

I just feel it…. It's a certain, it's a certain rush that you get sometimes. Nothing like on a football field or anything, but just your heart's racing, and I think that's the best sign of you knowing when to talk to someone. Even 235 if you say you don't have the courage or you say you don't want to, but deep down you really do because the only way to really solve anything is to talk to someone. (*Participant in treatment.*)

Engagement in religious or spiritual activities was 240 not a common response to feeling sad or hurt inside among this sample. This finding was striking given the historical role of spirituality and religion as a source for coping, support, and healing among African Americans. Only two of the 18 respondents, one from each 245 group, reported that they currently engaged in activities such as praying or going to church.

Table 2
Emerging Themes Regarding Help Seeking and Depression Among African American Adolescent Boys, by Treatment Status

Area	In treatment (*n* = 10)	Not in treatment (*n* = 8)
Problems experienced	Interpersonal conflict among peers Problems at school (behavioral or academic)	Family strain
Behaviors when dealing with a problem	Talks to family and friends Isolation	Talks to family only
People helping to identify the problem (other than family)	Self Teacher or other school personnel	No one
Preference for help	Family first, then professionals	Family only

Influences of Social Network on Help Seeking and Service Use

Network's Influence on Receipt of Formal Services. The respondents who were in treatment (*n* = 10) were asked to address questions regarding the process by which they were initially referred to formal mental health treatment. Five of the 10 respondents reported that they were referred to treatment by their school when teachers noted a decrease in functioning (academically and behaviorally) and parents or guardians agreed that professional help should be sought for these problems:

They [teachers and school officials] were like, maybe what you should do is and they were feeding her [mother]—and it's like more than one teacher saying it.... And they're like maybe you should do this. And then she put me in the program up at [outpatient treatment facility].

It was a recommendation.... It was a recommendation, yeah, from a lady at school...to my mother. And they had said, you know, try this out. They thought I had ADHD, they thought I was bipolar and all this stuff, but they couldn't put their finger on it. There was nothing that they could do to figure out exactly what was wrong with me.

Four of the 10 reported that a parent suggested or referred them for treatment:

My mom, yeah. Because she thought I had, you know, problems, issues or whatever. She just got me a counselor.

A parent's suggestion, however, should be distinguished here from a parental mandate. Several respondents (3 of 10) reported that a parent mandated formal mental health treatment, and they disagreed with this mandate:

She's making me [go to a MH professional]. If I had a choice or my say so, all this wouldn't be going on because I'm cool. I don't feel there's nothing wrong. I don't need no help. She asked me if I did. I laughed at her like, "What? Yeah, right."

Network Members' Thoughts about Respondent's Use of Formal Services. When asked whether family or friends would be supportive of their use of mental health services, respondents from both groups said that their family would support their use of formal mental health treatment:

They've [family] always been very supportive.... Even though a lot of them aren't really around me, aren't really that close to me. There's still enough love to go around. And with that, it makes it easier to come here [to treatment] instead of just being alone and coming here.... That [if family was not supportive] would definitely affect my mood at least. Maybe not necessarily coming here, but confidence-wise, it would definitely be a lot lower than what it is right now. (*Participant in treatment.*)

In contrast to those respondents not in treatment who reported that their family would support their use of mental health services, some from this group said that their family would not support their use of formal services. This finding should be further viewed in light of the problem the not-in-treatment group typically reported experiencing: family strain (problems related to family relations). Two respondents not in treatment reported that their family would want to handle problems regarding family relations among themselves without seeking professional help:

Because they feel as though why [should I] go to a counselor when I could come to them?

I think my mom would probably ask me why I didn't come to her first or something like that. "What's wrong with you?" She'd probably get mad. I don't know. But it's like, why didn't I come to her first and talk to her about it instead of me going to a therapist.

Respondents not in treatment also said that they would not talk to friends about their problems typically because their friends would not be supportive of their receipt of formal mental health services. In contrast, many respondents in treatment would talk to their friends when dealing with depressive symptoms. However, they would not tell their friends they were receiving mental health treatment—fearing that friends would laugh, joke, or tease them:

They'd probably think—they might joke around and say like, it's bad for me, you know, like I'm crazy or some-

231

330 thing, so I would like keep it to my family and myself. (*Respondent in treatment.*)

Attitudes toward Mental Health Care and Professionals

Respondents from both groups were asked to share their thoughts and perceptions regarding why it is diffi-
335 cult for mental health treatment providers to engage African American adolescent boys in mental health services. The respondents talked about the issue of stigma as a barrier associated with mental health ser-vice use. In particular, shame, embarrassment, and ex-clusion emerged from the interviews as themes regard-
340 ing the influences of the network on mental health ser-vice use:

> Because their friends might sometimes think like they're crazy and stuff like that. Wouldn't want to hang around them. And they'll just sit there and make up more ex-
345 cuses to stay away from them. It [mental health treat-ment] would draw all that person's friends away from him too. Then that person would just be, like, down in the dumps. (*Respondent in treatment.*)

Respondents from both groups said that many Afri-
350 can American adolescent boys sought to handle their problems on their own or had too much pride to go to formal mental health treatment:

> And I guess a lot of them would think, well, I don't need it. I'm this. I'm from here. I can do this. I can do that. So
355 they would…they have a certain feeling where they think they could get through it alone when they really couldn't. (*Respondent in treatment.*)

> (*Referring to pride.*) Like I'm not, you know, I'm too good to go to a counselor. Like I don't think I'm very
360 sick or I don't think nothing's wrong with me. I act nor-mal. I'm normal. You know, different things like that. False sense of themselves. (*Respondent not in treatment.*)

Furthermore, respondents shared their perceptions that talking to a mental health professional, for some
365 African American adolescent boys, meant that they would have to express their emotions associated with feeling sad or hurt inside, and that the expression of emotions was viewed as a sign of weakness among this population:

370 > Like they weren't manly enough. Like little girls. (*Re-spondent in treatment.*)

> (*Asking for help.*) …means that you're gay. That's what it means. That's how they [African American adolescent boys] interpret it. It means—well, I mean you go down
375 the line. If you ask for help, or if you cry, or if you look emotional, if you feel depressed, that means you're soft. If you're soft, then you're gay and you're not hard and not tough…. You can't let anybody know that you're soft. I swear it's like being in jail. (*Respondent in treat-*
380 *ment.*)

These comments reflect a certain machismo related to what may be defined among this population as a lack of strength when expressing emotions (i.e., crying) or asking for help. Similarly, use of the vernacular "gay"

385 among this group is part of a machismo culture that ascribed being weak or lacking strength to being femi-nine and further serves as an impediment to acknowl-edging the need for help and engaging in healthy forms of emotional expression.

390 When asked whether race of the provider affected mental health service utilization among African American adolescent boys, respondents said:

> They [African American adolescent boys] don't think that they [white professionals] can understand what
395 they're coming from. (*Respondent in treatment.*)

> And I mean it might be one of the…it might be a race is-sue because some—I think that there are some black peo-ple who close themselves off from white people. And, you know, in the mental health field, there is a majority
400 of white people, I think. (*Respondent in treatment.*)

Although the majority of the respondents said that race mattered, a few indicated that race of the provider was not as important; rather, what was important was how the provider treated them and how well the pro-
405 vider engaged them. One respondent said:

> I can't say it [race of the provider] would make a differ-ence at all because it's about getting help. It's about hav-ing someone that's there for you to understand what you're going through and to give you advice, to give you
410 encouragement, to help you sort out things that you're going through. So with me, white or black doesn't really make a difference. What matters is that we're trustworthy of each other. (*Respondent in treatment.*)

Discussion

The adolescent boys in this study were generally
415 similar to those in broader studies of nonclinical popu-lations (see Boldero & Fallon, 1995; Snell, 2002) in terms of seeking help first from family and at other times from friends and peers. In particular, peers ap-pear to have a powerful influence on this group regard-
420 ing the admission of emotional or psychological prob-lems, as well as the acknowledgment of the receipt of formal mental health services. Those who were in treatment said that they received emotional support from their friends, and that they were able to talk to
425 friends about their problems. However, additional analyses of this group revealed that most were reluctant to tell their friends that they were going to formal men-tal health services, fearing that friends would poke fun at them.

430 These contrasting findings reflect the importance of distinguishing between individually felt stigma (i.e., negative beliefs or perceptions of service use emanat-ing from within the individual) and network-induced stigma (i.e., negative beliefs or perceptions articulated
435 by friends regarding the affected individual's service use) when developing interventions and strategies to combat stigma related to service use for this group. Findings regarding the influence of peer networks also reflect the seemingly reasoned calculation about
440 friends by respondents in this study, such as when to

talk to them, what to share with them, and how supportive friends would be regarding the problem they are
facing.

This study gives a detailed description of the pathways to help seeking for African American adolescent
boys with depressive symptoms, in particular, the roles
of family, schools, and social agencies. For respondents receiving mental health care, identification of
their mental health problems was more likely to come
from family members and school personnel. Although
respondents in mental health treatment reported that
they initially tried to solve their problems on their own,
family members and school personnel still played an
active role in confirming their depressive symptoms
and facilitating their access to mental health services. It
is worth noting that the majority of the respondents
who were receiving mental health services reported
that the types of problems they experienced concerned
issues associated with the school environment (that is,
academic achievement or behavioral problems). This
finding highlights the important role teachers and other
school personnel (such as school social workers) play
in the assessment of mental health problems and making referrals to treatment.

Challenges for Social Work

Adolescent boys with high levels of depressive
symptoms who are not in treatment, however, may
pose a special challenge. Respondents who were not in
treatment in this study reported that the problems they
most often experienced concerned strained family relations. However, family members often counseled them
against going to a professional for help regarding these
emotional problems.

The predicament of the subgroup of respondents in
this study who were experiencing high levels of depressive symptoms but were not in mental health
treatment raises concern. At the time of the interview,
each respondent was involved in community-based
programs targeting high-risk youths, including a youth
employment program, a violence prevention program,
a truancy abatement program, and a homeless shelter.
However, no one in these settings engaged them about
their emotional and psychological struggles by attending to their needs or referring them to care. Although it
is important that social work practitioners and other
mental health professionals target the development of
strategies to address the attitudes of youths toward
mental illness and treatment, the situation for this subgroup of youths also reveals that those involved with
serving them need to be more sensitive to their mental
health needs. These professionals could provide assistance to youths by being referral agents and sources of
personal support.

For this high-risk group, religious congregations
and affiliated organizations that address contemporary
youth problems from a spiritual perspective may serve
as an alternative to seeking formal professional help

when dealing with mental health problems. However,
unlike earlier literature (e.g., Varon & Riley, 1999) that
documented the importance of spirituality and the
church in the lives of African Americans, problem
solving through prayer or seeking support from the
church did not play a significant role in the lives of
respondents in this study. This finding could be mis-
leading and illustrates the need for more empirical research to examine the extent to which the general
population of African American adolescent boys seeks
help from lay and ministry counselors and other adult
spiritual figures.

Functional impairment as a result of experiencing
depressive symptoms may clarify the issue of why two
subgroups of youths with similar depressive symptom
scores have disparate treatment trajectories. Based on
the self-report of problems experienced between the
two subgroups, respondents in treatment said that their
problems related to interpersonal conflict and problems
at school—behavioral or academic—whereas respondents not in treatment said that their problems related
to family strain. Depressive symptoms and associated
problems seemed to be recognized or identified by
network members when there was an accompanying
issue related to functionality. Thus, the perceptions of
network members regarding what constitutes impairment needs to be understood as a potential facilitator or
barrier to formal mental health treatment.

Limitations of the Study

Because this study focused on depressive symptoms as an indicator of mental health need, we cannot
determine how other mental health problems, for example, behavioral disorders (such as conduct disorder
and ADHD), in addition to depressive disorders might
differentially or concomitantly affect service referral or
service use.

Confirmatory and comparative analyses from the
perspective of actual network members would have
been desirable, but limitations of time and funding dictated that this study be restricted to the adolescents'
perceptions of their social network's influences on
mental health services use or nonuse. Although the
findings are based on the perspectives of a subgroup of
African American adolescent boys, this study laid the
groundwork for a more extensive investigation of these
issues in follow-up studies and for the design of an
outreach and an engagement strategy for depressed
African American adolescents.

Implications for Practice

Findings from this study have important implications regarding the recognition and identification of
depressive symptoms among African American adolescent boys. Strategies to improve the identification and
recognition of depressive symptoms among members
of this group are needed, especially in schools and
other community-based organizations. Social workers
and mental health services providers might be looking

for depressive symptom expression that fits the *Diagnostic and Statistical Manual of Mental Disorders* (DSM-IV-TR) criteria (American Psychiatric Association, 2000) and may miss the more subtle forms of expression unique to this group. Social workers and mental health service providers need to work collaboratively with community-based organizations serving this group. For example, social workers may provide training and education to staff regarding the signs and symptoms of depression, target strategies that attempt to ameliorate the perceived stigma among this group and those in their network, and develop intervention models that better engage families by incorporating them into the treatment process throughout the course of care. Better identification of mental health problems (i.e., depression) by social network members and those who provide treatment needs to become a targeted education strategy.

Quite often, professional help is a source of mental health care of last resort. There are multiple barriers regarding the help-seeking behaviors among adolescents enrolled in community-based programs, including stigma associated with mental illness, machismo and pride, and families and adolescents who believe that depression can be resolved without professional help. Therefore, it is necessary to reframe help seeking as a positive, proactive behavior among African American adolescent boys and their families.

Implications for Research

Future research needs to address the role of family and peers in the help-seeking process. Interventions that are effective for African American youths are particularly needed because social and family networks are not likely to be active users of mental health services, except when these are initiated through school. Survey research is needed to determine the extent to which the attitudes shown by youths in the single community studied are consistent across the country and the extent to which these attitudes are similar to or different from those of youths from other racial and ethnic groups. Particular attention should be given to determining the extent to which parents, especially mothers, and peers may inhibit help-seeking among this group. Once a better understanding of the network members' role in inhibiting the help-seeking process is ascertained, strategies for removing these barriers can be developed.

Studies examining the impact of referral type (mandated versus choice) on perceptions and use of mental health services have been done with adults (Pescosolido, Gardner, & Lubell, 1998). However, future research needs to examine this issue among adolescents of color, as well as the extent to which parent and child disagreement regarding problem identification and definition negatively affect the engagement process and utilization of mental health services.

Finally, findings from this study indicate that race of the provider was seen as an important issue among some respondents, particularly the belief that providers who were not African American would be unable to effectively treat this population. Thus, future research regarding the mental health treatment experiences of this group is necessary to determine how provider characteristics (i.e., race and gender) affect engagement and mental health treatment.

References

American Psychiatric Association. (2000). *Diagnostic and statistical manual of mental disorders (text revision)* (DSM-IV-TR). Washington, DC: American Psychiatric Press.

Angold, A., Erkanli, A., Farmer, E. M. Z., Fairbank, J. A., Burns, B. J., Keeler, G., & Costello, E. J. (2002). Psychiatric disorder, impairment, and service use in rural African American and white youth. *Archives of General Psychiatry, 59*, 893–901.

Birmaher, B., Ryan, N. D., Williamson, D. E., Brent, D. A., Kaufman, J., Dahl, R. E., Perel, J., & Nelson, B. (1996). Childhood and adolescent depression: A review of the past 10 years. Part I. *Journal of the American Academy of Child & Adolescent Psychiatry, 35*, 1427–1439.

Boldero, J., & Fallon, B. (1995). Adolescent help-seeking: What do they get help for and from whom? *Journal of Adolescence, 18*, 193–209.

Bussing, R., Zima, B. T., Gary, F. A., Mason, D. M., Leon, C. E., Sinha, K., & Garvan, C. W. (2003). Social networks, caregiver strain, and utilization of mental health services among elementary school students at high risk for ADHD. *Journal of the American Academy of Child & Adolescent Psychiatry, 42*, 842–850.

Chatters, L., Taylor, R., & Neighbors, H. (1989). Size of informal helper network mobilized during a serious personal problem among black Americans. *Journal of Marriage and the Family, 51*, 667–676.

DuRant, R. H., Getts, A., Cadenhead, C., Emans, S. J., & Woods, E. R. (1995). Exposure to violence and victimization and depression, hopelessness, and purpose in life among adolescents living in and around public housing. *Developmental and Behavioral Pediatrics, 16*, 233–237.

Garrison, C., Jackson, K., Marsteller, F., McKeown, R., & Addy, C. (1990). A longitudinal study of depressive symptomotology in young adolescents. *Journal of the American Academy of Child & Adolescent Psychiatry, 29*, 581–585.

Gibbs, J. (1990). Mental health issues of black adolescents: Implications for policy and practice. In A. Stiffman & L. Davis (Eds.), *Ethnic issues in adolescent mental health* (pp. 21–52). Newbury Park, CA: Sage Publications.

Hawkins, W., Hawkins, M., Sabatino, C., & Ley, S. (1998). Relationship of perceived future opportunity to depressive symptomotology of inner-city African-American adolescents. *Children and Adolescent Services, 20*, 757–764.

Hutchinson, E. (1996). *The assassination of the black male image.* Los Angeles: Middle Passage Press.

Lindsey, M. (2002). *Social network influences on African-American adolescents' mental health service use.* Unpublished doctoral dissertation, University of Pittsburgh.

Majors, R., & Billson, J. (1992). *Cool pose—The dilemmas of black manhood in America.* New York: Lexington Books.

McKay, M., Nudelman, R., McCadam, K., & Gonzales, J. (1996). Involving inner-city families in mental health services: First interview engagement skills. *Research on Social Work Practice, 6*, 462–472.

Miles, M., & Huberman, A. (1994). *Qualitative data analysis: An expanded source book* (2nd ed.). Thousand Oaks, CA: Sage Publications.

Offer, D., Howard, K., Schonert, K., & Ostrov, E. (1991). To whom do adolescents turn for help? Differences between disturbed and nondisturbed adolescents. *Journal of the American Academy of Child & Adolescent Psychiatry, 30*, 623–630.

Pescosolido, B. (1991). Illness careers and network ties: A conceptual model of utilization and compliance. *Advances in Medical Sociology, 2*, 161–184.

Pescosolido, B., & Boyer, C. (1999). How do people come to use mental health services? Current knowledge and changing perspectives. In A. Horwitz & T. Scheid (Eds.), *A handbook for the study of mental health: Social contexts, theories, and systems* (pp. 392–411). New York: Cambridge University Press.

Pescosolido, B., Gardner, C., & Lubell, K. (1998). How people get into mental health services: Stories of choice, coercion, and "muddling through" from "first timers." *Social Science and Medicine, 46*, 275–286.

Pescosolido, B., Wright, E., Alegria, M., & Vera, M. (1998). Social networks and patterns of use among the poor with mental health problems in Puerto Rico. *Medical Care, 36*, 1057–1072.

Petersen, A. C., Compas, B. E., Brooks-Gunn, J., Stemmler, M., Ey, S., & Grant, K. (1993). Depression in adolescence. *American Psychologist, 48*, 155–168.

Radloff, L. S. (1977). The CES-D Scale: A self-report depression scale for research in the general population. *Applied Psychological Measurement, 1*, 385–401.

Richardson, L. (2001). Seeking and obtaining mental health services: What do parents expect? *Archives of Psychiatric Nursing, 15*, 223–231.

Roberts, R., Roberts, C., & Chen, R. (1997). Ethnocultural differences in prevalence of adolescent depression. *American Journal of Community Psychology, 25*, 95–110.

Rogler, L., & Cortes, D. (1993). Help-seeking pathways: A unifying concept in mental health care. *American Journal of Psychiatry, 150*, 554–561.

Saunders, S., Resnick, M., Hobermann, H., & Blum, R. (1994). Formal help-seeking behavior of adolescents identifying themselves as having mental health problems. *Journal of the American Academy of Child and Adolescent Psychiatry, 33*, 718–728.

Snell, C. (2002). Help-seeking and risk-taking behavior among black street youth; Implications for HIV/AIDS prevention and social policy. *Journal of Health and Social Policy, 16*, 21–32.

Stevenson, H. (1998). Raising safe villages: Cultural–ecological factors that influence the emotional adjustment of adolescents. *Journal of Black Psychology, 24*, 44–59.

U.S. Department of Health and Human Services. (2001). *Mental health: Culture, race, and ethnicity—A supplement to mental health: A report of the surgeon general.* Rockville, MD: Author.

Varon, S., & Riley, A. (1999). Relationship between maternal church attendance and adolescent mental health and social functioning. *Psychiatric Services, 50*, 799–805.

Wu, P., Hoven, C., Bird, H., Moore, R., Cohen, P., Alegria, M., Dulcan, M., Goodman, S., Horwitz, S., Lichtman, J., Narrow, W., Rae, D., Regier, D., & Roper, M. (1999). Depressive and disruptive disorders and mental health service utilization in children and adolescents. *Journal of the American Academy of Child & Adolescent Psychiatry, 38*, 1081–1090.

Acknowledgments: This study was funded by the National Institute of Mental Health through a dissertation grant (1 RO3 MH63593-01), the W. K. Kellogg Foundation (Community Health Scholars Program), Michael A. Lindsey, Ph.D., principal investigator; as well as the Grants for National Academic Centers of Excellence on Youth Violence Prevention (R49/CCR318627-01), Philip J. Leaf, Ph.D., principal investigator. An earlier version of this article was presented at the meeting of the Society for Social Work and Research, January 2004, New Orleans.

About the authors: *Michael A. Lindsey*, Ph.D., MSW, MPH, is assistant professor, School of Social Work, University of Maryland, 525 West Redwood Street, Baltimore, MD 21201 (e-mail: mlindsey@ssw.umaryland.edu). *Wynne S. Korr*, Ph.D., is dean and professor, School of Social Work, University of Illinois, Urbana-Champaign. *Marina Broitman*, Ph.D., is scientific review administrator, Division of Extramural Affairs, National Institute of Mental Health, Bethesda, MD. *Lee Bone*, MPH, RN, is associate public health professor, Bloomberg School of Public Health, Johns Hopkins University; *Alan Green*, Ph.D., is assistant professor, School of Counseling and Professional Services, Johns Hopkins University; and *Philip J. Leaf*, Ph.D., is professor, Bloomberg School of Public Health, Johns Hopkins University.

Exercise for Article 34

Factual Questions

1. What is the explicitly stated purpose of this research?

2. What is the total number of participants in this study?

3. What is the name of the scale used to assess depressive symptoms?

4. In determining the categories and subcategories of themes, did the researchers convene to arrive at a consensus?

5. Which group ("those in treatment" *or* "those not in treatment") typically sought the advice and counsel of only their family members?

6. Do the researchers explicitly discuss the limitations of their study?

Questions for Discussion

7. Is it important to know that the researchers obtained informed consent? Explain. (See lines 130–133.)

8. Is it important to know where the interviews were conducted? Explain. (See lines 154–158.)

9. In your opinion, are there advantages to tape-recording the interviews? Are there disadvantages? Explain. (See lines 171–173.)

10. The researchers state that three readers independently reviewed and coded transcripts. Is it important to know that this was done independently? Explain. (See lines 173–176.)

11. To what extent did the sample questions in Table 1 help you understand this research?

12. In your opinion, are the suggestions for future research important? Explain. (See lines 580–615.)

13. If you had planned a study on this topic, would you have planned a qualitative study (as the authors of this article did) *or* a quantitative study (e.g., a survey with closed-ended questions)? Explain.

Quality Ratings

Directions: Indicate your level of agreement with each of the following statements by circling a number from 5 for strongly agree (SA) to 1 for strongly disagree (SD). If you believe an item is not applicable to this research article, leave it blank. Be prepared to explain your ratings. When responding to criteria A and B below, keep in mind that brief titles and abstracts are conventional in published research.

A. The title of the article is appropriate.

SA   5   4   3   2   1   SD

B. The abstract provides an effective overview of the research article.

SA   5   4   3   2   1   SD

C. The introduction establishes the importance of the study.

SA   5   4   3   2   1   SD

D. The literature review establishes the context for the study.

SA   5   4   3   2   1   SD

E. The research purpose, question, or hypothesis is clearly stated.

SA   5   4   3   2   1   SD

F. The method of sampling is sound.

SA   5   4   3   2   1   SD

G. Relevant demographics (for example, age, gender, and ethnicity) are described.

SA   5   4   3   2   1   SD

H. Measurement procedures are adequate.

SA   5   4   3   2   1   SD

I. All procedures have been described in sufficient detail to permit a replication of the study.

SA   5   4   3   2   1   SD

J. The participants have been adequately protected from potential harm.

SA   5   4   3   2   1   SD

K. The results are clearly described.

SA   5   4   3   2   1   SD

L. The discussion/conclusion is appropriate.

SA   5   4   3   2   1   SD

M. Despite any flaws, the report is worthy of publication.

SA   5   4   3   2   1   SD

Article 35

Evaluating the Use of Reflective Counseling Group Supervision for Military Counselors in Taiwan

PETER JEN DER PAN
Chung Yuan Christian University,
Chung-Li, Taiwan

LIANG-YU F. DENG
Chung Yuan Christian University,
Chung-Li, Taiwan

SHIOU-LING TSAI
Chung Yuan Christian University,
Chung-Li, Taiwan

ABSTRACT. The purpose of this study is to examine the effects of reflective counseling group supervision (RCGS) for military counselors. A convenience sampling method is adopted. Twenty-two military counselors participated in this study. Both qualitative and quantitative research methods were used for collecting and analyzing data. The results support our hypothesis that participants who received the RCGS would show a significant increase in their counseling competences. Four primary categories related to supervisory style, supervisory alliance, self-assessment, and supervising outcomes emerge as prominent and consistent from participants' learning experiences. RCGS can be an effective supervision model for participants. Implications of the findings for group supervision and further research are discussed.

From *Research on Social Work Practice, 18*, 346–355. Copyright
© 2008 by Sage Publications, Inc. Reprinted with permission.

Counseling supervision is central to both counselor education and the ongoing professional development of counselors. Although considerable attention has been paid to counseling supervision in a variety of counsel-
5 ing professions, counseling supervision by military counselors has not been extensively studied. Military counselors work in the Military Mental Hygiene Center and have been working with troops in Taiwan since 1991. They are responsible for assisting officers, non-
10 commissioned officers, and soldiers with adjustment issues, prevention of self-destruction, and enhancement of mental health (Ministry of National Defense, 2006). However, because of the frequent incidence of mental disorders, accidents, and self-injury that have occurred
15 in the military, the nature of the military mental hygiene work has been recently challenged by public discussions on the proper educational role of soldiers in the military system. Such discussions also led to a call for enhancing military counselors' competences.
20   In response to new needs in military mental hygiene work, the military system has had to alter their traditional strategies and actions in training counselors (Hu, 2006). Hu demonstrated an index system of mili-

tary counselor competence that includes professional
25 knowledge, professional commitment, and professional techniques. Only one study has explored the impact of solution-focused supervision related to military counselors (Chen, 2004). Chen's findings indicated that the experiences of developing group projects and strate-
30 gies, learning from supervisors' characteristics and aptitudes, enhancement of counseling skills and intervention, self-awareness of personal issues, and feelings with regard to the supervisory method and process influenced a military counselor's role and professional
35 development (Chen, 2004). Undoubtedly, the need to be supervised exists to enhance professional development of military counselors and ensure the client's welfare.
    Previous literature has demonstrated (Bernard &
40 Goodyear, 2004; Holloway, 1999) that supervision, in addition to helping counselors offer professional services, can also assist them in achieving maximum personal and professional growth. The goal of effective supervision is to develop a facilitative supervisory rela-
45 tionship characterized by empathy, warmth, trust, mutual respect, and flexibility (Worthen & McNeill, 2001). The tasks of supervision include teaching counseling skills, case conceptualization, professional role and practice, emotional awareness, and self-evaluation
50 (Holloway, 1999). Supervisors can teach supervisees professional knowledge in their roles as instructors, supporters, trainers, and consultants (Holloway, 1999). Watkins (1997) pointed out that supervision provides the supervisees with vital feedback about their per-
55 formance in the counseling session, offers guidance during periods of confusion, allows for alternative views, and offers a secure base for the supervisees. Supervisors were perceived as more trustworthy when they helped to establish clear goals for supervision,
60 gave direct feedback about the trainee's work, helped the supervisee develop his or her own style, suggested alternative ways of conceptualizing cases, and called the supervisee by name (Heppner & Handley, 1981). There was general agreement with regard to the top six

65 interpersonal skills that appeared most salient: providing direction, providing constructive feedback, building supervisee confidence, helping supervisees assess own strengths and growth areas, confronting when appropriate, and responding to supervisee concerns
70 (Wetchler & Vaughn, 1991). Tsui (2005) further indicated that social work supervision has been identified as one of the most important factors in determining the job satisfaction levels of social workers and the quality of service to clients.

75 Ward and House (1998) developed specific procedures regarding how to conduct a model of counseling supervision that integrates reflective learning theory with the concurrent development of counselor-in-training and supervisory relationship. Reflective learning
80 is contingent on the quality of the supervisory relationship (Sexton & Whiston, 1994). It is through this "constructed interaction" that active learning occurs and knowledge of how to change behavior develops (Shih, 1995; Shou & Shih, 1995). This implies a cyclical
85 supervisory interaction that aids a counselor-in-counseling context with a meaningful change in perception and practice. The supervisory relationship becomes a container to review a counselor's intentionality, belief, and base assumptions surrounding disorienting
90 professional events (Ward & House, 1998). In this relationship, a reexamination of professional assumptions assists the supervisee in developing a metaperspective of the counseling process. Therefore, a counseling supervisor is challenged to create a learning context
95 text that enhances supervisees' skills as they construct relevant frames from which to devise effective strategies in working with clients (Holloway, 1999). The learning alliance of reflective counseling group supervision (RCGS) is illustrated as a series of four phases
100 representing the developmental process of counseling supervision: contextual orientation, trust establishment, conceptual development, and clinical independence (Ward & House, 1998). Each phase of the supervisory relationship illustrates the learning experiences of the
105 participants and the central focus for the reflective learning experiences of the supervisees. The model represents a dynamic interchange that demonstrates the concurrent development of supervisory relationships, which in turn leads to the clinical independence of the
110 counselor trainees. Griffith and Frieden (2000) provided support for the notion that counselor educators can facilitate reflective thinking in students through the practices of Socratic questioning, journal writing, interpersonal process recall, and reflecting teams. Cor-
115 coran (2001) asserted that structural, process, and individual factors within the supervision environment were identified as intervening conditions to reflective process. Moreover, the consequences of reflective process included changes in condition, skills and behaviors,
120 and the personhood of trainee (Corcoran, 2002).

The group supervision model is the most popular model of supervision in a variety of professions, including psychotherapy (Holloway, 1999), counseling (Christensen & Kline, 2001), and social work
125 (Kadushin & Harkness, 2002). Group supervision is often used as a supplement to, rather than a substitute for, individual supervision. As defined by Kadushin and Harkness (2002), group supervision uses a group setting to fulfill the responsibilities of social work su-
130 pervision. In addition, there are more teaching and learning experiences available in a group context because the participants share their difficulties and experiences. Support for using group supervision is based on the belief that it offers opportunities for vicarious
135 learning in a supportive group environment (Christensen & Kline, 2001). It is stressed that, once established, this environment contributes to decreased supervisee anxiety, increased self-efficacy and confidence, and enhanced learning opportunities (Brown & Bourne,
140 1996; Starling, 1996). In addition, group supervision is seen as having the potential to reduce the issues of hierarchy and dependency found in individual supervision (Bernard & Goodyear, 2004). This has a particular meaning to military counselors because the first prior-
145 ity obligation of soldiers is obedience to orders and conformity to rules. In most cases, military counselors are not only soldiers who assume multiple obligations of military policy and superintendent's expectancy but also counselors who serve clients, clients' families, and
150 society at large. These multiple obligations can, and often do, come into conflict, and a major task of group supervision is to help military counselors address such conflicts. Finally, group supervision is advocated because it is an efficient use of supervisory time and ex-
155 pertise (Christensen & Kline, 2001; Hawkins & Shohet, 1989; Holloway & Johnston, 1985).

Despite a proliferation of research on the supervision and its related issues, little attention has been given to RCGS. Although procedures for conducting
160 RCGS appeared in the literature (Griffith & Frieden, 2000; Shih, 1995; Shou & Shih, 1995; Ward & House, 1998), there has been no reported evaluation of this model. There are a number of reasons why RCGS for military counselors is needed in the field of supervi-
165 sion. First, little group supervision is available to military counselors in any setting (Chen, 2004). Second, military counselors, as officers, have, more or less, their professional hierarchical ethics in the process of administration supervision. Therefore, they may not be
170 able to report directly to their counseling supervisors in their offices or comment freely to their officers because of rank. Third, military counselors already spend a significant portion of their time working with the military troops. Acting within the military counselor's role
175 function in the troops, they are used to teaching, asking, admonishing, and advising clients to change. The RCGS, however, by providing a context for the critical analysis of base assumptions and beliefs about clients, change, and one's practice may be able to offer a new
180 conceptualization of supervisory working alliance for

military counselors. The provision of a context that encourages supervisees to willingly explore the dissonant counseling experiences and move to the center of the learning situation is the essence of a reflective supervisory relationship. This is necessary to enable counselors to shift to a higher order of conceptual processing (Ward & House, 1998).

Because of the lack of basic research in the effects of RCGS, Shih (1995) suggested that future qualitative and quantitative research is necessary. In response to such requests and suggestions, the effects of RCGS are examined by both qualitative exploration and quantitative method in this study. However, the entire study was categorized as exploratory, as the quantitative research design is preexperimental. The purposes of this study were to examine quantitatively the effects of group supervision based on RCGS for military counselors and also to highlight findings from a qualitative exploration. Our hypothesis was that military counselors who received RCGS would show significant increase in their counseling competences between pretest and posttest.

Method

Participants and Procedures

A convenience sample was used in this study. Twenty-two military counselors, based on the availability of their time, participated in RCGS as part of an in-service counseling training program. One young counselor dropped out of this program because of a new task assignment. Twenty-one military counselors completed this training program. Thirty-three percent of the participants were female ($n = 7$), and 67% were male ($n = 14$). Ages ranged from 28 to 49, with a mean and modal age of 35. Eighty-one percent of the participants graduated from counseling-related majors ($n = 17$), and 19% of participants had received noncounseling-related majors ($n = 4$). Twenty-four percent of the participants have master's degrees ($n = 5$), 62% of the participants have bachelor's degrees ($n = 13$), and 14% graduated from junior colleges ($n = 3$). During the 2-year period, a monthly 2-hour group supervision session based on the RCGS model was conducted for the participants. Twenty-four sessions were completed.

Measures

Demographic questionnaire. The demographic form asked for the participants' gender, major, and educational background.

The Counseling Competence Inventory (CCI). The CCI (S. H. Liu & Wang, 1995) was used to measure the level of counseling competences for supervisee participants. The CCI is a 49-item, 7-point Likert-type measure (1 = *strongly disagree*, 7 = *strongly agree*). The CCI comprises eight subscales, including Professional Behavior, Depth Interaction, Message Interaction, Basic Communication, Conceptualization Skill, Personalization Skill, Personal Traits, and Methodological Foundation. Each subscale ranges from five to

seven items, High scores on the CCI indicate good counseling competences in specific subscales mentioned above. The Cronbach alpha is reported at .89 for the total score and .81 to .90 for the subscales. The test-retest reliability is reported at .91 over a period of 4 weeks. The concurrent validity, based largely on its correspondence with the Self-Rating Measures, has a correlation coefficient of .92 (Liu, 1999).

Counseling Group Supervision Feedback (CGSF). The CGSF was developed from open-ended descriptions of significant learning experiences from counseling group supervision for this study. Chou (1997) found that becoming an effective counselor is a complicated process for novice counselors. Based on his findings, a key factor that affects counselors' professional development is probably related to the quality of the counseling training they received (Lee, 2000). Therefore, in addition to the CCI, it was considered necessary to add open-ended questions to collect more precise information. This was accomplished by conducting a focus group interview 2 weeks after the program was completed. The current investigation is a preliminary effort to understand supervisees' perceived experiences by employing a qualitative research method. In reviewing previous research findings (C. J. Liu, 1997; Shih, 1995), the first question was to ask what they feel about the supervision program. The second question was to examine the supervisees' own experiences in the supervision program that benefited their professional development. Finally, the supervisees were asked to "list three important things learned from the process of supervision."

The RCGS Format

In this framework, military counselors are encouraged to reflect on the moment of action when situations do not present themselves as given, and clinical direction must be constructed from events that are puzzling, troubling, and uncertain. During the first meeting, the supervisor directs supervisees to formulate and share learning goals and facilitates an exploration of the roles and procedures supervisees would enact during the supervision group meeting. This discussion facilitates the development of supervision norms and is also the first step in the supervisors' ongoing efforts to establish a supportive learning environment in the supervision group. It is crucial to build up a supportive environment because learning is assumed to rely on effective feedback exchanges of the supervisees (Ward & House, 1998).

In each supervision session, one or two military counselors take turns presenting a case report. The presenting supervisee, group members, and the supervisor participate in a series of interactive activities according to a reflection on the civilian and military counselors' supervisory framework. This model implies that military counselors learn from observing and discussing clinical issues with the supervisor, offering and soliciting feedback, and addressing emotional and cognitive reactions to the here-and-now process of group supervision.

295 A primary characteristic of a reflective supervisory dialogue is a focus on themes rather than content patterns of the supervisees' report of the counseling session (Ward & House, 1998). Open-ended thematic observations can prompt a shift from content review to

300 process-oriented supervisory conversation. To promote self-assessment, supervisors address the following questions:

1. What hypotheses are possible for explaining the client needs?

305 2. Do you have the skills to address these effectively and ethically?

3. If not, what do you need to do to fill in this gap?

Data Collection and Analysis

Participants were asked to complete the CCI before the first session and immediately after the final session. A series of one-way repeated measures ANOVA were

310 used to determine the differences between the timing variables (see Table 1). Significance of difference between means was tested at the .01 level. In addition, the CGSF was collected shortly after the final session.

The participants' responses to these open-ended

315 questions were analyzed with a qualitative research method developed by Strauss and Corbin (1990) and Christensen and Kline (2001). We first read all of the participants' responses to provide us with a general sense of their contents ($N = 296$). Subsequently, each

320 of the participants' responses was written on an index card based on different questions. Two research team members then read these cards, clustered responses, and put them into meaningful domains and categories through careful discussion. At this point, the assess-

325 ment of interrater reliability was conducted. After the first test and retest, the interrater reliabilities were .89 and .92, respectively. Open coding was completed by separating, identifying, labeling, and categorizing data in terms of general themes. In open coding, based on

330 participants' responses, a theme surrounding "outcome" was developed by researchers. Subsequently, we grouped all data that seemed to relate to "outcome" into one large group named "supervising outcomes." Then, we further used participants' responses to build

335 properties and provide characteristics within the domain to help describe it. For example, as participants responded to interview questions and shared their perceptions, we identified affect, cognition, behavior, and attitude as four interrelated properties characterizing

340 "supervising outcomes" in group supervision. Thus, initial categories emerged from significant learning experiences generated by the participants.

Next, axial coding was used to reconnect data and highlight relations between categories and subcatego-

345 ries (Christensen & Kline, 2001). In axial coding, we explored those aspects that seemed to contribute to

participants' "outcome," such as awareness of self and interactions, increased clarification of personal assumptions about the counseling process, mastering

350 counseling skills, and military counselor's limits and strengths.

In selective coding, all information attained through previous data analysis was integrated and employed to develop a clearer, more abstract explanation and de-

355 scription of themes and relations emerged in the research. For this purpose, data were examined for changes in conditions that influenced actions, interactions, and participants' responses over time (Christensen & Kline, 2001; Strauss & Corbin, 1990). To do

360 this, each of the domains and categories were then reviewed, and data were coded or deleted as appropriate. For example, we explored data by means of explicating a story line that consisted of relations between all categories, identification of a core category and validation

365 of existing concepts, and refinement of properties and domains was used to define categories and concepts. Finally, four primary categories related to supervisory style, supervisory alliance, self-assessment, and supervising outcomes were constructed.

370 Maxwell (1996) indicated that each type of the qualitative research has its potential validity threat in the process of data description, interpretation, and theoretical selection. In this study, throughout the process of data collection and analysis, prolonged engagement

375 as well as researcher and method triangulation were used to ensure the credibility of findings (Christensen & Kline, 2001). For triangulation, this study involved peer researchers' interpretation of the data at different times. The prolonged engagement consisted of a 30-

380 minute group interview that was conducted by the researchers, which served as a final form of clarification and verification.

Results

Differences Between Pretests and Posttests on the CCI

A series of one-way repeated measures ANOVA was used to determine if military counselors' perceived

385 counseling competence could be explained by selected timing variables. The timing variables examined in this study were the pretest and posttest. The dependent variables were the CCI. The independent variables were the timing variables.

390 Means and standard deviations on participants' perceptions of the CCI during the pretest and posttest were calculated for Professional Behavior, $F(1, 20) = 11.64$, $p < .01$; Depth Interaction, $F(1, 20) = 51.26$, $p < .01$; Message Interaction, $F(1, 20) = 34.73$, $p < .01$; Basic

395 Communication, $F(1, 20) = 31.97$, $p < .01$; Conceptualization Skill, $F(1, 20) = 55.17$, $p < .01$; Personalization Skill, $F(1, 20) = 19.61$, $p < .01$; Personal Traits, $F(1, 20) = 36.53$, $p < .01$; and Methodological Foundation ($p < .01$). The results indicate that after conducting

400 24 sessions of GCGS, military counselors' perceived counseling competences have significantly increased in

240

Table 1
Summary of One-Way Repeated Measures ANOVA of the CCI

Subscale	M	SD	F	p	Effect size
Professional behavior					
Pretest	28.19	5.77	11.64	.003*	.368
Posttest	32.62	4.86			
Process skill					
Depth interaction					
Pretest	26.10	6.81	51.26	.000*	.719
Posttest	36.00	7.04			
Message interaction					
Pretest	24.33	6.98	34.73	.000*	.635
Posttest	31.19	6.60			
Basic communication					
Pretest	17.76	4.33	31.97	.000*	.615
Posttest	22.10	4.04			
Conceptualization skill					
Pretest	28.05	5.26	55.17	.000*	.734
Posttest	36.38	7.17			
Personalization skill					
Pretest	25.81	6.02	19.61	.000*	.495
Posttest	30.62	7.03			
Personal traits					
Pretest	37.33	6.74	36.53	.000*	.646
Posttest	44.05	5.47			

Note. CCI = Counseling Competence Inventory. $N = 21$. Effect sizes are reported for statistically significant differences ($p < .01$).
*$p < .01$.

all subscales of the CCI. Finally, the eta-squared was used to calculate effect size. Large effect sizes for all subscales found from the current study reveal significant practical meaning of the results.

Responses to the CGSF

Final data collection and analyses yield four primary categories related to supervisory style, supervisory alliance, self-assessment, and supervising outcomes, which emerged as prominent and consistent in the RCGS. Supervisory style referred to the supervisor's leader style. It was defined as supervisor-generated directions, feedback, information, and a unique approach to facilitate a reflective learning process. Supervisory alliance was characterized as the supervisor's developing and maintaining a positive supervisory alliance, which was crucial for enhancing the supervisee's willingness to reflect on the dissonant counseling experiences as well as on conceptual and clinical demands. Self-assessment was defined as the supervisees' development of insight regarding sense of contextual urgency in counseling relationships, ambiguity associated with the application of overall principles to crisis intervention, and ability to self-supervise. Supervising outcomes referred to what supervisees perceived in the group supervision. These outcomes included awareness of self and interactions, increased clarification of personal assumptions about counseling process, mastering counseling skills, and military counselor's limits and strengths.

Supervisory style. Participants found the supervisory style to be highly facilitative. The supervisor was frequently described as positive, safe, nonjudgmental, and a thoughtful person with whom they could take risks and learn to develop their own style of being a helper and counselor. One participant talked about being comfortable in supervision for the first time, making statements such as, "I have no idea what to do with this person.... This is a whole new ball game for me." She attributed her increased openness and lack of defensiveness to the supervisor's statement: "This is a learning environment, and let me go with each one of you." Participants described the supervisor's involvement on a continuum that ranged from the facilitator (e.g., observing and encouraging interaction) to the director (e.g., providing directions, offering unsolicited conceptual input, and giving feedback). Participants perceived the facilitative roles of the supervisor more positively than directive participation: "I really enjoy this approach because it allows us as students to observe the process and give our own feedback, rather than hear from an instructor to tell us what we need to improve"; "Through interactions in the group, I gained a lot of insight about how I relate to my clients"; and "I've realized that a supervisory group is a place where I can go to express myself and receive others' feedback." At this point, the supervisor is most effective when he or she assumes less directive and more facilitative roles. The supervisor is, however, also imparting knowledge and integrating information in the supervisory process. One participant indicated, "I really enjoy the amount of information we are getting." Specifically, supervisors' provision of information regarding the counseling strategies, mental disorders, and clinical situations increased awareness of themselves, their roles, and role behaviors. Another stated, "Information dissemination by the supervisor was especially helpful."

Supervisory alliance. In the beginning of the supervision, clarification of the supervisory relationship was the major issue, and quality supervision was discriminated by perceived trustworthiness and expertise of the supervisor. The supervisor supplied initial structure and highlighted the collaborative relationships between interactions, feedback, positive atmosphere, and skill development. When supervisees began group supervision, they were anxious about how they would be judged by other supervisees and by the supervisor. As a result, they became observers and avoided giving feedback. Over time, supervisees became more interested in their relationships with other participants and the supervisor because they increasingly valued, trusted, and respected the feedback they received. "I began to trust others' feedback. That trust helps me take more risks, share my comments in the supervision process, ask questions, and basically stay engaged in the process," said one supervisee. "Interactions with members and the supervisor are the most valuable part of group supervision," said another one. Another supervisee said, "I realize that my tension was reduced once I pushed myself to interact more in group supervision. Consequently, I learned more, trusted others, and enhanced my relationships with everyone in group supervision." Others had this to say: "I think, by encouraging us to take responsibility for learning from one another, the supervisor has allowed me to grow as a counselor. We have a wonderful environment to learn, as all have learned from one another"; "This is a positive atmosphere for me to grow and step out to do things differently in role play"; "It is a special experience to know no matter how badly we acted in role-playing situations, we all know that a supervisor is always there with us." Participants indicated engagement and group support as the two beneficial components: "I could not believe how quickly I've felt like doing teamwork with my group members and supervisors; they are very supportive—yet challenging, which makes me feel comfortable to share and to be myself." Participants pointed out that it was helpful to receive feedback during the supervisory process.

Self-assessment. Supervisees realized that learning was minimized when they were not actively involved in the feedback exchange process in group supervision. This was a process of participants' self-assessment. One supervisee indicated, "I got frustrated because I wasn't learning anything. When I was confronted I realized I interacted minimally and refrained from giving and soliciting feedback. I finally got it: I wasn't

involved in feedback and I was not learning." There was a growing awareness that participants examined the reflection in different ways. One participant mentioned,

> For me, the most important part of reflection in a general way, is to reflect: how is my work with clients, how is my personal life, how are these factors influencing my psychological status…for me, I evaluate my stress level. How is that balance going? Now I see professional and personal identity as part of one thing. They are just different parts, but inseparable.

As supervisees attained awareness during supervision, they gained a better understanding of counseling work concepts. By learning about themes, theories, and philosophical assumptions and by paying attention to the learning experiences, supervisees began to understand the counseling process in both supervision and the client's contexts, "I've realized that the struggle of dealing with personal issues is what group supervision and individual counseling are all about," said one supervisee.

Supervising outcomes. Three domains emerged from supervisees' perspectives: cognitive changes, skill developments, and personal growth. The cognitive domain included awareness of the military counselor's limits and strengths, moving away from dichotomous thinking, awareness of counselor's development as a lengthy process, and those related to one's knowledge base. Knowing the military counselors' limits and strengths are essential for all mental hygiene workers in military systems. Many participants stated, "I accept feeling frustrated and disappointed with my superintendent, but it's okay to have a 'bad working environment' as long as I am learning from it." Another participant expressed,

> Each superintendent has different leader style and therefore has a variety of expectations. Following his rules or creating good relationships with clients under the professional ethics was really tough to me. The most important thing is to learn how to adjust yourself. As long as I'm learning or getting better, I don't have to be perfect.

Many supervisees expressed,

> What came out for me at this period of time is that there isn't one answer. All things have two sides and it depends on where the client is and how you present it. So there is not just one intervention. It is more complex.

For some supervisees, a more complex understanding of clients naturally led them to the recognition of the need for more creative decision making with regard to interventions. A supervisee shared his opinion: "Looking at the supervisory sessions, one thing I've learned is that each case is unique and what works with one is not necessarily going to work with another." The skill domain included listening skills, goal-setting skills, and basic counseling skills. Supervisees also learned about specific skills to be employed in supervision and in their groups. As supervisees used techniques to interact

575 more effectively in supervision, they learned how to conduct their individual counseling more effectively. Similarly, as they gained awareness of themselves and used themes, theories, and philosophical assumptions throughout their learning process, they came to under-
580 stand counseling theories, counseling processes, and counseling skills more clearly. One supervisee indicated, "Fortunately, I learned about skills I can use in counseling, in RCGS, or in my real life." Another supervisee said, "I was suffering from being confronted
585 and I got frustrated because I felt I wasn't learning new things. I finally got it: I wasn't involved in interactions and I was not learning." The personal domain included openness to feedback, empathetic understanding to clients, and increased awareness of the need for self-
590 reflection. Many participants clearly expressed confidence in themselves as growing to become counselors. For example, one of the participants stated, "I am confident that I will become more skilled in my counseling encounters and I will be able to benefit others." When
595 participants were actively involved in group supervision, they gained increased awareness of themselves, conceptual development, relationships with others, and understanding of client issues.

Discussion and Applications to Social Work

According to the results of this study, significant
600 differences were found on the CCI between pretests to posttests, and the responses to open-ended questions also revealed meaningful supervisory experiences. Because the CCI is designed to assess a diverse range of competences including Professional Behavior, Depth
605 Interaction, Message Interaction, Basic Communication, Conceptualization Skills, Personalization Skill, Personal Traits, and Methodological Foundation, the results seem to fully support the hypothesis that military counselors who received RCGS would show a
610 significant increase in their counseling competences from pretests to posttests. Although previous research on group supervision (Christensen & Kline, 2001; S. H. Liu, 1999; McMahon & Simons, 2004) indicated that group supervision has effects on the training of super-
615 visees during their supervisory experience, the results in this study need to be examined more carefully. The use of pretest and posttest test design may have provided some spurious effects because of some uncontrollable threats to internal validity.
620 A number of explanations can be provided with regard to the changes reported after RCGS experiences. First, the model outlines the sequence of supervisee development as well as the interactive reflective learning cycle between the supervisor and supervisee.
625 Hence, developing and maintaining a positive learning alliance is crucial for enhancing the supervisee's willingness to reflect on the dissonant counseling experiences as well as on the conceptual and clinical demands that are essential for further counselor develop-
630 ment. Second, as trust is experienced within the super-

visory dyad, the dissonant experiences of supervisees are transformed into meaningful schemas and corresponding counseling skills. The supervisee develops in concert with the progression of the on-site supervision
635 relationship (Shih, 1995; Ward & House, 1998). Third, the supervisory relationship provides a context in which supervisees become more confident in professional risk-taking behaviors and strategies related to counseling relationships. Fourth, observing how fellow
640 members conduct an individual counseling may aid in learning counseling skills. As a person watches peers learn a skill, he or she feels more empowered to practice that skill. Observing a peer completing a task instills confidence in the person's ability to perform the
645 same task (Christensen & Kline, 2001).

Based on the data collected from the open-ended questions, results were congruent with previous findings regarding supervisory experiences, which include the following: (a) RCGS provides an opportunity to
650 learn through both participation and observation (Brown & Bourne, 1996; Ward & House, 1998), (b) supervisors must assume a facilitative role as an information integrator in the supervision process (Corcoran, 2001), (c) supervisors can also promote self-awareness
655 in supervisees (Chen, 2004; Christensen & Kline, 2001), (d) developing a positive learning alliance is crucial for the quality of the supervisory relationship (Holloway & Johnston, 1985), and (e) the more supervisees perceived supervisors as supportive, the more
660 both perceived level of trust and the supervisee's learning and growth (Shih, 1995; Wark, 1995; Worthen & McNeill, 1996).

In addition, theoretical constructs derived from this investigation highlight new perspectives directed at the
665 understanding of self-assessment. Self-assessment was related to supervisees' development of insight regarding the sense of contextual urgency in counseling relationships and ability to self-supervise. Based on RCGS, an emphasis on constructing professional experiences
670 is to believe that meaningful learning occurs only through self-examination of assumptions, patterns of interactions, and the operating premises of an action. Thus, providing a systematic and detailed account of the important experiences throughout the group super-
675 vision can evolve supervisees' experiences and knowledge. Learning from the supervisory process was consistently valued as the most important benefit, which is congruent with earlier findings (Chen, 2004; Liu, 1997; Shih, 1995; Tsui, 2005). This may be indicative of a
680 reflective supervisory dialogue, which is the primary nature of RCGS. One of the characteristics of reflective dialogue is an emphasis on self-assessment. Central to reflective learning theory, this internal process is characterized by the trainee's ability to reflect objectively
685 on the counseling process in relation to the needs of clients. The supervisees observed and learned from supervisory interactions directly and continually. Hence, participants' dissonant experiences can be

243

transformed into meaningful schemas. From this perspective, supervisors can promote self-assessment in supervisees by encouraging (a) an identification of goals regarding client issues and the counseling process, and (b) an increased self-direction in identifying professional gaps and strategies for development of the skills. The result provides insight into the developmental process of RCGS from this point of view. It is meaningful and valuable for military counselors when situations do not present themselves as given, and clinical direction must be constructed from events that are puzzling, troubling, and uncertain in the troops.

Information about ethical practice and legal challenges is not included in this study. Krushinski (2005) and McGlothlin, Rainey, and Kindsvatter (2005) reported that supervisors should know how to make their supervisees aware of professional and ethical standards and legal responsibilities of the counseling profession. This may reflect a controversial issue of military counselors' tasks. The role function of military counselors is to promote military officers' mental hygiene, and if necessary, to protect client welfare. It appears that military counselors were suffering from role conflicts and role confusion in Taiwan. Though conflicts of obligation are unavoidable for most members in complex societies, it seems clear that we ought to avoid assuming obligations we know will put us in frequent or irreconcilable conflict. Therefore, in advanced supervision, we can begin to analyze the moral situation of military counselors by reviewing some of their fundamental obligations and considering whether these obligations create special difficulties or irreconcilable conflicts. Bernard and Goodyear (2004) saw this as the supervisor's paramount responsibility. Because the purpose of supervision is to foster the supervisees' professional development, to ensure clients' welfare, and to improve the clinical outcome of the supervisee (Bernard & Goodyear, 2004), some risks have existed for military counselors in the supervisory process. Thus, future studies should include role conflict as a factor in the investigation of professional development. Furthermore, there is an enormous need for effective, qualified military counselors to deal with family and individual issues occurring in military families, especially during times of war. An ethical guideline may provide a framework for supervision of military counselors working with troubled clients. As a result, a qualified military counselor can provide services of good quality.

Of course, group supervision has advantages and disadvantages. Based on the findings of current qualitative research, group supervision provides a wide variety of learning experiences, including supervisory style, supervisory alliance, self-assessment, and supervising outcomes perceived by the participants in the group supervision sessions. However, as Brown and Bourne (1996) cautioned, group supervision focuses on issues that have relevance to the largest number of group members in social work. Specific and urgent needs cannot be handled immediately. In many cases, it may seem easier to opt out of responsibility to engage in exploration, problem solving, and decision making. Finally, conformity to group norms may be harmful to the creativity and productivity of the work team (Tsui, 2005).

Although supervision has been identified as one of the most important factors in determining the quality of service to clients in a variety of professions, it is surprising that supervision has not received as much attention as other components in social work practice, such as social work research or administration (Tsui, 2005). This is the first study that provides a comprehensive and in-depth exploration of the use of an important supervision model, RCGS, for military counselors. As it appears that RCGS can be an effective supervision tool for supervisees and supervisors, it is important that future research expands, confirms, and/or negates these initial conceptualizations. In particular, future researchers are encouraged to explore (a) supervisors' perceptions of this modality of supervision, (b) the difference of the supervisory working alliance between RCGS and a variety of supervisory models, (c) RCGS experiences with diverse populations of supervisees, and (d) clients' perceptions of the military counselor's role function of following the supervisory development.

Although these findings have generated several research questions for future research, this study is not without its limitations, and results should be interpreted with caution. First, a single-subject (one-group) design was chosen to examine the changes of operation in RCGS. Although this design provided the clearest means to describe the group, specify changes in the behavior or actions of the group over time, and link one or more selected process variables to outcome (Heppner, Kivlighan, & Wampold, 1992), the repeated use of measures without a comparative group might cause some methodological problems. Second, the use of pretest and posttest design has its weaknesses and limitations because threats to internal validity cannot be easily controlled. Finally, based on the findings of McMahon and Simons's (2004) study, a 3- to 6-month follow-up evaluation is recommended to test the ongoing progress and enduring changes. With these limitations in mind, the generalizability of the findings and the replication of this study should be undertaken with care. These limitations, however, provide opportunities for further exploration of RCGS.

References

Bernard, J. M., & Goodyear, R. K. (2004). *Fundamentals of clinical supervision* (3rd ed.). New York: Allyn & Bacon.

Brown, A., & Bourne, I. (1996). *The social work supervisor*. Buckingham, UK: Open University Press.

Chen, S. Z. (2004.). *An exploratory study on solution-focusing group supervision impacts of the counselor: An example of counselors in military*. Unpublished master's thesis, Fu Hsing Kang Political College, Taiwan.

Chou, Y. C. (1997). *A study of influential factors of counseling training process: An example of the practice of the brief counseling training.* Unpublished doctoral dissertation, National Changhua University, Taiwan.

Christensen, T. M., & Kline, W. B. (2001). The qualitative exploration of process-sensitive peer group supervision. *Journal for Specialists in Group Work, 26,* 81–99.

Corcoran, K. B. (2001). *An ethnographic study of therapist development and reflective within the context of postmodern supervision and training.* Unpublished doctoral dissertation, University of Akron.

Griffith, B. A., & Frieden, G. (2000). Facilitating reflective thinking in counselor education. *Counselor Education and Supervision, 40,* 82–93.

Hawkins, P., & Shohet, R. (1989). *Supervision in the helping professions.* Buckingham, UK: Open University Press.

Heppner P. P., & Handley, P. G. (1981). A study of the interpersonal influence process in supervision. *Journal of Counseling Psychology, 28,* 437–444.

Heppner, P. P., Kivlighan, D. M., Jr., & Wampold, B, E. (1992). *Research design in counseling.* Pacific Grove, CA: Brooks/Cole.

Holloway, E. L. (1999). *The strategic approach to supervision.* London, Sage.

Holloway, E. L., & Johnston, R. (1985). Group supervision: Widely practiced but poorly understood. *Counselor Education and Supervision, 24,* 332–340.

Hu, Z. S. (2006). Building an index system of military counselor's professional competence. *Military Science Journal, 38,* 318–439.

Kadushin, A., & Harkness, D. (2002). *Supervision in social work.* New York: Columbia University Press.

Krushinski, M. (2005). A comparison of the perceptions of the importance of formal supervision training between formally trained counselor supervisors and nonformally trained counselor supervisors. *Dissertation Abstracts International: Section B: The Sciences and Engineering, 65*(10-B), 5408.

Lee, H. H. (2000). *A qualitative research of the process of counselors' development.* Unpublished doctoral thesis, National Changhua University of Education, Taiwan.

Liu, C. J. (1997). *The verbal behaviors of supervisors and supervisees in the supervision process of the cyclical developmental model.* Unpublished doctoral thesis, National Changhua University of Education, Taiwan.

Liu, S. H. (1999). The verification of the self-rating version of Counseling Competence Inventory and the analyses of self-rated change pattern. *Chinese Annual Report of Guidance and Counseling, 7,* 201–244.

Liu, S. H., & Wang, S. T, (1995). An evaluation of individual counseling competence and analysis of category. *Chinese Annual Report, 3,* 1–40.

Maxwell, J. A. (1996). *Qualitative research design: An interactive approach.* Thousand Oaks, CA: Sage.

McGlothlin, J. M., Rainey, S., & Kindsvatter, A. (2005). Suicidal clients and supervisees: A model for considering supervisor roles. *Counselor Education and Supervision, 45,* 135–146.

McMahon, M., & Simons, R. (2004), Supervision training for professional counselors: An exploratory study. *Counselor Education and Supervision, 43,* 301–320.

Ministry of National Defense. (2006). Retrieved February 20, 2006, from http://www.mnd.gov.tw/eng/ROC/gpwb/pcp/index.htm

Sexton, T. L., & Whiston, S. C. (1994). The status of the counseling relationship: An empirical review, theoretical implications, and research directions. *Counseling Psychologist, 22,* 6–78.

Shih, S. J. (1995). *The construct of counseling supervision process: Analysis of the cyclical developmental model.* Unpublished doctoral thesis, National Changhua University, Taiwan.

Shou, W., & Shih, S. J. (1995). Comments and suggestions for establishing the cyclical developmental counseling supervision model. *Journal of Guidance and Counseling, 31,* 34–40.

Starling, P. V. (1996). The impact of peer supervision in a structured group on first-time practicum supervisees. *Dissertation Abstracts International Section A: Humanities and Social Sciences, 57*(1-A), 118.

Strauss, A., & Corbin, J. (1990). *Basics of qualitative research: Grounded theory procedures and techniques.* Newbury Park, CA; Sage.

Tsui, M. S. (2005). *Social work supervision: Contexts and concepts.* Thousand Oaks, CA: Sage.

Ward, C. C., & House, R. M. (1998). Counseling supervision: A reflective model. *Counselor Education and Supervision, 38,* 23–33.

Wark, L. (1995). Live supervision in family therapy: Qualitative interviews of supervision events as perceived by supervisors and supervisees. *American Journal of Family Therapy, 23,* 25–37.

Watkins, C. E., Jr. (1997). Defining psychotherapy supervision and understanding supervisor functioning. In C. E. Watkins, Jr. (Ed.), *Handbook of psychotherapy supervision* (pp. 3–10). New York: John Wiley & Sons.

Wetchler, J. L., & Vaughn, K. A. (1991). Perceptions of primary supervisor interpersonal skills: A critical incident analysis. *Contemporary Family Therapy, 13,* 61–69.

Worthen, V. E., & McNeill, B. W. (1996). A phenomenological investigation of "good" supervision events. *Journal of Counseling Psychology, 43,* 25–34.

Worthen, V. E., & McNeill, B. W. (2001). *What is effective supervision? A national survey of supervision experts.* Retrieved January 13, 2008, from http://0-search.epnet.com.cylis.lib.cycu.edu.tw:80/login.aspx?direct=true&db=eric&an=ED455466& lang=zh-t

Acknowledgments: The authors wish to express their deepest appreciation to Y. J. Wang, Jenny S. S. Yuan, and Wendy H. Y. Yu, research assistants, for their contributions to this study.

Address correspondence to: Peter Jen Der Pan, College of Humanities and Education, Chung Yuan Christian University, Chung-Li, Taiwan. E-mail: jender@cycu.edu.tw

Exercise for Article 35

Factual Questions

1. What was the researchers' explicitly stated hypothesis?

2. When was the CGSF used?

3. What was the pretest mean for Personal Traits on the pretest? What was the pretest mean for Personal Traits on the posttest?

4. Was the difference between the two means in your answer to Question 3 above statistically significant? If yes, at what probability level?

5. Do the researchers consider the lack of a control group to be a limitation of their study?

Questions for Discussion

6. What is your understanding of the meaning of the term "preexperimental"? (See lines 193–195.)

7. The researchers state that they used a "convenience sample." In your opinion, is this a desirable form of sampling? Explain. (See lines 203–206.)

8. In this study, counseling competencies were measured with a structured questionnaire and open-ended questions. In your opinion, is one type of measure better than the other? Explain. (See lines 225–266.)

9. In your opinion, is the analysis of the qualitative data described in sufficient detail? Explain. (See lines 314–382.)

10. Do you regard the quantitative results (lines 383–405) *or* the qualitative results (lines 406–598) to be more informative? Explain.

245

Quality Ratings

Directions: Indicate your level of agreement with each of the following statements by circling a number from 5 for strongly agree (SA) to 1 for strongly disagree (SD). If you believe an item is not applicable to this research article, leave it blank. Be prepared to explain your ratings. When responding to criteria A and B below, keep in mind that brief titles and abstracts are conventional in published research.

A.   The title of the article is appropriate.

SA   5   4   3   2   1   SD

B.   The abstract provides an effective overview of the research article.

SA   5   4   3   2   1   SD

C.   The introduction establishes the importance of the study.

SA   5   4   3   2   1   SD

D.   The literature review establishes the context for the study.

SA   5   4   3   2   1   SD

E.   The research purpose, question, or hypothesis is clearly stated.

SA   5   4   3   2   1   SD

F.   The method of sampling is sound.

SA   5   4   3   2   1   SD

G.   Relevant demographics (for example, age, gender, and ethnicity) are described.

SA   5   4   3   2   1   SD

H.   Measurement procedures are adequate.

SA   5   4   3   2   1   SD

I.   All procedures have been described in sufficient detail to permit a replication of the study.

SA   5   4   3   2   1   SD

J.   The participants have been adequately protected from potential harm.

SA   5   4   3   2   1   SD

K.   The results are clearly described.

SA   5   4   3   2   1   SD

L.   The discussion/conclusion is appropriate.

SA   5   4   3   2   1   SD

M.   Despite any flaws, the report is worthy of publication.

SA   5   4   3   2   1   SD

Article 36

Bullying and Aggression on the School Bus: School Bus Drivers' Observations and Suggestions

ELLEN W. deLARA
Syracuse University

ABSTRACT. Every school day, bus drivers are responsible for transporting children safely over many miles, yet they are rarely polled for their opinions or contributions to school safety. School bus drivers are in a unique position to inform the discussion on aggressive behavior during the school day. This exploratory study collected information from school bus drivers about student behavior on their buses and drivers' perceptions of school administrators' interest in their input. Thirty bus drivers from suburban and rural school districts in upstate New York participated in this action research inquiry. Data were gathered from surveys and semistructured individual interviews. Participants provided recommendations to school personnel to decrease bullying and aggressive behavior on the buses.

From *Journal of School Violence*, 7, 48–70. Copyright © 2008 by The Haworth Press. Reprinted with permission.

School bus drivers are often the first and the last school personnel to come in contact with students during the school day. They are in a unique position to contribute to our understanding about student violence and aggression based on their observations. Although their first charge is to drive safely, they are called on to deal with incidents of harassment, bullying, and other forms of violence during the ride. They interact not only with students but also with parents, school administrators, and teachers. Bus drivers have a distinct perspective on who and what contributes to school violence or school safety. This exploratory study investigates school bus drivers' observations on aggressive behavior on buses, their perceptions about school administrators' interest in their input, and the drivers' suggestions for improving school safety and the climate on buses.

While there is a great deal of interest in the topic of bullying at school, one area of research that has been largely ignored is aggression at the beginning and end of the school day—on the school bus. This is basically an undersupervised part of the school day, increasing the chances of children engaging in or witnessing bullying or other violent behavior (Doll, Murphy, & Song, 2003; Smith, Shu, & Madsen, 2001). A few studies have focused on the types and nature of school bus bullying (Allen, Young, Ashbaker, Heaton, & Parkinson, 2003; Raskaukas, 2005) but school bus drivers are rarely involved in the discussion.

Some research has specifically addressed various aspects of school busing concerns (deLara, 2000, 2002; Howley, 2001; Howley & Howley, 2001; Killeen & Sipple, 2000; Thurman, 2000) and school bus culture (Jewett, 2005). However, drivers' perceptions of their experience of bullying on the buses as well as their ideas for improvement have been neglected—an important resource since they are the only adults present on school buses.

Of the approximately 24 million children who are transported each weekday in the U.S. (National Association of State Directors of Pupil Transportation Services, NASDPTS, 2005), it is not unusual for rural and some suburban school bus drivers to carry students from kindergarten through high school on the same bus. This is referred to as "double routed" (Howley, 2001), and while it may make sense economically, it subjects younger children to the behaviors of older children. Many of these behaviors may be inappropriate for younger riders to witness (Jewett, 2005). Children who ride the bus to school may be targeted directly for harassing and abusive behavior on the bus and others are subjected as observers (Allen et al., 2003; deLara, 2002; Garbarino & deLara, 2002; Meyer & Astor, 2002). Raskauskas (2005) found that approximately two incidents of bullying occurred on each bus ride and that a full bus and undersupervised conditions are prime environmental factors for bullying. Another contributing variable is that during the bus ride, children are able to see the living accommodations of one another. According to some research, this provides ample opportunity to harass and torment those who seem to have less (Glover, Gough, Johnson, & Cartwright, 2000).

Bullying Prevalence, Definitions, and Impact

Bullying among students is a recalcitrant problem in U.S. schools (American Association of University Women, 2001; Devine & Lawson, 2004; Espelage &

Swearer, 2004; Garbarino & deLara, 2002; Nansel, Overpeck, Pilla, Ruan, Simons-Morton, & Scheidt, 2001) as well as abroad (Smith, 2003). In the U.S.,
70 prevalence varies depending on the definition and type of bullying being discussed. However, between 30% and 80% of all students in the U.S. are typically acknowledged to be involved as bullies, victims, onlookers, or some combination (American Association of
75 University Women [AAUW], 2001; Nansel, Overpeck, Pilla, Ruan, Simons-Morton, & Scheidt, 2001; U.S. Department of Education, 1998). Over 90% of students who are gay or lesbian are bullied during the school day according to the Gay, Lesbian, and Straight Educa-
80 tion Network (Harris Interactive and GLSEN, 2005). Sexual harassment, in particular, appears to be rampant among students in U.S. secondary schools (AAUW, 2001; Fineran, 1998, 2002; Grube, 2003), with 80% of students reporting personal sexual harassment and half
85 of all students admitting that they sexually harass others (AAUW, 2001). Sadly, educators and other school personnel contribute to this phenomenon through bullying students or by not intervening (AAUW, 2001; Human Rights Watch, 2001; Shakeshaft, 2004). While
90 there is some research investigating bullying on the school bus (Allen et al., 2003; deLara, 2002; Raskauskas, 2005), more is needed to establish prevalence rates separate from other venues during the school day.
95 A complex form of aggression, bullying needs to be taken seriously and should not be considered harmless (Astor, 1995; Mishna & Alaggia, 2005). Most schools in the U.S. have adopted the definition of bullying first proposed by Olweus (1993). This definition states that
100 for an action to be considered bullying it must be chronic and perpetrated by one or more individuals with more power than the victim. However, other research is beginning to question this definition by asking students directly for their definitions of what con-
105 stitutes bullying and aggressive behavior (Fatum & Hoyle, 1996; Garbarino & deLara, 2002) and by looking more deeply into systemic variables that support aggressive behavior by children (see Astor, Benbenishty, & Marachi, 2004; Espelage & Swearer, 2004).
110 Interestingly, while a few school districts take a systemic approach in their assessment of behavioral problems on the school bus (Hirsch, Lewis-Palmer, & Sugai, 2004), the majority of school districts do not. Most see the problems on the school bus as standing
115 alone, independent of the rest of the school day.

The continuum of bullying and aggression during the school day "ranges from psychological intimidation (e.g., group exclusion, starting rumors, sexual gestures) to verbal abuse (name-calling) to physical abuse (hit-
120 ting, kicking, inappropriate touching, sexual abuse) to life-threatening violence (threatening with a weapon, attempted homicide or suicide)" (deLara, 2006, p. 335). In a recent study of three rural schools, 82% of students reported experiencing some form of bullying at least

125 once in the three months preceding the inquiry (Dulmus, Theriot, Sowers, & Blackburn, 2004). In research conducted with high school students, more students reported being fearful of their peers on the school bus than they were during any other time of their school
130 day (deLara, 2000; 2002).

Media reports indicate that the nature and frequency of the problems on school buses are increasing (Williamson & Aratani, 2005). Some research supports that the most frequent form of bullying or inappropriate
135 behavior witnessed by bus drivers is sexual harassment, such as middle schoolers describing sex acts to first-graders (Allen et al., 2003). Sexual harassment and sexual assaults on school buses are a concern because they are among the fastest-growing forms of
140 school violence, according to Professor Robert Shoop at Kansas State University. He advises, "Sexual harassment is a much more serious issue in public schools than most people have been willing to admit and it's much more likely to occur in unsupervised venues like
145 buses or bathrooms" (Williamson & Aratani, 2005, p. B01).

Consequences for Drivers

Children are not alone in being bullied, intimidated, or worse on the school bus. Bus drivers, too, report aggressive behavior toward them (personal communi-
150 cation, Jim Ellis, Pupil Transportation Safety Institute, PTSI, 9-15-05). The first murder of a school bus driver took place on March 2, 2005, when Joyce Gregory was shot and killed by a student on her bus in Tennessee. A 14-year-old boy was angry because the driver reported
155 his use of smokeless tobacco and his anger led to homicide. The school bus transportation industry has begun a comprehensive investigation to see what can be done to prevent a similar event from happening in the future (School Bus Fleet, 2005).

Legal Issues

160 School administrators must be concerned not only for the safety of children in their charge but also for the local, state, and federal legislation that governs issues of safety. A district's funding resources may be impacted as a result of violations. Bullying in the form of
165 sexual harassment during the school day was addressed in the legal decision of Davis v. Monroe County Board of Education. In that case, the Supreme Court found "any school receiving Federal money can face a sex-discrimination suit for failing to intervene energetically
170 enough when a student complains of sexual harassment by another student" (Gorney, 1999, p. 44). (See Title IX [Federal Title IX of the Education Amendments (1972)]. US Code, vol. 20, section 1681 [P.L. 92–318]).
175 The Eden Prairie, Minnesota, case is typically cited as one of the first of its kind where a school district was not vigilant enough in protecting a 7-year-old from name-calling and unwanted touch on the school bus and at school (see Murdock & Kysilko, 1993, 1998).

180 The district was forced to pay restitution to the family and this set an important precedent for other school districts (Committee for Children, 2005).

Sometimes, legislation and obligation can collide. At the same time that administrators must protect stu-
185 dents from harassment and bullying, they must also protect the rights of privacy for students and their families under the Family Educational Right to Privacy Act (FERPA), otherwise known as the Buckley Amendment (20 USC S. 1232g, S. 1232g.). Currently, New
190 York State has a law pertaining to student information that is an amendment to Vehicle and Traffic Law VT 375.20. It requires information to be carried on the bus at all times about students with disabilities. However, parental consent must be obtained first for each stu-
195 dent. The law is in part the result of a long battle with the New York State Education Department (NYSED) to sanction the sharing of safety—critical information about students with transporters. Prior to this amendment, the NYSED did not share the nature of the
200 child's disability with transportation personnel (personal communication with Jim Ellis, PTSI, 9-29-05).

The Purpose

School bus rides with little direct supervision may result in inappropriate behavior by some children. Bus drivers observe and interact with students each school
205 day, yet there is very little research investigating their opinions and experiences. This study was conducted to collect information from school bus drivers about their observations of student behavior on the buses, their perceptions of school administrators' interest in ag-
210 gression on the bus, and their suggestions for decreasing bullying or other aggressive behavior.

Method

Procedure

A cover letter describing the research and survey were distributed to school bus drivers in attendance at a workshop required by New York State on general bus
215 safety issues. Thirty drivers from two rural and two suburban school districts completed the survey and volunteered for individual interviews. During all phases, drivers were able to consent or decline to participate freely. The two rural school districts met the
220 criteria for "rural" used by the Economic Research Service of the U.S. Department of Agriculture. The study fulfilled all requirements of the university's Internal Review Board.

Participants

A convenience sample of 30 bus drivers represent-
225 ing two suburban and two rural school districts was obtained for this exploratory study. The drivers' experience ranged from 2 months on the job to more than 20 years. The range in age of the bus drivers was from 38 years to 58 years with a mean age of 49. The aver-
230 age years of bus experience was 7.7 with a range that included neophytes of 2 months to the very experi-

enced of 29 years. The ratio of female to male was 3:1. All respondents were Caucasian. All but one had participated in training specifically for school bus drivers
235 dealing with children's illnesses or disabilities and emergency medical procedures. Seventeen drivers had received some kind of training on how to deal with disruptive, aggressive children on the bus. Drivers transported students from kindergarten through grade
240 12 and most drove a combination of routes (e.g., high school, middle school, and alternative school or K–12 both a.m. and p.m. along with one activity bus). Approximately 5% of the students in each of the four school districts were minority students and the mean of
245 students eligible for free or reduced lunch program was 30%. The demographics of school district size and socioeconomic status of students' families were roughly equivalent among the four districts.

Instrumentation

This inquiry was a mixed-methods study utilizing
250 an action-research and ecological/general systems theory framework. Action research is iterative and lends itself to discovering trends and meaning from the participants (Greenwood & Levin, 1998). Action research has been gaining popularity in public school education
255 because of its underlying philosophy of democracy and empowerment (Cranton, 1996). General systems theory informs us that the whole is always greater than the sum of its individual parts (von Bertalanffy, 1968; Whitchurch & Constantine, 1993). Consequently, for
260 schools as systems, this means viewing various groups and subsets as contributing to the overall functioning of the system (Allen-Meares, 2004). For this study, the bus drivers, the students, and the school administrators were conceptualized as active members of the system.
265 The study was interested in some of the interactions among them from the bus drivers' perspective.

Quantitative data were collected through a survey focused on drivers' observations on school bus bullying and aggression, drivers' perceptions about school
270 personnel on this topic, and drivers' suggestions for improvements. Qualitative data were collected through the surveys and individual interviews. The survey was distributed to a convenience sample of school bus drivers and was intended to elicit their observations of bul-
275 lying on the bus as well as their suggestions for decreasing it. Participants were asked to comment on their experiences with school administrators on the issue of school bus bullying. Bullying was not defined for the participants in order to elicit the broadest possi-
280 ble responses. The survey consisted of 16 Likert-type questions, 7 yes-no questions, and 11 open-ended questions. Basic demographic information was requested including number of years driving school bus and type of routes traveled. Several questions were asked to
285 determine the drivers' observations of bullying and other aggressive behavior. The responses were framed in a 4-point Likert-like scale (*Never, Once in a while,*

Often, Every day). An example of a typical question was: "How often does bullying occur on your bus?" Several questions were posed to determine the drivers' perceptions of interest by school personnel in bullying on the bus. One example: "Do you feel that school personnel are interested when you want to make a report of trouble on the bus?" For the questions that explored drivers' perceptions of school administrators' interest in their input, a 4-point response scale was used (*Not at all, Somewhat, Often, Always*). The survey included open-ended questions such as "Are there students who are chronic problems on your bus? If yes, please explain." "What do school officials do about these students?" "Why did you become a school bus driver?"

Qualitative data were gathered through the open-ended questions on the surveys and in the individual interviews with the bus drivers. The interviews used a semi-structured format lasting approximately 45 minutes each. Transportation managers in two of the districts and pupil transportation industry specialists were also interviewed for this inquiry.

Analysis

Because of the size of the sample for this study, the quantitative data were analyzed using descriptive statistics. Because the research was iterative, data collected from the surveys and from the interviews were presented, in aggregate, to bus drivers, transportation managers, and transportation industry personnel for their feedback. Qualitative data were analyzed using action research, grounded theory, and interpretivist approaches (Glaser & Strauss, 1967; Greenwood & Levin, 1998; Guba & Lincoln, 1989; Patton, 1990; Tesch, 1990; Wolcott, 1994). The survey and semi-structured format interview were pilot tested with transportation managers and transportation industry personnel prior to the start of the study.

Trustworthiness of qualitative data is dependent upon credibility, authenticity, and coherence (Greene & Caracelli, 1997; Guba & Lincoln, 1989). To ensure credibility, authenticity, and coherence, member checks were employed by presenting the data as they were collected to the school bus drivers as research partners. During member checks, the drivers would confirm or revise the findings and voice their own interpretations. According to Guba and Lincoln (1989), subjectivity can be minimized through member checks with research partners. To further substantiate credibility, authenticity, and coherence, triangulation was practiced. As stated above, aggregated data were presented to transportation managers and transportation industry personnel, also, as a form of triangulation. Two colleagues with a background in the area of education and transportation reviewed the findings and interpretations. Triangulation is another mechanism that is helpful for maintaining coherence in the qualitative data analysis.

Action research and interpretivist approaches were employed in looking at the data gleaned from the individual interviews. The concepts of dealing with real-life problems, data collection for the possibility of change, and participation of stakeholders in the research process are the essence of the action research model (Cranton, 1996; Greenwood & Levin, 1998) and were central to this project. Action research is a cogenerative learning process in which the "outsiders" are the researchers who facilitate the process of learning with the "insiders" or stakeholders who own the local issue or problem (Greenwood & Levin, 1998). In this study, the school bus drivers were the insiders viewed as having the expert knowledge on the critical issue of aggression on the school bus.

Interpretivist inquiry is exploratory and iterative allowing that there may be more than one way of viewing an issue or a problem. Questions in the semi-structured interviews were guided by knowledge that came forward during interviews with the school bus drivers. In an interpretivist inquiry, what is meaningful emerges from the data; consequently, the process is dependent on the perspective of the participants and is inductive (Schultz & Hatch, 1996). During the process of the inquiry, the school bus drivers actively engaged in the interpretation of all collected data. The aggregated data were reported to each driver at the conclusion of the individual interview. At that point, their opinions were solicited about what had been gathered from their colleagues.

Following a grounded theory approach, qualitative data were classified and categorized using a constant comparative strategy (Glaser & Strauss, 1967). After transcription of the individual interviews, themes emerged and were categorized guided by both categorical analysis strategies and by analysis of content.

Results

Because of the small sample size of this exploratory study, this article reports some quantitative data but focuses primarily on the results of the qualitative data. All of the drivers reported that bullying and aggression took place on their buses and most considered these behaviors problematic. According to the drivers, bullying and other forms of violence on the school bus can be put into two categories that describe the parameters of the problem:

1. Behavior of Students and Parents
2. Perceptions by Drivers of School Administrators

Behavior of Students and Parents

Types of Bullying Behavior. Drivers observed verbal bullying, psychological intimidation, physical bullying, fights, and sexual harassment. Verbal bullying was noticed by 90% (27) of the drivers and psychological intimidation by 70% (21). Eight drivers reported physical bullying and fights on their buses and 6 (20%) said they observed sexual harassment. Though most of the drivers said they heard the students call each other "faggot" or "gay" on a regular basis, the drivers did not consider this sexual harassment. They said: "The kids say that all the time; they don't mean anything sexual by it."

The rural bus drivers, in particular, saw children who came to school every day with dirty faces and dirty clothes. Drivers observed firsthand what children had to put up with from other students. These children became the most prominent and easiest targets for chronic bullying and harassment. One driver with five or six minority children on each bus said: "It's more acceptable to be mixed-race than to be 'a smelly kid'."

One family I had was bullied for years; it wasn't the kids' fault. The parents let them get on the bus with filthy clothes, dirty faces, and their hair uncombed" (female driver, 16 years experience, K-12 rural routes).

In the example above, the bus driver, the family, and the principal eventually solved the problem together by busing the children into school before the other students so that they could bathe at school. They had no running water at home. The driver cited this as a good example of how bus drivers can provide information to school administrators and work effectively as part of the safety and violence prevention team.

Frequency and Intervention. In terms of frequency, 70% (21) of drivers reported that bullying and other aggression happened once in a while. The other 30% said bullying occurred often on their buses. Drivers who said bullying occurred every day also said they intervened to stop it on a daily basis. Those who said bullying occurred once in a while said they only needed to intervene once in a while to curtail aggression on their bus. Drivers believed that they were quite vigilant about student behavior. Only one-quarter believed that bullying occurred on their bus that went unnoticed by them.

It's not always bullying, sometimes it's just meanness. I have to pull over the bus 3 times a week for low blows like kids saying to each other "Do you ever wash your hair?" or "You smell." They say it and they mean it, most especially to the really poor kids, the ones from way out or from the trailer parks (female driver, 15 years' experience, K-12 rural routes).

More than half of all participants reported that, in general, bullying occurred daily on buses. As the majority of drivers said bullying occurred on their own buses only once in a while, it is possible that drivers believe their peers have more difficulty with bullying behavior than they do personally.

Chronic Concerns. Drivers were asked if any students were chronic concerns for them. There were some students who tended to be problematic on the bus as bully, victim, or both. Students classified as victims were: "the poor kids," "the kids from trailer parks," and "kids with disabilities (either physical or emotional)." Consequently, those with disabilities and the poorest children were at the greatest risk of all types of bullying during the bus rides, according to the drivers. (The finding that children with vulnerabilities [e.g., emotional, physical, and learning] are victimized during the school day is consistent with other research studies; see Mishna & Alaggia, 2005.) Children who were physically neglected by their families were bullied on the school bus. Students were tormented for their disheveled appearance and poorly kept clothing. Often, children with special emotional needs were both targeted for bullying and acted as bullies themselves. The drivers also indicated that the following students acted as bullies on the bus (ranked by drivers in descending order): those with emotional problems, athletes, unpopular students, special education students, and middle school students. Further, they specified that hostile verbal exchanges were the norm and that physical fights were just as likely between girls as between boys.

Strategies to Moderate Bullying and Aggression. In general, when asked what they did to interrupt or prevent violence on their buses, the bus drivers had a variety of strategies. The strategies they used were to:

1. Seat children close to the driver who are susceptible to bullying or being victimized;
2. Separate children who are fighting or having difficulty and assign seats;
3. Be "aware of everything" and watch for the moods and signs of troubled kids;
4. Talk with bullies about being respectful on the bus;
5. Intervene before anything happens, and discuss the day with the kids;
6. Maintain a good relationship with each child;
7. Ask about interests and hobbies;
8. Try to engage potential bullies in positive conversations; and
9. Above all, talk to the students with respect.

Basically, their specific strategies build on the inner strengths of aggressive children and distract them from disrespectful, disruptive behavior. When these interventions failed or where there was a serious or ongoing problem, the drivers reported this to their transportation managers and to school administrators. One rural driver shared her sense of exasperation trying to explain to students the relationship of respectful behavior to safety on the bus. She communicates to the students: "It isn't ok to treat me with disrespect." To which, she often hears: "Well, you haven't earned my respect."

Holding Parents and Students Accountable. To decrease bullying and violent behavior on the school buses, both before and after school, drivers believed both students and their parents must be held accountable for their actions. When students didn't treat the drivers with respect, drivers stated this impaired their ability to control the behavior of individual children on the bus, and sometimes affected overall bus climate.

When students behave badly, drivers suggested school administrators should:

1. Involve parents immediately;
2. Hold parents accountable for their child's poor behavior on the bus;
3. Take quick and decisive action;
4. Be prepared to involve the police at times;
5. Label assault when an action is assault; and
6. "Stop handling it (assault) internally."

Bus drivers asked for specific training and workshops on how to deal with parents who do not accept that their own child has any responsibility for problem behavior on the bus. One driver said: "I would like to know how to get parents to take ownership of their child's negative behavior and work from there" (female driver, 1 year experience, suburban route). One female driver with 19 years of rural K–12 experience said, "The teachers in our district are going to have a Stress Management Workshop Day. I think that would be a good idea for the kids, too. And the bus drivers really need it. Sometimes the kids bully me!"

Perceptions by Drivers of School Administrators

Interest of Administrators. When asked if school administrators were interested in what happened on the buses or made an effort to find out, the great majority (90%) of the drivers responded "somewhat" to these questions. Similarly, the majority of drivers (70%) believed that school personnel were only "somewhat" interested when they reported trouble on the bus. In the qualitative portion of the study, the drivers included the teachers as only somewhat interested in reports about problems on the bus. This was an area of major concern for the drivers. Drivers with less experience expected school administrators to take an active interest in what happened on the school bus. Drivers with more experience no longer seemed to have the expectation that administrators would be interested but were frustrated at what they perceived to be their inattention to problems on the school bus. Several drivers confided that they had stopped filing discipline reports due to lack of response from school administrators. This leaves significant information on certain individuals and collective problems on buses out of circulation in the system. The majority of poor marks were directed to middle school and high school administrators regarding their level of concern and follow up on bus bullying. Drivers complained that school administrators at the middle and high school levels rarely took their referrals for disciplinary action seriously. However, approximately one-quarter of the drivers believed that elementary school administrators and teachers were interested in problems on the bus and that they provided good follow-through about the drivers' concerns. Principals at the lower grade levels often took immediate action on the referrals and provided needed feedback to the drivers, according to the participants.

Support from Administrators. About one-third of the drivers said their school administrators were not supportive of their efforts to control bullying on their buses. They cited principals' lack of follow-up as evidence for their lack of support for the drivers' efforts. Approximately one-third of the drivers thought school principals could do a much better job of providing support to them and the last third said school administrators were supportive and reinforced their efforts to control bullying.

When the bus drivers were asked if school officials did anything about students who chronically caused problems on the bus, 20% (6) answered "not at all" and 20% (6) answered "often." The other 60% (18) answered "sometimes." No one answered "always." This may be indicative of a problem or it may indicate that the drivers were not aware of follow-up that occurred by school officials after a problem was reported. The majority of the drivers expressed disappointment and dissatisfaction that school administrators did not hold accountable students who were consistently problematic.

Kids are less respectful now; they don't care what they say to you. You could say the kids bully me! (Female driver, 21 years' experience, suburban routes).

To reduce chronic problems, the bus drivers were in agreement that there should be minimum standards for good behavior on the bus. Two drivers recommended that districts implement programs in Pre-K and 1st grade that teach children the difference between respectful interactions and hurtful behavior. All of the bus drivers suggested that administrators set clear expectations, at the beginning of the school year, for behavior on the school bus. Several drivers put forward the idea of having a recognizable school authority figure actually board the buses to delineate the rules. It was seen as a good way to set out appropriate conduct for the students. Further, they recommended that administrators communicate the specific follow-up actions that would be taken by the school for failure to meet the behavioral standards. This was considered to constitute a show of solidarity of school administrators with the bus drivers.

One-way Communication and Legislative Prohibitions. The majority of participants agreed that communication between drivers and school administrators needed improvement. The study participants reported that there was a disconnection between the information shared among the Transportation Manager or Supervisor of the district, school personnel, and the transporters. This information-sharing was often only one-way (from the drivers) and drivers said this represented a serious problem in communication. Further, drivers reported that school administrators did not provide enough, or consistent, follow-up on discipline referrals.

An important ongoing issue for these drivers was that school districts expect bus drivers to deal with many serious health problems of the children on their routes. These problems include anaphylactic shock due to severe nut allergies or diabetes, seizures due to epilepsy, and other neurological disorders, etc. At the same time, the districts did not give drivers enough information about children with special needs because of emotional or family problems. They stated that this information is necessary to provide safety to individual children and to maintain a calm atmosphere on their buses.

One veteran driver offered a powerful example. He disclosed that a boy he had driven every day for 4 years got off his bus one day and didn't show up the next at the bus stop. When this driver, with 10 years' experience on rural routes, asked the other students, "Where's Jim [not his real name] today?" The students responded, "He's dead. He committed suicide." The driver was shocked and his shock has been compounded by the fact that in the years that have elapsed since the incident, no one from the district has ever contacted him about this traumatic event. The driver said repeatedly during the interview, "I was the last person from the school to ever see him." He was able to ascertain later that the boy had been experiencing a great deal of bullying in school. Though this bus driver prided himself as someone the kids could come to, the boy never gave a hint of his unhappiness. Thus, without any information from the school before the fact, there was no way for the driver to be aware or vigilant for similar situations that might have occurred on the bus. Without any information after the fact, there was no way to make sense of what happened or to consider any way to help prevent a similar tragedy in the future.

Although the state education department mandates bus drivers take continuing education courses each year for such things as peanut allergies and other physical conditions, drivers were not given information on the psychological well-being of the children in their charge. Despite the fact that this is the result of federal and state legislation to protect the privacy of children and families (Family Educational Right to Privacy Act, Buckley Amendment), 20 U.S.C. Section 1232g (2005), the drivers believed it is an indication that they are held in poor regard by their school districts and are not really considered to be part of the educational team.

This is a controversial issue based on boundary concerns. The drivers believed that they needed more information to do their jobs effectively for all of the children. At the same time, families have the right to privacy. The drivers are called upon to be medical responders, but the definition of what constitutes medical need appeared unclear to them at times.

Supervision. Drivers described the difficulty of safely transporting the children and supervising them at the same time. Creative ways to provide more supervision on the school bus such as soliciting volunteer adult riders or implementing a "Buddy System" were suggested. A "Buddy System" pairs older, responsible students who volunteer to mentor younger ones specifically for the time on the bus. This model works well in terms of academic mentoring or tutoring and could be applied to the sociocultural environment of the bus that younger students have difficulty navigating.

School Safety Team. Only 6 of the 30 drivers said they were included in the school district's planning efforts to reduce bullying. This seemed particularly distressing to the drivers. As the first and the last school employee to see a child during the school day, the drivers believed they had an opportunity to connect with children. They cited their role as a unique way to make a contribution as part of the school team to prevent violence. Aggressive behavior can be interrupted if it is caught and dealt with early enough, according to the participants' experience. To do so effectively means improved communication among all stakeholders, but particularly between transporters and school administrators. Teamwork, according to the drivers, consists of backup, follow-up, and participating as part of an ongoing team charged with school safety planning.

Discussion

Bus drivers considered bullying on the bus a significant problem. They indicated that bullying and other forms of violence occurred on their own bus routes and that bullying and aggression were problems on their own bus routes. They concurred that bullying and aggression were problems on school buses in general. Drivers cited several categories and types of bullying or aggressive behavior on their buses. They pointed to verbal bullying and psychological intimidation as the most prevalent forms of aggression in their experience, though sexual harassment, physical bullying, and physical fighting were cited as problematic also.

In terms of frequency, they said it is important for administrators and educators to be cognizant of the fact that bullying and other forms of aggressive behavior are occurring on school bus rides much of the time. An interesting finding from the research was that drivers did not consider words such as "faggot" or "gay" that were used repeatedly by the students to be sexual harassment. Another important result was that only a small portion of the drivers were involved as members of their district's overall school safety planning efforts.

The bus drivers were able to enumerate their own strategies to curtail bullying, and they put forward several suggestions for working together with school administrators. The suggestions addressed student behavior and also expressed driver concerns with the behavior of administrators that fell along a continuum from inadequate communication to ineffective or inconsistent follow-up on discipline.

Responses from the drivers point to a systemic problem. Though it is the students' behavior that is the focus for adults, the data indicate that bullying and

253

aggression on the bus may be perpetuated inadvertently by the actions or inaction of all school stakeholders.

Limitations

740 The drivers in this study provided valuable information and suggestions for reducing bullying and aggression on school buses. However, this exploratory study involved a small convenience sample of bus drivers in upstate New York. Clearly, a larger sample of drivers is required before any generalizability of 745 themes can be claimed. Due to the small number of participants in this study, results may be indicative of problems on suburban and rural school buses or merely a reflection of local school district issues. The school bus survey is in development form and because of its 750 limited distribution, reliability and validity cannot be determined at this time.

Conclusion

This study presents the school bus drivers' voice on the critical issue of bullying or aggressive behavior on the school bus and proposes that their perspective and 755 input are critical to the resolution of these concerns. This small inquiry indicates that creative solutions and practices can be devised to interrupt chronic bullying and aggression on the school bus. The school bus drivers had numerous suggestions to offer and, individu- 760 ally, they implemented practices they considered effective. The study demonstrates that school districts need to establish policy that includes school bus drivers in ongoing discussion and planning efforts for safe schools.

765 Typically, school bus drivers are the only adults present on school buses. For effective anti-bullying programming, more research with school bus drivers, utilizing mixed-methods inquiry including surveys, focus groups, and individual interviews, is needed. 770 Following this small exploratory study, a larger group of participants representing all levels of experience and various types of school districts is called for. Comparing and contrasting the input of drivers from rural, suburban, and urban schools would add to the literature on 775 the phenomenon of bullying and aggression on the school bus. This study begs the questions: Are there bus routes where the issue of bullying is marginal? If so, does the driver's experience or personality play a major role? What are the practices and programs util- 780 ized in school districts that are successfully minimizing bullying or other forms of aggression on their school buses? A large comprehensive comparative study may provide information that could be applied more generally to school bus anti-bullying practices and programs.

785 The psychological consequences of bullying on children (e.g., anxiety and depression) are well established in the literature (Cullerton-Sen & Crick, 2005; Rigby, 2000; Slee, 1995; Salmon, James, & Smith, 1998; Storch & Brassard, 2003). From this study, the 790 following questions arise: What, if any, is the effect of school bus bullying and aggression on a child's will-

ingness to attend school? On school absences? On a child's ability to concentrate at school? The possible impact on school attachment and school achievement 795 as a result of witnessing bullying episodes or being victimized directly is worthy of future research. In order to access this, subsequent research needs to investigate students' perceptions of safety on the school bus and their experiences of bullying or aggression. School 800 bus drivers are critical to the understanding and remediation of these potential problems.

From their own understanding of children, their own creativity, and from listening to fellow drivers, the school bus drivers generated strategies they found use- 805 ful in controlling some forms of problematic behaviors on the bus. Many of the strategies the school bus drivers used to interrupt or prevent bullying and aggression derived from their own resources, assets, and inner strengths as well as those of the children (e.g., asking 810 about interests or hobbies). Taking a strengths-based approach in future studies looking for solutions to aggressive behavior on the bus could make an important contribution to the literature on this topic. Investigating these strategies for efficacy could reveal useful data for 815 successful program planning.

The drivers in this study identified parents' unwillingness to hold their children accountable for disrespectful behavior as significant concern contributing to problems on the school bus. Some parents behaved 820 defensively and hampered driver efforts to effect changes on the bus, according to the drivers. Parents have a unique perspective on school bus issues from their children's comments and experiences. Parents should be involved as concerned stakeholders in dis- 825 trictwide dialogue about school bus behavior issues and need to be included in future research studies.

School administrators' lack of interest or followthrough on problematic behaviors, according to the bus drivers, was a major concern. Convening collective 830 discussion groups for school bus drivers, transportation managers, and school administrators could reduce this criticism. In attempting to do their jobs well, school bus drivers need and should be afforded full support from school administrators. All school personnel (e.g., 835 bus drivers, transportation managers, school administrators, and teachers) can profit from more effective communication. One-way communication is not beneficial in solving systemic problems.

The school bus drivers emphasized the issue of re- 840 spect—adults treating children with respect and teaching children, from the first days of primary education, how to behave respectfully toward others. Drivers cited children with disabilities and children who were poor as chronic targets of bullying and aggressive behavior 845 on the bus. School programs promoting tolerance for difference may not be extending their reach to the school bus ride or should be evaluated for this venue. Though not all school districts or administrators consider the teaching of respect to be under the purview of

850 public education, effective programs aimed at conveying these principles may contribute to a safer bus ride for all students.

855 Bus drivers observe interactions between and among students that perhaps no one else will see during the school day. Therefore, they are in a unique position to identify types of bullying and other aggressive or inappropriate behavior that take place during their part of the school day. They can help prevent this behavior not only on their buses but also potentially during the

860 rest of the day through the implementation of effective communication mechanisms with school personnel. Further, as a portal into the school day, school bus drivers can be an integral part of the school safety planning effort in every school district.

References

Allen, M., Young, E. L., Ashbaker, B. Y., Heaton, E., & Parkinson, M. (2003). Sexual harassment on the school bus: Supporting and preparing bus drivers to respond appropriately. *Journal of School Violence, 2*(4), 101–109.

Allen-Meares. P. (2004). An ecological perspective of social work and services in schools. In P. Allen-Meares (Ed.). *Social work services in schools* (pp. 71–94). Boston: Pearson Education.

American Association of University Women (AAUW). (2001). *Hostile hallways: Bullying, teasing, and sexual harassment in school.* Washington, DC: Author.

Aronson, E. (2000). *No one left to hate: Teaching compassion after Columbine.* New York: W. H. Freeman.

Astor, R. A. (1995). School violence: A blueprint for elementary school interventions. *Social Work in Education, 17*, 101–115.

Astor, R., Benbenishty, R., & Marachi, R. (2004). Violence in schools. In P. Allen-Meares (Ed.), *Social work services in schools* (4th ed., pp. 149–182). New York: Pearson.

Brent, Perper, Moritz, Friend, Roth, Schweers, Balach, & Baugher. (1993). Adolescent witnesses to a peer suicide. *Journal of the American Academy of Child and Adolescent Psychiatry, 32*(6), 1184–1188.

Committee for Children (2005). *Intervention efforts: Sexual harassment.* Retrieved October 16, 2005, from http://www.cfchildren.org/articlef/wallslf/harassment

Cranton, P. (1996). *Professional development as transformative learning: New perspectives for teachers of adults.* San Francisco, CA: Jossey-Bass.

Culberton-Sen, C., & Crick, N. R. (2005). Understanding the effects of physical and relational victimization: The utility of multiple perspectives in predicting social-emotional adjustment. *School Psychology Review, 34*(2), 147–160.

deLara, E. W. (2000). *Adolescents' perceptions of safety in rural high schools and their solutions for enhancing safety and decreasing school violence: A rural case study.* Doctoral dissertation, Cornell University.

deLara, E. W. (2002). Peer predictability: An adolescent strategy for enhancing a sense of safety at school. *Journal of School Violence, 1*(3), 31–56.

deLara, E. W. (2006). Bullying and violence in U.S schools. In N. E. Dowd, D. G. Singer, & R. F. Wilson (Eds). *Children, Culture and Violence.* Thousand Oaks, CA: Sage Publishers.

Doll, B., Murphy, P., & Song, S. Y. (2003). The relationship between children's self-reported recess problems and peer acceptance and friendships. *Journal of School Psychology, 41*, 113–130.

Dulmus, C., Theriot, M. T., Sowers, K. M., & Blackburn, J. A. (2004). Student reports of peer bullying victimization in a rural school. *Stress, Trauma and Crisis: An International Journal, 17*(1), 1–16.

Espelage, D. L., & Swearer, S. M. (Eds). (2004). *Bullying in American schools: A social-ecological perspective on prevention and intervention.* Mahwah, NJ: Erlbaum.

Family Educational Right to Privacy Act (Buckley Amendment), 20 U.S.C. Section 1232g (2005). United States Code Service. Retrieved October 7, 2005, from http://web.lexis-nexis.com

Fatum, W. R., & Hoyle, J. C. (1996). Is it violence? School violence from the student perspective: Trends and interventions. *The School Counselor, 44*(1), 28–34.

Fineran, S. (1998). Teenage peer sexual harassment: Implications for social work practice in education, *Social Work, 43*(1), 55–64.

Fineran, S. (2002). Sexual harassment between same-sex peers: Intersection of mental health, homophobia, and sexual violence in schools. *Social Work, 47*(1), 65–74.

Garbarino, J., & deLara, E. (2002). *And words can hurt forever: How to protect adolescents from bullying, harassment, and emotional violence.* NY: Simon and Schuster/The Free Press.

Gaughan, E., Cerio, J. D., & Myers, R. A. (2001). Lethal violence in schools: A national survey final report (pp. 3–39). Alfred, NY: Alfred University.

Glaser, B. G., & Strauss, A. L. (1967). *The discovery of grounded theory: Strategies for qualitative research.* NY: Aldine De Gruyter Publishing.

Glover, D., Gough, G., & Johnson, M. with N. Cartwright (2000). Bullying in 25 secondary schools: Incidence, impact and intervention. *Educational Research, 42*(2), 141–156.

Gorney, C. (1999). Teaching Johnny the appropriate ways to flirt. *The New York Times Magazine* (June 13, 1999) pp. 43–47, 67, 73, 80–83.

Greene, J., & Caracelli, V. (1997). Advances in mixed-method evaluation: The challenges and benefits of integrating diverse paradigms. *New Directions for Evaluation,* No. 74. San Francisco: Jossey-Bass.

Greenwood, D., & Levin, M. (1998). *Introduction to action research: Social research for social change.* Thousand Oaks, CA: Sage.

Grube, B., & Lens, V. (2003). Student-to-student harassment: The impact of Davis v. Monroe. *Children and Schools, 25*(3), 173–185.

Guba, E. G., & Lincoln, Y. S. (1989). *Fourth generation evaluation.* Newbury Park, CA: Sage Publications.

Harris Interactive and Gay Lesbian and Straight Education Network (GLSEN) (2005). *From Teasing to Torment: School Climate in America, A survey of students and teachers.* NY: GLSEN. Retrieved October 12, 2005, from www.glsen.org

Hirsch, E. J., Lewis-Palmer, T., & Sugai, G. (2004). Using school bus discipline referral data in decision making: Two case studies. *Preventing School Failure, 48*(4), 4–9.

Howley, C. (2001). The rural school bus ride in five states: A report to the rural school and community trust. *ERIC Clearinghouse on Rural Education and Small Schools* (AEL, Inc.) and Ohio University. Retrieved October 1, 2005, from http://www.ruraledu.org/docs/howley_bus.htm

Howley, A., & Howley, C. (2001). *Rural school busing.* U.S. Department of Education, Office of Educational Research and Improvement under contract # ED-99-CO-0027. Retrieved October 1, 2005, from http://acclaim.coe.ohioedu

Jewett, L. (2005). Power beads, body glitter, and backseat bad-asses: Girls, power, and position on the school bus. In N. G. Adams & P. J. Bettis (Eds.), *Geographies of girlhood identities in-between* (pp. 35–52). Mahwah, NJ: Lawrence Erlbaum Associates Publishers.

Killeen, K., & Sipple, J. (2000). *School consolidation and transportation policy: An empirical and institutional analysis.* Randolph, VT: Rural School and Community Trust. Retrieved October 30, 2005, from www.ruraledu.org/docs/killeen_sipple.pdf

Kingery, P., Pruitt, B. E., Brizzola, J., & Heuberger, G. (1996). Violence prevention in rural areas: Evidence of the need for educational reform and community action. *International Journal of Educational Reform, 5*(1), 26–34.

Meyer, H. A., & Astor, R. A. (2002). Child and parent perspectives on routes to and from school in high crime neighborhoods. *Journal of School Violence, 1*(4), 101–128.

Mishna, F., & Alaggia, R. (2005). Weighing the risks: A child's decision to disclose peer victimization. *Children and Schools, 27*(4), 217–226.

Murdock, K. W., & Kysilko, D. (1993, 1998). *Sexual harassment in schools: What it is. What to do. A policy guide.* Alexandria, VA: National Association of State Boards of Education.

National Association of Attorneys General. (2000). *Bruised inside: What our children say about youth violence, what causes it and what we need to do about it.* A Project of Washington Attorney General Christine Gregoire's Presidential Initiative on Our Children in the New Millennium. Washington, DC: National Association of Attorneys General.

National Association of State Directors of Pupil Transportation Services (NASDPTS). (2002). *History of School Bus Safety.* Report produced by the National Association of State Directors of Pupil Transportation Services. Retrieved June 5, 2006, from http://www.nasdpts.org/paperSHistor.html

Olweus, D. (1993). *Bullying at school: What we know and what we can do.* Malden, MA: Blackwell.

Patton, M. Q. (1990). *Qualitative evaluation and research methods, 2nd Edition.* Newbury Park, CA: Sage Publications.

Pupil Transportation Safety Institute. (2005). *Growing Respect on Your Bus* [VIDEO] (2005). Produced by Pupil Transportation Safety Institute, Syracuse, NY. Available at: www.ptsi.org

Rashkauskas, J. (2005). Bullying on the school bus: A video analysis. *Journal of School Violence, 4*(3), 93–107.

Rigby, K. (2000). Effects of peer victimization in schools and perceived social support on adolescent well-being. *Journal of Adolescence, 23*, 57–68.

Salmon, G., James, A. & Smith, D. M. (1998). Bullying in schools: Self-reported anxiety, depression, and self-esteem in secondary school children. *British Medical Journal, 317*, 924–925.

School Bus Fleet. (2005). Slain bus driver mourned by 1,500 (April, 2005). Retrieved June 9, 2005, from http://www.schoolbusfleet.com/t_print.cfm?action=art_det&storyID=1069

Schultz, M., & Hatch, M. J. (1996). Living with multiple paradigms: The case of paradigm interplay in organizational culture studies. *Academy of Management Review, 21*(2), 529–557.

Shakeshaft, C. (2004). *Educator sexual misconduct: A synthesis of the existing literature*. Washington, DC: The United States Department of Education, Office of the Undersecretary, Policy and Program Studies Service.

Slee, P. T. (1995). Peer victimization and its relationship to depression among Australian primary school students. *Personality and Individual Differences, 18*(1), 57–62.

Smith, P. K. (2003). *Violence in schools: The response in Europe*. London: Falmer Routledge.

Smith, P. K., Shu, S., & Madsen, K. (2001). Characteristics of victims of school bullying: Developmental changes in coping strategies and skills. In J. Juvonen & S. Graham (Eds.), *Peer harassment in school: The plight of the vulnerable and victimized* (pp. 332–351). New York: Guilford Press.

Spence, B. (2000). Long school bus rides: Their effect on school budgets, family life, and student achievement. *Rural Education Issue Digest*. ED 448 955. Retrieved October 5, 2005, from www.ael.org/rel/rural/pdf/digestl.pdf

Storch, E. A., & Brassard, M. R. (2003). The relationship of peer victimization to social anxiety and loneliness in adolescence. *Child Study Journal, 33*(1), 1–18.

Tesch, R. (1990). *Qualitative research: Analysis types and software tools*. NY: The Falmer Press.

Thurman, S. W. (2000). *A rolling town: The long bus ride in a rural southern Appalachian county*. Unpublished Doctoral Dissertation, Western Carolina University.

U.S. Department of Education. (1998). *Preventing bullying: A manual for schools and communities*. Washington, D.C: United States Department of Education.

von Bertalanffy, L. (1968). *General system theory: Foundations, development, applications* (Rev. ed.). New York: George Braziller, Inc.

Vossekuil, B., Reddy, M., Fein, R., Borum, R., & Modzeleski, W. (2000). *USSS Safe School Initiative: An interim report on the prevention of targeted violence in schools*. Washington, DC: US Secret Service, National Threat Assessment Center.

Whitchurch, G. G., & Constantine, L. L. (1993). Systems theory. In P. G. Boss, W. J. Doherty, R. LaRossa, et al. (Eds.), *Sourcebook of Family Theories and Methods: A Contextual Approach*. New York: Plenum Press.

Williamson, E., & Aratani, L. (2005). As school bus assaults rise, danger often overlooked. *The Washington Post*, June 14, 2005, p. B01.

Wolcott, H. (1994). *Transforming qualitative data: Description, analysis, and interpretation*. Thousand Oaks, CA: Sage Publications.

Acknowledgments: The author would like to acknowledge assistance in preparing this paper from Kathy Furneaux and Jim Ellis, Pupil Transportation Safety Institute (PTSI) in Syracuse, NY; Albert Neal, School Bus Fleet Journal; and Robin Parks, T.S.T. BOCES-NYS. The research was funded by grants from the USDA and Syracuse University.

Address correspondence to: Ellen W. deLara, School of Social Work, Syracuse University, 400 Sims Hall, Syracuse, NY 13244. E-mail: edelara@syr.edu

Exercise for Article 36

Factual Questions

1. Most schools use the definition of bullying that says for an action to be considered bullying it must be what?

2. Were the drivers required to participate in this study?

3. The sample consisted of how many bus drivers?

4. "Member checks" were employed by presenting the data as they were collected to whom?

5. What percentage of the participants said that bullying occurred "often" on their buses?

6. What percentage of the participants said that school personnel were only "somewhat" interested when they reported trouble on the bus?

Questions for Discussion

7. The researcher states, "Bullying was not defined for the participants in order to elicit the broadest possible responses." If you had conducted this study, would you have defined bullying for the participants? Why? Why not? (See lines 278–280.)

8. Would you be interested in knowing the specific questions asked during the interviews? Explain. (See lines 302–308.)

9. In your opinion, is the analysis of the qualitative data described in sufficient detail? Explain. (See lines 309–378.)

10. Is the fact that the sample included only drivers in upstate New York an important limitation of this study? Explain. (See lines 741–751.)

11. Are the quantitative results (i.e., percentages) *or* the qualitative results more interesting to you? Explain. (See lines 379–702.)

12. Do you think it would be worthwhile to conduct another study on this topic with a larger, more representative sample? Explain. (See lines 741–751.)

Quality Ratings

Directions: Indicate your level of agreement with each of the following statements by circling a number from 5 for strongly agree (SA) to 1 for strongly disagree (SD). If you believe an item is not applicable to this research article, leave it blank. Be prepared to explain your ratings. When responding to criteria A and B below, keep in mind that brief titles and abstracts are conventional in published research.

A. The title of the article is appropriate.

    SA   5   4   3   2   1   SD

B. The abstract provides an effective overview of the research article.

    SA   5   4   3   2   1   SD

C. The introduction establishes the importance of the study.

    SA   5   4   3   2   1   SD

D. The literature review establishes the context for the study.

        SA 5 4 3 2 1 SD

E. The research purpose, question, or hypothesis is clearly stated.

        SA 5 4 3 2 1 SD

F. The method of sampling is sound.

        SA 5 4 3 2 1 SD

G. Relevant demographics (for example, age, gender, and ethnicity) are described.

        SA 5 4 3 2 1 SD

H. Measurement procedures are adequate.

        SA 5 4 3 2 1 SD

I. All procedures have been described in sufficient detail to permit a replication of the study.

        SA 5 4 3 2 1 SD

J. The participants have been adequately protected from potential harm.

        SA 5 4 3 2 1 SD

K. The results are clearly described.

        SA 5 4 3 2 1 SD

L. The discussion/conclusion is appropriate.

        SA 5 4 3 2 1 SD

M. Despite any flaws, the report is worthy of publication.

        SA 5 4 3 2 1 SD

Article 37

Unretired and Better Than Ever:
Older Adults As Foster Parents for Children

DONALD H. GOUGHLER
Family Services of Western Pennsylvania

ANNETTE C. TRUNZO
Family Services of Western Pennsylvania

ABSTRACT. The authors explore issues concerning employing older adults as foster parents for children. A survey of agencies in the United States suggests that agencies that utilize older adults as foster parents experience benefits, including elders' abilities to impart life experience and to offer a high degree of tolerance and time flexibility. Older foster parents, when surveyed, reported that fostering benefited them, citing pleasures they derived and defining contributions gained to their own welfare. The authors recommend strategies for agencies to recruit older adults as foster parents as well as public consciousness-raising efforts that promote the value gained by society and the older adults when they choose second careers in child care.

From *Families in Society: The Journal of Contemporary Social Services*, 86, 393–400. Copyright © 2005 by Children and Families. Reprinted with permission.

Foster parents are a vital part of the child welfare system and are asked to fulfill all the role responsibilities of natural parents. Each year, family foster care is being provided to an estimated 542,000 children who
5 have been abused or neglected (Adoption and Foster Care Analysis and Reporting System [AFCARS], 2003). Two significant factors contribute to the challenge of foster care placement for social service agencies. On one hand, continuing high numbers of children
10 are entering the child welfare system whereas, on the other hand, the number of available foster care homes is declining. Although the total number of licensed family foster homes in the United States is not known, 38 states reported a total of 133,503 homes on the last
15 day of 1998 (Child Welfare League of America [CWLA], 2000). When compared with the number of children in out-of-home placement, it becomes clear that the number of foster homes has been insufficient to accommodate the demand. Of the children in out-of-
20 home care, 19% were cared for in a group home or institutional placement, with the remaining children primarily being cared for in a nonrelative foster home or relative placement (AFCARS, 2003). Unfortunately, the lack of foster homes sometimes leads child welfare
25 agencies to place the child in a more restrictive level of care than needed.

Foster Care: The Literature
Changes in Foster Care Service Arena

Shifts arose in the foster care system with the passage of the Adoption Assistance and Child Welfare Act of 1980, an amendment to the Social Security Act of
30 1935. This law emphasized family reunification and permanency planning for children who are in out-of-home placement (Pecora, Whittaker, Maluccio, & Barth, 2000), and with the inception of this law, the population of children in foster care was reduced by
35 nearly one-half (CWLA, 2002). However, with the rate of co-occurring mental health disorders and substance abuse in the adult population estimated to have ranged from 29% to 59% in 1978 (Regier et al., 1990), alcohol and drug abuse issues in the birth parents were factors
40 for out-of-home placement in nearly 75% of all children entering care (Child Welfare Partnership, 1999). In spite of the decrease of the number of children in out-of-home care as a result of this legislation, the number of children who are not living with their par-
45 ents has grown, requiring more foster home families. Between 1986 and 1995, there was a 44% increase in children in out-of-home placements in the United States (Child Welfare Partnership, 1999). In addition to the number of children involved in the child welfare
50 system, there were, and continue to be, many children who are being cared for by grandparents or other relatives not placed through formal mechanisms. There are approximately 6 million children living in the United States who are being cared for in a household headed
55 by a grandparent or other relative who is not a birth parent (Brown, 2003).

Adoption was renewed as a viable option for a child to achieve permanency with the passage of the Adoption and Safe Families Act of 1997. The foster parents
60 who were already caring for the child in their home were often looked upon as the first option to achieving permanency. When they adopted children, these foster parents typically left the resource pool of foster care providers, leaving a shortage of experienced and capa-
65 ble foster families for many agencies. In addition, changes in economics and social customs over the past several decades have exacerbated the shortage. Throughout earlier generations in American history

258

when there was a different economic climate, two-parent households could afford one wage earner and a parent at home. On the contrary, most modern households need two wage earners. In addition, with the rise of single-parent-headed households over recent years, the pool of families with time to assume the role of foster parent has decreased.

The Role of Older Adults in Foster Care

Traditionally, older adults have served a vital role in the lives of children, whether as grandparents or community members. In the field of foster care, older adults could become a major resource in providing the necessary stable homes for the child who is in need of a temporary home. Older adults bring with them a perspective on life and life experiences that makes them uniquely suitable for the task of foster parents. They have been recognized in a volunteer capacity as being more flexible and spontaneous in their interactions with others and for their ability to contribute to a program's services (Strom & Strom, 1999). At the voluntary level, they have demonstrated notable capacities to provide care for children in such national programs as the Foster Grandparent Program. Older foster parents may also be more committed to providing foster care services once involved with an agency. In a study of predictors of foster parents' satisfaction, older foster mothers tended to be more satisfied in their role as foster parents and more content in continuing to be foster parents than younger foster mothers (Denby, Rindfleisch, & Bean, 1999).

Benefits derived from continued work or volunteer experience for the older adult have been demonstrated in the literature. In Dulin and Hill (2003), altruistic activity in older adults was predictive of positive affect. The older adult worker who engaged in providing services to others reported better psychological functioning than their nonaltruistic cohorts. In a large sample of members of a church, those who engaged in altruistic social behaviors experienced higher levels of mental health functioning than those who did not engage in these activities (Schwartz, Meisenhelder, Ma, & Reed, 2003). Other findings suggest that older adults who participated in community service work derived benefits of positive social integration and the activity served as a buffer against stress (Piliavin, 2003). Older adults who participated in The Foster Grandparent Program reported less depression, more social support, and enhanced life satisfaction than did adults who were not foster grandparents (Sweeney, 2000).

Older Americans

Changes in the Older Population

In 1965, the United States Congress passed the Older Americans Act, which established a strong policy of support for ten important social objectives that addressed concerns of older people. Among those objectives was the declaration that "older people should have the opportunity for employment with no discriminatory practices because of age" (Older Americans Act of 1965). At the time when the act was passed, a relatively small proportion (9.2%) of the United States population was 65 years of age or older (U.S. Department of Commerce, Bureau of the Census, 1960, Table 45). At the same time, an unusually high proportion of Americans (39%) were younger than 20 and were filling schools and colleges at unprecedented rates (U.S. Department of Commerce, Bureau of the Census, 1960, Table 45). American society built new structures and developed new resources based on the ascendancy of that group of young people, the so-called baby boom generation.

Today, 40 years after the passage of the Older Americans Act, the first born of the baby boom generation are nearly 60 years old, now number 77 million people, and soon will become the subjects of this legislation. In some ways, these new elders will represent importantly different demographic characteristics from their grandparents of the mid-1960s. For one, they constitute a larger proportion of the total population than the earlier older generation (12.4% as compared with 9.2%), and by 2040, this group will peak at 19.5% of the population (Hobbs & Damon, 2004). They also differ from their grandparents because they can expect to live longer, experience better health, are better educated, and have more retirement income.

Panek (1997) notes that the current aging generation will be expected to remain in the workforce longer for a variety of reasons, including increased longevity. This group has experienced improvements in health and life expectancy, which could allow them to remain active in the work force until older ages (Johnson, 2004). In the area of education, the American population as a whole, as well as older adults specifically, has a higher level of educational achievement than was the case 40 years ago. Only 6.5% of the older adults of 1965 had graduated from college (U.S. Department of Commerce, Bureau of the Census, 1960, Table 173), as compared with 10.0% of persons who were 65 in 2002 (U.S. Department of Commerce, Bureau of the Census, 2002). Although economic security is still an important concern for older adults, they are better off than their cohorts of the past. In contrast to the older adults of the 1960s, today's elders have benefited from the development of Medicare and the increases in Social Security and enjoy a stronger base of retirement income than their predecessors had. The Social Security program has been key to bringing the poverty rate among the elderly down from 28% in 1967 to about 12% today (Zimmerman, 2000).

Potential for Future Worker Shortages

In fact, economic advances represented by Social Security and pension advances have significantly improved the retirement prospective, and some believe that employer and government pensions and health plans will prompt them to leave the labor force and stay out, causing shortages in the labor force (Penner, Perun, & Steuerle, 2003). This trend has already been recognized in Europe and is the subject of major employment policy research and planning (Employment Task Force of the European Union, 2003). Dychtwald, Erickson, and Morison (2004) observed,

While the ranks of the youngest workers (16–24) are growing at 15% this decade, the 25- to 34-year-old segment is growing at just half that, and the workforce population between ages 35 and 44, which are the prime executive development years, is actually declining. (p. 1)

Much has been written about the impact this retired generation will impose on the economy. Some draw the conclusion that as the income provided by this retired generation recedes, some level of continued work by them is needed to contribute to the support of American society (Ekerdt, 2004; Kleyman, 2003; Penner et al., 2003; Steuerle & Carasso, 2001). The Older Americans Act of 1965 recognized that work might continue to retain a role in the lives of older adults. Although the Act focused on community service employment, administration of this employment program over the years has featured an effort to develop unsubsidized employment across all sectors of the economy.

Self-Actualization Through Work

Another reason to encourage able and willing elders to continue to work is that work is a positive lifestyle option for many. Gradual retirement via part-time jobs or new careers can be compatible with better health and self-actualization (Dahlherg, 2004; Dychtwald et al., 2004). Older adults in the 21st century are now and will continue to be more educated and physically and mentally active; these factors will have significant implications for both the quality and quantity of older adults as a labor force in the coming years (Besl & Kale, 1996; McManus, 2004). Many of these individuals will seek to continue working in endeavors that provide self-actualization as a primary benefit even if financial rewards are more limited. In recent research by the American Association for Retired Persons, 2,000 preretirees confirmed that for them, retirement work will need to "keep you mentally active" (80%), "make you feel useful" (74%), and "provide fun and enjoyment" (73%) (Brown, 2003).

Resource for Social Services

Social service agencies are among those employers that need to consider the attractive characteristics of these new elders in terms of future staffing needs. Agencies should evaluate the potential of older workers to be employed in those categories of jobs that currently present agencies with a recruitment challenge, as well as those categories expected to challenge recruitment in the future. The focus should be on retaining people beyond normal retirement or proactively developing strategies to recruit older adults into some of these jobs. Agencies need to examine myths about the capacity of older adults to perform effectively in specific social service job categories.

The field of child foster care is an example of a social service area in which older adults in the 21st century may seek and find a rewarding experience that offers them a direct opportunity to contribute to the social good. This field is also being challenged to recruit a workforce in the 21st century.

Method

Participants and Procedures

In gathering background information for this article, we were interested in the experiences of foster care agencies and older adults who are foster parents, so we drew a stratified random sample of foster care agencies from the Alliance for Children and Families and the Foster Family Treatment Association membership lists. The original sample size contained 132 agencies, with 66 agencies coming from states with the highest percentage of older adult residents (13.8% to 17.6% of older adults in the population) and the remaining 66 agencies dispersed across the United States. Of the 132 agencies surveyed, 44 returned the questionnaire (33%). In these agencies, there were a total of 2,387 foster families with 261 individuals who were identified as being aged 60 or older. The agency foster care programs varied in size from two foster families to 443 families, with the average agency having 55 foster families.

We also distributed 261 surveys to older foster parents who were identified by the agencies, and from these, we received 67 (26%) responses. The average age of these respondents was 64, with 22% being male and 78% female; 68% were married, and the responding foster parents had provided an average of 23 years of foster care services. The minimum time of providing services in this population was 6 months and the maximum time was 36 years.

All potential participants were sent a letter explaining the purpose of the study to encourage their participation. Respondents were asked to complete a one-page questionnaire and return the completed questionnaire in a self-addressed, stamped envelope. In addition to the agency surveys, a foster parent questionnaire was supplied for the older adults serving as foster parents. Agencies that were sent the agency surveys were asked to distribute the foster parent surveys to their foster parents who were 60 and older. Overall, the questionnaires were mailed and collected over a period of 8 weeks.

Measures

The agency questionnaire contained 10 questions relating to the foster care program. Specifically, we were interested in the number of older adults who were employed as foster parents, any recruitment efforts they utilized to enroll older adults, and their perception of challenges and benefits in utilizing older adults as foster parents. The foster parent questionnaire had 4 questions about providing foster care services that were rated on a 5-point scale, with 5 being the highest positive response. In addition, there was an open-ended question regarding the foster parents' "favorite thing" about being a foster parent; there were also two satisfaction questions and demographic information questions.

Findings

Of the agencies responding, 32% acknowledged a concern or challenge related to the prospect of using older adults as foster parents. The identified challenges tended to be centered on concerns over the foster parent's health or physical capabilities (43%) and negative personality characteristics such as "being set in own ways" (35%). The agencies reported 58% positive responses in the question of benefits associated in having an older adult as a foster parent. Many of the respondents (48%) identified the older adult's experience and wisdom as a benefit for the children and program. Other responses cited the older adult's time and flexibility afforded by being retired as a positive aspect (13%); others noted favorable characteristics such as patience, understanding, and tolerance (15%); and others felt that the older foster parents provided more stability and dependability (10%). Another beneficial element that was noted was the tendency of birth families to relate differently to older foster parents, feeling less challenged by a foster parent who is in the age range of a grandparent (8%; see Table 1). Only two of the agencies had age requirements not allowing people older than 65 to serve as foster parents, whereas most of the agencies had requirements that a foster parent had to be at least 21 years of age. Only three agencies specifically focused on recruiting older adults as foster parents.

Table 1
Challenges and Benefits of Older Adults as Foster Parents

		N	%
Challenges (N = 23)	Health/lifespan issues	10	43
	Negative characteristics	8	35
	Technology use/ documentation	2	9
	Need for more support/ training	2	9
	Other	1	4
Benefits (N = 52)	Experience/wisdom	25	48
	Patience/tolerance	8	15
	Flexibility with time schedules	7	13
	Stability/dependability	5	10
	Decreased role confusion	4	8
	Other	3	6

The foster parents responded quite positively concerning their feelings about providing foster care services. Such questions as, "How much do you like providing foster care?" yielded a 4.71 rating, and "How often are your main interests and pleasures in life con-

nected with doing foster care?" yielded a rating of 4.08. Foster parents felt very strongly that providing foster care was valuable (4.82), and they were very satisfied with doing foster care (4.37; see Table 2).

Table 2
Mean Score for Foster Parent Survey

	N	M	SD
1. How much do you like providing foster care?	65	4.71	.46
2. How often do you feel satisfied with doing foster care?	65	4.37	.57
3. How often are your main interests and pleasures in life connected with doing foster care?	63	4.08	.75
4. How often do you feel it is valuable to provide foster care?	65	4.82	.39

In determining a foster parent's perceptions about being a foster parent, respondents indicated several categories of responses. Many identified an altruistic desire or pleasure in seeing changes or growth in the child (44%), and the pursuit of providing care and love to a child emerged as being almost equally important (33%; see Table 3).

Table 3
Foster Parents' Favorite Things About Providing Foster Care (N = 57)

	N	%
Changes/growth in child	25	44
Providing/caring for child	19	33
Companionship	7	12
Challenge	3	5
Other	3	5

Qualitative Research: Foster Parent Interviews

Survey data were augmented by qualitative interviews of 12 foster parents. The interviews were conducted in person with older foster parents from the foster care program at Family Services of Western Pennsylvania. All foster parents 55 years of age or older from the agency were telephoned by an agency researcher who asked whether an interview could be arranged. Of the 16 foster parents who met this criterion, 12 agreed to be interviewed. All interviews were conducted by a master's-level clinician in the respondent's home, with one interview in an agency office; all interviews occurred between September 24 and October 11, 2004. In homes where there was a spouse, both foster parents were invited to participate in the interview. The interviews were approximately 60 to 90 minutes in length and involved an exploration of the foster parents' experiences, including their perceptions of the benefits and difficulties in providing foster care to children. Several areas related to foster care were discussed, such as why they became foster parents, what they find valuable about being foster parents, struggles or difficulties they experience, and the supports and resources they have used to manage the difficulties. All interviews were tape-recorded and transcribed for analysis, and two independent raters reviewed transcripts of the interviews to determine common themes.

Qualitative Findings

An analysis of the transcripts identified four topical areas relevant to a foster parent's experience: (a) motivation to be a foster provider, (b) values in the provision of foster care services, (c) struggles or difficulties in providing foster care, and (d) issues of resources and supports. Examples of typical reactions in each of these areas are presented.

Motivation to Be Foster Parents

In discussing the motivation for providing foster care, foster parents tended to express their desire and delight in being around children and wanting to help them. Other times, it was noted that providing foster care involved dealing with the empty nest syndrome or addressing deeper self-actualization needs or fulfilling religious ones. Most of the foster parents were able to recall a specific time in their lives when they were motivated to decide to become a foster parent. What appeared to be the motivating factor appeared also to sustain these foster parents to continue to provide care.

Enjoyment of children. Mrs. T is a 76-year-old married Caucasian woman who has been providing foster care services for 11 years with her husband, who is 79 years old. This couple talked about their love for children and enjoying a home filled with children.

When my own youngest child, who is now 34, started school I wanted foster care then. We do nothing and we go nowhere. I liked kids all my life. I had my neighbor's kids over all the time. I think I should have children in the house.

Another foster parent, twice-widowed Mrs. B, Caucasian, 63, who started providing foster care at the age of 55, said, "I never enjoyed or found anything more rewarding than having those kids."

Mrs. H, a widowed African American woman of 57, said, "I became a foster parent because I love kids; I got gangs of grandkids, but I just love kids. I'd rather be in a house full of kids than adults." A single African American woman of 66, who has been providing foster care for 4 years, said, "I love kids. I never had none. I figured maybe this is my job to help kids in need, and I enjoy doing it."

Religious reasons. Another foster parent, a 79-year-old Caucasian widowed woman, Mrs. S, was motivated by a deal she had made with God when she was going through a medical crisis with her daughter and herself:

I thought I was pregnant in my 40s and I was tickled to death. I went to the doctor and I wasn't pregnant.... They told me that I had leukemia and I had approximately 9 months to live. My daughter came down with spinal meningitis. They kept her in isolation...I screamed. I didn't pray. I screamed at God above and told him he couldn't do that, take my crippled child and take me. The doctor told me that I couldn't bargain with God. I told him I am not making a bargain. I am telling him that if he doesn't take my kid, I will do anything for his children. I will take care of his children. Dr. Young didn't understand, but my husband did. Kate [her daughter] came out OK with no severe problems. Our church had a foster mother, and she told me to go down to this agency. I went down and I became a foster mother.

Another foster parent, Mrs. C, African American, divorced, 70, phrased it like this, "It is because that is why God has me here. That is the mission that he put me on this earth to do." Mr. and Mrs. D, 68 and 72, Caucasian, said, "It is a wonderful ministry of love. You cannot be a selfish person and do this because if you are, there is no place. So your life, half the time, is put on the back burner."

Value of Providing Foster Care

The foster parents interviewed identified similar values in providing foster care to those of the foster parents who responded to the questionnaire. Typical responses centered on the desire to make a difference in a child's life and to care for children. Other responses also indicated that the foster parent benefited from the foster care relationship. To some respondents, being a foster parent gives them purpose and adds meaning to their lives.

Contributions to others. A married couple in their 70s stated the importance of giving something to the child. The wife said, "I think if I can save one child, one is better than none at all. If everybody could just save one of these little kids, that makes a difference." The husband added that it was valuable to "give them something that their own family couldn't give them, which may be love and affection."

A 79-year-old African American foster mother viewed her service of foster care as an opportunity for teaching children. She said, "I teach the kids these things so it will stick with them for the rest of their life. I plant seeds."

Contributions to self. A foster mother (age 79) said, "I am not alone in this big house. It gives me something to do. I have to get up in the morning whether I want to or not." A 70-year-old divorced African American woman said, "[Being a foster parent] helped me a lot because it kept me busy after my mother passed. The children...helped keep my mind off of my mother passing. It helped me to keep myself busy." Another single foster mother (age 79, African American) said, "Yes, because I don't want to just sit here and do nothing, worry about just me and get old by myself."

Struggles or Difficulties of Providing Foster Care

The foster parents consistently talked about having difficulties with saying goodbye to the children whom they have cared for when it is time to return them to their birth families. They also noted the difficulties in their relationships with the birth parents; they struggled

470 with the birth parents over parenting issues. They also struggled to manage the child's torn feelings of loyalty between the foster parent and the birth parent.

Conflict with birth parents. Widowed foster mother Mrs. C (age 74) said, "The mothers sometimes can be 475 difficult. I got some mothers that have really been a headache. They are mad at the system. They are upset with the foster parent. They blame us that we have their children."

Child's feelings. Ms. MJ (age 67) said,

480 They [the children] can be rebellious because they want to be with their mother. It is a struggle to let them know that I am here to help them and give them support and love till they can go back to their mother.

An African American widowed woman of 67 said,

485 It is hard. It is hard. It is hard on them. It is harder on them than you because you are the adult. But the kids, it is a shame that they have to leave, pushed and moved around like that; it is not fair. They are depending all on an adult until they can depend on themselves.

490 A widowed Mrs. S identified the struggle for a child: "But can you imagine the torn morale in this kid—the love for her mother and still the love and respect for the foster mother that raised her."

Factors Contributing to Success

The foster parents spoke about the importance of 495 having support and resources available to them from the agency and the community. They appeared willing to acknowledge that they cannot do the work of foster care without assistance from others. It is apparent that when the foster care agency provides the day-to-day 500 assistance for the foster parents, they are appreciative and are able to fulfill their roles. When the children have special needs, assistance from professionals, whether it is from mental health or physical health providers, is necessary to assist these families. Friends and 505 family members also appear to play an important role in providing the social support needed to carry out this challenging work.

Mrs. W, a widowed woman of 71, said, "I have a friend who told me that if I get to the point I obviously 510 need a break, she will watch the kids for me." She went on to explain that she also utilizes the respite services of the agency when she needs a longer break from the "work." Mrs. G stated that she also utilized respite services after an operation when she "just couldn't keep 515 up with them [the children]." Mr. and Mrs. D said, "We left one church and joined another church, which was loving and accepting. This is an absolute must because if you do not have this support, you cannot go out in public."

520 Ms. M, a single African American woman of 67, said,

Oh, I have phone numbers of whom to call. CYF [Children, Youth and Families]...tells me where to go and what to do, and usually they help me to go. Well, CYF

525 and Family Services helps me a whole lot; at least they show me the way to go.

She noted the following about when she cared for a child with behavioral health needs: "The therapist was with him in school during the day, and then he came to 530 the house every evening for 2 hours. So really, I am learning from them; this is teaching me, too."

Discussion

Older adults can be an important resource for social service agencies by working as foster parents. Their experience and life perspective appear to be advanta- 535 geous qualities for any foster care agency. As many older adults are retired, they may have more time available to devote themselves to the care of children, which is an asset because available time is necessary in completing the many tasks associated with child care, 540 such as attending doctor appointments, enrolling for school, and attending court hearings. Whereas working foster parents often struggle when a new child comes into their home for emergency placement in the middle of the night when there is little time to secure babysit- 545 ting so that they can attend work the following day, a retired adult does not have to grapple with that situation.

The contributions of older adults working as foster parents appear not only to have a beneficial effect for 550 the foster care program but also to enhance the elder's own sense of well-being. It is understood in the literature that older adults who seek work after retirement do so to contribute their experience in a meaningful way and to feel valued. These individuals may seek em- 555 ployment that provides self-actualization as a primary benefit and not for financial rewards. An older adult who provides foster care appears to experience similar benefits of self-actualization.

Older adults serving as foster parents also make an 560 important contribution to society as a whole. An altruistic goal to give of oneself for the benefit of another is a higher level human experience. Individuals whose work enables them to give profoundly to children who have been neglected or abused find an avenue for 565 achieving this goal. The value of the contribution made by the foster parent is beyond any monetary compensation.

Limitations

The ability to generalize the results of this study is limited due to the relatively small agency sample size 570 ($N = 44$) and foster parent sample size ($N = 67$), yielding a relatively modest response rate to the total number of surveys mailed (33% and 26%, respectively). The study was conducted on a very small budget that did not include the possibility of an incentive to either 575 the agency or the foster parents for their participation. The study was limited to only those foster care agencies and foster parents who responded to the request to participate. These factors limit the generalizability and

263

580 interpretation of the findings. The possibility that the limited results could be attributed to chance cannot be ruled out and thus would need replication before interpretative value can be given. The qualitative study, though yielding a response rate of 75%, also has limited generalizability as the population of foster parents 585 was from Western Pennsylvania and connected with a single provider agency.

Recommendations for Practice

The United States currently has the largest older population in its history; this population possesses great potential to continue to contribute to the economic and social wealth of the nation and the betterment of conditions for fellow citizens. At the same time, the United States needs older adults' continued contribution. In the social arena, child foster care offers a sterling opportunity for older people to pass the best of their experience to a new generation that needs someone to care for them. To capitalize on this resource, foster care agencies need to consider several recommendations relating to recruitment of older adults as foster parents and tailoring supports for them, as well as boosting public awareness of productive aging alternatives.

Recruitment. First, foster care agencies should look at marketing directly to the older population to provide the additional foster care homes that society requires. An important target would be associations where educated and skilled older adults may have natural connections, such as retired nurse or teacher associations. It would also be beneficial to acknowledge directly the benefits the agency and the older person may experience by forming the foster care relationship. Other marketing tools should depict older adults serving in the capacity of foster parents, and current older foster parents can be utilized directly in recruiting efforts.

Tailored training and support. For older adults who decide to become foster parents, foster care agencies may need to provide additional support to help them cope with the stress of caring for young children and to deal with the demands placed on them by the placing agency. Training that acknowledges their unique perspectives on parenting should be provided and should include additional lessons on how to manage the complex details of foster parenting. If they are on a limited income and the small stipend that is provided for foster care services causes difficulty, they may face challenges in managing economics. They also may need to utilize respite services more often as they take time to attend to their own medical or health situations if additional family support is not available. This additional support may also increase the odds that an experienced foster parent who enters older life may continue being a foster parent.

Productive aging options. Finally, public information sources need to publicize more comprehensive options for healthy aging. Since the time when the

635 Older Americans Act (1965) was adopted, a great amount of attention to preretirement education programs has developed in the United States. In addition, the popular media frequently feature information related to planning for retirement. Typically, these programs emphasize the rich potential of leisure activities to fill the retirement years and are based on the notion that older adults want to withdraw from work and relax. Although this is often true, some older adults, for various reasons, would like to continue to work, and some of these would like to enter a second or different type of career. Because this larger, new generation of older adults is so well prepared to continue their contribution to society, it behooves planners of preretirement programs and providers of information on aging in the present and future to make a greater effort to incorporate information on new careers.

References

Adoption and Safe Families Act, 105 U.S.C.§89. (1997).

Adoption Assistance and Child Welfare Act, 96 U.S.C.§272. (1980).

Adoption and Foster Care Analysis and Reporting System. (2003). *The AFCARS Report: Preliminary FY 2001 Estimates as of March 2003 (8)*. Retrieved on October 10, 2004, from http://www.acf.hhs.gov/programs/cb/publications/afcars/report8.htm

Besl, J. R., & Kale, B. D. (1996, June). Older workers in the 21st century: Active and educated, a case study. *Monthly Labor Review, 119*, 18–28.

Brown, K. (2003). *Staying ahead of the curve 2003: The AARP working in retirement study*. Retrieved April 20, 2005, from http://www.aarp.org/research/reference/publicopinions/aresearch-import-417.html

Child Welfare League of America. (2000). Licensed homes and facilities, 1998. Retrieved March 13, 2001, from http://ndas.cwla.org/data_stats/access/predefined/Report.asp?ReportID=49

Child Welfare League of America. (2002). *Research Roundup: Family Reunification*. Retrieved March 14, 2003, from http://www.cwla.org/programs/r2p/rrnews0203.pdf

Child Welfare Partnership. (1999). *Cohort IV report. An examination of longer-term foster care in Oregon between 1995–1997*. Retrieved August 2, 2004, from www.cwp.pdx.edu/assets/Long_Term_Cohort_IV_Report.pdf

Dahlberg, S. (2004, February). The new elderhood. *Training, 141*, 46–47.

Denby, R., Rindfleisch, N., & Bean, G. (1999). Predictors of foster parents' satisfaction and intent to continue to foster. *Child Abuse & Neglect, 23*, 287–303.

Dulin, P. L., & Hill, R. D. (2003). Relationships between altruistic activity and positive and negative affect among low-income older adult service providers. *Aging & Mental Health, 7*, 294–299.

Dychtwald, K., Erickson, T., & Morison, B. (2004, March). It's time to retire retirement. *Harvard Business Review, 82*, 1.

Ekerdt, D. J. (2004). Born to retire: The foreshortened life course. *The Gerontologist, 44*, 3–9.

Employment Task Force of the European Union. (2003). *Jobs, jobs, jobs: Creating more employment in Europe*. Retrieved April 20, 2005, from http://europa.eu.int/comm/employment_social/employment_strategy/pdf/etf_en.pdf

Hobbs, F. B., & Damon, B. L. (2004). *65+ in the United States*. Retrieved on September 24, 2004, from http://www.census.gov/prod/1/pop/p23-190/p23-190.html

Johnson, R. W. (2004, July). Trends in job demands among older workers. *Monthly Labor Review, 127*, 48–56.

Kleyman, P. (2003, July/August). Phased retirement will ease many into active older years [Electronic version]. *Aging Today: The Bimonthly Newspaper of the American Society for Aging*, 1.

Panek, P. E. (1997). The older worker. In A. D. Fisk & W. A. Rogers (Eds.), *Handbook of human factors and the older adult* (pp. 363–387). New York: Academic.

Pecora, P. J., Whittaker, J. K., Maluccio, A. N., & Barth, R. P. (2000). *The child welfare challenge*. New York: Aldine de Gruyter.

Penner, R. G., Perun, P., & Steuerle, C. E. (2003). *Letting older workers work*. Retrieved April 20, 2005, from http://www.urban.org/url.cfm?ID=310861

Piliavin, J. A. (2003). Doing well by doing good: Benefits for the benefactor. In C. L. M. Keyes & J. Haidt (Eds.), *Flourishing: Positive psychology and the life well lived* (pp. 227–247). Washington, DC: American Psychological Association.

Regier, D. A., Farmer, M. E., Rae, D. S., Locke, B. Z., Keith, S. J., Judd, L. L., & Goodwin, F. K. (1990). Comorbidity of mental disorders with alcohol and other drugs: Results from the Epidemiologic Catchment Area (ECA) Study. *JAMA, 264*, 2511–2518.

Schwartz, C., Meisenhelder, J. B., Ma, Y., & Reed, G. (2003). Altruistic social interest behaviors are associated with better mental health. *Psychosomatic Medicine, 65*, 778–785.

Social Security Act, 42 U.S.C.§1320. (1935).

Steuerle, C. E., & Carasso, A. (2001). *A prediction: Older workers will work more in the future.* Retrieved April 20, 2005, from http://www.urban.org/url.cfm?ID=310258

Strom, R., & Strom, S. (1999). Establishing school volunteer programs. *Child and Youth Services, 20*, 177–188.

Sweeney, A. R. (2000). An evaluation of the foster grandparent program in Fresno, California. Dissertation abstracts international: Section BL the Sciences and Engineering. Vol 61 (1-B), July 2000, 550.

University of Michigan, Institute for Social Research. (2004). *Boomers unexpected ethos: Work until we drop?* Retrieved from http://www.umich.edu/news/index.html?Releases/2004/Jul04/r071504c

U.S. Department of Commerce, Bureau of the Census. (1960). *1960 Census of the population: Vol. 1. Characteristics of the population.* Washington, DC: U.S. Bureau of the Census.

U.S. Department of Commerce, Bureau of the Census. (2002). *Current population Survey.* Retrieved on September 24, 2004, from http://www.census.gov/population/socdemo/age/ppl-167/tab01.txt

Zimmerman, S. L. (2000). A family policy agenda to enhance families' transactional interdependencies over the life span. *Families in Society, 81*, 557–575.

About the authors: *Donald H. Goughler*, MSW, is chief executive officer, Family Services of Western Pennsylvania, and part-time faculty member at the University of Pittsburgh, School of Social Work, where he teaches courses in management. *Annette C. Trunzo*, MSW, is director of research and program evaluation, Family Services of Western Pennsylvania.

Address correspondence to: Donald H. Goughler at goughlerd@fswp.org or Family Services of Western Pennsylvania, 3230 William Pitt Way, Pittsburgh, PA 15238-1361.

Exercise for Article 37

Factual Questions

1. What percentage of the 261 surveys that were distributed to older foster parents were returned to the researchers?

2. What did the researchers do to encourage participation?

3. The researchers used an open-ended question regarding what?

4. How many of the responding agencies specifically focused on recruiting older adults?

5. How many of the 16 foster parents who were contacted by telephone agreed to be interviewed?

6. The mean (*M*) for the first question in Table 2 is 4.71. In light of the measure used, is this a high value?

Questions for Discussion

7. The literature review in this article is longer than the literature reviews in a number of the other arti-

cles in this book. In your opinion, is this relatively long review a special strength of this article? Explain. (See lines 27–240.)

8. The researchers state that they drew a "stratified random sample." What is your understanding of the meaning of this term? (See lines 243–244.)

9. Of the 132 agencies surveyed, 33% returned the questionnaire. Is this an important weakness of this research? Why? Why not? (See lines 251–253.)

10. The results shown in Table 1 are described in lines 296–314. How helpful is the table in helping you understand these results?

11. The qualitative part of this research was based on interviews. The participants who were interviewed were from one foster care program. In your opinion, does this limit the generalizability of the results? (See lines 337–341.)

12. The researchers present quantitative findings in lines 294–336 and qualitative findings in lines 364–531. In your opinion, are both types of findings equally informative? Is one type more informative than the other? Explain.

13. Unlike most of the other articles in this book, this article is based on both quantitative and qualitative research. Do you believe that this is a strength of this article? Explain.

Quality Ratings

Directions: Indicate your level of agreement with each of the following statements by circling a number from 5 for strongly agree (SA) to 1 for strongly disagree (SD). If you believe an item is not applicable to this research article, leave it blank. Be prepared to explain your ratings. When responding to criteria A and B below, keep in mind that brief titles and abstracts are conventional in published research.

A. The title of the article is appropriate.

SA   5   4   3   2   1   SD

B. The abstract provides an effective overview of the research article.

SA   5   4   3   2   1   SD

C. The introduction establishes the importance of the study.

SA   5   4   3   2   1   SD

D. The literature review establishes the context for the study.

SA   5   4   3   2   1   SD

E. The research purpose, question, or hypothesis is clearly stated.

SA   5   4   3   2   1   SD

F. The method of sampling is sound.

SA   5   4   3   2   1   SD

G. Relevant demographics (for example, age, gender, and ethnicity) are described.

SA   5   4   3   2   1   SD

H. Measurement procedures are adequate.

SA   5   4   3   2   1   SD

I. All procedures have been described in sufficient detail to permit a replication of the study.

SA   5   4   3   2   1   SD

J. The participants have been adequately protected from potential harm.

SA   5   4   3   2   1   SD

K. The results are clearly described.

SA   5   4   3   2   1   SD

L. The discussion/conclusion is appropriate.

SA   5   4   3   2   1   SD

M. Despite any flaws, the report is worthy of publication.

SA   5   4   3   2   1   SD

Article 38

Project D.A.R.E. Outcome
Effectiveness Revisited

STEVEN L. WEST
Virginia Commonwealth University

KERI K. O'NEAL
University of North Carolina, Chapel Hill

OBJECTIVES. We provide an updated meta-analysis on the effectiveness of Project D.A.R.E. in preventing alcohol, tobacco, and illicit drug use among school-aged youths.
METHODS. We used meta-analytic techniques to create an overall effect size for D.A.R.E. outcome evaluations reported in scientific journals.
RESULTS. The overall weighted effect size for the included D.A.R.E. studies was extremely small (correlation coefficient = 0.011; Cohen's d = 0.023; 95% confidence interval = –0.04, 0.08) and nonsignificant (z = 0.73, NS).
CONCLUSIONS. Our study supports previous findings indicating that D.A.R.E. is ineffective.

From *American Journal of Public Health*, 94, 1027–1029. Copyright © 2004 by American Journal of Public Health. Reprinted with permission.

In the United States, Project D.A.R.E. (Drug Abuse Resistance Education) is one of the most widely used substance abuse prevention programs targeted at school-aged youths. In recent years, D.A.R.E. has been 5 the country's largest single school-based prevention program in terms of federal expenditures, with an average of three-quarters of a billion dollars spent on its provision annually.[1] Although its effectiveness in preventing substance use has been called into question, its 10 application in our nation's schools remains very extensive.[2-6]

Given the recent increases in alcohol and other drug use among high school and college students,[7] the continued use of D.A.R.E. and similar programs seems 15 likely. In a meta-analysis examining the effectiveness of D.A.R.E., Ennett et al.[3] noted negligible yet positive effect sizes (ranging from 0.00 to 0.11) when outcomes occurring immediately after program completion were considered. However, this analysis involved 2 major 20 limitations. First, Ennett et al. included research from nonpeer-reviewed sources, including annual reports produced for agencies associated with the provision of D.A.R.E. services. While such an inclusion does not necessarily represent a serious methodological flaw, 25 use of such sources has been called into question.[8]

Second, Ennett and colleagues included only studies in which postintervention assessment was conducted immediately at program termination. As noted by Lynam et al.,[6] the developmental trajectories of drug 30 experimentation and use vary over time. Thus, if individuals are assessed during periods in which rates of experimentation and use are naturally high, any positive effects that could be found at times of lower experimentation will be deflated. Likewise, assessments 35 made during periods in which experimentation and use are slight will exaggerate the overall effect of the intervention.

Ideally, problems such as those just described could be solved by the use of large-scale longitudinal studies 40 involving extensive follow-up over a period of years. There have been several longer-term follow-ups, but the cost of such efforts may limit the number of longitudinal studies that can be conducted. In the present analysis, we attempted to overcome this difficulty by 45 including a wider range of follow-up reports, from immediate posttests to 10-year postintervention assessments, in an updated meta-analysis of all currently available research articles reporting an outcome evaluation of Project D.A.R.E.

Methods

We conducted computer searches of the *ERIC*, 50 *MEDLINE*, and *PsycINFO* databases in late fall 2002 to obtain articles for the present study. In addition, we reviewed the reference lists of the acquired articles for other potential sources. We initially reviewed roughly 55 40 articles from these efforts; 11 studies appearing in the literature from 1991 to 2002 met our 3 inclusion criteria, which were as follows:

1. The research was reported in a peer-reviewed journal; reports from dissertations/theses, books, and 60 unpublished manuscripts were not included. We selected this criterion in an attempt to ensure inclusion of only those studies with rigorous methodologies. As noted, a previous meta-analysis of Project D.A.R.E. included research from nonre- 65 viewed sources, a fact that critics have suggested may have added error to the reported findings.[8]
2. The research included a control or comparison group (i.e., the research must have involved an experimental or quasi-experimental design).

Table 1
Primary Articles Included in the Meta-Analysis

Study (year)	Sample	r	d	95% confidence interval
Ringwalt et al. (1991)[18]	5th and 6th graders (n = 1270; 52% female/48% male; 50% African American/40% Anglo/10% other), posttested immediately	0.025	0.056	−0.06, 0.16
Becker et al. (1992)[19]	5th graders (n = 2878), posttested immediately	−0.058	−0.117	−0.19, −0.04
Harmon (1993)[20]	5th graders (n = 708), posttested immediately	0.015	0.030	−0.12, 0.18
Ennett et al. (1994)[21]	7th and 8th graders (n = 1334; 54% Anglo/22% African American/9% Hispanic/15% other), 2 years post-D.A.R.E.	0.000	0.000[a]	−0.11, 0.11
Rosenbaum et al. (1994)[22]	6th and 7th graders (n = 1584; 49.7% female/50.3% male; 49.9% Anglo/24.7% African American/8.9% Hispanic/16.5% other), 1 year post-D.A.R.E.	0.000	0.000[a]	−0.10, 0.10
Wysong et al. (1994)[23]	12th graders (n = 619), 5 years post-D.A.R.E.	0.000	0.000[a]	−0.16, 0.16
Dukes et al. (1996)[24]	9th graders (n = 849), 3 years post-D.A.R.E.	0.035	0.072	−0.06, 0.21
Zagumny & Thompson (1997)[25]	6th graders (n = 395; 48% female/52% male), 4–5 years post-D.A.R.E.	0.184	0.376	0.07, 0.68
Lynam et al. (1999)[6]	6th graders (n = 1002; 57% female/43% male; 75.1% Anglo/20.4% African American/0.5% other), 10 years post-D.A.R.E.	0.000	0.000[a]	−0.15, 0.15
Thombs (2000)[26]	5th through 10th graders (n = 630; 90.4% Anglo/5.5% African American/4.1% other), posttested at least 1 to 6 years post-D.A.R.E.	0.025	0.038	−0.15, 0.23
Ahmed et al. (2002)[14]	5th and 6th graders (n = 236; 50% female/50% male/69% Anglo/24% African American/7% other), posttested immediately	0.198	0.405	0.01, 0.80

Note. r = correlation coefficient; *d* = difference in the means of the treatment and control conditions divided by the pooled standard deviation. Negative signs for *r* and *d* indicate greater effectiveness of control/comparison group.
[a]Assumed effect size.

70   3. The research included both preintervention and postintervention assessments of at least 1 of 3 key variables: alcohol use, illicit drug use, and tobacco use. We chose to include only those effect sizes that concerned actual substance use behaviors,
75   since the true test of a substance use prevention effort is its impact on actual rates of use.

Using these criteria, we refined the original list of studies to 11 studies (Table 1). We calculated effect sizes using the procedures outlined by Rosenthal.[9]
80   Meta-analysis results are commonly presented in the form of either a correlation coefficient (r) or the difference in the means of the treatment and control conditions divided by the pooled standard deviation (Cohen's d).[10] Since both are ratings of effect size, they
85   can readily be converted to one another, and, if not provided in the original analyses, they can be calculated via F, t, and χ^2 statistics as well as means and standard deviations.[9] We calculated both estimations for the individual
90   included studies and for the overall analysis. As discussed by Amato and Keith,[11] tests of significance used in meta-analyses require that effect sizes be independent; therefore, if 2 or more effect sizes were generated within the same outcome category, we used the mean
95   effect size. We also used the procedure for weighting effect sizes suggested by Shadish and Haddock[12] to ensure that all effect sizes were in the form of a common metric. In addition, we calculated 95% confidence intervals (CIs) for each study and for the overall
100   analysis.

Results

The average weighted effect size (r) for all studies was 0.011 (d = 0.023; 95% CI = −0.04, 0.08), indicating marginally better outcomes for individuals participating in D.A.R.E. relative to participants in control
105   conditions. The fact that the associated CI included a negative value indicates that the average effect size was not significantly greater than zero at $p < .05$. According to the guidelines developed by Cohen,[13] both of the effect sizes obtained were below the level nor
110   mally considered small. Four of the included studies noted no effect of D.A.R.E. relative to control conditions, and 1 study noted that D.A.R.E. was less effective than the control condition.

Furthermore, the 6 reports indicating that D.A.R.E.
115   had more positive effects were for the most part small (Figure 1). The largest effect size was found in a report in which the only outcome examined was smoking. Finally, we conducted a test of cumulative significance to determine whether differences existed between
120   D.A.R.E. participants and non-D.A.R.E. participants. This test produced nonsignificant results (z = 0.73, NS).

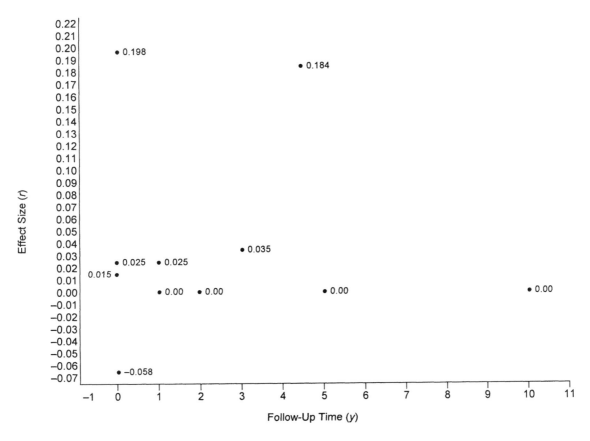

Figure 1. Plot of effect sizes, by follow-up time.

Discussion

Our results confirm the findings of a previous meta-analysis[3] indicating that Project D.A.R.E. is ineffective. This is not surprising, given the substantial information developed over the past decade to that effect. Critics of the present analysis might argue that, despite the magnitude of our findings, the direction of the effect of D.A.R.E. was generally positive. While this is the case, it should be emphasized that the effects we found did not differ significantly from the variation one would expect by chance. According to Cohen's guidelines,[13] the effect size we obtained would have needed to be 20 times larger to be considered even small. Given the tremendous expenditures in time and money involved with D.A.R.E., it would appear that continued efforts should focus on other techniques and programs that might produce more substantial effects.

Our findings also indicate that D.A.R.E. was minimally effective during the follow-up periods that would place its participants in the very age groups targeted. Indeed, no noticeable effects could be discerned in nearly half of the reports, including the study involving the longest follow-up period. This is an important consideration for those involved in program planning and development.

As noted earlier, progression in regard to experimentation and use varies over time. Use of alcohol and other drugs reaches a peak during adolescence or young adulthood and decreases steadily thereafter.[7,15] Such a developmental path would be expected of all individuals, regardless of their exposure to a prevention effort. Ideally, individuals enrolled in a program such as D.A.R.E. would report limited or no use during their adolescent and young adult years. The fact that half of the included studies reported no beneficial effect of D.A.R.E. beyond what would be expected by chance casts serious doubt on its utility.

One shortcoming of our analysis should be noted. In many of the studies we included, individual students were the unit of analysis in calculating effects. As noted by Rosenbaum and Hanson,[16] this practice tends to lead to overestimates of program effectiveness since the true unit of analysis is the schools in which the students are "nested." Because our meta-analysis was limited to the types of data and related information available from the original articles, the potential for such inflation of program effectiveness exists. However, the overall effect sizes calculated here were small and non-significant, and thus it is unlikely that inclusion of studies making this error had a significant impact on the current findings.

An additional caveat is that all of the studies included in this analysis represent evaluations of what is commonly referred to as the "old D.A.R.E.": programs generally based on the original formulations of the D.A.R.E. model. In response to the many critiques of

the program, the D.A.R.E. prevention model was sub-
stantially revamped in 2001, thanks in part to a $13.6
180 million grant provided by the Robert Wood Johnson
Foundation.[17] The revisions to the model have since
given rise to programs working under the "new
D.A.R.E." paradigm. However, at the time of the writing of this article we were unable to find any major
185 evaluation of the new D.A.R.E. model in the research
literature, and the effectiveness of such efforts has yet
to be determined.

References

1. McNeal RB, Hanson WB. An examination of strategies for gaining convergent validity in natural experiments: D.A.R.E. as an illustrative case
study. *Eval Rev.* 1995;19:141–158.
2. Donnermeyer J, Wurschmidt T. Educators' perceptions of the D.A.R.E.
program. *J Drug Educ.* 1997;27:259–276.
3. Ennett ST, Tobler NS, Ringwalt CL, Flewelling RL. How effective is
Drug Abuse Resistance Education? A meta-analysis of Project D.A.R.E.
outcome evaluations. *Am J Public Health.* 1994;84:1394–1401.
4. Hanson WB. Pilot test results comparing the All Stars Program with
seventh-grade D.A.R.E.: Program integrity and mediating variable
analysis. *Subst Use Misuse.* 1996;31:1359–1377.
5. Hanson WB, McNeal RB. How D.A.R.E. works: An examination of
program effects on mediating variables. *Health Educ Behav.*
1997;24:165–176.
6. Lynam DR, Milich R, Zimmerman R, et al. Project D.A.R.E: No effects
at 10-year follow-up. *J Consult Clin Psychol.* 1999;67:590–593.
7. Johnston LD, O'Malley PM, Bachman JG. *National Survey Results on
Drug Use from the Monitoring the Future Study, 1975–1998. Volume 1:
Secondary School Students.* Rockville, Md: National Institute on Drug
Abuse; 1999. NIH publication 99–4660.
8. Gorman DM. The effectiveness of D.A.R.E. and other drug use prevention programs. *Am J Public Health.* 1995;85:873.
9. Rosenthal R. *Meta-Analytic Procedures for Social Research.* 2nd ed.
Thousand Oaks, CA: Sage Publications; 1991.
10. DasEiden R, Reifman A. Effects of Brazelton demonstrations on later
parenting: A meta-analysis. *J Pediatr Psychol.* 1996;21:857–868.
11. Amato PH, Keith B. Parental divorce and well-being of children: A
meta-analysis. *Psychol Bull.* 1991;110:26–46.
12. Shadish WR, Haddock CK. Combining estimates of effect size. In: Cooper H, Hedges LV, eds. *The Handbook of Research Synthesis.* New
York, NY: Russell Sage Foundation; 1994:261–281.
13. Cohen J. *Statistical Power Analysis for the Behavioral Sciences.* 2nd ed.
Hillsdale, NJ: Lawrence Erlbaum Associates; 1998.
14. Ahmed NU, Ahmed NS, Bennett CR, Hinds JE. Impact of a drug abuse
resistance education (D.A.R.E.) program in preventing the initiation of
cigarette smoking in fifth- and sixth-grade students. *J Natl Med Assoc.*
2002;94:249–256.
15. Shedler J, Block J. Adolescent drug use and psychological health: A
longitudinal inquiry. *Am Psychol.* 1990;45:612–630.
16. Rosenbaum DP, Hanson GS. Assessing the effects of a school-based
drug education: A six-year multilevel analysis of Project D.A.R.E. *J Res
Crime Delinquency.* 1998;35:381–412.
17. Improving and evaluating the D.A.R.E. school-based substance abuse
prevention curriculum. Available at: http://www.rwjf.org/programs/
grantDetail.jsp?id=040371. Accessed January 8, 2003.
18. Ringwalt C, Ennett ST, Holt KD. An outcome evaluation of Project
D.A.R.E. (Drug Abuse Resistance Education). *Health Educ Res.*
1991;6:327–337.
19. Becker HK, Agopian MW, Yeh S. Impact evaluation of drug abuse resistance education (D.A.R.E.). *J Drug Educ.* 1992;22:283–291.
20. Harmon MA. Reducing the risk of drug involvement among early adolescents: An evaluation of drug abuse resistance education (D.A.R.E.).
Eval Rev. 1993;17:221–239.
21. Ennett ST, Rosenbaum DP, Flewelling RL, Bieler GS, Ringwalt CL,
Bailey SL. Long-term evaluation of drug abuse resistance education.
Addict Behav. 1994;19:113–125.
22. Rosenbaum DP, Flewelling RL, Bailey SL, Ringwalt CL, Wilkinson DL.
Cops in the classroom: A longitudinal evaluation of drug abuse resistance education (D.A.R.E.). *J Res Crime Delinquency.* 1994;31:3–31.
23. Wysong E, Aniskiewicz R, Wright D. Truth and D.A.R.E.: Tracking
drug education to graduation and as symbolic politics. *Soc Probl.*
1994;41:448–472.
24. Dukes RL, Ullman JB, Stein JA. Three-year follow-up of drug abuse
resistance education (D.A.R.E.). *Eval Rev.* 1996;20:49–66.
25. Zagumny MJ, Thompson MK. Does D.A.R.E. work? An evaluation in
rural Tennessee. *J Alcohol Drug Educ.* 1997;42:32–41.
26. Thombs DL. A retrospective study of D.A.R.E.: Substantive effects not
detected in undergraduates. *J Alcohol Drug Educ.* 2000;46:27–40.

Acknowledgments: Portions of this research were presented at the
Eighth Annual Meeting of the Society for Prevention Research,
Montreal, Quebec, Canada, June 2000.

About the authors: *Steven L. West* is with the Department of Rehabilitation Counseling, Virginia Commonwealth University, Richmond. *Keri K. O'Neal* is with the Center for Developmental Science,
University of North Carolina, Chapel Hill. Drs. West and O'Neal
contributed equally to all aspects of study design, data analysis, and
the writing of this article. No protocol approval was needed for this
study.

Address correspondence to: Steven L. West, Ph.D., Virginia Commonwealth University, Department of Rehabilitation Counseling,
1112 East Clay St., Box 980330, Richmond, VA 23298-0330.
E-mail: slwest2@vcu.edu

Exercise for Article 38

Factual Questions

1. To identify the articles for this meta-analysis, the
researchers conducted computer searches of which
three databases?

2. Which study had the largest effect size (r)? (Identify it by the name of the author and year of publication.) What was the value of r in this study?

3. What was the average weighted effect size (r) for
all studies included in this meta-analysis?

4. The study with the largest effect size examined
only one outcome. What was the outcome?

5. According to Figure 1, the study with the longest
follow-up time had what effect size?

6. Were the researchers able to find any major
evaluations of the *new* D.A.R.E. paradigm?

Questions for Discussion

7. The researchers do not describe the D.A.R.E. program components. In your opinion, would it have
been desirable for them to do so? Explain.

8. What is your opinion of the researchers' decision
to include only research reported in peer-reviewed
journals? (See lines 58–66.)

9. What is your opinion of the researchers' decision
to include only evaluations that included a control
or comparison group? (See lines 67–69.)

10. Does it surprise you that the study by Becker et al. in Table 1 has negative effect sizes? Explain.

11. In Table 1, 95% confidence intervals are reported. What is your understanding of the meaning of these intervals?

12. What is your opinion on the researchers' suggestion in lines 134–138? Is your opinion based on the data in this meta-analysis? Explain.

Quality Ratings

Directions: Indicate your level of agreement with each of the following statements by circling a number from 5 for strongly agree (SA) to 1 for strongly disagree (SD). If you believe an item is not applicable to this research article, leave it blank. Be prepared to explain your ratings. When responding to criteria A and B below, keep in mind that brief titles and abstracts are conventional in published research.

A. The title of the article is appropriate.

SA   5   4   3   2   1   SD

B. The abstract provides an effective overview of the research article.

SA   5   4   3   2   1   SD

C. The introduction establishes the importance of the study.

SA   5   4   3   2   1   SD

D. The literature review establishes the context for the study.

SA   5   4   3   2   1   SD

E. The research purpose, question, or hypothesis is clearly stated.

SA   5   4   3   2   1   SD

F. The method of sampling is sound.

SA   5   4   3   2   1   SD

G. Relevant demographics (for example, age, gender, and ethnicity) are described.

SA   5   4   3   2   1   SD

H. Measurement procedures are adequate.

SA   5   4   3   2   1   SD

I. All procedures have been described in sufficient detail to permit a replication of the study.

SA   5   4   3   2   1   SD

J. The participants have been adequately protected from potential harm.

SA   5   4   3   2   1   SD

K. The results are clearly described.

SA   5   4   3   2   1   SD

L. The discussion/conclusion is appropriate.

SA   5   4   3   2   1   SD

M. Despite any flaws, the report is worthy of publication.

SA   5   4   3   2   1   SD

Appendix A

Reading Research Reports: A Brief Introduction

DAVID A. SCHROEDER   DAVID E. JOHNSON   THOMAS D. JENSEN

To many students, the prospect of reading a research report in a professional journal elicits so much fear that no information is, in fact, transmitted. Such apprehension on the part of the reader is not necessary, and we
5 hope that this article will help students understand more clearly what such reports are all about and will teach them how to use these resources more effectively. Let us assure you that there is nothing mystical or magical about research reports, although they may be somewhat
10 more technical and precise in style, more intimidating in vocabulary, and more likely to refer to specific sources of information than are everyday mass media sources. However, once you get beyond these intimidating features, you will find that the vast majority of research
15 reports do a good job of guiding you through a project and informing you of important points of which you should be aware.

A scientific research report has but one purpose: to communicate to others the results of one's scientific
20 investigations. To ensure that readers will be able to appreciate fully the import and implications of the research, the author of the report will make every effort to describe the project so comprehensively that even a naïve reader will be able to follow the logic as he or she
25 traces the author's thinking through the project.

A standardized format has been developed by editors and authors to facilitate effective communication. The format is subject to some modification, according to the specific needs and goals of a particular author for
30 a particular article, but, in general, most articles possess a number of features in common. We will briefly discuss the six major sections of research articles and the purpose of each. We hope that this selection will help you take full advantage of the subsequent articles and to
35 appreciate their content as informed "consumers" of social psychological research.

Heading

The heading of an article consists of the title, the name of the author or authors, and their institutional affiliations. Typically, the title provides a brief descrip-
40 tion of the primary independent and dependent variables

that have been investigated in the study. This information should help you begin to categorize the study into some implicit organizational framework that will help you keep track of the social psychological material. For
45 example, if the title includes the word *persuasion*, you should immediately recognize that the article will be related to the attitude-change literature, and you should prepare yourself to identify the similarities and differences between the present study and the previous litera-
50 ture.

The names of the authors may also be important to you for at least two reasons. First, it is quite common for social psychologists to use the names of authors as a shorthand notation in referring among themselves to
55 critical articles. Rather than asking, "Have you read 'Videotape and the attribution process: Reversing actors' and observers' points of view'?," it is much easier to say, "Have you read the Storms (1973) article?" In addition, this strategy gives the author(s) credit for the
60 material contained in the article. Second, you will find that most researchers actively pursue programs of research that are specific to a particular area of interest. For example, you will eventually be able to recognize that an article written by Albert Bandura is likely to be
65 about social learning processes, while an article by Leonard Berkowitz is probably going to discuss aggression and violence. Once you begin to identify the major researchers in each area, you will find that you will be able to go beyond the information presented within an
70 article and understand not only how a piece of research fits into a well-defined body of literature but also how it may be related to other less obvious topics.

Abstract

The Abstract is a short (often less than 150 words) preview of the contents of the article. The Abstract
75 should be totally self-contained and intelligible without any reference to the article proper. It should briefly convey a statement of the problem explored, the methods used, the major results of the study, and the conclusions reached. The Abstract helps to set the stage and to pre-
80 pare you for the article itself. Just as the title helps you place the article in a particular area of investigation, the Abstract helps pinpoint the exact question or questions to be addressed in the study.

Introduction

The Introduction provides the foundation for the

85 study itself and therefore for the remainder of the article. Thus, it serves several critical functions for the reader. First, it provides a context for the article and the study by discussing past literature that is relevant to and has implications for the present research. Second, it per-
90 mits a thorough discussion of the rationale for the research that was conducted and a full description of the independent and dependent variables that were employed. Third, it allows the hypotheses that were tested to be stated explicitly, and the arguments on which these
95 predictions were based to be elucidated. Each of these functions will be considered in detail.

The literature review that is typically the initial portion of the Introduction is not intended to provide a comprehensive restatement of all the published articles
100 that are tangentially relevant to the present research. Normally, a selective review is presented—one that carefully sets up the rationale of the study and identifies deficiencies in our understanding of the phenomena being investigated. In taking this approach, the author is
105 attempting to provide insights into the thought processes that preceded the actual conducting of the study. Usually, the literature review will begin by discussing rather broad conceptual issues (e.g., major theories, recognized areas of investigation) and will then gradually narrow its
110 focus to more specific concerns (e.g., specific findings from previous research, methods that have been employed). It may be helpful to think of the Introduction as a funnel, gradually drawing one's attention to a central point that represents the critical feature of the article.

115 Following the review of the past literature, the author typically presents the rationale for his or her own research. A research study may have one of several goals as its primary aim: (1) It may be designed to answer a question specifically raised by the previous lit-
120 erature but left unanswered. (2) It may attempt to correct methodological flaws that have plagued previous research and threaten the validity of the conclusions reached. (3) It may seek to reconcile conflicting findings that have been reported in the literature, typically
125 by identifying and/or eliminating confounding variables by exerting greater experimental control. (4) It may be designed to assess the validity of a scientific theory by testing one or more hypotheses that have been deduced or derived from that theory. (5) It may begin a novel
130 line of research that has not been previously pursued or discussed in the literature. Research pursuing any of these five goals may yield significant contributions to a particular field of inquiry.

After providing the rationale for the study, the au-
135 thor properly continues to narrow the focus of the article from broad conceptual issues to the particular variables that are to be employed in the study. Ideally, in experimental studies, the author clearly identifies the independent and dependent variables to be used; in correla-
140 tional studies, the predictor and criterion variables are specified. For those readers who do not have an extensive background in research methodology, a brief ex-

planation of experimental and correlational studies may be in order.

145 *Experimental studies.* An experimental study is designed to identify cause–effect relationships between independent variables that the experimenter systematically manipulates and the dependent variable that is used to measure the behavior of interest. In such a
150 study, the researcher controls the situation to eliminate or neutralize the effects of all extraneous factors that may affect the behavior of interest in order to assess more precisely the impact of the independent variables alone. In most instances, only the tightly controlled ex-
155 perimental method permits valid inferences of cause–effect relationships to be made.

Correlational studies. In some circumstances, the researcher cannot exert the degree of control over the situation that is necessary for a true experimental study.
160 Rather than giving up the project, the researcher may explore alternative methods that may still permit an assessment of his or her hypotheses and predictions. One such alternative is the correlational approach. In a correlational study, the researcher specifies a set of
165 measures that should be related conceptually to the display of a target behavior. The measure that is used to assess the target behavior is called the criterion variable; the measure from which the researcher expects to be able to make predictions about the criterion variable is
170 called the predictor variable. Correlational studies permit the researcher to assess the degree of relationship between the predictor variable(s) and the criterion variable(s), but inferences of cause-and-effect cannot be validly made because the effects of extraneous variables
175 have not been adequately controlled. Correlational studies are most frequently used in naturalistic or applied situations in which researchers must either tolerate the lack of control and do the best they can under the circumstances or give up any hope of testing their hy-
180 potheses.

After the discussion of these critical components of the study, the author explicitly states the exact predictions that the study is designed to test. The previous material should have set the stage sufficiently well for
185 you as a reader to anticipate what these hypotheses will be, but it is incumbent on the author to present them nonetheless. The wording of the hypotheses may vary, some authors preferring to state the predictions in conceptual terms (e.g., "The arousal of cognitive disso-
190 nance due to counterattitudinal advocacy is expected to lead to greater attitude change than the presentation of an attitude-consistent argument.") and others preferring to state their predictions in terms of the actual operationalizations that they employed (e.g., "Subjects who
195 received a $1 incentive to say that an objectively boring task was fun are expected to subsequently evaluate the task as being more enjoyable than subjects who were offered a $20 incentive to say that the task was interesting.").

200   In reading a research report, it is imperative that you pay attention to the relationship between the initial literature review, the rationale for the study, and the statement of the hypotheses. In a well-conceived and well-designed investigation, each section will flow logi-

205 cally from the preceding one; the internal consistency of the author's arguments will make for smooth transitions as the presentation advances. If there appear to be discontinuities or inconsistencies throughout the author's presentation, it would be wise to take a more critical

210 view of the study—particularly if the predictions do not seem to follow logically from the earlier material. In such cases, the author may be trying to present as a prediction a description of the findings that were unexpectedly uncovered when the study was being conducted.

215 Although there is nothing wrong with reporting unexpected findings in a journal article, the author should be honest enough to identify them as what they really are. As a reader, you should have much more confidence in the reliability of predictions that obtain than you do in

220 data that can be described by postdictions only.

Method

    To this point, the author has dealt with the study in relatively abstract terms, and has given little attention to the actual procedures used in conducting it. In the Method section, the author at last describes the opera-

225 tionalizations and procedures that were employed in the investigation. There are at least two reasons for the detailed presentation of this information. First, such a presentation allows interested readers to reconstruct the methodology used, so that a replication of the study can

230 be undertaken. By conducting a replication using different subject populations and slightly different operationalizations of the same conceptual variables, more information can be gained about the validity of the conclusions that the original investigator reached. Second,

235 even if a replication is not conducted, the careful description of the method used will permit you to evaluate the adequacy of the procedures employed.

    The Method section typically comprises two or more subsections, each of which has a specific function to

240 fulfill. Almost without exception, the Method section begins with a subject subsection, consisting of a complete description of the subjects who participated in the study.[1] The number of subjects should be indicated, and there should be a summary of important demographic

245 information (e.g., numbers of male and female subjects, age) so that you can know to what populations the findings can be reasonably generalized. Sampling techniques that were used to recruit subjects and incentives used to induce volunteering should also be clearly speci-

250 fied. To the extent that subject characteristics are of primary importance to the goals of the research, greater

detail is presented in this subsection, and more attention should be directed to it.

    A procedures subsection is also almost always in-

255 cluded in the Method section. This subsection presents a detailed account of the subjects' experiences in the experiment. Although other formats may also be effective, the most common presentation style is to describe the subjects' activities in chronological order. A thorough

260 description of all questionnaires administered or tasks completed is given, as well as any other features that might be reasonably expected to affect the behavior of the subjects in the study.

    After the procedures have been discussed, a full de-

265 scription of the independent variables in an experimental study, or predictor variables in a correlational study, is typically provided. Verbatim description of each of the different levels of each independent variable is presented, and similar detail is used to describe each pre-

270 dictor variable. This information may be included either in the procedures subsection or, if the description of these variables is quite lengthy, in a separate subsection.

    After thoroughly describing these variables, the author usually describes the dependent variables in an

275 experimental study, and the criterion variables in a correlational study. The description of the dependent and/or criterion variables also requires a verbatim specification of the exact operationalizations that were employed. When appropriate and available, information about the

280 reliability and validity of these measures is also presented. In addition, if the investigator has included any questions that were intended to allow the effectiveness of the independent variable manipulation to be assessed, these manipulation checks are described at this point.

285 All of this information may be incorporated in the procedures subsection or in a separate subsection.

    After you have read the Method section, there should be no question about what has been done to the subjects who participated in the study. You should try to

290 evaluate how representative the methods that were used were of the conceptual variables discussed in the Introduction. Manipulation checks may help to allay one's concerns, but poorly conceived manipulation checks are of little or no value. Therefore, it is important for you as

295 a reader to remember that you are ultimately responsible for the critical evaluation of any research report.

Results

    Once the full methodology of the study has been described for the reader, the author proceeds to report the results of the statistical analyses that were conducted on

300 the data. The Results section is probably the most intimidating section for students to read, and often the most difficult section for researchers to write. You are typically confronted with terminology and analytical techniques with which you are at best unfamiliar, or at

305 worst totally ignorant. There is no reason for you to feel bad about this state of affairs; as a neophyte in the world of research, you cannot expect mastery of all phases of

---

[1] *Editor's note*: Many researchers prefer the terms *participants* or *respondents* to the term *subjects*.

research from the start. Even experienced researchers are often exposed to statistical techniques with which
310 they are unfamiliar, requiring them either to learn the techniques or to rely on others to assess the appropriateness of the procedure. For the student researcher, a little experience and a conscientious effort to learn the basics will lead to mastery of the statistical skills necessary.
315 The author's task is similarly difficult. He or she is attempting to present the findings of the study in a straightforward and easily understood manner, but the presentation of statistical findings does not always lend itself readily to this task. The author must decide
320 whether to present the results strictly within the text of the article or to use tables, graphs, and figures to help convey the information effectively. Although the implications of the data may be clear to the researcher, trying to present the data clearly and concisely so that the
325 reader will also be able to discern the implications is not necessarily assured. In addition, the author is obligated to present all the significant results obtained in the statistical analyses, not just the results that support the hypotheses being tested. Although this may clutter the
330 presentation and detract from the simplicity of the interpretation, it must be remembered that the researcher's primary goal is to seek the truth, not to espouse a particular point of view that may not be supported by the data.

Discussion

335 The Discussion section is the part of the manuscript in which the author offers an evaluation and interpretation of the findings of the study, particularly as they relate to the hypotheses that were proposed in the Introduction. Typically, the author will begin this section
340 with a brief review of the major findings of the study and a clear statement of whether the data were consistent or inconsistent with the hypotheses. The Discussion will then address any discrepancies between the predictions and the data, trying to resolve these inconsisten-
345 cies and offering plausible reasons for their occurrence. In general, the first portion of the Discussion is devoted to an evaluation of the hypotheses that were originally set forth in the Introduction, given the data that were obtained in the research.
350 The Discussion may be seen as the inverse of the Introduction, paralleling the issues raised in that section in the opposite order of presentation. Therefore, after discussing the relationship of the data with the hypotheses, the author often attempts to integrate the new findings
355 into the body of research that provided the background for the study. Just as this literature initially provided the context within which you can understand the rationale for the study, it subsequently provides the context within which the data can be understood and inter-
360 preted. The author's responsibility at this point is to help you recognize the potential import of the research, without relying on hype or gimmicks to make the point.

The Discussion continues to expand in terms of the breadth of ideas discussed until it reaches the broad,
365 conceptual issues that are addressed by the superordinate theoretical work that originally stimulated the past research literature. If a particular piece of research is to make a significant contribution to the field, its findings must either clarify some past discrepancy in the litera-
370 ture, identify boundary conditions for the applicability of the critical theoretical work, reconcile differences of opinion among the researchers in the field, or otherwise contribute to a more complete understanding of the mechanisms and mediators of important social phenom-
375 ena.

Once the author has reached the goals that are common to most journal articles, attention may be turned to less rigorous ideas. Depending on a particular journal's editorial policy and the availability of additional space,
380 the author may finish the article with a brief section about possible applications of the present work, implications for future work in the area, and with some restraint, speculations about what lies ahead for the line of research. Scientists tend to have relatively little toler-
385 ance for conclusions without foundation and off-the-cuff comments made without full consideration. Therefore, authors must be careful not to overstep the bounds of propriety in making speculations about the future. But such exercises can be useful and can serve a
390 heuristic function for other researchers if the notions stated are well conceived.

Finally, particularly if the article has been relatively long or complex, the author may decide to end it with a short Conclusion. The Conclusion usually simply re-
395 states the major arguments that have been made throughout the article, reminding the reader one last time of the value of the work.

As we suggested earlier, not all articles will follow the format exactly. Some latitude is allowed to accom-
400 modate the particular needs of the author and the quirks of the research being described. Given that the goal is effective communication of information, it would not be reasonable for the format to dictate what could and could not be included in a manuscript. We hope that this
405 introduction will help to demystify research articles and provide you with some insights into what an author is trying to accomplish at various points in the report.

Let us end with a word of encouragement: Your enjoyment of social psychology will be enhanced by your
410 fuller appreciation of the sources of the information to which you are being exposed, and, to the extent that you are able to read and understand these original sources for yourself, your appreciation of this work will be maximized.

Reference

Storms, M. D. (1973). Videotape and the attribution process: Reversing actors' and observers' points of view. *Journal of Personality and Social Psychology, 27,* 165–175.

Exercise for Appendix A

Factual Questions

1. What four elements should the Abstract convey?

2. Which part of a report provides the "foundation" for the study and the remainder of the article?

3. Normally, should the literature review be "selective" *or* "comprehensive"?

4. If there is a research hypothesis, should it be explicitly stated in the Introduction?

5. Are "experimental" *or* "correlational" studies better for making inferences about cause-and-effect?

6. What is a *criterion variable* in a correlational study?

7. Which part of a report describes the operationalizations and procedures employed in the investigation?

8. The Method section usually begins with a description of what?

9. According to the authors, what is probably the most intimidating section of a research report for students?

10. Should experienced researchers expect to find statistical techniques with which they are unfamiliar when they read research reports?

11. How should the Discussion section of a research report typically begin?

12. Which part of a report usually simply restates the major arguments that have been made throughout the article?

Notes

Notes

Notes

Notes